THE MANAGEMENT OF STRESS AND ANXIETY IN MEDICAL DISORDERS

Edited by

DAVID I. MOSTOFSKY
DAVID H. BARLOW

Boston University

Allyn and Bacon

Boston   London   Toronto   Sydney   Tokyo   Singapore

Series Editor: Becky Pascal
Series Editorial Assistant: Susan Hutchinson
Marketing Manager: Stephen Smith

Copyright © 2000 by Allyn & Bacon
A Pearson Education Company
Needham Heights, MA 02494

Internet: www.abacon.com

Library of Congress Cataloging-in-Publication Data

The management of stress and anxiety in medical disorders / edited by
   David I. Mostofsky and David H. Barlow.
     p.   cm.
   Includes bibliographical references and index.
   ISBN 0-205-28704-2
   1. Stress management. 2. Stress (Psychology) 3. Medicine and
psychology. I. Mostofsky, David I. II. Barlow, David H.
   [DNLM: 1. Anxiety—therapy. 2. Disease—psychology. 3. Stress,
Psychological—therapy. WM 172 M2656 2000]
RA785.M35 2000
616.85′223—dc21
DNLM/DLC
for Library of Congress   99-32656
                                              CIP

Printed in the United States of America

10 9 8 7 6 5 4 3 2 1   04 03 02 01 00

CONTENTS

PART IV   CHRONIC DISORDERS AND PATHOPHYSIOLOGY

PART V   HEALTH PROMOTION/DISEASE PREVENTION

PREFACE

The relatively recent changes in the clinical activities of medicine and psychology have influenced both professions to reexamine some long-standing biases concerning the role of mental health concepts and intervention strategies in the "medical" care and treatment of patently nonmental health disorders. Such a reexamination has led to a recognition that sickness may be represented by elements that are biological and organic, by elements that are behavioral, emotional, and cognitive, and by elements that are predominantly interpersonal and psychosocial. For some sickness conditions, one or more of the elements may be absent or may strongly interact with other elements (Mostofsky, 1981). The unitary nature of a medical syndrome is thus preserved even when psychological dynamics are introduced to account for etiological factors, symptom manifestations, or therapeutic success.

Startling new findings in the past several years suggest that recognizing, assessing, and understanding the role of stress and anxiety in medical disorders may become some of the most important functions of clinicians in future years. This is due to several factors: First, anxiety and stress disorders *without* the complication of medical disorders are highly prevalent in medical settings, as thoroughly reviewed by Roy-Byrne and Katon (this volume). Also, anxiety and mood disorders go unrecognized in at least 50% of all cases. Second, a very clear understanding has emerged that stress and anxiety greatly complicate the presence of medical disorders, leading directly to exacerbations and, in some cases, to onset of the medical disorder. Fortunately we are now beginning to understand the neurobiological processes mediating the effects of stress and anxiety on physical functioning and disease. Explorations of the interaction of stress and anxiety with immune and endocrine system functioning reveal particularly exciting discoveries and are reviewed throughout this book. In part because of these findings, recent trends in behavioral medicine

and in the delivery of health care services are reversing the strategy of "carving out" mental health care from physical care, and instead strongly emphasizing the importance of collaborative efforts among clinicians treating mental and physical disorders. Thus, behavioral health care is being "carved back in" to medical settings (Hayes, Barlow, & Nelson-Gray, 1999).

In this book we bring together, for the first time, many of the leading clinical scientists working in these areas. The book begins with an illuminating chapter from Roy-Byrne and Katon on the imperative of focusing on stress and anxiety in primary care settings, describing recent systematic efforts in that direction. An important and up-to-the-minute chapter by Sullivan, Kent, and Coplan details surprising new information on the neurobiology of stress and anxiety in the context of its relation to disease processes. This is followed by chapters by notable and leading contributors outlining current, state-of-the-art procedures for the assessment and management of stress and anxiety in a variety of disorders, most usually treated in primary care or medical settings.

We consider this book to be a blueprint for practice and research for the first decade of the new century, and we are delighted to be part of this process. We hope that the wide variety of behavioral health and primary care providers, as well as those pursuing research in these areas, will find the chapters as practical and descriptively and theoretically rich as we have.

We would like to acknowledge the invaluable assistance of our publishers in the persons of Sue Hutchinson and Sean Wakely for facilitating the production of this book, and to thank Bette Selwyn for undertaking many of the administrative functions necessary to put this book together. We would like to extend our deepest appreciation to several of our doctoral students in clinical psychology who worked in a short time frame to produce a very useful and well-done subject and author index. To Molly Choate, Elizabeth Cohen, Jessica Grisham, Hyo-Jin Kim, and Susan Raffa. We hope others will benefit as much from your efforts as we have. We dedicate this book to future students, both from our own institution at Boston University and to others who we hope will pursue these ideas with determination and vigor, as we all strive to relieve the enormous suffering associated with the onset and course of these disorders.

David I. Mostofsky
David H. Barlow
Boston University

Hayes, S. C., Barlow, D. H., & Nelson-Gray, R. O. (1999). The scientist practitioner: Research and accountability in the age of managed care (2d ed.). Needham Heights, MA: Allyn and Bacon.

Mostofsky, D. I. (1997). Behavioral treatment. In M. R. Trimble & J. L. Cummings (Eds.), *Behavioral neurology* (pp. 327–336). Boston: Butterworth-Heinemann.

ABOUT THE EDITORS
AND CONTRIBUTORS

ABOUT THE EDITORS

David I. Mostofsky is Professor of Psychology at Boston University, where he was Chairman of the Experimental/Physiological Program in Brain, Behavior, and Cognition and is currently Director of the Laboratory for Experimental Behavioral Medicine. He was awarded a B.A. from Yeshiva College and a Ph.D. in Experimental Psychology from Boston University. The recipient of many awards, including the Switzer Fellow awarded by the Mary Switzer Memorial Foundation, Senior International Fellowship from the National Institutes of Health (Fogarty), Norway Marshall Fund Award, Einstein Fellow of the Israel Academy of Science, Distinguished Visitor of the American Psychological Association, and Fulbright Scholar. He was a Visiting Professor at the University of Modena in Italy. Other academic and professional affiliations include appointments as Adjunct Professor in the Boston University School of Medicine; Director of Research Services in the Department of Neurology at New England Hospital; Director, Behavioral Neurology Program, Children's Hospital Medical Center; Assistant Clinical Professor of Pediatrics, New England Medical Center, Boston; Research Associate, Medical Staff, Children's Hospital Medical Center; and Chair, International Interest Group on Neurobehavioral Aspects of Epilepsy.

He is the author and coauthor of more than a hundred articles in journals and contributed chapters, and he has edited thirteen books and monographs. His research interests include operant conditioning, behavioral medicine, epilepsy, pain, and the biobehavioral effects of essential fatty acids.

David H. Barlow received his Ph.D. from the University of Vermont in 1969 and has published over 400 articles and chapters and over 20 books, mostly in the areas of anxiety disorders, sexual problems, and clinical research methodology. Books include: D. H. Barlow and M. Hersen, *Single Case Experimental Designs: Strategies for Studying Behavioral Change* (2d ed.) (New York: Pergamon, 1984); D. H. Barlow, *Anxiety and Its Disorders: The Nature and Treatment of Anxiety and Panic* (New York: Guilford, 1988); D. H. Barlow (Ed.), *Clinical Handbook of Psychological Disorders* (2d ed.) (New York: Guilford, 1993); D. H. Barlow and V. M. Durand, *Abnormal Psychology: An Integrative Approach* (2d ed.) (Monterey, CA: Brooks/Cole, 1999); and most recently, S. C. Hayes, D. H. Barlow, and R. O. Nelson-Gray, *The Scientist Practitioner: Research and Accountability in the Age of Managed Care* (2d ed.) (Needham Heights, MA: Allyn and Bacon, 1999).

He is formerly Professor of Psychiatry at the University of Mississippi Medical Center and Professor of Psychiatry and Psychology at Brown University; he founded clinical psychology internships in both settings. He was also Distinguished Professor in the Department of Psychology and Director of the Phobia and Anxiety Disorders Clinic at the University at Albany, State University of New York. Currently he is Professor of Psychology, Research Professor of Psychiatry, and Director of Clinical Training Programs and Director of the Center for Anxiety and Related Disorders at Boston University.

Dr. Barlow is the recipient of the First Graduate Alumni Scholar Award from the Graduate College, The University of Vermont. Other awards include the Distinguished Scientist Award from Section III of the Division of Clinical Psychology of the American Psychological Association; the Excellence in Research Award from the State University of New York at Albany, and a Merit award from the National Institute of Mental Health for long-term contributions to the clinical research effort. He is past president of the Division of Clinical Psychology of the American Psychological Association, past president of the Association for the

Advancement of Behavior Therapy, Past Associate Editor of the *Journal of Consulting and Clinical Psychology*, and Past Editor of the journals *Behavior Therapy* and *Journal of Applied Behavior Analysis*. Currently he is Editor of the journal *Clinical Psychology: Science and Practice*. He was also Chair of the American Psychological Association Task Force of Psychological Intervention Guidelines, was a member of the DSM-IV Task Force of the American Psychiatric Association, and was Co-Chair of the work group for revising the anxiety disorder categories. He is also a Diplomate in Clinical Psychology of the American Board of Professional Psychology and maintains a private practice.

ABOUT THE CONTRIBUTORS

Carolyn Aibel is a graduate student at the University of Colorado at Boulder, where she does research on eating disorders. She has a B.A. in Psychology from Wesleyan University and an M.A. in Psychology from the University of Colorado.

Frank Andrasik received his doctorate in Clinical Psychology from Ohio University in 1979, after completing an Internship at Western Psychiatric Institute and Clinic, Department of Psychiatry, University of Pittsburgh School of Medicine. He presently holds the positions of Associate Vice Provost for Graduate Studies, Professor of Psychology, and Director of the Behavioral Medicine Laboratory at the University of West Florida.

Dr. Andrasik has been the recipient of several federal and foundation research grants, including a Research Career Development Award from the National Institute of Neurological Disorders and Stroke. He is a member of the Behavioral Medicine Study Section at NIH. He was the 1992 recipient of the Association for Applied Psychophysiology and Biofeedback's Merit Award for Long-Term Research and/or Clinical Achievements. Dr. Andrasik currently serves as Editor in Chief of *Applied Psychophysiology and Biofeedback* (formerly *Biofeedback and Self-Regulation*) and is a Past Editor for *Behavior Therapy*. He served as President of the Association for Applied Psychophysiology and Biofeedback in 1993–1994. He has published and presented extensively on the topics of pain, stress, biofeedback, applied psychophysiology, and behavioral medicine.

Philip R. Appel, Ph.D., is currently the Supervisor of Psychological Services at the National Rehabilitation Hospital in Washington, DC.

Sandra L. Baker, M.A., is an advanced Clinical Psychology doctoral student at Boston University. She is currently working at the Center for Anxiety and Related Disorders, specializing in the assessment and treatment of adult anxiety disorders, particularly panic disorder with agoraphobia and social phobia.

Marcia P. Bergtraum, M.D., is a Pediatric Neurologist on staff at the Schneider Children's Hospital of the Albert Einstein College of Medicine.

Dr. Bergtraum is the Medical Director of the Association for the Help of Retarded Children of Nassau County.

Per Björntorp, M.D., Ph.D., is Professor of Medicine at Sahlgren's University Hospital, Göteborg, Sweden. He earned his M.D. and Ph.D. at the University of Göteborg. He is also a Visiting Professor at Rockefeller, Columbia, and Barcelona Universities. Previously Chairman of the European and Swedish Associations for the Study of Obesity, he is currently Editor in Chief of the *International Journal of Obesity* and member of the International Obesity Task Force.

Edward B. Blanchard received his Ph.D. in Clinical Psychology in 1969 from Stanford University. After holding faculty positions at the University of Georgia, University of Mississippi Medical Center, and University of Tennessee Health Sciences Center, he came to the University at Albany, SUNY, in 1977. In 1989 he was named Distinguished Professor of Psychology. He has been investigating psychosocial aspects of irritable bowel syndrome since 1985, including nine different trials of various cognitive-behavioral treatments.

Joseph Bleiberg, Ph.D., is currently Chairman of the Behavioral Sciences Section at the National Rehabilitation Hospital in Washington, DC. He is also a Clinical Associate Professor in the Department of Neurology at Georgetown University School of Medicine.

Trudie Chalder currently works as a Senior Lecturer in the Department of Psychological Medicine at Guy's, King's and St. Thomas' School of Medicine (GKT), London. She is a cognitive behavioral psychotherapist and has an M.Sc. in Health Psychology and a Ph.D. in Psychology that is related to the area of fatigue in primary care. She has worked as a clinician and a researcher in the area of chronic fatigue and chronic fatigue syndrome for about 10 years.

John F. Chaves, Ph.D., is Professor and Head, Division of Behavioral Medicine and Bioethics, Department of Oral Biology, Indiana University School of Dentistry, Indianapolis, IN. He coedited *Hypnosis: The Cognitive Behavioral Perspective*, with N. P. Spanos and coauthored *Hypnosis, Imagination and Human Potentialities* with T. X. Barber and N. P. Spanos.

Anthony Cleare is currently a Senior Lecturer in the Department of Psychological Medicine at Guy's, King's and St. Thomas' School of Medicine and the Institute of Psychiatry, London. He also holds an honorary consultant position at the Maudsley Hospital in London. After obtaining a degree in Psychology from University College London, he trained in medicine at Guy's Hospital Medical School in London. In 1998 he obtained a Ph.D., looking at neuroendocrine aspects of affective disorders. His current clinical practice includes a special interest in chronic fatigue syndrome.

Jeremy D. Coplan, M.D., is Associate Professor in Clinical Psychiatry at Columbia University, College of Physicians and Surgeons, and Associate Director of the Biological Studies Unit, New York State Psychiatric Institute. Areas of research include the effects of adverse early rearing in nonhuman primates on behavioral, neuropeptide, neuroendocrine, and monoamine function. From a clinical standpoint, Dr. Coplan has conducted research into the neurobiology of anxiety disorders, specifically panic disorder, with particular emphasis on the sodium lactate infusion and serotonin function. More recent interests include the role of glutamate antagonists in stress modulation and neuroimaging of the anxiety patient.

Linda Wilcoxon Craighead is Professor of Psychology at the University of Colorado at Boulder. She has published numerous papers and presented workshops on the treatment of obesity and eating disorders. She is coeditor of *Cognitive and Behavioral Interventions: An Empirical Approach to Mental Health Problems* (Allyn and Bacon, 1994).

Susan E. Doron received her M.A. in Psychology from Boston University in 1996. She is currently a doctoral student in the Clinical Psychology program at Boston University and a Research Associate at the Women's Health Sciences Division of the National Center for PTSD, Boston VA Medical Center. Her research interests include physiological aspects of stress and emotion as well as behavioral medicine interventions for medical comorbidity.

Anke Ehlers, Ph.D., is a Wellcome Principal Research Fellow at the Department of Psychiatry, University of Oxford, U.K. Her research focuses on anxiety disorders and psychological aspects of dermatological and cardiovascular problems. She has worked at the universities of Stanford, CA (Research Scholar), Marburg, Germany (Assistant Professor), and Göttingen, Germany (Professor).

Jonathan M. Feldman is a graduate student in the doctoral Clinical Psychology program at Rutgers University. He is conducting research to identify behavioral factors that interfere with asthma self-management.

Joshua Fogel received his B.A. from Brooklyn College in 1993 and is currently a student in the Clinical Health Psychology Ph.D. program at the Ferkauf Graduate School of Psychology. His interests are in geriatrics, rehabilitation, and pain. He is currently doing research on motivation in geriatric stroke patients.

Robert Fried (Ph.D. 1964, Rutgers), is professor of Biopsychology, Hunter College, CUNY, and Director, Stress and Biofeedback Clinic, Albert Ellis Institute, New York. He has authored more than 50 scientific publications and *The Hyperventilation Syndrome* (Johns Hopkins University Press, 1987) and *The Psychology and Physiology of Breathing in*

Behavioral Medicine, Clinical Psychology and Psychiatry (Plenum, 1993).

Cheryl A. Frye, Assistant Professor, Psychology Department, the University of Albany, is a behavioral neuroscientist. Her graduate work was in the Department of Psychology at Tufts University; postdoctoral training was in the Biology Department at Boston University. Her research examines functional consequences of steroids on cognitive, affective, and reproductive behavior.

Nicholas D. Giardino received his M.S. in Clinical Psychology at Rutgers University and is currently pursuing his Ph.D. at the same institution. He has been involved in psychophysiologic and treatment studies of asthma, as well as more general research on the relationship between emotional and somatic disorders.

Jennifer Hoffman Goldberg is a doctoral candidate in Counseling Psychology at Stanford University. Her research interests include behavioral medicine, anxiety, and depression.

K. Gunnar Götestam, M.D. 1968, Ph.D. in Psychology 1973. He has been Professor of Psychiatry, Norwegian University of Science and Technology (NTNU) Trondheim since 1977 and is Chief Psychiatrist at Sör-Tröndelag Psychiatric Hospitals (STPS). He has authored four books and 150 articles for international publications.

Kamala A. I. Greene, M.A., is a Clinical Psychology doctoral student at Boston University. She is currently working at the Center for Anxiety and Related Disorders doing research, assessment, and treatment of patients with anxiety disorders.

Peter J. Hauri is currently a Professor of Psychology at the Mayo Medical School and the Director of the Mayo Clinic Sleep Disorders Center in Rochester, MN. A native of Switzerland, he has been in research and clinical sleep work for the past 38 years.

A. Brooke Hinkson is Data Manager at the New England Research Institute. Her baccalaureate degree is in Psychology from Wheaton College. While at Wheaton, Hinkson's honor's thesis examined effects of anxiety on health behavior compliance.

Göran Holm, M.D., Ph.D., is Associate Professor of Medicine at Sahlgren's University Hospital, Göteborg, Sweden, He earned his M.D. and Ph.D. at the University of Göteborg. He was previously head of the Department of Medicine at Sahlgren's Hospital.

Wayne Katon, M.D., is a Professor of Psychiatry, Director of the Division of Health Services and Epidemiology, and Vice-Chair of the Department of Psychiatry and Behavioral Sciences, University of Washington Medical School. He is Director of an NIMH-funded National Research Service Award Primary Care fellowship that has successfully trained psychiatrists and primary care physicians for academic leadership positions. Dr. Katon is internationally renowned for his research on the prevalence of anxiety and depressive disorders in primary care, and the relationship of psychiatric disorders to medically unexplained symptoms such as headache and fatigue. In recent years his research has focused on developing innovative models of integrating mental health professionals into primary care to improve the care of patients with major depression and panic disorder. Dr. Katon has written over 200 journal articles and chapters as well as *Panic Disorder in the Medical Setting*, a book for primary care physicians.

Dr. Katon has won the American Academy of Family Practice Award for Excellence in Teaching in Primary Care numerous times. He has also been awarded the Academy of Psychosomatic Medicine Research Award (1993).

Susan Kennedy is Associate Professor of Psychology at Denison University. She received her Ph.D. in Psychobiology from Ohio State University and subsequently completed postdoctoral training in Behavioral Immunology at the Ohio State University College of Medicine, Department of Medical Microbiology and Immunology.

Justine M. Kent, M.D., is a Clinical Research Fellow in anxiety and affective disorders and an Assistant Attending Psychiatrist at Columbia University College of Physicians and Surgeons. Her primary areas of research are neuroimaging and biologic challenge studies in anxiety disorders.

Paul M. Lehrer, Ph.D., is Professor of Psychiatry and Director of the Center for Stress Management and Behavioral Medicine, UMDNJ—Robert Wood Johnson Medical School. He is also a respiratory psychophysiologist and is a major contributor to research on the psychophysiology of asthma, as well as the specific effects of various relaxation techniques.

Barbara G. Melamed, Ph.D., is Professor of Psychology in the Departments of Clinical Health Psychology—Ferkauf Graduate School of Psychology, Psychiatry, and Epidemiology and Social Medicine of Yeshiva University at the Albert Einstein College of Medicine. She was a founder of Behavioral Dentistry through her research funded by the National Institutes of Dental Research. She has served as President of the American Psychological Association's Division of Health Psychology. She is a Diplomate in Health Psychology awarded by the American Board of Professional Psychology and practices in Mamaroneck, New York.

Tamara L. Newton received her Ph.D. in Clinical Psychology from Rutgers University in 1992 and completed postdoctoral training at the Ohio State University College of Medicine, Division of Health Psychology. She is currently Clinical Research Psychologist at the Women's Health Sciences Division of the National Center for PTSD, Boston VA Medical Center. She has published in the areas of emotion, gender, and biological stress responses and currently is principal investigator on a grant from the National Heart, Lung, and Blood Institute and coinvestigator on a grant from the Department of Defense, Women's Health Research Program. Clinically she specializes in the treatment of women's stress-related and medical disorders.

Cynthia T. M. H. Nguyen, M.D., completed her internship, residency, and NIMH fellowship at Stanford University and is ABD in Languages and Civilizations at Harvard University. She is a psychiatrist in private practice in Palo Alto, CA. Her interests include anxiety disorders, cross-cultural psychiatry, and writing.

Raymond W. Novaco, Ph.D., is Professor of Psychology and Social Behavior at the University of California, Irvine. He has long-standing interests in anger dyscontrol and interventions for it. His recent treatment research concerns treatment-resistant patients having severe anger, including veterans with combat-related PTSD and highly assaulting psychotic patients in forensic hospitals.

Peter P. Roy-Byrne, M.D., received his training at the UCLA Neuropsychiatric Institute and at the National Institute of Mental Health (NIMH) Intramural Research Program. Following his stay at NIMH, he went to the University of Washington in Seattle, where he is currently Professor and Vice-Chair of the Department of Psychiatry and Behavioral Sciences and Chief of Psychiatry at the university's Harborview Medical Center.

Dr. Roy-Byrne has published over 200 articles and book chapters, and has lectured extensively both nationally and internationally on various clinical and research issues. His research has focused on the phenomenology and neurobiology of mood and anxiety disorders, with a special interest in benzodiazepine tranquilizers and the role of the benzodiazepine receptor in mood and anxiety disorders. More recently, Dr. Roy-Byrne has focused some of his research efforts on the outcomes of health services as they impact academic managed care environments, and on strategies to improve the treatment of anxiety in primary care patients.

Shani Robins received his Ph.D. in Psychology from the University of California, Santa Barbara. He is currently an NIMH Research Fellow at the University of California, Irvine. His research program examines the influence of wisdom-related cognitive appraisals on anger and the effect of metaphorical reasoning on the resolution of everyday dilemmas.

Roland Rosmond, M.D., Ph.D., is a Research Fellow at Sahlgren's University Hospital, Göteborg, Sweden. He earned his M.D. and Ph.D. at the University of Göteborg.

Neil Schneiderman, Ph.D., is James L. Knight Professor of Psychology, Medicine, Psychiatry and Behavioral Sciences, and Biomedical Engineering at the

University of Miami, Coral Gables, FL. He has received the American Psychology Association's Distinguished Scientific Contribution Award.

Javaid I. Sheikh, M.D., M.B.A., is Associate Professor of Psychiatry, Stanford University School of Medicine, and Chief of Psychiatry, Veterans Affairs Palo Alto Health Care System. He has conducted research in the area of anxiety disorders in late life for the last several years and is the author of numerous original articles in the field.

Geir Smedslund, Ph.D. in Psychology 1996, Norwegian University of Science and Technology, Clinical Psychologist 1991, University of Oslo. His research has focused on the effects of smoking, personality, and lifestyle on diseases and illness.

David A. Spiegel, M.D., is a Research Professor and Associate Director for Clinical and Medical Programs at the Center for Anxiety and Related Disorders at Boston University. Previously, he was Chairman of the Department of Psychiatry and Behavioral Medicine at the University of Illinois College of Medicine at Peoria.

Ulrich Stangier, Ph.D., is Assistant Professor of Clinical Psychology and Managing Director of Clinical Training at the University of Frankfurt/Main, Germany. The psychological assessment and behavioral treatment of skin disorders, somatoform disorders, and social phobia are his major research interests. He worked as a Research Clinical Psychologist at the Department of Dermatology, University of Marburg, Germany, between 1984 and 1993.

Gregory M. Sullivan, M.D., is a Clinical Research Fellow in anxiety and affective disorders and an Assistant Attending Psychiatrist at Columbia University College of Physicians and Surgeons. His primary research is on the roles of stress and autonomic dysregulation in panic disorder pathogenesis and the development of a rodent model of panic disorder.

Shannon M. Turner, Ph.D., earned her degree in Clinical Psychology from the State University of New York at Albany in 1997 and completed her residency at the University of Mississippi/Jackson VA Consortium. She is now the Research Scientist in the Department of Family Medicine at the Oklahoma State University College of Osteopathic Medicine in Tulsa, OK.

Risa B. Weisberg is a Postdoctoral Fellow at Brown University, Department of Psychiatry and Human Behavior. She received her Ph.D. in Clinical Psychology from the University at Albany. Her areas of specialization are anxiety disorders and sexual health. She presently serves as Project Director on the Primary Care Anxiety Project, a naturalistic, longitudinal study of anxiety disorders in primary care patients.

Simon Wessely is Professor of Epidemiological and Liaison Psychiatry at King's College School of Medicine and the Institute of Psychiatry, and Honorary Consultant Psychiatrist at King's and Maudsley Hospitals. He is Director of the Chronic Fatigue Syndrome Research Unit and also the Gulf War Illnesses Research Unit, both at the new Guy's, King's and St. Thomas' Medical School.

His main research interests are in various aspects of epidemiology, and also in the gray areas between medicine and psychiatry. He has published over 200 pages on many subjects, including the epidemiology of schizophrenia, crime and mental illness, posttraumatic stress, medicine and law, history of psychiatry, chronic pain, somatization, Gulf War illness, and deliberate self-harm. He has a particular interest in chronic fatigue syndrome; as well as running a clinical service specializing in the care of patients with the condition. He has published on most aspects of the topic.

Markus Wiegel, M.A., is a Clinical Psychology doctoral student at Boston University. He is employed by the Center for Anxiety and Related Disorders, where he is involved in research and clinical activities, specializing in adult anxiety disorders and sexual dysfunctions.

Daniel T. Williams, M.D., is Clinical Professor of Psychiatry at the Columbia University College of

Physicians and Surgeons. He is also Attending Psychiatrist at the Columbia-Presbyterian Medical Center in New York, where he serves as Consultant to the Comprehensive Epilepsy Center, to the Center for Parkinson's Disease and Other Movement Disorders, and to the Pediatric Neuro-Psychiatry Service.

Ray W. Winters, Ph.D., is Professor of Psychology at the University of Miami, Coral Gables, FL. Dr. Winters is a biological psychologist whose research interests include central nervous system control of the cardiovascular system, stress and coronary heart disease, and the neurobiology of affective disorders.

CHAPTER 1

ANXIETY MANAGEMENT IN THE MEDICAL SETTING: Rationale, Barriers to Diagnosis and Treatment, and Proposed Solutions

Peter P. Roy-Byrne

Wayne Katon

The words *stress* and *anxiety* are often used interchangeably in the popular press to describe human psychological reactions to various life events. However, the term *stress* is considerably broader and more inclusive than *anxiety,* encompassing a range of reactions, some disabling and some not, characterized by a mixture of anxiety and depressive symptoms. By contrast, the term *anxiety,* like *depression,* is more narrow and more specifically associated with discrete syndromes and diagnosable mental disorders, usually causing some degree of disability and often thought to require therapeutic intervention.

The anxiety disorders are the most prevalent group of disorders in the community, according to the two major U.S. epidemiologic studies completed over the last two decades (Regier et al., 1993; Kessler et al., 1994b). Although the DSM diagnostic manuals have traditionally listed five types of disorders under the anxiety disorder rubric (panic, generalized anxiety, phobic disorders, obsessive-compulsive disorder [OCD], and posttraumatic stress disorder [PTSD]), it is the first three that are most traditionally associated with the term *anxiety.* In contrast, OCD is now known to have clinical, biological, genetic, and treatment response characteristics that differ significantly from those seen in other anxiety disorders, and thus to be in a class of its own. Similarly, PTSD, because of the central role of the symptom of dissociation, as well as biological characteristics that distinctly differ from

those seen in depressive and anxiety disorders also occupies a unique place in the nomenclature. For these reasons, as well as the fact that there is little published information available on the prevalence and characteristics of these last two disorders in primary care, we will focus on the first three types of anxiety disorders (panic disorder, generalized anxiety disorder, and the spectrum of phobic disorders) in discussing the role of anxiety in the medical setting. We will also include studies that have examined "subthreshold" expressions of these disorders, as recent work has established that such syndromes are also associated with functional impairment (Weiller et al., 1998). Because findings from psychiatric settings cannot be generalized to the primary care setting, we will focus on studies in the latter setting, supplemented by data from community studies when applicable.

RATIONALE FOR FOCUSING ON ANXIETY IN THE MEDICAL SETTING

Prevalence

Although the figures vary, both the Epidemiologic Catchment Area (ECA) (Regier et al., 1993) and National Comorbidity Survey (NCS) (Kessler et al., 1994) studies show that the prevalence of anxiety disorders in the community, whether considered as lifetime or current 12-month prevalence, is greater than that of any other group of disorders. The majority of patients with a current or lifetime psychiatric diagnosis have multiple disorders, and over half of the affected people have an anxiety disorder. The majority of patients with mental disorders do not receive any treatment at all, and for those who do, only a minority are seen in specialty mental health settings. About half of the anxiety disorder patients who receive treatment are seen in the general medical, as opposed to mental health specialty, setting (Ford, 1994; Kessler et al., 1998; Regier et al., 1993).

Although diagnostic prevalence studies have only recently been completed in medical settings, previous reports have noted that anxiety was the most common problem family practice doctors felt they saw (Orleans et al., 1985), that between 20 and 30% of patients in these settings had elevated anxiety scores on the Zung Scale (Zung, 1986), and that about one in five primary care patients were taking benzodiazepines (Wells et al., 1986).

The prevalence of anxiety disorders in primary care is generally thought to be higher than in the community, although only a few studies actually provide DSM diagnostic figures. The larger U.S. studies show rates of 18% for combined panic, generalized anxiety, and anxiety disorder NOS (Spitzer et al., 1995) and 9% including only panic and generalized anxiety (Leon et al., 1995), with neither study including the much larger phobia category. Another study that surveyed patients with general medical conditions of hypertension, diabetes, and heart disease showed a combined rate of 15% for panic, generalized anxiety, and phobic disorder (Sherbourne, Jackson, et al., 1996). An international WHO study of mental disorders in primary care settings showed rates of 10% for panic, generalized anxiety, and agoraphobia (Sartorious et al., 1996). A very large epidemiological study (Fifer et al., 1994) focusing more on anxiety symptoms than on specific disorders (although diagnoses were obtained on a subsample of anxious patients) showed rates of roughly 10% for undiagnosed and untreated nonpanic, nonphobic symptoms of anxiety. Because combined totals that would reveal the degree of overlap between disorders are not provided (and because the Fifer et al. study did not include already diagnosed patients in the rates), probable rates when the missing two conditions (i.e., panic and phobia) are included can only be estimated and are probably between 20 and 25%. Given the exclusion of some disorders in these studies, they certainly suggest that, at any one time, probably one in five to six patients seen in the primary care setting has an anxiety disorder. This is a considerable proportion with a potentially major impact on the physician's ability to interpret somatic symptoms and on the course and outcome of co-occurring medical disorders. It is for this very obvious reason that increased attention needs to be focused on the care of anxiety disorders in the primary care setting.

Association with Unexplained Physical Symptoms and/or Medical Illness

The prevalence of anxiety disorders rises even further when the population is narrowed beyond generic primary care patients to those with specific symptomatic complaints or medical illnesses. Studies have shown that many patients in primary care do not have a medical diagnosis; i.e., they have physical symptoms without an underlying physical explanation (Vázquez-Barquero et al., 1990). Approximately 40–50% of visits to primary care physicians are for 1 of 10 common physical symptoms; over a 1-year period only 10–15% of those patients are found to have a medical diagnosis that explains the physical symptoms (Kroenke & Mangelsdorff, 1989). Patients with unexplained medical symptoms, not surprisingly, have a higher rate of psychiatric illness than other primary care patients (Van Hemert et al., 1993). For example, Kroenke et al. (1994) showed that the presence of *any* physical symptom increases the likelihood of either a mood or anxiety disorder two- or threefold. If the symptoms had *no* physical explanation, the association was even stronger. As the number of physical symptoms rose, the probability of having a disorder increased so that, for example, the prevalence of anxiety disorder was 7% in patients with two or three unexplained physical symptoms but 48% in those with nine or more unexplained physical symptoms. The presence of physical symptoms, in general, increases the likelihood of anxiety disorders whether they are cardiac (Chignon et al., 1993; Klein et al. 1995), gastrointestinal (Walker et al., 1992), or otoneurologic (Drachman & Hart, 1982).

The rate of anxiety disorders is particularly high in specific subsets of patients with unexplained physical symptoms. Panic disorder is overrepresented in patient populations with chest pain and normal coronary arteries (40%—Katon et al., 1988), palpitations (45%—Barsky et al., 1994), unexplained syncope (20%—Linzer et al., 1992), irritable bowel syndrome (40%—Walker et al., 1990), unexplained vertigo and dizziness (20%—Stein et al., 1994), headache (27%—Marazziti et al., 1995), and labile hypertension tested for pheochromocytoma (40%—Fogarty et al., 1994). Generalized anxiety disorder (GAD) is also overrepresented in patients with normal coronary arteries (56%—Kane et al., 1988); with irritable bowel syndrome (11%— Walker et al., 1990; 26%—Lydiard et al., 1993), with headache (25%—Marazziti et al., 1995), with symptomatic hyperventilation (82%—de-Ruiter et al., 1989); and presenting to an emergency room and found not to have cardiac pathology (Wulsin et al., 1991). Among anxiety disorder patients, gastroenterologists are the medical specialists most often seen by patients with GAD, whereas otolaryngologists and neurologists are most often seen by patients with panic disorder (Kennedy & Schwab, 1997).

In addition to anxiety disorders providing an explanation for previously unexplained physical symptoms, anxiety can also coexist with bona fide medical illness and can alter its presentation, course, and treatment response. In these comorbid medical-psychiatric cases, anxiety may potentially represent a response to or effect of a medical illness, a factor that is aggravating the medical illness, or something totally separate. Again, much of the available data involves anxiety coexisting with cardiac, respiratory, gastrointestinal (GI), and otoneurologic illness, in which there is significant overlap with major clusters of autonomic-like anxiety symptoms. Some studies (Katon et al., 1986; Rogers et al., 1994) have suggested that there may be an increased rate of specific medical illnesses (migraine headache, hypertension, coronary artery disease, ulcer, thyroid disease, asthma) in certain patients with panic disorder.

The rate of panic disorder in cardiac patients is probably higher than that of the general population,

with studies documenting rates of 16% (Yinglin et al., 1993), 9% (Goldberg et al., 1990), and 23% (Katon et al., 1988). In one study, 60% of patients referred for an EKG had panic disorder, but these patients were equally likely to have abnormal or normal EKGs (Chignon et al., 1993). Hence, the presence of anxiety by no means rules out actual medical illness. Panic disorder can potentially worsen cardiac disease by provoking elevated heart rate, blood pressure, and smooth muscle constriction (Katon et al., 1990). In fact, longitudinal epidemiologic studies (Kawachi et al., 1994, 1995) show a clear-cut association of symptoms of phobic anxiety with sudden cardiac death, possibly due to decreased vagal tone and heart rate variability. Heart rate variability has been associated in prior studies with fatal ventricular arrhythmias. Interestingly, decreased vagal tone and heart rate variability are well known to occur in patients with panic disorder regardless of whether or not they have any cardiac problems (Yeragani et al., 1993; 1995). This decreased heart rate variability appears to be state-related as it was normalized in one study following effective anxiety treatment with the antidepressant paroxetine (Tucker et al., 1997). Another possible physiologic mediator of the anxiety–cardiac disease relationship is abnormal smooth muscle tone, which could well be CNS-mediated and cause dynamic coronary blood flow abnormalities that result in chest pain in both patients with panic disorder and those with chest pain and a normal angiogram (Roy-Byrne et al., 1989). A similar abnormality could contribute to an association between panic disorder and labile hypertension (Fogarty et al., 1994).

There also appears to be an increased rate of respiratory illness in patients with panic as well as increased anxiety disorders in patients with respiratory disorders. For example, studies have shown an increased prevalence of panic disorder in asthma, ranging from 6 to 24% (Carr et al., 1994; Perna et al., 1997; Shavitt et al., 1992), and in COPD (Karajgi et al., 1990; Smoller et al., 1996; Yellowlees et al., 1987), and an increased rate of panic attacks in patients referred for pulmonary testing (Pollack et al., 1996). Conversely, there appears to be an increased rate of lifetime respiratory illness in certain psychiatric disorders (Spinhoven et al., 1994), with panic disorder representing the highest proportion of these psychiatric patients (47%).

In patients with a childhood onset respiratory disease, a conditioning effect could be responsible for the development over time of progressive anxiety symptoms (Zandbergen et al., 1991). Many patients with asthma can have frightening near death episodes that provoke future anxiety with even mild symptoms. In fact, one study showed that 90% of patients with panic and asthma reported asthma attacks well before the onset of panic (Perna et al., 1997). Finally, the increased carbon dioxide sensitivity in panic disorder (Papp et al., 1997) has prompted researchers to speculate that the intermittent hypercapnea of COPD could sensitize some of these patients to develop panic disorder. Such interrelationships may be particularly prominent in later onset anxiety syndromes that develop in middle age in the context of medical illness and sudden physiological perturbation of the internal milieu. However, the occurrence of increased dynamic airways resistance in panic disorder without known respiratory disease (Perna et al., 1994) suggests the possibility of a psychophysiologic direction of cause and effect as well.

The association between functional GI symptoms and anxiety has been previously discussed. The decreased vagal tone often seen in anxiety disorder patients, as well as the generalized smooth muscle abnormality previously noted, may also exacerbate bona fide GI motility disturbances due, for example, to inflammatory bowel disease. Conversely, intermittent distension of intestine and colon in animals can increase the rate of central noradrenergic activity by increasing locus coeruleus firing rate (Svensson, 1987), which could in turn cause worsening anxiety. However, rates of anxiety disorder were not particularly elevated in patients with Crohn's disease or ulcerative colitis in two studies (Walker et al., 1990). However, patients taking steroids (and likely to be more severely ill) were not part of these studies, and other studies have shown greater anxiety symptoms in Crohn's patients (Addolorato et al., 1997).

Finally, there is an intriguing relationship between panic disorder and certain neurologic disturbances. In the otoneurologic area, studies have shown an increased rate of abnormality on vestibular testing in about 75% of panic patients (Jacob et al., 1985; Sklare et al., 1990). However, the particular findings did not conform to well-known patterns seen in familiar otologic disease entities, such as Ménière's disease

or vestibular neuronitis. There is also an increased rate of panic disorder in patients with actual vestibular disease (Spitzer et al., 1994), although the rate of panic in patients without known otologic disorder was significantly higher than in those with well-defined otoneurologic entity in one study (Sullivan et al., 1993). The association between anxiety and vestibular disturbance appears to be more prominent when there actually is evidence of vestibular dysfunction, even if it does not conform to familiar disease entities, in contrast to, for example, cardiac and GI symptoms. In addition to the increased rate of panic in headaches previously described, panic patients appear to have a particularly increased risk for migraine (Stewart et al., 1989) and are more likely to use medical services when they have migraines (Stewart et al., 1992). This has been documented in family studies in which panic patients' family members with panic appear to be at increased risk of migraine (Merikangas et al., 1990).

Association with Disability and High Medical Utilization

Studies have clearly demonstrated that anxious patients seen in general medical settings have significant disability. A recent study of patients with various medical disorders, focusing on anxious symptoms rather than disorders, showed that those with self-reported anxiety had a nearly fourfold greater length of disability than nonanxious respondents (18 vs. 4.8 bed days) (Marcus et al., 1997). Furthermore, after adjustment for differences in demographic characteristics and burden of general medical illness, anxiety was associated with an *additional* 3.8 bed days. Studies describing patients with discrete anxiety disorders have also shown similar disability. In the primary care setting, two studies (Katon, Hall et al., 1995; Sherbourne, Wells, et al., 1996) showed decrements in role and social functioning using the SF-36 comparable to that seen with major depression. Another study (Spitzer et al., 1995) found patients with anxiety disorders had a greater number of disability days than those with cardiac disorders, renal disorders, or diabetes. Studies focusing on more generalized symptoms of anxiety, or mixed anxiety and depression, have found similar disproportionate disability. In one study (Ormel et al., 1993), 40% of patients with sub-syndromal anxiety and 43% with subsyndromal mixed anxiety and depression had at least mild impairment in social role, while 30% and 57%, respectively, had at least mild impairment in occupational role. Another study (Fifer et al., 1994) using the SF-36 (Short Form Health Survey) showed that anxious patients compared with controls had lower functioning scores for both social functioning and role limitations due to physical illness. A third study (Roy-Byrne et al., 1994) focused on mixed anxiety and depression and showed that Global Assessment of Functioning scores were lower in these patients compared to controls. A final study (Olfson et al., 1996) focused on subthreshold anxiety symptoms (those not qualifying for a DSM diagnosis) and showed that patients with a variety of mood and anxiety subthreshold symptoms had greater disability, although after adjusting for the confounding effects of other Axis I disorders, other subthreshold symptoms, and demographic and physical factors, only panic symptoms were specifically associated with impairment. Nonetheless, this particular study does show the powerful effect that panic symptoms have on disability.

The association of anxiety disorders with unexplained somatic symptoms indirectly suggests that anxious patients are likely to overutilize medical services. However, several studies have addressed this issue more directly. Compared to patients with depression, patients with panic disorder are one and a half to four times as likely to have at least six visits to the general medical services (Simon, 1992). U.S. Department of Labor statistics (1985) show that in the community, patients with panic disorder use primary care services at a rate three times that of most other patients, and a similar figure was found for a proportion of patients seeking health care service, compared with the general population in the ECA study (Klerman et al., 1991). A study specifically focused on distressed high utilizers of medical services at a large HMO (Katon et al., 1990) showed that 22% of these individuals had panic disorder, while 40% had GAD. Another British study showed patients with panic remained undiagnosed for an average of 10 years, during which time they had an ever increasing rate of use of all types of services including doctor visits, ER units, hospital services, and diagnostic procedures (Simpson et al., 1994). Our recent study (Roy-Byrne

et al., in press) showed that patients with panic disorder in primary care, compared to the same primary care patients without a psychiatric diagnosis, had higher rates of doctor and ER visits, although not hospital days.

BARRIERS TO DIAGNOSIS AND TREATMENT

Poor Recognition of Anxiety

A prerequisite for effective treatment of any problem is efficient recognition, although recognition by itself does not guarantee that treatment will be adequate. Mental disorders are poorly recognized by primary care physicians (Pérez-Stable et al., 1990; Thompson et al., 1983), particularly when accompanied by unexplained somatic symptoms (Bridges & Goldberg, 1985; Kirmayer et al., 1993). While the prominence of anxiety symptoms might suggest that anxiety would be easier to recognize, or harder to ignore, than depression, Ormel et al. (1993) showed that physicians are much better at recognizing depression than anxiety, and that recognition of "borderline" anxiety was even worse, with only one in five of these cases being recognized. Because panic attacks so closely mimic medical disorders requiring immediate treatment, primary care physicians are often distracted by the concern that they will fail to recognize medical conditions requiring acute intervention. In one study a majority of 57 panic disorder patients saw an average of 10 physicians before finally being diagnosed (Sheehan, 1982). This is consistent with high rates of physician nonrecognition of panic disorder in other studies (61% in primary care—Spitzer et al., 1994; 98% in ER patients with chest pain—Fleet et al., 1996; 80% in general medical patients referred for psychiatric evaluation—Cowley & Roy-Byrne, unpublished). One study (Fifer et al., 1994) reported high rates of nonrecognition for the entire cluster of anxiety symptoms, regardless of the ultimate diagnosis, showing that only 44% of patients with clinically significant anxiety symptoms were recognized. Another study using a 1987 national hospital discharge survey data base for medical/surgical inpatients with principal medical diagnoses reported rates of anxiety disorder far lower than predicted by surveys of community-dwelling individuals or by anxiety symptoms screens among medical inpatients, whereas rates reported for mood disorder or substance use disorder are much more concordant with community and other estimates (Fulop, 1990). This suggests the possibility of physician rationalization that anxiety is an expected part of an acute medical hospital stay.

Reasons for Nonrecognition of Anxiety

Barriers to effective recognition of anxiety disorders in the medical setting can be divided into (1) patient-related barriers, (2) physician-related barriers, and (3) system/process of care barriers.

1. *Patient barriers* include the stigma of mental illness, which enhances the tendency of some patients to express psychiatric distress in an idiom of physical complaints (i.e., somatization); a lack of patient knowledge about the mind–body connection; and the natural tendency of patients, particularly in primary care, to present with mixed symptoms that may not be classic representations of well-described mood or anxiety disorders (Katon & Roy-Byrne, 1991). A further factor, not unique to the medical setting per se, is the presentation of anxiety by patients from different cultural backgrounds in a somewhat different manner (e.g., ataque de nervios—see Liebowitz et al., 1994).

2. *Physician barriers* include the well-known Cartesian dualism shared by Western individuals, which promotes a tendency to look for physical causes of somatic symptoms. Another physician barrier is that panic patients often present with cardiologic symptoms and signs (e.g., labile hypertension, tachycardia, ectopic beats), and the current U.S. medical legal atmosphere leads to overemphasis on not missing an MI or other cardiac disorders (paroxysmal atrial tachycardia, pheochromocytoma). In addition, anxious patients may be particularly difficult or frustrating for primary care physicians, provoking physician avoidance or aversion. For example, panic disorder was the most common diagnosis in patients seen by their physicians as "difficult" (Hahn et al., 1996), while another study showed that GAD was overrepresented in a sample of "frustrating" patients (Lin et al., 1991). This adversely impacts recognition; a

recent study showed that a negative attitude toward the patient is associated with inaccurate diagnosis (Giron et al., 1998). While there is also a clear-cut lack of knowledge about psychiatric disorders in general, it is currently thought that physician knowledge about depression is far greater than about anxiety (Wilson et al., 1997). It is of interest that both older and female physicians are more likely to make correct diagnoses (Ford, 1994). This finding may possibly be related to another study (Robbins et al., 1994) which indicated that physicians who are more sensitive to nonverbal expressions of emotion are more accurate diagnostically.

3. *System and process of medical care barriers* are perhaps most prominent in contributing to poor diagnosis and recognition, although their effect on treatment is proportionately much greater (see next section). There is, quite simply, a lack of adequate time for primary care physicians to assess psychiatric issues. Health care "reform" has further decreased the diverse primary care visit from 10 to 15 minutes to 7 to 10 minutes! This has never been more evident than in the difficulty primary care physicians have had in using primary care–based diagnostic systems such as the PRIME MD (Spitzer et al., 1994), even though these systems take at most 10 minutes to complete. Faced with many new disease guidelines and similar requests from other medical specialists to perform brief screenings for myriad other medical disorders, primary care physicians are overwhelmed and unable to accommodate everyone. Because of the focus on episodic acute care, there is a lack of close follow-up of patients in the primary care setting. This prevents physicians from evaluating patients longitudinally and better appreciating the constellation of their symptoms. Some authors have suggested that use of very simple one-question screens could help primary care physicians improve recognition. We recently tested such a screening instrument, adapted from one used originally by Katon, Hollifield et al. (1995), and found that it detected virtually all cases of panic ultimately identical by structured (CIDI) interview, although only about one-third of screen positive patients actually had panic disorder (Stein et al., in press). Use of this or a similar screener would be a necessary first step in improving outcome of anxiety in primary care, although recent reviews have clearly

shown that improved recognition alone is inadequate for improving outcome in primary care patients with mental disorders (Higgins, 1994).

Inadequate Treatment of Anxiety

A number of studies have shown that even when anxiety disorders are recognized, they are inadequately treated. For example, feedback given to the primary care physicians in the Fifer et al. (1994) study did not affect patient outcomes (Mathias et al., 1994; Yelin et al., 1996). Even in psychiatric specialty settings, effective treatments for anxiety disorders continue to be underutilized. In Katon et al.'s (1990) high utilizer study, the outcomes of patients (40% of whom had panic or GAD) did not improve despite giving physicians feedback about diagnosis *and* specific medication treatment algorithms. The review previously cited (Higgins, 1994) also concluded that recognition does little to improve patient outcome, probably because it does not guarantee that patients receive and adhere to appropriate treatment.

There is little data on utilization of anti-anxiety treatment in primary care. The one available study (Meredith et al., 1997) shows that minor tranquilizers were used more often (10–30%) than antidepressants (5–20%) for patients with either panic, GAD, or phobia. Psychotherapy was also relatively underutilized (20–35%). Recent data from our clinics also show a very low rate of use of medications or psychotherapy and an even lower rate of "adequate" treatment (correct medication and dose, or correct type of therapy, e.g., cognitive-behavioral, [Roy-Byrne et al., in press]). Even when treated, patients with panic disorder and depression, compared to patients with depression alone, more often terminate treatment prematurely and respond more poorly to both antidepressants and psychotherapy (Brown et al., 1996).

Reasons for Inadequate Treatment of Anxiety

The physician and patient factors that prevent effective recognition also operate to make treatment more difficult. However, system/process of care issues impact the likelihood of effective treatment far more powerfully than they do recognition. The factor of limited time is perhaps most important. Physicians quite simply do not have adequate time to explain to patients what is wrong with them, particularly when it involves a mental disorder presenting with somatic or physical symptoms. And yet, anxious patients have a profound need to understand what is wrong, as much of their symptomatology is aggravated by catastrophic thinking and hypochondriacal fears. In this regard, it is no accident that cognitive-behavioral therapy (CBT), with its very high patient educational content, is extremely well accepted by primary care anxiety patients (Sharp et al., 1997). In sum, an explanatory model needs to be presented that will not be overly focused on either mind or body, but will integrate both.

The importance and effectiveness of treatment need to be highlighted, and in the case of medication, the importance of adherence to treatment even after symptoms have improved needs to be repeatedly emphasized. However, the orientation toward acute care and treatment in most primary care medical settings means that the treatment of what are more chronic anxiety disorders is doomed to fail. For example, telling a patient following a diagnosis of panic, "Try this medication (50mg Zoloft) and come back in 1 month" without adequate explanation of the disorder often leads to poor adherence and loss of follow-up. An infectious disease model is usually followed in the evaluation and treatment of many patients (i.e., the problem is time-limited and will go away quickly with some simple medical intervention), guaranteeing that most patients with anxiety disorders, which tend to be more chronic, relapsing, and remitting, will suffer greatly.

The separate and distinct systems of care for medical versus mental disorders also makes treatment difficult. These systems of care mirror clear-cut differences in insurance benefits, with mental disorders systematically discriminated against and not receiving the same parity of coverage as medical disorders (Sharfstein et al., 1993). In the past few years, mental health benefits have been even more proportionately reduced (by over 50%) relative to medical illness benefits (6%) (Mental Health Report, 1998). This structural factor has a major effect on treatment. Primary care physicians clearly recognize the issue and try to circumvent it, often substituting medical for mental health diagnostic codes (Rost et al., 1994) and in effect "secretly" treating depression or anxiety by calling it something else. This "solution" may actually backfire, however, by perpetuating rather than challenging the current system.

PROPOSED SOLUTIONS

Health care outcomes are a direct effect of the interaction between the patient, the provider, and the health care process. These three variables ultimately influence the way medical illness is managed, and all strategies designed to improve patient care (so-called disease management) work by influencing them. The acute care orientation of most medical management of disease (e.g., management of acute symptoms during an office visit) has unfortunately been associated with poor outcome for chronic diseases with relapsing and remitting courses, such as anxiety disorder. Wagner et al. (1996) have described a need for more planned, organized, and ongoing care to improve treatment of chronic illness. More importantly, in chronic illness, day-to-day responsibility for disease management focuses more heavily on the patient, whose "self-management" must effectively incorporate adherence to the physician's and care process's "medical management" (VonKorff et al., 1997). This kind of disease management strategy, which of necessity would use physician extenders and provide more education for the patient, more contact with the patient, and more opportunity to self-manage, may explain the high placebo response rate reported in anxious patients. Although they are given no active medication, their disorder is diagnosed and explained, they come for multiple visits, and they fill out rating scales that enhance their ability to self-monitor. In fact, disorders with the highest placebo response rates (anxiety and milder depressions) are probably most amenable to disease management strategies.

Collaborative Care

Interventions that strengthen and support self-management by promoting physician–patient collaboration (i.e., collaborative care) have been used to improve outcome in cancer (Andersen, 1992), diabetes (Glasgow et al., 1989), arthritis (Lorig & Holman, 1993), and asthma (Clark et al., 1994).

These interventions have been developed based on social learning and self-regulation theories (Von-Korff et al., 1997). Contemporary social learning theory emphasizes that behavior is a product of cognitive processes and their interaction with the social and physical environment (Bandura, 1982) and highlights the importance of belief in one's own ability to produce a desired outcome (Tobin et al., 1986). Key principles are that (1) illness management skills are learned, (2) self-confidence (efficacy) will enhance these skills, (3) the social environment (e.g., health care environment) will enhance or impede self-management, and (4) the physician must be diligent in monitoring and responding to changes in illness (Von Korff et al., 1997). Bandura's theory has been expanded (Thoresen & Kirmil-Gray, 1983) to include a fourth physiologic (i.e., disease) dimension in addition to the cognitive, behavioral skill, and social environment dimensions, to acknowledge the important role of biological perturbations and medical treatment by the physician.

Collaborative care interventions focus on three areas: patient education, expert systems, and process planning:

1. *Patient education and activation:* Using the cognitive dimension to combat the traditional patient role as a passive recipient of care who may abandon care due to side effects, bewilderment, or demoralization, patients need to be activated to collaborate more in their care, to build self-efficacy, and to manage the impact of symptoms on life roles. Videotapes, pamphlets, and other educational programs can help to accomplish this. While these things are important, they are quite ineffective when used alone.

2. *Development and implementation of expert systems:* A disease-based focus will ensure that the physician's medication management is evidence-based by focusing not on only the provision of guidelines, but also on their successful implementation. Recent studies of the treatment of hypertension (Winikoff et al., 1985), diabetes (Weinberger et al., 1995), and hypercholestrolemia (Headrick et al., 1992), as well as a meta-analysis of 102 trials to improve physician practice (Oxman et al., 1995), suggest that on-site, case-by-case feedback given to the primary care provider by those with specialized knowledge

(medical specialists and physician extenders and proxies) may be the most effective form of provider education (i.e., improves knowledge and outcome), is superior to routine CME courses, and will facilitate rapid and timely specialty consultation when needed.

3. *Process of care:* The health care environment must provide advanced planning of more extended care, using physician extender visits and phone contacts to augment physician office visits. During visits, prevention of illness, education, psychosocial support, side-effect and outcome assessment, and active and sustained follow-up are emphasized. Again, studies in cancer, hypertension, diabetes, and depression (Katon, Kroff et al., 1995) show that these kinds of interventions are more successful in improving patient outcome than strategies designed to singularly affect provider behavior. This feedback will improve physicians' recognition of anxiety disorder, and by teaching them about its symptoms and side-effect experiences with medication, will enable physicians to more effectively resume long-term care of patients with this chronic, relapsing illness. In fact, a recent study (Lin et al., 1997) suggested that this "reorganization of service delivery" was the most important factor in promoting good outcomes for depressed patients, since physician education alone did nothing of a lasting nature.

Collaborative care strategies are supported not only by self-management theory, but also by two recent studies which have shown that the integration of mental health services into the primary care setting results in improved patient outcomes for patients with major depression (Katon, Korff, et al., 1995). An initial study shows that collaborative care with a psychiatrist and primary care physician meeting alternately for several sessions with the patient and improved patient education via videotapes and pamphlets resulted in improved patient adherence to antidepressant medication and higher patient and provider satisfaction with care and depression outcome, compared with care as usual (Katon, Hollifield, et al., 1995). A second study demonstrated that the use of a behavioral health specialist delivering brief CBT for four to six sessions and relaying the psychiatrist's suggestions about drug therapy to the primary care physician (based on weekly psychiatric reviews of

patient progress with the behavioral health specialist) resulted in improved patient outcome (Katon, Korff, et al., 1995). Both of these studies showed an improvement in cost-effectiveness (measured as improved outcome per unit cost) and incremental cost-effectiveness (cost of intervention minus cost of usual care divided by the effect of intervention minus the effect of usual care) for patients with major depression, although neither was able to demonstrate an absolute cost-offset effect (VonKorff et al., 1998). However, indirect costs, such as work absenteeism and lost work productivity and family burden, which are important costs to the employer and family, were not included in this analysis.

Multimodal Care

The theoretical considerations and recent depression studies discussed here strongly support the heuristic value of multimodal treatment intervention, particularly for persistent and relapsing disorders with disabling cognitive and behavioral aspects, such as anxiety. The value-added potential of CBT techniques is quite important. Cognitive-behavioral therapy contains many traditionally utilized self-management elements, such as techniques to enhance patient self-efficacy and allow self-corrective checks on progress, and an emphasis on health-promoting activities patients carry out on their own, which promote maintenance of initial acute treatment gains. Inclusion of a medication treatment component is also desirable, as medication is the main treatment in primary care and is necessary to maintain and potentiate the physician's role as a primary care provider. Physicians will continue to provide medication to many anxious patients, and it is best if they are helped to do this appropriately and effectively.

CONCLUSION

Anxiety disorders are among the most prevalent psychiatric disorders in the community and primary care settings and are associated with high medical utilization and costs; unexplained medical symptoms and hypochondriacal worry; significant impairment in familial, social, and work roles (indirect costs); and a good deal of patient suffering. Unfortunately, disorders are often not accurately diagnosed, and even when diagnosed correctly, few patients receive guide-line-level treatments. Disease management methods that integrate mental health professionals into primary care and improve patient education have been shown to improve primary care treatment and outcome of depression. Research based on these methods needs to be tested to improve the care and outcomes of anxiety disorders.

REFERENCES

Addolorato, G., Capristo, E., Stefanini, G., & Gasbarrini, G. (1997). Inflammatory bowel disease: A study of the association between anxiety and depression, physical morbidity, and nutritional state. *Scandinavian Journal of Gastroenterology, 32*(10), 1013–1021.

Andersen, B. (1992). Psychological interventions for cancer patients to enhance the quality of life. Special issue: Behavioral medicine: An update for the 1990's. *Journal of Consulting and Clinical Psychology, 60,* 552–568.

Bandura, A. (1982). Self-efficacy mechanism in human agency. *American Psychologist, 37,* 122–147.

Barsky, A., Cleary, P., Coeytaux, R., & Ruskin, J. (1994). Psychiatric disorders in medical outpatients complaining of palpitations. *Journal of General Internal Medicine, 9*(6), 306–1313.

Bridges, K., & Goldberg, D. (1985). Somatic presentation of DSM-III psychiatric disorders in primary care. *Journal Psychosomatic Research, 29,* 563–569.

Brown, C., Schulberg, H., Madonia, M., Shear, M., & Houck, P. R. (1996). PANIC: Treatment outcomes for primary care patients with major depression and lifetime anxiety disorders. *American Journal of Psychiatry, 153,* 1293–1300.

Carr, R., Lehrer, P., Rausch, L., & Hochron, S. (1994). Anxiety sensitivity and panic attacks in an asthmatic population. *Behavior Research and Therapy, 32,* 411–418.

Chignon, J., Lepine, J., & Ades, J. (1993). Panic disorder in cardiac outpatients. *American Journal of Psychiatry, 150,* 780–785.

Clark, N., Evans, D., Zimmerman, B., Levison, J., & Mellins, R. (1994). Patient and family management of asthma: Theory based techniques for the clinician. *Journal of Asthma, 31,* 427–435.

Cowley, D. S., & Roy-Byrne, P. (unpublished). Reasons for psychiatric referral in distressed primary care patients.

de-Ruiter, C., Garssen, B., Rijken, H., Kraaimaat, F. (1989). The hyperventilation syndrome in panic disorder, agoraphobia and generalized anxiety disorder. *Behavior Research Therapy, 27,* 447–452.

Drachman, D., & Hart, C. (1982). An approach to the dizzy patients. *Neurology, 22,* 323–330.

Fifer, S., Mathias, S., Patrick, D., Mazonson, P., Lubeck, D., & Buesching, D. (1994) Untreated anxiety among adult primary care patients in a health maintenance organization. *Archives of General Psychiatry, 51,* 740–750.

Fleet, R. P., Dupuis, G., Marchand, A., Burelle, D., Arsenault, A., & Beitman, B. D. (1996). Panic disorder in emergency department chest pain patients: Prevalence, comorbidity, suicidal ideation, and physician recognition. *American Journal of Medicine, 101,* 371–378.

Fogarty, C. E., Jr., Russo, J., Simon, G., & Katon, W. (1994). Hypertension and pheochromocytoma testing: The association with anxiety disorders. *Archives of Family Medicine, 3,* 55–60.

Ford, D. (1994). Recognition and under-recognition of mental disorders in adult primary care. In J. Miranda, A. Hohmann, C. Attkisson, & D. Larson (Eds.), *Mental Disorders in Primary Care* (pp. 186–205). San Francisco: Jossey-Bass.

Fulop, G. (1990). Anxiety disorders in the general hospital setting. *Psychiatric Medicine, 8*(3), 187–195.

Giron, M., Manjon-Arce, P., Pueato-Barber, J., Sanchez-Garcia, E., Gomez-Beneyo, M. (1998). Clinical interview skills and identification of emotional disorders in primary care. *American Journal of Psychiatry, 155,* 530–535.

Glasgow, R., Toobert, D., Riddle, M., Donnelly, J., Mitchell, D. L., & Calder. (1989). Diabetes-specific social learning variables and self-care behaviors among persons with Type II diabetes. *Health Psychology, 8,* 285–303.

Goldberg, R., Morris, P., Christian, F., Badger, J., Chabot, S., & Edlund, M. (1990). Panic disorder in cardiac outpatients. *Psychosomatics, 31,* 168–173.

Hahn, S., Kroenke, K., Spitzer, R., Brody, D., Williams, J., Linzer, M., & de Gruy, F. V., III. (1996). The difficult patient: Prevalence, psychopathology, and functional impairment. *Journal of General Internal Medicine, 11,* 1–8.

Headrick, L., Speroff, T., Pelecanos, H., & Cebul, R. (1992). Efforts to improve compliance with the National Cholesterol Education Program guidelines. Results of a randomized controlled trial. *Archives of Internal Medicine, 152,* 2490–2496.

Higgins, E. (1994). A review of unrecognized mental illness in primary care: Prevalence, natural history, and efforts to change the course [see comments]. *Archives of Family Medicine, 3*(10), 908–917.

Jacob, R., Moller, M., Turner, S., & Wall, C. I. (1985). Otoneurological examination of panic disorder and agoraphobia with panic attacks: A pilot study. *American Journal of Psychiatry, 142,* 715–720.

Kane, F. J., Harper, R., & Wittels, E. (1988). Angina as a symptom of psychiatric illness. *Southern Medical Journal, 81,* 1412–1416.

Karajgi, B., Rifkin, A., Doddi, S., & Kolli, R. (1990). The prevalence of anxiety disorders in patients with chronic obstructive pulmonary disease. *American Journal of Psychiatry, 147,* 200–201.

Katon, W., Hall, M., Russo, J., Cormier, L., Hollifield, M., Vitaliano, P., & Beitman, B. (1988). Chest pain: Relationship of psychiatric illness to coronary arteriographic results. *American Journal of Medicine, 84,* 1–9.

Katon, W., Hollifield, M., Chapman, T., Mannuzza, S., Ballenger, J., & Fyer, A. (1995). Infrequent panic attacks: Psychiatric comorbidity, personality characteristics and functional disability. *Journal of Psychiatric Research, 29*(2), 121–131.

Katon, W., Korff, M. V., Lin, E., Lipscomb, P., Russo, J., Wagner, E., & Polk, E. (1990). Distressed high utilizers of medical care. DSM III R diagnoses and treatment needs. *General Hospital Psychiatry, 12,* 355–362.

Katon, W., Korff, M. V., Lin, E., Walker, E., Simon, G., Bush, T. R., Robinson, P., & Russo, J. (1995). Collaborative management to achieve treatment guidelines. *JAMA, 273,* 1026–1031.

Katon, W., & Roy-Byrne, P. (1991). Mixed anxiety and depression. *Journal of Abnormal Psychology, 100,* 337–345.

Katon, W., Vitaliano, P., Russo, J., Cormier, L., Anderson, K., & Jones, M. (1986). Panic disorder: Epidemiology in primary care. *Journal of Family Practitioners, 23,* 233–239.

Kawachi, I., Sparrow, D., Vokonas, P., & Weiss, S. (1994). Symptoms of anxiety and risk of coronary heart disease: The Normative Aging Study. *Circulation, 90,* 2225–2229.

Kawachi, I., Sparrow, D., Vokonas, P., & Weiss, S. (1995). Decreased heart rate variability in men with phobic anxiety (data from the Normative Aging Study). *American Journal of Cardiology, 75,* 882–885.

Kennedy, B., & Schwab J. (1997). Utilization of medical specialists by anxiety disorder patients. *Psychosomatics, 38,* 109–112.

Kessler, R., McGonagle, K., Zhao, S., Nelson, C., Hughes, M., Eshleman, S., Wittchen, H. U., & Kendler, K. (1994). Lifetime and 12-month prevalence of DSM-III-R psychiatric disorders in the United States. Results from the National Comorbidity Study. *Archives of General Psychiatry, 51,* 8–19.

Kessler, R., Olfson, M., & Berglund, P. (1998). Patterns and predictors of treatment contact after first onset of psychiatric disorders. *American Journal of Psychiatry, 155,* 62–69.

Kirmayer, L., Robbins, J., Dworkind, M., & Yaffe, M. (1993). Somatization and the recognition of depression and anxiety in primary care. *American Journal of Psychiatry, 150,* 734–741.

Klein, E., Lin, S., Colin, V., Lang, R., & Lenox, R. (1995). Anxiety disorders among patients in a general emergency service in Israel. *Psychiatry Services, 46,* 488–492.

Klerman, G., Wissman, M., Quellette, R., Johnson, J., & Greenwald, S. (1991). Panic attacks in the community: Social morbidity and health care utilization. *JAMA, 265,* 742–746.

Kroenke, K., & Mangelsdorff, A. (1989). Common symptoms in ambulatory care: Incidence, evaluation, therapy, and outcome. *American Journal of Medicine, 86,* 262–266.

Kroenke, K., Spitzer, R. L., Williams, J. B. W., Linzer, M., Hahn, S. R., de Gruy, F. V., III, & Brody, D. (1994). Physical symptoms in primary care: Predictors of psychiatric disorders and functional impairment. *Archives of Family Medicine, 3,* 774–779.

Leon, A., Olfson, M., Broadhead, W., Barrett, J., Blacklow, R., Keller, M. Higgins, E., & Weissman, M. (1995). Prevalence of mental disorders in primary care: Implications for screening. *Archives of Family Medicine, 4,* 857–861.

Liebowitz, M., Salmán, E., Jusino, C., Garfinkel, R., Street, Cárdenas D., Silvestre, J., Fyer, A., Carrasco, J., Davies, S., Guarnaccia, P., & Kleind, F. (1994). Ataque de nervios and panic disorder. *American Journal of Psychiatry, 151*(6), 871–875.

Lin, E., Katon, W., Korff, M. V., Bush, T., Lipscomb, P., Russo, J., & Wagner, E. (1991). Frustrating patients: Physician and patient perspectives among distressed high users of medical services. *Journal of General Internal Medicine, 6,* 241–246.

Lin, E., Katon, W., Simon, G., Korff, M. V., Bush, T., Rutter, C., Saunders, K., & Walker, E. (1997). Achieving guidelines for the treatment of depression in primary care: Is physician education enough? *Medical Care, 35,* 831–842.

Linzer, M., Divine, G., & Estes, N. (1992). Medically unexplained syncope: Relationship to psychiatric illness. *American Journal of Medicine, 92*(suppl 1A), 18S–25S.

Lorig, K., & Holman, H. (1993). Arthritis self-management studies: A twelve-year review. *Health Education Quarterly, 20,* 17–28.

Lydiard, R., Fossey, M., Marsh, W., & Ballenger, J. C. (1993). Prevalence of psychiatric disorder patients with irritable bowel syndrome. *Psychosomatics, 34,* 229–234.

Marazziti, D., Toni, C., Pedri, S., Bonuccelli, U., Pavese, A., Muratorio, A., Cassano, G. B., & Adiskal, H. (1995). Headache, panic disorder, and depression: Comorbidity or a spectrum? *Neuropsychobiology, 31,* 125–129.

Marcus, S., Olfson, M., Pincus, H., Shear, M., & Zarin, D. (1997). Self-reported anxiety, general medical conditions, and disability bed days. *American Journal of Psychiatry, 154,* 1766–1768.

Mathias, S., Fifer, S., Mazonson, P., Lubeck, D., Buesching, D., & Patrick, D. (1994). Necessary but not sufficient: The effect of screening and feedback on outcomes of primary care patients with untreated anxiety. *Journal of General Internal Medicine, 9,* 606–615.

Mental Health Report. (1998). New study finds steep decline in mental health care coverage. Business Publishers Inc., Silver Springs, MD, *22,* 77.

Meredith, L., Sherbourne, C., Jackson, C., Camp, P., & Wells, K. (1997). Treatment typically provided for comorbid anxiety disorder. *Archives of Family Medicine, 6,* 231–237.

Merikangas, K., Angst, J., & Isler, H. (1990). Migraine and psychopathology: Results of the Zurich cohort study of young adults. *Archives of Psychiatry, 47,* 849–853.

Olfson, M., Broadhead, W., Weissman, M., Leon, A., Farber, L., Hoven, C., & Kathol, R. (1996). Subthreshold psychiatric symptoms in a primary care group practice. *Archives of General Psychiatry, 53,* 880–886.

Orleans, C., George, L., & Houpt, J. (1985). How primary physicians treat psychiatric disorders: A national survey of family practitioners. *Archives of General Psychiatry, 42,* 52–57.

Ormel, J., Oldehinkel, T., Brilman, E., & Vandenbrink, W. (1993). Outcome of depression and anxiety in primary care: A three-wave $3\frac{1}{2}$ year study of psychopathology and disability. *Archives of General Psychiatry, 50,* 759–766.

Oxman, A., Thomson, M., Davis, D., & Haynes, R. (1995). No magic bullets: A systematic review of 102 trials of interventions to improve professional practice. *Canadian Medical Association Journal, 153,* 1423–1431.

Papp, L., Martinez, J., Klein, D., Coplan, J., Norman, R., Cole, R., de-Jesus, J., Ross, D., Goetz, R., & Gorma, J. (1997). Respiratory psychophysiology of panic disorder: Three respiratory challenges in 98 subjects. *American Journal of Psychiatry, 154,* 1557–1565.

Pérez-Stable, E., Miranda, J., Munoz, R., & Ying, Y. (1990). Depression in medical outpatients: Under recognition and misdiagnosis [see comments]. *Archives of Internal Medicine, 150,* 1083–1088.

Perna, G., Bertani, A., Politi, E., Columbo, G., & Bellodi, L. (1997). Asthma and panic attacks. *Biological Psychiatry, 42,* 625–630.

Perna, G., Marconi, C., Battaglia, M., Bertani, A., Panzacchi, A., & Bellodi, L. (1994). Subclinical impairment of lung airways in patients with panic disorder. *Biological Psychiatry, 36,* 601–605.

Pollack, M., Kradin, R., Otto, M., Worthington, J., Gould, R., Sabatino, S., & Rosenbaum, J. (1996). Prevalence of panic in patients referred for pulmonary function testing at a major medical center. *American Journal of Psychiatry, 153,* 110–113.

Regier, D., Narrow, W., Rae, D., Manderscheid, R., Locke, B., & Goodwin, F. (1993). The defacto US mental and addictive disorders service system. *Archives of General Psychiatry, 50,* 85–94.

Robbins, J., Kirmayer, L., Cathébras, P., Yaffe, M., & Dworkind, M. (1994). Physician characteristics and the recognition of depression and anxiety in primary care. *Medical Care, 32,* 795–812.

Rogers, M., White, K., Warshaw, M., Yonkers, K., Rodriguez-Villa, F., Chang, G., & Keller, M. (1994). Prevalence of medical illness in patients with anxiety disorders. *International Journal of Psychiatry in Medicine, 24,* 83–96.

Rost, K., Smith, G., Matthews, D., & Guise, B. (1994). The deliberate misdiagnosis of major depression in primary care. *Archives of Family Medicine, 3,* 333–337.

Roy-Byrne, P., Katon, W., Broadhead, W., Lepine, J., Richards, J., Brantley, P., Russo, J., Zinbarg, R., Barlow, D., & Liebowitz, M. (1994). Subsyndromal ("mixed") anxiety depression in primary care [see comments]. *Journal of General Internal Medicine, 9,* 507–512.

Roy-Byrne, P., Schmidt, P., Cannon, R., Diem, H., & Rubinow, D. (1989). Microvascular angina and panic disorder. *International Journal of Psychiatry in Medicine, 19,* 315–325.

Roy-Byrne, P., Stein, M., Russo, J., Mercier, E., Thomas, R., McQuaid, J., Katon, W., Craske, M., Bystrisky, S., & Sherbourne, C. (1999). Panic disorder in the primary care setting: Comorbidity, disability, service utilization, and treatment. *Journal Clinical Psychiatry, 60,* 492–499.

Sartorius, N., Ustun, T., Lecrubier, Y., & Wittchen, H. (1996). Depression comorbid with anxiety: Results from the WHO study on Psychological Disorders in Primary Health Care. *British Journal of Psychiatry, 168* (suppl 30), 38–43.

Sharfstein, S., Stoline, A., & Goldman, H. (1993). Psychiatric care and health insurance reform. *American Journal of Psychiatry, 150,* 7–18.

Sharp, D., Power, K., Simpson, R., Swanson, V., & Anstee, J. (1997). Global measures of outcome in a controlled comparison of pharmacological and psychological treatment of panic disorder and agoraphobia in primary care. *British Journal of General Practice, 47,* 136–137.

Shavitt, R., Gentil, B., & Mandetta, R. (1992). The association of panic/agoraphobia and asthma: Contributing factors and clinical implications. *General Hospital Psychiatry, 14,* 420–423.

Sheehan, D. (1982). Current concepts in psychiatry: Panic attacks and phobias. *New England Journal of Medicine, 307*(3), 156–158.

Sherbourne, C., Jackson, C., Meredith, L., Camp, P., & Wells, K. (1996). Prevalence of comorbid anxiety disorders in primary care outpatients. *Archives of Family Medicine, 5,* 27–34.

Sherbourne, C., Wells, K., & Judd, L. (1996). Functioning and well being of patients with panic disorder. *American Journal of Psychiatry, 153*(2), 213–218.

Simon, G. (1992). Psychiatric disorder and functional somatic symptoms as predictors of health care use. *Psychiatric Medicine, 10*(3), 49–59.

Simpson, R., Kazmierczak, T., Power, K., & Sharp, D. M. (1994). Controlled comparison of patients with panic disorder. *British Journal of General Practitioners,* 352–356.

Sklare, D., Stein, M., Pikus, A., Uhde, T. (1990). Dysequilibrium and audiovestibular function in panic disorder: Symptom profiles and test findings. *American Journal of Otolaryngology, 11,* 338–341.

Smoller, J., Pollack, M., Otto, M., Rosenbaum, J., & Kradin, R. (1996). Panic, anxiety, dyspnea, and respiratory disease: Theoretical and clinical considerations. *American Journal of Respiratory Critical Care Medicine, 154,* 6–17.

Spinhoven, P., Ros, M., Westgeest, A., & Does, A. V. (1994). The prevalence of respiratory disorders in panic disorder, major depressive disorder and V-code patients. *Behavior Research and Therapy, 32,* 647–649.

Spitzer, R., Kroenke, K., Linzer, M., Hahn, S., Williams, J., deGruy, F. R., III, Brody, D., & Davies, M. (1995). Health related quality of life in primary care patients with mental disorders: Results from the PRIME MD 1000 Study [see comments]. *JAMA, 274*(19), 1511–1517.

Spitzer, R., Williams, J., Kroenke, K., Linzer, M., deGruy, F. R., III, Hahn, S., Brody, D., & Johnson, J. (1994). Utility of a new procedure for diagnosing mental disorders in primary care: The PRIME MD 1000 study [see comments]. *JAMA, 272*(22), 1749–1756.

Stein, M., Asmundson, G., Ireland, D., & Walker, J. (1994). Panic disorder in patients attending a clinic for vestibular disorders. *American Journal of Psychiatry, 151,* 1697–1700.

Stein, M., Roy-Byrne, P., McQuaid, J., Laffoy, C., Russo, J., McCabill, M., Katon, W., Craske, M., Bystrisky, A., & Sherbourne, C. (in press). Development of a brief diagnostic screen for panic disorder in primary care.

Stewart, W., Linet, M., & Cenentano, D. (1989). Migraine headaches and panic attacks. *Psychosomatic Medicine, 51,* 559–569.

Stewart, W., Shechter, A., & Liberman, J. (1992). Physician consultation for headache pain and history of pain results from a population-based study. *American Journal of Medicine, 92* (suppl 1a), 355–405.

Sullivan, M., Clark, M., Katon, W., Fishchl, M., Russo, J., Dobie, R., & Voorhees, R. (1993). Psychiatric and otologic diagnoses in patients complaining of dizziness. *Archives of Internal Medicine, 153,* 1479–1484.

Svensson, T. (1987). Peripheral, autonomic regulation of locus coeruleus noradrenergic neurons in brain: Putative implications for psychiatry and psychopharmacology. *Psychopharmacology 92,* 1–7.

Thompson, T., Stoudemire, A., Mitchell, W., & Grant, R. (1983). Under recognition of patients' psychosocial distress in a university hospital medical clinic. *American Journal of Psychiatry, 140,* 158–161.

Thoresen, C., & Kirmil-Gray, K. (1983). Self-management psychology and the treatment of childhood asthma. *Journal of Allergy and Clinical Immunology, 72,* 596–606.

Tobin, D., Reynolds, R., Holroyd, K., & Creer, T. (1986). Self-management and social learning theory. In K. A. Holroyd & T. L. Creer, (Eds.), *Self-management of chronic disease.* Academic Press.

Tucker, P., Adamson, P., Miranda, R., Jr., Scarborough, A., Williams, D., Groff, J., & McLean, H. (1997). Paroxetine increases heart rate variability in panic disorder. *Journal of Clinical Psychopharmacology, 17*(5), 370–376.

U.S. Department of Health and Human Services. (1985). Public Health Service National Center for Health Statistics, *National Medical Care Utilization and Expenditure Survey (NMCUES).* Washington, D.C.: US Government Printing Office.

Van Hemert, A., Hengevald, M. W., Bolk, J., Rooijmans, H., & Vandenbroucke, J. (1993). Psychiatric disorders in relation to medical illness among patients of a general medical outpatient clinic. *Psychological Medicine, 23*(1), 167–173.

Vázquez-Barquero, J., Wilkinson, G., Williams, P., Diez-Manrique, J., & Pena, C. (1990). Mental health and medical consultation in primary care settings. *Psychological Medicine, 20*(3), 681–694.

VonKorff, M., Gruman, J., Schaefer, J., Curry, S., & Wagner, E. (1997). Collaborative management of chronic illness. *Annals of Internal Medicine, 127*(12), 1097–1102.

VonKorff, M., Katon, W., Bush, T., Lin, E., Simon, G., Saunders, K., Ludman, E., Walker, E., & Unitzer, J. (1998). Treatment costs, cost offset and cost effectiveness of collaborative management of depression. *Psychosomatic Medicine, 60,* 143–149.

Wagner, E. H., Austin, B. T., & VonKorff, M. (1996). Organizing care for patients with chronic illness. *Milbank Quarterly, 14,* 511–540

Walker, E., Katon, W., Jemelka, R., Roy-Byrne, P. (1992). Comorbidity of gastrointestinal complaints, depression, and anxiety in the Epidemiologic Catchment Area Study. *American Journal of Medicine, 92*(1A), 265–305.

Walker, E., Roy-Byrne, P., Katon, J., & Amosd, L. L. (1990). Psychiatric illness and irritable bowel syndrome: A comparison with inflammatory bowel disease. *American Journal of Psychiatry, 147,* 1656–1661.

Weiller, E., Bisserbe, J., Maier, W., & Lecrubier, Y. (1998). Prevalence and recognition of anxiety syndromes in five European primary care settings. *British Journal of Psychiatry, 173*(suppl 34), 18–23.

Weinberger, M., Kirkman, M., Samsa, G., Shortliffe, E., Landsman, P., Cowper, P., Simel, D., & Feussner, J. (1995). A nurse coordinated intervention for primary care patients with non–insulin-dependent diabetes mellitus. *Journal of General Internal Medicine 10,* 59–66.

Wells, K., Goldberg, G., Brook, R., & Leake, B. (1986). Quality of care of psychotropic drug use in internal medicine group practices. *Western Journal of Medicine, 145,* 710–714.

Wilson, J., Ross, J., & DuPont, R. (1997). Anxiety disorders in managed care. *Behavioral Health Management,* March/April, 33–38.

Winikoff, R., Wilner, S., Neisuler, R., & Barnett, G. (1985). Limitations of provider interventions in hypertension quality assurance. *American Journal of Public Health, 75,* 43–46.

Wulsin, L., Arnold, L., & Hillard, J. (1991). Axis I disorders in ER patients with atypical chest pain. *International Journal of Psychiatry Medicine, 21,* 37–46.

Yelin, E., Mathias, S., Buesching, D., Rowland, C., Caluscin, R., & Fifer, S. (1996). The impact on employment of an intervention to increase recognition of previously untreated anxiety among primary care physicians. *Social Sciences Medicine, 42,* 1069–1075.

Yellowlees, P., Alpers, J., Bowden, J., Bryant, G., & Ruffin, R. (1987). Psychiatric morbidity in patients with chronic airflow obstruction. *Medical Journal of Australia, 149,* 246–249.

Yeragani, V., Pohl, R., Berger, R., Balon, R., Ramesh, C., Glitz, D., Srinivasan, K., & Weinberg, P. (1993). Decreased heart rate variability in panic disorder patients: A study of power-spectral analysis of heart rate. *Psychiatry Research, 46,* 89–103.

Yinglin, K., Wulsin, L., Arnold, L., & Rouan, G. (1993). Estimated prevalences of panic disorder and depression among consecutive patients seen in an emergency department with acute chest pain. *Journal of General Internal Medicine, 8,* 231–235.

Zandbergen, J., Bright, M., Pols, H., Fernandez, I., Loof, C. D., & Griez, F. (1991). Higher lifetime prevalence of respiratory diseases in panic disorder? *American Journal of Psychiatry, 148,* 1583–1585.

Zung, W. (1986). Prevalence of clinically significant anxiety in a family practice setting. *American Journal of Psychiatry, 143,* 1471–1472.

CHAPTER 2

THE NEUROBIOLOGY OF STRESS AND ANXIETY

Gregory M. Sullivan
Justine M. Kent
Jeremy D. Coplan

STRESS AND THE DEVELOPMENT OF ANXIETY

Conceptions of Stress

The term *stress* can be broadly defined as a state of challenge or threat to an organism. In the nineteenth century, Claude Bernard introduced the concept that organisms exist in a state of dynamic internal physiologic equilibrium (or *milieu intérieur*), a state Walter Cannon later referred to as *homeostasis* (Chrousos & Gold, 1992). Cannon (1914) was also the first to describe the "fight or flight" response observed in response to acute stress. In this model the challenging force to an organism's homeostasis is termed the *stressor,* and the counterbalancing force elicited in the organism is the *adaptive response.*

In the twentieth century, Hans Seyle described the "stress syndrome." He observed that noxious preparations (chemical stressors) of diverse natures injected into the rat would cause identical responses in the animals. Specifically, the adrenal glands, known to produce stress hormones such as epinephrine and cortisol, would enlarge while immune system tissues, such as the thymus gland and lymph nodes, would involute (Berczi, 1998). Seyle further demonstrated that the thymus involution was mediated by the adrenals by showing this effect was absent in animals with adrenals removed. Of utmost significance in Seyle's observations was that the responses to various stressors were essentially uniform. Therefore, they were not specific to the stressor but, rather, a general mechanism of adaptation. Seyle proposed the novel concept that certain disease states are paradoxically the result of the adaptive response to a stress and thus are "diseases of adaptation." The current conceptualization of stress holds that adaptive responses may be either appropriate and balancing or, alternately, may fail to reestablish homeostasis because they are insufficient or excessive. With tremendous foresight, Seyle went on to describe a diverse array of endocrine, immune, metabolic, and behavioral aspects of the stress response.

An understanding of the stress response has proceeded relatively slowly, perhaps due to the complexity of interconnections between systems that Seyle predicted 50 years ago. Comprehensively, the stress response can be viewed as a stereotyped cascade of physiologic changes throughout the body following stimuli that are either dangerous or perceived of as dangerous. These changes can be protective or pathologic. The current conceptualization of the stress response offers a window into the *milieu intérieur* that includes essentially every major system in the body and may have treatment implications for an array of psychiatric and medical disorders.

Defining a Stressor

A major difficulty in the study of stress and stress response is the varying conceptions of a stressor. Animal models of stress have included such stressors as induced hunger, exposure to cold, physical restraint, noxious chemical administration, exposure to a predator or a socially dominant member of the same species, inescapable electric shocks, or near drowning. Human stressors are generally more broadly defined to also include complex life events such as adversity in relationships, health, work, finances, and within the social structure. Although there is some evidence that psychological stress activates the same pathways as observed in animal models, caution must be taken not to overgeneralize.

With that in mind, we will nevertheless attempt in this chapter to construct a human model of stress and anxiety based mainly on animal models. Much of the current conceptualization of the stress response has been pioneered by Chrousos and Gold (1992), who have synthesized a cogent model of the behavioral, neuroendocrine, and autonomic nervous systems' response to stress. We will attempt to build on this seminal work a developmental model that includes a hypothesis on the development of anxiety and anxiety disorders.

The Stress Response

The stress response is characterized by behavioral and physical adaptations that prepare an organism for response to an external challenge. Behaviorally there is a redirection of attention to the threat and the assumption of characteristic defensive postures or movements. At the same time there are physical adaptations that involve a shifting of energy utilization to body systems necessary for immediate action (Chrousos & Gold, 1992). The cardiovascular and pulmonary systems are stimulated. Blood supply is preferentially directed to the brain and musculoskeletal systems. And the liver mobilizes emergency energy currency by producing glucose and breaking down fats. Systems that are unnecessary during a challenge, such as the reproductive and digestive systems, are suppressed. These changes result in a state of increased mental and physical arousal necessary for survival actions in response to the challenge.

The brain is informed of stressors by two major routes: by way of neural pathways including afferent nerves from sensory modalities and the viscera; and through signal molecules carried by blood, such as toxins, immune cell molecules, and hormones. Importantly, seemingly innocuous cues in the environment may also be considered stressors to the degree that they have previously been associated with adversity. Such cues activate fear memory pathways in such a way as to elicit a stress response, as will be discussed later in the chapter.

Two central constituents of the brain's response to stressors are the corticotropin-releasing factor (CRF) system and the norepinephrine (NE) system (Chrousos & Gold, 1992). CRF is a peptide hormone originally identified in the hypothalamus. More recently, CRF and its receptors have been shown to be widely distributed throughout the brain (Gray, 1993). The activity of CRF is clearly altered during an adaptive response (Kalin et al., 1994). Norepinephrine-producing neurons originate in the locus ceruleus (LC), as well as other nuclei in the medulla and pons, and they project to the cortex, subcortical sites, cerebellum, and spinal cord. These NE neurons are activated during the stress response and play a role in regulating the spontaneous discharge of neurons in diverse areas. This second system has been termed the LC-NE system by Chrousos and Gold.

The CRF system and the LC-NE system have known effects outside the central nervous system by way of two peripheral effector pathways. For the CRF system the pathway is the hypothalamic-pituitary-adrenal (HPA) axis. For the LC-NE system the pathway is the autonomic nervous system (ANS), including the sympathetic-adrenomedullary branch and the parasympathetic branch. The adrenal gland responds to stress-induced activity of these two arms by releasing corticosteroids and epinephrine. The ANS has diverse effects on multiple systems including the cardiovascular, pulmonary, urogenital, and gastrointestinal systems. Components of the HPA axis and the ANS also have direct effects on the immune system.

CRF has emerged as a neurotransmitter that plays a central role in stress, anxiety, and depression. The cell bodies, terminals, and receptors for CRF, and its more recently identified homolog urocortin (UC), have a pattern of distribution that anatomically maps onto key structures involved in response to adversity (Gray, 1993). Regions in which CRF neurons are predominantly found include the paraventricular nuclei (PVN) of the hypothalamus, the central nucleus of the amygdala (CNA), and the lateral bed nucleus of the stria terminalis (BNST). CRF neurons project not only to regions of neuroendocrine regulation but also to monoaminergic brainstem nuclei involved in modulation of the stress response and to regions that initiate or modify components of a musculoskeletal response to threat. When CRF is artificially administered to the ventricles of experimental animals, the characteristic physical and behavioral adaptations of the stress response are produced (Heilig et al., 1994). Further, CRF is now hypothesized to serve as a facilitator of both the cognitive and the physical symptoms of anxiety by enhancing transmission through key structures in the stress response system.

CRF neurons of the PVN of the hypothalamus project to the hypophysial portal system in the median eminence. They release CRF into portal blood, which stimulates the pituitary gland to secrete adrenocorticotropic hormone (ACTH) into the main bloodstream (Chrousos, 1995). At the level of the hypothalamus there is a synergistic interplay with another PVN hormone known as arginine-vasopressin (AVP) such that during stress there is increased amplitude and synchronization of CRF and AVP pulsation into the portal circulation, resulting in increased pituitary-adrenal activity. Pituitary ACTH circulating in the blood stimulates the adrenal glands to release corticosteroids, the final effector hormones of the HPA axis. Corticosteroids act at a cellular level in diverse organs and tissues. They bind to intracellular receptors and have direct and indirect effects on DNA transcription as well as effects on messenger RNA translation (Chrousos, 1998). Corticosteroids also limit the HPA axis and the stress response through a feedback mechanism by direct actions on the frontal cortex, amygdala, hippocampus, hypothalamus, and pituitary.

PVN CRF neurons also project to NE neurons of the brainstem, such as those in the LC, which reciprocally project back to the PVN, linking the two main constituents of the stress system (Chrousos, 1998). Dopaminergic pathways, such as one from the ventral tegmentum to the prefrontal cortex, are stimulated by the CRF and LC-NE systems as well as corticosteroids during stress. The dopamine pathways are believed to be involved in anticipation and vigilance during stress and also to have a reciprocal inhibitory effect on the stress system. The CRF and LC-NE systems also reciprocally innervate opioid peptide-producing neurons of the arcuate nucleus of the hypothalamus. This pathway appears to be involved in analgesia during stress and also reciprocally inhibits the main constituents of the stress system. Also deserving of mention are serotonergic pathways originating in the raphe nuclei, which have both stimulating effects on CRF and NE neurons as well as complex effects at the level of the amygdala

(Chrousos & Gold, 1992; Graeff et al., 1996; Tork & Hornung, 1990).

Anxiety

Anxiety is a somewhat nebulous term as it is routinely applied to quite diverse phenomena. The term is often applied to the feeling of difficult-to-describe discomfort in anticipation of some poorly defined threatening situation. In humans the term *fear* is more often used when the threatening situation is more delineated, although the distinctions between these terms are often not clear. *Anxiety* can also refer to a symptom reported in various disorders, including depression, psychotic disorders, endocrine disorders, delirium, dementia, toxic/metabolic disorders, and drug withdrawal. Beyond the subjective feeling that can only be described with words that give little further information ("keyed up," "jittery," "nervous," "tense"), anxiety is associated with an array of cognitive, perceptual, somatic, and behavioral symptoms. Certain cognitive symptoms include catastrophic misappraisals, confusion, and the urge to escape from a location or situation. Perceptual disturbances include derealization, depersonalization, and hyperesthesia. Somatic symptoms include shortness of breath, chest pressure or tightness, palpitations, muscle tension, sweating, chills, hot flashes, dry mouth, choking, nausea, diarrhea, urge to micturate, and numbness or tingling. Behavioral symptoms include fearful facial expressions, irritability, and pacing or immobility.

An *anxiety disorder* is a psychiatric disorder in which a feeling of anxiety is considered to be the major or dominant component. Specific examples of anxiety disorders will be discussed in detail later in this chapter. To date there has been a paucity of rigorous study on anxiety secondary to medical disorders. Yet presently there is a convergence of data from stress studies, neuroscience fear literature, and anxiety disorders research that indicates common anatomical and neurotransmitter pathways for anxiety generation. It is likely that anxiety associated with medical disorders is often generated through the same pathways.

Fear Pathways and Their Relation to Stress and Anxiety

Tremendous advances have been made in the elucidation of the neural circuitry underlying fear behavior, and most evidence points to the amygdala as the central component (Davis, 1992; LeDoux, 1996). Much of this circuitry has been identified by the study of Pavlovian conditioning. One such paradigm studied in detail in the rat involves the pairing of an innocuous tone, the conditioned stimulus (CS), with a mild yet aversive foot shock, the unconditioned stimulus (US). Even after only one such pairing the rat will later respond to the CS alone with behavioral, neuroendocrine, and autonomic changes indicative of fear of an impending shock. This response to the tone includes freezing, stress hormone release, cardiovascular and pulmonary activation, and somatic reflex potentiation. The rat can also learn an association between the foot shock and a representation of the environment (the context) in which the shock was received. When placed back in that environment, it will respond with the same fear responses. This is known as *contextual fear conditioning*. A conditioned fear response to cue or context can therefore be elicited by stimuli indicative of real danger or stimuli that are, rather, simply predictive of danger. *Higher-order conditioning* refers to the pairing of a new innocuous stimulus with a past CS such that the new stimulus will elicit a fear response when later presented alone. This indicates further that fear associations can be added to fear memory without the occurrence of adversity (the US).

Pioneering studies in the monkey by Kluver and Bucy (1939) demonstrated that lesions in the temporal lobe, including the amygdala area, basically abolished fear of natural dangers, such as snakes, as well as fear behavior typical when confronted with novelty. Later lesioning studies demonstrated that the amygdala is critical to the normal fear response to natural enemies (an anesthetized cat) or a CS previously paired with a shock (Blanchard & Blanchard, 1972). The amygdala is a region located in the medial temporal lobe that is made up of structurally and functionally heterogeneous nuclei. In the case of auditory conditioning, auditory CS information proceeds from the ear through the brainstem to the auditory relay in the thalamus, known as the medial geniculate body (LeDoux, 1996). From there the information is relayed to the amygdala by two parallel pathways. A quick monosynaptic thalamo-amygdala pathway and a slower polysynaptic thalamic-cortical-amygdala pathway both converge on the lateral nucleus of the amygdala (LA). The former pathway is believed to provide a fast, yet unprocessed, representation of stimuli necessary for immediate action, whereas the latter pathway contains cortically processed information that may provide for a more appropriate action when the stimuli is measured against cortical memory from past experience. The amygdala appears to process information in series and in parallel through an organized array of intra-amygdaloid circuits formed by individual amygdalar nuclei (Pitkanen et al., 1997). These intra-amygdala pathways allow a stimulus representation to be modulated by different functional systems such as those mediating memories from past experience and information about the hormonal and homeostatic milieu of the organism. The CNA is considered the main output station of the amygdala as it is critical for the expression of the conditioned fear response (LeDoux, 1996). The CNA projects to and activates regions that initiate the specific components of a fear response. CNA projections to the periaqueductal gray (PAG) are involved in freezing behavior and pain modulation; those to the bed nucleus of the stria terminalis and PVN are involved in HPA axis activation; and those to the parabrachial nucleus, lateral hypothalamus, and dorsal motor nucleus of the vagus are involved in cardiorespiratory stimulation (Davis, 1992; Manning, 1998). The CNA also projects to the ventral tegmental area, the LC, and the raphe nuclei and is thus connected with key dopaminergic, noradrenergic, and serotonergic loci, respectively.

Recent evidence indicates that auditory and contextual fear conditioning occur by different intra-amygdala pathways (Figure 2.1). An auditory cue relayed through the thalamus enters the LA where it is associated with the shock. This information is then relayed to the CNA. For contextual fear conditioning the hippocampus is first necessary for creating a representation of the environment, utilizing information received from the entorhinal cortex and subiculum (LeDoux et al., 1990). This information is relayed through the basal/accessory basal (B/AB) nuclei of the amygdala and then to the CNA. Lesions of the LA block auditory fear conditioning (LeDoux et al., 1990), while lesions of the B/AB attenuate contextual fear conditioning but have no effect on auditory fear conditioning (Majidishad et al., 1996).

Stress can influence functioning of various components of the fear system. Social isolation, a stressful

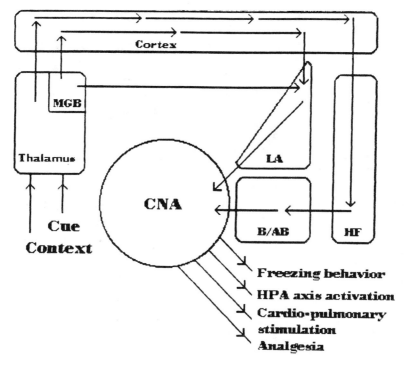

FIGURE 2.1. Diagram of identified pathways by which environmental cues and contexts become associated with adverse stimuli in such a way as to elicit future fear responses without further adversity. MGB = medial geniculate body; CNA = central nucleus of the amygdala; LA = lateral nucleus of the amygdala; B/AB = basal and accessory basal nuclei of the amygdala; HF = hippocampal formation

situation in the rat, causes deficient auditory fear conditioning (Rudy & Pugh, 1996). Normally such conditioning is specific to the frequency of the tone (the CS), but under such stress the rat exhibits fear behavior when re-presented with tones of different frequencies. Also, corticosteroid administered to a CS on the day of testing of fear behavior results in potentiated learned fear behavior to a given auditory cue (Corodimas et al., 1994). Social isolation decreases contextually elicited fear behavior (Rudy, 1996; Rudy & Pugh, 1996). Thus, there is evidence that stress or stress hormones can increase generalization to a discrete cue, cause supranormal fear responses, and impair contextual fear expression. It can therefore be imagined how stress may make learned fear responses less specific and yet greater in magnitude.

Evidence of the amygdala's role in human fear and anxiety comes from electrophysiological studies, neuroimaging, and assessment of individuals with bilateral amygdala damage. Stereotaxic electrical stimulation of the amygdala in conscious humans has been reported to elicit symptoms of anxiety disorders including fear, anxiety, depersonalization, visceral sensations in the chest and epigastric region, and changes in autonomic function (Halgren, 1992). Imaging studies indicate amygdala involvement in human conditioned fear as well as conscious and unconscious responses to fearful facial expressions (LaBar et al., 1998; Morris et al., 1998; Whalen et al., 1998). Individuals with bilateral amygdala damage have a poor ability to judge unfamiliar faces as not trustworthy or not approachable compared to such judgments made by individuals without such damage (Adolphs et al., 1998). Therefore, evidence to date in the human indicates a phylogenetic conservation of function of the amygdala across mammals with respect to its role in predicting adversity and coordinating the fear response.

A Model of Stress and Anxiety Interaction

In order to develop a cogent model of the interaction of stress and anxiety in the human, it is helpful to divide development into two discrete periods in which both the types of threats and the archetectonics of the response systems are very different. There is a wealth of evidence that will not be reviewed here indicating a strong genetic component to fearful traits, anxious behavior, and the development of anxiety disorders. For this model we assume a strong genetic component that is without environmental influence at the point of conception.

In utero there is the potential for stressors such as toxins, malnutrition, and physical trauma, although here too we leave these as assumptions. There is much evidence from animal research that during the postnatal period the thresholds for future activation of the stress response system are sculpted by the environment. One model is that of "handling" of rat pups. Pups that are handled by their human caregivers for short periods of time and then returned to their mothers have long been noted to appear more resilient in the face of stress and to demonstrate less anxiety-like behavior. It has been shown that mothers of handled pups more frequently display licking/grooming and arched-back nursing (LG-ABN) (Liu et al., 1997). It has also been noted that in the absence of handling there are variations between rats in the frequency of LG-ABN while nursing. As adult rats the group that received high levels of such maternal behavior during the first 10 days of life showed reduced plasma ACTH and cortisol in response to restraint stress. It was further demonstrated that CRH mRNA expression in the PVN negatively correlated and glucocorticoid receptor mRNA in the hippocampus positively correlated with the frequency of such licking and grooming. It is believed that increased sensitivity to glucocorticoid feedback at the level of the hippocampus is at least partially responsible for the decreased levels of ACTH and CRF observed in response to stress. One explanation for such phenomena is that the handling process (which includes the maternal behavioral response) triggers thyroid hormone release in the pups; thyroid hormone, in turn, activates serotonergic projections to the hippocampus that affect glucocorticoid receptor number (Francis et al., 1996). The adult offspring of mothers that displayed high frequency LG-ABN have also been shown to have increased benzodiazepine receptor density in the amygdala and LC, decreased CRF receptor density in the LC, and increased a2-adrenergic receptor density in the LC (Caldji et al., 1998). These findings indicate that the early environment has dramatic effects on the CRF system, the amygdala, and the LC and directly shapes future response to stress.

Another animal model with potential relevance to stress and anxiety is the nonhuman primate. Manipulations of the early psychosocial environment of infant bonnet macaques have been shown to result in anxious-like behavioral profiles in youth and adult life (Rosenblum & Paully, 1984). When nursing mothers of such infant monkeys are subjected to unpredictable demands when foraging for food, as opposed to predictable low demand and predictable high demand control environments, they adversely alter their behavior toward the infant (Rosenblum & Andrews, 1994). Remarkably, the infants raised in the unpredictable environment have heightened anxious-like behavior during development. They have increased behavioral inhibition in response to separation, to fear stimuli, and to new social groups and environments (Coplan, Rosenblum, et al., 1995), analogous to children described by Jerome Kagan as behaviorally inhibited to the unfamiliar (Kagan et al., 1987). Of utmost significance, the cerebrospinal fluid (CSF) of these monkeys has CRF levels that are persistently elevated (Coplan et al., 1996) while CSF cortisol levels are depressed. Further, these monkeys show significant correlation, not seen in controls, between CSF CRF and heightened CSF levels of serotonin and dopamine metabolites and the growth hormone axis peptide somatostatin (Coplan, Trost, et al., 1998). It is hypothesized that increased adversity in the mother–infant interaction results in CRF overexpression, which secondarily results in alteration in other systems relevant to stress and anxiety. In other work, electroencephalogram recording has demonstrated relatively higher right frontal lobe activity in abnormally fearful rhesus macaques, supporting the notion that a fearful phenotype is related to grossly altered brain activity (Kalin et al., 1998). Taken together, the described animal models support the notion that the stress response and anxiety pathways are at least partially sculpted by the early environment; a view propounded over a century ago by Freud (1966 [1886–1899]).

Kagan has shown in prospective child studies that 4-month-old infants who show a low threshold for becoming distressed and motorically aroused in reaction to unfamiliar stimuli are more likely than others to become fearful and subdued during early childhood (Kagan, 1997). Further, children originally identified as behaviorally inhibited at 21 months and who remained inhibited at 4.0, 5.5, and 7.5 years old had higher rates of anxiety disorders than children who were not consistently inhibited (Hirshfeld et al., 1992).

We propose that early environmental stress interacts with the genotype of individuals such that general thresholds for activation are set for systems such as the CRF and LC-NE systems. The genetics of the individual are thus on a spectrum from facilitating to ameliorating the development of maladaptive responses to stress. Indeed, with the handling model of rats and the unpredictable psychosocial environment model in monkeys there are the unexpectedly resilient and the unexpectedly poorly adapted individuals whose reactivity does not correspond with the group response to the environment. In the human early environment the factors responsible for the environmental sculpting could be adverse circumstances such as unpredictability of caregiver nurturing, prolonged separations, neglect, and abuse.

The second period of life, which continues up until death, has the general reactivity of the stress response that was set in the postnatal stage, but stressful life events continue to elicit stress responses and can cumulatively add to fear memory. Such memory can have effects on future stress response, and thus, even though thresholds have been set, there is the potential for facilitated responses due to memory of past adverse experience. In other words, a response to a stressful situation at this stage is the sum of the severity of the current stress plus the memory of cues and contexts from past stresses. This may lead to an appropriate stress response or an excessive or prolonged stress response.

In this model, anxiety is observed in two forms, acute and chronic. Acute anxiety can be elicited by cues in the present environment that are associated with previous stress-inducing experience. Chronic anxiety is a result of repetitive cuing that has been associated with stress response. For example, a person who has lost several close relatives to cancer may become anxious each time he or she hears the word *cancer*. Then, when told of an abnormal cancer screening result, several visits to a doctor for the work-up may induce a state of chronic anxiety that continues despite the work-up ultimately demonstrating no evidence of cancer. In this case the expectation of a deadly outcome continues despite sound evidence to the contrary.

The stress response is clearly a necessity for survival in an environment full of challenges to homeostasis. Yet it appears not to be finely tuned for appropriately gauged responses to all permutations of environmental challenge. The combination of a "jumpy" CRF and LC-NE system due to early environmental sculpting and increased amygdala-mediated cue and contextual fear memories due to past adversity may make future responses much less specific, such that anxious and/or avoidant behavior predominates.

The term *allostasis* has been coined to refer to the process of reestablishing homeostasis in the face of a challenge (Sterling & Eyer, 1981). While homeostasis implies a set point to which a system returns, allostasis means stabilization through change. Thus, activation of both the CRF system and the NE-LC system in response to stress are examples of allostasis. Further, the term *allostatic load* has been developed to refer to excessive activity of an allostatic system that causes damage and resulting pathophysiology in an organism (Schulkin et al., 1998). The general types of allostatic load include frequent overstimulation by stress, failure to shut off the allostatic responses when no longer necessary, and inability to turn on the allostatic responses when necessary. Because the stress response has effects on so many of the body's systems, allostatic load is a potential danger for perhaps every organ system, including the brain. For example, monkeys that live for several years in a colony in which they are socially subordinate to a dominant male develop stomach ulcers and have marked degeneration of the hippocampus, both evidence of allostatic load (Uno et al., 1989). The expectation of negative events, as in the cancer work-up previously described, is an example of allostatic load in which cognition has been adversely altered such that catastrophic misappraisals persist.

Figure 2.2 summarizes this model of stress and anxiety interaction. The level of reactivity to stress during early development is a result of an individual's genetics and early environmental stressors. This period results in individuals who can be classified on a spectrum from social/bold to behaviorally inhibited (depicted as two pathways rather than a spectrum). Later, further stressors can impact in two ways. Stress alone can make the individual feel "stressed," or stress plus cued/contextual memories can elicit a summed response that includes anxiety. Anxiety can result from stress along either pathway; it is the degree to which cued/contextual memories are activated that determines the level of anxiety. If the stress is severe, repeated, or chronic and there are fear-laden associations to present cues or context, the behaviorally inhibited group is more likely to develop anxiety than the social/bold group. The development

of allostatic load can occur secondary to the nature of the stress response (i.e., severe stress) or as a result of chronic anxiety (repeated or persistent cues and context). Anxiety disorders are seen as developing due to an interaction of allostatic load, developmental thresholds for stress response, and genetics. Because anxiety itself can activate allostatic systems, anxiety disorders can lead to further allostatic load.

Such a model is certainly speculative, but it may be of heuristic value when considering the heterogeneity of anxiety responses to seemingly similar stressful stimuli. Implicit in this model is the variability of systemic effects such responses can have on the functioning of various body systems. In the following section, effects of the stress response on selected body systems will be summarized, and examples of allostatic load will also be mentioned.

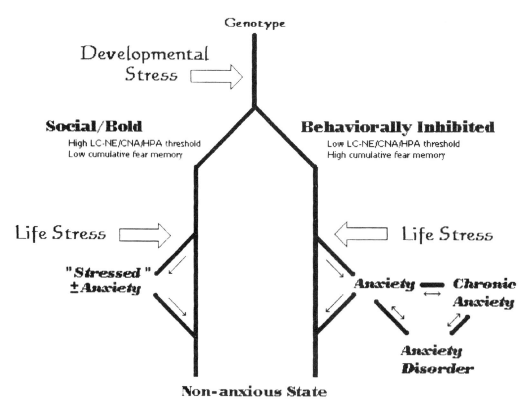

FIGURE 2.2. Representation of the hypothetical effects of stress on behavioral state in early development and adult life.

Stress and the Endocrine Systems

The hypothalamic-pituitary-thyroid (HPT) axis activity is inhibited by stress at several levels. Stress is associated with decreased pituitary production of thyroid-stimulating hormone (TSH) (Chrousos & Gold, 1992). In fact, hydrocortisone infusions in healthy humans at doses mimicking moderate and severe stress result in a decrease in TSH pulse amplitude by 60% and abolition of the normal nocturnal TSH surge for both moderate and severe stress doses (Samuels et al., 1994). Nocturnal serum TSH surge is also abolished in patients with adrenocorticotropin (ACTH)-dependent or ACTH-independent Cushing's syndrome (Bartalena et al., 1991). Activation of the HPA axis is also associated with the "euthyroid sick" syndrome, in which the conversion of thyroid hormone to its metabolically more active form is inhibited in peripheral tissues (Chrousos, 1998). In clinical depression blunted TSH response to thyrotropin-releasing hormone is more frequent in depressed subjects who are nonsuppressors of dexamethasone (a synthetic corticosteroid) (Rush et al., 1997), indicating possible allostatic load on the thyroid axis due to a chronically activated HPA axis.

The growth hormone (GH) axis is similarly inhibited by activation of the stress response. During prolonged stress there is suppression of GH secretion and inhibition of somatomedin C, apparently secondary to glucocorticoid effect. There is also both preclinical and clinical evidence for an inhibitory role of CRF on GH secretion (Nemeroff, 1992; Holsboer et al., 1994). CRF administration to humans both before or concomitant with growth hormone–releasing factor (GHRF) inhibits the GHRF-induced release of GH, suggesting the possible mechanism (Barbarino et al., 1990). The GH axis is also clearly dysregulated in states of pathologic anxiety, as will be discussed shortly (Sullivan et al., 1998). One child study found that anxiety disorder during childhood prospectively predicted relatively short stature in early adulthood among females, but not males, accounting for more than 5% of the variance in adult height (Pine et al., 1996).

The reproductive axis is also inhibited at several levels by stress-induced activation of the HPA axis (Chrousos, 1998). Both CRF and glucocorticoid activation suppress gonadotropin-releasing hormone secretion. As well, glucocorticoids inhibit pituitary gonadotroph secretion and gonadal tissues themselves. Individuals who are highly physically trained, such as distance runners, show evidence of both hyperactivation of the HPA axis and suppression of the gonadal system. Ultimately males show a reduction in testosterone levels and females have loss of the menstrual cycle (amenorrhea). Such suppression of the gonadal axis is also seen in anorexia nervosa and starvation.

Stress and the Cardiovascular System

Cardiovascular response to an auditory CS in the rat appears to be dependent on both sympathetic and parasympathetic components, with vagal influences serving to suppress heart rate acceleration to a certain degree (Sakaguchi et al., 1983). Studies in the human, using heart transplantation as a model, have shown that during psychological stress the major factor responsible for the elicited tachycardia is not circulating hormones but rather a change in the ratio of sympathetic to parasympathetic control of the heart (Sloan et al., 1990). The parasympathetic control over the heart can be measured by beat-to-beat variability in heart rate. Several studies have shown that anxiety is associated with reduced heart period variability. For example, it has been demonstrated that there is reduced heart period variability in panic disorder patients compared to normal controls (Klein et al., 1995; Yeragani et al., 1998). Further, in a large epidemiologic study it was shown that patients with a high level of "phobic anxiety," a construct that appears to overlap substantially with panic disorder, have both reduced heart period variability and an increased risk of cardiovascular morbidity (Kawachi et al., 1995). Therefore, reduction in heart period variability in certain anxiety states may represent altered autonomic control of the heart and may also be pathologic.

Stress and the Gastrointestinal and Genitourinary Systems

Gastrointestinal disorders of unclear etiology such as irritable bowel syndrome have been shown to be associated with affective and anxiety disorders (Walker et al., 1992). Evidence is now emerging that CRF can have profound effects on gut motility, and, reciprocally, colonic distension can activate the LC by a CRF-dependent mechanism (Fukudo et al., 1998; Lechner et al., 1997). Further, the pontine micturition center, also known as Barrington's nucleus, appears to have complex interconnections with the LC, PAG, and forebrain; and evidence is emerging that this center may be involved in particular stress and anxiety-related dysfunction in the gastrointestinal and genitourinary systems (Ding et al., 1998; Pavcovich et al., 1998).

Stress and the Immune System

Although a close connection between stress and immune function has long been recognized, only recently have the mediators of this connection been elucidated (Dunn, 1995). Immune system activation leads to activation of the HPA axis, and stress system response leads to significant modulation of the immune response, indicating bi-directional communication. Cytokines such as IL-1, IL-6, and TNF-a, well known for functions in the immune response, have recently been revealed also to activate CRF release in the brain. Although corticosteroids certainly have immunosuppressive effects, there is evidence that the CRF system has a corticosteroid-independent mechanism of immune system modulation (Sullivan et al., 1997).

It has been proposed that the purpose of CRF system activation by cytokines is to suppress the immune response and thus avoid an overreaction that would lead to an autoimmune state. This is partly based upon work with two strains of rats, Fisher 344 and Lewis, which differ in their susceptibility to inflammatory disease (Dunn, 1995). The Lewis rats, which easily develop autoimmune responses when exposed to particular antigens, appear to have deficient activation of the HPA axis in response to circulating cytokines. This is an example of allostatic load due to failure to appropriately turn on an allostatic system.

The immune system has two major types of response to antigenic challenge: the T helper 1 (TH_1), or cell-mediated immune response, and the T helper 2 (TH_2), or antibody-mediated immune response. The pattern of cytokines and immune cell surface proteins expressed during the inflammatory response indicates which type is predominant. It has been shown that glucocorticoids and catecholamines favor TH_2 over TH_1 immune cells and mediators by controlling the production of specific key regulatory cytokines. However, certain infectious diseases require an intact TH_1 response for successful immune defense. Surgical stress induces a shift from a TH_1 pattern to TH_2 commensurate to the trauma of the surgery (Decker et al., 1996). It has been hypothesized that "Gulf War syndrome" involves an interaction of antigenic (vaccination) challenge and psychological stress that results in a pathologic shift from TH_1 to TH_2 reactivity (Rook & Zumla, 1997). Hypothetically, both the antigenic challenge and the psychological stress have a combined effect on the activation of CRF, resulting in both immune and affective/anxiety sequelae.

Stressful life events have been associated with reductions of cytotoxic T lymphocytes and natural killer cells in asymptomatic HIV infection as well as with early progression of HIV disease (Evans et al., 1997; Leserman et al., 1997). High cytokine states well known in all stages of HIV infection (Tyor et al., 1992) theoretically may contribute to a centrally mediated (CRF-dependent) immunosuppressive message at a time when full lymphocyte function is necessary to check the cellular virulence of HIV. Further elucidation of such neuroimmune communication would seem of utmost relevance to the understanding of certain infectious diseases, cancers, and autoimmune diseases.

ANXIETY DISORDERS

For nearly two decades, research on anxiety disorders has largely been conducted based on illness categories defined by the American Psychiatric Association's *Diagnostic and Statistical Manual* (DSM). Diagnoses were made operational in the third edition of DSM (DSM-III), published in 1980, and refined in subsequent editions (DSM-III-R and the current DSM-IV). The introduction of criteria-based diagnoses permitted for the first time a rational approach to anxiety studies and the possibility of replication. Yet what has also emerged from such diagnoses-based separation of study groups is the often apparent biological overlap between groups. This is seemingly indicative of certain common functional-anatomic pathways of pathologic anxiety that cut across diagnostic boundaries and may also be relevant to anxiety states in medical disorders.

Pharmacological challenge involves assessing the difference in response to an administered chemical agent between individuals with a disorder compared to a control group. This method generally offers two possible responses to measure: (1) the level of a particular body biochemical, such as a hormone or monoamine metabolite; or (2) the induction of cognitive, behavioral, and autonomic symptoms resembling those of particular anxiety disorders. This approach has yielded valuable pioneering data on neuroendocrine and monoaminergic systems involvement in certain anxiety disorders. The second major research method has been neuroimaging, which, although still in its infancy, has yielded valuable functional, anatomic, and receptor density data. Currently various hypothetical pathways involved in pathological anxiety are being proposed guided by pharmacological challenge studies, neuroimaging, and the extensive preclinical knowledge base on fear pathways (Charney et al., 1998a and b; Graeff et al., 1996; LeDoux, 1996). We will summarize selected biological findings for several representative anxiety disorders that have pathology that may be accounted for by the hypothetical mechanisms proposed in the first part of this chapter.

Panic Disorder

Panic disorder (PD) is characterized by the occurrence of unexpected and rapidly progressing panic attacks. An individual attack, which should peak in intensity within 10 minutes, has cognitive components such as severe feelings of fear, distress, and depersonalization. An attack is also marked by somatic components such as palpitations, shortness of breath, gastrointestinal distress, sweating, chills, and tingling sensations. Necessary for a diagnosis of panic disorder, as per DSM-IV (APA, 1994) diagnostic criteria, is the presence of disabling sequelae of such attacks, including worry about future attacks, worry about the mental or physical implications of the attacks, or phobic avoidance of situations associated with the attacks. Most attacks are clinically observed to have a short time course ranging from about 5 to 30 minutes.

Various agents have been used to induce panic-like reactions at higher rates in PD patients than in normal controls. These include sodium lactate, sodium bicarbonate, inhaled carbon dioxide (CO_2, generally 5% or greater), isoproterenol, doxapram, yohimbine, m-chlorophenylpiperazine, fenfluramine, β-carboline, caffeine, and cholecystokinin (CCK) agonists (Coplan & Klein, 1996). The diversity of agents would seem to imply a low threshold for the triggering of the panic pathway by a variety of mechanisms.

Challenge with clonidine, an α2-agonist, results in the replicable finding of a blunted GH response in PD patients (Sullivan et al., 1998), often interpreted to indicate postsynaptic α2-adrenergic receptor subsensitivity in PD. Yohimbine, an α2-antagonist that stimulates firing of the LC, elicits high rates of panic-like anxiety in PD patients accompanied by increases in serum level of the principal noradrenergic metabolite, 3-methoxy 4-hydroxyphenylglycol (MHPG). Particular adrenergic agonists and the carotid chemoreceptor stimulator doxapram may in part act via peripheral receptors that relay information via vagal and glossopharyngeal afferents to the nucleus tractus solitarius (NTS). The NTS is known to have connections with the amygdala and hypothalamus through the parabrachial nucleus as well as indirect connections with the LC (Berkley & Scofield, 1990; Gorman et al., 1989).

Challenge studies with the mixed serotonin agonist-antagonist mCPP and the indirect serotonin agonist fenfluramine have demonstrated increased rates of anxiety, though not necessarily overt panic attacks, to these agents, particularly in PD patients (Wetzler et al., 1996). This may indicate postsynaptic 5-HT hypersensitivity in PD. Preclinical studies implicate serotonergic neurons originating in the raphe nuclei in modulation of an evolved complex response to threat. A 5-HT pathway originating in the dorsal raphe nucleus (DRN) and running along the medial forebrain bundle innervates the amygdala and frontal cortex and is hypothesized to facilitate active escape or avoidance behaviors in response to distal threat (Graeff et al., 1996). It is assumed that such resultant behavior relies on learning and relates to conditioned or anticipatory anxiety. A DRN pathway innervates the periventricular and PAG region such that 5-HT neurons inhibit inborn fight or flight reactions in response to proximal danger, acute pain, or asphyxia.

It has been demonstrated that clonidine induces a greater percentage decrease in serum cortisol in PD patients compared with controls (Coplan, Pine, et al., 1995). There is also an apparent uncoupling of the LC-NE system and the HPA axis as correlations observed in controls between MHPG and cortisol, at baseline or maximal change to clonidine, are significantly reduced in PD. Analysis of a decade of sodium lactate studies at one institution indicates that the strongest predictors of panic during the baseline period before lactate infusion were fear, high cortisol, and low pCO_2 (Coplan, Goetz, et al., 1998). Such predictors are consistent with a hypothetical CRF-mediated amygdaloid system effecting changes in cortical areas (cognitive misappraisal), the PVN of the hypothalamus (HPA axis activation), and the parabrachial nucleus (hyperventilation), respectively.

To date, dynamic brain imaging studies in panic disorder have yielded somewhat inconsistent results. A single photon emission computed tomography (SPECT) imaging study of cerebral blood flow in PD patients at rest demonstrated bilateral hippocampal area hypoperfusion (De Cristofaro et al., 1993), although another study demonstrated no significant regional differences compared to comparison subjects (Lucey et al., 1997). Positron emission tomography (PET) studies of cerebral blood flow utilizing ^{15}O-H$_2$O suggest a decrease in the left-to-right parahippocampal blood flow ratio in panic patients (Reiman et al., 1984, 1986). The first study of glucose metabolism in panic disorder (utilizing ^{18}F-FDG) reported a similar reduction in the left-to-right blood flow ratio in the hippocampal region, along with a decrease in metabolism in the left inferior parietal lobe (Nordahl et al., 1990). A more recent study of cerebral glucose metabolism in a sample of women with panic disorder also reported a significant difference between patients and female controls in metabolism in the hippocampal and parahippocampal regions; however, contrary to earlier studies, increases were greater in the left-versus right-sided regions (Bisaga et al., 1998). It is difficult to draw definitive conclusions from these studies in light of numerous methodologic and technical issues including nonquantitation, lack of coregistration with magnetic resonance imaging (MRI), and individual variability in the anatomy of the hippocampal region. Also, resolution of specific structures of interest such as the amygdala is quite limited.

However, in sum, these data provide support for a possible resting baseline abnormality in blood flow and metabolism in the hippocampal and parahippocampal regions of PD patients.

Few investigators have attempted challenge studies in concert with imaging in PD patients. Results from two early SPECT studies suggest that panic patients may exhibit a decrease in frontal cortical cerebral blood flow during panic provocation. In one study utilizing Tc-labeled hexamethylpropyleneamino oxide SPECT imaging, panic patients challenged with yohimbine demonstrated increased anxiety and decreased frontal cerebral blood flow when compared to controls (Woods et al., 1988). In another study, PD patients were challenged with lactate infusions and imaged utilizing SPECT with the ^{133}Xenon inhalation technique (Stewart et al., 1988). The investigators reported that panicking PD subjects showed either a smaller increase or a decrease in hemispheric blood flow in response to lactate compared to a robust increase in blood flow in the comparison subjects and nonpanicking panic subjects. One explanation for this finding is that the vasoconstrictive effect of hypocapnia secondary to hyperventilation during panic may have overcome the expected increase in blood flow due to lactate load. Regional analyses revealed greater increases in the right occipital area and a tendency toward decreased CBF in the frontal regions. Utilizing ^{15}O-H$_2$O PET to measure cerebral blood flow, panic patients have also been challenged with lactate infusions, and increases in blood flow in the insular cortex and claustrum/lateral putamen were reported (Reiman et al., 1989).

There is preclinical evidence that attenuation of local inhibitory GABAergic transmission in the basolateral amygdala or dorsomedial hypothalamus is capable of eliciting panic-like physiological and behavioral responses in rats (Sanders et al., 1995; Shekhar et al., 1996). Human receptor studies employing SPECT imaging have shown in PD patients decreased benzodiazepine binding in the right hippocampus and left temporal lobe (Feistel, 1993; Kaschka et al., 1992) and increased binding in the right middle frontal gyrus (Kuikka et al., 1995). More recently investigators reported a global reduction in benzodiazepine binding in PD patients, with the largest regional decreases seen in the right orbitofrontal cortex and right insula. This study, utilizing highly sensitive quantitative PET imaging, suggests that these structures, also implicated in other anxiety disorders, may play a significant role in panic disorder (Malizia et al., 1998).

Generalized Anxiety Disorder

According to DSM-IV, generalized anxiety disorder (GAD) is characterized by excessive and difficult-to-control anxiety or worry persisting for at least 6 months combined with at least three additional symptoms such as restlessness, being easily fatigued, difficulty concentrating, irritability, muscle tension, and sleep disturbance.

One study of women with GAD demonstrated an attenuated skin conductance response to stress as well as a slower recovery to baseline skin conductance poststress (Hoehn-Saric et al., 1989), suggesting both hyporesponsive and prolonged autonomic response in GAD. Clonodine challenge in GAD demonstrated a blunted growth hormone response in GAD, suggesting, as in PD, possible a_2-adrenoceptor subsensitivity (Abelson et al., 1991). Dexamethasone challenge, which normally suppresses cortisol, showed nonsuppression rates in about a third of GAD patients, although baseline cortisol levels appear normal in GAD (Avery et al., 1985; Tiller et al., 1988). Thus, there is limited evidence of HPA and NE dysregulation in GAD.

Evidence for serotonin involvement in GAD is suggested by clinical studies showing anxiolytic effect with 5-HT1A agonists and 5-HT2 antagonists (Katz et al., 1993; Laakmann et al., 1998). Also, one study demonstrated that urinary levels of the serotonin metabolite 5-hydroxyindoleacetic acid (5-HIAA) predicted the severity of several anxiety symptoms in GAD (Garvey et al., 1995). A challenge study with mCPP, the mixed 5-HT agonist-antagonist that has greatest agonist activity for $5-HT_{2C}$ and $5-HT_3$ receptors and to a lesser extent $5-HT_{1A/1}D$, demonstrated greater rates of anxiety and anger in GAD patients than in controls (Germine et al., 1992).

There have been few neuroimaging studies to date in GAD. An early PET study examined glucose metabolism in GAD patients pre- and posttreatment with a benzodiazepine (Buchsbaum et al., 1987). Brain regions known to have the highest benzodiazepine (gamma-aminobutyric acid [GABA]) receptor density

(particularly the occipital cortex) showed the greatest decreases in metabolic rate posttreatment. A later study by the same investigators demonstrated lowered glucose metabolism in the basal ganglia and elevated metabolism in the occipital, temporal, and frontal lobes of GAD subjects versus healthy controls (Wu et al., 1991).

More recently, drug-naive GAD patients were studied using SPECT imaging to measure benzodiazepine receptor binding (Tiihonen, Kuikka, Rasanen, et al., 1997). Results showed significantly decreased receptor binding in the left temporal pole among GAD patients, an area also implicated in PD patients as having lowered receptor density. Interestingly, the overall heterogeneity of receptor density distribution in the left temporal cortex appeared to be lost in GAD patients, leading the authors to propose that maintaining high regional heterogeneity of receptor density may be critical for adaptation to situations of heightened anxiety or stress.

Social Phobia

According to DSM-IV, social phobia (SP) is characterized by fear of exposure to unfamiliar people or to scrutiny in social or performance situations combined with fear of acting in an embarrassing or humiliating way. Such exposure also almost invariably provokes an anxiety reaction that may have prominent cognitive and autonomic components similar to a situationally bound or predisposed panic attack. The situations must be avoided or else endured with intense anxiety or distress, and the fears must be recognized as excessive or unreasonable.

Although studies are limited by small numbers of subjects, SP patients appear to panic to lactate infusion and CO_2 inhalation at lower rates in comparison to patients with PD (Papp et al., 1993; Leibowitz et al., 1985), whereas challenge with the selective CCK_B receptor agonist pentagastrin induced a high rate of panic attacks in SP (Uhde et al., 1997). Orthostatic challenge has demonstrated elevated supine and standing NE levels compared with PD patients and controls (Stein et al., 1992). Similarly, increased blood pressure response to Valsalva maneuver and exaggerated vagal withdrawal in response to isometric exercise have also been identified in SP (Stein et al., 1994). Clonidine challenge has shown a blunted growth hormone response in SP (Tancer et al., 1993). Social phobics do not appear to have an abnormal urinary cortisol or nonsuppression on the DST, suggesting no gross HPA axis abnormality in SP (Uhde et al., 1994).

It has been hypothesized that SP responds favorably to the monoamine oxidase inhibitors due to their enhancement of dopaminergic transmission. The dopamine metabolite homovanillic acid has been shown to be low in the CSF in one study of PD patients with SP, but unfortunately diagnostic specificity is unclear for this finding (Johnson et al., 1994). A SPECT study in SP utilizing the labeled cocaine analog [^{123}I]β-CIT did demonstrate decreased dopamine reuptake site density in the striatum (Tiihonen, Kuikka, Bergstrom et al., 1997). Also, decreased cellular energy activity and neuronal activity and abnormal membrane function in regions that include the basal ganglia have been suggested by magnetic resonance spectroscopy studies in SP (Davidson et al., 1993). MRI demonstrated that there is a greater reduction putamen size with aging in SP compared with controls (Potts et al., 1994). Thus, there is preliminary evidence pointing to dopaminergic dysfunction in SP.

Posttraumatic Stress Disorder

According to the DSM-IV, a diagnosis of posttraumatic stress disorder (PTSD) requires the occurrence of an event or events that threatened death or serious injury or threatened the physical integrity of self or others. The response to such threat includes intense fear, helplessness, or horror. Symptoms include persistent (greater than 1 month) reexperiencing of the trauma in the form of thoughts, images, or dreams; behaving or feeling the trauma is recurring; and intense psychological or physiological reactivity to cues that are reminders of the trauma. There should be avoidance of stimuli associated with the trauma and numbing of general emotional responsiveness. Symptoms of increased arousal should also be present and can include sleep disturbance, irritability, poor concentration, and exaggerated startle reflex.

When auditory and visual cues are utilized as challenge material in subjects with PTSD, plasma epinephrine and norepinephrine have been shown to rise in temporal relation to subjective psychophysiologic arousal elicited by the material (Blanchard et al., 1991; McFall et al., 1990). Both in veterans and in abused girls with PTSD there is increased urinary excretion of catecholamines (Kosten et al., 1987; Yehuda et al., 1992). Yohimbine induces panic at moderate rates in PTSD as well as flashbacks in about a third of subjects (Southwick et al., 1997). As well, the serotonergic agent mCPP induced panic in a third of PTSD subjects. It was noted in this study that 81% of the PTSD subjects had a panic attack to yohimbine or mCPP, but not both, raising the possibility of subtypes of PTSD with either more serotonergic or more noradrenergic dysfunction.

Some of the more striking biological findings in PTSD have been found in the CRF system. Plasma and urinary cortisol have been found to be low, and lymphocytes have increased glucocorticoid receptor number (Yehuda et al., 1990, 1995). CRF in the CSF has been found to be elevated in PTSD (Bremner, Licinio, et al., 1997). Challenge with exogenous CRF in PTSD results in a blunted ACTH response (DeBellis, Chrousos, et al., 1994; Smith et al., 1989), whereas challenge with low-dose dexamethasone has been found to cause enhanced suppression of cortisol in PTSD (Yehuda et al., 1993, 1995). Such findings in PTSD indicate a "hyperregulation" of the HPA axis in PTSD in which there is possible CRF hypersecretion while glucocorticoid receptors are increased in number and appear more sensitive.

Plasma b-endorphin levels have been reported to be reduced in PTSD, implicating abnormality in the opioid system (Hoffman et al., 1989). Combat veterans with PTSD also have an analgesic response to combat-related stimuli that is reversed by the opiate antagonist naloxone (Pitman et al., 1990). Yet, at baseline, patients with chronic PTSD have been demonstrated to have reduced pain threshold (Friedman, 1991). This raises the possibility that the opioid system is also hyperregulated due to a chronically activated CRF system such that there is still an adequate opioid response to further CRF elevation due to the stress and anxiety caused by the combat-related stimuli.

Abnormalities in HPT axis have also been identified in PTSD, including significant elevations in mean total triiodothyronine (T3) (Mason et al., 1996). This raises the possibility that the unique HPA axis profile leads to an increase in conversion of thyroxine (T4) to T3, opposite to what is seen during an acute stress response. A blunted TSH response to TRH stimulation has been reported in

PTSD (Reist et al., 1995). Also, positive correlations between thyroid hormone measures and novelty seeking as well as hyperarousal have been identified, suggesting a link between behavior and neurohormonal abnormalities (Wang et al., 1997).

Preclinical research first illuminated a potentially important feature of PTSD: hippocampal atrophy. Heightened glucocorticoid levels provoked in animal models of stress are associated with hippocampal damage (Sapolsky, 1990; Uno et al., 1989). As PTSD by definition is a disorder resulting from exposure to an immeasurably stressful event, the question has been raised as to whether PTSD patients would also manifest hippocampal damage as a result of stress-induced glucocorticoid release. PTSD patients have been found to have memory deficits in declarative memory, a function believed to require the hippocampus, suggesting dysfunction of the hippocampus (Bremner et al., 1993; Uddo et al., 1993).

More recently, four MRI studies have confirmed hippocampal atrophy in PTSD patients including combat veterans (Bremner et al., 1995; Gurvits et al., 1996) and victims of physical and/or sexual abuse (Bremner, Randall, et al., 1997; Stein et al., 1997). Although hippocampal damage in PTSD is speculated to be due to glucocorticoid effects, PTSD patients have not been definitively shown to have had a surge in cortisol. An alternate explanation is that those who go on to develop PTSD after a trauma have congenitally smaller hippocampi that predisposed them to the disorder.

PET studies have provided complementary information about dynamic brain function in PTSD patients both in the resting state and during the provocation of PTSD symptoms. A resting state study examining brain metabolism with FDG-PET revealed a decrease in metabolism in the temporal cortex, an area important in memory and attention (Bremner, Innis, et al., 1997), whereas yohimbine challenge demonstrated decreased hippocampal metabolism in PTSD subjects compared to healthy individuals. Other investigators have measured changes in cerebral blood flow (CBF), as a reflection of metabolism and neuronal activation, during provocation paradigms. These studies have implicated increased flow in limbic regions along with decreased flow in the middle temporal, inferior frontal, orbitofrontal, and medial prefrontal cortices (Bremner et al., 1999; Rauch et al., 1996; Shin et al., 1997).

In the rodent an intact medial prefrontal cortex has been shown to be critical to the extinction of fear response to repeated presentations of a conditioned stimulus (Morgan & LeDoux, 1995). Thus, the failure of activation of the medial prefrontal cortex in PTSD patients in response to trauma-related stimuli raises the question of faulty extinction in PTSD.

CONCLUSION

Research on the neurobiology of stress and anxiety is at an exciting stage in which there is a convergence of data from diverse disciplines such as psychology, neuroscience, internal medicine, and psychiatry. Previously unrecognized connections between body systems are being elucidated, allowing more comprehensive models of stress, the stress response, and the emergence of anxiety. As such research progresses, the pathologic implications of excessive stress and anxiety are becoming more clear. Optimally this improved understanding will soon lead to better management strategies and therapeutics for stress and anxiety as well as their sequelae.

REFERENCES

Abelson, J. L., Glitz, D., Cameron, O. G., Lee, M. A., Bronzo, M., & Curtis, G. C. (1991). Blunted growth hormone response to clonidine in patients with generalized anxiety disorder. *Archives of General Psychiatry, 25,* 141–152.

Adolphs, R., Tranel, D., & Damasio, A. R. (1998). The human amygdala in social judgment. *Nature, 393,* 470–474.

American Psychiatric Association. (1994). *Diagnostic and statistical manual of mental disorders* (4th ed.). Washington, DC: Author.

Avery, D. H., Osgood, T. B., Ishiki, D. M., Wilson, L. G., Kenny, M., & Dunner, D. L. (1985). The DST in psychiatric outpatients with generalized anxiety disorder, panic disorder, or primary affective disorder. *American Journal of Psychiatry, 142,* 844–848.

Barbarino, A., Corsello, S. M., Della Casa, S., Tofani, A., Sciuto, R., Rota, C. A., Bollanti, L., & Barini, A. (1990). Corticotropin-releasing hormone inhibition of growth hormone–releasing hormone-induced growth hormone release in man. *Journal of Clinical Endocrinology and Metabolism, 71,* 1368–1374.

Bartalena, L., Martino, E., Petrini, L., Velluzzi, F., Loviselli, A., Grasso, L., Mammoli, C., & Pinchera, A. (1991). The nocturnal serum thyrotropin surge is abolished in patients with adrenocorticotropin (ACTH)-dependent or ACTH-independent Cushing's syndrome. *Journal of Clinical Endocrinology and Metabolism, 72,* 1195–1199.

Berczi, I. (1998). The stress concept and neuroimmuno-regulation in modern biology. *Annals of the New York Academy of Sciences, 851,* 3–12.

Berkley, K. J., & Scofield, S. L. (1990). Relays from the spinal cord and solitary nucleus through the parabrachial nucleus to the forebrain in the cat. *Brain Research, 529,* 333–338.

Bisaga, A., Katz, J. L., Antonini, A., Wright, C. E., Margouleff, C., Gorman, J. M., & Eidelberg, D. (1998). Cerebral glucose metabolism in women with panic disorder. *American Journal of Psychiatry, 155,* 1178–1183.

Blanchard, E. B., Kolb, L. C., & Prins, A. (1991). Changes in plasma norepinephrine to combat-related stimuli among Vietnam veterans with posttraumatic stress disorder. *Journal of Nervous and Mental Disease, 79,* 371–373.

Blanchard, R. J., & Blanchard, D. C. (1972). Innate and conditioned reactions to threat in rats with amygdaloid lesions. *Journal of Comparative and Physiological Psychology, 81,* 281–290.

Bremner, J. D., Innis, R. B., Ng, C. K., Staib, L. H., Salomon, R. M., Bronen, R. A., Duncan, J., Southwick, S. M., Krystal, J. H., Rich, D., Zubal, G., Dey, H., Soufer, R., & Charney, D. S. (1997). Positron emission tomography measurement of cerebral metabolic correlates of yohimbine administration in combat-related posttraumatic stress disorder. *Archives of General Psychiatry, 54,* 246–254.

Bremner, J. D., Licinio, J., Darnell, A., Krystal, J. H., Owens, M. J., Southwick, S. M., Nemeroff, C. B., & Charney, D. S. (1997). Elevated CSF corticotropin-releasing factor concentration in posttraumatic stress disorder. *American Journal of Psychiatry, 154,* 624–629.

Bremner, J. D., Randall, P., Scott, T. M., Bronen, R. A., Seibyl, J. P., Southwick, S. M., Delaney, R. C., McCarthy, G., Charney, D. S., & Innis, R. B. (1995). MRI-based measurement of hippocampal volume in posttraumatic stress disorder. *American Journal of Psychiatry, 152,* 973–981.

Bremner, J. D., Randall, P., Vermetten, E., Staib, L., Bronen, R. A., Mazure, C., Capelli, S., McCarthy, G., Innis, R. B., & Charney, D. S. (1997). MRI-based measurement of hippocampal volume in posttraumatic stress disorder related to childhood physical and sexual abuse: A preliminary report. *Biological Psychiatry, 41,* 23–32.

Bremner, J. D., Scott, T. M., Delaney, R. C., Southwick, S. M., Mason, J. W., Johnson, D. R., Innis, R. B., McCarthy, G., & Charney, D. S. (1993). Deficits in short-term memory in post-traumatic stress disorder. *American Journal of Psychiatry, 150,* 1015–1019.

Bremner, J. D., Staib, L., Kaloupek, D., Southwick, S. M., Soufer, R., & Charney, D. S. (1999). Positron emission tomographic (PET)–based measurement of cerebral blood flow correlates of traumatic reminders in Vietnam combat veterans with and without posttraumatic stress disorder. *Biological Psychiatry.*

Buchsbaum, M. S., Wu, J., Haier, R., Hazlett, E., Ball, R., Katz, M., Sokolski, K., Lagunas-Solar, M., & Langer, D. (1987). Positron emission tomography assessment of effects of benzodiazepines on regional glucose metabolic rate in patients with anxiety disorder. *Life Sciences, 40,* 2393–2400.

Caldji, C., Tannenbaum, B., Sharma, S., Francis, D., Plotsky, P. M., & Meaney, M. J. (1998). Maternal care during infancy regulates the development of neural systems mediating the expression of fearfulness in the rat. *Proceedings of the National Academy of Sciences of the USA, 95,* 5335–5340.

Cannon, W. B. (1914). Emergency function of the adrenal medulla in pain and major emotions. *American Journal of Physiology, 3,* 356–372.

Charney, D. S., Grillon, C., & Bremner, J. D. (1998a). The neurobiological basis of anxiety and fear: Circuits, mechanisms, and neurochemical interactions (Part I). *Neuroscientist, 4,* 35–44.

Charney, D. S., Grillon, C., & Bremner, J. D. (1998b). The neurobiological basis of anxiety and fear: Circuits, mechanisms, and neurochemical interactions (Part II). *Neuroscientist, 4,* 122–132.

Chrousos, G. P. (1995). The hypothalamic-pituitary-adrenal axis and immune-mediated inflammation. *New England Journal of Medicine, 332,* 1351–1362.

Chrousos, G. P. (1998). Stressors, stress, and neuroendocrine integration of the adaptive response. *Annals of the New York Academy of Sciences, 851,* 311–335.

Chrousos, G. P., & Gold, P. W. (1992). The concept of stress and stress system disorders: Overview of physical and behavioral homeostasis. *JAMA, 267,* 1244–1252.

Coplan, J. D., Andrews, M. W., Rosenblum, L. A., Owens, M. J., Gorman, J. M., & Nemeroff, C. B. (1996). Increased cerebrospinal fluid CRF concentrations in adult non-human primates previously exposed to adverse experiences as infants. *Proceedings of the National Academy of Sciences of the USA, 93,* 1619–1623.

Coplan, J. D., Goetz, R., Klein, D. F., Papp, L. A., Fyer, A. J., Liebowitz, M. R., Davies, S. O., & Gorman, J. M. (1998). Plasma cortisol concentrations preceding lactate-induced panic: Psychological, biochemical, and physiological correlates. *Archives of General Psychiatry, 55,* 130–136.

Coplan, J. D., & Klein, D. F. (1996). Pharmacologic probes in panic disorder. In H. G. M. Westenberg, J. A. Den Boer, & D. L. Murphy (Eds.), *Advances in the neurobiology of anxiety disorders* (pp. 179–204). New York: Wiley.

Coplan, J. D., Pine, D., Papp, L., Martinez, J., Cooper, T., Rosenblum, L. A., & Gorman, J. M. (1995). Uncoupling of the noradrenergic-hypothalamic-pituitary-adrenal axis in panic disorder patients. *Neuropsychopharmacology, 13,* 65–73.

Coplan, J. D., Rosenblum, L. A., & Gorman, J. M. (1995). Primate models of anxiety: Longitudinal perspectives. *Psychiatric Clinics of North America, 18,* 727–743.

Coplan, J. D., Trost, R. C., Owens, M. J., Cooper, T. B., Gorman, J. M., Nemeroff, C. B., & Rosenblum, L. A. (1998). Cerebrospinal fluid concentrations of somatostatin and biogenic amines in grown primates reared by mothers exposed to manipulated foraging conditions. *Archives of General Psychiatry, 55,* 473–477.

Corodimas, K. P., LeDoux, J. E., Gold, P. W., & Schulkin, J. (1994). Corticosterone potentiation of learned fear. *Annals of the New York Academy of Sciences, 746,* 392–393.

Davidson, J. R., Krishnan, K. R., Charles, H. C., Boyko, O., Potts, N. L., Ford, S. M., & Patterson, L. (1993). Magnetic resonance spectroscopy in social phobia: Preliminary findings. *Journal of Clinical Psychiatry, 54* (suppl.), 19–25.

Davis, M. (1992). The role of the amygdala in conditioned fear. In J. P. Aggleton (Ed.), *The amygdala: Neurobiological aspects of emotion, memory, and mental dysfunction* (pp. 255–306). New York: Wiley-Liss.

DeBellis, M. D., Lefter, L., Trickett, P. K., & Putnam, F. W. (1994). Urinary catecholamine excretion in sexually abused girls. *Journal of the American Academy of Child and Adolescent Psychiatry, 33,* 320–327.

De Cristofaro, M. T., Sessarego, A., Pupi, A., Biondi, F., & Faravelli, C. (1993). Brain perfusion abnormalities in drug-naive, lactate-sensitive panic patients: A SPECT study. *Biological Psychiatry, 33,* 505–512.

Decker, D., Schondorf, M., Bidlingmaier, F., Hirner, A., & von Ruecker, A. A. (1996). Surgical stress induces a shift in the type-1/type-2 T-helper cell balance, suggesting down-regulation of cell-mediated and up-regulation of antibody-mediated immunity commensurate to the trauma. *Surgery, 119,* 316–325.

Ding, Y. Q., Wang, D., Nie, H., Guan, Z. L., Lu, B. Z., & Li, J. S. (1998). Direct projections from the periaqueductal gray to pontine micturition center neurons projecting to the lumbosacral cord segments: An electron microscopic study in the rat. *Neuroscience Letters, 242,* 97–100.

Dunn, A. J. (1995). Interactions between the nervous system and the immune system: Implications for psychopharmacology. In F. E. Bloom & D. J. Kupfer (Eds.), *Psychopharmacology: The fourth generation of progress.* New York: Raven Press.

Evans, D. L., Leserman, J., Perkins, D. O., Stern, R. A., Murphy, C., Zheng, B., Gettes, D., Longmate, J. A., Silva, G. S., van der Horst, C. M., Hall, C. D., Folds, J. D., Golden, R. N., & Petitto, J. M. (1997). Severe life stress as a predictor of early disease progression in HIV infection. *American Journal of Psychiatry, 154,* 630–634.

Feistel, H. (1993). Assessment of cerebral benzodiazepine receptor distribution in anxiety disorders: A study with I-123-iomazenil [Abstract]. *Journal of Nuclear Medicine, 34,* 47.

Francis, D., Diorio, J., LaPlante, P., Weaver, S., Seckl, J. R., & Meaney, M. J. (1996). The role of early environmental events in regulating neuroendocrine development. *Annals of the New York Academy of Science, 794,* 136–152.

Friedman, M. J. (1991). Biological approaches to the diagnosis and treatment of post-traumatic stress disorder. *Journal of Traumatic Stress, 4,* 67–91.

Freud, S. (Ed.). (1966). The standard edition of the complete psychological works of Sigmund Freud (vol. 1, 1886–1899) (pp. 281–343). London: Hogarth Press.

Fukudo, S., Nomura, T., & Hongo, M. (1998). Impact of corticotropin-releasing hormone on gastrointestinal motility and adrenocorticotropic hormone in normal controls and patients with irritable bowel syndrome. *Gut, 42,* 845–849.

Garvey, M. J., Noyes, R., Jr., Woodman, C., & Laukes, C. (1995). Relationship of generalized anxiety symptoms to urinary 5-hydroxyindoleacetic acid and vanillylmandelic acid. *Psychiatry Research, 57,* 1–5.

Germine, M., Goddard, A. W., Woods, S. W., Charney, D. S., & Heninger, G. R. (1992). Anger and anxiety responses to m-chlorophenylpiperazine in generalized anxiety disorder. *Biological Psychiatry, 32,* 457–461.

Gorman, J. M., Fyer, M. R., Goetz, R., Askanazi, J., Liebowitz, M. R., Fyer, A. J., Kinney, J., & Klein, D. F. (1998). Ventilatory physiology of patients with panic disorder. *Archives of General Psychiatry, 45,* 31–39.

Gorman, J. M., Liebowitz, M. R., Fyer, A. J., & Stein, J. (1989). A neuroanatomical hypothesis for panic disorder. *American Journal of Psychiatry, 146,* 148–161.

Graeff, F. G., Guimaraes, F. S., DeAndrade, T. G., & Deakin, J. F. (1996): Role of 5-HT in stress, anxiety, and depression. *Pharmacology Biochememistry and Behavior, 54,* 129–141.

Gray, T. S. (1993). Amygdaloid CRF pathways: Role in autonomic, neuroendocrine, and behavioral response to stress. *Annals of the New York Academy of Science, 697,* 53–60.

Gurvits, T. V., Shenton, M. E., Hokama, H., Ohta, H., Lasko, N. B., Gilbertson, M. W., Orr, S. P., Kikinis, R., Jolesz, F. A., McCarley, R. W., & Pitman, R. K. (1996). Magnetic resonance imaging study of hippocampal volume in chronic combat-related posttraumatic stress disorder. *Biological Psychiatry, 40,* 192–199.

Halgren, E. (1992). Emotional neurophysiology of the amygdala within the context of human cognition. In J. P. Aggleton (Ed.), *The amygdala: Neurobiological aspects of emotion, memory, and mental dysfunction* (p. 191). New York: Wiley-Liss.

Heilig, M., Koob, G. F., Ekman, R., & Britton, K. T. (1994). Corticotropin-releasing factor and neuropeptide Y: Role in emotional integration. *Trends in Neurosciences, 17,* 80–85.

Hirshfeld, D. R., Rosenbaum, J. F., Biederman, J., Bolduc, E. A., Faraone, S. V., Snidman, N., Reznick, J. S., & Kagan, J. (1992). Stable behavioral inhibition and its association with anxiety disorder. *Journal of the American Academy of Child and Adolescent Psychiatry, 31,* 103–111.

Hoehn-Saric, R., McLeod, D. R., & Zimmerli, W. D. (1989). Somatic manifestations in women with generalized anxiety disorder. *Archives of General Psychiatry, 46,* 1113–1119.

Hoffman, L., Watson, P. D., Wilson, G., & Montgomery, J. (1989). Low plasma beta-endorphin in post-traumatic stress disorder. *Australian and New Zealand Journal of Psychiatry, 29,* 268–273.

Holsboer, F., Grasser, A., Friess, E., & Wiedemann, K. (1994). Steroid effects on central neurons and implications for psychiatric and neurological disorders. *Annals of the New York Academy of Science, 746,* 345–359.

Johnson, M. R., Lydiard, R. B., Zealberg, J. J., Fossey, M. D., & Ballenger, J. C. (1994). Plasma and CSF HVA levels in panic patients with comorbid social phobia. *Biological Psychiatry, 36,* 426–427.

Kagan, J. (1997). Temperament and the reactions to unfamiliarity. *Child Development, 68,* 139–143.

Kagan, J., Reznick, J. S., & Snidman, N. (1987). The physiology and psychology of behavioral inhibition in children. *Child Development, 58,* 1459–1473.

Kalin, N. H., Shelton, S. E., Rickman, M., & Davidson, R. J. (1998). Individual differences in freezing and cortisol in infant and mother rhesus monkeys. *Behavioral Neuroscience, 112,* 251–254.

Kalin, N. H., Takahashi, L. K., & Chen, F. L. (1994). Restraint stress increases corticotropin-releasing hormone mRNA content in the amygdala and paraventricular nucleus. *Brain Research, 656,* 182–186.

Kaschka, W. P., Feistel, H., Ebert, D., Joraschky, P., & Marienhagen, J. (1992). Cerebral gaba-a benzodiazepine receptor distribution in anxiety disorders. *Clinical Neuropharmacology, 15* (suppl.), 27B.

Katz, R. J., Landau, P. S., Lott, M., Bystritsky, A., Diamond, B., Hoehn-Saric, R., Rosenthal, M., & Weise, C. (1993). Serotonergic (5-HT2) mediation of anxietytherapeutic effects of serazepine in generalized anxiety disorder. *Biological Psychiatry, 34,* 41–44.

Kawachi, I., Sparrow, D., Vokonas, P. S., & Weiss, S. T. (1995). Decreased heart rate variability in men with phobic anxiety (data from the Normative Aging Study). *American Journal of Cardiology, 75,* 882–885.

Klein, E., Cnaani, E., Harel, T., Braun, S., & Beh-haim, S. A. (1995). Altered heart rate variability in panic disorder patients. *Biological Psychiatry, 37,* 18–24.

Kluver, H., & Bucy, P. C. (1939). Preliminary analysis of functions of the temporal lobes in monkeys. *Archives of Neurology and Psychiatry, 42,* 979–1000.

Kosten, T. R., Mason, J. W., & Giller, E. L. (1987). Sustained urinary norepinephrine and epinephrine elevation in posttraumatic stress disorder. *Psychoneuroendocrinology, 12,* 13–20.

Kuikka, J. T., Pitkanen, A., Lepola, U., Partanen, K., Vainio, P., Bergstrom, K. A., Wieler, H. J., Kaiser, K. P., Mittelbach, L., & Koponen, H. (1995). Abnormal regional benzodiazepine receptor uptake in the prefrontal cortex in patients with panic disorder. *Nuclear Medicine Communications, 16,* 273–280.

Laakmann, G., Schule, C., Lorkowski, G., Baghai, T., Kuhn, K., & Ehrentraut, S. (1998). Buspirone and lorazepam in the treatment of generalized anxiety disorder in outpatients. *Psychopharmacology* (Berl), *136,* 357–366.

LaBar, K. S., Gatenby, J. C., Gore, J. C., LeDoux, J. E., & Phelps, E. A. (1998). Human amygdala activation during conditioned fear acquisition and extinction: A mixed-trial fMRI study. *Neuron, 20,* 937–945.

Lechner, S. M., Curtis, A. L., Brons, R., & Valentino, R. J. (1997). Locus coeruleus activation by colon distention: Role of corticotropin-releasing factor and excitatory amino acids. *Brain Research, 756,* 114–124.

LeDoux, J. E. (Ed.). (1996). *The emotional brain.* New York: Simon and Schuster.

LeDoux, J. E., Cicchetti, P., Xagoraris, A., & Romanski, L. M. (1990). The lateral amygdaloid nucleus: Sensory interface of the amygdala in fear conditioning. *Journal of Neuroscience, 10,* 1062–1069.

Leserman, J., Petetto, J. M., Perkins, D. O., Folds, J. D., Golden, R. N., & Evans, D. L. (1997). Severe stress, depressive symptoms, and change in lymphocyte subsets in human immunodeficiency virus–infected men. *Archives of General Psychiatry, 54,* 279–285.

Liebowitz, M. R., Fyer, A. J., Gorman, J. M., Dillon, D., Davies, S., Stein, J. M., Cohen, B. S., & Klein, D. F. (1985). Specificity of lactate infusion in social phobia vs. panic disorder. *American Journal of Psychiatry, 142,* 947–950.

Liu, D., Diorio, J., Tannenbaum, B., Caldji, C., Francis, D., Freedman, A., Sharma, S., Pearson, D., Plotsky, P. M., & Meaney, M. J. (1997). Maternal care, hippocampal glucocorticoid receptors, and hypothalamic-pituitary-adrenal response to stress. *Science, 277,* 1659–1662.

Lucey, J. V., Costa, D. C., Busatto, G., et al. (1997). Caudate regional cerebral blood flow in obsessive-compulsive disorder, panic disorder and healthy controls on single photon emission computerized tomography. *Psychiatry Research, 74,* 25–33.

Majidishad, P., Pelli, D. G., & LeDoux, J. E. (1996). Disruption of fear conditioning to contextual stimuli but not to tone by lesions of the accessory basal nucleus of the amygdala [Abstract]. *Society for Neuroscience, 22,* 1116.

Malizia, A. L., Cunningham, V. J., Bell, C. J., Liddle, P. F., Jones, T., & Nutt, D. J. (1998). Decreased brain GABA(A)-benzodiazepine receptor binding in panic disorder: Preliminary results from a quantitative PET study. *Archives of General Psychiatry, 55,* 715–720.

Manning, B. H. (1998). A lateralized deficit in morphine antinociception after unilateral inactivation of the central amygdala. *Journal of Neuroscience, 18,* 9453–9470.

Mason, J., Weizman, R., Laor, N., Wang, S., Schujovitsky, A., Abramovitz-Schneider, P., Feiler, D., & Charney, D. (1996). Serum triiodothyronine elevation in posttraumatic stress disorder: A cross-cultural study. *Biological Psychiatry, 39,* 835–838.

McFall, M. E., Murburg, M. M., Ko, G. N., & Veith, R. C. (1990). Autonomic responses to stress in Vietnam combat veterans with posttraumatic stress disorder. *Biological Psychiatry, 27,* 1165–1175.

Morgan, M. A., & LeDoux, J. E. (1995). Differential contribution of dorsal and ventral medial prefrontal cortex to the acquisition and extinction of conditioned fear in rats. *Behavioral Neuroscience, 109,* 681–688.

Morris, J. S., Ohman, A., & Dolan, R. J. (1998). Conscious and unconscious emotional learning in the human amygdala. *Nature, 393,* 467–470.

Nemeroff, C. B. (1992). New vistas in neuropeptide research in neuropsychiatry: Focus on corticotropin-releasing factor. *Neuropsychopharmacology, 6,* 69–75.

Nordahl, T. E., Semple, W. E., Gross, M., Mellman, T. A., Stein, M. B., Goyer, P., King, A. C., Uhde, T. W., &

Cohen, R. M. (1990). Cerebral glucose metabolic differences in patients with panic disorder. *Neuropsychopharmacology, 3,* 261–272.

Papp, L. A., Klein, D. F., Martinez, J., Schneier, F., Cole, R., Liebowitz, M. R., Hollander, E., Fyer, A. J., Jordan, F., & Gorman, J. M. (1993). Diagnostic and substance specificity of carbon-dioxide-induced panic. *American Journal of Psychiatry, 150,* 250–257.

Pavcovich, L. A., Yang, M., Miselis, R. R., & Valentino, R. J. (1998). Novel role for the pontine micturition center, Barrington's nucleus: Evidence for coordination of colonic and forebrain activity. *Brain Research, 784,* 355–361.

Pine, D. S., Cohen, P., & Brook, J. (1996). Emotional problems during youth as predictors of stature during early adulthood: Results from a prospective epidemiologic study. *Pediatrics, 97,* 856–863.

Pitkanen, A., Savander, V., & LeDoux, J. E. (1997). Organization of intra-amygdaloid circuitries in the rat: An emerging framework for understanding functions of the amygdala. *Trends in Neuroscience, 20,* 517–523.

Pitman, R. K., van der Kolk, B. A., Orr, S. P., & Greenberg, M. S. (1990). Naloxone-reversible analgesic response to combat-related stimuli in posttraumatic stress disorder. *Archives of General Psychiatry, 47,* 541–544.

Potts, N. L., Davidson, J. R., Krishnan, K. R., & Doraiswamy, P. M. (1994). Magnetic resonance imaging in social phobia. *Psychiatry Research, 52,* 35–42.

Rauch, S. L., van der Kolk, B. A., Fisler, R. E., Alpert, N. M., Orr, S. P., Savage, C. R., Fischman, A. J., Jenike, M. A., & Pitman, R. K. (1996). A symptom provocation study of posttraumatic stress disorder using positron emission tomography and script driven imagery. *Archives of General Psychiatry, 53,* 380–387.

Reiman, E. M., Raichle, M. E., Butler, F .K., Herscovitch, P., & Robins, E. (1984). A focal brain abnormality in panic disorder, a severe form of anxiety. *Nature, 310,* 683–685.

Reiman, E. M., Raichle, M. E., Robins, E., Butler, F. K., Herscovitch, P., Fox, P., & Perlmutter, J. (1986). The application of positron emission tomography to the study of panic disorder. *American Journal of Psychiatry, 143,* 469–477.

Reiman, E. M., Raichle, M. E., Robins, E., Mintun, M. A., Fusselman, M. J., Fox, P. T., Price, J. L., & Hackman, K. A. (1989). Neuroanatomical correlates of a lactate-induced anxiety attack. *Archives of General Psychiatry, 46,* 493–500.

Reist, C., Kauffmann, C. D., Chicz-Demet, A., Chen, C. C., & Demet, E. M. (1995). REM latency, dexamethasone suppression test, and thyroid releasing hormone stimulation test in posttraumatic stress disorder. *Progress in*

Neuropsychopharmacology and Biological Psychiatry, 19, 433–443.

Rook, G. A., & Zumla, A. (1997). Gulf War syndrome: Is it due to a systemic shift in cytokine balance towards a Th$_2$ profile? *Lancet, 349,* 1831–1833.

Rosenblum, L. A., & Andrews, M. W. (1994). Influences of environmental demand on maternal behavior and infant development. *Acta Paediatrica Supplement, 397,* 57–63.

Rosenblum, L. A., & Paully, G. S. (1984). The effects of varying environmental demands on maternal and infant behavior. *Child Development, 55,* 305–314.

Rudy, J. W. (1996). Postconditioning isolation disrupts contextual conditioning: An experimental analysis. *Behavioral Neuroscience, 110,* 238–246.

Rudy, J. W., & Pugh, C. R. (1996). A comparison of contextual and generalized auditory cue fear conditioning: Evidence for similar memory processes. *Behavioral Neuroscience, 110,* 1299–1308.

Rush, A. J., Giles, D. E., Schlesser, M. A., Orsulak, P. J., Weissenburger, J. E., Fulton, C. L., Fairchild, C. J., & Roffwarg, H. P. (1997). Dexamethasone response, thyrotropin-releasing hormone stimulation, rapid eye movement latency, and subtypes of depression. *Biological Psychiatry, 41,* 915–928.

Sakaguchi, A., LeDoux, J. E., & Reis, D. J. (1983). Sympathetic nerves and adrenal medulla: Contributions to cardiovascular-conditioned emotional responses in spontaneously hypertensive rats. *Hypertension, 5,* 728–738.

Samuels, M. H., Luther, M., Henry, P., & Ridgway, E. C. (1994) Effects of hydrocortisone on pulsatile pituitary glycoprotein secretion. *Journal of Clinical Endocrinology and Metabolism, 78,* 211–215.

Sanders, S. K., Morzorati, S. L., & Shekhar, A. (1995). Priming of experimental anxiety by repeated subthreshold GABA blockade in the rat amygdala. *Brain Research, 699,* 250–259.

Sapolsky, R. M. (1990). Stress in the wild. *Scientific American, 262,*116–123.

Schulkin, J., Gold, P. W., & McEwen, B. S. (1998). Induction of corticotropin-releasing hormone gene expression by glucocorticoids: Implications for understanding the states of fear and anxiety and allostatic load. *Psychoneuroendocrinology, 23,* 219–243.

Shekhar, A., Keim, S. R., Simon, J. R., & McBride, W. J. (1996). Physiological arousal elicited by sodium lactate infusion in rats with dorsomedial hypothalamic GABA dysfunction. *Pharmacology Biochemistry and Behavior, 55,* 249–256.

Shin, L. M., Kosslyn, S. M., McNally, R. J., Alpert, N. M., Thompson, W. L., Rauch, S. L., Macklin, M. L., & Pitman, R. K. (1997). Visual imagery and perception in posttraumatic stress disorder: A positron emission tomographic investigation. *Archives of General Psychiatry, 54,* 233–237.

Sloan, R. P., Shapiro, P. A., & Gorman, J. M. (1990). Psychophysiological reactivity in cardiac transplant recipients. *Psychophysiology, 27,* 187–194.

Smith, M. A., Davidson, J., Ritchie, J. C., Kudler, H., Lipper, S., Chappell, P., & Nemeroff, C. B. (1989). The corticotropin releasing hormone test in patients with posttraumatic stress disorder. *Biological Psychiatry, 26,* 349–355.

Southwick, S. M., Krystal, J. H., Bremner, J. D., Morgan, C. A., III, Nicolaou, A. L., Nagy, L. M., Johnson, D. R., Heninger, G. R., & Charney, D. S. (1997). Noradrenergic and serotonergic function in posttraumatic stress disorder. *Archives of General Psychiatry, 54,* 749–758.

Stein, M. B., Asmundson, G. J., & Chartier, M. (1994). Autonomic responsivity in generalized social phobia. *Journal of Affective Disorders, 31,* 211–221.

Stein, M. B., Koverola, C., Hanna, C., Torchia, M. G., & McClarty, B. (1997). Hippocampal volume in women victimized by childhood sexual abuse. *Psychological Medicine, 27,* 951–959.

Stein, M. B., Tancer, M. E., & Uhde, T. W. (1992). Heart rate and plasma norepinephrine responsivity to othostatic challenge in anxiety disorders: Comparison of patients with panic disorder and social phobia and normal control subjects. *Archives of General Psychiatry, 49,* 311–317.

Sterling, P., & Eyer, J. (1981). Allostasis: A new paradigm to explain arousal pathology. In S. Fisher & H. S. Reason (Eds.), *Handbook of life stress, cognition and health.* New York: Wiley.

Stewart, R. S., Devous, M. D., Rush, A. J., Lane, L., & Bonte, F. J. (1988). Cerebral blood flow changes during sodium-lactate-induced panic attacks. *American Journal of Psychiatry, 145,* 442–449.

Sullivan, G. M., Canfield, S. M., Lederman, S., Xiao, E., Ferin, M., & Wardlaw, S. L. (1997). Intracerebroventricular injection of interleukin-1 suppresses peripheral lymphocyte function in the primate. *Neuroimmunomodulation, 4,* 12–18.

Sullivan, G. M., Coplan, J. D., & Gorman, J. M. (1998). The psychoneuroendocrinology of anxiety disorders. *Psychiatric Clinics of North America, 2,* 397–412.

Tancer, M. E., Stein, M. B., & Uhde, T. W. (1993). Growth hormone response to clonidine in social phobia: Comparison to patients with panic disorder and healthy volunteers. *Biological Psychiatry, 34,* 591–595.

Tiihonen, J., Kuikka, J., Bergstrom, K., Lepola, U., Koponen, H., & Leinonen, E. (1997). Dopamine reuptake site densities in patients with social phobia. *American Journal of Psychiatry, 54,* 239–242.

Tiihonen, J., Kuikka, J., Rasanen, P., Lepola, U., Koponen, H., Liuska, A., Lehmusvaara, A., Vainio, P., Kononen, M. et al. (1997). Cerebral benzodiazepine receptor binding and distribution in generalized anxiety disorder: A fractal analysis. *Molecular Psychiatry, 2*(6), 463–471.

Tiller, J. W., Biddle, N., Maguire, K. P., & Davies, B. M. (1988). The dexamethasone suppression test and plasma dexamethasone in generalized anxiety disorder. *Biological Psychiatry, 23,* 261–270.

Tork, I., & Hornung, J. P. (1990). Raphe nuclei and the serotonergic system. In G. Paxinos (Ed.), *The human nervous system* (pp. 1001–1022). San Diego, CA: Academic Press.

Tyor, W. R., Glass, J. D., Griffin, J. W., Becker, P. S., McArthur, J. C., Bezman, L., & Griffin, D. E. (1992). Cytokine expression in the brain during the acquired immunodeficiency syndrome. *Annals of Neurology, 31,* 349–360.

Uddo, M., Vasterling, J. T., Brailey, K., & Sutker, P. B. (1993). Memory and attention in posttraumatic stress disorder. *Journal of Psychopathology and Behavioral Assessment, 15,* 43–52

Uhde, T. W. (1997). A comparison of the effects of intravenous pentagastrin on patients with social phobia, panic disorder, and healthy subjects. *Neuropsychopharmacology, 16,* 229–237.

Uhde, T. W., & Tancer, M. E. (1994). Normal urinary free cortisol and post dexamethasone cortisol in social phobia. *Journal of Affective Disorders, 30,* 155–161.

Uno, H., Ross, T., Else, J., Suleman, M., & Sapolsky, R. (1989). Hippocampal damage associated with prolonged and fatal stress in primates. *Journal of Neuroscience, 9,* 1705–1711.

Walker, E. A., Katon, W. J., Jemelka, R. P., & Roy-Bryne, P. P. (1992). Comorbidity of gastrointestinal complaints, depression, and anxiety in the Epidemiologic Catchment Area (ECA) study. *American Journal of Medicine, 92,* 26S–30S.

Wang, S., Mason, J., Charney, D., Yehuda, R., Riney, S., & Southwick, S. (1997). Relationships between hormonal profile and novelty seeking in combat-related posttraumatic stress disorder. *Biological Psychiatry, 41,* 145–151.

Wetzler, S., Asnis, G. M., DeLecuona, J. M., & Kalus, O. (1996). Serotonin function in panic disorder: Intravenous administration of meta-chlorophenylpiperazine. *Psychiatry Research, 62,* 77–82.

Whalen, P. J., Rauch, S. L., Etcoff, N. L., McInerney, S. C., Lee, M. B., & Jenike, M. A. (1998). Masked presentations of emotional facial expressions modulate amygdala activity without explicit knowledge. *Journal of Neuroscience, 18,* 411–418.

Woods, S. W., Koster, K., Krystal, J. K., Smith, E. O., Zubal, I. G., Hoffer, P. B., & Charney, D. S. (1988). Yohimbine alters regional cerebral blood flow in panic disorder. *Lancet, 2,* 678.

Wu, J. C., Buchsbaum, M. S., Hershey, T. G., Hazlett, E., Sicotte, N., & Johnson, J. C. (1991). PET in generalized anxiety disorder. *Biological Psychiatry, 29,* 1181–1199.

Yehuda, R., Boisoneau, D., Lowy, M. T., & Giller, E. L. (1995). Dose-response changes in plasma cortisol and lymphocyte glucocorticoid receptors following dexamethasone administration in combat veterans with and without posttraumatic stress disorder. *Archives of General Psychiatry, 52,* 583–593.

Yehuda, R., Southwick, S. M., Nussbaum, G., Wahby, V., Giller, E. L., Jr., & Mason, J. W. (1990). Low urinary cortisol excretion in patients with PTSD. *Journal of Mental Diseases, 178,* 366–409.

Yehuda, R., Southwick, S., Giller, E. L., Ma, X., & Mason, J. W. (1992). Urinary catecholamine excretion and severity of PTSD symptoms in Vietnam combat veterans. *Journal of Nervous and Mental Disease, 180,* 321–325.

Yehuda, R., Southwick, S. M., Krystal, J. M., Charney, D. S., & Mason, J. W. (1993). Enhanced suppression of cortisol following dexamethasone administration in combat veterans with posttraumatic stress disorder and major depressive disorder. *American Journal of Psychiatry, 150,* 83–86.

Yeragani, V. K., Sobolewski, E., Igel, G., Johnson, C., Jampala, V. C., Kay, J., Hillman, N., Yeragani, S., & Vempati, S. (1998). Decreased heart-period variability in patients with panic disorder: A study of Holter ECG records. *Psychiatry Research, 78,* 89–99.

CHAPTER 3

PHARMACOLOGICAL MANAGEMENT OF ANXIETY DISORDERS

David A. Spiegel
Markus Wiegel
Sandra L. Baker
Kamala A. I. Greene

Anxiety disorders are among the most common and challenging illnesses seen by primary care practitioners. Fortunately, they are also among the most treatable. The marketing of new medicinal agents during the last decade, as well as the continuing refinement of empirically validated psychosocial therapies, has greatly improved the outlook for most anxiety sufferers. At the same time, the increasing array of available treatments requires clinicians to choose among options whose relative advantages and disadvantages for a particular patient may not be entirely clear. The situation is further complicated by the fact that patients are often seeing other caregivers concurrently for the same problems (Gray, 1987; Sanderson & Wetzler, 1993) or may desire a combination of medication and psychotherapy (Rapaport et al, 1996; Waikar et al., 1994/1995). Very little is known about how different treatments interact with each other, although as Gray (1987) observed, the interactions may not always be beneficial.

In this chapter we discuss the pharmacological management of the major anxiety disorders and, where data are available, the combination of pharmacotherapy with forms of psychosocial treatment. The psychosocial treatments themselves are described elsewhere in this book.

GENERAL CONSIDERATIONS FOR PHARMACOTHERAPY

The selection of an appropriate pharmacological treatment for an anxious patient requires consideration of a number of factors. Chief among these is the establish-

ment of an accurate diagnosis. Anxiety disorders have many features in common; however, they often respond differently to drugs. For example, panic attacks occur in the context of panic disorder, phobias, obsessive-compulsive disorder (OCD), and posttraumatic stress disorder (PTSD) (American Psychiatric Association [APA], 1994), but, as we shall discuss, benzodiazepines, which are effective for the treatment of panic disorder and probably social phobia, are of little help for OCD and PTSD and actually may be detrimental when used for specific phobias.

Second, it is uncommon for anxiety disorders to exist in isolation. More often, two or more disorders will be present together, or an anxiety disorder will coexist with a mood or substance-related disorder or a complicating medical condition. Among individuals with panic disorder, for example, an estimated 15–30% also have social phobia, 25% generalized anxiety disorder, 10–20% specific phobias, 8–10% OCD, and 50–65% major depression (*DSM-IV*). When possible, it makes sense to select a medication that is likely to be efficacious for other present conditions as well as for the primary disorder. Table 3.1 summarizes the disorders for which there is good evidence of efficacy for various medications (these are discussed in more detail later in this chapter). The table may be helpful in choosing an agent when conditions occur together.

The prevalence of substance use disorders among patients with anxiety disorders is estimated to be 10–20% (Bibb & Chambless, 1986; Cox et al., 1990; DuPont, 1997; Thyer et al., 1986), and individuals

TABLE 3.1. Medications with Empirically Established Efficacy for Specific Anxiety Disorders

MEDICATION CLASS	ANXIETY DISORDER						
	PANIC DISORDER[a]	GAD	PTSD	SOCIAL PHOBIA[b] (GENERALIZED)	SOCIAL PHOBIA[b] (PERFORMANCE)	SPECIFIC PHOBIA[c]	OCD
Benzodiazepines	alprazolam (++) clonazepam (++) lorazepam (+)	most (+)		clonazepam (+)			
TCAs	imipramine (++) clomipramine (++)	imipramine (++)	imipramine (+) amitriptyline (+)				clomipramine (++)
SSRIs[d]	paroxetine (++) sertraline (++) fluoxetine (+) citalopram (+) fluvoxamine (+)		fluoxetine (++)	paroxetine (++)			paroxetine (++) sertraline (++) fluoxetine (++) fluvoxamine (++)
MAOIs	phenelzine (++)		phenelzine (+)	phenelzine (++)			
Azapirones		buspirone (++)					
Beta blockers					propranolol (+) atenolol (+)		
Other		venlafaxine (++) trazodone (+)	nefazodone (+)				

[a]Combine with exposure instructions for patients with significant agoraphobia.
[b]Combine with exposure instructions.
[c]Pharmacotherapy is generally not indicated for specific phobia.
[d]If one SSRI is effective, others probably are as well.
(+) Probably effective. Efficacy demonstrated in at least one large, well-designed, double-blind trial or in several uncontrolled trials by different investigators.
(++) Effective. Efficacy demonstrated in at least two large, well-designed, double-blind trials conducted at multiple sites or by different investigators comparing with placebo or to a drug with established efficacy.
TCAs = tricyclic antidepressants; SSRIs = selective serotonin reuptake inhibitors; MAOIs = monoamine oxidase inhibitors.

with alcohol abuse or dependence are two to three times more likely than others to have anxiety disorders (Swendsen et al., 1998). The relation of alcohol use to anxiety is complex and appears to be different for different disorders. When present with phobias, alcoholism typically occurs secondarily (Swendsen et al., 1998) and may be a consequence of drinking as a form of self-medication (Kushner, Sher, & Beitman, 1990; Marshall, 1995; Schneier et al., 1989). However, alcoholism is as likely to precede as to follow panic disorder, suggesting that in some cases it may increase the risk of panic disorder or share common etiologic factors with it (Swendsen et al., 1998). Consistent with that, comorbid alcoholism is associated with increased severity of panic disorder but not phobias (Swendsen et al., 1998). Those relationships suggest that when alcoholism develops secondarily to a pervasive phobia, one might reasonably treat the phobia first. But when it is present with panic disorder, the two conditions should be treated together or the alcoholism first (DuPont, 1997). Of course, in choosing a medication, possible alcohol–medication interactions must be considered.

A patient's past psychiatric history and family history also often provide useful information with respect to treatment decisions. For example, patients with a personal or family history of major depression might do best on an antidepressant medication with efficacy for the presenting problem, and a history of substance abuse would argue against the use of benzodiazepines. Other factors that influence the choice of a medication regimen include the patient's age, current health, use of other medications, and preferences, as well as medication costs.

PHARMACOLOGICAL AGENTS

As indicated in Table 3.1, medications from several classes have been shown to be effective for the treatment of certain anxiety disorders, and many are effective for more than one disorder. In this section we briefly review some features of the major classes of these medications as they pertain to the treatment of anxiety disorders in general. Information relevant to the treatment of specific disorders and about other agents used to treat anxiety is presented in the next section. Readers should consult the *Physician's Desk Reference,* package insert, or a recent psychopharma-

cology textbook (e.g., Schatzberg, Cole, & DeBattista, 1997; Schatzberg & Nemeroff, 1998) for more detailed information about specific drugs.

Benzodiazepines

Introduced in the early 1960s as a safer and better-tolerated alternative to barbiturates, benzodiazepines have for decades been the most frequently prescribed medications for anxiety and anxiety-related disorders. Eight agents in this class are currently approved by the Food and Drug Administration (FDA) for the treatment of general anxiety, and two (alprazolam and clonazepam) for the treatment of panic disorder. In addition to their anxiolytic effects, benzodiazepines also have hypnotic, myorelaxant, and anticonvulsant properties and are useful for the treatment of alcohol withdrawal syndromes (Ballenger, 1998).

Benzodiazepines are thought to work by enhancing the natural effect of gamma-aminobutyric acid (GABA) on chloride conductance through cell membranes, which inhibits cellular excitability (for detailed discussions of the mechanisms of action of psychopharmacological agents see Stahl, 1996). Compared with other drugs used to treat anxiety disorders, benzodiazepines are safe, act quickly, and have relatively few side effects. The principal side effect is sedation; others include ataxia, weakness, psychomotor impairment, confusion, and anterograde amnesia. These effects are dose-dependent and generally transient.

Concerns about the potential of benzodiazepines to induce tolerance, abuse, and dependence have been the source of considerable controversy and confusion, leading some patients and practitioners to shy away from these agents (for a review of this topic see Shader & Greenblatt, 1993). Although tolerance does develop to the sedative side effects of benzodiazepines, there is little evidence that it does to their anxiolytic effects (Hayward, Wardle, & Higgitt, 1989; Romach et al., 1992). Instances of benzodiazepine abuse are also uncommon and occur primarily as part of a polysubstance abuse pattern (APA, 1990).

In contrast to tolerance and abuse, physiological dependence on benzodiazepines develops in most patients with prolonged therapy, as evidenced by the occurrence of characteristic withdrawal symptoms when the medication is reduced or discontinued. Withdrawal symptoms such as nervousness, irritability, sleep disturbance, dizziness, and tremor (Pecknold et al., 1988; Schweizer, Rickels, et al., 1990) overlap considerably with symptoms of anxiety and may be misinterpreted as a return of the disorder being treated, leading to unnecessary reinstatement of pharmacotherapy. In practice this problem can generally be avoided by the use of a very slow, flexible drug taper (Spiegel & Bruce, 1997).

Serotonin 1A (5-HT$_{1A}$) Receptor Partial Agonists

Receptor partial agonists are agents that act similarly to natural receptor ligands (e.g., neurotransmitters) but with weaker effects. Theoretically, that property gives them opposite effects in the presence of an excess or deficiency of the natural ligand. In the former case, by competitively displacing the excess ligand from some of its receptor sites, they produce a functional decrease in its effect; in the latter, by occupying empty receptors, they partially compensate for the deficient ligand and thus produce a functional increase in its effect. Serotonergic excess has long been suspected to play a role in anxiety, because drugs that increase serotonin tend to exacerbate anxiety, and drugs that decrease it tend to reduce anxiety (Stahl, 1996). Consistent with those observations, several drugs that act as partial agonists at 5-HT$_{1A}$ receptors have been found to have anxiolytic properties.

The first 5-HT$_{1A}$ partial agonist to be developed was buspirone, which received FDA approval for generalized anxiety disorder in 1986. Several related compounds are presently being tested (e.g., gepirone, ipsapirone). Buspirone has no affinity for the benzodiazepine receptor and lacks the benzodiazepines' sedative, muscle relaxant, and anticonvulsant properties as well as their ability to potentiate the effects of alcohol (Ninan, Cole, & Yonkers, 1998). Moreover, it has no apparent abuse potential and does not cause a dependence syndrome (Rickels, 1990). Side effects, including dizziness, headaches, nausea, and nervousness, are generally manageable by a temporary dosage reduction. One disadvantage of buspirone relative to the benzodiazepines is its slower onset of action, similar to that of antidepressant medications.

As previously noted, partial agonists should theoretically be helpful for conditions attributable to neurotransmitter deficiencies as well as excesses.

Accordingly, one might expect that serotonin receptor partial agonists might be helpful for depression in addition to anxiety. Indeed, buspirone has been shown to have antidepressant activity at doses of 40–60 mg/d, somewhat higher than generally required for its antianxiety effect (Fabre, 1990; Rickels, 1990; Robinson et al., 1990).

In view of its many advantages over the benzodiazepines, it is perhaps surprising that buspirone has not enjoyed greater popularity. This appears to be due in part to the impression of psychiatrists and other physicians that buspirone is less effective than benzodiazepines and does not work in patients who have taken benzodiazepines in the past (Schatzberg et al., 1997). To the extent that patients associate the effectiveness of benzodiazepines with their sedative side effects or the promptness of their action, they may report a lack of benefit from buspirone. Therefore, when buspirone is prescribed, it is important to ensure that patients have appropriate expectations regarding side effects and response time (Hales, Hilty, & Wise, 1997; Schweizer & Rickels, 1997b).

Tricyclic Antidepressants

Tricyclic antidepressants (TCAs) have a role in the treatment of several anxiety disorders, although with notable differences. Imipramine was the first agent noted to suppress panic attacks (Klein & Fink, 1962) and is still the gold standard for pharmacotherapeutic efficacy in panic disorder. Clomipramine is the only TCA with significant efficacy in OCD, and it is currently the standard among treatments for that disorder. TCAs have a variety of actions in the central nervous system (CNS). Their therapeutic efficacy is thought to result from inhibition of the postrelease reuptake of norepinephrine or serotonin into presynaptic nerve terminals. However, their side effects (e.g., sedation, weight gain, dry mouth, blurred vision, tachycardia, constipation, urinary hesitancy, postural hypotension, dizziness) arise primarily from blockade of postsynaptic adrenergic, muscarinic, histamine, or dopamine receptors. TCAs differ in the degrees to which they exert these various effects, which is useful to consider when changing medications because of intolerance or poor response (for a comparative table see Potter, Manji, & Rudorfer, 1998, p. 202). The unique efficacy of clomipramine in OCD is attributed to its exceptionally potent effect on serotonin reuptake relative to norepinephrine reuptake.

In a substantial minority of patients with panic disorder, TCAs also cause CNS activation, a side effect known as the "jitteriness syndrome" and characterized by increased anxiety and panic, shakiness, irritability, and insomnia (Pohl et al., 1988). This side effect also occurs with other antidepressants and is a common cause of treatment discontinuation. It occurs at the onset of treatment, generally is time-limited, and can be minimized by starting with low medication doses and increasing slowly.

Monoamine Oxidase Inhibitors

Monoamine oxidase inhibitors (MAOIs) are rarely prescribed by primary care physicians owing to concern about potential untoward interactions with certain foods, beverages, and medications. However, their efficacy for anxiety conditions such as panic disorder and generalized social phobia is undisputed. MAOIs are believed to exert their therapeutic effects by inhibiting monoamine oxidase A (MAO-A), the enzyme that metabolizes the neurotransmitters most closely linked to anxiety and depression (e.g., norepinephrine and serotonin). Classic MAOIs (e.g., phenelzine, tranylcypromine) irreversibly deactivate MAO-A (as well as MAO-B), producing potent and long lasting effects. However, recently a new class of MAOIs has been developed that bind reversibly to MAO-A with little affinity for MAO-B. Called *reversible inhibitors of MAO-A (RIMAs)*, these agents, which include moclobemide and brofaromine, have less potential for causing hypertensive episodes and are therefore safer than currently available MAOIs. RIMAs appear to be effective for the treatment of anxiety and mood disorders, but it is not clear when they will be available commercially in the United States.

Selective Serotonin Reuptake Inhibitors

Initially developed as antidepressants, the selective serotonin reuptake inhibitors (SSRIs) have also become favored agents for the treatment of several anxiety disorders, including OCD, panic disorder, social phobia, and PTSD. As a class these agents (which include fluoxetine, paroxetine, sertraline, fluvoxamine, and citalopram) have several advantages over previously available drugs for anxiety; they are safer, better tolerated, and easier to dose than the TCAs and MAOIs, and they lack the abuse and dependence potentials of the benzodiazepines. Moreover, they have a broad spectrum of therapeutic activity, which may be useful when comorbid conditions are present (see Table 3.1).

Pharmacologically, SSRIs inhibit the postrelease reuptake of serotonin into presynaptic nerve terminals in the same way that TCAs block reuptake of a wider range of neurotransmitters. However, they have substantially less affinity for the various postsynaptic receptors that are associated with most of the adverse effects of TCAs. Nevertheless, because serotonergic neurons are widely distributed in the brain and body, SSRIs have a number of side effects, including gastrointestinal symptoms, CNS activation, tremor, headaches, and sexual impairment. CNS activation (including the jitteriness syndrome discussed above) may be especially problematic for anxiety-disordered patients, requiring greater than usual informational preparation and support; lower initial drug doses; slower dose increases; and, occasionally, brief administration of a benzodiazepine or trazodone early in treatment.

Although the SSRIs have many features in common, there are clinically relevant differences among them with regard to their functional half-lives, their potential for drug interactions, and their distribution in special populations such as the elderly (Tollefson & Rosenbaum, 1998). Some SSRIs (e.g., fluoxetine, paroxetine, and fluvoxamine) can interfere with the metabolism of triazolo compounds such as alprazolam or triazolam, necessitating extra caution when these agents are used with them.

PHARMACOTHERAPY OF SPECIFIC DISORDERS

Panic Disorder with or without Agoraphobia

As noted earlier, panic attacks occur in a variety of contexts, both normal and pathological. Panic disorder is diagnosed when a person has experienced panic attacks recurrently and unexpectedly and has developed complications such as persistent concern about having additional attacks, worry about the implications of attacks, or altered behavior because of the attacks (*DSM-IV*). Approximately one-third to one-half of individuals with panic disorder also have agoraphobia.

Historically, pharmacological treatment of panic disorder and agoraphobia has focused on the suppression of panic attacks, with the expectation that when those are controlled, reductions in anticipatory anxiety, agoraphobic avoidance, and the other cognitive and behavioral aspects of the disorder will follow. However, that view has been challenged recently (e.g., Bandelow et al., 1995; Davidson & Moroz, 1998; Spiegel, 1998b), and it is now increasingly recognized that broader measures of treatment efficacy must be used. A simple measure that can be used in primary care settings is the Panic Disorder Severity Scale (PDSS), a clinician-completed, seven-item scale that rates the core features of panic disorder as well as interference with work and social activities (Shear et al., 1997).

Several classes of medications have been shown to be effective for the treatment of panic disorder, as reviewed in the following subsections. For more detailed information the reader is referred to the recently published "Practice Guideline for the Treatment of Patients with Panic Disorder" (APA, 1998). The guideline provides an informative summary of scientific data and professional opinion about the care of patients with panic disorder as well as treatment recommendations.

Benzodiazepines

Despite early observations suggesting that benzodiazepines might not be helpful for panic disorder (e.g., Klein, 1964), their efficacy has since been demonstrated conclusively. Alprazolam was the first pharmacological agent to receive FDA approval for the treatment of panic disorder (see Spiegel, 1998a, for a review of efficacy studies). In the pivotal multicenter trials, alprazolam at an average dose of approximately 6 mg/d was superior to placebo on a range of measures including panic attacks, anticipatory anxiety, panic-related phobias, disability, depressive symptoms, and global improvement (Ballenger et al., 1988; Cross-National Collaborative Panic Study,

1992; Lesser et al., 1988; Noyes et al., 1988). In a subsequent 6-month maintenance study, acute treatment improvements were sustained, with no evidence of tolerance to the therapeutic effects of the drug (Schweizer et al., 1993).

More recently, clonazepam at doses of 1 to 4 mg/d was efficacious on nearly all measures in two large clinical trials (Davidson & Moroz, 1998; Moroz & Rosenbaum, 1998; Rosenbaum, Moroz, & Bowden, 1997). Following 6 to 9 weeks of treatment, nearly half of the patients were evaluated as normal or only borderline ill on the Clinical Global Impressions scale (CGI; Guy, 1976). Other benzodiazepines, including diazepam (Noyes et al., 1996) and lorazepam (Charney & Woods, 1989; Schweizer, Pohl et al., 1990), have also been shown to be effective for panic disorder.

Although the initial alprazolam efficacy studies used average doses of nearly 6 mg/d, subsequent fixed-dose trials have found that many patients benefit from as little as 2 mg/d (Lydiard et al., 1992; Uhlenhuth et al., 1989). This appears to be due primarily to reductions in general and anticipatory anxiety and unexpected (spontaneous) panic attacks as opposed to situationally related anxiety and panic attacks (Lesser et al., 1992; Uhlenhuth et al., 1997). Drug concentration studies suggest that unexpected attacks have a flat blood concentration–response relationship above 20–40 ng/ml (corresponding roughly to doses of 2–4 mg/d) (Greenblatt, Harmatz, & Shader, 1993). In the clonazepam fixed-dose trial, response was flat above 1 mg/d not only for unexpected panics but for most measures, indicating that for most patients 1 mg/d is sufficient (Davidson & Moroz, 1998).

As noted earlier, concerns about possible adverse effects of long-term benzodiazepine therapy have rarely been realized in panic disorder patients. Naturalistic studies of patients treated with alprazolam for up to 4 years (Nagy et al., 1989) or clonazepam for 2 years (Worthington et al., 1998) have found maintenance of gains with no evidence of abuse or dose escalation over time. On the other hand, discontinuance of therapy has been associated with high rates of relapse—typically 50–75%—even after as long as 8 months of treatment (Ballenger, 1994; Spiegel, 1998a). Whether a longer period of maintenance therapy would improve that outcome is unknown, but prolonged benzodiazepine use has been associated with a greater return to drug use in one study (Wardle et al., 1994).

TCAs

The ability of imipramine to suppress panic attacks was demonstrated by Klein and Fink more than 30 years ago, long before the formal delineation of panic disorder as a unique subtype of anxiety (Klein, 1964, 1967; Klein & Fink, 1962). Since then, its efficacy for panic disorder has been demonstrated in at least 15 controlled trials (APA, 1998). In the largest study to date, imipramine (mean dose = 155 mg/d) was superior to placebo and comparable to alprazolam (mean dose = 5.7 mg/d) on a wide range of measures after 8 weeks of treatment, although improvement began earlier with alprazolam (Cross-National Collaborative Panic Study, 1992; Klerman, 1992). Clomipramine has been evaluated in several controlled trials and appears to be at least as effective as imipramine (Cassano et al., 1988; Modigh, Westberg, & Eriksson, 1992) and SSRIs (Lecrubier et al., 1997; Lydiard, Pollack, et al., 1997), and possibly at lower doses (Lecrubier et al., 1997; Roy-Byrne et al., 1993). Although not well studied, other TCAs, including desipramine (Lydiard et al., 1993) and nortryptyline (Roy-Byrne et al., 1993), are also probably effective.

As does alprazolam, imipramine appears to selectively suppress unexpected as opposed to situationally cued panic attacks (Uhlenhuth et al., 1997). Whether it has any direct effect on agoraphobic fear and avoidance is unclear. In an intriguing study, Mavissakalian and Perel (1995) found that panic attacks had a relatively flat drug concentration–response relationship above 140 ng/ml, whereas phobic anxiety and avoidance appeared to have an inverted U-shaped relationship centered narrowly on concentrations in the range of 120–140 ng/ml. If that is so, it suggests that imipramine may have a therapeutic window for optimal response in panic disorder. The investigators have proposed a target dose of 1.75 to 2.0 mg/kg/d, or about 130 mg/d (Mavissakalian & Perel, 1997).

Improvement with TCA therapy typically begins within 3 to 4 weeks and may increase for several months. As with benzodiazepines, termination of therapy is associated with high rates of relapse, even after 6 to 9 months of treatment (Clark et al., 1994;

Katschnig et al., 1995; Mavissakalian & Perel, 1992a; Rickels et al., 1993; Wiborg & Dahl, 1996). However, in one study (Mavissakalian & Perel, 1992a), patients who had been treated successfully for 6 months with imipramine at a dose of 2.25 mg/kg/d were able to be maintained thereafter without relapsing at half that dose. A nonrandomized comparison found that patients so treated for a total of 18 months relapsed at a significantly lower rate following drug discontinuance than patients who had received only 6 months of full-dose therapy (Mavissakalian & Perel, 1992b).

SSRIs

Paroxetine was the first nonbenzodiazepine to receive FDA approval for panic disorder. Its efficacy for panic disorder has been demonstrated in three multicenter trials (Ballenger et al., 1998; Lecrubier et al., 1997; Oehrberg et al., 1995). The minimum effective dose appears to be 40 mg/d, at which dose it was comparable to clomipramine (mean dose = 92 mg/d) and superior to placebo on several panic measures as well as measures of overall illness severity and improvement (for a review of efficacy studies, see Lydiard et al., 1998).

Sertraline, at a mean dose of 122 mg/d, was superior to placebo in two controlled trials (Pohl, Wolkow, & Clary, 1998; Rapaport, Wolkow, & Clary, 1998). Significant differences were found on measures of panic attacks, anxiety, mood, and functioning, as well as on global measures including the PDSS, CGI, and a quality-of-life scale. A separate fixed-dose study found that doses of 50, 100, and 200 mg/d were equally effective (DuBoff et al., 1995). Other controlled trials have found fluoxetine 20 mg/d and citalopram 20–30 or 40–60 mg/d to be better than placebo, and citalopram 20–30 mg/d to be comparable to clomipramine (Lydiard, Pollack, et al., 1997; Wade et al., 1997). Fluvoxamine was better than placebo in one study at a mean dose of 230 mg/d (Black et al., 1993) but not in another study at a mean dose of 171 mg/d (Nair et al., 1996).

Response to SSRIs appears to take somewhat longer than it does to TCAs. There is little information about the optimal duration of treatment. In an extension of the paroxetine fixed-dose study (Ballenger et al., 1998), responders were continued on paroxetine for a total of 22 weeks, after which half were crossed over to placebo. Thirty percent of those switched to placebo relapsed within 12 weeks (Lydiard et al, 1998). In contrast, improvement was maintained among patients continued on paroxetine for a total of 48 weeks in an extension of the LeCrubier et al. (1997) study. Relapse rates after long-term treatment with SSRIs have not been reported.

MAOIs

It is commonly believed that MAOIs are effective for the treatment of panic disorder; however, there are few controlled trials. In the most rigorous study of a currently available MAOI, Sheehan, Ballenger, and Jacobsen (1980) compared phenelzine (45 mg/d), imipramine (150 mg/d), and placebo in 57 patients with panic attacks and agoraphobia. After 12 weeks of treatment, phenelzine was superior to placebo on a variety of measures and was slightly, but not significantly, better than imipramine on most of them. Other studies have suggested that higher doses (e.g., 60–90 mg/d) may be required for optimal response (Roy-Byrne et al., 1993). A controlled trial of brofaromine, a reversible inhibitor of MAO-A, found it to be effective for both panic and phobic symptoms in individuals with panic disorder (Bakish et al., 1993).

Other Antidepressants

Venlafaxine, at a mean dose of 150 mg/d, was effective for panic disorder in a small controlled trial (Pollack et al., 1996), and data from two case series suggest that doses in the range of 50–75 mg/d may be sufficient for many patients (Geracioti, 1995; Papp et al., 1998). Trazodone was more effective than placebo in a small single-blind study (Mavissakalian et al., 1987) but was less effective than either imipramine or alprazolam in a double-blind comparison (Charney et al., 1986). The related compound, nefazodone, has shown some efficacy in depressed patients with panic attacks (DeMartinis, Schweizer, & Rickels, 1996; Zajecka, 1996), but its efficacy for panic disorder is unknown.

Other Agents

Valproic acid has been reported to be effective in several cases of panic disorder (Woodman & Noyes, 1994) and was superior to placebo in a small crossover study (Lum et al., 1990). Propranolol was as effective as alprazolam in one trial (Ravaris et al., 1991) but was ineffective in two others (Noyes et al., 1984; Munjack et al., 1989). Inositol, a second messenger precursor, was effective in a small placebo-controlled trial (Benjamin et al., 1995). The efficacies of other drugs, including calcium channel blockers, clonidine, and buspirone, have yet to be established.

Combined Pharmacotherapy and Psychotherapy

Several early trials of patients with agoraphobia found a short-term advantage for the combination of imipramine and situational exposure therapy over either treatment alone, although the advantage was lost by 2-year follow-up (for reviews, see Mavissakalian, 1993; Telch & Lucas, 1994). Subsequently, deBeurs and colleagues found that fluvoxamine plus exposure therapy was better than exposure alone at reducing agoraphobic avoidance in patients with panic disorder (deBeurs et al., 1995). A study of buspirone plus cognitive-behavioral therapy (CBT) found that the drug enhanced the effects of CBT on generalized anxiety and agoraphobia in the short term (16 weeks) but had no advantage over CBT alone a year after both treatments had ended (Cottraux et al., 1995). The largest combined treatment study to date compared the combination of imipramine and CBT to each treatment alone, a pill placebo, and CBT plus a pill placebo in approximately 300 patients with no more than mild agoraphobia (Barlow, 1998). Preliminary reports indicate that the combined treatment was slightly better than imipramine or CBT alone on some measures as long as pharmacotherapy was continued (9 months) (Gorman, 1998; Shear, 1998) but lost its advantage over CBT after drug treatment was stopped (Woods, 1998).

The combination of benzodiazepines with psychotherapy is more controversial (Wardle, 1990). A review of combined treatment studies involving patients with panic disorder found little evidence that such combinations are better than CBT alone (Spiegel & Bruce, 1997), and there are some data suggesting that concurrent benzodiazepine therapy may undermine the long-term outcome of exposure therapy (Marks et al., 1993) or CBT (Brown & Barlow, 1995; Otto, Pollack, & Sabatino, 1996). In contrast to that, several small studies have found that the administration of CBT to panic disorder patients being withdrawn from benzodiazepine therapy facilitates successful drug discontinuance and reduces relapse during the subsequent 2 to 4 years (Bruce, Spiegel, & Hegel, in press; Hegel, Ravaris, & Ahles, 1994; Otto et al., 1993; Spiegel et al., 1994). There is also a single report that the addition of dynamic psychotherapy during the first 3 months of a 9-month course of clomipramine reduced relapse when that drug was discontinued (Wiborg & Dahl, 1996).

Clinical Management

It is important for patients to know that they have a choice of effective treatments for panic disorder. Both pharmacotherapy and CBT (see Hofmann & Spiegel, 1999) have been shown to be effective, and at present there is no convincing evidence that one modality is better than the other in general or for specific patients (APA, 1998). Neither is there convincing evidence that combined treatments are sufficiently better than pharmacotherapy or CBT alone to justify their routine use for panic disorder.

The usual starting dose, initial target dose, and maximum recommended dose for the major pharmacological agents used to treat panic disorder are summarized in Table 3.2. There is no clear best agent for uncomplicated panic disorder; selections are usually made on the basis of preferences, side effects, cost,

and comorbidity. In recent years the SSRIs have become the favored drugs among pharmacotherapy experts, with benzodiazepines taking second place and TCAs third (Uhlenhuth, 1998). In the event of an unsatisfactory response to single agents, a combination of a benzodiazepine and an antidepressant is preferred before an MAOI is considered.

Because many patients with panic disorder experience an initial hyperstimulatory reaction to antidepressant medications (see medication overviews), antidepressants are usually started at a low dose and increased every few days as tolerated until the target dose is reached. Some physicians administer a benzodiazepine, trazodone, or a beta blocker temporarily if stimulation is excessive. If there is no response after 4 weeks on a TCA or 6 weeks on an SSRI, further increases may be made. Benzodiazepines may be increased more quickly, the limiting factor being sedative side effects. Improvement is usually apparent within the first week but may take several weeks to reach a plateau. Periodic administration of the PDSS may facilitate assessment of treatment response.

If pharmacotherapy is being given as the sole treatment, it should be continued for at least a year before a slow drug taper is attempted. As panic attacks subside, the patient should be encouraged to reenter avoided situations as a means of testing the adequacy of the drug dose, building confidence, and resuming a normal lifestyle (Ballenger, 1991; Pollack & Otto, 1994). In our experience, support and encouragement

TABLE 3.2. Typical Doses for the Major Panic Disorder Medications in Healthy Adults with No Concurrent Medications

MEDICATION	USUAL STARTING DOSE (mg/d)	INITIAL TARGET DOSE (mg/d)	MAXIMUM RECOMMENDED DOSE (mg/d)
Benzodiazepines:			
alprazolam[a]	0.75	2–3	10
clonazepam[b]	0.25–0.5	1	4
TCAs:[c]			
imipramine[d]	10	100–150	300
clomipramine	25	50–100	250
SSRIs:[c]			
paroxetine	10	40	60
sertraline	25	50	200
fluoxetine	5–10	20	80
fluvoxamine	25	100	300
citaloprom	10	20	60

[a] Alprazolam is usually taken in divided doses 3–4 times daily to avoid between-dose symptoms.
[b] Clonazepam is usually taken in divided doses 2–3 times daily.
[c] Low starting doses may be required to avoid initial hyperstimulation.
[d] There may be a therapeutic window for imipramine for overall response.

to challenge avoided situations can often substitute for increases in the medication dose and result in a better long-term outcome. For patients with residual agoraphobia or persistent fear of panic sensations and for those who have difficulty discontinuing pharmacotherapy, referral for CBT may be helpful (Clark et al., 1994; Bruce et al., 1995).

Social Phobia

Persons with social phobia have marked fear of certain social or performance situations, exposure to which almost invariably evokes an immediate anxiety or panic response (*DSM-IV*). Traditionally treatment of these individuals has emphasized interventions such as skills training and graded exposure to the feared situations. However, data are accumulating that some medications may be helpful as well, either in their own right or as adjuncts to psychotherapy (Fahlén, 1995; Marshall et al., 1994). In selecting a pharmacological agent for social phobia, it is important to distinguish people who fear most social situations (generalized social phobia) from those with more circumscribed fears such as public speaking or performance anxiety, because it is now apparent that these subtypes respond differently to medications. Unfortunately, many early trials included patients with a mixture of these subtypes, making interpretation of the results difficult.

MAOIs

There is good evidence that the traditional MAOIs (e.g., phenelzine, tranylcypromine) are effective for the generalized subtype of social phobia. Liebowitz et al. (1990, 1992) compared phenelzine (mean dose = 76 mg/day) to atenolol (mean dose = 73 mg/day) and a pill placebo in 74 patients with social phobia, most of whom (76%) had generalized social distress. After 8 weeks of treatment, phenelzine was significantly more effective than placebo, with 64% of the phenelzine-treated patients showing moderate to marked improvement compared with 23% of the controls. Atenolol was intermediate between these two groups and not significantly different from either. A separate analysis of only the generalized social phobics showed the same pattern of response. A similarly good response rate (79% moderately to markedly improved) was obtained in a smaller uncontrolled trial of tranylcypromine (Versiani et al., 1988).

More recently, attention has turned to the safer reversible inhibitors of MAO-A. In an early controlled trial, moclobemide was found to be significantly better than placebo and comparable on most measures to phenelzine in efficacy (Versiani et al., 1992); however, two subsequent multicenter studies were more discouraging. Although one found moclobemide to be modestly better than placebo at a dose of 600 mg/d (Katschnig et al., 1997), the other found no benefit over placebo at doses ranging from 75 to 900 mg/d (Noyes et al., 1997). Controlled trials of brofaromine have yielded similarly mixed results (e.g., Fahlén et al., 1995; Lott et al., 1997).

SSRIs

Because of the potential adverse effects of the currently available MAOIs, the SSRIs have become the drugs of choice for generalized social phobia for many pharmacotherapists. To date, most studies of these agents have been small or uncontrolled; however, the consistency of their findings suggests that all SSRIs are probably efficacious for that disorder. There are preliminary reports of two large controlled trials of paroxetine in which it was superior to placebo on a range of measures after 12 weeks of treatment (Allgulander, 1998; Pitts et al., 1998). The optimal dosage was 20 mg/d. Improvement appears to be maintained with continued treatment, but in one study, substitution of placebo for paroxetine after 11 weeks resulted in relapse in five of eight patients (Stein et al., 1996).

Van Ameringen, Mancini, and Streiner (1993, 1994) reported moderate to marked improvement in 16 of 20 patients treated openly with sertraline (mean dose = 148 mg/d) and in 10 of 13 treated openly with fluoxetine (mean dose = 54 mg/d). Sertraline (mean dose = 134 mg/day) was also effective in a small, placebo-controlled crossover study (Katzelnick et al., 1995). Good separation from placebo (46% vs. 7% substantially improved) was also obtained with fluvoxamine (150 mg/d) in a small controlled trial (van Vliet, den Boer, & Westenberg, 1994).

Benzodiazepines

Although generally not first-choice agents for social phobia, the high-potency benzodiazepines have been effective in a number of small uncontrolled trials (e.g., Davidson et al., 1991; Lydiard et al., 1988; Munjack et al., 1990; Ontiveros & Fontaine, 1990) and at least one double-blind, placebo-controlled study (Davidson, Potts, et al., 1993). Most of these trials used clonazepam at mean doses of 2–3 mg/d (range = 0.5–6.0 mg/d). In one, Davidson et al. (1991) obtained moderate to marked improvement in 22 of 26 patients who were followed for an average of 11.3 months. During that time, 20 were able to decrease their dosages while maintaining their gains, including 5 patients who were able to discontinue their clonazepam altogether. However, in another study, 8 of 16 responders who were switched to placebo after 4 months of clonazepam treatment relapsed within 10 weeks (Ontiveros et al., 1998).

Beta Blockers

Socially anxious individuals are often acutely aware of adrenergically mediated manifestations of anxiety such as tachycardia, sweating, blushing, dry mouth, or tremor and may fear that they are obvious to others as well or that they will interfere with the person's ability to perform in public. Such symptoms can become the center of an increasing spiral of anxiety (Marshall, 1995; Rosenbaum & Pollock, 1994). The rationale for the use of beta blockers is to reduce those symptoms and thus prevent a debilitating spiral.

Initial enthusiasm for beta blockers in the treatment of social phobia resulted from studies of individuals with performance anxiety (Barlow, 1988; Jefferson, 1995). In 1985, Liebowitz et al. reviewed 11 controlled trials involving nonclinical samples with performance anxiety and found 8 in which beta blockers (alprenolol, oxprenolol, propranolol, atenolol, and pindolol) were superior to placebo. In contrast to those findings, beta blockers appear to be ineffective for the treatment of the generalized form of social phobia (Marshall, 1995). At least two studies of atenolol at doses up to 100 mg/d found it to be no better than placebo for that disorder (Liebowitz et al., 1992; Turner, Beidel, & Jacob, 1994).

Other Agents

There is a report of the successful use of clonidine 0.2 mg/d in a socially phobic individual who had not responded to phenelzine, alprazolam, or propranolol (Goldstein, 1987). Good results have also been reported in patients with generalized social phobia in a

small case series using venlafaxine, at a mean dose of 146 mg/d (Kelsey, 1995), and in a series using sustained-release bupropion, at doses of 200–400 mg/d (Emmanuel et al., 1998). Buspirone (mean dose = 48 mg/d) was helpful for general anxiety but not phobic symptoms in patients with unspecified social phobias (Munjack et al., 1991) and was not significantly better than placebo on most measures at a mean dose of 32 mg/d in musicians with performance anxiety (Clark & Agras, 1991).

Combined Pharmacotherapy and Psychotherapy

There are very few data on the combination of pharmacotherapy and psychotherapy for social phobia. In a small early trial, Falloon, Lloyd, and Harpin (1981) compared 4 weeks of social skills training plus either propranolol (range = 160–320 mg/day) or placebo in 16 individuals with unspecified social phobias. Patients in both groups improved, with no significant between-group differences. In a study cited in the preceding section, Clark and Agras (1991) compared the efficacies of buspirone, placebo, five sessions of cognitive behavioral group therapy (CBGT) plus buspirone, and five sessions of CBGT plus placebo in the treatment of 34 musicians with performance anxiety. Across groups, subjects who received CBGT (with either buspirone or placebo) showed a significant decrease in anxiety and increases in confidence and performance. Paired comparisons favored CBGT plus placebo over CBGT plus buspirone. Finally, Gelernter et al. (1991) compared 12 weeks of phenelzine (mean dose = 55 mg/d) plus self-directed exposure, alprazolam (mean dose = 4.2 mg/d) plus self-exposure, placebo plus self-exposure, and CBGT without medication in a sample of 65 patients, most of whom had fear of one or two specific social situations. All four groups were significantly improved at posttreatment, with no consistent differences among them. In each instance, these studies failed to show an advantage of combined therapy over cognitive-behavioral treatments alone.

Clinical Management

Pharmacological treatment of generalized social phobia typically begins with one or more trials of an SSRI, followed by a trial of clonazepam or, in patients who can manage the necessary dietary and drug restrictions, an MAOI. As with agoraphobia, patients should be encouraged to engage in avoided social activities as treatment proceeds. There is little information as to what constitutes an adequate drug trial in social phobia or how long treatment should be continued in responders. In the absence of such data, the guidelines for SSRI-treatment of OCD would seem reasonable here as well (see below). For excessive performance anxiety the as-needed use of a beta blocker is generally sufficient. Typical doses are 20–40 mg of propranol taken an hour before performing or 50–100 mg of atenolol taken 2 to 4 hours before, but the optimal dose and timing should be determined individually. A test dose is recommended prior to use with a performance (Jefferson, 1995).

Specific Phobias

Specific phobias are characterized by excessive and persistent fear of circumscribed objects or situations such as harmless animals or insects, heights, storms, enclosed spaces, flying, injections, or the sight of blood (*DSM-IV*). Fears of this kind are common in the general population and rarely cause sufficient distress or impairment to warrant treatment. The principal treatment for specific phobias is in vivo exposure therapy, in which patients are assisted to face the feared object or situation until their anxiety subsides. Most of the empirical work on drug treatments for these disorders has involved the use of pharmacological agents as adjuncts to exposure therapy and thus involves combined treatment studies. Most often the agents employed have been sedatives (for a review of drug studies with theoretical implications for pharmacotherapy of specific phobia, see Liebowitz, 1991).

Benzodiazepines

Findings have been mixed regarding the effects of benzodiazepines on exposure therapy. In a novel early trial, Marks et al. (1972) examined the timing of drug administration relative to exposure therapy in a group of individuals with a mixture of specific phobias. Subjects received diazepam at a dose of 0.1 mg/kg of body weight either 1 hour ("peak effect") or 4 hours ("waning effect") prior to exposure sessions, or a pill placebo prior to exposure. Participants

in the waning effect group had a significantly better response to exposure therapy than placebo recipients, with the peak effect group being intermediate. Subsequently, Bernadt, Silverstone, and Singleton (1980) compared diazepam 10 mg, tolamolol (a beta blocker) 200 mg, or a pill placebo given prior to exposure therapy in a group of women with snake, mice, or spider phobia. Tolamolol reduced tachycardia during exposure but did not affect patients' willingness to approach the feared stimuli or their subjective fear and avoidance ratings. In contrast, diazepam increased approach behavior but had no effect on heart rate.

In a recent study, Wilhelm and Roth (1997) examined the use of alprazolam prior to exposure therapy for the treatment of flying phobia. Twenty-eight women with fear of air travel flew twice, 1 week apart. Before the first flight, participants received either a 1-mg dose of alprazolam or a pill placebo. No pills were administered before the second flight. Consistent with the previous studies, alprazolam reduced subjective anxiety and general symptomatology during the first flight, relative to placebo. However, during the second flight the previous alprazolam recipients reported marked increases in anxiety and panic attacks, whereas the previous placebo recipients reported declines in anxiety and panic from the first flight. The investigators suggested that receiving alprazolam prior to the first flight interfered with the therapeutic effects of facing the feared situation and concluded that the use of benzodiazepines on an "as-needed" basis may be detrimental to the long-term outcome of exposure therapy.

TCAs

There are a few reports of the use of clomipramine (Carey et al., 1975; Escobar & Landbloom, 1976), phenelzine (Solyom et al., 1981), or nifedipine (Klein, Geraci, & Uhde, 1990) in the treatment of phobias; however, these are difficult to interpret because the samples included subjects with agoraphobia or social phobia as well as specific phobia. In a controlled trial, Zitrin and colleagues compared imipramine plus behavior therapy, a pill placebo plus behavior therapy, and imipramine plus supportive therapy in a sample of individuals with various phobias (Zitrin, Klein, & Woerner, 1978; Zitrin et al., 1983). Overall, the only effect of imipramine was a higher early dropout rate than occurred with placebo. However, in a personal communication to Fyer (1987), Klein distinguished a subgroup of individuals from that study who, when confronting a feared object or situation, experienced repeated limited symptom attacks (autonomic symptomatology); for those individuals, imipramine was superior to placebo. It is possible that those subjects had subclinical or clinical panic disorder, which had not been defined at the time the study was conducted.

Clinical Management

When treatment is indicated, behavior therapy, specifically in vivo exposure therapy, is the treatment of choice for specific phobias. There is little empirical support for the use of pharmacotherapy for these disorders. Although administration of a low dose of a benzodiazepine prior to exposure sessions may reduce discomfort during sessions, it may also undermine the therapeutic effects of exposure.

Obsessive-Compulsive Disorder

The essential feature of obsessive-compulsive disorder is the presence of obsessions or compulsions of sufficient intensity to be time-consuming, cause marked distress, or significantly impair functioning (*DSM-IV*). Until recently the only effective treatment for OCD was a form of behavior therapy known as exposure and response prevention (ERP). However, the appearance of pharmacological agents with powerful effects on serotonin reuptake (i.e., clomipramine and the SSRIs) has dramatically increased the options available to OCD sufferers. Still, even with the best current treatments, complete remission of OCD symptoms rarely occurs. Therefore, clinical management often consists of efforts to optimize improvement through comparative trials of different treatments or by augmenting or combining treatments. A useful reference for clinicians engaged in that process is "Expert Consensus Guidelines: Treatment of Obsessive-Compulsive Disorder" (March et al., 1997). The guidelines summarize the opinions of world experts about clinical situations that may arise during the management of patients with OCD, and the article includes a handout designed for patients and their families.

To facilitate assessment of treatment response, it is helpful to have a quantitative measure of improvement. The leading measure is the Yale-Brown Obsessive Compulsive Scale (Y-BOCS; Goodman, Price, Rasmussen, Mazure, Fleischmann, et al., 1989; Goodman, Price, Rasmussen, Mazure, Delgado, et al., 1989), a 10-item clinician-administered instrument that can be completed in a few minutes. A patient self-report version of this scale is also available (Baer, 1991, pp. 210–214). A reduction of 25–35% on the Y-BOCS is generally considered a clinically meaningful improvement (Pigott & Seay, 1998).

Clomipramine

The most extensively studied and best-validated pharmacological agent for OCD is clomipramine, a tricyclic antidepressant with a uniquely potent effect on serotonin reuptake and the only one with appreciable efficacy in OCD. By 1993 it had been shown to be effective in more than 20 controlled trials in children and adults (Jenike, 1993). The pivotal trials of clomipramine—two placebo-controlled, flexible-dose studies involving a total of 520 patients—were reported in 1991 (Clomipramine Collaborative Study Group). In those studies the average reductions in the Y-BOCS score after 10 weeks of treatment were 38% and 44% for clomipramine-treated patients (mean final dose = approximately 225 mg/d) versus 3% and 5% for placebo-treated patients. Overall, more than half of the clomipramine-treated patients had at least a 35% reduction in symptoms.

SSRIs

Following the success of clomipramine for the treatment of OCD, large-scale multicenter trials were conducted for several SSRIs. Tollefson, Rampey, et al. (1994) examined the efficacy and safety of fluoxetine in fixed doses of 20, 40, or 60 mg/d in two trials involving a total of 355 patients. All three dosages were superior to placebo from week 5 onward, with a slight but statistically significant trend toward greater improvement at higher doses. Overall, approximately one-third of fluoxetine-treated patients achieved at least a 35% reduction in Y-BOCS scores by week 13, compared with 8.5% of placebo-treated patients.

In a similar study, Greist, Chouinard, et al. (1995) evaluated three fixed dosages of sertraline (50, 100, and 200 mg/d) in 324 patients. There were no significant differences among the three dosage groups during the 12-week study. Overall, Y-BOCS scores decreased by 23.4% in sertraline-treated patients compared with 14.6% in placebo-treated patients. Treatment effects were evident from week 2 onward for Y-BOCS scores and from week 4 onward for most other outcome measures. Fluvoxamine (mean final dose = 249 mg/d) was superior to placebo in a 10-week, flexible-dose study involving 320 patients (Rasmussen et al., in press). The average decrease in Y-BOCS scores was 20%. A separate long-term study in children also found fluvoxamine to be effective, with acute treatment gains maintained or enhanced during a 1-year continuation period (Walkup et al., 1998).

Finally, Zohar and colleagues compared paroxetine to both clomipramine and placebo in a 12-week, flexible-dose study involving 406 patients (Zohar, Judge, & the OCD Paroxetine Study Investigators, 1996). The majority (53%) of patients in the paroxetine group received a maximum daily dose of 60 mg, with approximately equal proportions (9–14%) of the remaining patients receiving 50, 40, 30, or 20 mg. Both active medications were superior to placebo from week 6 onward, with no significant differences between drugs. Fifty-five percent of patients in both groups, compared with 35% of placebo-treated patients, achieved at least a 25% [sic] reduction in Y-BOCS scores.

Relative Efficacies of Serotoninergic Antidepressants

Although a meta-analysis of data from the multicenter trials suggested that clomipramine may be more effective than the SSRIs for OCD (Greist, Jefferson, et al., 1995), direct comparisons have not supported that notion (e.g., Freeman et al., 1994; Koran et al., 1996; Pigott et al., 1990; Smeraldi, Erzegovesi, & Bianchi, 1992; Zohar, Judge, & the OCD Paroxetine Study Investigators, 1996). At the present time it appears that all of the first-line agents have similar efficacy (Pigott & Seay, 1998).

Long-Term Treatment

Long-term continuation of treatment with clomipramine or SSRIs has been associated with maintenance or enhancement of acute treatment improvements (Greist, Jefferson, et al., 1995; Tollefson, Birkett, et al., 1994; Wheadon & Gergel, 1995). However, when pharmacotherapy is given as the only treatment for OCD, the majority of patients relapse within a few weeks to a few months after it is discontinued (Leonard et al., 1991; Pato et al., 1988; Tollefson, Birkett, et al., 1994; Wheadon & Gergel, 1995).

Other Pharmacological Agents

A variety of other compounds occasionally are used either as augmentative agents for patients who have responded only partially to standard drug therapies or have comorbid psychiatric conditions or as third-line monotherapies for patients who have not responded to standard drugs or ERP. The best-supported augmentation strategy is the addition of a neuroleptic agent (e.g., pimozide, haloperidol, or risperidone) to a serotonergic drug for patients with comorbid tic disorders (McDougal et al., 1990, 1994, 1995). Augmentation with clonazepam has been helpful in some cases and may be useful in patients with prominent anxiety or agitation (Hewlett, Vinogradov, & Agras, 1992; Leonard et al., 1994; Pigott, L'Heureux, Bernstein, et al., 1992). Buspirone has been reported to enhance response to standard drugs in some OCD patients (Jenike, Baer, & Buttolph, 1991; Markowitz, Stagnos, & Calabresa, 1990), although controlled studies have failed to demonstrate a superiority over placebo augmentation (Grady et al., 1993; McDougal et al., 1993; Pigott, L'Heureux, Hill, et al., 1992). For further information about strategies for treatment-resistant patients, see current references or the expert guidelines.

Combined Pharmacotherapy and Psychotherapy

Many experts (e.g., Greist, Jefferson, et al., 1995) recommend treating OCD with the combination of a serotonin reuptake inhibitor and ERP, although that strategy has not been well studied. A review of three published combined treatment studies found modest advantages for the addition of clomipramine or flu-voxamine to ERP in patients with comorbid depression; however, the most robust finding was that the addition of ERP to pharmacotherapy substantially reduced relapse when drugs were discontinued (Spiegel, in press). A more recent study found no advantage of adding fluvoxamine to ERP or cognitive therapy for OCD (van Balkom et al., 1998).

Clinical Management

Table 3.3 summarizes the usual starting dose, initial target dose, and maximum recommended dose for the major first-line drugs for OCD in adults. Most pharmacotherapists begin treatment with an SSRI rather than clomipramine because of its more favorable side effect profile and safety. Typically the dose is advanced to the average dose within the first month of treatment and to the maximum dose by the end of the second month. Improvement is usually apparent by 4–6 weeks, although the full extent of improvement may take several months. Experts recommend switching to a different medication if there is no response after 4–6 weeks at a maximum dose (March et al., 1997). Patients should not be considered medication-refractory until they have failed trials of at least two SSRIs and clomipramine. At that point, referral to a specialist is recommended.

Patients who respond to pharmacological or combined treatment should be maintained on the acute treatment dose of medication for at least a year (longer if they are not receiving ERP). A gradual drug taper can then be cautiously attempted. Experts recommend a taper rate of not more than 25% every 2 months (March et al., 1997). The best protection against relapse is concurrent ERP. In the case of repeated relapses despite ERP, long-term prophylactic drug maintenance therapy may be needed.

Generalized Anxiety Disorder

According to some studies, generalized anxiety disorder (GAD) is the anxiety disorder most commonly seen in primary care settings (Brawman-Mintzer & Lydiard, 1996) and in the elderly (Mintzer & Brawman-Mintzer, 1996). The diagnostic criteria for GAD have undergone several revisions since they first appeared in *DSM-III* (APA, 1980). As currently defined (*DSM-IV*), the disorder is characterized by excessive and uncontrollable anxiety and worry for a period of at least 6 months, accompanied by physical symptoms of restlessness, fatigue, difficulty concentrating, irritability, muscle tension, and sleep disturbance. GAD is distinguished conceptually from transient anxiety that occurs in response to a life stressor, although practically, until 6 months have passed without resolution, the distinction is difficult to make.

The identification of effective pharmacological treatments for GAD has been hampered by high placebo response rates in most studies (Schweizer & Rickels, 1997a), which suggests that factors such as empathy and the doctor–patient alliance may be very important in the treatment of this disorder (Schweizer & Rickels, 1997a,b). Nevertheless, several agents have been shown to be effective in some trials.

Benzodiazepines

The benzodiazepines have been the gold standard for the acute treatment of generalized anxiety for more than three decades (Cutler et al., 1994). Their efficacy has been well established in numerous controlled trials in comparison with a host of other agents (see following paragraphs). Because of their myorelaxant and sedative properties, benzodiazepines are helpful for some of the somatic symptoms of GAD (e.g., muscle tension and sleep disturbance), as well as anxiety and

TABLE 3.3. Typical Doses for the Major OCD Medications in Healthy Adults with No Concurrent Medications

MEDICATION	USUAL STARTING DOSE (mg/d)	INITIAL TARGET DOSE (mg/d)	MAXIMUM RECOMMENDED DOSE (mg/d)
clomipramine	25–50	150	250
fluoxetine	20	20	80
fluvoxamine	50	150	300
paroxetine	20	40	60
sertraline	50	50	200

worry (Bourin & Malinge, 1995). In addition, their rapid onset of action may increase compliance with therapy. However, due to the concerns discussed earlier about benzodiazepines, there has been interest in developing other treatment options.

Buspirone

Buspirone currently is the only pharmacological agent with an FDA-approved indication for the treatment of GAD. Its efficacy and safety relative to benzodiazepines and placebo have been demonstrated in several well-controlled trials (see Rickels, 1990, for a review). In one of the largest trials, Rickels et al. (1982) compared buspirone (20–25 mg/d) with diazepam (20–25 mg/d) and a pill placebo over a 4-week period in 212 patients. Moderate to marked improvement was observed in approximately 70% of the buspirone- and diazepam-treated patients, compared with 29% of the placebo-treated patients. Other studies have found buspirone to be as effective for generalized anxiety as clorazepate (Cohn et al., 1986; Rickels, Fox et al., 1988), alprazolam (Cohn & Wilcox, 1986; Enkelmann, 1991), oxazepam (Anssea et al., 1990; Strand et al., 1990), and lorazepam (Bourin & Milinge, 1995; Chiaie et al., 1995; Cohn & Wilcox, 1986; Petracca et al., 1990). Buspirone also appears to be effective in reducing some of the associated features of GAD, including depressive symptoms (Fabre, 1990; Sramek et al., 1996) and agitation in patients with dementia (Mintzer & Brawman-Mintzer, 1996; Sheikh & Salzman, 1995). Its onset of action is somewhat slower (2–4 weeks) than that of benzodiazepines (Enkelmann, 1991; Rickels, 1990).

Tricyclic Antidepressants

At least three studies have found imipramine to be superior to placebo for the treatment of GAD (Hoehn-Saric, McLeod, & Zimmerli, 1988; Kahn et al., 1986; Rickels et al., 1993). In a large well-controlled study, Rickels et al. (1993) compared imipramine (mean dose = 143 mg/d) to trazodone (mean dose = 245 mg/d), diazepam (mean dose = 26 mg/d), and a pill placebo in 230 patients. During the first 2 weeks, diazepam was superior to the two antidepressants in reducing anxiety, but from week 3 onward, all three active drugs were comparable. Among

study completers ($N = 149$), moderate to marked improvement was seen in approximately 69% of those taking an active drug compared with 39% taking placebo. In a recent small open trial, clomipramine (up to 250 mg/d) was effective in 5 of 10 patients, 2 of whom had previously failed to improve with a benzodiazepine (Wingerson, Nguyen, & Roy-Byrne, 1992). Four of the nonresponders discontinued treatment due to stimulatory side effects.

Other Antidepressants

The efficacy of SSRIs for GAD has yet to be determined, although clinical experience suggests that they may be helpful if excessive stimulation can be avoided (Lydiard et al., 1996). Preliminary reports of two large multicenter trials of an extended-release form of venlafaxine indicate that it is effective for GAD at doses as low as 75 mg/d, with declines in anxiety being evident in some cases by the end of the first week of treatment (Aguiar et al., 1998; Entsuah et al., 1998). As noted previously, trazodone was as effective as imipramine and diazepam in a double-blind, placebo-controlled trial (Rickels et al., 1993). Positive results have also been reported in small open trials of nefazodone (Hedges et al., 1996) and mirtazapine, a novel antidepressant (Goodnick, Puig, & Devane, 1998).

Other Agents

Abecarnil, a beta-carboline that acts as a partial agonist at benzodiazepine receptors, has shown some promise in the treatment of GAD (Lydiard, Ballenger, & Rickels, 1997; Pollack et al., 1997; Small & Bystritsky, 1997). In one study, abecarnil (mean dose = 7.4 mg/d) was as effective as alprazolam (mean dose = 2.6 mg/d) at posttreatment, and abecarnil-treated patients sustained their improvements better after drug discontinuation (Lydiard, Ballenger, & Rickels, 1997). Ipsapirone, an azapirone with somewhat greater affinity and selectivity for the 5-HT$_{1A}$ receptor and fewer side effects than buspirone (Fanelli et al., 1990) was superior to placebo and comparable to lorazepam in an 8-week multicenter trial (Cutler et al., 1993). Ondansetron, a selective antagonist of 5-HT$_3$ receptors, was also effective in a small placebo-controlled study (Freeman et al., 1997).

Combined Pharmacotherapy and Psychotherapy

Almost nothing is known about combined treatment approaches for GAD, although they are used commonly in clinical practice. There is one published trial comparing CBT, diazepam (15 mg/d), a pill placebo, CBT plus diazepam, or CBT plus placebo in a primary care clinic sample (Power, Simpson, Swanson, & Wallace, 1990; Power, Simpson, Swanson, Wallace, et al., 1990). At posttreatment (10 weeks) and follow-up (6 months), all three CBT conditions were superior to the placebo and diazepam conditions. Improvement ranged from 56 to 70% in the former groups and from 18 to 30% in the latter. Although the CBT groups did not differ significantly from each other on any single measure, the CBT plus diazepam group improved earliest and had the largest percentage of patients achieving clinically significant change on all measures.

Clinical Management

In view of the high placebo response rate in GAD, it is important to consider whether pharmacological treatment for a particular patient is warranted. If the complaints are relatively minor or are directly related to a situational stressor, brief psychotherapy and support may be the treatment of choice (Schweizer & Rickels, 1996). In a World Health Organization (WHO) study, patients who initially reported physical or minor emotional complaints responded better to counseling than to diazepam, even when counseling was limited to only 3 hours (WHO, 1988, as cited in Boulenger et al., 1997).

If the presentation is more severe and urgent intervention is needed, the temporary use (up to a few weeks) of a benzodiazepine may be helpful as an adjunct to psychotherapy. The drug should be tapered as therapy proceeds. In less urgent cases a trial of buspirone is a good initial choice. The typical starting dose is 15 mg/d in divided doses, which is increased by 5 mg/d every few days to a target dose of 30 mg/d. If the response is insufficient after 2–4 weeks at that amount, the dose may be advanced gradually to a maximum of 60 mg/d. Improvement may continue for up to 3 months. It is important to inform patients of the expected side effects and time for response, especially if they have taken benzodiazepines previously (see previous comments under pharmacological agents). When switching from a benzodiazepine to buspirone, it may be helpful to continue the benzodiazepine during the first month of buspirone therapy before initiating a gradual taper (Rickels, 1990).

Failing a course of buspirone, trials of antidepressant medications (e.g., imipramine, venlafaxine, trazodone) would be a reasonable second choice if time permits, followed by a more extended course of a benzodiazepine. Generally, longer half-life benzodiazepines (e.g., diazepam, clonazepam), which can be taken once or twice daily, are preferred when extended therapy is required (Rickels et al., 1988; Schweizer, Rickels et al., 1990). Treatment responders should be continued on medication for at least 6 months before a gradual drug taper is attempted. Even so, a substantial proportion, perhaps even a majority, will relapse after drug discontinuance. The proportion relapsing may be lower after treatment with buspirone than with a benzodiazepine (Rickels, Schweizer, et al., 1988), although the occurrence of withdrawal symptoms in the latter case may confuse the assessment of relapse (Roy-Byrne et al., 1993).

Posttraumatic Stress Disorder

Posttraumatic stress disorder (PTSD) develops in individuals as a consequence of experiencing a frightening or horrifying event. Its characteristic features include recurrent reexperiencing of the event, for example through nightmares, intrusive recollections, or flashbacks; avoidance of things the person associates with the trauma or of emotional experiences in general; and persistent hyperarousal (*DSM-IV*). Occasionally hallucinations or dissociative episodes occur as part of reliving the experience.

Research on pharmacological treatments for PTSD has lagged behind work on other anxiety disorders (van der Kolk et al., 1994). One of the challenges is the multidimensional nature of the disturbance. In 1992, Davidson outlined six main goals for the pharmacotherapy of PTSD: reduction of intrusive symptoms, improvement of avoidance, reduction of persistent hyperarousal, relief of depression, improvement of impulse regulation, and control of acute dissociative and psychotic features. Assessment of treatment efficacy should include consideration of each of these dimensions. Currently there is no definitive pharmacological treatment for PTSD (Hertzberg et al., 1998; Shalev, Bonne, & Eth, 1996); however, several agents have shown promise.

MAOIs

Studies have yielded inconsistent findings regarding the efficacy of MAOIs for PTSD (e.g., Davidson, Walker, & Kilts, 1987; Demartino, Mollica, & Wilk, 1995; Hogben & Cornfield, 1981; Lerer et al., 1987; Milanes et al., 1984; Shestatsky, Greenberg, & Lerer, 1988), although it is possible that in some instances the duration of treatment may have been insufficient (Lydiard et al., 1996). In an 8-week, double-blind trial, Frank et al. (1988) compared phenelzine (mean dose = 71 mg/d) to imipramine (mean dose = 240 mg/d) and placebo in 34 veterans with PTSD and found that both active medications reduced intrusive symptoms but not avoidance. On an overall measure of severity, phenelzine was nonsignificantly better than imipramine.

TCAs

Results with TCAs have also been mixed. In controlled trials, improvements have been observed in some PTSD symptoms following treatment with imipramine (Burstein, 1984; Frank et al., 1988) or amitriptyline (Davidson et al., 1990; Davidson, Kudler, et al., 1993). Davidson et al. (1990) found amitriptyline (up to 300 mg/d) to be significantly better than placebo on several measures, including avoidance, among completers of an 8-week trial. However, improvements were modest, and at posttreatment, 64% of the amitriptyline-treated patients still met diagnostic criteria for PTSD. In a 4-week crossover study, desipramine (up to 200 mg/d) was no more effective than placebo for PTSD symptoms (Reist et al., 1989). Other TCAs, including clomipramine, nortriptyline, and doxepin, have reportedly been useful in isolated cases (Marshall et al., 1996).

SSRIs and Other Antidepressants

Preliminary studies of newer antidepressants that have prominent serotonergic properties have been more encouraging. Positive open trials have been reported with several SSRIs, including fluoxetine (McDougle et al., 1991; Nagy et al., 1993), sertraline (Kline et al., 1994), and fluvoxamine (Tucker, Smith, Miranda et al., 1998). Fluoxetine at doses up to 60 mg/d has been superior to placebo in at least two randomized controlled trials (Connor et al., 1998; van der Kolk et al., 1994). In the van der Kolk study, improvement in overall PTSD symptomatology was evident after 5 weeks of treatment and was most pronounced in the arousal and emotional numbing domains and for depression. The study concluded after 5 weeks, so it is unknown whether further improvement would have occurred with continued treatment.

Most recently, nefazodone has been studied in several open trials, with efficacy reported at doses of 200–600 mg/d (Davis et al., 1998; Tucker, Smith, Jones et al., 1998; Zisook et al., 1998). The Zisook report was particularly noteworthy. Subjects were 18 Vietnam combat veterans with chronic PTSD (mean duration 22 years) who had failed an average of seven previous medication trials, including at least one trial of an SSRI. After 12 weeks of treatment with nefazodone, the group evidenced significant improvements in PTSD symptoms of intrusive recollections, avoidance, and hyperarousal, as well as depression, sleep, sexual functioning, and quality of life. Most patients required relatively high doses of nefazodone; the mean dose was 400 mg/d. This impressive result, along with the other open trials, is promising, but controlled trials are needed. The related antidepressant trazodone was also effective in a small open trial (Hertzberg et al., 1996).

Other Agents

Lithium and anticonvulsant drugs with efficacy in bipolar disorder (e.g., carbamazepine, valproate, lamotrigine) have been used with some success in PTSD, possibly acting through reduction of kindling (Fesler, 1991; Hertzberg et al., 1998; Lipper et al., 1986; Wolf, Alavi, & Mosnaim, 1988). Beta blockers (e.g., propranolol) and clonidine have also been helpful in some cases (Vargas & Davidson, 1993), although possibly more so in combination with antidepressants (Kinzie & Leung, 1989). In one report, the addition of resperidone to stable antidepressant therapy was deemed helpful in reducing psychotic symptoms in veterans with combat-related PTSD (Hammer & Ulmer, 1998).

Naltrexone was helpful for flashbacks in a small open trial (Bills & Kreisler, 1993). Alprazolam, at doses up to 6 mg/d, has not been effective for PTSD symptoms in two small trials, aside from some reduction in general anxiety (Braun et al., 1990; Gelpin et al., 1996). Moreover, benzodiazepines have been reported to increase anger in some PTSD patients (Feldman, 1987).

Clinical Management

Although data are limited, the very promising early findings with the SSRIs and nefazodone make these agents the drugs of first choice when pharmacotherapy for PTSD is indicated. It appears that many patients may require doses toward the upper end of the approved therapeutic range for optimal response and that trials should be continued for at least 8 weeks. Adjunctive therapy with other agents may be helpful for residual symptoms, for example, beta blockers for persistent symptoms of autonomic arousal (Taylor, 1998), anticonvulsants for anger and aggressive outbursts (Lipper et al., 1986; Wolf et al., 1988), or resperidone for psychotic symptoms (Hammer & Ulmer, 1998). In addition, referral for conjunctive, trauma-focused psychotherapy is recommended for most patients (Marshall et al., 1996). Failing trials of SSRIs and nefazodone, other agents (e.g., imipramine, phenelzine) may be tried.

REFERENCES

Aguiar, L. M., Haskins, T., Rudolph, R. L., Pallay, A., & Derivan, A. T. (1998, May). Double-blind, placebo-controlled study of once-daily venlafaxine extended release in outpatients with GAD. Poster session presented at the annual meeting of the American Psychiatric Association, Toronto.

Allgulander, C. (1998, June). Efficacy of paroxetine in social phobia—a single-center double-blind study of 96 symptomatic volunteers randomized to treatment with paroxetine 20–50 mg or placebo for 3 months. Poster session presented at the annual meeting of the New Clinical Drug Evaluation Unit (NCDEU) Program, Boca Raton, FL.

American Psychiatric Association. (1980). *Diagnostic and statistical manual of mental disorders* (3d ed.). Washington, DC: Author.

American Psychiatric Association. (1990). *Benzodiazepine dependence, toxicity, and abuse*. Washington, DC: Author.

American Psychiatric Association. (1994). *Diagnostic and statistical manual of mental disorders* (4th ed.). Washington, DC: Author.

American Psychiatric Association. (1998). Practice guideline for the treatment of patients with panic disorder. *American Journal of Psychiatry, 155* (5, suppl.).

Anssea, M., Papart, P., Gerard, M. A., von Frenckell, R., & Franck, G. (1990). Controlled comparison of buspirone and oxazepam in generalized anxiety. *Neuropsychobiology, 24,* 74–78.

Baer, L. (1991). *Getting control: Overcoming your obsessions and compulsions*. Boston: Little, Brown.

Bakish, D., Saxena, B. M., Bowden, R., & D'Souza, J. (1993). Reversible monoamine oxidase-A inhibitors in panic disorder. *Clinical Neuropsychopharmacology, 16* (suppl. 2), S77–S82.

Ballenger, J. C. (1991). Long-term pharmacologic treatment of panic disorder. *Journal of Clinical Psychiatry, 52* (2, suppl.), 291–298.

Ballenger, J. C. (1994). Overview of the pharmacotherapy of panic disorder. In B. E. Wolfe & J. D. Maser (Eds.), *Treatment of panic disorder: A consensus development conference* (pp. 69–72). Washington, DC: American Psychiatric Press.

Ballenger, J. C. (1998). Benzodiazepines. In A. F. Schatzberg & C. B. Nemeroff (Eds.), *Textbook of psychopharmacology* (2d ed.) (pp. 271–286). Washington, DC: American Psychiatric Press.

Ballenger, J. C., Burrows, G. D., DuPont, R. L., Lesser, I. M., Noyes, R., Pecknold, J. C., Rifkin, A., & Swinson, R. P. (1988). Alprazolam in panic disorder and agoraphobia: Results from a multicenter trial, I: Efficacy in short-term treatment. *Archives of General Psychiatry, 45,* 413–422.

Ballenger, J. C., Wheadon, D. E., Steiner, M., Bushnell, W., & Gergel, I. (1998). Double-blind fixed-dose, placebo controlled study of paroxetine in the treatment of panic disorder. *American Journal of Psychiatry, 155,* 36–42.

Bandelow, B., Hajak, G., Holzrichter, S., Kunert, H. J., & Ruther, E. (1995). Assessing the efficacy of treatments for panic disorder and agoraphobia, I: Methodological problems. *International Clinical Psychopharmacology, 10,* 83–93.

Barlow, D. H. (1988). *Anxiety and its disorders*. New York: Guilford Press.

Barlow, D. H. (1998, June). Design, sample, and pretreatment attrition. In S. W. Woods (Chair), *First line treatment of panic disorder—cognitive behavior treatment vs. imipramine vs. their combination: A multi-center study*. Symposium conducted at the annual meeting of the New Clinical Drug Evaluation Unit (NCDEU) Program, Boca Raton, FL.

Benjamin, J., Levine, J., Fux, M., Aviv, A., Levy, D., & Belmaker, R. H. (1995). Double-blind, placebo-controlled, crossover trial of inositol treatment for panic disorder. *American Journal of Psychiatry, 152,* 1084–1086.

Bernadt, M. W., Silverstone, T., & Singleton, W. (1980). Behavioural and subjective effects of beta-adrenergic blockade in phobic subjects. *British Journal of Psychiatry, 137,* 452–457.

Bibb, J., & Chambless, D. L. (1986). Alcohol use and abuse among diagnosed agoraphobics. *Behaviour Research and Therapy, 24,* 49–58.

Bills, L. J., & Kreisler, K. (1993). Treatment of flashbacks with naltrexone. *American Journal of Psychiatry, 150,* 1430.

Black, D. W., Wesner, R., Bowers, W., & Gabel, J. (1993). A comparison of fluvoxamine, cognitive therapy, and placebo in the treatment of panic disorder. *Archives of General Psychiatry, 50,* 44–50.

Boulenger, J., Fournier, M., Rosales, D., & Lavallée, Y. (1997). Mixed anxiety and depression: From theory to practice. *Journal of Clinical Psychiatry, 58* (suppl. 8), 27–34.

Bourin, M., & Malinge, M. (1995). Controlled comparison of the effects and abrupt discontinuation of buspirone and lorazepam. *Progress in Neuro-psychopharmacology and Biological Psychiatry, 19,* 567–575.

Braun, P., Greenberg, D., Dasberg, H., & Lerer, B. (1990). Core symptoms of posttraumatic stress disorder unimproved by alprazolam treatment. *Journal of Clinical Psychiatry, 51,* 236–238.

Brawman-Mintzer, O., & Lydiard, R. B. (1996). Generalized anxiety disorder: Issues in epidemiology. *Journal of Clinical Psychiatry, 57* (suppl. 7), 3–8.

Brown, T. A., & Barlow, D. H. (1995). Long-term outcome of cognitive-behavioral treatment of panic disorder: Clinical predictors and alternative strategies for assessment. *Journal of Consulting and Clinical Psychology, 63,* 754–765.

Bruce, T. J., Spiegel, D. A., Gregg, S. F., & Nuzzarello, A. (1995). Predictors of alprazolam discontinuation with and without cognitive behavior therapy in panic disorder. *American Journal of Psychiatry, 152,* 1156–1160.

Bruce, T. J., Spiegel, D. A., & Hegel, M. T. (1999). Cognitive behavior therapy helps prevent relapse and recurrence of panic disorder following alprazolam discontinuation: A long-term follow-up of the Peoria and Dartmouth studies. *Journal of Consulting and Clinical Psychology, 67,* 151–156.

Burstein, A. (1984). Treatment of post-traumatic stress disorder with imipramine. *Psychosomatics, 25,* 3681–3687.

Carey, M. S., Hawkinson, R., Kornhaber, A., & Wellish, C. S. (1975). The use of clomipramine in phobic patients: Preliminary research report. *Current Therapeutic Research, 17,* 107–110.

Cassano, G. B., Petracca, A., Perugi, G., Nisita, C., Musetti, L., Mengali, F., & McNair, D. M. (1988). Clomipramine for panic disorder; I: The first 10 weeks of a long-term comparison with imipramine. *Journal of Affective Disorders, 14,* 123–127.

Charney, D. S., & Woods, S. W. (1989). Benzodiazepine treatment of panic disorder: A comparison of alprazolam and lorazepam. *Journal of Clinical Psychiatry, 50,* 418–423.

Charney, D. S., Woods, S. W., Goodman, W. K., Rifkin, B., Kinch, M., Aiken, B., Quadrino, L. M., & Heninger, G. R. (1986). Drug treatment of panic disorder: The comparative efficacy of imipramine, alprazolam, and trazodone. *Journal of Clinical Psychiatry, 47,* 580–586.

Chiaie, R. D., Pancheri, P., Casacchia, M., Stratta, P., Kotzalidis, G. D., & Zibellini, M. (1995). Assessment of the efficacy of buspirone in patients affected by generalized anxiety disorder, shifting to buspirone from prior treatment with lorazepam: A placebo controlled study. *Journal of Clinical Psychopharmacology, 15,* 12–19.

Clark, D. B., & Agras, W. S. (1991). The assessment and treatment of performance anxiety in musicians. *American Journal of Psychiatry, 148,* 598–605.

Clark, D. M., Salkovskis, P. M., Hackman, A., Middleton, H., Anastasiades, P., & Gelder, M. (1994). A comparison of cognitive therapy, applied relaxation, and imipramine in the treatment of panic disorder. *British Journal of Psychiatry, 164,* 759–769.

Clomipramine Collaborative Study Group. (1991). Clomipramine in the treatment of patients with obsessive-compulsive disorder. *Archives of General Psychiatry, 48,* 730–738.

Cohn, J. B., Bowden, C. L., Fisher, J. G., & Rodos, J. J. (1986). Double-blind comparison of buspirone and clorazepate in anxious outpatients. *American Journal of Medicine, 80* (suppl. 3B), 10–16.

Cohn, J. B., & Wilcox, C. S. (1986). Low-sedation potential of buspirone compared with alprazolam and lorazepam in the treatment of anxious outpatients: A double-blind study. *Journal of Clinical Psychiatry, 47,* 409–412.

Connor, K. M., Davidson, J. R. T., Sutherland, S., Malik, M., Tupler, L., Smith, R., & Davison, R. (1998, June). Pharmacotherapy for civilians with posttraumatic stress disorder: Differential response patterns to fluoxetine and placebo. Poster session presented at the annual meeting of the New Clinical Drug Evaluation Unit (NCDEU) Program, Boca Raton, FL.

Cottraux, J., Note, I-D., Cungi, C., Légeron, P., Heim, F., Chneiweiss, L., Bernard, G., & Bouvard, M. (1995). A controlled study of cognitive behaviour therapy with buspirone or placebo in panic disorder with agoraphobia. *British Journal of Psychiatry, 167,* 635–641.

Cox, B. J., Norton, G. R., Swinson, R. P., & Endler, N. S. (1990). Substance abuse and panic-related anxiety: A critical review. *Behaviour Research and Therapy, 28,* 385–393.

Cross-National Collaborative Panic Study, Second Phase Investigators. (1992). Drug treatment of panic disorder: Comparative efficacy of alprazolam, imipramine, and placebo. *British Journal of Psychiatry, 160,* 191–202.

Cutler, N. R., Keppel-Hesselink, J. M., & Sramek, J. J. (1994). A phase II multicenter dose-finding, efficacy and safety trial of ipsapirone in outpatients with generalized anxiety disorder. *Progress in Neuro-psychopharmacology and Biological Psychiatry, 18,* 447–463.

Cutler, N. R., Sramek, J. J., Keppel-Hesselink, J. M., Krol, A., Roes, J., Rickels, K., & Schweizer, E. (1993). A double-blind, placebo-controlled study comparing the efficacy and safety of ipsapirone versus lorazepam in patients with generalized anxiety disorder: A prospective multicenter trial. *Journal of Clinical Psychopharmacology, 13,* 429–437.

Davidson, J. (1992). Drug therapy of post-traumatic stress disorder. *British Journal of Psychiatry, 160,* 309–314.

Davidson, J., Kudler, H., Smith, R., Mahorney, S. L., Lipper, S., Hammett, E., Saunders, W. B., & Cavenar, J. O. (1990). Treatment of posttraumatic stress disorder with amitriptyline and placebo. *Archives of General Psychiatry, 47,* 259–266.

Davidson, J., Walker, J. I., & Kilts, C. (1987). A pilot study of phenelzine in the treatment of posttraumatic stress disorder. *British Journal of Psychiatry, 150,* 252–255.

Davidson, J. R. T., & Moroz, G. (1998). Pivotal studies of clonazepam in panic disorder. *Psychopharmacology Bulletin, 34,* 169–174.

Davidson, J. R. T., Ford, S. M., Smith, R. D., & Potts, N. L. S. (1991). Long-term treatment of social phobia with clonazepam. *Journal of Clinical Psychiatry, 52* (suppl. 11), 16–20.

Davidson, J. R. T., Kudler, H., Saunders, W. B., Erickson, L., Smith, R. D., Stein, R. M., Lipper, S., Hammett, E. B., Mahorney, S. L., & Cavenar, J. O. (1993). Predicting response to amitriptyline in posttraumatic stress disorder. *American Journal of Psychiatry, 150,* 1024–1029.

Davidson, J. R. T., Potts, N., Richichi, E., Krishnan, R., Ford, S. M., Smith, R., & Wilson, W. H. (1993).

Treatment of social phobia with clonazepam and placebo. *Journal of Clinical Psychopharmacology, 13,* 423–428.

Davis, L. L., Nugent, A., Clark, M., Murray, J., Kramer, G., & Petty, F. (1998, June). Nefazodone treatment for chronic posttraumatic stress disorder: An open trial. Poster session presented at the annual meeting of the New Clinical Drug Evaluation Unit (NCDEU) Program, Boca Raton, FL.

deBeurs, E., van Balkom, A. J. L. M., Lange, A., Koele, P., & van Dyck, R. (1995). Treatment of panic disorder with agoraphobia: Comparison of fluvoxamine, placebo, and psychological panic management combined with exposure and exposure in vivo alone. *American Journal of Psychiatry, 152,* 683–691.

DeMartinis, N. A., Schweizer, E., & Rickels, K. (1996). An open-label trial of nefazodone in high comorbidity panic disorder. *Journal of Clinical Psychiatry, 57,* 245–248.

Demartino, R., Mollica, R. F., & Wilk, V. (1995). Monoamine oxidase inhibitors in posttraumatic stress disorder: Promise and problems in Indochinese survivors of trauma. *Journal of Nervous and Mental Disease, 183,* 510–515.

DuBoff, E., England, D., Ferguson, J. M., Londborg, P. D., Rosenthal, M. H., Smith, W., Weise, C., & Wolkow, R. M. (1995, September). *Sertraline in the treatment of panic disorder.* Presentation at the 8th Congress of the European College of Neuropsychopharmacology, Venice.

DuPont, R. L. (1997). Panic disorder and addiction: The clinical issues of comorbidity. *Bulletin of the Menninger Clinic, 61* (2, suppl. A), A54–A65.

Emmanuel, N. P., Cosby, C., Brawman-Mintzer, O., Morton, A., Book, S., Johnson, M., Lorberbaum, J., Crawford, M., Kapp, R., & Lydiard, B. (1998, June). Open-label treatment of social phobia using sustained-release bupropion. Poster session presented at the annual meeting of the New Clinical Drug Evaluation Unit (NCDEU) Program, Boca Raton, FL.

Enkelmann, R. (1991). Alprazolam versus buspirone in the treatment of outpatients with generalized anxiety disorder. *Psychopharmacology, 105,* 428–432.

Entsuah, R., Derivan, A. T., Haskins, T., Rudolph, R. L., & Aguiar, L. M. (1998, May). Double-blind, placebo-controlled study of once-daily venlafaxine extended release and buspirone in outpatients with GAD. Poster session presented at the annual meeting of the American Psychiatric Association, Toronto.

Escobar, J. I., & Landbloom, R. P. (1976). Treatment of phobic neurosis with clomipramine: A controlled clinical trial. *Current Therapeutic Research, 20,* 680–685.

Fabre, L. F. (1990). Buspirone in the management of major depression: A placebo-controlled comparison. *Journal of Clinical Psychiatry, 51* (suppl. 9), 55–61.

Fahlén, T. (1995). Personality traits in social phobia, II: Changes during drug treatment. *Journal of Clinical Psychiatry, 56,* 569–573.

Fahlén, T., Nilsson, H. L., Borg, K., Humble, M., & Pauli, U. (1995). Social phobia: The clinical efficacy and tolerability of the monoamine oxidase-A and serotonin uptake inhibitor brofaromine. *Acta Psychiatrica Scandinavica, 92,* 351–358.

Falloon, I. R. H., Lloyd, G. G., & Harpin, R. E. (1981). The treatment of social phobia: Real life rehearsal with nonprofessional therapists. *Journal of Nervous and Mental Disease, 169,* 180–184.

Fanelli, R. J., Schuurman, T., Glaser, T., & Traber, J. (1990). Ipsapirone: A novel anxiolytic and selective 5-HT_{1A} receptor ligand. *Progress in Clinical and Biological Research, 361,* 461–467.

Feldman, T. B. (1987). Alprazolam in the treatment of post-traumatic stress disorder (letter). *Journal of Clinical Psychiatry, 48,* 216–217.

Fesler, F. A. (1991). Valproate in combat-related posttraumatic stress disorder. *Journal of Clinical Psychiatry, 52,* 361–364.

Frank, J. B., Kosten, T. R., Giller, E. L., & Dan, E. (1988). A randomized clinical trial of phenelzine and imipramine for posttraumatic stress disorder. *American Journal of Psychiatry, 145,* 1289–1291.

Freeman, A. M., Westphal, J. R., Norris, G. T., Roggero, B. A., Webb, P. B., Freeman, K. L., Rush, J. A., Hearne, E. M., & Evoniuk, G. (1997). Efficacy of ondansetron in the treatment of generalized anxiety disorder. *Depression and Anxiety, 5,* 140–141.

Freeman, C. P. L., Trimble, M. R., Deakin, F. W., Stokes, T. M., & Ashford, J. J. (1994). Fluvoxamine versus clomipramine in the treatment of obsessive compulsive disorder: A multicenter, randomized double-blind parallel group comparison. *Journal of Clinical Psychiatry, 55,* 301–305.

Fyer, A. J. (1987). Simple phobia. In T. A. Ban, P. Pichot, & W. Poldinger (Eds.), *Modern problems of pharmacopsychiatry* (pp. 174–192). New York: Karger.

Gelernter, C. S., Uhde, T. W., Cimbolic, P., Arnkoff, D. B., Vittone, B. J., Tancer, M. E., & Bartko, J. J. (1991). Cognitive-behavioral and pharmacological treatments of social phobia. *Archives of General Psychiatry, 48,* 938–945.

Gelpin, E., Bonne, O., Peri, T., Brandes, D., & Shalev, A. (1996). Treatment of recent trauma survivors with benzodiazepines: A prospective study. *Journal of Clinical Psychiatry, 57,* 390–394.

Geracioti, J. D. (1995). Venlafaxine treatment of panic disorder: A case series. *Journal of Clinical Psychiatry, 56,* 408–410.

Goldstein, S. (1987). Treatment of social phobia with clonidine. *Biological Psychiatry, 22,* 369–372.

Goodman, W. K., Price, L. H., Rasmussen, S. A., Mazure, C., Fleischmann, R. L., Hill, C. L., Henniger, G. R., & Charney, D. S. (1989). The Yale-Brown Obsessive Compulsive Scale (Y-BOCS), I: Development, use, and reliability. *Archives of General Psychiatry, 46,* 1006–1011.

Goodnick, P. J., Puig, A., & Devane, C. L. (1998, May). Mirtazapine in generalized anxiety and depression. Poster session presented at the annual meeting of the American Psychiatric Association, Toronto.

Gorman, J. M. (1998, June). Continuation treatment outcomes. In S. W. Woods (Chair), First line treatment of panic disorder—cognitive behavior treatment vs. imipramine vs. their combination: A multi-center study. Symposium conducted at the annual meeting of the New Clinical Drug Evaluation Unit (NCDEU) Program, Boca Raton, FL.

Grady, T. A., Pigott, T. A., L'Heureux, F., Hill, J. L., Bernstein, S. E., & Murphy, D. L. (1993). Double-blind study of adjuvant buspirone for fluoxetine-treated patients with obsessive-compulsive disorder. *American Journal of Psychiatry, 150,* 819–821.

Gray, J. A. (1987). Interactions between drugs and behavior therapy. In H. J. Eysenck & I. Martin (Eds.), *Theoretical foundations of behavior therapy,* New York: Plenum Press.

Greenblatt, D. J., Harmatz, J. S., & Shader, R. I. (1993). Plasma alprazolam concentrations: Relation to efficacy and side effects in the treatment of panic disorder. *Archives of General Psychiatry, 50,* 715–722.

Greist, J., Chouinard, G., DuBof, E., Halaris, A., Won Kim, S., Koran, L., Liebowotiz, M., Lydiard, B., Rasmussen, S., White, K., & Sikes, C. (1995). Double-blind parallel comparison of three dosages of sertraline and placebo in outpatients with obsessive-compulsive disorder. *Archives of General Psychiatry, 52,* 289–295.

Greist, J. H., Jefferson, J. W., Kobak, K. A., Katzelnik, D. J., & Serlin, R. C. (1995). Efficacy and tolerability of serotonin transport inhibitors in obsessive-compulsive disorder: A meta-analysis. *Archives of General Psychiatry, 52,* 53–60.

Guy, W. (1976). Clinical global impressions (028-CGI). In *ECDEU assessment manual for psychopharmacology* (pp. 217–222). DHEW Publication No. (ADM)76-338. Rockville, MD: National Institute of Mental Health. [See also National Institute of Mental Health. Special feature: Rating scales and assessment instruments for use in pediatric psychopharmacology research. *Psychopharmacology Bulletin, 21* (4)].

Hales, R. E., Hilty, D. A., and Wise, M. G. (1997). A treatment algorithm for the management of anxiety in primary care practice. *Journal of Clinical Psychiatry, 58* (suppl. 3), 76–80.

Hammer, M., & Ulmer, H. (1998, June). Resperidone for positive symptoms of psychosis in PTSD: A preliminary open trial. Poster session presented at the annual meeting of the New Clinical Drug Evaluation Unit (NCDEU) Program, Boca Raton, FL.

Hayward, P., Wardle, J., & Higgitt, A. (1989). Benzodiazepine research: Current findings and practical consequences. *British Journal of Clinical Psychology, 28,* 307–327.

Hedges, D. W., Reimherr, F. W., Strong, R. E., Halls, C. H., & Rust, C. (1996). An open trial of nefazodone in adult patients with generalized anxiety disorder. *Psychopharmacology Bulletin, 32,* 671–676.

Hegel, M. T., Ravaris, C. L., & Ahles, T. A. (1994). Combined cognitive-behavioral and time-limited alprazolam treatment of panic disorder. *Behavior Therapy, 25,* 183–195.

Hertzberg, M. A., Butterfield, M. I., Feldman, M., Beckham, J., Sutherland, S. M., Conner, K. M., & Davidson, J. R. T. (1998, June). A study of lamotrigine in the treatment of posttraumatic stress disorder (PTSD). Poster session presented at the annual meeting of the New Clinical Drug Evaluation Unit (NCDEU) Program, Boca Raton, FL.

Hertzberg, M., Feldman, M. E., Beckham, J. C., & Davidson, J. R. T. (1996). Trial of trazodone for posttraumatic stress disorder using a multiple baseline group design. *Journal of Clinical Psychopharmacology, 16,* 294–298.

Hewlett, W. A., Vinogradov, S., & Agras, W. S. (1992). Clomipramine, clonazepam, and clonidine treatment of obsessive-compulsive disorder. *Journal of Clinical Psychopharmacology, 12,* 175–178.

Hoehn-Saric, R., McLeod, D. R., & Zimmerli, W. D. (1988). Differential effects of alprazolam and imipramine in generalized anxiety disorder: Somatic versus psychic symptoms. *Journal of Clinical Psychiatry, 49,* 293–301.

Hofmann, S. G., & Spiegel, D. A. (1999). Panic Control Treatment and its applications. *Journal of Psychotherapy Practice and Research, 8,* 3–11.

Hogben, G. L., & Cornfield, R. B. (1981). Treatment of traumatic war neurosis with phenelzine. *Archives of General Psychiatry, 38,* 440–445.

Jefferson, J. W. (1995). Social phobia: A pharmacologic treatment overview. *Journal of Clinical Psychiatry, 56* (suppl. 5), 18–24.

Jenike, M. A. (1993). Obsessive-compulsive disorder: Efficacy of specific treatments as assessed by controlled trials. *Psychopharmacology Bulletin, 29,* 487–499.

Jenike, M. A., Baer, L., & Buttolph, L. (1991). Buspirone augmentation of fluoxetine in patients with obsessive-compulsive disorder. *Journal of Clinical Psychiatry, 1,* 13–14.

Kahn, R. J., McNair, D. M., Lipman, R. S., Covi, L., Rickels, K., Downing, R., Fisher, S., & Frankenthaler, L. M. (1986). Imipramine and chlordiazepoxide in depressive and anxiety disorders; II: Efficacy in anxious outpatients. *Archives of General Psychiatry, 43,* 79–85.

Katschnig, H., Amering, M., Stolk, J. M., Klerman, G. L., Ballenger, J. C., Briggs, A., Buller, R., Cassano, G., Garvey, M., Roth, M., & Solyom, C. (1995). Long-term follow-up after a drug trial for panic disorder. *British Journal of Psychiatry, 167,* 487–494.

Katschnig, H., Stein, M. B., & Buller, R., on behalf of the International Multicenter Clinical Trial Group on Moclobemide in Social Phobia. (1997). Moclobemide in social phobia: A double-blind, placebo-controlled clinical study. *European Archives of Psychiatry and Clinical Neuroscience, 247,* 71–80.

Katzelnick, D. J., Kobak, K, A., Greist, J. H., Jefferson, J. W., Mantle, J. M., & Serlin, R. C. (1995). Sertraline for social phobia: A double-blind, placebo-controlled crossover study. *American Journal of Psychiatry, 152,* 1368–1371.

Kelsey, J. E. (1995). Venlafaxine in social phobia. *Psychopharmacology Bulletin, 31,* 767–771.

Kinzie, J. D., & Leung, P. (1989). Clonidine in Cambodian patients with posttraumatic stress disorder. *Journal of Nervous and Mental Disorders, 177,* 546–550.

Klein, D. F. (1964). Delineation of two drug-responsive anxiety syndromes. *Psychopharmacologia, 5,* 397–408.

Klein, D. F. (1967). Importance of psychiatric diagnosis in prediction of clinical drug effects. *Archives of General Psychiatry, 16,* 118–126.

Klein, D. F., & Fink, M. (1962). Psychiatric reaction patterns to imipramine. *American Journal of Psychiatry, 119,* 432–438.

Klein, E., Geraci, M., & Uhde, T. W. (1990). Inefficacy of single-dose nifedipine in the treatment of phobic anxiety. *Israel Journal of Psychiatry and Related Sciences, 27,* 119–123.

Klerman, G. L. (1992). Drug treatment of panic disorder: Reply to comment by Marks and associates. *British Journal of Psychiatry, 161,* 465–471.

Kline, N. A., Dow, B. M., Brown, S. A., & Matloff, S. L. (1994). Sertraline efficacy in depressed combat veterans with posttraumatic stress disorder (letter). *American Journal of Psychiatry, 151,* 621.

Koran, L. M., McElroy, S. L., Davidson, J. R., Rasmussen, S. A., Hollander, E., & Jenike, M. A. (1996). Fluoxetine versus clomipramine for obsessive-compulsive disorder: A double-blind comparison. *Journal of Clinical Psychopharmacology, 16,* 121–129.

Kushner, M. G., Sher, K. J., & Beitman, B. D. (1990). The relation between alcohol problems and the anxiety disorders. *American Journal of Psychiatry, 147,* 685–695.

Lecrubier, Y., Bakker, A., Dunbar, G., Judge, R., and the Collaborative Panic Study Investigators. (1997). A comparison of paroxetine, clomipramine, and placebo in the treatment of panic disorder. *Acta Psychiatrica Scandinavica, 95,* 145–152.

Leonard, H. L., Swedo, S. E., Lenane, M. D., Rettew, D. C., Cheslow, D. L., Hamburger, S. D., & Rapoport, J. L. (1991). A double-blind desipramine substitution during long-term clomipramine treatment in children and adolescents with obsessive-compulsive disorder. *Archives of General Psychiatry, 48,* 922–927.

Leonard, H., Topol, D., Bukstein, O., Hindmarsh, D., Allen, A., & Swedo, S. (1994). Clonazepam as an augmenting agent in the treatment of childhood-onset obsessive-compulsive disorder. *Journal of the American Academy of Child and Adolescent Psychiatry, 33,* 792–794.

Lerer, B., Bleich, A., Kotler, M., Garb, R., Hertzberg, M., & Levin, B. (1987). Posttraumatic stress disorder in Israeli combat veterans: Effect of phenelzine treatment. *Archives of General Psychiatry, 44,* 976–981.

Lesser, I. M., Lydiard, R. B., Antal, E., Rubin, R. T., Ballenger, J. C., & DuPont, R. (1992). Alprazolam plasma concentrations and treatment response in panic disorder and agoraphobia. *American Journal of Psychiatry, 149,* 1556–1562.

Lesser, I. M., Rubin, R., Pecknold, J. C., Rifkin, A., Swinson, R. P., Lydiard, R. B., Burrows, G. D., Noyes, R., & DuPont, R. L. (1988). Secondary depression in panic disorder and agoraphobia, I: Frequency, severity, and response to treatment. *Archives of General Psychiatry, 45,* 437–453.

Liebowitz, M. R. (1991). Psychopharmacological management of social and simple phobias. In W. Coryell & G. Winokur (Eds.), *The clinical management of anxiety disorders* (pp. 63–78). New York: Oxford University Press.

Liebowitz, M. R., Gorman, J. M., Fyer, A. J., & Klein, D. F. (1985). Social phobia: Review of a neglected anxiety disorder. *Archives of General Psychiatry, 42,* 729–736.

Liebowitz, M. R., Schneier, F., Campeas, R., Gorman, J., Fyer, A., Hollander, E., Hatterer, J., & Papp, L. (1990). Phenelzine and atenolol in social phobia. *Psychopharmacology Bulletin, 26,* 123–125.

Liebowitz, M. R., Schneier, F., Campeas, R., Hollander, E., Jatterer, J., Fyer, A., Gorman, J., Papp, L., Davies, S., Gully, R., & Klein, D. (1992). Phenelzine vs atenolol in social phobia: A placebo-controlled comparison. *Archives of General Psychiatry, 49,* 290–300.

Lipper, S., Davidson, J. R., Grady, T. A., Edinger, J. D., Hammett, E. B., Mahorney, S. L., & Cavenar, J. O., Jr. (1986). Preliminary study of carbamazepine in posttraumatic stress disorder. *Psychosomatics, 27,* 849–854.

Lott, M., Greist, J. H., Jefferson, J. W., Kobak, K. A., Katzelnick, D. J., Katz, R. J., & Schaettle, S. C. (1997). Brofaromine for social phobia: A multicenter, placebo-controlled, double-blind study. *Journal of Clinical Psychopharmacology, 17,* 255–260.

Lum, M., Fontaine, R., Elie, R., & Ontiveros, A. (1990). Divalproex sodium's antipanic effect in panic disorder: A placebo-controlled study. *Biological Psychiatry, 27* (9A), 164.

Lydiard, R. B., Ballenger, J. C., & Rickels, K. (1997). A double-blind evaluation of the safety and efficacy of abecarnil, alprazolam, and placebo in outpatients with generalized anxiety disorder. *Journal of Clinical Psychiatry, 58* (suppl. 11), 11–18.

Lydiard, R. B., Brawman-Mintzer, O., & Ballenger, J. C. (1996). Recent developments in the psychopharmacology of anxiety disorders. *Journal of Consulting and Clinical Psychology, 64,* 660–668.

Lydiard, R. B., Laraia, M. T., Howell, E. F., & Ballenger, J. C. (1988). Alprazolam in the treatment of social phobia. *Journal of Clinical Psychiatry, 49,* 17–19.

Lydiard, R. B., Lesser, I. M., Ballenger, J. C., Rubin, R. T., Laraia, M. T., & DuPont, R. (1992). A fixed-dose study of alprazolam 2 mg, alprazolam 6 mg, and placebo in panic disorder. *Journal of Clinical Psychopharmacology, 12,* 96–103.

Lydiard, R. B., Morton, W. A., Emmanuel, N. P., Zealberg, J. J., Laraia, M. T., Stuart, G. W., O'Neil, P. M., & Ballenger, J. C. (1993). Preliminary report: Placebo-controlled, double-blind study of the clinical and metabolic effects of desipramine in panic disorder. *Psychopharmacology Bulletin, 29,* 183–188.

Lydiard, R. B., Pollack, M. H., Judge, R., Michelson, D., & Tamura, R. (1997, September). *Fluoxetine in panic disorder: A placebo-controlled study.* Presentation at the 10th Congress of the European College of Neuro-psychopharmacology, Vienna.

Lydiard, R. B., Steiner, M., Burnham, D., & Gergel, I. (1998). Efficacy studies of paroxetine in panic disorder. *Psychopharmacology Bulletin, 34,* 175–182.

March, J. S., Frances, A., Carpenter, D., & Kahn, D. A. (Eds.). (1997). Expert consensus guidelines: Treatment of obsessive-compulsive disorder. *Journal of Clinical Psychiatry, 58* (suppl. 4).

Markowitz, P. J., Stagnos, J., & Calabresa, J. R. (1990). Buspirone augmentation of fluoxetine on obsessive compulsive disorder. *American Journal of Psychiatry, 147,* 798–800.

Marks, I. M., Swinson, R. P., Basoglu, M., Kuch, K., Noshirvani, H., O'Sullivan, G., Lelliott, P. T., Kirby, M., McNamee, G., Sengun, S., & Wickwire, K. (1993). Alprazolam and exposure alone and combined in panic disorder with agoraphobia: A controlled study in London and Toronto. *British Journal of Psychiatry, 162,* 776–787.

Marks, I. M., Viswanthan, R., Lipsedge, M. S., & Gardner, R. (1972). Enhanced relief of phobias by flooding during waning diazepam effect. *British Journal of Psychiatry, 121,* 493–505.

Marshall, J. R. (1995). Integrated treatment of social phobia. *Bulletin of the Menninger Clinic, 59* (2, suppl. A), A27–A37.

Marshall, R. D., Schneier, F. R., Fallon, B. A., Feerick, J., & Liebowitz, M. R. (1994). Medication therapy for social phobia. *Journal of Clinical Psychiatry, 55* (6, suppl), 33–37.

Marshall, R. D., Stein, D. J., Liebowitz, M. R., & Yehuda, R. (1996). A pharmacotherapy algorithm in the treatment of posttraumatic stress disorder. *Psychiatric Annals, 26,* 217–226.

Mavissakalian, M. (1993). Combined behavioral therapy and pharmacotherapy of agoraphobia. *Journal of Psychiatric Research, 22* (suppl. 1), 179–191.

Mavissakalian, M., & Perel, J. M. (1992a). Clinical experiments in maintenance and discontinuation of imipramine therapy in panic disorder with agoraphobia. *Archives of General Psychiatry, 49,* 318–323.

Mavissakalian, M., & Perel, J. M. (1992b). Protective effects of imipramine maintenance treatment in panic disorder with agoraphobia. *American Journal of Psychiatry, 149,* 1053–1057.

Mavissakalian, M. R., & Perel, J. M. (1995). Imipramine treatment of panic disorder with agoraphobia: Dose ranging and plasma level–response relationships. *American Journal of Psychiatry, 152,* 673–682.

Mavissakalian, M. R., & Perel, J. M. (1997). Optimal target dose of imipramine in panic disorder with agoraphobia [Abstract]. *Biological Psychiatry, 41,* 91S–92S.

Mavissakalian, M., Perel, J., Bowler, K., & Dealy, R. (1987). Trazodone in the treatment of panic disorder and agoraphobia with panic attacks. *American Journal of Psychiatry, 144,* 785–787.

McDougal, C. J., Fleischmann, R. L., Epperson, C. N., Wasylink, S., Leckman, J. F., & Price, L. H. (1995). Risperidone addition in fluvoxamine-refractory obsessive compulsive disorder: Three cases. *Journal of Clinical Psychiatry, 56,* 526–528.

McDougal, C. J., Goodman, W. K., Leckman, J. F., Holzer, J. C., Barr, L. C., McCance-Katz, E., Heninger, G. R., & Price, L. H. (1993). Limited therapeutic effect of addition of buspirone in fluvoxamine-refractory obsessive-compulsive disorder. *American Journal of Psychiatry, 150,* 647–649.

McDougal, C. J., Goodman, W. K., Leckman, J. F., Lee, N. C., Heninger, G. R., & Price, L. H. (1994). Haloperidol addition in fluvoxamine-refractory obsessive compulsive disorder: A double-blind, placebo-controlled study in patients with and without tics. *Archives of General Psychiatry, 51,* 302–308.

McDougal, C. J., Goodman, W. K., Price, L. H., Delgado, P. L., Krystal, J. H., Charney, D. S., & Heninger, G. R. (1990). Neuroleptic addition in fluvoxamine-refractory obsessive-compulsive disorder. *American Journal of Psychiatry, 147,* 652–654.

McDougal, C. J., Southwick, S. M., Charney, D. S., & St. James, R. L. (1991). An open trial of fluoxetine in the treatment of posttraumatic stress disorder. *Journal of Clinical Psychopharmacology, 11,* 325–327.

Milanes, F. J., Mack, C. N., Dennison, J., & Slater, V. L. (1984, June). Phenelzine treatment in post-Vietnam stress syndrome. *VA Practitioner,* pp. 40–49.

Mintzer, J. E., & Brawman-Mintzer, O. (1996). Agitation as a possible expression of generalized anxiety disorder in the demented elderly patients: Toward a treatment approach. *Journal of Clinical Psychiatry, 57* (suppl. 7), 55–63.

Modigh, K., Westberg, P., & Eriksson, E. (1992). Superiority of clomipramine over imipramine in the treatment of panic disorder: A placebo-controlled trial. *Journal of Clinical Psychopharmacology, 12,* 251–261.

Moroz, G., & Rosenbaum, J. F. (1998). Efficacy, safety, and gradual discontinuation of clonazepam in panic disorder: A placebo-controlled multicenter study using optimized doses. Manuscript submitted for publication.

Munjack, D. J., Baltazar, P. L., Bohn, P. B., Cabe, D. D., & Appleton, A. A. (1990). Clonazepam in the treatment of social phobia: A pilot study. *Journal of Clinical Psychiatry, 51* (5, suppl), 35–40.

Munjack, D. J., Bruns, J., Baltazar, P. L., Brown, R., Leonard, M., Nagy, R., Koek, R., Crocker, B., & Schafer, S. (1991). A pilot study of buspirone in the treatment of social phobia. *Journal of Anxiety Disorders, 5,* 87–98.

Munjack, D. J., Crocker, B., Cabe, D., Brown, R., Usigli, R., Zulueta, A., McManus, M., McDowell, D., Palmer, R., & Leonard, M. (1989). Alprazolam, propranolol, and placebo in the treatment of panic disorder and agoraphobia with panic attacks. *Journal of Clinical Psychopharmacology, 9,* 22–27.

Nagy, L. M., Krystal, J. H., Woods, S. W., & Charney, D. S. (1989). Clinical and medication outcome after short-term alprazolam and behavioral group treatment of panic disorder and agoraphobia with panic attacks. *Archives of General Psychiatry, 46,* 993–999.

Nagy, L. M., Morgan, C. A., Southwick, S. M., & Charney, D. S. (1993). Open prospective trial of fluoxetine for posttraumatic stress disorder. *Journal of Clinical Psychopharmacology, 13,* 107–113.

Nair, N. P. V., Bakish, D., Saxena, B., Amin, M., Schwartz, G., & West, T. E. G. (1996). Comparison of fluvoxamine, imipramine, and placebo in the treatment of outpatients with panic disorder. *Anxiety, 2,* 192–198.

Ninan, P. T., Cole, J. O., & Yonkers, K. A. (1998). Nonbenzodiazepine anxiolytics. In A. F. Schatzberg & C. B. Nemeroff (Eds.), *Textbook of psychopharmacology* (pp. 287–300). Washington, DC: American Psychiatric Press.

Noyes, R. J., Anderson, D. J., Clancy, J., Crowe, R. R., Slymen, D. J., Ghoneim, M. M., & Hinrichs, J. V. (1984). Diazepam and propranolol in panic disorder and agoraphobia. *Archives of General Psychiatry, 41,* 287–292.

Noyes, R., Burrows, G. D., Reich, J. H., Judd, F. K., Garvey, M. J., Norman, T. R., Cook, B. L., & Marriott, P. (1996). Diazepam versus alprazolam for the treatment of panic disorder. *Journal of Clinical Psychiatry, 57,* 349–355.

Noyes, R., DuPont, R. L., Pecknold, J. C., Rifkin, A., Rubin, R. T., Swinson, R. P., Ballenger, J. C., & Burrows, G. D. (1988). Alprazolam in panic disorder and agoraphobia: Results from a multicenter trial, II: Patient acceptance, side effects, and safety. *Archives of General Psychiatry, 45,* 423–428.

Noyes, R., Moroz, G., Davidson, J. R. T., Liebowitz, M. R., Davidson, A., Siegel, J., Bell, J., Cain, J. W., Curlik, S. M., Kent, T. A., Lydiard, R. B., Mallinger, A. G., Pollack, M. H., Rapaport, M., Rasmussen, S. A., Hedges, D., Schweizer, E., & Uhlenhuth, E. H. (1997). Moclobemide in social phobia: A controlled dose-response trial. *Journal of Clinical Psychopharmacology, 17,* 247–254.

Oehrberg, S., Christiansen, P. E., Behnke, K., Borup, A. L., Severin, B., Soegaard, J., Calberg, H., Judge, R., Ohrstrom, J. K., & Manniche, P. M. (1995). Paroxetine in the treatment of panic disorder: A randomized, double-blind, placebo-controlled study. *British Journal of Psychiatry, 167,* 374–379.

Ontiveros, A., Costilla, A., Rojas, A., & Diaz, R. (1998, June). Clonazepam long-term efficacy in social phobia. Poster session presented at the annual meeting of the American Psychiatric Association, Toronto.

Ontiveros, A., & Fontaine, R. (1990). Social phobia and clonazepam. *Canadian Journal of Psychiatry, 35,* 439–441.

Otto, M. W., Pollack, M. H., & Sabatino, S. A. (1996). Maintenance of remission following cognitive behavior therapy for panic disorder: Possible deleterious effects of concurrent medication treatment. *Behavior Therapy, 27,* 473–482.

Otto, M. W., Pollack, M. H., Sachs, G. S., Reiter, S. R., Meltzer-Brody, S., & Rosenbaum, J. F. (1993). Discontinuation of benzodiazepine treatment: Efficacy of cognitive behavioral therapy for patients with panic disorder. *American Journal of Psychiatry, 150,* 1485–1490.

Papp, L. A., Sinha, S. S., Martinez, J. M., Coplan, J. D., Amchin, J., & Gorman, J. M. (1998). Low-dose venlafaxine treatment in panic disorder. *Psychopharmacology Bulletin, 34,* 207–209.

Pato, M. T., Zohar-Kadouch, R., Zohar, J., & Murphy, D. L. (1988). Return of symptoms after discontinuation of clomipramine in patients with obsessive-compulsive disorder. *American Journal of Psychiatry, 145,* 1521–1525.

Pecknold, J. C., Swinson, R. P., Kuch, K., & Lewis, C. P. (1988). Alprazolam in panic disorder and agoraphobia: Results from a multicenter trial; III. Discontinuation effects. *Archives of General Psychiatry, 45,* 429–436.

Petracca, A., Nisita, C., McNair, D., Melis, G-B., Guerani, G., & Cassano, G. B. (1990). Treatment of generalized anxiety disorder: Preliminary clinical experience with buspirone. *Journal of Clinical Psychiatry, 51* (suppl. 9), 31–39.

Pigott, T., L'Heureux, F., Bernstein, S., Rubenstein, C., Dubbert, B., & Murphy, D. (1992). A controlled trial of adjuvant clonazepam in clomipramine and fluoxetine treated patients with OCD. *Proceedings of the 145th Annual American Psychiatric Association Meeting, 144,* 82.

Pigott, T. A., L'Heureux, F., Hill, J. L., Bihari, K., Bernstein, S. E., & Murphy, D. L. (1992). A double-blind study of adjuvant buspirone hydrochloride in clomipramine-treated patients with obsessive compulsive disorder. *Journal of Clinical Psychopharmacology, 12,* 11–18.

Pigott, T. A., Pato, M., Bernstein, S. E., Grover, G. N., Hill, J. L., Tolliver, T. J., & Murphy, D. L. (1990). Controlled comparisons of clomipramine and fluoxetine in the treatment of obsessive-compulsive disorder. *Archives of General Psychiatry, 47,* 926–932.

Pigott, T. A., & Seay, S. (1998). Biological treatments for obsessive-compulsive disorder: Literature review. In R. P. Swinson, M. M. Antony, S. Rachman, & M. A. Richter (Eds.), *Obsessive-compulsive disorder: Theory, research, and treatment* (pp. 298–326). New York: Guilford Press.

Pitts, C. D., Carpenter, D. J., Oakes, R., Gergel, I. P., & Travers, J. (1998, June). A randomized, double-blind, fixed-dose comparison of paroxetine (20 mg, 40 mg, 60 mg) and placebo in the treatment of social anxiety disorder. Poster session presented at the annual meeting of the New Clinical Drug Evaluation Unit (NCDEU) Program, Boca Raton, FL.

Pohl, R. B., Wolkow, R. M., & Clary, C. M. (1998). Sertraline in the treatment of panic disorder: A double-blind multicenter trial. *American Journal of Psychiatry, 155,* 1189–1195.

Pohl, R., Yeragani, K. V., Balon, R., & Lycaki, H. (1988). The jitteriness syndrome in panic disorder patients treated with antidepressants. *Journal of Clinical Psychiatry, 49,* 100–104.

Pollack, M. H., & Otto, M. W. (1994). Long-term pharmacologic treatment of panic disorder. *Psychiatric Annals, 24,* 291–298.

Pollack, M. H., Worthington, J. J., Manfro, G. G., Otto, M. W., & Zucker, B. G. (1997). Abecarnil for the treatment of generalized anxiety disorder: A placebo-controlled comparison of two dosage ranges of abecarnil and buspirone. *Journal of Clinical Psychiatry, 58* (suppl. 11), 19–23.

Pollack, M. H., Worthington, J. J., Otto, M. W., Maki, K. M., Smoller, J. W., Manfro, G. G., Rudolph, R., & Rosenbaum, J. F. (1996). Venlafaxine for panic disorder: Results from a double-blind, placebo-controlled study. *Psychopharmacology Bulletin, 32,* 667–670.

Potter, W. Z., Manji, H. K., & Rudorfer, M. V. (1998). Tricyclics and tetracyclics. In A. F. Schatzberg & C. B. Nemeroff (Eds.), *Textbook of psychopharmacology* (2d ed.) (pp. 199–218). Washington, DC: American Psychiatric Press.

Power, K. G., Simpson, R. J., Swanson, V., & Wallace, L. A. (1990). Controlled comparison of pharmacological and psychological treatment of generalized anxiety disorder in primary care. *British Journal of General Practice, 40,* 289–294.

Power, K. G., Simpson, R. J., Swanson, V., Wallace, L. A., Feistner, A. T. C., & Sharp, D. (1990). A controlled comparison of cognitive-behaviour therapy, diazepam, and placebo, alone and in combination, for the treatment of generalized anxiety disorder. *Journal of Anxiety Disorders, 4,* 267–292.

Rapaport, M. H., Frevert, T., Babior, S., Seymour, S., Zisook, S., Kelsoe, J., & Judd, L. L. (1996). Comparison of descriptive variables for symptomatic volunteers and clinical patients with anxiety disorders. *Anxiety, 2,* 117–122.

Rapaport, M. H., Wolkow, R. M., & Clary, C. M. (1998). Methodologies and outcomes from the sertraline multicenter flexible-dose trials. *Psychopharmacology Bulletin, 34,* 183–189.

Rasmussen, S., Goodman, W., Greist, J., Jenike, M., & Kozak, M. (in press). Fluvoxamine in the treatment of OCD: A multi-center double-blind, placebo-controlled study in outpatients. *American Journal of Psychiatry.*

Ravaris, C. L., Friedman, M. J., Hauri, P. J., & McHugo, G. J. (1991). A controlled study of alprazolam and propranolol in panic-disordered and agoraphobic outpatients. *Journal of Clinical Psychopharmacology, 11,* 344–350.

Reist, C., Kauffmann, C. D., Haier, R. J., Sangdahl, C., DeMet, E. M., Chicz-DeMet, A., & Nelson, J. N. (1989). A controlled trial of desipramine in 18 men with posttraumatic stress disorder. *American Journal of Psychiatry, 146,* 513–516.

Rickels, K. (1990). Buspirone in clinical practice. *Journal of Clinical Psychiatry, 51* (suppl. 9), 51–54.

Rickels, K., Downing, R., Schweizer, E., & Hassman, H. (1993). Antidepressants for the treatment of generalized anxiety disorder: A placebo-controlled comparison of imipramine, trazodone, and diazepam. *Archives of General Psychiatry, 50,* 884–895.

Rickels, K., Fox, I. L., Greenblatt, D. J., Sandler, K. R., & Schless, A. (1988). Clorazepate and lorazepam: Clinical improvement and rebound anxiety. *American Journal of Psychiatry, 145,* 312–317.

Rickels, K., Schweizer, E., Csanalosi, I., Case, W. G., & Chung, H. (1988). Long-term treatment of anxiety and risk of withdrawal. *Archives of General Psychiatry, 45,* 444–450.

Rickels, K., Schweizer, E., Weiss, S., & Zavodnick, S. (1993). Maintenance drug treatment of panic disorder, II: Short- and long-term outcome after drug taper. *Archives of General Psychiatry, 50,* 61–68.

Rickels, K., Weisman, K., Norstad, N., Singer, M., Stoltz, D., Brown, A., & Danton, J. (1982). Buspirone and diazepam in anxiety: A controlled study. *Journal of Clinical Psychiatry, 43* (12, sec. 2), 81–86.

Robinson, D. S., Rickels, K., Feighner, J., Fabrelf, L. F., Jr., Gammans, R. E., Shrotriya, C., Alms, D. R., Andary, J. J., & Messina, M. E. (1990). Clinical effects of the 5-HT$_{1A}$ partial agonists in depression: A composite analysis of buspirone in the treatment of depression. *Journal of Clinical Psychopharmacology, 10* (suppl. 3), 67S–76S.

Romach, M. K., Somer, G. R., Sobell, S. C., Sobell, M. B., Kaplan, H. L., & Sellers, E. M. (1992). Characteristics of long-term alprazolam users in the community. *Journal of Clinical Psychopharmacology, 12,* 316–332.

Rosenbaum, J. F., & Pollock, R. A. (1994). The psychopharmacology of social phobia and comorbid disorders. *Bulletin of the Menninger Clinic, 5* (2, suppl. A), A67–A83.

Rosenbaum, J. F., Moroz, G., & Bowden, C. L. for the Clonazepam Panic Disorder Dose-Response Study Group. (1997). Clonazepam in the treatment of panic disorder with or without agoraphobia: A dose-response study of efficacy, safety and discontinuance. *Journal of Clinical Psychopharmacology, 17,* 390–400.

Roy-Byrne, P., Wingerson, D., Cowley, D., & Dager, S. (1993). Psychopharmacologic treatment of panic, generalized anxiety disorder, and social phobia. *Psychiatric Clinics of North America, 16,* 719–735.

Sanderson, W. C., & Wetzler, S. (1993). Observations on the cognitive behavioral treatment of panic disorder: Impact of benzodiazepines. *Psychotherapy, 30,* 125–132.

Schatzberg A. F., & Nemeroff, C. B. (Eds.). (1998). *Textbook of psychopharmacology* (2d ed.). Washington, DC: American Psychiatric Press.

Schatzberg A. F., Cole, J. O., & DeBattista, C. (1997). *Manual of clinical psychopharmacology* (3d ed.). Washington, DC: American Psychiatric Press.

Schneier, F. R., Martin, L. Y., Liebowitz, M. R., Gorman, J. M., & Fyer, A. J. (1989). Alcohol abuse in social phobia. *Journal of Anxiety Disorders, 3,* 15–23.

Schweizer, E., & Rickels, K. (1996). The long-term management of generalized anxiety disorder: Issues and dilemmas. *Journal of Clinical Psychiatry, 57* (suppl. 7), 9–12.

Schweizer, E., & Rickels, K. (1997a). Placebo response in generalized anxiety: Its effect on the outcome of clinical trials. *Journal of Clinical Psychiatry, 58* (suppl. 11), 30–38.

Schweizer, E., & Rickels, K. (1997b). Strategies for treatment of generalized anxiety in primary care setting. *Journal of Clinical Psychiatry, 58* (suppl. 3), 27–31.

Schweizer, E., Pohl, R., Balon, R., Fox, I., Rickels, K., & Yeragani, K. (1990). Lorazepam vs. alprazolam in the treatment of panic disorder. *Pharmacopsychiatry, 23,* 90–93.

Schweizer, E., Rickels, K., Case, W. G., & Greenblatt, D. J. (1990). Long-term therapeutic use of benzodiazapines; II: Effects of gradual taper. *Archives of General Psychiatry, 47,* 908–915.

Schweizer, E., Rickels, K., Weiss, S., & Zavodnick, S. (1993). Maintenance drug treatment of panic disorder, I: Results of a prospective, placebo-controlled comparison of alprazolam and imipramine. *Archives of General Psychiatry, 50,* 51–60.

Shader, R. I., & Greenblatt, D. J. (1993). Use of benzodiazepines in anxiety disorders. *New England Journal of Medicine, 328,* 1398–1405.

Shalev, A. Y., Bonne, O., & Eth, S. (1996). Treatment of posttraumatic stress disorder: A review. *Psychosomatic Medicine, 58,* 165–182.

Shear, M. K. (1998, June). Acute treatment outcomes. In S. W. Woods (Chair), *First line treatment of panic disorder—cognitive behavior treatment vs. imipramine vs. their combination: A multi-center study.* Symposium conducted at the annual meeting of the New Clinical Drug Evaluation Unit (NCDEU) Program, Boca Raton, FL.

Shear, M. K., Brown, T. A., Barlow, D. H., Money, R., Sholomskas, D. E., Woods, S. W., Gorman, J. M., & Papp, L. A. (1997). Multicenter collaborative panic disorder severity scale. *American Journal of Psychiatry, 154,* 1571–1575.

Sheehan, D. V., Ballenger, J., & Jacobsen, G. (1980). Treatment of endogenous anxiety with phobic, hysterical, and hypochondriacal symptoms. *Archives of General Psychiatry, 37,* 51–59.

Sheikh, J. I., & Salzman, C. (1995). Anxiety in the elderly: Course and treatment. *Psychiatric Clinics of North America, 18,* 871–883.

Shestatsky, M., Greenberg, D., & Lerer, B. (1988). A controlled trial of phenelzine in posttraumatic stress disorder, *Psychiatry Research, 24,* 149–155.

Small, G. W., & Bystritsky, A. (1997). Double-blind, placebo-controlled trial of two doses of abecarnil for geriatric anxiety. *Journal of Clinical Psychiatry, 58* (suppl. 11), 24–29.

Smeraldi, E., Erzegovesi, S., & Bianchi, I. (1992). Fluvoxamine versus clomipramine treatment in OCD: A preliminary study. *New Trends in Experimental and Clinical Psychiatry, 8,* 63–65.

Solyom, C., Solyom, L., LaPierre, Y., Pecknold, J., & Morton, L. (1981). Phenelzine and exposure in the treatment of phobias. *Biological Psychiatry, 16,* 239–247.

Spiegel, D. A. (1998a). Efficacy studies of alprazolam in panic disorder. *Psychopharmacology Bulletin, 34,* 191–195.

Spiegel, D. A. (1998b, May). Is reduction in panic attacks a sufficient measure of treatment efficacy in panic disorder? In J. M. Gorman (Chair), *Treatment strategies for successful outcomes in patients with panic disorder.* Symposium conducted at the annual meeting of the American Psychiatric Association, Toronto.

Spiegel, D. A. (in press). Combined drug and behavioral treatments for OCD: Early findings. In W. K. Goodamn, M. V. Rudorfer, & J. D. Maser (Eds.), *Treatment challenges in obsessive compulsive disorder.* Hillsdale, NJ: Erlbaum.

Spiegel, D. A., & Bruce, T. J. (1997). Benzodiazepines and exposure-based cognitive behavior therapies for panic disorder: Conclusions from combined treatment trials. *American Journal of Psychiatry, 154,* 773–780.

Spiegel, D. A., Bruce, T. J., Gregg, S. F., & Nuzzarello, A. (1994). Does cognitive behavior therapy assist slow-taper alprazolam discontinuation in panic disorder? *American Journal of Psychiatry, 151,* 876–881.

Sramek, J. J., Tansman, M., Suri, A., Hornig-Rohan, M., Amsterdam, J. D., Stahl, S. M., Weisler, R. H., & Cutler, N. R. (1996). Efficacy of buspirone in generalized anxiety disorder with coexisting mild depressive symptoms. *Journal of Clinical Psychiatry, 57,* 287–291.

Stahl, S. M. (1996). *Essential psychopharmacology.* Cambridge, UK: Cambridge University Press.

Stein, M. B., Chartier, M. J., Hazen, A. L., Kroft, C. D. L., Chale, R. A., Cote, D., & Walker, J. R. (1996). Paroxetine in the treatment of generalized social phobia: Open-label treatment and double-blind placebo-controlled discontinuation. *Journal of Clinical Psychopharmacology, 16,* 218–222.

Strand, M., Hetta, J., Rosen, A., Sörensen, S., Malmström, R., Fabian, C., Marits, K., Vetterskog, K., Liljestrand, A-G., & Hegen, C. (1990). A double-blind, controlled trial in primary care patients with generalized anxiety: A comparison between buspirone and oxazepam. *Journal of Clinical Psychiatry, 51* (suppl. 9), 40–45.

Swendsen, J. D., Merikangas, K. R., Canino, G. J., Kessler, R. C., Rubio-Stipec, M., & Angst, J. (1998). The comorbidity of alcoholism with anxiety and depressive disorders in four geographic communities. *Comprehensive Psychiatry, 39,* 176–184.

Taylor, C. B. (1998). Treatment of anxiety disorders. In A. F. Schatzberg & C. B. Nemeroff (Eds.), *Textbook of psychopharmacology* (pp. 775–789). Washington, DC: American Psychiatric Press.

Telch, M. J., & Lucas, R. A. (1994). Combined pharmacological and psychological treatment of panic disorder: Current status and future directions. In B. E. Wolfe & J. D. Maser (Eds.), *Treatment of panic disorder: A consensus development conference* (pp. 177–197). Washington, DC: American Psychiatric Press.

Thyer, B. A., Parrish, R. T., Himle, J., Cameron, O. G., Curtis, G. C., & Nesse, R. M. (1986). Alcohol abuse among clinically anxious patients. *Behaviour Research and Therapy, 24,* 357–359.

Tollefson, G., Birkett, M., Koran, L., & Genduso, L. (1994). Continuation treatment of OCD: Double-blind and open-label experience with fluoxetine. *Journal of Clinical Psychiatry, 55,* 69–78.

Tollefson, G. D., Rampey, A. H., Potvin, J. H., Jenike, M. A., Rush, A. J., Dominguez, R. A., Koran, L. M., Shear, M. K., Goodman, W., & Genduso, L. A. (1994). A multicenter investigation of fixed-dose fluoxetine in the treatment of obsessive-compulsive disorder. *Archives of General Psychiatry, 51,* 559–567.

Tollefson, G. D., & Rosenbaum, J. F. (1998). Selective serotonin reuptake inhibitors. In A. F. Schatzberg & C. B. Nemeroff (Eds.), *Textbook of psychopharmacology* (2d ed.) (pp. 219–237). Washington, DC: American Psychiatric Press.

Tucker, P. M., Smith, K., L., Jones, D., Carson, M., & Bhupathiraju, R. (1998, June). Nefazodone in PTSD: Effects on symptoms and physiological reactivity. Poster session presented at the annual meeting of the New Clinical Drug Evaluation Unit (NCDEU) Program, Boca Raton, FL.

Tucker, P. M., Smith, K. L., Miranda, R., & Marx, B. (1998, June). Fluvoxamine in PTSD: Do physiological and subjective improvement coincide?. Poster session presented at the annual meeting of the New Clinical Drug Evaluation Unit (NCDEU) Program, Boca Raton, FL.

Turner, S. M., Beidel, D. C., & Jacob, R. G. (1994). Social phobia: A comparison of behavior therapy and atenolol. *Journal of Consulting and Clinical Psychology, 62,* 350–358.

Uhlenhuth, E. H. (1998). Treatment strategies in panic disorder: Recommendations of an expert panel [Abstract]. *Psiquiatria Biológica, 6* (1, suppl. 1), 96.

Uhlenhuth, E. H., Matuzas, W., Glass, R. M., & Easton, C. (1989). Response of panic disorder to fixed doses of alprazolam or imipramine. *Journal of Affective Disorders, 17,* 261–270.

Uhlenhuth, E. H., Matuzas, W., Warner, T. D., & Thompson, P. M. (1997). Methodological issues in psychopharmacological research; Growing placebo response rate: The problem in recent therapeutic trials. *Psychopharmacology Bulletin, 33,* 31–39.

Van Ameringen, M., Mancini, C., & Streiner, D. L. (1993). Fluoxetine efficacy in social phobia. *Journal of Clinical Psychiatry, 54,* 27–32.

Van Ameringen, M., Mancini, C., & Streiner, D. (1994). Sertraline in social phobia. *Journal of Affective Disorders, 31,* 141–145.

van Balkom, A. J. L. M., de Haan, E., van Oppen, P., Spinhoven, P., Hoogduin, K. A. L., & van Dyck, R. (1998). Cognitive and behavioral therapies alone versus in combination with fluvoxamine in the treatment of obsessive compulsive disorder. *Journal of Nervous and Mental Disease, 186,* 492–499.

van der Kolk, B. A., Dreyfuss, D., Michael, M., Shera, D., Berkowitz, R., Fisler, R., & Saxe, G. (1994). Fluoxetine in posttraumatic stress disorder. *Journal of Clinical Psychiatry, 55,* 517–522.

Van Vliet, I. M., den Boer, J. A., & Westenberg, H. G. M. (1994). Psychopharmacological treatment of social phobia; a double blind placebo controlled study with fluvoxamine. *Psychopharmacology, 115,* 128–134.

Vargas, M. A., & Davidson, J. R. T. (1993). Post-traumatic stress disorder. *Psychiatric Clinics of North America, 16,* 737–748.

Versiani, M., Mundim, F. D., Nardi, A. E., & Liebowitz, M. R. (1988). Tranylcypromine in social phobia. *Journal of Clinical Psychopharmacology, 8,* 279–283.

Versiani, M., Nardi, A. E., Mundim, F. D., Alves, A. B., Liebowitz, M. R., & Amrein, R. (1992). Pharmacotherapy of social phobia: A controlled study with moclobemide and phenelzine. *British Journal of Psychiatry, 161,* 353–360.

Wade, A. G., Lepola, U., Koponen, H. J., Pedersen, V., & Pedersen, T. (1997). The effect of citalopram in panic disorder. *British Journal of Psychiatry, 170,* 549–553.

Waikar, S. V., Bystritsky, A., Craske, M. G., & Murphy, K. M. (1994/1995). Etiological beliefs and treatment preferences in anxiety-disordered patients. *Anxiety, 1,* 134–137.

Walkup, J. T., Reeve, E., Yaryura-Tobias, J., Wong, L. F., Claghorn, J., Gaffney, G., Greist, J., Holland, D., McConville, B., Pigott, T., Pravetz, M., & Riddle, M. (1998, June). Fluvoxamine for childhood obsessive compulsive disorder: Long-term treatment. Poster session presented at the annual meeting of the New Clinical Drug Evaluation Unit (NCDEU) Program, Boca Raton, FL.

Wardle, J. (1990). Behavior therapy and benzodiazepines: Allies or enemies. *British Journal of Psychiatry, 156,* 163–168.

Wardle, J., Hayward, P., Higgitt, A., Stabl, M., Blizard, R., & Gray, J. (1994). Effects of concurrent diazepam treatment on the outcome of exposure therapy in agoraphobia. *Behaviour Research and Therapy, 32,* 203–215.

Wheadon, D., & Gergel, I. (1995). Long-term treatment with paroxetine for outpatients with OCD: An extension of the fixed dose study. Manuscript submitted for publication.

Wiborg, I. M., & Dahl, A. V. (1996). Does brief dynamic psychotherapy reduce the relapse rate of panic disorder? *Archives of General Psychiatry, 53,* 689–694.

Wilhelm, F. H., & Roth, W. T. (1997). Acute and delayed effects of alprazolam on flight phobics during exposure. *Behaviour Research and Therapy, 35,* 831–841.

Wingerson, D., Nguyen, C., & Roy-Byrne, P. P. (1992). Clomipramine treatment for generalized anxiety disorder (letter to the editor). *Journal of Clinical Psychopharmacology, 12,* 214–215.

Wolf, M. E., Alavi, A., & Mosnaim, A. D. (1988). Post-traumatic stress disorder in Vietnam veterans: Clinical and EEG findings; possible therapeutic effects of carbamazepine. *Biological Psychiatry, 23,* 642–644.

Woodman, C. L., & Noyes, R. (1994). Panic disorder: Treatment with valproate. *Journal of Clinical Psychiatry, 55,* 134–136.

Woods, S. W. (1998, June). No-treatment followup outcomes. In S. W. Woods (Chair), *First line treatment of panic disorder—cognitive behavior treatment vs. imipramine vs. their combination: A multi-center study.* Symposium conducted at the annual meeting of the New Clinical Drug Evaluation Unit (NCDEU) Program, Boca Raton, FL.

Worthington, J. J., Pollack, M. H., Otto, M. W., McLean, R. Y. S., Moroz, G., & Rosenbaum, J. F. (1998). Long-term experience with clonazepam in patients with a primary diagnosis of panic disorder. *Psychopharmacology Bulletin, 34,* 199–205.

Zajecka, J. M. (1996). The effect of nefazodone on comorbid anxiety symptoms associated with depression: Experience in family practice and psychiatric outpatient clinics. *Journal of Clinical Psychiatry, 57* (suppl. 2), 10–14.

Zisook, S., Chentsova-Dutton, Y., Ellenor, G., Kodsi, A., Smith-Vaniz, A., & Kline, N. A. (1998, June). Nefazodone in patients with treatment-refractory PTSD. Poster session presented at the annual meeting of the American Psychiatric Association, Toronto.

Zitrin, C. M., Klein, D. F., & Woerner, M. G. (1978). Behavior therapy, supportive psychotherapy, imipramine, and phobias. *Archives of General Psychiatry, 35,* 307–316.

Zitrin, C. M., Klein, D. F., Woerner, M. G., & Ross, D. C. (1983). Treatment of phobias; I: Comparison of imipramine hydrochloride and placebo. *Archives of General Psychiatry, 40,* 125–138.

Zohar, J., Judge, R., & the OCD Paroxetine Study Investigators. (1996). Paroxetine versus clomipramine in the treatment of obsessive-compulsive disorder. *British Journal of Psychiatry, 169,* 468–474.

CHAPTER 4

BIOFEEDBACK

Frank Andrasik

Olson (1995), after examining various operational and teleological definitions and considering proposed underlying theoretical models, offers a comprehensive definition of applied biofeedback that is based on a synthesis:

> As a process, applied biofeedback is (1) a group of therapeutic procedures that (2) utilizes electronic or electromechanical instruments (3) to accurately measure, process, and "feed back" to persons (4) information with reinforcing properties (5) about their neuromuscular and autonomic activity, both normal and abnormal, (6) in the form of analogue or binary, auditory and/or visual feedback signals. (7) Best achieved with a competent biofeedback professional, (8) the objectives are to help persons develop greater awareness and voluntary control over their physiological processes that are otherwise outside awareness and/or under less voluntary control, (9) by first controlling the external signal, (10) and then with internal psychophysiological cues. (p. 29)

The biofeedback movement in general can be traced back to the 1960s, when a number of converging scientific findings and sociocultural trends fostered development of what was then a radically new approach to behavior change (Schwartz & Olson, 1995). At this time, empirical studies (Engel, 1972; Harris & Brady, 1974; Kamiya, 1969; Kimmel, 1967, 1979; Kristt & Engel, 1975; Miller, 1969, 1978; Miller & DiCara, 1967; Shapiro, Tursky, & Schwartz, 1970; Surwit, Shapiro, & Feld, 1976) were beginning to show that both human and animal subjects could be conditioned to control certain autonomic nervous system functions, such as blood pressure, salivation, gastrointestinal contractions, urine formation, sweat gland activity, vasomotor response, and cardiac activity. The possibility that glandular and visceral responses, heretofore thought to function automatically and even unconsciously, could be influenced by the conscious attempts of individuals opened the eyes of many medical and psychological visionaries. It was only a matter of time before clinical applications began to surface. These applications are the focus of this chapter.

Before proceeding with this review, it will be helpful to distinguish between the "general practice" (GP) biofeedback clinician and the "biofeedback specialist" (Andrasik & Blanchard, 1983). The GP biofeedback clinician treats conditions that typically share certain characteristics. The symptoms in this first cluster are generally related to heightened arousal or excessive sympathetic nervous system (SNS) activity and have some association to stress or anxiety. Examples include anxiety disorders, recurrent headaches, elevated blood pressure, and irritable bowel syndrome. For these types of conditions a host of other behavioral approaches have been attempted with similar success. The "workhorse" tools for the GP biofeedback practitioner include (1) electromyographic (EMG) biofeedback to reduce tension states in targeted muscles, (2) temperature biofeedback to increase peripheral blood flow and skin surface temperature, and (3) skin conductance biofeedback to reduce sweat gland activity. These procedures will be described in greater detail as select disorders are reviewed. In practice the GP biofeedback clinician regularly augments treatment by collateral arousal reduction procedures (such as diaphragmatic breathing, guided imagery, autogenic training, progressive muscle relaxation training, meditation, etc.). In the literature, treatments range from 8 to 20 sessions on average.

Other conditions treated by biofeedback require more specialized approaches and often extended training trials (40–80 sessions). Examples for this second cluster include modifying certain brain rhythms (electroencephalographic biofeedback) for deterring epilepsy, for improving cognitive functioning in individuals who have experienced head trauma, and for enhancing attention and concentration in children who are diagnosed with attention deficit hyperactivity disorder; increasing muscle tone for people experiencing paralysis due to stroke; and enhancing muscle tone and coordination for people having disorders of intestinal motility (fecal incontinence). Stress and anxiety may or may not be involved in the clinical presentation, and there is little evidence that relaxation or arousal reduction plays a large role in the clinical gains obtained. These specialized approaches and the conditions they target will not be addressed further.

A SELECTIVE REVIEW AND EVALUATION OF THE LITERATURE

There is a vast array of medical conditions, with or without a concurrent anxiety or stress component, to which biofeedback has been applied, and summarizing and critiquing this literature could easily require a text the size of this volume. For example, in the mid-1980s the Biofeedback Society of America (now the Association for Applied Psychophysiology and Biofeedback [AAPB]) commissioned experts to prepare critical reviews of applications judged by various segments of the membership to warrant such a review. At every step along the way, additional expert commentary was obtained from individuals from varied professional backgrounds. The following disorders were judged to merit review and to contain adequate supporting data for the beneficial role of biofeedback: headache (vascular and tension-type), hypertension, dental (temporomandibular and bruxism), motor function, gastrointestinal, chronic pain, and Raynaud's syndrome (Hatch, Fisher, & Rugh, 1987). More recently the AAPB published a document that attempted, among other things, to identify

TABLE 4.1. Efficacy Criteria for Clinical Biofeedback

Biofeedback therapy is considered appropriate for treatment of a disorder when the following criteria are met:

1. The therapy is clinically efficacious in comparison to appropriate control groups, and the results of treatment are statistically significant.
2. Replication studies report similar efficacious results.
3. Efficacy is demonstrated in long-term follow-up studies that are conducted in clinical settings using clinical treatment protocols.
4. The therapy has no contraindications.

Source: Shellenberger et al., 1994.

TABLE 4.2. Diagnostic Conditions Meeting Efficacy Criteria

Anxiety disorders	Incontinence: Urinary
Asthma	Insomnia
Attention deficit and hyperactivity	Motion sickness
Cerebral palsy	Myofascial pain, TMJ pain, and mandibular dysfunction
Disorders of intestine motility (irritable bowel syndrome, rectal pain, rectal ulcer)	Neuromuscular disorders (i.e., Bell's palsy, whiplash, muscle-tendon transfers, low back strain, joint repair, torticollis, peripheral nerve problems, spasm, incomplete spinal cord lesion and lower motor neuron lesion, ataxia, dystonia, and paralysis)
Enuresis	
Epilepsy	
Essential hypertension	Pain: Chronic
Headache: Migraine	Pain: Rheumatoid arthritis
Headache: Mixed	Raynaud's disease
Headache: Tension	Stroke
Incontinence: Fecal	

Source: From Shellenberger et al., 1994.

conditions for which biofeedback had met criteria for clinical efficacy (Shellenberger et al., 1994). The criteria utilized by this review committee are spelled out in Table 4.1, and the resulting list for diagnostic conditions is presented in Table 4.2. The efficacy criteria employed by the AAPB review panel admittedly are not as rigorous as those employed by the APA Division 12 Task Force on Promotion and Dissemination of Psychological Procedures (Chambless et al., 1998); nonetheless, they provide a rationale for limiting the review content for this chapter. With respect to the APA task force, headache was the only disorder judged to meet the criteria for a "well-established" treatment; chronic pain and Raynaud's were judged as having "probably efficacious" treatments. The task force acknowledged it had not focused in depth on health psychology/behavioral medicine, so other applications may have been overlooked.

Taking these considerations into account, the present author has chosen to review a very limited number of conditions, selected according to the following guidelines: Ample literature exists to permit a careful assessment of clinical benefits and research issues, the application has been judged to be efficacious by one or more panels designed to make such a determination, the condition has a definite link to stress and anxiety, and the condition is not addressed elsewhere in this text. This leads to selection of the three following conditions for more in-depth discussion: recurrent headache, Raynaud's syndrome, and hypertension.

The biofeedback approaches utilized for these disorders vary enough to permit the author to illustrate an array of applications, and the literatures address diverse clinical and research issues that provide multiple insights and examples that have broad applicability.

RECURRENT HEADACHE

Headache affects 90% of all males and 95% of all females during their lifetime (Linet, Stewart, & Celentaño, 1989; Silberstein & Lipton, 1993). It is the seventh-leading presenting complaint in ambulatory care in the United States, accounting for about 18 million visits a year (Barrett, 1996; Smith, 1992). Headaches are typically benign; however, for 1–3% of patients the underlying cause can be life-threatening (Evans, 1996). The most common forms of headache are migraine, tension-type, and combinations of the two, with diagnoses being made according to criteria specified by the International Headache Society (Headache Classification Committee of the International Headache Society, 1988). Approximately 23 million people in the United States experience severe migraine headaches, with a sizable number of these individuals being markedly disabled or in need of bed rest during attacks (Stewart, Lipton, Celentano, et al., 1992). In primary care practice the most commonly diagnosed variety of headache is tension-type, with migraine headaches occurring approximately half as frequently (McGrady et al., 1999). Headaches can begin at a very young age. Prevalence increases steadily through the late teen years, at which point it begins to stabilize and subsequently slowly decline (Andrasik, Blake, & McCarran, 1986; Bille, 1961, 1981; Hockaday & Barlow, 1993; Lipton & Stewart, 1997). Stress is closely associated with recurrent migraine and tension-type headache, as a trigger, exacerbator, and consequence that can further intensify psychological distress (Andrasik, in press; Drummond, in press). The majority of individuals experiencing headache seek no or minimal formal treatment, suffering greatly in silence (Lipton & Stewart, 1997). Those seeking treatment most often utilize over-the-counter preparations and prescription medications, designed to palliate, abort, or prevent attacks (see McGrady et al., 1999). However, a growing number of individuals have begun to seek nonmedical treatments as adjuncts or alternatives.

Behavioral or nonpharmacological treatments have been pursued for nearly 30 years for recurrent headache, with the first applications consisting of biofeedback. The initial applications were distinct and applied specifically, according to headache type.

Tension-Type Headache

In the typical biofeedback approach for tension-type headache, EMG electrodes are attached to the surface of the forehead area, the patient is given easily processed information about the ongoing level of muscle activity in this area (via an auditory tone that is directly proportional to the detected tension level) and is coached in strategies to facilitate relaxation and reductions in tension levels (Budzynski, Stoyva, & Adler, 1970). At the time this procedure was developed (late 1960s and early 1970s) it was widely believed that sustained muscular contractions were the main cause of tension-type headache and that the tension level in the frontal area served as a good barometer for tension elsewhere in the body, especially for head, neck, and shoulder muscles. Current-day EMG biofeedback approaches to tension-type headache include more extensive, individualized assessment of muscle locations (bilateral frontal-posterior neck electrode placement and scanning of multiple sites) as well as the use of dynamic (recordings taken during movement and postural changes as well as at rest) and in vivo or ambulatory monitoring (Andrasik, 1992).

Research has shown that a number of cognitive as well as behavioral changes occur when patients undergo biofeedback (enhanced confidence and self-efficacy, which promote more active and varied attempts to cope), in addition to improved abilities to regulate tension levels (Andrasik & Holroyd, 1980; Holroyd et al., 1984). These changes may serve important mediating functions (Bandura, 1997). This may also help explain the positive treatment effects observed for tension-type headache patients who lack evidence of heightened muscle involvement, yet nonetheless benefit from EMG treatment. Other biofeedback approaches have been attempted in pilot investigations (feedback of electro-encephalogram [EEG] parameters and electrodermal response), but data are too limited at present to permit any firm conclusions about their utility.

Migraine Headache

Three distinct biofeedback approaches have been developed for migraine headache: autogenic feedback, which is used most commonly; blood volume pulse biofeedback; and transcranial doppler biofeedback.

Autogenic feedback originated from a serendipitous finding at the Menninger Clinic in Topeka, Kansas (Sargent, Green, & Walters, 1972). During a standard laboratory evaluation at the clinic it was noticed that spontaneous termination of a migraine was accompanied by flushing in the hands and a rapid, sizable rise in surface hand temperature. This astute observation, combined with clinical creativity, led researchers to pilot-test whether teaching migraine sufferers how to increase peripheral temperature voluntarily might afford patients some improved abilities to regulate their headaches. In early research conducted at Menninger, highly sensitive temperature probes were attached to a patient's index finger and to the middle of the forehead. The temperature differential between the two probes was displayed to the participant, who then was instructed in ways to increase hand temperature relative to forehead temperature (in the hopes of shunting blood flow in the head and redirecting it to the extremities). This thermal biofeedback was combined with components of autogenic therapy, resulting in what was termed "autogenic feedback." Initially it was not known whether the temperature change occurring in patients was due to forehead cooling, hand warming, or both. Subsequent study revealed that most of the effect was due to hand warming, so most present-day biofeedback therapists typically monitor temperature from single peripheral sites. The mechanism underlying hand warming is not known. Current theoretical accounts speculate that hand warming (1) derives its effect *indirectly* from the decreased sympathetic nervous system arousal that must occur in order for peripheral dilation and subsequent hand warming to take place and/or (2) helps to stabilize the vascular system and counteract vasomotor instability and perturbations (much like some prophylactic medications (Dalessio et al., 1979; Gauthier et al., 1981; Sovak et al., 1978). If the first account is true, then autogenic feedback may be a versatile, generalized relaxation procedure. (This issue will be reexamined in the section on Raynaud's syndrome).

Hand warming biofeedback combined with autogenic training remains the predominant nonpharmacological approach for migraine, but a second type of biofeedback is being studied. This treatment evolved from a more straightforward rationale and involves monitoring blood volume pulse (BVP) from the temporal artery to teach patients how to reduce or constrict blood flow, much as occurs with pharmacological abortive agents. This technique for coping with migraine attacks is based on the research of Tunis and Wolff (1952), who found an association between pain and both extra- and intracranial artery dilatation during the migraine attack. More recently, Haynes et al. (1991) found a significant correlation between induced headache activity and cephalic BVP amplitude measurements.

The initial effectiveness of this biofeedback treatment was evaluated by Friar and Beatty (1976). Nineteen migraine patients, 18 of whom had reported prior treatment success with ergotamine tartrate (abortive agent), were carefully selected from a pool of 74 potential patients. Measures of blood flow were taken from pressure-transducing plethysmographs attached at two sites: (1) directly above the temporal artery or to one of its main ramifications and (2) on the ventral surface of the index finger. Subjects were matched and assigned randomly to receive pulse amplitude feedback from the temporal area (experimental group) or the finger (control group), both in the direction of decreased blood flow. After eight training sessions, experimental subjects were able to decrease blood flow in the temporal region by 20% during nonheadache periods. (It is impossible to train patients directly during an attack, so patients needed to learn the vasoconstriction strategies during the interval period.) No significant changes in temporal blood flow occurred for the control subjects. Experimental subjects improved by approximately 45%, versus 14% by control subjects.

Although BVP biofeedback has support, measurement problems (varying reliability, inability to quantify values in an absolute sense) have led some to investigate other autoregulation parameters in the treatment of migraine attacks, specifically those based on the *transcranial doppler technique (TCD)* (see Andrasik & Gerber, 1993). This approach targets the middle cerebral artery (MCA), based on the observations of Friberg et al. (1991) that migraine pain was due to, or at least closely associated with, intracranial large artery dilatation. Moreover, they demonstrated that sumatriptan treatment significantly constricted the dilated MCA on the headache side. Development of the MCA-training technology was preceded by comprehensive examinations that showed TCD was quite safe and possessed high reliability with migraine patients (reliability coefficients ranging from .75 to .95). There are two different parameters that can be targeted for MCA training: (1) mean blood velocity (MBV) and (2) peripheral resistance index (Pourcelot index, RI), which is the quotient of systolic minus diastolic value divided by diastolic value. RI measurement has some clear advantages over MBV, in that it is uninfluenced by age and TCD sound angle. However, it has the disadvantage of being influenced by respiration, which is why mean blood flow velocity (MFV) is included as well. This approach requires special instrumentation beyond that typically available to the GP biofeedback clinician. Because of this and the limited data base available to support its use, this approach will not be discussed further. (More detailed information about nonpharmacological treatment procedures for headache may be found in Andrasik, 1986; Andrasik & Gerber, 1993; Blanchard & Andrasik, 1985; and Gerber, Andrasik, & Schoenen, in press).

Meta-analytic Reviews of Treatment

Outcome investigations abound in the headache literature and are so numerous that recent reviews have resorted to quantitative approaches or meta-analysis. Included in these analyses are the various forms of relaxation and cognitive stress management treatments that have been studied. Table 4.3 contains summaries of the meta-analyses conducted to date for nonpharmacological treatments for both tension-type and migraine headache. In these evaluations, all studies were pooled for analysis; poorly designed studies were included along with expertly designed studies. Most research investigations evaluate single modalities (occasionally two), but, in practice, clinicians incorporate multiple modalities to capitalize on the strengths of each. For these reasons the quantitative results in Table 4.3 may be best viewed as demarcating the lower-bound estimate of treatment effects.

From this table it is learned that (1) symptom improvement from autogenic feedback, EMG biofeedback (excluding treatment of migraine), relaxation, and cognitive therapy ranges from 36 to 65%; (2) results of these nonpharmacological treatments exceed effects obtained from control procedures (psychological, pharmacological, and waiting list); (3) the combination of biofeedback and relaxation consistently yields improvement rates close to 60%; (4) thermal biofeedback is less effective in the absence of autogenic therapy; and (5) BVP and EMG biofeedback may be somewhat less effective overall than other forms of treatment for migraine. An NIH Technology Assessment Panel (1996), addressing chronic pain and insomnia, concluded that EMG biofeedback was superior to psychological placebo but equivalent to relaxation for tension-type headache, which is consistent with findings from the extant meta-analyses. Finally, in 1994 the Agency for Health Care Policy and Research (AHCPR) commissioned a meta-analysis to serve as the scientific basis for their Headache Treatment Guideline Project. This analysis was designed not only to update previous meta-analyses, but also to provide a highly rigorous, independent analysis of the published literature. Although the AHCPR has not yet released their final report (Goslin et al., in press), preliminary reports (McCrory et al., 1996) reach conclusions similar to those reported here.

The similar outcomes for biofeedback and relaxation have led some to conclude that these procedures may be interchangeable clinically. Research employing aspects of crossover methodology suggests this may not be true and that biofeedback may afford certain patients distinct advantages over relaxation (Blanchard et al., 1982). The fact that the combination of the two procedures is somewhat superior to either alone argues against the notion of interchangeability as well. Most of the studies included in the meta-analyses have limited their posttreatment evaluation period to brief intervals, typically 6 months or less. Approximately a dozen studies have examined maintenance beyond 1 or more years. These reveal that initial effects do tend to endure rather well; brief, periodic contacts may help gains become even more durable (e.g., Andrasik, Blanchard et al., 1984; Blanchard, 1987; Blanchard et al., 1987, 1988).

Holroyd and Penzien (1990) reported the first meta-analytic comparison of drug and nondrug treatments.

TABLE 4.3. Average Improvement Rates from Separate Meta-Analyses

A. *Tension-Type Headache*

	EMG	REL	EMG + REL	BFCT	COG	PHARM	OTHER	PTCT	MDCT	WTLT
Blanchard, Andrasik, et al. (1980)	61	59	59					35	35	–05
Holroyd & Penzien (1986)	46	45	57							–04
Bogaards & ter Kuile (1994)	47	36	56	15	53	39	38	20		–05

B. *Migraine Headache*

	ATFB	THBF	REL	VMBF	THBF + REL	EMG	PTCT	MDCT	WTLT
Blanchard, Andrasik, et al. (1980)	65	52	53				17		11
Holroyd (1986)		28	44	31	57			13	
Blanchard & Andrasik (1987)	49	27	48	43		29	26		

EMG = electromyographic biofeedback, generally provided from the frontal/forehead muscles.
REL = relaxation therapy, generally of the muscle tensing and relaxing variety.
BFCT = biofeedback control procedure, generally false or noncontingent biofeedback.
COG = cognitive therapy, stress coping training, or problem-solving therapy.
PHARM = various medications, ranging from aspirin and nonsteroidal inflammatories to prophylactics to narcotics.
OTHER = various approaches, other than BF, REL, or COG.
PTCT = psychological or pseudotherapy control procedure.
MDCT = medication control procedure; results taken from double-blind, placebo-controlled medication trials.
WTLT = waiting list control procedure; no treatment.
ATFB = thermal biofeedback augmented by components of autogenic training, as developed at the Menninger Clinic.
THBF = thermal biofeedback by itself.
VMBF = vasomotor biofeedback provided from the temporal artery.

71

For this analysis, results from 35 clinical trials of self-regulatory treatment (relaxation, biofeedback, or the two combined), 25 clinical trials of propranolol, 20 placebo investigations, and 17 untreated control groups were statistically compared. Average patient response to self-regulatory treatment was virtually identical to that to propranolol (43.3% vs. 43.7%), with both treatments statistically and clinically exceeding placebo (14.3%) and no treatment (2.1%). Bogaards and ter Kuile (1994), as shown in Table 4.3, found that EMG biofeedback, EMG combined with relaxation training, and cognitive therapy were superior to medication for tension-type headache, once again supporting the comparative efficacy of biofeedback and related procedures.

The nonpharmacological treatments that have been researched extensively with adults have all been studied with children and adolescents who experience these same forms of headache. Although the literature is not as extensive as that for adults, research with pediatric migraine is developed sufficiently that it has been the subject of a meta-analysis that also included quantitative analyses of various pharmacological treatments. This meta-analysis (Hermann, Kim, & Blanchard, 1995) evaluated how various nonpharmacological treatments compared to one another, how various pharmacological prophylactic approaches compared to one another, and how these two forms of treatment compared to each other. The major findings are discussed here and are summarized succinctly in Table 4.4, which has been reproduced from their article. To illustrate how to interpret this table, first consider thermal biofeedback. Comparing down the column, it is learned that outcomes from this treatment exceeded those obtained by multicomponent treatments (at least three or more distinct behavioral treatments combined), active medications (calcium channel blockers and serotonergic agents), psychological and drug placebos, and no treatment controls. The addition of relaxation training (BFB+ PMR) did not add appreciably to effectiveness, but this combination exceeded all other treatment and control conditions. Of additional interest is the finding that both active medications exceeded drug placebo. Data for other medications (propranolol, dopaminergic drugs, ergotamine, and clonidine) were too limited to permit meaningful analyses in the primary comparisons. Thus, evidence is mounting that various

treatments can be of considerable clinical value to pediatric migraine patients and that approaches incorporating behavioral components fare especially well. Some have argued that children may be particularly well suited to such nonmedical approaches (Attanasio et al., 1985). More recently, Allen and Shriver (1998) showed that effects for biofeedback could be increased significantly by additionally teaching parents how best to respond to their children's pain symptoms (based on operant principles).

Although there is strong support for the efficacy of biofeedback and related procedures for alleviating recurrent headache, little is known about predictor variables. Research tentatively suggests the following. Patients with pathogenic, cluster, or posttraumatic headaches; individuals whose headaches are continuous, refractory, or influenced greatly by hormonal factors; and patients who reveal moderate elevations on scales assessing anxiety, depression, and related psychological distress may require longer, more comprehensive, and multidisciplinary treatment (see Rowan & Andrasik, 1996, for a review). Even for relatively refractory cases, biofeedback and related treatments still may be of value by helping patients cope more effectively with the psychological sequelae that often accompany chronic pain ("headache-related distress"). It is likely that a number of the patients reporting continuous headache are abusing analgesic or ergot medications and need to be weaned from these substances. However, compliance and attrition frequently surface as problems when this course is recommended. Wittchen (1983) successfully counteracted these problems by combining intensive relaxation training with medication reduction. Thus, a structured program for reducing excessive use of medications might be facilitated if accompanied by nonpharmacological treatment in concert with appropriate prophylactic medication. Self-regulation therapy may also be helpful for treating women whose migraines continue throughout pregnancy, when pharmacological therapy options are necessarily limited. Children appear to be especially good candidates for biofeedback and often respond more quickly and with greater improvement (Andrasik, Blake, & McCarran, 1986; Attanasio et al., 1985). Older patients often require more time to master self-regulation skills (Arena et al., 1991; Kabela et al., 1989).

TABLE 4.4. Significance of the Within-Group Effect Size Differences across the Different Behavioral and Pharmacological Treatments[a]

	THERMAL		BFB + PMR	MULTICOMPONENT TREATMENT	PSYCHOLOGICAL PLACEBO	WAIT LIST	CALCIUM BLOCKERS	SEROTONERGIC DRUGS	DRUG PLACEBO
	BFB	PMR							
Thermal BFB	—								
PMR	>**	—							
BFB + PMR	n.s.	<**	—						
Multicomponent treatment	>**	n.s.	>**	—					
Psychological placebo	>**	>**	>**	>**	—				
Wait list	>**	>**	>**	>**	n.s.	—			
Calcium blockers	>**	n.s.	>**	n.s.	<**	<**	—		
Serotonergic drugs	>**	n.s.	>**	n.s.	<**	<**	n.s.	—	
Drug placebo	>**	>**	>**	>**	n.s.	n.s.	>*	>**	—

Source: Reprinted from Hermann, Kim, & Blanchard, Behavioral and prophylactic pharmacological intervention studies of pediatric migrane: An exploratory meta-analysis, Copyright © 1995, 239–256, with permission from Elsevier Science.

[a]The unequality signs refer to the comparison between columns and rows (e.g., Thermal BFB > PMR). The comparisons were based on the mean ES for each treatment category after removal of outliers.

$*P < 0.05$; $**P < 0.01$.

BFB = biofeedback; PMR = progressive muscle relaxation.

In summary, biofeedback and related procedures have ample empirical support for treating headaches, and few contraindications or untoward side effects have been reported. Perhaps the most significant drawback to these procedures is their expense (time and costs). The behavioral treatments described here have been shown to be adaptable to less intensive delivery models, without any loss in effectiveness, making them more cost-effective and cost-competitive (Haddock et al., 1997; Rowan & Andrasik, 1996). The typical home-based or reduced contact treatment involves three to five office visits, with treatment supplemented by written training manuals and audiocassettes to use in home instruction. Indeed, there are a number of distinct advantages to reduced contact treatment models and few disadvantages (Andrasik, 1996). Most of these treatments may be administered effectively in groups, which also conserves therapist time and patient expense (Napier, Miller, & Andrasik, 1997).

RAYNAUD'S DISEASE

The primary symptom of Raynaud's disease is episodic vasospasms in the digits of the hands and feet. Attacks are typically brief (several minutes' duration), progressing from blanching to cyanosis (dark bluish or purplish coloration due to deficient oxygenation of the blood) and rubor (red coloration, resulting from inflammation). Raynaud (1988) believed that increased activity of the SNS caused this exaggerated response to cold stimuli. Subsequent theorizing (Lewis, 1929) and recently accumulated evidence (see Freedman, 1995) support the notion that Raynaud's disease is due to a basal hypersensitivity in the peripheral vascular system of the digits. Catecholamine elevations, which normally occur during emotional stress, and reflex cooling can trigger these vasospastic attacks. Raynaud's disease is four times more common in females than in males; overall prevalence is estimated to be approximately 4.3% in the United States (Weinrich et al., 1990). When it is not possible to identify a disease process for the vasospasms, such as scleroderma (thickening of the skin caused by swelling and thickening of fibrous tissue, with eventual atrophy of the epidermis) or other collagen vascular diseases, the condition is termed Raynaud's disease. When the condition occurs secondary to another disease, it is labeled Raynaud's phenomenon. The medication of first choice

for Raynaud's symptoms is nifedipine, a calcium channel blocker, which produces marked decreases in frequency, intensity, and duration of attacks in approximately two-thirds of patients (Coffman, 1979, 1991). Surgical sympathectomies have also been utilized (Freedman, 1995).

Biofeedback treatment has focused on the primary form of the disorder, Raynaud's disease. Investigators have attempted various biofeedback and behavioral approaches for treatment (see Freedman, 1995). The study conducted by Freedman, Ianni, and Wenig (1983), which describes a direct comparison of the more common approaches, will be discussed in detail, as it serves as an exemplar for many reasons—careful participant screening, clear description of methodology, comprehensive assessment that involved data collection in the natural environment, comparison of several intervention approaches, and close monitoring of progress over time.

Four men and 28 women, ranging in age from 20 to 65, were carefully screened by the co-investigator rheumatologist to ensure they met explicit diagnostic criteria (developed by Allen & Brown, 1932), evidenced negative serological tests for antinuclear antibodies, and were absent of evidence of connective tissue disease (normal nailfold capillaries).

Extensive assessments were completed at home and in the laboratory prior to initiation of treatment and 1 year hence. Home assessments had two parts. First, participants were asked to maintain detailed records for each vasospastic attack (date, time, place, perceived cause, and visual description) for 1 month prior to treatment and 1 year thereafter. Second, hand temperatures were recorded for 12 continuous hours on 2 consecutive days in the natural environment. Participants were cued to provide activity and stress ratings each hour and to depress an event recorder on the Medilog ambulatory temperature recording device at the onset of any attack. Symptom report cards were completed for each attack as well. Laboratory assessments were performed in a sound-proofed room where it was possible to attain a high degree of control over temperature and humidity. Laboratory assessments prior to treatment focused on the preexisting ability of participants to increase hand temperature (participants were instructed to raise hand temperature, but no techniques or feedback was provided, which afforded a measure of "voluntary" control) and the response of participants to presentation of a cold stressor. To accomplish this, participants were asked to place the middle phalange of their dominant middle finger directly on top of a thermoelectric module, while temperature decreased from 30 to 20 degrees Centigrade, at a rate of 1 degree Centigrade for 10 minutes, after which the terminal temperature was maintained for 6 additional minutes.

Upon completion of the assessment, participants were randomly assigned to one of four conditions: autogenic training, frontal EMG biofeedback, finger temperature biofeedback as normally administered, and finger temperature biofeedback administered during cold stress. Each participant received 10 treatments over 5 weeks. Each session consisted of the following phases: adaptation (10 minutes), resting baseline (16 minutes), and treatment (16 minutes). Finger temperature, forehead EMG, and skin conductance levels were monitored for all subjects during treatment. Treatment was identical for both temperature biofeedback conditions for the first five sessions. Beginning in session six, participants assigned to training under cold stress were subjected to increasingly cold temperatures, following the procedures used during assessment. Additionally, one-half of participants in each condition received concurrent cognitive stress management. Cognitive stress management followed the approach of Meichenbaum (1977) and was administered in two 10-minute segments, one segment occurring before and one immediately after the other treatment was completed. The first segment focused on identifying environmental and stressful precipitants of attacks and accompanying cognitions. The second segment discussed strategies for preventing and/or aborting attacks in everyday life. Participants were asked to practice at home only those strategies assigned to them (so as not to confound treatments).

Following treatment and 1 year later, only the individuals receiving temperature biofeedback were able to increase hand temperature during voluntary control assessments; the increases shown by the participants trained under cold stress were of the greatest magnitude. Further, 1-year ambulatory monitoring revealed that greater temperature differentials (difference between ambient and finger temperature) were required to produce attacks in participants who had received temperature biofeedback versus the other two treatments. Reported attack frequencies for baseline

and the last 5 months of the 1-year follow-up period are shown in Figure 4.1. Both temperature biofeedback treatments produced significant reductions in symptom attacks, with the greatest reductions occurring for patients trained under cold stress (92.5% vs. 66.8% reduction). No appreciable improvement was reported for patients receiving autogenic training (32.6%) or frontal EMG biofeedback (17.0%). Participants who received EMG biofeedback and autogenic training showed signs of becoming more relaxed (revealed declines in muscle tension, heart rate, and reported stress), but they did not show significant increases in hand temperature or decreases in Raynaud's symptoms. Thus, treatment effects were not mediated by general or overall relaxation, nor by reductions in SNS activation. Rather, the training effects for temperature biofeedback were specific to the hands. These findings raise questions about the mechanism of action when temperature biofeedback is used for other conditions. No effects were found for the addition of cognitive stress management, but this may be due in part to the limited number of participants receiving this treatment component. Two- and 3-year follow-up assessments revealed continued gains for patients receiving thermal biofeedback (Freedman, Ianni, & Wenig, 1985).

Elsewhere Freedman (1993) has outlined clinical and methodological recommendations when administering temperature biofeedback to individuals who have been diagnosed with Raynaud's disease. These recommendations are summarized briefly here:

1. During biofeedback, temperature elevations typically occur quickly and, before too much time has passed, patients reach a point at which no further gains are possible (after 15–20 minutes). Continuing much beyond that point can be counterproductive and lead to vasoconstriction and frustration. Clinicians need to alert subjects to this possibility and keep training trials to a moderate length. The author has noted similar effects (Andrasik et al., 1984; Otis et al., 1995).

2. Finger temperature is affected greatly by ambient temperature, so reasonable control over room temperature is important, especially in the early phases of training.

3. Once initial self-regulation abilities are established, training under more demanding or stressful

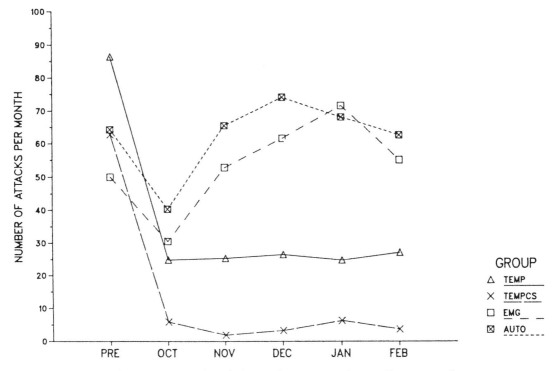

FIGURE 4.1. Reported Headache Attack Frequencies during Follow-up Period

Source: Freedman et al., 1983. Copyright © 1983 by the American Psychological Association. Reprinted with permission.
TEMP = finger temperature feedback; TEMPCS = finger temperature feedback under cold stress; EMG = frontalis EMG
feedback; AUTO = autogenic training.

conditions can enhance treatment effects and make them more generalizable and durable. The stimulus of choice for Raynaud's treatment has been gradual exposure to cold stress, as cold temperature is a common precipitator for attacks. Lynn and Freedman (1979) discuss other ways to facilitate transfer of training effects, such as adding booster sessions, fading treatment over time, incorporating stimulus control procedures, varying stimuli associated with training, simulating "real world" conditions in other ways, and using multiple intervention approaches.

HYPERTENSION

Hypertension is a significant risk factor for a host of cardiovascular diseases (myocardial infarction, stroke, congestive heart failure), which constitute the leading cause of morbidity and mortality in the United States (Rosen, Brondolo, & Kostis, 1993). Approximately one-fifth of the population (50 million or so) experiences hypertension, defined as a systolic blood pressure (SBP) exceeding 140 mmHg or a diastolic blood pressure (DBP) above 90 mmHg (Joint National Committee on Detection, Evaluation, and Treatment of High Blood Pressure, 1993). Blood pressure rises steadily with age, and elevation is increasingly present in certain minorities. The most recent classification system proposes a four-stage model that varies as a function of increasing elevations in both SBP and DBP (see Table 4.5), wherein increased scores reflect increased risk, in order to provide a more useful classification scheme to guide future research efforts and tailor clinical management. Long-term care, however, is recommended for individuals in any of the risk categories.

High blood pressure is the end result of multiple factors, which may be both quantitatively and qualitatively different for individuals (Pickering, 1995). In clinical practice it is rare for therapists to use single

TABLE 4.5. High Blood Pressure Classification System

DIASTOLIC BP (mmHg)	SYSTOLIC BP (mmHg)				
	<140	140–159	160–179	180–209	>210
<90		1	2	3	4
90–99	1	1	2	3	4
100–109	2	2	2	3	4
110–119	3	3	3	3	4
>120	4	4	4	4	4

Source: Joint National Committee on Detection, Evaluation, and Treatment of High Blood Pressure, 1993.

or isolated interventions. The more typical approach involves numerous components, such as lifestyle alteration (exercise, diet [weight reduction, sodium restriction, moderation of alcohol intake, etc.]) and various stress management techniques (progressive muscle relaxation training, yoga, transcendental meditation, autogenic training, biofeedback, and cognitive therapy), usually in conjunction with some type of medication (Rosen, Brondolo, & Kostis, 1993). Early biofeedback efforts involved direct control over BP parameters alone. Problems with instrumentation and failures to replicate led to the search for alternative, less direct approaches. For purposes of illustration, the study by Fahrion et al. (1986) will be described in detail, for it provides thorough descriptions of a trial that involved a large number of individuals all treated in a fairly common manner that chiefly employed a biofeedback-based approach similar to those currently in use.

The "multicomponent psychophysiologic therapy" of Fahrion et al. (1986) involved (1) patient education, which discussed the physiology of BP increases and decreases, provided a rationale for biofeedback training, and described how voluntary control of physiologic responses can be achieved; (2) thermal biofeedback to increase both hand and foot temperature, the latter target being added to better promote peripheral vasodilation; (3) frontal EMG biofeedback; (4) diaphragmatic breathing exercises; (5) autogenic phrases; (6) home relaxation practice; and (7) home monitoring of hand and foot temperatures and BP before and after practice. Hourly sessions were held once a week in the clinic and participants were asked to practice relaxation each day for 15–20 minutes.

Seventy-seven consecutive patients, with physician-diagnosed hypertension, began treatment and con-

tinued until participants either (1) met all of the rigorously established training goals (able to sustain hand temperatures at or above 95°F and foot temperatures at or above 93°F for 10 minutes per practice session; sustain muscle tension levels at or below 3 microvolts for 10 minutes; breath diaphragmatically; and become normotensive [prerelaxation BPs at or below 140/90 while reducing any antihypertensive medication to 0]), (2) achieved BP stabilization over several weeks, or (3) ceased participation. At these points, participants were categorized as "complete success," defined as a return to average pressures at or below 140/90 mmHg in the absence of antihypertensive medication; "partial success" for medicated patients defined either as return to average pressure at or below 140/90 while the patient remained on some degree of medication or, if pressures were initially controlled on medication at or below 140/90, maintaining such control on reduced medication; "partial success" for unmedicated patients defined as achieving "clinically significant reductions" in SBP, DBP, or both although not achieving the criterion level at or below 140/90; or "failure," defined as no reduction in either BP or medication level. Patients were followed for varying periods, with the average follow-up period being nearly 3 years.

Several findings merit discussion. First, the number of sessions varied considerably among the participants, ranging from a low of 4 to a high of 71, with a mean of 17.8 sessions (calculated from their table 1). Second, the majority of participants, when provided unlimited training sessions, were able to achieve all or most of the training goals established. Third, substantial short-term improvements in control of blood pressure were achieved and these endured rather well for the patients the authors were able to follow (61 of the original 77). For example, of the 54 patients who began on medication, 58% were able to eliminate their medication while at the same time reducing their BPs an average of 15/10 mmHg. An additional 35% of the medicated patients were able to decrease their medications by approximately half as their BP readings decreased by 18/10 mmHg. The remaining 7% of medicated patients showed no improvement in BP or medication reductions. Similar reductions in BP were evidenced in patients who were not on medication upon entering the study. The major findings for the follow-up assessment are summarized in Table 4.6, where it is seen that 51% of patients remained well controlled off medication, 41% remained partially controlled, and 8% were unsuccessful. Similar findings have been reported by Blanchard et al. (1984, 1986) and Glasgow, Engel, and D'Lugoff (1989).

Biofeedback and related stress management approaches to blood pressure control do not appear as prominently in the literature as they once did. This seems to be related in part to the publication of various reviews suggesting less favorable outcomes for these approaches when implemented in isolation (e.g., Eisenberg et al., 1993; Jacob et al., 1986, 1991, 1992; Kaufmann et al., 1988). Other reasons perhaps involve cost economics, which have been exacerbated by the forces of managed care.

The meta-analysis of cognitive behavior therapy (CBT) conducted by Eisenberg et al. (1993) merits close review because conclusions drawn were based in part on two quantitative analyses of pharmacological treatments conducted by other authors (Collins et al., 1990; MacMahon et al., 1990). The main findings of Eisenberg et al., for the present discussion, were: (1) CBT for hypertension produced statistically significant reductions in both DP and SP (9.0 and 13.4 mmHg, respectively) relative to wait-list or no-treatment conditions when baseline BP was assessed during a single session; (2) these differences were much smaller in magnitude and not statistically significant when baseline BP was based on readings collected over multiple sessions (4.0 and 4.1 mmHg, respectively); (3) CBT for hypertension did not differ statistically significantly from attention placebo for either method of determining baseline BP (differences

of 4.5 and 6.5 mmHg for single-session baseline (BL) and 1.3 and 2.8 for multiple-session BL); and (4) these effects did not rival those for similar statistical analyses conducted for randomized controlled trials of pharmacotherapy versus placebo (mean DBP reductions of 5–6 mmHg).

The author served as president of the AAPB when Eisenberg et al. was published and drafted a comment, outlining problems apparent in the review: inappropriate and confounded comparisons across the pharmacological and CBT literatures, failure to consider effects from differential attrition, failure to consider whether CBT resulted in less need for medication, and failure to equate treatment doses. (The full text of these comments appears in another source, Andrasik, 1994.)

A more current meta-analysis compared pharmacological and nonpharmacological treatments directly (unlike Eisenberg et al., who drew comparisons across meta-analyses that were not conducted identically) and arrived at somewhat different conclusions. Linden and Chambers (1994) analyzed 166 randomized clinical trials, evaluating the effects of various medications (diuretics, beta blockers, and calcium channel blockers), weight reduction, sodium and alcohol restriction, physical exercise, calcium and potassium supplements, standard single-method (progressive muscle relaxation training, autogenic training, meditation, and biofeedback) and standard multimethod relaxation therapy (combinations of the aforementioned treatments), and individualized therapies (CBT, marital communication training, anger management, etc.). Analysis focused on pre to post within-treatment changes, rather than comparisons between treatment and control conditions, as the authors wanted to address

TABLE 4.6. Summary of Follow-up Outcome Status for 61 of 77 Initially Treated Patients

OUTCOME CLASSIFICATION	FOLLOW-UP AVAILABLE	FOLLOW-UP OUTCOME STATUS		
		SUCCESS	PARTIAL	UNSUCCESSFUL
Medicated				
Success	25	20	5	0
Partial Success	15	0	15	0
Unsuccessful	2	0	1	1
Unmedicated				
Success	14	10	4	0
Partial Success	4	0	3	1
Unsuccessful	1	1	0	0

Source: Data from Fahrion et al., 1986.

TABLE 4.7. Effects of Pharmacological, Weight Loss, Physical Exercise, Nutrition, and Relaxation and Individualized Treatments for Hypertension

SYSTOLIC BLOOD PRESSURE		DIASTOLIC BLOOD PRESSURE	
TYPE OF TREATMENT	ADJUSTED EFFECT SIZE	TYPE OF TREATMENT	ADJUSTED EFFECT SIZE
Individualized therapy	.65	Calcium channel blockers	.79
Physical exercise	.65	Diuretics	.77
Diuretics	.59	Beta blockers	.76
Weight reduction	.57	Individualized therapy	.69
Multimethod relaxation therapy	.51	Weight reduction	.59
Betablockers	.50	Physical exercise	.56
Calcium channel blockers	.49	Sodium restriction	.49
Single-method relaxation therapy	.47	Multimethod relaxation therapy	.41
Sodium restriction	.45	Single-method relaxation therapy	.40
Potassium supplementation	.36	Potassium supplementation	.35
Alcohol restriction	.34	Alcohol restriction	.34
Calcium supplementation	.13	Calcium supplementation	.02

Source: Linden and Chambers, 1994.

the question of main relevance to patients and practitioners: How much better will a patient get when he or she receives treatment X? Effect sizes were reported in two different ways, raw and adjusted. Adjusted effect sizes (to control for pretreatment BP differences, which are known to set a limit on the amount of change that can subsequently occur) for the various treatment conditions are presented in Table 4.7, according to magnitude, for SBP and DBP. Individualized therapy was found to be highly effective for SBP and DBP, with the magnitude of this effect being similar to that for medication and lifestyle modification. Multimethod relaxation treatment was of moderate effectiveness for lowering SBP, but less so for DBP. Single-method relaxation treatment fared less well. Potassium and calcium supplementation and alcohol restriction showed the least effects.

These results help pinpoint the incremental utility of various treatments, indicate that multicomponent and individualized, tailored treatments are preferable, and support the practice of combining treatments from varied domains. Little is known, however, about which combinations are optimal for which patients and the extent to which improvements from nondrug treatments, especially for individualized approaches, generalize outside the research setting and the degree to which they impact other health indices. The findings of Linden and Chambers (1994) indicate that further investigation of nondrug treatments is clearly warranted.

REFERENCES

Allen, E., & Brown, G. (1932). A critical review of minimal requisites for diagnosis. *American Journal of Medical Science, 183,* 187–195.

Allen, K. D., & Shriver, M. D. (1998). Role of parent-mediated pain behavior management strategies in biofeedback treatment of childhood migraines. *Behavior Therapy, 29,* 477–490.

Andrasik, F. (1986). Relaxation and biofeedback for chronic headaches. In A. D. Holzman & D. C. Turk (Eds.), *Pain management: A handbook of psychological treatment approaches* (pp. 213–239). New York: Pergamon Press.

Andrasik, F. (1992). Assessment of patients with headaches. In D. C. Turk & R. Melzack (Eds.), *Handbook of pain assessment* (pp. 344–361). New York: Springer.

Andrasik, F. (1994). Twenty-five years of progress: Twenty-five more? *Biofeedback and Self-Regulation, 19,* 311–324.

Andrasik, F. (1996). Behavioral management of migraine. *Biomedicine and Pharmacotherapy, 50,* 52–57.

Andrasik, F. (in press). Psychological mechanisms of tension-type headache. In K. M. A. Welch, J. Olesen, & P. Tfelt-Hansen (Eds.), *The headaches* (2d ed.). New York: Lippincott-Raven.

Andrasik, F., Blake, D. D., & McCarran, M. S. (1986). A biobehavioral analysis of pediatric headache. In N. A. Krasnegor, J. D. Arasteh, & M. F. Cataldo (Eds.), *Child health behavior: A behavioral pediatrics perspective* (pp. 394–433). New York: Wiley.

Andrasik, F., & Blanchard, E. B. (1983). Applications of biofeedback to therapy. In C. E. Walker (Ed.), *Handbook* of clinical psychology: Theory, research and practice (pp. 1123–1164). Homewood, IL: Dorsey.

Andrasik, F., Blanchard, E. B., Neff, D. F., & Rodichok, L. D. (1984). Biofeedback and relaxation training for chronic headache: A controlled comparison of booster treatments and regular contacts for long-term maintenance. Journal of Consulting and Clinical Psychology, 52(4), 609–615.

Andrasik, F., & Gerber, W. D. (1993). Relaxation, biofeedback, and stress-coping therapies. In J. Olesen, P. Tfelt-Hansen, & K. M. A. Welch (Eds.), The headaches (pp. 833–841). New York: Raven Press.

Andrasik, F., & Holroyd, K. A. (1980). A test of specific and nonspecific effects in the biofeedback treatment of tension headache. Journal of Consulting and Clinical Psychology, 48, 575–586.

Andrasik, F., Pallmeyer, T. P., Blanchard, E. B., & Attanasio, V. (1984). Continuous versus interrupted schedules of thermal biofeedback: An exploratory analysis with clinical subjects. Biofeedback and Self-Regulation, 9, 291–298.

Arena, J. G., Hannah, S. L., Bruno, G. M., & Meador K. J. (1991). Electromyographic biofeedback training for tension headache in the elderly: A prospective study. Biofeedback and Self-Regulation, 16(4), 379–390.

Attanasio, V., Andrasik, F., Burke, E. J., Blake, D. D., Kabela, E., & McCarran, M. S. (1985). Clinical issues in utilizing biofeedback with children. Clinical Biofeedback and Health, 8(2), 134–141.

Bandura, A. (1997). Self-efficacy: The exercise of control. New York: Freeman.

Barrett, E. J. (1996). Primary care for women: Assessment and management of headache. Nurse Midwifery, 41(2), 117–124.

Bille, R. (1961). Migraine in school children. Acta Pediatrica Scandinavica, 51 (suppl. 136), 1–151.

Bille, R. (1981). Migraine in children and its prognosis. Cephalalgia, 1, 71–75.

Blanchard, E. B. (1987). Long-term effects of behavioral treatment of chronic headache. Behavior Therapy, 18, 375–385.

Blanchard, E. B., & Andrasik, F. (1985). Management of chronic headaches: A psychological approach. New York: Pergamon Press.

Blanchard, E. B., Andrasik, F., Neff, D. F., Teders, S. J., Pallmeyer, T. P., Arena, J. G., Jurish, S. E., Saunders, N. L., Ahles, T. A., & Rodichok, L. D. (1982). Sequential comparisons of relaxation training and biofeedback in the treatment of three kinds of chronic headache or, the machines may be necessary some of the time. Behaviour Research and Therapy, 20, 469–481.

Blanchard, E. B., Appelbaum, K. A., Guarnieri, P., Morrill, B., & Dentinger, M. P. (1987). Five year prospective follow-up on the treatment of chronic headache with biofeedback and/or relaxation. Headache, 27, 580–583.

Blanchard, E. B., Appelbaum, K. A., Guarnieri, P, Neff, D. F., Andrasik, F., & Jaccard, J. (1988). Two studies of long-term follow-up of minimal therapist contact treatments of vascular and tension headache. Journal of Consulting and Clinical Psychology, 56(3), 427–431.

Blanchard, E. B., McCoy, G. C., Andrasik, F., Acerra, M., Pallmeyer, T. P., Gerardi, R., Halpern, M., & Musso, A. (1984). Preliminary results from a controlled evaluation of thermal biofeedback as a treatment for essential hypertension. Biofeedback and Self-Regulation, 9, 471–495.

Blanchard, E. B., McCoy, G. C., Musso, A., Gerardi, M. A., Pallmeyer, T. P., Gerardi, R., Cotch, P. A., Siracusa, K., & Andrasik, F. (1986). A controlled comparison of thermal biofeedback and relaxation training in the treatment of essential hypertension: I. Short-term and long-term outcome. Behavior Therapy, 17, 563–579.

Bogaards, M. C., & ter Kuile, M. M. (1994). Treatment of recurrent tension headache: A meta analytic review. Clinical Journal of Pain, 10, 174–190.

Budzynski, T., Stoyva, J., & Adler, C. (1970). Feedback-induced relaxation: Application to tension headache. Journal of Behavior and Experimental Psychiatry, 1, 205–211.

Chambless, D. L., Baker, M. J., Baucom, D. H., Beutler, L. E., Calhoun, K. S., Crits-Christoph, P., Daiuto, A., DeRubeis, R., Detweiler, J., Haaga, D. A. F., Johnson, S. B., McCurry, S., Mueser, K. T., Pope, K. S., Sanderson, W. C., Shoham, V., Stickle, T., Williams, D. A., & Woody, S. R. (1998). Update on empirically validated therapies, II. The Clinical Psychologist, 51, 3–16.

Coffman, J. D. (1979). Vasodilator drugs in peripheral vascular disease. New England Journal of Medicine, 300, 713–717.

Coffman, J. D. (1991). Raynaud's phenomenon. Hypertension, 17, 593–602.

Collins, R., Peto, R., MacMahon, S., Hebert, P., Fiebach, N. H., Eberlein, K. A., Godwin, J., Qizilbash, N., Taylor, J. O., & Hennekens, C. H. (1990). Blood pressure, stroke and coronary heart disease. Part 2. Short-term reductions in blood pressure: Overview of randomized drug trials in their epidemiological context. Lancet, 335, 827–838.

Dalessio, D. J., Kunzel, M., Sternbach, R., &, Sovak, M. (1979). Conditioned adaptation-relaxation in migraine therapy. JAMA, 242, 2102–2104.

Eisenberg, D. M., Delbanco, T. L., Berkey, C. S., Kaptchuk, T. J., Kupelnick, B., Kuhl, J., & Chalmers, T. C. (1993). Cognitive behavioral techniques for hypertension: Are they effective? *Annals of Internal Medicine, 118,* 964–972.

Engel, B. T. (1972). Operant conditioning of cardiac function: A status report. *Psychophysiology, 9,* 161–177.

Evans, R. W. (1996). Diagnostic testing for the evaluation of headaches. *Neurology Clinic, 14*(1), 1–26.

Fahrion, S., Norris, P., Green, A., Green, E., & Snarr, C. (1986). Biobehavioral treatment of essential hypertension: A group outcome study. *Biofeedback and Self-Regulation, 11,* 257–277.

Freedman, R. R. (1993). Raynaud's disease and phenomenon. In R. J. Gatchel & E. B. Blanchard (Eds.), *Psychophysiological disorders: Research and clinical applications* (pp. 245–267). Washington, DC: American Psychological Association.

Freedman, R. R. (1995). Raynaud's disease and phenomenon. In A. J. Goreczny (Ed.), *Handbook of health and rehabilitation psychology* (pp. 117–131). New York: Plenum.

Freedman, R. R., Ianni, P., & Wenig, P. (1983). Behavioral treatment of Raynaud's disease. *Journal of Consulting and Clinical Psychology, 51,* 539–549.

Freedman, R. R., Ianni, P., & Wenig, P. (1985). Behavioral treatment of Raynaud's disease: Long-term follow-up. *Journal of Consulting and Clinical Psychology, 53,* 136.

Friar, L. R., & Beatty, I. (1976). Migraine: Management by trained control of vasoconstriction. *Journal of Consulting and Clinical Psychology, 44,* 46–53.

Friberg, L., Olesen, J., Iversen, H. K., & Sperling, B. (1991). Migraine pain associated with middle cerebral artery dilatation: Reversal by sumatriptan. *Lancet, 338,* 13–17.

Gauthier, J., Bois, R., Allaire, D., & Drolet, M. (1981). Evaluation of skin temperature biofeedback training at two different sites for migraine. *Journal of Behavioral Medicine, 4,* 407–419.

Gerber, W. D., Andrasik, F., & Schoenen, J. (in press). *Tension-type headache: Diagnosis and management.* European Headache Foundation.

Glasgow, M. S., Engel, B. T., & D'Lugoff, B. C. (1989). A controlled study of a standardized behavioral stepped treatment for hypertension. *Psychosomatic Medicine, 51,* 10–26.

Goslin, R. E., Gray, R. N., McCrory, D. C., Penzien, D. B., Rains, J. C., & Hasselblad, V. (in press). *Evidence report: Behavioral and physical treatments for migraine.* Rockville, MD: Agency for Health Care Policy and Research.

Haddock, C., Rowan, A. B., Andrasik, F., Wilson, P. G., Talcott, G. W., & Stein, R. J. (1997). Home-based behavioral treatments for chronic benign headache: A meta-analysis of controlled trials. *Cephalalgia, 17,* 113–118.

Harris, A. H., & Brady, J. V. (1974). Animal learning—visceral and autonomic conditioning. *Annual Review of Psychology, 25,* 107–133.

Hatch, J. P., Fisher, J. G., & Rugh, J. D. (Eds.). (1987). *Biofeedback: Studies in clinical efficacy.* New York: Plenum.

Haynes, S. N., Gannon, L. R., Bank, J., Shelton, D., & Goodwin, J. (1991). Cephalic blood flow correlates of induced headaches. *Journal of Behavioral Medicine, 13,* 467–480.

Headache Classification Committee of the International Headache Society. (1988). Classification and diagnostic criteria for headache disorders, cranial neuralgias and facial pain. *Cephalalgia, 8,* 1–97.

Hermann, C., Kim M., & Blanchard, E. B. (1995). Behavioral and prophylactic pharmacological intervention studies of pediatric migraine: An exploratory meta-analysis. *Pain, 60,* 239–256.

Hockaday, J. M., & Barlow, C. F. (1993). Headache in children. *The Headaches,* 795–808.

Holroyd, K. A. (1986). Recurrent headache. In K. A. Holroyd & T. Creer (Eds.), *Self-management of chronic disease: Handbook of clinical interventions and research* (pp. 373–413). New York: Academic.

Holroyd, K. A., & Penzien, D. B. (1986). Client variables and the behavioral treatment of recurrent tension headache: A meta-analytic review. *Journal of Behavioral Medicine, 9,* 515–536.

Holroyd, K., & Penzien, D. (1990). Pharmacological versus non-pharmacological prophylaxis of recurrent migraine headache: A meta-analytic review of clinical trials. *Pain, 42,* 1–13.

Holroyd, K. A., Penzien, D. B., Hursey, K. G., Tobin, D. I., Rogers, L., Holm, J. E., Marcille, P. J., Hall, J. R., & Chila, A. G. (1984). Change mechanisms in EMG biofeedback training: Cognitive changes underlying improvements in tension headache. *Journal of Consulting and Clinical Psychology, 52,* 1039–1053.

Jacob, R. G., Chesney, M. A., Williams, D. M., Ding, Y., & Shapiro, A. P. (1991). Relaxation therapy for hypertension: Design effects and treatment effects. *Annals of Behavioral Medicine, 13,* 5–17.

Jacob, R. G., Shapiro, A. P., O'Hara, P., Portser, S., Kruger, A., Gatsonis, C., & Ding, Y. (1992). Relaxation therapy for hypertension: Setting-specific effects. *Psychosomatic Medicine, 54,* 87–101.

Jacob, R. G., Shapiro, A. P., Reeves, R. A., Johnsen, A. M., McDonald, R. H., & Coburn, C. (1986). Relaxation therapy for hypertension: Comparisons of effects with concomitant placebo, diuretic, and beta-blocker. *Archives of Internal Medicine, 146,* 2335–2340.

Joint National Committee on Detection, Evaluation, and Treatment of High Blood Pressure (JNC-V). (1993). Fifth report. *Archives of Internal Medicine, 67,* 48–59.

Kabela, E., Blanchard, E. B., Appelbaum, K. A., & Nicholson, N. (1989). Self-regulatory treatment of headache in the elderly. *Biofeedback and Self-Regulation, 14*(3), 219–228.

Kamiya, J. (1969). Operant control of the EEG alpha rhythm and some of its reported effects on consciousness. In C. T. Hart (Ed.), *Altered states of consciousness: A book of readings.* New York: Wiley.

Kaufmann, P. G., Jacob, R. G., Ewart, C. K., Chesney, M. A., Muenz, L. R., Doub, N., & Mercer, W. (1988). Hypertension intervention pooling project. *Health Psychology, 7* (suppl.), 209–224.

Kimmel, H. O. (1967). Instrumental conditioning of autonomically mediated responses behavior. *Psychological Bulletin, 67,* 337–345.

Kimmel, H. O. (1979). Instrumental conditioning of autonomically mediated responses in human beings. *American Psychologist, 29,* 325–335.

Kristt, D. A., & Engel, B. T. (1975). Learned control of blood pressure in patients with high blood pressure. *Circulation, 51,* 370–378.

Lewis, T. (1929). Experiments relating to the peripheral mechanism involved in spasmodic arrest of circulation in the fingers: A variety of Raynaud's disease. *Heart, 15,* 7–101.

Linden, W., & Chambers, L. (1994). Clinical effectiveness of non-drug treatment for hypertension: A meta-analysis. *Annals of Behavioral Medicine, 16,* 35–45.

Linet, M. S., Stewart, W. F., Celentano, D. D., et al. (1989). An epidemiologic study of headache among adolescents and young adults. *JAMA, 261,* 2211–2216.

Lipton, R. B., & Stewart, W. F. (1997). Prevalence and impact of migraine. In N. T. Mathew (Ed.), *Neurologic clinics: Advances in headache* (vol. 15) (pp. 1–13). Philadelphia: Saunders.

Lynn, S., & Freedman, R. R. (1979). Transfer and evaluation of biofeedback treatment. *Maximizing treatment gains: Transfer enhancement in psychotherapy.* New York: Academic Press.

MacMahon, S., Peto, R., Cutler, J., Collins, R., Sorlie, P., Neaton, J., Abbott, R., Godwin, J., Dyer, A., & Stamler, J. (1990). Blood pressure, stroke, and coronary heart disease. Part 1. Prolonged differences in blood pressure: Prospective observational studies corrected for the regression dilution bias. *Lancet, 335,* 765–774.

McCrory, D. C., Penzien, D. B., Rains, J. C., & Hasselblad, V. (1996). Efficacy of behavioral treatments for migraine and tension-type headache: Meta-analysis of controlled trials. *Headache, 36,* 272.

McGrady, A. V., Andrasik, F., Baskin, S. M., Penzien, D. B., Striefel, S., Tietjen, G., Davies, T., & Wickramasekera, I. (1999). Psychophysiological therapy for chronic headache in primary care. Manuscript under review.

Meichenbaum, D. (1977). Cognitive Behavior Modification. New York: Plenum.

Miller, N. E. (1969). Learning of visceral and glandular responses. *Science, 163,* 434–445.

Miller, N. E. (1978). Biofeedback and visceral learning. *Annual Review of Psychology, 29,* 373–404.

Miller, N. E., & DiCara, L. (1967). Instrumental learning of heart rate changes in curarized rats: Shaping and specificity to discriminative stimulus. *Journal of Comparative and Physiological Psychology, 63,* 12–19.

Napier, D., Miller, C., & Andrasik, F. (1997). Group treatment for recurrent headache. *Advances in Medical Psychotherapy, 9,* 21–31.

NIH Technology Assessment Panel. (1996). Integration of behavioral and relaxation approaches into the treatment of chronic pain and insomnia. *JAMA, 276,* 313–318.

Olson, R. P. (1995). Definitions of biofeedback and applied psychophysiology. In M. S. Schwartz & Associates (Ed.), *Biofeedback: A practitioner's guide* (2d ed.) (pp. 27–31). New York: Guilford Press.

Otis, J. D., Rasey, H. W., Vrochopoulos, S., Wincze, J. P., & Andrasik, F. (1995). Temperature acquisition as a function of the computer-based biofeedback system utilized: An exploratory analysis. *Biofeedback and Self-Regulation, 20,* 185–190.

Pickering, T. G. (1995). Hypertension. In A. J. Goreczny (Ed.), *Handbook of health and rehabilitation psychology* (pp. 219–237). New York: Plenum.

Raynaud, M. (1888). *New research on the nature and treatment of local asphyxia of the extremities* (T. Barlow, Trans.). London: New Syndenham Society.

Rosen, R. C., Brondolo, E., & Kostis, J. B. (1993). Non-pharmacological treatment of essential hypertension: Research and clinical applications. In R. J. Gatchel & E. B. Blanchard (Eds.), *Psychophysiological disorders: Research and clinical applications* (pp. 63–110). Washington, DC: American Psychological Association.

Rowan, A. B., & Andrasik, F. (1996). Efficacy and cost-effectiveness of minimal therapist contact treatments of chronic headaches: A review. *Behavior Therapy, 27,* 207–234.

Sargent, J. D., Green, E. E., & Walters, E. D. (1972). The use of autogenic feedback training in a pilot study of migraine and tension headaches. *Headache, 12,* 120–124.

Schwartz, M. S., & Olson, R. P. (1995). A historical perspective on the field of biofeedback and applied psychophysiology. In M. S. Schwartz & Associates (Ed.), *Biofeedback: A practitioner's guide* (2d ed.) (pp. 3–18). New York: Guilford Press.

Shapiro D., Tursky, B., & Schwartz, G. E. (1970). Differentiation of heart rate and systolic blood pressure in man by operant conditioning. *Psychosomatic Medicine, 32,* 417–423.

Silberstein, S. D., & Lipton, R. B. (1993). Epidemiology of migraine. *Neuroepidemiology, 12*(3), 179–194.

Smith, R. (1992). Chronic headaches in family practice. *Journal of American Board of Family Practice, 5*(6), 589–599.

Sovak, M., Kunzel, M., Sternbach, R. A., & Dalessio, D. J. (1978). Is volitional manipulation of hemodynamics a valid rationale for biofeedback therapy of migraine? *Headache, 18,* 197–202.

Stewart, W. F., Lipton, R. B., Celentano, D. D., et al. (1992). Prevalence of migraine headache in the United States. *JAMA, 267,* 64–69.

Surwit, R. S., Shapiro, E., & Feld, J. L. (1976). Digital temperature autoregulation and associated cardiovascular changes. *Psychophysiology, 13,* 242–248.

Tunis, M. M., & Wolff, H. G. (1952). Analysis of cranial artery pulse waves in patients with vascular headache of the migraine type. *American Journal of Medical Sciences, 244,* 565–568.

Weinrich, M. C., Marieq, H. R., Keil, J. E., McGregor, A. R., & Diat, F. (1990). Prevalence of Raynaud's phenomenon in the adult population of South Carolina. *Journal of Clinical Epidemiology, 43,* 1343–1349.

Wittchen, H. U. (1983). A biobehavioral treatment program (SEP) for chronic migraine patients. In K. A. Holroyd, B. Schlote, & H. Zenz (Eds.), *Perspectives in research on headache* (pp. 183–197). Toronto: Hogrefe.

CHAPTER 5

COGNITIVE-BEHAVIORAL PROCESSES IN MANAGING THE STRESS AND ANXIETY OF MEDICAL ILLNESS

Tamara L. Newton
Susan E. Doron

THE BIOPSYCHOSOCIAL IMPACT OF MEDICAL ILLNESS

Occurrence of a serious medical illness poses many psychological threats and challenges (e.g., Moyer & Salovey, 1996). The possibility of untimely death or permanent and sometimes progressive physical and cognitive debilitation challenges core assumptions that the world is just and that people have control over whether bad things happen (Janoff-Bulman, 1992). Recurrent or chronic symptoms, sometimes accompanied by pain, may dramatically reduce physical, social, and occupational functioning. Normative, anticipated unfolding of life roles is often interrupted, threatening the sense of meaning, identity, and personal worth derived from these roles and from one's physical integrity. These changes can spill into social relationships, causing strain and feelings of social isolation at a time when individuals are in great need of support from others.

When this cascade of cognitive, physical, and social changes exceeds a person's internal and external resources, stress and emotional responses including depression and anxiety may result (Lazarus & Folkman, 1984). These emotional responses add markedly to the burden of illness. For instance, when depressive symptoms accompany advanced coronary artery disease, reduction in social functioning is doubled relative to that associated with coronary artery disease alone (Wells et al., 1989). Moreover, emotional distress may confer elevated risk for subsequent morbidity; anxiety and current or lifetime history of depression are associated with significant increases in the probability of

adverse cardiac events in the year following a heart attack (Frasure-Smith, Lespérance, & Talajic, 1995). For these reasons there is strong interest in developing psychosocial interventions that are effective as adjuvant treatments for persons with medical conditions, in order both to improve quality of life and to decrease suffering (Spiegel, 1994) and possibly to enhance physical health outcomes.

COGNITIVE-BEHAVIORAL INTERVENTIONS FOR MEDICAL CONDITIONS

In the present chapter we focus on cognitive-behavioral interventions used to treat and manage emotional distress associated with medical conditions.[1] More specifically, we consider methods designed to change cognition, a fundamental component of biopsychosocial responses to medical conditions. Cognition is central to how people appraise, or evaluate, internal (e.g., physical sensations and symptoms) and external

---

1. Widely utilized in the management of diverse aspects of medical conditions, cognitive-behavioral principles play a prominent role in the modification of health behaviors (e.g., Lerman & Glanz, 1997) and in the management of reactions to stressful medical procedures such as chemotherapy or surgery (e.g., Burish & Tope, 1992). In contrast to these applications, the present chapter focuses on broad-based cognitive-behavioral interventions utilized to manage emotional reactions that accompany specific medical illnesses and syndromes.

(e.g., communications from medical providers) information relevant to well-being, and it is vital to generating goals and plans in response to this information (Leventhal, 1982). Moreover, cognition is essential to the formation of internal, mental representations of illness and the self (Leventhal, 1982). Operating largely outside of awareness, these emotion-laden representations are instrumental in efforts to make meaning out of the bodily changes and other losses that frequently accompany medical illness (Brewin, 1989; Leventhal, 1986). In cognitive-behavioral interventions for medical conditions, methods designed to facilitate cognitive change sometimes constitute the main focus of treatment (e.g., Greene & Blanchard, 1994), but more often they are one part of multicomponent treatments that include additional methods such as instruction in relaxation and training in communication or interpersonal skills (e.g., Lutgendorf et al., 1998). Thus, in the present chapter, we use the term *cognitive-behavioral* to refer to treatments that either solely or as part of a multicomponent treatment package include methods designed to achieve cognitive change.

Aims and Outcomes

Cognitive-behavioral interventions have been evaluated in the management of emotional distress associated with catastrophic and potentially life-threatening illnesses, including human immunodeficiency virus (HIV), cancer, and heart disease (e.g., Hill, Kelleher, & Shumaker, 1992), as well as distress associated with chronic illnesses that severely compromise quality of life, such as rheumatoid arthritis (Keefe & Caldwell, 1997), or that may ultimately decrease life expectancy, such as hypertension (Shapiro et al., 1997). In all cases, these interventions are intended to accompany and complement, not replace, medical interventions. In general, there are three separate, but interrelated, goals of cognitive-behavioral interventions for medical conditions: quality of life, health outcomes, and health care utilization and cost.

Quality of Life

Most commonly cognitive-behavioral interventions for medical conditions aim to decrease the emotional toll of illness and increase quality of life. This goal includes enhancing psychological functioning and decreasing emotional distress (e.g., Lutgendorf et al., 1997), but it also encompasses increasing functional status (e.g., activity level) and reducing disease- and treatment-related symptoms (e.g., pain; Keefe et al., 1990a).

Health Outcomes

Because emotional responses that accompany medical conditions have been associated with increased risk for subsequent morbidity (e.g., Frasure-Smith, Lespérance, & Talajic, 1995), there is interest in whether cognitive-behavioral interventions designed to reduce emotional distress can also enhance biomedical status, slow disease progression, reduce the probability of recurrence, and perhaps extend longevity. Although the processes that link emotional distress and morbidity/mortality are not well understood, there are several hypothesized pathways (Cohen & Rodriguez, 1995). One plausible pathway concerns the impact of emotional distress on health behaviors and health practices, including reductions in physical exercise and sleep quality; increases in use of substances such as alcohol, caffeine, and nicotine; and decreased adherence to medical regimens (Andersen, Kiecolt-Glaser, & Glaser, 1994; Goldston et al., 1995; Keefe & Caldwell, 1997). Another hypothesized pathway concerns biological stress responses. This pathway is predicated upon associations between emotional distress, such as depression and anxiety, and neuroendocrine and immunological alterations (Calabrese, Kling, & Gold, 1987; Herbert & Cohen, 1993). For example, among women treated surgically for invasive breast cancer, those who report a hallmark stress response (Horowitz, Wilner, & Alvarez, 1979) characterized by cycles of emotional intrusion (e.g., dreams and intrusive thoughts about having cancer) and avoidance (e.g., keeping feelings secret, pushing away thoughts of cancer), are more likely to have reductions in basic immune cell function, such as decreased peripheral blood lymphocyte proliferation and decreased natural killer (NK) cell lysis (Andersen et al., 1998). Whether such changes in immune response profiles have significant health consequences is a question that remains to be empirically evaluated.

Health Care Utilization and Cost

Finally, cognitive-behavioral interventions for medical conditions may help contain health care utilization and costs (Friedman et al., 1995; Sobel, 1995). For example, high-utilizing primary care patients who participated in one of two 6-week, group-based cognitive-behavioral interventions significantly decreased their number of medical visits over a 6-month follow-up period compared to patients in an information-only control group. This effect represented an average decrease of 2.8 visits in the treated groups as compared to a decrease of .6 visits in the control group, with an estimated net health care cost savings of $85 per patient in the same 6-month period (Friedman et al., 1995; Hellman et al., 1990). These cost savings and reductions in health care utilization occurred in the context of enhanced patient-centered outcomes; compared to control group members, participants in the cognitive-behavioral intervention reported significant reductions in general psychological distress and distress over physical symptoms at the 6-month follow-up.

Conceptual Roots

The conceptual origins of many, if not most, cognitive-behavioral interventions for medical conditions can be traced to one of two theories, or their combination: the transactional model of stress and coping (Lazarus & Folkman, 1984) and the cognitive theory of emotional disorders (Beck et al., 1979). As will be described subsequently, these two theories differ with regard to the specific phenomena they were developed to explain and the constructs they employ, but both are based on a cognitive-mediational model of stress and emotion. That is, they posit that cognitive processes and representations mediate emotional responses to external events, such as life stressors, and internal events, such as physical symptoms or sensations. In general terms, interventions derived from these theories are designed to reduce negative emotional responses by altering cognition.

Transactional stress theory seeks to explain the cognitive origins of stress, a constellation of cognitive, emotional, and biological changes that arises out of the relationship between the person and his or her environment (Lazarus & Folkman, 1984). According to this theory, stress occurs when a person perceives that his or her resources, whether psychological, social, or cultural, are insufficient to manage environmental demands that are perceived as potentially endangering his or her well-being. Two cognitive processes, appraisal and coping, are central to this model. *Appraisals* are an individual's cognitive evaluation of the personal significance (e.g., threat, loss, challenge) of an environmental demand, followed by a judgment as to whether there is a coping response that will curtail the demand and that can be successfully executed. In contrast, *coping* refers to actual efforts to manage stressful environmental demands. The many different coping strategies that have been identified are often categorized according to two general functions: problem-focused and emotion-focused coping (Lazarus, 1993). *Problem-focused coping* refers to efforts to reduce stress by actually changing the environment. In contrast, *emotion-focused coping* refers to efforts to regulate one's emotional response to the environmental demand, for example by reappraising the situation or looking at it in a different way.

Cognitive theory seeks to explain the cognitive origins of emotional disorders such as depression (Beck et al., 1979) and anxiety (Beck, Emery, & Greenberg, 1985). In this approach, key constructs include automatic thoughts, schemata, and cognitive distortions. *Automatic thoughts* refer to fleeting thoughts or images that are available to conscious introspection, although individuals may have learned to disattend to them and may need to develop skills for recognizing them. Such thoughts reveal individual evaluations of the self, the world, or the future and are proposed to mediate subsequent emotional and behavioral responses to internal and external events. According to cognitive theory, automatic thoughts are products of *schemata,* internal representations of the self and the world that develop through experience and that serve as "filters" through which individuals perceive and recall information about themselves and the social world. For example, some evidence suggests that persons with anxiety disorders are biased toward perceiving and recalling self-relevant information in terms of danger and threat (e.g., Foa et al., 1991). Finally, *cognitive distortions* refer to biased ways of evaluating new information, such as selectively attending to negative aspects of the self or the world, discounting positive aspects, or catastrophically overestimating the probability of a negative outcome for some future event (Beck, 1995).

Cognitive Change Processes

In 1989 Brewin identified some 20 or so separate therapies, all labeled "cognitive-behavioral," but many with different "brand names." While the brand names implied that the therapies differed from one another, the cognitive-behavioral label implied similarities. Most likely the therapies were neither identical nor entirely different, but missing were the dimensions along which the similarities and dissimilarities could be evaluated. In response to this, Brewin (1989) proposed three cognitive change processes, or "mechanisms of action harnessed by different cognitive and behavior procedures" (p. 379). These processes describe much of what appears to actually occur during different cognitive-behavioral therapies. They serve as dimensions along which various cognitive-behavioral treatments can be compared, unifying therapies with distinct brand names while simultaneously providing a view of cognitive change that is more informative than the label "cognitive-behavioral."

A situation similar to that described by Brewin (1989) faces the field of cognitive-behavioral interventions for medical conditions today. By serving as a conceptual foundation and by directly informing clinical methods, transactional stress theory and cognitive theory have significantly influenced the development of cognitive-behavioral interventions for medical conditions. This has been a productive influence, yielding evidence that such interventions have the potential to favorably affect a broad range of biomedical and health care outcomes (e.g., Compas et al., 1998). Nonetheless, there is a need for a component analysis approach in order to disaggregate these interventions and identify the actual cognitive change processes that are targeted during therapy. An analytic approach such as this will foster linkages between cognitive-behavioral interventions and basic theory and research concerning cognition, emotion, and biological stress responses, an endeavor that eventually could facilitate identification of change processes that generate the most robust enhancements of health outcomes. For these reasons we have chosen to organize our discussion of cognitive-behavioral interventions for medical conditions around Brewin's (1989) conceptual analysis of three

cognitive change processes: correcting misconceptions or omissions in verbally accessible knowledge, modifying nonconscious schemata, and modifying self-regulation.

Correcting Misconceptions or Omissions in Verbally Accessible Knowledge

One of the three cognitive change processes proposed by Brewin (1989) concerns correcting misconceptions or omissions in verbally accessible knowledge (i.e., conscious beliefs that are available to introspection), particularly with regard to unfamiliar situations or stressors. Individuals facing a new medical diagnosis sometimes lack important information about their illness and its treatment. Even when they have been aware of their diagnosis for quite some time, individuals may have incomplete knowledge obtained from friends, family members, or the media, or they may have difficulty understanding or retaining information provided by their medical team. Further, based on observation of their own symptoms over time, they may form their own theories of the cause and consequences of their illness. Indeed, individuals develop their own unique illness theories, or "commonsense" models of illness, which are characterized by five distinct attributes: (1) disease identity, represented by labels (e.g., "high blood pressure") and symptoms (e.g. shortness of breath, fatigue); (2) perceived cause (e.g., viral exposure, stress, personal behavior, family history); (3) perceived consequences (e.g., physical, social, and economic outcomes); (4) anticipated time line, including onset, course, and duration of the illness; and (5) curability or control (Leventhal, Meyer, & Nerenz, 1980; Leventhal & Nerenz, 1985; Leventhal, 1986). These lay models of illness are developed by encoding symptom experiences, information from medical providers and other sources such as family, friends, and the media, and other illness-related information into existing schemata, or memory representations, of past illnesses or illness episodes. This process leads to significant individual variation in commonsense illness theories (Leventhal, 1982).

A person's commonsense illness theory is critical to successful adaptation to medical illness; it has implications for emotional responses to the medical condition and for coping efforts (Leventhal, 1982). For example, when individuals with hypertension enter medical treatment for this condition, they are more likely to drop out of treatment if they view their condition as acute or episodic, as opposed to chronic (Meyer, Leventhal, & Gutmann, 1985). Among pain patients, those who believe their pain will be a chronic condition show reduced adherence to physical therapy and behavioral therapy assignments (Williams & Thorn, 1989). Further, when dissonance develops between an individual's illness theory and the actual course of the illness, emotional distress and reduced coping efforts may result. For instance, among patients with the chronically painful and physically debilitating condition rheumatoid arthritis, those whose illness models are characterized by perceptions of arthritis as curable and caused by personal behavior report the highest levels of depression over a subsequent 4-month time period (Schiaffino, Shawaryn, & Blum, 1998).

The results of some treatment-outcome studies indicate that adjuvant interventions that are solely educational or informational do not yield outcomes as substantial as those generated by multicomponent cognitive-behavioral treatments (e.g., Hellman et al., 1990; Keefe et al., 1990a). Nonetheless, research on lay illness theories suggests that providing information to correct misconceptions or omissions in illness knowledge is an aspect of cognitive-behavioral interventions that may contribute to favorable adaptation to medical conditions. Indeed, many of the effective multicomponent cognitive-behavioral interventions include an educational phase (e.g., Keefe et al., 1990a; Lutgendorf et al., 1997). The impact of educational components might be bolstered by drawing on research concerning lay illness theories. For example, educational components could be designed to provide information that addresses the five dimensions of lay illness models (i.e., identity, perceived cause, perceived consequences, anticipated time line, and control). Moreover, the delivery of educational components might be enhanced by assessment of individuals' preexisting illness models. Medical providers are only one source of information encoded into illness representations; information derived from past illness experiences, daily experiences with symptoms, or from friends and family may compete and conflict with information from medical providers,

impeding accurate encoding of information that could enhance adaptation. Awareness of potential conflicts between existing illness schemata and new information might facilitate encoding of corrective information. In this way, educational components would not only provide information, but would do so in a way that is sensitive to psychological barriers to encoding. As Brewin (1989) suggests, the effectiveness of this change process "depends on the plausibility with which the new information is delivered and its ability to provide a satisfactory explanation for the individual's experience" (p. 386).

Modifying Nonconscious Schemata

Most people have extensive histories of encountering various physical symptoms, whether related to their own injuries, medical procedures, acute or chronic illnesses or to exposure to others' symptoms and illnesses (Bishop, 1987). These experiences are encoded into internal representations, or schemata, in terms of concrete physical sensations and symptoms (e.g., lumps, soreness), affective responses (e.g., fear, distress, disgust), and meaning (e.g., "cancer" or "cyst"). In contrast to verbally accessible knowledge, many aspects of these experientially based memories are not fully available to conscious introspection. Nonetheless, they may dramatically influence emotional and behavioral responses to subsequent symptoms and illness episodes, particularly when they are activated by situational triggers or cues (Brewin, 1989; Leventhal, 1986). Thus, similar to the danger schemata of anxious individuals, illness schemata are assumed to be nonconscious representations of past experiences that are situationally, but not verbally, accessible (Brewin, 1989; Leventhal, 1986).

As an example, a person who has experienced debilitating episodes of fatigue following a viral illness may develop a schema comprising sensations of muscle weakness, loss of muscle tone, breathlessness, and subjective loss of energy, along with emotions such as fear of losing bodily strength and dejection over continued decrements in physical functioning. These concrete and affective components may be accompanied by an interpretation of certain bodily sensations as indicative of impending loss of bodily strength and inability to function physically. This schema may be activated by ordinary experiences of breathlessness or muscle strain that occur in response to day-to-day exertion long after resolution of the viral illness, leading to continued marked reductions in physical functioning.

The content of illness schemata may be inferred through careful attention to illness cognition (i.e., automatic thoughts and images) available to conscious introspection, or through attention to changes in behavioral patterns such as reductions in or restructuring of physical activity, or avoidance of certain activities. Cognitive therapists summarize these inferences in terms of general rules or "core beliefs" (Brewin, 1989). Verbal persuasion or education will not suffice to change these core beliefs because they are based upon strongly encoded schemata that themselves control the perception and encoding of information in a biased fashion; confirmatory evidence will be sought, attended to, and encoded, whereas evidence that contradicts the basic tenets of schemata will be ignored. In such cases the therapy goal is not to provide information or to improve self-regulation abilities. Rather, the goals are to generate experiential evidence that is contrary to the illness schemata, to assist patients with integrating this evidence, and to teach patients to uncover and challenge automatic illness cognition that reactivates their illness schemata and maintains dysfunctional behavior patterns.

Cognitive-behavioral interventions for chronic fatigue syndrome (CFS) that employ graded exposure provide a good example of this change process. Symptoms associated with CFS include ". . . debilitating fatigue, low-grade fever, lymph node pain and tenderness, pharyngitis, myalgias, arthralgias, cognitive difficulties, and mood changes" (Antoni et al., 1994, p. 573). These symptoms can lead to severe limitations in the lives of those who suffer with them, often professional, highly successful individuals (Abbey, 1996). Deale et al. (1997) tested whether a 13-session cognitive-behavioral intervention, administered individually, was significantly superior to relaxation in reducing CFS symptoms. The cognitive-behavioral intervention emphasized gradual increases in physical activity (graded activity), gradual decreases in rest, and cognitive restructuring in order to provide experiential evidence that activity could be increased without exacerbating fatigue symptoms. Compared to patients who received relaxation training, a significantly greater proportion of patients who received the cognitive-behavioral intervention showed improved functional physical status at the 6-month follow-up. In addition, patients who received cognitive-behavioral therapy reported significantly greater increases in work and social adjustment, and decreases in fatigue and fatigue-related problems.

This change process has also been employed in cognitive-behavioral treatments for irritable bowel syndrome, a gastrointestinal disorder characterized by abdominal pain and changes in bowel habits, for which no physiological explanation can be found and that is often accompanied by anxiety or mood disorders (Greene & Blanchard, 1994). Interventions directed toward schemata change via experiential disconfirmation and cognitive restructuring are particularly effective in reducing gastrointestinal physiological symptoms and patients' reports of behavioral avoidance, yielding more robust results than multicomponent cognitive-behavioral interventions (Blanchard & Malamood, 1996; Payne & Blanchard, 1995).

Modifying Self-Regulation

A person who has been newly diagnosed with a medical condition or who faces a chronic or recurrent condition is challenged to find new ways to regulate thoughts, feelings, and behaviors. Familiar ways of self-regulation may be ineffective for this new stressor, or they may be no longer feasible due to changes in physical or psychological functioning. A cornerstone of many cognitive-behavioral interventions for medical conditions, modifying self-regulation generally consists of "altering the conscious appraisal of coping options, teaching more effective coping strategies, and encouraging greater persistence in their use" (Brewin, 1989, p. 385).

The centrality of this change process to cognitive-behavioral interventions is consistent with extensive empirical documentation of the importance of coping and self-regulation for successful adaptation to diverse medical conditions. For example, among individuals diagnosed with CFS, those who rely mainly on self-regulation strategies characterized by denial and disengagement report greater illness burden, or disruption in psychosocial and physical life domains due to fatigue (Antoni et al., 1994). Among patients heterogeneous with respect to medical condition (e.g., chronic pain, cardiovascular and gastroenterologic disorders, fatigue), coping accounts for a significant proportion of variance in adjustment to illness, as assessed by self-reported depressive and physical symptoms, along with self-reported physical and psychosocial impairment. After controlling for physician-rated severity of disease, individuals who adopt an emotion-focused coping style characterized by avoidance, self-blame, and wishful thinking show the poorest adjustment to their illness (Bombardier, D'Amico, & Jordan, 1990). Moreover, an illness appraisal of "hold back" appears to play a role in this process. Specifically, individuals who believe that, because of their illness, they must hold back from doing what they want are the most likely to employ emotion-focused forms of coping, have the highest level of depressive symptoms, and have the poorest psychosocial adjustment. These associations hold even after controlling for level of physical impairment. This suggests that the "hold back" appraisal is associated with adjustment independent of disorder-based physical limitations, perhaps reflecting the development of a fear-avoidance response to illness, a response that might be effectively targeted by cognitive-behavioral interventions (Bombardier, D'Amico, & Jordan, 1990).

Self-regulation is also a particularly powerful ingredient in functional adaptation to chronic pain, such as osteoarthritic knee pain. For example, reports of pain and psychological distress are lower and health status is better among individuals who refrain from overly negative thinking when they have knee pain and who feel confident in their ability to manage their experience of pain. These individuals experience less difficulty in overall functioning and demonstrate superior speed when assessed for specific physical capabilities, such as walking a 5-mile course or moving from a standing to a sitting position, than patients who use irrational coping methods such as catastrophizing. These associations between self-regulation and functional capacity hold even after controlling for pain severity, age, gender, and medical variables (i.e., obesity and X-ray indicators of disease severity; Keefe et al., 1987).

Adaptation to catastrophic, life-threatening illnesses that overwhelm the coping capacities of most people is also enhanced by certain self-regulation strategies. Among women with breast cancer and cancer patients heterogeneous with respect to type and severity of cancer, self-regulation characterized by cognitive and behavioral avoidance and denial is associated with high levels of emotional distress, whereas focusing on the positive and seeking social support is associated with low levels of distress (Dunkel-Schetter et al., 1992; Stanton & Snider, 1993). Preliminary evidence also links self-regulation to disease progression and biological markers. Avoidant coping strategies are associated with more rapid cancer progression over the course of a 1-year period (Epping-Jordan, Compas, & Howell, 1994). Among seropositive gay men finding out about their HIV serostatus, increases in denial from pre- to postnotification of serostatus are associated with greater likelihood of disease progression 2 years later and greater likelihood of progression to symptom status, after controlling for CD4 counts assessed upon entry into the study (Ironson et al., 1994). In addition, these same increases in denial are negatively correlated with CD4 cell number and proliferative responses of peripheral blood lymphocytes at 1-year follow-up (Ironson et al., 1994).

With regard to cognitive-behavioral interventions, modification of self-regulation skills has played a central role in treatments for chronic, debilitating disorders and for catastrophic, potentially life-threatening disorders. We would like to highlight three randomized, controlled treatment-outcome studies that exemplify the importance of teaching self-regulation skills. These three studies reveal that cognitive-behavioral interventions can modify participants' use of specific self-regulation strategies and can also bolster their general confidence in their coping ability, both of which appear to be pathways to enhanced health outcomes.

Lutgendorf et al. (1997) evaluated the efficacy of a cognitive-behavioral stress management (CBSM) group intervention for managing chronic stress in symptomatic, HIV-seropositive gay men who had been diagnosed with HIV for at least 6 months. The CBSM intervention was a multicomponent treatment that included progressive muscle relaxation, psychoeducation about the human stress response and about HIV transmission and related health behaviors, cognitive restructuring, assertiveness training, and other strategies for behavioral change. A portion of the group time was used to role play CBSM strategies with other members. At the conclusion of the 10-week intervention, self-reported depression, anxiety, and total distress were significantly reduced among participants in the CBSM intervention, but not among members of the assessment-only control group. A subsequent analysis of mediators indicated that the CBSM intervention was associated with improvements in specific self-regulation abilities (Lutgendorf et al., 1998). Members of the CBSM intervention showed significant increases in positive reframing, acceptance, active coping, and perceived social support (a composite of feelings of attachment, social integration, reliable alliance, and guidance), whereas for the members of the control group, positive reframing and acceptance declined over the 10-week period and active coping and perceived social support were unchanged. Further, there was some evidence that these enhancements in self-regulatory abilities mediated the effect of the CBSM intervention on emotional distress: Among CBSM participants, increased perceptions of social support and enhanced cognitive coping skills were significantly associated with decreased self-reported anxiety, depression, and total mood disturbance.

The importance of teaching self-regulatory skills is also highlighted by a group cognitive-behavioral intervention designed to manage postsurgical distress in patients with malignant melanoma who had early diagnoses and good prognoses (Fawzy, Cousins, et al., 1990; Fawzy, Kemeny, et al., 1990; Fawzy et al., 1993). In addition to teaching coping skills, the structured 6-week multicomponent group intervention was designed to provide health education, teach relaxation techniques, and enhance psychological support. The coping skills treatment module focused on three general self-regulation strategies: active-cognitive, active-behavioral, and avoidant coping. Although the negative effects of avoidant coping were reviewed, the overarching approach was characterized by a focus on the power of coping flexibility, or learning to willfully choose and apply coping strategies best suited to the immediate problem at hand. Participants were presented with coping scenarios that depicted situations commonly encountered by cancer patients, ranging from diagnosis and treatment issues to problems communicating with friends and coworkers and planning for the future. A positive coping scenario and a negative coping scenario were illustrated for each problem situation, and patients were then encouraged to apply these

scenarios to problems they currently faced (Fawzy & Fawzy, 1994).

Compared to members of the assessment-only control group, participants in the treatment group reported more vigor immediately following completion of the intervention. At 6-months postintervention they reported less depression, fatigue, and overall negative mood and more vigor, along with an increased percentage of natural killer cells (Fawzy, Cousins, et al., 1990; Fawzy, Kemeny, et al., 1990). Assessment of stress mediators revealed that, compared to control group members, participants in the cognitive-behavioral intervention used more active behavioral coping at the end of the intervention and 6 months later. Moreover, intervention participants decreased their use of passive resignation and increased their use of distraction. Finally, among members of the intervention group the use of active coping was associated with more vigor and decreased fatigue, anger, and overall negative mood, whereas the use of avoidant strategies was associated with more anxiety, depression, and overall negative mood. When recurrence and survival were assessed 5 to 6 years later among participants with Stage I disease, participants in the cognitive-behavioral intervention had a significantly better survival rate than control participants, an effect that held after controlling for biomedical disease indices. Further, increases in active-behavioral coping from pretreatment to 6 months postintervention were significantly and positively related to survival (Fawzy et al., 1993).

Finally, Keefe et al. (1990a) compared the efficacy of the following three interventions in a group of patients with osteoarthritic knee pain: pain coping skills training, arthritis education, or standard care. Both the pain coping skills training and the arthritis education interventions met for 90-minute sessions each week in groups of six to nine patients. During the course of the 10-week multicomponent treatment, patients in the coping skills intervention learned and practiced application of a cognitive-behavioral "menu" of coping skills designed to help control and decrease pain by modifying thoughts, beliefs, feelings, and actions that affect pain (Keefe, 1986). The coping skills menu included cognitive restructuring, in which participants were first taught to identify automatic negative thought distortions experienced during pain episodes, and then to replace them with realistic, objective thoughts or calming self-statements. The coping intervention also incorporated experiential disconfirmation methods, in which patients learned to pace cycles of activity and rest. Like many experiential disconfirmation methods, this one was designed to reduce activity avoidance caused by anxious anticipation of activity-induced pain. In addition, this disconfirmation method served to bolster coping efficacy by illustrating to patients that they could control, rather than be controlled by, the amount of pain they experienced during activities. Other components of the coping skills training included progressive relaxation, and distraction techniques, such as imagery and novel activities. Final coping training sessions focused on problem solving, in which patients learned to apply a combination of these coping skills when faced with a problem situation.

Following treatment, patients in the pain coping training reported significantly lower levels of psychological disability, as well as lower levels of pain, compared to those in the arthritis education or standard care groups. Among the pain coping treatment participants, those who believed that their ability to decrease and control pain had improved during the 10-week intervention showed less physical disability following treatment (Keefe et al., 1990a). While some posttreatment advances were not maintained at the 6-month follow-up, overall, patients who experienced the best long-term improvements in pain and pain behavior as well as physical and psychological disability were the patients who also showed the greatest improvements in perceived coping efficacy during the 10-week intervention (Keefe et al., 1990b).

Efficacy of Cognitive-Behavioral Interventions for Medical Conditions

There is increasing emphasis on assessing the efficacy of psychological treatments and communicating these findings to health care policy makers to facilitate the development of clinical practice guidelines for widespread use in the delivery of health care (Barlow, 1996; Chambless & Hollon, 1998). To this end, psychological treatments are evaluated against a set of criteria (e.g., superiority to no treatment, placebo, or alternative treatment established in a randomized, controlled

clinical trial and in independent research settings; research conducted with treatment manuals) and, based on the results, categorized according to the level of confidence with which efficacy can be established (e.g., efficacious, probably efficacious, well-established; Chambless et al., 1996; Chambless & Hollon, 1998). While it would be beyond the scope of this chapter to provide a comprehensive discussion of data bearing on empirical validation of cognitive-behavioral interventions for medical conditions, we would like to make two general points.

First, in a recent selective review of this topic, Compas et al. (1998) concluded that the efficacy of cognitive-behavioral interventions for several medical conditions could be supported with varying degrees of confidence. For example, for interventions designed to treat the chronic pain of rheumatic disorders and migraine headaches, supporting evidence from randomized, controlled treatment-outcome studies was strong and consistent, and efficacy for pain reduction was characterized as well established. Behavioral interventions for managing the physical side effects of chemotherapy for cancer were similarly well supported. In contrast, the efficacy of interventions designed to manage the emotional distress of cancer more broadly was less well established. Although preliminary evidence appears promising, there is a great need for replication using larger samples composed of individuals with specific types of cancer. In sum, although much work remains to be done, a substantial body of evidence suggests that the continued development of cognitive-behavioral interventions as adjuvant treatments for medical conditions has the potential to yield favorable outcomes.

Second, identifying the specific "active ingredients" of cognitive-behavioral interventions, and their relative contributions to efficacy, is an area in need of additional research (Keefe, Dunsmore, & Burnett, 1992, p. 534). Multicomponent interventions for medical conditions are common, often including all of the three cognitive change processes discussed previously, along with more strictly behavioral methods such as progressive muscle relaxation, thereby making it difficult to disentangle the contributions of the specific treatment components (Emmelkamp & van Oppen, 1993). The treatment-outcome literature for migraine headaches provides an example of the value of such a component analysis approach.

Comparisons of behavioral (e.g., thermal biofeedback plus relaxation training) and cognitive treatment methods for migraine headaches have yielded the general consensus that cognitive, or cognitive-behavioral, treatments do not add significantly to the efficacy of purely behavioral interventions (Compas et al., 1998). The contributions of specific change processes to outcomes such as enhanced quality of life, improved biomedical status, and reduced health care utilization remain to be addressed in future research. Component analysis will enable interventions to harness the most effective therapeutic change processes, thereby generating concentrated interventions that are not diluted by less effective processes (Keefe, Dunsmore, & Burnett, 1992).

SUMMARY AND FUTURE DIRECTIONS

The occurrence of a medical illness represents a major, sometimes catastrophic, life event that may severely tax one's coping abilities and culminate in a complex biopsychosocial response. Cognition is central to this response, from attending to and appraising symptoms, to generating coping behaviors and forming internal illness representations comprising symptom experiences, emotion, and meaning. Accordingly, cognitive-behavioral interventions have been evaluated with regard to their ability to ameliorate emotional distress associated with a range of medical conditions. In addition, there is growing interest in assessing their efficacy for improving biomedical status and decreasing health care utilization and costs. Given preliminary support for the efficacy of cognitive-behavioral interventions for certain medical conditions, one important goal of future research will be to refine interventions by examining the relative contribution of specific change processes to treatment outcomes.

Despite this optimistic appraisal of cognitive-behavioral interventions for medical conditions, some caveats are in order. First, it is important to note that for some medical conditions, preliminary examination of cognitive-behavioral interventions has yielded inconsistent, null, or even reverse effects. For example, in a randomized, controlled clinical trial, Schwarz and Blanchard (1991) compared the efficacy of a multicomponent cognitive-behavioral intervention to that of a symptom-monitoring control for reducing self-reported symptoms of inflammatory bowel diseases. Outcome assessments revealed that control participants fared better than treatment participants in terms of symptom reduction, even though treatment participants reported a greater level of subjective emotional improvement.

In another example, Frasure-Smith et al. (1997) employed a randomized, controlled trial to evaluate the efficacy of a nursing intervention for enhancing adaptation to myocardial infarction (MI). The nursing intervention consisted of monitoring levels of psychological distress by telephone each month for 1 year, combined with home nursing visits in response to high levels of distress. Patients identified as experiencing increased psychological distress received approximately five to six 1-hour in-home nursing visits. Each visit was a case management–style intervention that included provision of advice, support, reassurance, and referral to other health care resources in the community. Compared with members of the standard medical care control group, neither men nor women who participated in the nursing intervention showed significant reductions in anxiety or depression after 1 year. Among men, participation in the intervention did not affect survival, resulting in no significant differences in either cardiac mortality, or all-cause mortality, compared to men in the control group. In contrast, compared to women who received standard care, women who participated in the nursing intervention had significantly higher rates of cardiac mortality, in particular deaths due to arrhythmia, and significantly higher rates of all-cause mortality over the course of the one-year intervention.

Although this nursing intervention is not cognitive-behavioral in the strictest sense, the authors raised the possibility that the dramatic and unexpected findings for women MI patients could in part be due to the effect of the study's methods upon cognitive-affective processes, ultimately resulting in increased distress in some female patients. In particular, the authors expressed concern about the higher number of deaths due to arrhythmia among women in the intervention group, citing evidence that psychological factors may play a meaningful role in deaths due to arrhythmia in post-MI patients. The authors suggested that telephone checks on low mortality risk patients could have resulted in patients thinking more about their MI and may have increased their psychological distress by triggering erroneous appraisals of poor prognosis. In addition, they suggested that, rather than enhancing patients' coping abilities, the systematic approach used by the study for addressing small elevations in psychological distress may have interfered with patients' usual coping skills, such as denial. Furthermore, they hypothesized that multiple home nursing visits could have exposed or stirred familial and social stressors that remain uncovered in outpatient care settings, and may have increased expectations for the improvement of enduring problems that went beyond the limitations of the study. Although post hoc, these explanations underscore potentially powerful associations between cognitive-affective processes and health that have been brought to light by this investigation. Harnessing the power of these processes may eventually lead to more effective cognitive-behavioral treatments for medical conditions. Finally, in closing, we would like to raise a number of issues for future consideration.

Psychiatric Vulnerabilities

The prevalence of psychiatric conditions, such as affective and anxiety disorders and substance use disorders, is significantly elevated among persons with chronic medical conditions (Banks & Kerns, 1996; Hill, Kelleher, & Shumaker, 1992; Melamed, 1995; Wells, Golding, & Burnam, 1988). Thus, a critical question for cognitive-behavioral approaches to medical conditions concerns the impact of psychiatric comorbidity on treatment efficacy. To date, many treatment-outcome studies have specifically excluded individuals with current Axis I disorders or with psychiatric histories, making it unclear if results will generalize to individuals with comorbid psychiatric conditions. Indeed, one of the few studies to address this issue suggests that they may not. Blanchard et al. (1992), in a study of individuals with irritable bowel syndrome, found that a comorbid diagnosable Axis I psychiatric disorder significantly reduced the likelihood of gastrointestinal symptom improvement after participation in cognitive-behavioral treatment. Given the prevalence of psychiatric/medical comorbidities, there is a need for research that assesses the impact of a current or lifetime psychiatric history on the efficacy of cognitive-behavioral interventions for

medical conditions (Keefe & Caldwell, 1997). If psychiatric comorbidity does reduce treatment efficacy, then research will need to be directed toward the design of different, more effective, interventions. For example, treatments of longer duration might be considered, as might sequences of interventions in which the Axis I condition is targeted first, followed by the specific cognitive-affective response to the medical condition. Alternatively, treatments that target the Axis I condition only may be sufficient in these cases (Blanchard et al., 1992).

Emotionally Avoidant Coping

Across a number of medical conditions, denial and minimization of stress and emotions are associated with decreased quality of life and compromised adaptation (e.g., Antoni et al., 1994; Dunkel-Schetter et al., 1992), and there is emerging evidence that they are also correlated with poorer biomedical outcomes (e.g., Fawzy et al., 1993). Thus, individuals who habitually employ such avoidant strategies may be among those most in need of psychosocial interventions.[2] However, they also may be among those most difficult to recruit into cognitive-behavioral interventions because they may not perceive such interventions as necessary or because they may have less willingness or emotional capacity to confront and acknowledge their health threat. Thus, research should assess the rate at which such individuals volunteer for treatment studies, and, if necessary, special attention should be directed to developing strategies for recruiting them into treatment (Fawzy et al., 1993).

With regard to the modification of emotionally avoidant self-regulation, to date, cognitive-behavioral interventions for medical conditions have focused on teaching active coping skills. However, a recent study designed to assess the process of coping suggests an alternative intervention. Miller et al. (1996) provide evidence that, in response to a serious health threat, self-regulation by denial and disengagement is

---

2. The literature is not wholly consistent in this regard. Avoidant coping strategies may be beneficial in some situations (e.g., Suls & Fletcher, 1985), and Frasure-Smith et al. (1997) hypothesized that the disruption of denial may have played a role in the negative health outcomes observed in their study.

associated with recurrent cycles of intrusive and emotionally charged images, along with cognitive attempts to inhibit such intrusions. More specifically, the authors hypothesize that patients resort to global denial and disengagement when their cognitive efforts to inhibit specific images and intrusions fail. Thus, because denial and disengagement appear to be driven in part by intrusions of overwhelming emotions, this process analysis suggests that one way to treat avoidant coping might be to employ interventions that target the underlying intrusive ideation. For example, cognitive-behavioral interventions designed to treat anxiety disorders characterized by a similar stress response might be effective in this regard (e.g., Resick & Schnicke, 1992). One possible mitigating factor is that some of these interventions are designed to treat emotional responses to acute stressors, whereas many medical stressors are chronic and ongoing.

Affective Change Processes

The cognitive change processes discussed in this chapter involve alteration of emotion, in addition to cognition, and thus, in some ways they may be thought of as "affective change processes" (Greenberg & Safran, 1987, p. 171). However, these change processes are predicated upon a cognitive-mediational model of emotion, which posits that cognitive processes mediate emotional responses to internal and external events. Recent theoretical developments in the study of human emotion suggest the existence of noncognitive pathways for activation of emotion, a proposition supported by experimental research (Izard, 1993). For example, sensorimotor and motivational processes that accompany pain may activate emotion without the involvement of cognition (Izard, 1993). Although speculative, this suggests that cognitive change processes may be insufficient to target and modify all emotional responses. In this regard, Greenberg and Safran (1987) reviewed the psychotherapy literature and identified six different affective change processes, including acknowledging emotion, arousal of emotional responses, expression of feelings, modifying dysfunctional affective responses, taking responsibility for emotion, and creation of meaning. The venerable research tradition concerning emotions and health (e.g., Leventhal & Patrick-Miller, 1993) raises the possibility that some of these affective change processes

may be important additions to interventions for medical conditions. As one example, the health effects of writing about emotionally stressful life events (intervention group) versus daily plans (control group) were compared in patients with rheumatoid arthritis and asthma (Smyth et al., 1999). At 4 months post-treatment, patients who wrote about stressful events showed significantly greater rates of clinically meaningful health improvement than did patients in the control group. The mechanisms responsible for this clinical improvement are currently unknown, but the study investigators note the relevance of prior research in which similar writing interventions were associated with enhanced proliferative responses of peripheral blood lymphocytes in healthy young adults (Pennebaker, Kiecolt-Glaser, & Glaser, 1988).

Interpersonal Context of Self-Regulation

Social relationships are key ingredients of well-being, forming the biopsychosocial context for one's efforts to cope with the stress of medical illness. Individuals who have intimate social ties, and those who have others to turn to for emotional support and material assistance, are at lower risk of physical health problems than are those with less extensive interpersonal resources (House, Landis, & Umberson, 1988). On the other hand, when characterized by strife, strain, and conflict, close relationships may impair well-being, to an even greater degree than supportive ties enhance it (Rook, 1984). Furthermore, emotion communication patterns in close relationships are associated broadly with biological stress responses, including alterations in immunological (Kiecolt-Glaser et al., 1993), neuroendocrine (Kiecolt-Glaser et al., 1996), and cardiovascular (Ewart et al., 1991) response systems. One future direction for research on cognitive-behavioral treatments for medical conditions will be to develop interventions that draw upon close relationships in support of cognitive change. A noteworthy example concerns the integration of spousal support with cognitive-behavioral therapy for the treatment of osteoarthritic knee pain (Keefe et al., 1996). This study compared three interventions: (1) cognitive-behavioral therapy (CBT), (2) spouse-assisted cognitive-behavioral therapy, and (3) a control condition consisting of arthritis education with spouse present. In the spouse-assisted

CBT group, both patients and spouses attended sessions that included marital relational training in communications, behavioral rehearsal, solving problems, and maintenance, as well as pain coping skills training. Following treatment, patients in the spouse-assisted CBT group, as compared with patients in the arthritis education group, obtained better outcomes for levels of pain, psychological disability, and self-efficacy coping attempts, as well as marital adjustment. For nearly all outcome measures there were no substantial differences between the spouse-assisted CBT and conventional CBT interventions. However, there was an overall pattern for spouse-assisted CBT to yield the most optimal results, followed by conventional CBT and arthritis education. In addition, for patients in the spouse-assisted CBT group, improvement in marital relationship was associated with improvement in psychological disability (Keefe et al., 1996), highlighting potential connections between social relationships and cognitive change that should be explored in future research.

Specificity versus Shared Determinants

In this chapter we focused on three cognitive change processes and their application to the management of a wide range of medical conditions that differ in terms of degree of life threat, likely psychological impact, and underlying biological system. This raises interesting questions about the need for disease-specific interventions. With regard to this, two contrasting, implicit points of view can be identified. One point of view assumes specificity with regard to psychosocial factors and illness (e.g., Cohen & Rodriguez, 1995) and is characterized by attention to the etiological and pathophysiological differences among diseases, along with differences in course (e.g., chronic, progressive, recurrent flare-ups), stage, and outcome. In its extreme form this approach suggests that specific cognitive-affective change processes need to be targeted to treat specific pathophysiological processes and diseases and that the effectiveness of change processes may not generalize across medical disorders.

A contrasting point of view draws on converging evidence that certain psychosocial factors contribute

to the prediction of health outcomes across different diseases. This point of view is concerned with "shared psychosocial determinants" of health and illness, factors that do not appear to be disease-specific but that instead have been linked to multiple medical conditions (Sobel, 1995). This approach implies that there may be particular change processes that effectively target a range of diseases, involving different biological systems, across their course. Such an approach may be particularly relevant to the development of psychosocial interventions for medical comorbidity, or the presence of more than one diagnosed medical disorder. Medical comorbidity, a phenomenon that has been largely neglected by behavioral medicine researchers, involves multiple pathophysiological systems, occurs across the life span, and is associated with dramatic elevations in costs of direct health care services (Doron et al., 1998; Hoffman, Rice, & Sung, 1996). Although further research will be necessary to assess the merits of targeting shared psychosocial determinants versus disease-specific processes, it seems likely that, ultimately, the most powerful adjuvant interventions for medical conditions will be synergistic, combining methods designed to alter cognitive-affective pathways common to many illnesses with those designed to target disease-specific processes.

REFERENCES

Abbey, S. E. (1996). Psychotherapeutic perspectives on chronic fatigue syndrome. In M. A. Demitrack & S. E. Abbey (Eds.), *Chronic fatigue syndrome: An integrative approach to evaluation and treatment* (pp. 185–211). New York: Guilford Press.

Andersen, B. L., Farrar, W. B., Golden-Kreutz, D., Kutz, L. A., MacCallum, R., Courtney, M. E., & Glaser, R. (1998). Stress and immune responses after surgical treatment for regional breast cancer. *Journal of the National Cancer Institute, 90,* 30–36.

Andersen, B. L., Kiecolt-Glaser, J. K., & Glaser, R. (1994). A biobehavioral model of cancer stress and disease course. *American Psychologist, 49,* 389–404.

Antoni, M. H., Brickman, A., Lutgendorf, S., Klimas, N., Imia-Fins, A., Ironson, G., Quillian, R., Miguez, M. J., Riel, F. V., Morgan, R., Patarca, R., & Fletcher, M. A. (1994). Psychosocial correlates of illness burden in chronic fatigue syndrome. *Clinical Infectious Diseases, 18,* S73–S78.

Banks, S. M., & Kerns, R. D. (1996). Explaining high rates of depression in chronic pain: A diathesis-stress framework. *Psychological Bulletin, 119,* 95–110.

Barlow, D. H. (1996). Health care policy, psychotherapy research, and the future of psychotherapy. *American Psychologist, 51,* 1050–1058.

Beck, A. T., Emery, G., & Greenberg, R. L. (1985). *Anxiety disorders and phobias: A cognitive perspective.* New York: Basic Books.

Beck, A. T., Rush, A. J., Shaw, B. F., & Emery, G. (1979). *Cognitive therapy of depression.* New York: Guilford Press.

Beck, J. S. (1995). *Cognitive therapy: Basics and beyond.* New York: Guilford Press.

Bishop, G. D. (1987). Lay conceptions of physical symptoms. *Journal of Applied Social Psychology, 17,* 127–146.

Blanchard, E. B., & Malamood, H. S. (1996). Psychological treatment of irritable bowel syndrome. *Professional Psychology: Research and Practice, 27,* 241–244.

Blanchard, E. B., Scharff, L., Payne, A., Schwarz, S. P., Suls, J. M., & Malamood, H. (1992). Prediction of outcome from cognitive-behavioral treatment of irritable bowel syndrome. *Behaviour Research and Therapy, 30,* 647–650.

Bombardier, C. H., D'Amico, C., & Jordan, J. S. (1990). The relationship of appraisal and coping to chronic illness adjustment. *Behaviour Research and Therapy, 28,* 297–304.

Brewin, C. R. (1989). Cognitive change processes in psychotherapy. *Psychological Review, 96,* 379–394.

Burish, T. G., & Tope, D. M. (1992). Psychological techniques for controlling the adverse side effects of cancer chemotherapy: Findings from a decade of research. *Journal of Pain and Symptom Management, 7,* 287–301.

Calabrese, J. R., Kling, M. A., & Gold, P. W. (1987). Alterations in immunocompetence during stress, bereavement, and depression: Focus on neuroendocrine regulation. *American Journal of Psychiatry, 144,* 1123–1134.

Chambless, D. L., & Hollon, S. D. (1998). Defining empirically supported therapies. *Journal of Consulting and Clinical Psychology, 66,* 7–18.

Chambless, D. L., Sanderson, W. C., Shoham, V., Bennett Johnson, S., Pope, K. S., Crits-Christoph, P., Baker, M., Johnson, B., Woody, S. R., Sue, S., Beutler, L., Williams, D. A., & McCurry, S. (1996). An update on empirically validated therapies. *The Clinical Psychologist, 49,* 5–18.

Cohen, S., & Rodriguez, M. S. (1995). Pathways linking affective disturbances and physical disorders. *Health Psychology, 14,* 374–380.

Compas, B. E., Haaga, D. A. F., Keefe, F. J., Leitenberg, H., & Williams, D. A. (1998). Sampling of empirically supported psychological treatments from health psychology: Smoking, chronic pain, cancer, and bulimia nervosa. *Journal of Consulting and Clinical Psychology, 66,* 89–112.

Deale, A., Chalder, T., Marks, I., & Wessely, S. (1997). Cognitive behavior therapy for chronic fatigue syndrome: A randomized controlled trial. *American Journal of Psychiatry, 154,* 408–414.

Doron, S. E., Newton, T. L., Caulfield, M. B., & Huang, M. T. (1998, March). The prevalence of comorbidity among women veteran medical users. Poster session presented at the annual meeting of the Society of Behavioral Medicine, New Orleans, LA.

Dunkel-Schetter, C., Feinstein, L. G., Taylor, S. E., & Falke, R. L. (1992). Patterns of coping with cancer. *Health Psychology, 11,* 79–87.

Emmelkamp, P. M. G., & van Oppen, P. (1993). Cognitive interventions in behavioral medicine. *Psychotherapy and Psychosomatics, 59,* 116–130.

Epping-Jordan, J. E., Compas, B. E., & Howell, D. C. (1994). Predictors of cancer progression in young adult men and women: Avoidance, intrusive thoughts, and psychological symptoms. *Health Psychology, 13,* 539–547.

Ewart, C. K., Taylor, C. B., Kraemer, H. C., & Agras, W. S. (1991). High blood pressure and marital discord: Not being nasty matters more than being nice. *Health Psychology, 10,* 155–163.

Fawzy, F. I., Cousins, N., Fawzy, N. W., Kemeny, M. E., Elashoff, R., & Morton, D. (1990). A structured psychiatric intervention for cancer patients, I. Changes over time in methods of coping and affective disturbance. *Archives of General Psychiatry, 47,* 720–725.

Fawzy, F. I., & Fawzy, N. W. (1994). A structured psychoeducational intervention for cancer patients. *General Hospital Psychiatry, 16,* 149–192.

Fawzy, F. I., Fawzy, N. W., Hyun, C. S., Elashoff, R., Guthrie, D., Fahey, J. L., & Morton, D. L. (1993). Malignant melanoma: Effects of an early structured psychiatric intervention, coping, and affective state on recurrence and survival 6 years later. *Archives of General Psychiatry, 50,* 681–689.

Fawzy, F. I., Kemeny, M. E., Fawzy, N. W., Elashoff, R., Morton, D., Cousins, N., & Fahey, J. L. (1990). A structured psychiatric intervention for cancer patients, II. Changes over time in immunological measures. *Archives of General Psychiatry, 47,* 729–735.

Foa, E. B., Feske, U., Murdock, T. B., Kozak, M. J., & McCarthy, P. R. (1991). Processing of threat-related information in rape victims. *Journal of Abnormal Psychology, 100,* 156–162.

Frasure-Smith, N., Lespérance, F., Prince, R. H., Verrier, P., Garber, R. A., Juneau, M., Wolfson, C., & Bourassa, M. G. (1997). Randomised trial of home-based psychosocial nursing intervention for patients recovering from myocardial infarction. *Lancet, 350,* 473–479.

Frasure-Smith, N., Lespérance, F., & Talajic, M. (1995). The impact of negative emotions on prognosis following myocardial infarction: Is it more than depression? *Health Psychology, 14,* 388–398.

Friedman, R., Sobel, D., Myers, P., Caudill, M., & Benson, H. (1995). Behavioral medicine, clinical health psychology, and cost offset. *Health Psychology, 14,* 509–518.

Goldston, D. B., Kovacs, M., Obrosky, D. S., & Iyengar, S. (1995). A longitudinal study of life events and metabolic control among youths with insulin-dependent diabetes mellitus. *Health Psychology, 14,* 409–414.

Greenberg, L. S., & Safran, J. D. (1987). *Emotion in psychotherapy.* New York: Guilford Press.

Greene, B., & Blanchard, E. B. (1994). Cognitive therapy for irritable bowel syndrome. *Journal of Consulting and Clinical Psychology, 62,* 576–582.

Hellman, C. J. C., Budd, M., Borysenko, J., McClelland, D. C., & Benson, H. (1990). A study of the effectiveness of two group behavioral medicine interventions for patients with psychosomatic complaints. *Behavioral Medicine, 16,* 165–173.

Herbert, T. B., & Cohen, S. (1993). Depression and immunity: A meta-analytic review. *Psychological Bulletin, 113,* 472–486.

Hill, D. R., Kelleher, K., & Shumaker, S. A. (1992). Psychosocial interventions in adult patients with coronary heart disease and cancer. *General Hospital Psychiatry, 14* (suppl.), 28S–42S.

Hoffman, C., Rice, D., & Sung, H. (1996). Persons with chronic conditions: Their prevalence and costs. *JAMA, 276,* 1473–1479.

Horowitz, M., Wilner, N., & Alvarez, W. (1979). Impact of events scale: A measure of subjective stress. *Psychosomatic Medicine, 41,* 209–218.

House, J. S., Landis, K. R., & Umberson, D. (1988). Social relationships and health. *Science, 241,* 540–545.

Ironson, G., Friedman, A., Kliman, N., Antoni, M., Fletcher, M. A., LaPerriere, A., Somoneau, J., & Schneiderman, N. (1994). Distress, denial, and low adherence to behavioral interventions predict faster disease progression in gay men infected with human immunodeficiency virus. *International Journal of Behavioral Medicine, 1,* 90–105.

Izard, C. E. (1993). Four systems for emotion activation: Cognitive and noncognitive processes. *Psychological Review, 100,* 68–90.

Janoff-Bulman, R. (1992). *Shattered assumptions: Towards a new psychology of trauma.* New York: Free Press.

Keefe, F. J. (1986). *Cognitive behavioral treatment of arthritis pain.* Unpublished treatment manual, Duke University Medical Center.

Keefe, F. J., & Caldwell, D. S. (1997). Cognitive behavioral control of arthritis pain. *Medical Clinics of North America, 81,* 277–290.

Keefe, F. J., Caldwell, D. S., Baucom, D., Sailey, A., Robinson, E., Timmons, K., Beaupre, P., Weisberg, J., & Helms, M. (1996). Spouse-assisted coping skills training in the management of osteoarthritis knee pain. *Arthritis Care Research, 9,* 279–291.

Keefe, F. J., Caldwell, D. S., Queen, K. T., Gil, C., Martinez, S., Crisson, J. E., Ogden, W., & Nunley, J. (1987). Pain coping strategies in osteoarthritis patients. *Journal of Consulting and Clinical Psychology, 55,* 208–212.

Keefe, F. J., Caldwell, D. S., Williams, D. A., Gil, K. M., Mitchell, D., Robertson, C., Martinez, S., Nunley, J., Beckham, J. C., Crisson, J. E., & Helms, M. (1990a). Pain coping skills training in the management of osteoarthritic knee pain: A comparative study. *Behavior Therapy, 21,* 49–62.

Keefe, F. J., Caldwell, D. S., Williams, D. A., Gil, K. M., Mitchell, D., Robertson, C., Martinez, S., Nunley, J., Beckham, J. C., & Helms, M. (1990b). Pain coping skills training in the management of osteoarthritic knee pain: Follow-up results. *Behavior Therapy, 21,* 435–447.

Keefe, F. J., Dunsmore, J., & Burnett, R. (1992). Behavioral and cognitive-behavioral approaches to chronic pain: Recent advances and future directions. *Journal of Consulting and Clinical Psychology, 60,* 528–536.

Kiecolt-Glaser, J. K., Malarkey, W. B., Chee, M., Newton, T. L., Cacioppo, J. T., Mao, H., & Glaser, R. (1993). Negative behavior during marital conflict is associated with immunological down-regulation. *Psychosomatic Medicine, 55,* 395–409.

Kiecolt-Glaser, J. K., Newton, T. L., Glaser, R., Cacioppo, J. T., & Malarkey, W. B. (1996). Marital conflict and endocrine function: Are men more physiologically affected than women? *Journal of Consulting and Clinical Psychology, 64,* 324–332.

Lazarus, R. S. (1993). Coping theory and research: Past, present, and future. *Psychosomatic Medicine, 55,* 234–247.

Lazarus, R. S., & Folkman, S. (1984). *Stress, appraisal, and coping.* New York: Springer.

Lerman, C., & Glanz, K. (1997). Stress, coping, and health behavior. In K. Glanz, F. M. Lewis, & B. K. Rimer (Eds.), *Health behavior and health education: Theory, research, and practice* (2d ed.) (pp. 113–138). San Francisco: Jossey-Bass.

Leventhal, H. (1982). Behavioral medicine: Psychology in health care. In D. Mechanic (Ed.), *Handbook of health care policies and the health professions* (pp. 709–743). New York: Free Press.

Leventhal, H. (1986). Symptom reporting: A focus on process. In S. McHugh & T. M. Vallis (Eds.), *Illness behavior: A multidisciplinary model* (pp. 219–237). New York: Plenum.

Leventhal, H., Meyer, D., & Nerenz, D. (1980). The common sense representation of illness danger. In S. Rachman (Ed.), *Medical psychology* (vol. 2). New York: Pergamon Press.

Leventhal, H., & Nerenz, D. R. (1985). The assessment of illness cognition. In P. Karoly (Ed.), *Measurement strategies in health psychology* (pp. 517–554). New York: Wiley.

Leventhal, H., & Patrick-Miller, L. (1993). Emotion and illness: The mind is in the body. In M. Lewis & J. M. Haviland (Eds.), *Handbook of emotions* (pp. 365–379). New York: Guilford Press.

Lutgendorf, S. K., Antoni, M. H., Ironson, G., Klimas, N., Kuman, M., Starr, K., McCabe, P., Cleven, K., Fletcher, M. A., & Schneiderman, N. (1997). Cognitive-behavioral stress management decreases dysphoric mood and herpes simplex virus-type 2 antibody titers in symptomatic HIV-seropositive gay men. *Journal of Consulting and Clinical Psychology, 65,* 31–43.

Lutgendorf, S. K., Antoni, M. H., Ironson, G., Starr, K., Costello, N., Zuckerman, M., Klimas, N., Fletcher, M. A., & Schneiderman, N. (1998). Changes in cognitive coping skills and social support during cognitive behavioral stress management intervention and distress outcomes in symptomatic human immunodeficiency virus (HIV)-seropositive gay men. *Psychosomatic Medicine, 60,* 204–214.

Melamed, B. G. (1995). The interface between physical and mental disorders: The need to dismantle the biopsychosocialneuroimmunological model of disease. *Journal of Clinical Psychological in Medical Settings, 2,* 225–231.

Meyer, D., Leventhal, H., & Gutmann, M. (1985). Common-sense models of illness: The example of hypertension. *Health Psychology, 4,* 115–135.

Miller, S. M., Rodoletz, M., Schroeder, C. M., Mangan, C. E., & Sedlacek, T. V. (1996). Applications of the monitoring process model to coping with severe long-term medical threats. *Health Psychology, 15,* 216–225.

Moyer, A., & Salovey, P. (1996). Psychosocial sequelae of breast cancer and its treatment. *Annals of Behavioral Medicine, 18,* 110–125.

Payne, A., & Blanchard, E. B. (1995). A controlled comparison of cognitive therapy and self-help support groups in the treatment of irritable bowel syndrome. *Journal of Consulting and Clinical Psychology, 63,* 779–786.

Pennebaker, J. W., Kiecolt-Glaser, J. K., & Glaser, R. (1988). Disclosure of traumas and immune function: Health implications for psychotherapy. *Journal of Consulting and Clinical Psychology, 56,* 239–245.

Resick, P. A., & Schnicke, M. K. (1992). Cognitive processing therapy for sexual assault victims. *Journal of Consulting and Clinical Psychology, 60,* 748–756.

Rook, K. S. (1984). The negative side of social interaction: Impact on psychological well-being. *Journal of Personality and Social Psychology, 39,* 1135–1148.

Schiaffino, K. M., Shawaryn, M. A., & Blum, D. (1998). Examining the impact of illness representations on psychological adjustment to chronic illnesses. *Health Psychology, 17,* 262–268.

Schwarz, S. P., & Blanchard, E. B. (1991). Evaluation of a psychological treatment for inflammatory bowel disease. *Behaviour Research and Therapy, 29,* 167–177.

Shapiro, D., Hui, K. K., Oakley, M. E., Pasic, J., & Jamner, L. D. (1997). Reduction in drug requirements for hypertension by means of a cognitive-behavioral intervention. *American Journal of Hypertension, 10,* 9–17.

Smyth, J. M., Stone, A. A., Hurewitz, A., & Kaell, A. (1999). Effects of writing about stressful experiences on symptom reduction in patients with asthma or rheumatoid arthritis. *JAMA, 14,* 1304–1309.

Sobel, D. S. (1995). Rethinking medicine: Improving health outcomes with cost-effective psychosocial interventions. *Psychosomatic Medicine, 57,* 234–244.

Spiegel, D. (1994). Health caring: Psychosocial support for patients with cancer. *Cancer, 74,* 1453–1457.

Stanton, A. L., & Snider, P. R. (1993). Coping with a breast cancer diagnosis: A prospective study. *Health Psychology, 12,* 16–23.

Suls, J., & Fletcher, B. (1985). The relative efficacy of avoidant and nonavoidant coping strategies: A meta-analysis. *Health Psychology, 4,* 249–288.

Wells, K. B., Golding, J. M., & Burnam, M. A. (1988). Psychiatric disorder in a sample of the general population with and without chronic medical conditions. *American Journal of Psychiatry, 145,* 976–981.

Wells, K. B., Stewart, A., Hays, R. D., Burnam, A., Rogers, W., Daniels, M., Berry, S., Greenfield, S., & Ware, J. (1989). The functioning and well-being of depressed patients. *JAMA, 262,* 914–919.

Williams, D. A., & Thorn, B. E. (1989). An empirical assessment of pain beliefs. *Pain, 36,* 351–358.

CHAPTER 6

BREATHING AS A CLINICAL TOOL

Robert Fried

Breath is the horse and mind is the rider.
—Tibetan saying

We have long identified breathing with life: The Book of Genesis tells us, "And the Lord God formed man of the dust of the ground, and breathed into his nostrils the breath of life; and the man became a living being." Thus, in Western tradition all life begins with breath. It is also perceived to end that way: Common metaphors for dying are "He breathed his last" or "He expired."

In the tradition of India, for instance, the basic force of life, *prana,* is mediated by breathing-related meditation, and the ultimate interaction with that force is through "pranic breathing." In Chinese traditional medicine, *Qi,* pronounced "tschi," is the vital energy of life. One component, *natural air Qi,* is extracted from the air we breathe by the lungs. Both of these Eastern traditions have given a unique flavor to the modern study of the role of breathing in the physiology of behavior and its application in clinical therapies now actively being pursued in research and clinical treatment centers worldwide. Thus, it is altogether appropriate to begin by crediting these traditions with increasing our awareness of the role of breathing in behavior physiology and in the treatment of a wide range of medical and psychological disorders.

Yet, as important as breathing behavior is and as central as it seems to be to physical and mental well-being, it has somehow eluded attention from all but a relatively small number of behavioral scientists, most of whom, parenthetically, belong to the International Society for Advancement of Respiratory Psychophysiology (ISARP), an organization that does not even have a permanent home base.

Historically it was generally assumed that breathing is so fundamental to life processes that it basically takes care of itself. Yet, there is incontrovertible evidence that, despite its apparent automaticity, it is subject to the influences of many physiopathological and psychopathological processes—a fact about which, it seems, only scientists remain somehow skeptical.

Abnormalities in breathing patterns have long been sought as the cause of physiological and psychological problems with varying degrees of "hard" scientific evidence ensuing. I have detailed *The Psychology and Physiology of Breathing in Behavioral Medicine* (Fried & Grimaldi, 1993), so the purpose of this chapter is to more briefly acquaint health sciences professionals concerned with contributing to the reduction of medical disorders and treating stress-related, emotion-based, and psychophysiological disorders (previously called "psychosomatic") with:

1. The nature of normal breathing and detection of abnormal breathing patterns
2. The aim of breathing training
3. How to do breathing training in accordance with our best understanding of a good therapeutic outcome

NORMAL AND ABNORMAL BREATHING

Breathing differs much from other behaviors connected to the psychophysiology of illness, stress and anxiety: It is under both voluntary control and control of systemic pulmonary reflexes, chemoreceptor-mediated reflexes responding to blood-gas composition at different anatomical sites, and brain mechanisms. Although recent research now casts doubt on the supposition, breathing may also respond to modulation by the sympathetic and parasympathetic branches of the autonomic nervous system. But, remarkably, these regulatory processes are readily bypassed when breathing is voluntary.

Breathing affects ventilation (the movement of air in and out of the alveoli), oxygen (O_2) delivery to body tissues and elimination of carbon dioxide (CO_2) from the blood, and the maintenance of the body's acid-base balance at an optimum pH—7.4, slightly alkaline (Comroe, 1974). Of course, it also affects all other body functions including energy metabolism, heart function and blood circulation, and brain and cognitive function. In some organisms such as the dog, breathing also affects the control of body temperature. All of the breathing-related processes in the body interact in complex ways.

The Lungs

Blood is oxygenated from atmospheric air entering the alveoli in the lungs; there CO_2 that accumulated during the metabolic conversion of glucose to energy is removed. Figure 6.1 shows the airways (the trachea, bronchi, and bronchioles) that conduct atmospheric air into the right and left lobes of the lungs, terminating in the alveoli during inspiration, and back out of the lungs during expiration.

The trachea (windpipe) extends downward from the esophagus, dividing at the sternal angle into the right and left primary bronchi. It consists of stacked cartilaginous incomplete rings—like stacked *C*'s— and connective tissue that allow it to expand in the esophagus during swallowing. Striated muscle fibers "close" the cartilage rings. The walls of the trachea are smooth muscle. The inner wall forming the lumen is lined with ciliated epithelial cells.

The primary bronchi become the secondary (lobar bronchi), which, in turn, divide into the bronchioles in the lobes of the lungs—the whole thing forming the "bronchial tree" of the lungs. As the bronchiolar branching becomes more extensive, cartilage rings are gradually replaced by smooth muscle in the bronchioles.

In inspiration, O_2 in atmospheric air in the lungs diffuses into the blood stream circulating in capillaries surrounding the alveolar membrane because its pressure (concentration) in atmospheric air is greater than

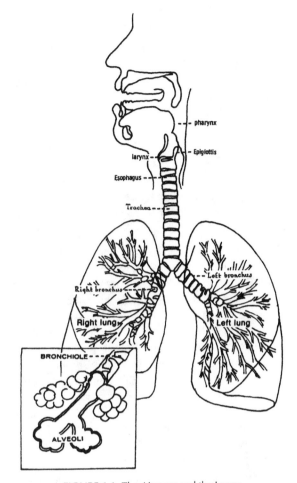

FIGURE 6.1. The Airways and the Lungs

Source: Fried & Grimaldi (1993), *The Psychology and Physiology of Breathing in Behavioral Medicine, Clinical Psychology and Psychiatry* (New York: Plenum Publishing).

in blood, in accordance with Henry's law: The quantity of a gas that will dissolve in a liquid is proportional to the partial pressure of the gas (P; see below) and its solubility coefficient (temperature held constant). Conversely, the partial pressure (concentration) of CO_2 is greater in blood and so it diffuses into the atmospheric air in the alveoli of the lungs.

Although some O_2 and CO_2 is carried dissolved in blood plasma, both are mostly bound to hemoglobin in the red blood cells. The hemoglobin is said to have an "affinity" for O_2, with which it combines to form oxihemoglobin (O_2Hb). That affinity varies with several critical variables:

1. Blood pH
2. O_2 concentration in blood
3. Concentration of organic phosphates (see Benesch & Benesch, 1976)
4. Concentration of nitric oxide (see Barnes, 1986; Barnes & Belvisi, 1993; Belvisi et al., 1992; Stamler et al., 1997)

Lung "Volumes" at Rest

Common Terms Describing Lung Volumes (Comroe, 1974; Fried, 1993; Tortora & Anagnostakos, 1984):

Tidal volume (Vt): Depth of breathing or volume of air that moves into the lungs in inspiration and out (*end-tidal,* or *ET*) in expiration. Normal Vt is about 500 milliliters (ml), of which about 350 ml reaches the alveoli due to the alveolar "dead air space." Breathing is commonly measured in Vt per minute, or *minute volume (Vmin):* Normal Vmin is estimated to be about 12 (normal respiration rate) *times* Vt (500 ml) *equals* 6,000 milliliters of air for men, and it is a little bit less in women.

Inspiratory reserve volume (IRV): The maximum amount of air that can be inspired from the ET expiratory position. The IRV is about 3,600 ml, or 3,100 ml more than Vt.

Expiratory reserve volume (ERV): The maximum amount of air that can be forcibly exhaled after normal inhale. ERV is about 1,200 ml.

Residual volume: Air remaining in the lungs after expulsion of expiratory reserve volume—1,200 ml.

Common Terms Describing Lung "Capacities" in Clinical Application

FEV$_1$ and FVC: When the client first inhales maximally, then exhales as forcefully as he or she can, the volume expired in the first second is called *1-second forced expiratory volume (FEV$_1$).* The total volume exhaled is the *forced vital capacity (FVC).*

Both FEV$_1$ and FVC are measured with a spirometer. The Vitalograph model 2100 spirometer is porta-ble, simple to use, and inexpensive.[1] The instrument comes with a booklet that provides expected values for client populations. I recommend it highly to any professional who appreciates the role of breathing in stress-related emotional and medical disorders. It is virtually impossible to determine whether observed breathing patterns fall within or exceed normal expected limits without a spirometer. A table detailing lung volumes and capacities can be found in Comroe, et al. (1962), *The Lung* 2nd ed. Year Book Medical Publishers, and the relationship between principal volumes and capacity is illustrated in Ruch & Fulton (1960), *Medical Physiology and Biophysics.* W. B. Saunders.

Breathing Frequency

In a healthy person at rest the respiratory frequency (breathing rate) is principally determined by the momentary activity level (metabolism) and by height, weight, and gender. One good way to determine that expected value for a given client is to consult a standard nomograph such as the one that can be found in Radford (1955), Ventilation standards for use in artificial respiration. *Journal of Applied Physiology, 7,* 451–450.

A nomograph is a multiscale figure that allows you to determine a third expected value by drawing a straight line through any two others. For instance, if you know the client's weight and respiratory frequency, you can predict expected tidal volume. Any deviation from the expected value is to be considered abnormal.

For example, a man weighing 150 lb who breathes at 25 breaths per minute (b/min) would be expected to have an end-tidal volume of 300 ml, well below normal value. Another example: An average man at rest, weighing 150 lb, would have an expected breathing rate of about 10 b/min and end-tidal volume (Vt) of about 550 ml of air. For an average woman weighing about 130 lb the corresponding breathing rate would be about 11 b/min and Vt would be about 450 ml.

---

1. Vitalograph Inc., 8347 Quivira Road, Lenexa, Kansas 66215; 800-255-6626.

Breathing Patterns

Common Terms Describing Breathing Patterns (adapted from Comroe, 1974):

Eupnea: Normal breathing, consisting of repeated rhythmic inspiratory and expiratory cycles without inspiratory or expiratory pause, and in which inspiration is active and expiration passive.

Hyperpnea: Increased breathing rate. May refer to increased tidal volume with or without increased frequency.

Tachypnea: Increased frequency of breathing.

Hyperventilation: Increased alveolar ventilation in relation to metabolic rate (i.e., decreases alveolar carbon dioxide concentration [PCO_2] to less than 4.8%, or 37 torr).

Hypoventilation: Decreased alveolar ventilation in relation to metabolic rate (i.e., permits alveolar carbon dioxide concentration to rise above 43 torr [5.6%]).

Apnea: Cessation of respiration in the resting expiratory position.

Apneusis: Cessation of respiration in the inspiratory position.

Apneustic breathing: Apneusis interrupted periodically by expiration; may be rhythmic.

Gasping: Spasmodic inspiratory effort, usually maximal, brief, and terminating abruptly; may be rhythmic or irregular.

Cheyne-Stokes respiration: Cycles of gradually increasing tidal volume followed by gradually decreasing tidal volume.

Biot's respiration: Irregular respiration with pauses; sequences of uniformly deep gasps, apnea, then deep gasps.

Clinicians have long hoped to find breathing patterns that reliably distinguish between psychopathological states, just as many breathing patterns may distinguish between organic and metabolic diseases. Their efforts have been valiant, but they have not met with unqualified success. However, evidence suggests that breathing patterns have a certain individual consistency (Shea et al., 1987), although they do not really constitute an individual signature as fingerprints do.

Studies of respiratory patterns were conventionally made with a pneumograph, an air-filled tubular structure made to encircle the thorax, connected to an air pressure recording device. Expansion and contraction of the chest change the air pressure in the tube and that change is recorded as a change in breathing. A spirometer, on the other hand, measures air flow in and out of the lungs, usually through the mouth or nose. The pressure on the chest exerted by the pneumograph confounded compliance of the lungs. *Compliance* is the ease with which the lungs and the chest wall can expand.

The pneumograph is cumbersome and offers considerable mechanical resistance to thoracic expansion and excursion; consequently various other devices collectively called "plethysmograph" are also in use. Some of these are devices with electrodes placed on the arms or on the chest to pick up changes in the electrical impedance to a small electrical current coursing through the chest as it expands and contracts. Chest impedance, a measure of the resistance to the small ac current passing through the chest between the electrodes, changes predictably with breathing and can be calibrated to provide volume changes. In fact, the amplified change in the baseline of the conventional electrocardiogram (ECG), or even the electromyograph (EMG), can be used that way because it reflects impedance changes.

Figure 6.2 shows chest impedance change in a 60-second recording made during deep diaphragmatic breathing training. Breathing rate is about 3 b/min with equal inhale and exhale intervals. Heart rate varies with breathing in the well-known pulse rhythm called RSA (see Figure 6.2), and the EMG baseline with unfiltered pulse signal also varies with breathing, as thoracic excursion reflects inhaled volume change.

Alveolar and Blood Gas Composition

In most individuals free of organic disease, stress-related disorders, or emotional or psychiatric illness the mode of breathing may actually make very little difference. Individuals with more or less "normal"

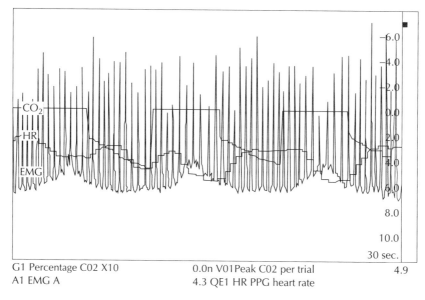

FIGURE 6.2. Change in EMG Baseline with Chest Impedance Change

Source: Fried & Grimaldi (1993), *The Psychology and Physiology of Breathing in Behavioral Medicine, Clinical Psychology and Psychiatry* (New York: Plenum Publishing).

breathing may show considerable between-subject variation in breathing mode, pattern, and frequency. Those with abnormal breathing may likewise show considerable variation in pattern and frequency. But, in the latter case, there will also be a significant departure from the expected values that index normal metabolism and healthy functioning.

Breathing subserves two different basic but interrelated physiological functions: First, it ventilates the body, and second, it maintains the acid-base homeostasis.

The body is intolerant of any departure from the acid-base balance, which maintains most, though not all, body tissue at a pH of 7.4—somewhat alkaline. While the kidneys are commonly thought responsible for that function, they do only about 15% of the job; breathing accounts for 85% by eliminating bicarbonate.

A note about the concept of partial pressure (Dalton's law): Each gas in a mixture of gases exerts its own pressure. The pressure of a gas in a mixture of gases is called the partial pressure (P). The total pressure of a mixture of gases is the sum of the partial pressures of its components.

A note on pressure nomenclature: Air pressure is ordinarily expressed in lb per square inch. In physiol-

ogy, air pressure is commonly expressed in units called torr (named after Toricelli). We learn early that air pressure varies with elevation above sea level.

Air is composed of different gases including oxygen (21%), carbon dioxide (0.03%), and the most plentiful, nitrogen (78.6%). In addition, air contains water vapor and other gases and pollutants. Each component exerts its proportional share of the total air pressure. Thus, the portion of the total pressure that is exerted by any one component is called the partial pressure and is represented by the symbol P.

The partial pressure of gases in atmospheric air is of tangential concern to physiologists, but not so the partial pressure of carbon dioxide in alveolar air (PCO_2), and the partial pressure of oxygen (PaO_2) and of carbon dioxide ($PaCO_2$) bound to hemoglobin in arterial blood.

Air exhaled from the lungs, usually considered "alveolar air" for the sake of simplicity, is different in gas composition from atmospheric air. It consists of:

.14% O_2
.5% CO_2
.6% water vapor
.69% N_2 and other gases and pollutants

Most physiology textbooks refer to the partial pressure of gases in units of torr, and psychophysiologists usually refer to it in percent, so there is bound to be a certain element of confusion. Psychophysiologists refer to percent alveolar CO_2, or end-tidal CO_2, as PCO_2 or $PETCO_2$.

To convert atmospheric pressure to the conventional barometric "inches":

1. 1 millimeter = 0.3937 in.
2. Atmospheric pressure at sea level is 760 mm Hg (or 760 torr).
3. $760 \times 0.03937 = 29.92$ in.

Normal alveolar PCO_2 is 38.0 torr; $PETCO_2$ is $38 \div 730 = 0.05$, or 5%.

There is usually a close correlation between alveolar CO_2 (PCO_2) and arterial blood CO_2 content, or saturation ($PaCO_2$). The concentration, or partial pressure, of alveolar CO_2 is commonly measured with an infrared capnometer. I recommend the unit distributed by Applied Physiology Instruments (API).[2] API also distributes an oximeter that can be used to measure $PaCO_2$. Both units are inexpensive, portable, and user-friendly.

Oxygenation

Each 100 ml of oxygenated blood holds about 20 ml of O_2. Ninety-seven percent of it is held by hemoglobin (Hb). Saturation is the volume, or the percentage, of Hb combined with O_2 to form oxyhemoglobin (O_2Hb), the form in which it is transported in the red blood cells, in the blood stream. The principal factor that determines saturation is the amount of O_2 available. But the principal factor that determines its release from Hb is pH (see section on the Bohr effect, below).

Two other substances are crucial in determining oxyhemoglobin saturation and its transport to body tissues. One of these is the gas nitric oxide, and the other is a product of glucose metabolism, 2,3-diphosphoglycerate (DPG), which competes with O_2 for binding to Hb. The concentration of DPG also varies with pH.

Respiratory Control of the Acid-Base Balance

Physiologists usually refer to CO_2 as the variable controlling the body acid-base balance, but, actually, it is the hydrogen ion (H^+): When CO_2 dissolves in blood, it combines with water to form carbonic acid (H_2CO_3). The enzyme carbonic anhydrase causes carbonic acid to break down rapidly to form H^+ and bicarbonate (HCO_3^-). Obviously any increase in CO_2 will cause an increase in H^+. Although there are CO_2 chemoreceptors throughout the body, it is hydrogen ions that mainly control breathing rate.

The acid-base balance, thus, depends on the retention or elimination of hydrogen ions, and it is crucial to all metabolic processes. The body is far less tolerant of the alkalosis that results from excess CO_2 loss (hypocarbia) than of the hypoxia that results from a comparable and even greater reduction in oxygen.

A pH of 7.0 is neutral, neither acid nor alkaline (base). Values of pH greater than 7.0 indicate alkaline, and values of pH below 7.0 indicate acid. When arterial blood pH rises from the normal value of 7.38: breathing frequency rises, Vmin rises, and $PaCO_2$ declines (Comroe, 1974). This is a typical "hyperventilation" (HV) pattern. In physiology the principle of homeostasis dictates that you cannot "lose" components: If one thing goes up, another must be going down. An otherwise healthy client cannot reasonably be thought to maintain chronic rapid breathing and HV for "psychological" reasons. Look for acidosis.

Hyperventilation may, in the extreme case, be a life-saving compensatory mechanism intended to enlist the lungs in reducing the acid load of the body by eliminating hydrogen ions. The medical conditions that cause clinical acidosis include diabetes; heart disease and kidney failure; and eating disorders such as fasting, anorexia, and bulimia, which can produce ketoacidosis. Some prescription and over-the-counter drugs also cause acidosis—aspirin is prominent among them. Slowing rapid breathing could be hazardous to the client.

Chronic abnormal breathing is *invariably* driven by abnormal metabolism. It is thus essential to pay careful attention to blood gas indices suggesting compensation for metabolic acidosis. There is no evidence supporting a "psychogenic" basis to chronic HV. Studies in which HV is putatively assigned a

---

2. Applied Physiology Instruments, 9200 Hemlock Ave., Bainbridge Island, WA, 98110. Phone: 296-855-9770, e-mail: DanDyno@aol.com.

"functional" origin invariably rely on fanciful psychodynamic rather than on organic/metabolic sources and explanations.

Oxygen is a dangerous substance. It oxidizes—when this process rises to a certain level, we call it fire. Thus, the acid-base homeostasis is a built-in safeguard to limit excess physiological oxygen. That affinity of hemoglobin for oxygen helps to determine arterial blood O_2 saturation, and it is kept in check by the pH of blood.

A decrease in alveolar CO_2, and consequently in $PETCO_2$, causes a proportional increase in alkalinity and, in the long run, alkalosis. Alkalinity raises the affinity of hemoglobin for oxygen, while acidosis lowers it. The more alkaline the hemoglobin, the more it holds onto oxygen, while less alkaline hemoglobin gives it up more readily. In healthy individuals low blood pH is usually the result of lactic acid resulting from muscle activity.

The Bohr Effect

In an acid environment, Hb more readily dissociates, or releases, O_2. Figure 6.3 illustrates this Bohr effect.

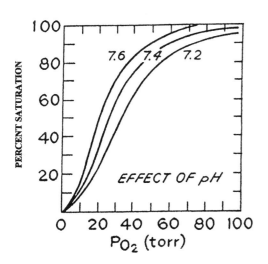

**Bohr effect: Oxygen saturation for
different values of pH**

FIGURE 6.3. The Bohr Effect: O_2Hb Dissociation
at Constant Temperature and Different pH Levels

Source: Fried & Grimaldi (1993), *The Psychology and Physiology of Breathing in Behavioral Medicine, Clinical Psychology and Psychiatry* (New York: Plenum Publishing).

Hemoglobin affinity rises with alkalinity and decreases with acidity. Note that oxygen saturation drops from 50% to 45% as pH rises from 7.38 (normal) to 7.6 (alkalosis).

Paradigm Shift in Understanding of Respiratory Physiology

In 1980 Robert F. Furchgott (co-winner of the *1996 Lasker Award in Basic Medical Research*) and John V. Zawadzki of Downstate Medical Center, Brooklyn, New York, published their finding in *Nature* that the paradoxical vasoconstriction of strips of rabbit artery stimulated with acetylcholine (Ach) was attributable to often occurring but inadvertent damage done to the endothelium lining in laboratory preparations. After further study, they concluded that Ach can only induce vessel relaxation if the endothelium is intact and if acetylcholine can stimulate it to release an unidentified endothelium-dependent relaxing factor dubbed EDRF. In 1988 Moncada, Palmer, and Higgs determined that EDRF is the gas nitric oxide (see also Moncada & Higgs, 1990; Moncada, Palmer, & Higgs, 1991).

Subsequently the sequence of neurotransmitters involved in the arterial blood vessel relaxation pathway was delineated by Murad (1996), co-winner with Furchgott of the *Lasker Award*). Ach signals the cells of the endothelium to synthesize NO from the amino acid L-arginine with the constitutive isoform of the enzyme, nitric oxide synthase (NOS). NO then signals the smooth muscle cells to release cyclic guanosine monophosphate (cGMP). The cGMP is a powerful vasodilator that acts as a neurotransmitter whose activity is terminated by the take-up enzyme type-5 phosphodiesterase.

Once the role of NO in the process of smooth muscle relaxation was delineated, other physiological functions of NO were quickly discovered. These are detailed in Fried and Merrell (1999) and in Moncada and Higgs (1990). But it was not long after the seminal work of Furgott and of Moncada that NO's implications in breathing were uncovered.

The first significant clue was published in 1986, when Barnes reported that "in addition to classical cholinergic and adrenergic neural mechanisms, a third division of autonomic control has been recognized in human airways. Non-adrenergic inhibitory nerves are the dominant inhibitory neural pathway in human airway smooth muscle." While this early publication correctly identified the existence of a nonadrenergic, noncholinergic (NANC) function in breathing, it incorrectly attributed it to a third ANS pathway. Belvisi et al. (1992) subsequently reported that there is a prominent nonadrenergic neural bronchodilator mechanism mediated entirely by nitric oxide. Subsequently Stamler and others reported that NO regulates not only systemic but also pulmonary vascular resistance in healthy humans (Cooper et al., 1996; Stamler et al., 1994).

That NO, and not an NANC neural mechanism, regulates norm-oxic pulmonary vascular tone constitutes a paradigm shift in our understanding of airways and associated vascular control in respiratory physiology. It goes far toward explaining the unreliability of present theories of airways and associated vascular control, and the often hit-or-miss nature of the treatment method used to correct certain breathing disorders.

These new findings about the role of NO in respiratory function have led to recognition of a number of clues about certain forms of pathophysiology: In healthy adult "controls," most of the NO in exhaled air apparently comes from the nasal airways with relatively little of it coming from the lower airways and from the mouth. But in asthmatics exhaled NO was two- to threefold greater than in controls. This increase in NO was attributed to production of NO in the lower airways by an inflammatory process in which macrophages synthesize large amounts of NO with the inducible isoform of nitric oxide synthase (iNOS). Kharitonov (Kharitonov et al., 1994) has suggested that high exhaled NO production in asthmatic patients reflects increased iNOS activity, because it is known that steroids inhibit iNOS.

Other applications such as NO inhalation therapy have been reported: in treatment of "blue baby syndrome" and in reducing adult respiratory distress syndrome (ARDS) (Bone, 1993; Rossaint et al., 1993) and pulmonary hypertension (Frostrell et al., 1991; Goldman, Rees, & Macrae, 1995; Mehta et al., 1995; Pepke-Zaba et al., 1991).

It is not yet clear where this research will finally lead, but it represents a new approach to our understanding of fundamental respiratory airways control mechanisms and a new approach to the treatment of some specific disorders such as asthma and ARDS. It suggests, however, that development of clinically useful instrumentation to detect exhaled NO levels (where 30 ppb is normal in healthy adults) may be a logical next step in implementing any treatment, because NO production may be an essential outcome variable.

Breathing Assessment

Mental health practitioners who plan to teach relaxation to a client suffering a medical disorder may find it helpful, indeed essential in some cases, to obtain a breathing profile. Such an assessment should include at least the parameters of breathing frequency, breathing mode, (alveolar) $PETCO_2$, and (arterial) PaO_2. Such a profile and the instrumentation required to obtain it are detailed in a number of my previous publications (Fried, 1993), but, in general, with the client recumbent in a recliner:

- Breathing frequency and PCO_2 are both obtained, using a capnometer collecting end-tidal air with a small nasal catheter.
- Breathing mode: Chest versus abdominal mode is observed visually. Pneumograph or plethysmograph sensors surrounding the chest are undesirable because they impede natural breathing motion.
- $PaCO_2$ is measured with a finger sensor–type oximeter.
- A cardiotachometer analyzes pulse time distribution.

I have found the I-330 physiological monitoring units made by J & J Instruments very helpful for this profiling. The units and their software interface readily with a conventional PC. The units are rugged and reliable and their cost is relatively modest. Visual analog traces of these parameters can be displayed for the patient on a video monitor.

Figure 6.4 illustrates a breathing profile of a healthy middle-age woman during deep diaphragmatic breathing training. This figure shows a 1-minute "captured" screen. The $PETCO_2$ tracing is upside down for the convenience of the client: It is easier to follow breathing when the trace rises with inhale and drops with exhale. An SaO_2 tracing is superimposed on $PETCO_2$. Thoracic and abdominal plethysmograph tracings of

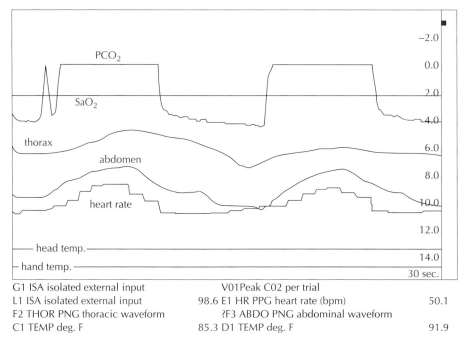

FIGURE 6.4. Psychophysiological Breathing Profile

Source: Fried & Grimaldi (1993), *The Psychology and Physiology of Breathing in Behavioral Medicine, Clinical Psychology and Psychiatry* (New York: Plenum Publishing).

chest and abdomen excursion show that one cannot invariably gauge breathing from these commonly used measures, as indicated by the deep inhale/exhale reversal seen at the beginning of the tracing. A pulse tachometer tracing displays heart rate. Hand and head-apex temperature are detected with a finger-contact and a scalp-contact thermistor.

Note that in this subject, breathing is regular (except the brief reversal at the front of the tracing) at about 4 b/min to 5 b/min; PETCO$_2$ is low, at about 4.5%; and both chest and abdomen move more or less at the same time, although they correspond to chest and abdomen excursions except in reversals—abdominal and chest excursion tracings show that breathing is not effortless and that chest motion is still dominant even though breathing outwardly appears to be "deep."

Thermal traces of hand temperature are often helpful indices because low PaCO$_2$ is associated with vasoconstriction. Thus, as PETCO$_2$ rises, PaCO$_2$ should follow, and increase in hand temperature is a good indication that this is happening.

A thermistor on the scalp apex is used to confirm that training does not inadvertently result in idiosyncratic circulatory changes: When breathing training improves blood gas composition, both hand and scalp temperature should rise. However, the hand temperature should rise more than the scalp temperature, because hand temperature is commonly lower than head temperature. When breathing training is successful, hand and head temperature will come to within about 1 degree F, around 92° to 94°F.

BREATHING TRAINING

The need for breathing training may be indicated by the presence of certain signs or symptoms in addition to medical disorders:

- Chronic shortness of breath and sighing respiration
- Asthmatic breathing
- Chronic tiredness
- Sleeplessness
- Headache

- Migraine
- Anxiety
- Inability to concentrate
- Impaired memory
- Depression
- Irritability
- Muscle tension and pain
- Unexplained pain

The following guidelines for the goal of breathing training in a resting or recumbent position may prove helpful:

Mode: "Easy," deep, predominantly abdominal, nasal breathing
Rhythm: Equal inhale and exhale intervals
PETCO$_2$: Around 5.0% for men and 4.5% for women (not less than 4.3% or more than 5.3% for either men or women)
SaO$_2$: Between 95% and 98% for both men and women
Pulse pattern: RSA

Regarding breathing frequency, it is unwise to "teach to a rate" because the behavior that gives rise to rate may lead to improper client compliance such as breath holding to please the trainer or to avoid perceived failure. If the client is encouraged to breathe through the nose and slowly fill the lungs as the diaphragm contracts (as evidenced by outward abdominal excursion) and then to slowly exhale (pulling in the abdomen at the end of exhale), the rate will automatically slow down by itself. With training, it will drop to between three and five breaths per minute. PETCO$_2$ may not normalize at first, and the breathing behavior may seem unnatural to the client, but with short periods of slow and easy practice over time the pieces will fall into place.

General Training Procedures

In most instances, training proceeds by steps:

1. *Relaxation training:* A modified systematic muscle relaxation program can be taught first, and the breathing is then integrated into it.
2. *Breathing training:* The client is taught deep diaphragmatic breathing with physiological moni-

toring, as well as biofeedback, when appropriate, from session to session until he or she can sustain about 10 consecutive deep diaphragmatic breaths with comfort and normal PETCO$_2$ (normocapnia) (Fried, 1990a,b, 1994; Fried & Grimaldi, 1993).
3. *Advanced maneuvers:* Respiration is combined with imagery.

While the "trainer" watches the client and the instruments:

First test of "receptivity": The client is asked to sit up and lean back in the recliner, head resting comfortably against the back of the recliner. Then he or she is asked to close the eyes. If a slight decrease in breathing rate occurs now, lasting perhaps one or two breaths, sometimes accompanied by a slight increase in finger temperature, it strongly predicts that the client will have little difficulty learning deep diaphragmatic breathing.
Second test of "receptivity": The client is told, "Now when you inhale, hold your breath and count to two. As you exhale, hold it and count to two."

If the client cannot do this simple task, it may be that there are problems with the mechanics of breathing, perhaps an inability to control respiratory muscles. In asthma clients especially, there may be what appears to be a reluctance to exhale. This restriction of end-tidal volume impairs inspiration because there is still more air left in the lungs than one would normally expect. I have noted in many cases that PCO$_2$ is near normal in asthma clients and often even elevated because this increase in the volume of dead air space favors CO$_2$ retention. Such a mechanism has some adaptive value because it tends to keep the oxygen dissociation curve (see previous discussion of the Bohr effect) near normal. However, if there is even a slight elevation in PCO$_2$, there will also be an increase in respiratory drive causing diaphragmatic fatigue.

Breathing Training with Physiological Monitoring

Physiological (bio-) feedback is usually an open loop system, in which feedback actually provides "knowledge of results" in the traditional style of Thorndike's "law of effects" for performance correction. We recognize this empirically when, in thermal biofeedback, we ascribe initial drop in hand temperature to performance anxiety.

A modified breathing profile is obtained before training begins, and a decision is made about which modalities will be monitored. The modified profile in part **a** of Figure 6.5 is the initial psychophysiological breathing profile (30-second screen duration) of a professional woman in her early 40s who sought help for tension, anxiety, and headaches. Breathing rate is approximately 18 b/min; $PETCO_2$ is 4.6% (as read directly from the capnometer) (33 torr); SaO_2 is 97.9%; pulse rate is about 68; hand temperature is 79.5°F; and scalp apex temperature is 92.8°F (room temperature is 76°F). Breathing rate is elevated with low CO_2 (hypocapnia). Peripheral vasoconstriction is likely since her hands are cold, but because she is a runner, her pulse rate is relatively low.

Breathing Training—Day 1

The client is coupled to the physiological interface by the electrodes, sensors, and cables, and the general training procedure is explained in detail. The traces on the video monitor are explained and the client is then instructed as follows:

> Please put this book flat on your abdomen, spine up, and push it out as far as you can. That's good. Now relax. Thank you. Did you feel any pain or discomfort? No. Good.

The degree of outward excursion is noted, the screen is "frozen," and the monitor trace changes are discussed.

A note of caution to the client (and therapist):

> Most people are unused to deep abdominal/diaphragmatic excursion. It may be strenuous. If training proceeds too quickly, you may experience painful diaphragmatic cramps. Should such cramps occur, stop the exercise immediately. If an exercise causes you pain or discomfort, stop it immediately, and bring it to my attention.

> Now you will be doing an abdominal breathing training exercise that has been very helpful in getting people to do more deep, slow abdominal breathing and relax. It helps reduce muscle tension, pulse rate, and blood pressure and helps people get a general sense of alert well-being, relaxation, and comfort.

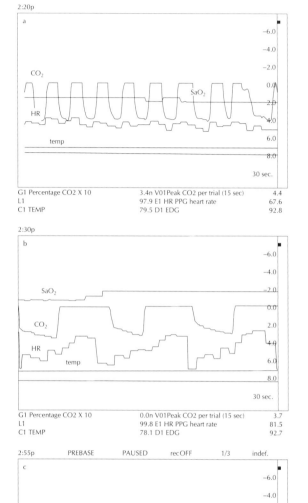

FIGURE 6.5. Breathing Profile

Source: Fried & Grimaldi (1993), *The Psychology and Physiology of Breathing in Behavioral Medicine, Clinical Psychology and Psychiatry* (New York: Plenum Publishing).

Here is what happens during diaphragmatic breathing, when you breathe with your abdomen. Your diaphragm, which separates your lungs and heart from your stomach and digestive system, contracts, and in so doing, it alters its shape from a dome, vaulted upward, to a more or less flat sheet.

When this occurs, two things happen simultaneously: First, the space created in the chest cavity permits the lungs to expand and fill with air. Second, it appears to you that your abdomen is pushed outward. Then, as you exhale, the diaphragm, no longer directed to contract, relaxes and resumes its upward vaulted shape. Because of its elasticity, the air is pushed out of your lungs and your abdomen returns to its original shape.

Because you haven't done anything like this before, I have divided the training procedures over several sessions so that your muscles will have time to adjust and become toned for this task.

It is generally a good idea to do deep abdominal breathing exercises in short segments of only three or four breaths, without straining the diaphragm, and with repeated emphasis on comfort.

This exercise is really aerobic. You are trying to increase oxygenation of the body by increasing the efficiency of breathing. You do not need to plunge, like a health freak, into pain as a measure of success. If you experience pain and discomfort, you are overdoing it.

Do you feel dizzy? If not, good. If you feel dizzy, you are overbreathing—hyperventilating. You are putting too much effort into it, too early in the game. Make the motions a little more subtle: Not so far out on inhale, and not so far in on exhale. If you feel dizzy, stop and rest a little while until it passes, which it usually does quickly. Close your mouth. Breathe in and out only through your nose. Breathing through your mouth tends to promote hyperventilation. Look at your hands.

As you inhale, keep your chest down. Let the hand on your abdomen rise as the air fills your abdomen.

Now let's look at the screen and see how you're doing.

If there is difficulty in client compliance, try:

Place this book on your lap [*spine up, so that it won't slide off*]. Now, without coordinating it with your breath at all, push the book out as far as you can with your abdomen.

When you inhale, your abdomen should move out about as far as it did when you pushed the book. If it did not move out much, don't worry; you may be tense, that's to be expected. It will improve with practice.

On exhale:

Slowly—but never so slowly that it creates discomfort—pull your abdomen back as far as it will go, but do not let it raise your chest. Good. Now don't stop. Don't pause; repeat the inhale and exhale procedure once more. Rest for a moment.

Now let's look at the screen and see how you are doing.

Now, once again: Inhale . . . fill up. And, exhale . . . pull all the way back.

Repeat this procedure three times, then stop.

Let's see how you are doing. Here is what's happened to your breathing and to your oxygen and carbon dioxide levels. . . . Your hand and head temperature now are. . . . That's all for today.

Doing much more than this may be counterproductive, possibly causing cramps or dizziness. There may be a slight tendency to hyperventilate at first. Many of my clients do. It will pass and, with practice, it will disappear.

Breathing Training—Day 2

The client is prepared the same way for the exercise as on Day 1:

Please sit back in your chair. Place your hands on your knees for a moment. Let yourself relax. Close your mouth.

Place your hands on your chest and abdomen as you did yesterday. Once you get the knack, you can do it without your hands.

Now, looking at your hands, inhale, holding down your chest and letting your abdomen fill up. Then exhale slowly, and pull your abdomen all the way back.

Now let's look at the traces on the monitor.

Then the procedure is repeated several times and the performance explained and discussed.

That's enough for today.

> Did you find it to be any easier? Did your abdomen move further out when you inhaled? Did the hand on your chest remain more or less motionless? Can you pull your abdomen a little further in?

I recommend only very short exercise sessions the first few days. Diaphragm and abdominal muscles need time to tone up.

Breathing Training—Day 3

> Let's see you do the exercise without your hands. Prepare yourself in your chair, as you did yesterday. Try it.

After three consecutive deep breaths, performance is explained and discussed.

> Does your chest remain more still as you inhale, and is your abdomen moving outward? If it is, good. If not, go back to using your hands. But, if you can, proceed breathing in and out four times in a row— close your eyes.
>   If you still need to use your hands, then proceed, eyes closed, and imagine what your hands are doing. Good.
>   That's it for today.

I usually make it a practice to review the pre- and posttraining profile and to review signs and symptom frequency and severity after a session. As soon as the client can sustain deep diaphragmatic breathing for at least 10 to 15 consecutive breaths without hypocapnia, the breathing exercise can be integrated with a modified form of muscle relaxation, imagery, and music. (See also *The Breath Connection,* Fried, 1990c.)

There is the possibility of diaphragmatic fatigue. Figures 6.5 **b** and 6.5 **c** show consecutive screens during the training procedure. Figure 6.5 **b** shows a good breathing configuration at about 6 b/min, and pulse rate is prominently synchronized with breathing. Figure 6.5 **c** shows 2 b/min to 3 b/min and trace reversal due to fatigue at the beginning of the last inspiration in the capnogram. Note: Sometimes trace reversal indicates swallowing, but it is more commonly an indication of fatigue and calls for terminating the training trial. It is counterproductive to push the client to continue the exercise when there is evidence of diaphragm muscle fatigue. What may be true in building muscle bulk does not hold for breathing training: Too little is almost always better than too much.

A note on pulse/breath synchronization: For an individual at rest, doing deep diaphragmatic breathing, a particular pulse distribution pattern will often appear: Heart rate will rise with inspiration and fall with expiration, but the mean pulse rate will change little. This breath-synchronized rising and falling heart rate is called respiratory sinus arrhythmia (RSA). It is not an indication of pathology as the term *arrhythmia* suggests—on the contrary; RSA is an indication of the restoration of vagal tone by heart/lung reflexive synchrony. The term *arrhythmia* dates back to the time when physiologists thought that consecutive pulse interbeat time intervals should be equal in a person at rest. The RSA pattern is readily observed in Figure 6.5 **b**. Note the HR trace: Pulse rises with inspiration and declines with expiration. The HR and PCO_2 traces are a little out of phase because the HR trace is "real time." But there is a slight delay—about $\frac{1}{2}$ to $\frac{3}{4}$ sec—due to end-tidal transit time through the catheter measuring about 30 in the capnometer.

The physiological traces on the monitor are the best means for making sure that you, the practitioner, are in control of what your client is learning. I have often criticized studies in which the instructions to the client are wrong, vague, or absent.

The trainer/therapist must take responsibility for training and guiding the client so that the resultant behavior is the best that all of his or her knowledge plus experience and technology can produce. Think about what is required to produce the anatomical mechanics of deep diaphragmatic breathing behavior: It is you who are teaching it to that client.

The computer displays traces representing breathing, PCO_2, SaO_2, and so on. You should watch it carefully and your client as well, and you can stop the screen and then discuss the traces and the data with the client, after short training segments of a few consecutive breaths, allowing a brief rest period.

When the client improves, training segments may be lengthened. Occasionally the client may have difficulty with abdominal breathing. Instructions then include:

> As you inhale, fill up your abdomen as much as you can. That's it. Good, keep going.
>   You've got lots of room in there. Keep going. Keep filling. Good.
>   Now see how the trace has changed?

The procedure described here has been published elsewhere (Fried, 1999). It is adapted for the treatment of hyperventilation in a variety of clinical subpopulations and is an integral program for devising a strategy of breathing training with physiological monitoring (biofeedback).

Occasionally the client may show an initial inability to contract the diaphragm without also raising the chest in breathing. If this is the case, it is possible also to monitor the activity of the muscles in the neck region above the scalenes. EMG electrodes can be attached over the trapezius muscles, right and left, where these are met by the neck. Figure 6.6 shows such an arrangement. It shows clearly that the client is lifting the chest with each breath. One goal of breathing training is to eliminate such chest lifting in deep diaphragmatic (abdominal) breathing.

Guided Imagery and Physiological Monitoring

Meditation (especially transcendental meditation [TM]), yoga, modified versions of yoga, and the relaxation response (Benson, Beary, & Carol, 1974) tend to promote a relaxed hypometabolic state with many of the components that seem desirable to counter stress, tension, and anxiety. But for most people, they do not provide it quickly enough. Many clients would benefit from such exercises but become discouraged or impatient. The more rapid and profound the change, the more the client will be motivated to practice a training procedure.

The most effective of the yoga-derived techniques, in achieving diaphragmatic breathing, is probably TM. But clients are not equally adept at it, and there is no immediate knowledge of results—an absolutely essential component of self-regulation strategies.

A review of the available biofeedback techniques by Glueck and Stroebel (1975) recommended the "mantra-type passive meditation" of TM. Many of the previous findings on breathing alterations in TM were also confirmed by Wolkove et al. (1984), whose observations suggested an alteration in wakefulness, more subtle than sleep or the unconscious state, thought to be able to significantly affect chemical and neural regulation of breathing.

In view of such findings, I decided to teach my clients to induce a wakeful relaxed state in which

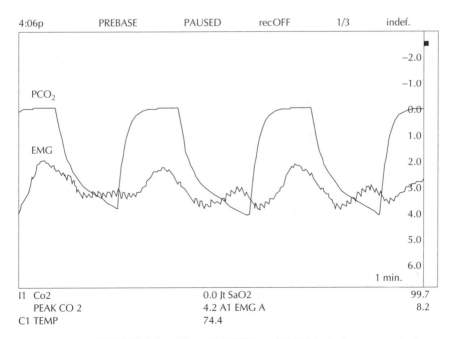

FIGURE 6.6. Breathing with $PETCO_2$ and EMG Monitoring

Source: Fried & Grimaldi (1993), *The Psychology and Physiology of Breathing in Behavioral Medicine, Clinical Psychology and Psychiatry* (New York: Plenum Publishing).

breathing is in synchrony with a self-discovered "natural physiological rhythm," using biofeedback, not to self-monitor but as an adjunct to fine-tune the induction of this state. That is, I monitor the effect of the induction and adjust the instructions to clients in accordance with the outcome of their efforts to engage in a hypo-aroused behavior.

In order to convince myself that I was on the right track, I used a frequency spectrum analyzer to monitor the EEG on-line and "dumped" the momentary power-spectral composition of the EEG onto a hard copy. (Conventional electrode placement is described in Fried, 1993.)

Thus, during the breathing maneuvers both the client and I can simultaneously watch breathing pattern and PETCO$_2$, as well as the composition of the "brain waves" changing with each phase of inhale and exhale.

A conventional average normal frequency distribution of the EEG in the delta (dc to 3 Hz), theta (4 to 7 Hz), alpha (8 Hz to 14 Hz), and beta bands can be found in Kooi (1971). Normally, there is an elevation in activity in alpha (8 Hz to 9 Hz).

Figure 6.7 shows the average frequency distribution in a client before and during breathing training: Before training, there is increased activity in theta, around 6 Hz, while during breathing training, theta activity decreases while alpha activity rises.

Elevated EEG theta activity is commonly associated with tension, anxiety, mental unrest, and even with seizures (Fried, Fox, & Carlton, 1990). On the other hand, alpha activity is associated with calm and relaxation. Breathing training is said to raise alpha activity level and was a prominent feature in early physiological studies of yogic exercises.

Inducing a response inhibiting sympathetic ANS arousal by the induction of hypoarousal requires the client to acquire both a different mind-set and a change in muscle tension pattern. This is accomplished by instructions to imagine the following:

Do you like the beach? Good.

I will give you instructions to imagine that you are on your favorite beach. Are you comfortable? Good. Please close your eyes.

During the time that you are imagining the scene that I will suggest to you, I will be watching these instruments, and I will be giving you information about what they tell me that you are doing and what is happening to you. Periodically I will ask you to

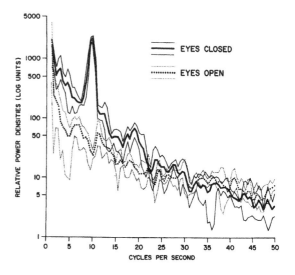

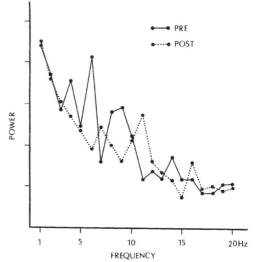

FIGURE 6.7. Pre– and Post–Breathing Training EEG in Four Migraine Sufferers

Source: Fried & Grimaldi (1993), *The Psychology and Physiology of Breathing in Behavioral Medicine, Clinical Psychology and Psychiatry* (New York: Plenum Publishing).

open your eyes and to look at these instruments also so that you can see for yourself how you are doing.

OK? Let's begin.

If there is evidence of exceptional tension, I instruct the client in a modified form of Jacobsonian relaxation (e.g., alternately squeezing or contracting and relaxing the brow, nose, and cheeks; shrugging the head into the shoulders; squeezing and relaxing the shoulders, upper arms, fists, chest muscles, stomach, and thighs; and stretching the calves). Then, I proceed:

> Now, please imagine that you are on your favorite beach. Look around you. You are standing on the beach. There are a few people about. You can just make out some people out of the corner of your eyes, but you can't see them clearly and you can't hear them talk.
> The sun is shining. It is midmorning. It is warm but not hot. Feel the sun warming your shoulders and your arms. Let the warmth flow right into your body. Feel the relaxation of being on this pleasant warm beach, and let it flow right through your body. Good.
> Now then, look at the ocean before you. Feel the sun? See the beach? Look at the ocean again: It is calm. Look at the surf now: It is gently coming up on the beach and receding. See it gently coming up on the beach? And receding? Nod your head if the answer is "yes." Good.
> When the surf comes up on the beach next, take a breath and let it out slowly as the surf is receding from the beach. Good.
> You are relaxed, alert, awake.

The next action is coordinated with the $PETCO_2$ trace on the video monitor. As the trace indicates that inspiration is beginning, I say:

> Now, the surf is coming up on the beach.

And as expiration begins:

> Now the surf is receding from the beach.

Thus, the motion of the surf is synchronous with the inspiration and expiration phases of breathing and feedback is given during the first few breaths:

> That's good. Very good. Here is the surf coming in now. Good. And now, going out. Good.

When the client is breathing slowly, as almost invariably happens, about 3 b/min to 5 b/min or less, $PETCO_2$ may rise somewhat in those in whom it was previously depressed (if deep breathing is sustained, it will drop again). The instructions are now altered:

> You are doing well. Your breathing is rhythmic and slow, and your lung CO_2 level is adjusting well. I will now stop the action on the screen so that you can see this for yourself. Please open your eyes.

The screen is "frozen" and I can then discuss the pattern with the client:

> Here is when you were breathing in, and here is when you were exhaling. You can see how nice and smooth the pattern is. Good.
> Let's begin again: It is midmorning. You are on the beach, and the sun is shining. The sun is warm but not hot. Feel the warmth on your shoulders, relaxing your body. Let it flow through your arms . . . and to your hands. Look at the ocean in front of you. It is calm. You are relaxed, comfortable, alert. Alert and not at all sleepy. Awake and alert.
> Look at the surf gently coming up on the beach. Good. And now receding. Good.

At this point the client is usually synchronizing breathing with the imaginary action of the surf as it returns to the slow, rhythmic pattern. In some cases I have noted that breathing automatically shifts to the abdominal mode, but this is not frequent. In persons in whom thoracic breathing prevails, I add:

> As you are breathing in with the tide, push out your belly. Breathe by pushing out your belly as far as it will go when you breathe in. Good. Now, pull back your belly to breathe out. Good.
> As you are standing on the beach and breathing with the surf, put your right hand on your belly and push your hand out as you breathe in. Good. And pull your belly in as you breathe out with the receding tide.

Each session consists of three to four such image-related exercises, lasting from 2 to 3 minutes each. At the end of the session a printout of the capnograph, as well as other details, including EEG and finger and head temperature changes, are discussed. On subsequent sessions the previous record is discussed before training begins, and some goals of that day's training session are established.

I have found this procedure to be exceptionally rapid in inducing slow, deep breathing, and the concomitant EEG is astonishingly similar to that reported in TM. Some clients, though not all, have produced the pattern on the first training session in as little as 3 to 5 minutes.

When EEG is monitored simultaneously with breathing, I will also stop the client and freeze the spectrum analyzer screen when there is a substantial elevation in *alpha,* to discuss the meaning and implication of the elevation:

Good. And now you are showing a strong alpha response and there is no theta. How do you feel?

When the client shows a good breathing configuration and there is alpha elevation and mean theta reduction and end-tidal CO_2 is decreasing, the instructions are changed again:

Now you are doing very well. You are relaxed and alert. Why don't you go ahead and set the pace yourself? And as you are breathing in with the surf and out as the surf recedes from the beach, tell yourself, "I am relaxed and alert, warm and comfortable and alert."

I have found it important to use the words "alert" and/or "awake and not at all sleepy" on the inspiration phase of breathing. And I use "relaxed, warm, comfortable," on the expiration phase. I consider it important for the client to associate the proper words with the energizing and the passive phases of breathing, as contraction of the diaphragm is active and breathing out is passive.

Second, as noted previously, at no time do I set a respiration rate for the client. I give no indication that there is a desired breathing rate. Yet the client tends to adjust automatically to the 3 b/min to 5 b/min rate of TM and Zen. It is also common that after several minutes of this breathing, using surf imagery as the "metronome," as it were, there will be a decrease in $PETCO_2$, signifying a decrease in metabolism. When this does not occur, the client is probably not really relaxing.

During training I do not generally permit $PETCO_2$ to decrease beyond a certain point without checking the client's blood pressure. If it drops below 4%, I will ask the client if she or he is experiencing dizziness, faintness, or any discomfort. Lower PCO_2 can be taken to mean hypoarousal, but it can also signify hypocapnia. It is important to differentiate between the two.

Chronic hypocapnia is often accompanied by elevated theta and symptoms of hyperventilation syndrome (HVS), whereas hypoarousal is an asymptomatic state of reported well-being and alert comfort. If the client reports feeling good, relaxed, and alert, I will usually continue the training for another 30 seconds, always watching for sudden changes in breathing rate, rhythm, and percentage of end-tidal CO_2, as well as theta EEG.

In extreme cases, syncope is usually preceded by a sharp drop in blood pressure and a significant increase in theta (Engel, Romano, & McLin, 1944). None of my clients experienced syncope with this training procedure, probably because hypotensives are excluded from training, but breathing training has been shown to have a profound effect on blood pressure (Benson, Beary, & Carol, 1974; Blackwell et al., 1976; Datey et al., 1969; Stone & DeLeon, 1976).

Diaphragmatic Breathing and Hypometabolism

It is a basic tenet of physiology that respiration determines metabolism at any given instant, activity level considered. Consequently, numerous investigators have asked why meditation, unlike relaxation, most forms of biofeedback, and hypnosis, produces a hypoaroused, hypometabolic state. Fenwick et al. (1977) reported a decrease of about 16% in CO_2 output with TM. Wallace (1970a,b) reported about 20% reduction in O_2 consumption after about 5 minutes of TM, and there are many other similar reports. These observations have not been reported in connection with most forms of biofeedback, relaxation, or hypnosis.

But if respiration rate in my clients decreased and PCO_2 decreased, then metabolic rate must have decreased as well. Otherwise, PCO_2 would have had to increase. The validity of this assumption is best demonstrated by evidence in one client who "faked it": This 34-year-old woman controlled her breathing to about 3 b/min. But $PETCO_2$ rose to about 5.9%. This is commonly observed in hyperventilators when their breathing rate is controlled by counting, another reason why a capnometer is indispensable.

SUMMARY

The breathing training method described here appears to produce a pattern that looks like the one in the hypometabolic state of TM and Zen meditation. It is psychophysiologically characterized by:

- A reported state of alert relaxation and comfort
- Reduced stress and anxiety
- A sense of well-being
- Decreased PCO_2, suggesting hypometabolism
- Increased finger temperature, suggesting improved peripheral blood circulation

- RSA pulse interbeat pattern accompanying deep diaphragmatic breathing
- An EEG in which alpha is coherent and predominant and theta is depressed, with the exception of "transients" known to be associated with improved brain blood flow' and relaxation.

The psychophysiology of the various meditative states has been described in detail by numerous investigators since its initial study by Das and Gasteau (1957). The almost universal connection to breathing either as an active component or as a passive outcome speaks to how fundamental proper breathing is to relaxation and to therapies to counter tension and anxiety.

REFERENCES

Alving, K., Weitzberg, E., & Lundberg, J. M. (1993). Increased amount of nitric oxide in exhaled air of asthmatics. *European Respiratory Journal, 6,* 1368–1370.

Barnes, P. J. (1986). Non-adenergic non-cholinergic neural control of human airways. *Archives of Internal Pharmacodynamics, 280* (suppl.), 208–228.

Barnes, P. J., & Belvisi, M. G. (1993). Nitric oxide and lung disease. *Thorax, 48,* 1034–1043.

Belvisi, M. G., Stretton, C. D., Yacoub, M., & Barnes, P. J. (1992). Nitric oxide is the endogenous neurotransmitter of bronchodilator nerves in humans. *European Journal of Pharmacology, 210,* 221–222.

Benesch, R., & Benesch, R. E. (1976). The effect of organic phosphates from the human erythrocyte on the allosteric properties of hemoglobin. *Biochemistry & Biophysics Research Committee, 26,* 162–167.

Benson, H., Beary, J. E., & Carol, M. P. (1974). The relaxation response. *Psychiatry, 37,* 37–47.

Blackwell, B., Bloomfield, S., Gartside, P., Robinson, A., Hanenson, I., Magenheim, H., Nidich, A., & Zigler, R. (1976). Transcendental meditation in hypertension. *Lancet, 1,* 223–236.

Bone, R. C. (1993). A new therapy for the adult respiratory distress syndrome. *New England Journal of Medicine, 328,* 431–432.

Comroe, J. H. (1974). *Physiology of respiration* (2d ed.). Chicago: Yearbook Medical Publishers.

Comroe, J. H. Jr., Forster, R. E. II, DuBois, A. B., Briscoe, W. A. & Carlsen, E. (1962). *The lung: Clinical physiology and pulmonary function tests* (2nd ed.) Chicago, IL: Year Book Medical Publishers, Inc.

Cooper, C. J., Landzberg, M. J., Anderson, T. J., Todd, T. J., Charbonneau, F., Creager, M. A., Ganz, P., & Selwyn, A. P. (1996). Role of nitric oxide in the local regulation of pulmonary vascular resistance in humans. *Circulation, 93,* 266–271.

Das, N. N., & Gasteau, H. (1957). Variations de l'activité, electrique du cerveau, du coeur, et des muscles squeletiques au cours de la meditation et de l'extase yogique. *EEG and Clinical Neurophysiology, 6* (suppl.), 211–219.

Datey, K. K., Deshmukh, S. N., Dalvi, C. P., & Vinekar, S. L. (1969). "Shavasan": A yogic exercise in the management of hypertension. *Angiology, 20,* 325–333.

Engel, G. L., Romano, J., & McLin, T. R. (1944). Vasodepressor and carotid sinus syncopy. *Archives of Internal Medicine, 74,* 100–119.

Fenwick, P. B. C., Donaldson, S., Gillis, L., Bushman, J., Fenton, G. W., Tilsley, I. P., & Serafinowicz, H. (1977). Metabolic and EEG changes during transcendental meditation: An explanation. *Biological Psychology, 5,* 101–118.

Fried, R. (1990a). Integrating music in breathing training and relaxation: I. Background, rationale, and relevant elements. *Biofeedback and Self-Regulation, 15,* 161–169.

Fried, R. (1990b). Integrating music in breathing training and relaxation: II. Applications. *Biofeedback and Self-Regulation, 15,* 171–177.

Fried, R. (1990c). *The breath connection.* New York: Insight/Plenum Press.

Fried, R. (1994). Respiration in clinical psychophysiology: How to assess clinical parameters in breathing and their change with treatment. In J. G. Carlson, A. R. Seifert, & N. Birbaumer (Eds.), *Clinical applied psychophysiology.* New York: Plenum Press.

Fried, R. (1999). *Breathe well . . . be well—a holistic approach.* New York: Wiley.

Fried, R., Fox, M. G., & Carlton, R. M. (1990). Effect of diaphragmatic respiration with end-tidal CO_2 biofeedback on respiration, EEG, and seizure frequency in idiopathic epilepsy. *Annals of the New York Academy of Sciences, 602,* 67–96.

Fried, R., & Grimaldi, J. (1993). *The psychology and physiology of breathing in behavioral medicine, clinical psychology and psychiatry.* New York: Plenum.

Fried, R., & Merrell, W. C. (1999). *The arginine solution.* New York: Warner Books.

Frostell, C., Fratacci, M.-D., Wain, J. C., Jones, R., & Zapol, W. M. (1991). Inhaled nitric oxide. A selective pulmonary vasodilator reversing hypoxic pulmonary vasoconstriction. *Circulation, 83,* 2038–2047.

Furchgott, R. F., & Zawadzki, J. V. (1980). The obligatory role of endothelial cells in the relaxation of arterial smooth muscle by acetylcholine. *Nature, 288,* 373–376.

Glueck, B. S., & Stroebel, C. F. (1975). Biofeedback and meditation in the treatment of psychiatric illness. *Comparative Psychiatry, 16,* 303–321.

Goldman, A. P., Rees, P. G., & Macrae, D. J. (1995). Is it time to consider domiciliary nitric oxide? *Lancet, 345,* 199–200.

Kharitonov, S. A., Yates, D., Robbins, R. A., Logan-Sinclair, R., Shinebourne, E. A., & Barnes, P. J. (1994). Increased nitric oxide in exhaled air of asthmatic patients. *Lancet, 343,* 133–135.

Kooi, K. A. (1971). *Fundamentals of electroencephalography.* New York: Harper & Row.

Mehta, S., Stewart, D. J., Langleben, D., & R. D. Levy (1995). Short-term pulmonary vasodilation with L-arginine in pulmonary hypertension. *Circulation, 92,* 1539–1545.

Moncada, S., & Higgs, E. A. (Eds.). (1990). *Nitric oxide from L-arginine: A bioregulatory system.* Amsterdam: Elsevier Science Publishers.

Moncada, S., Palmer, R. M. J., & Higgs, E. A. (1988). The discovery of nitric oxide as the endogenous nitrovasodilator. *Hypertension, 12,* 365–372.

Moncada, S., Palmer, R. M. J., & Higgs, E. A. (1991). Nitric oxide: Physiology, pathophysiology, and pharmacology. *Pharmacological Reviews, 43,* 109–142.

Murad, F. (1996). Signal transduction using nitric oxide and cyclic guanosine monophosphate. *JAMA, 276,* 1189–1192.

Pepke-Zaba, J., Higenbottam, T. W., Dinh-Xuan, A. T., Stone, D., & Wallwork, J. (1991). Inhaled nitric oxide as a cause of selective pulmonary vasodilatation in pulmonary hypertension. *Lancet, 338,* 1173–1174.

Rossaint, R., Falke, K. J., Lopez, F., Slama, K., Pison, U., & Zapol, W. M. (1993). Inhaled nitric oxide for the adult respiratory distress syndrome. *New England Journal of Medicine, 328,* 399–405.

Ruch, T. C., & Fulton, J. F. (1960). *Medical physiology and biophysics* (18th ed.). Philadelphia: Saunders.

Shea, S. A., Walter, J., Murphy, K., & Guz, A. (1987). Evidence for individuality of breathing patterns in resting healthy man. *Respiratory Physiology, 68,* 331–344.

Stamler, J. S., Jia, L., Eu, J. P., McMahon, T. J., Demchenko, I. T., Bonaventura, J., Gerbert, K., & Piantadosi, C. A. (1997a). Blood flow regulation by S-nitrosohemoglobin in the physiological oxygen gradient. *Science, 276,* 2034–2036.

Stamler, J. S., Loh, E., Roddy, M.-A., Currie, K. E., & Creager, M. A. (1994). Nitric oxide regulates basal systemic and pulmonary vascular resistance in healthy humans. *Circulation, 89,* 2035–2040.

Stone, R. A., & DeLeon, J. (1976). Psychotherapeutic control of hypertension. *New England Journal of Medicine, 294,* 80–84.

Tortora, G. J., & Anagnostakos, N. P. (1984). *Principles of anatomy and physiology* (4th ed.). Philadelphia: Harper & Row.

Wallace, R. K. (1970a). Physiological effects of transcendental meditation. *Science, 167,* 1751–1754.

Wallace, R. K. (1970b). *Physiological effects of transcendental meditation.* Los Angeles: Students International Meditation Society.

West, J. B. (1995). *Respiratory physiology—the essentials* (5th ed.). Baltimore, MD: Williams & Wilkins.

Wolkove, N., Kreisman, H., Darragh, D., Cohen, C. V., & Frank, H. (1984). Effect of transcendental meditation on breathing and respiratory control. *Journal of Applied Physiology, 56,* 607–612.

CHAPTER 7

HYPNOSIS IN THE MANAGEMENT OF ANXIETY ASSOCIATED WITH MEDICAL CONDITIONS AND THEIR TREATMENT

John F. Chaves

Anxiety accompanies a wide variety of acute and chronic medical conditions and is often heightened by the diagnostic and treatment protocols associated with these conditions. Patients catastrophize, dwelling on and amplifying the fearful and worrisome aspects of their experiences, further augmenting their symptoms or the stress, pain, and other aversive aspects of the clinical procedures to which they are subjected (Chaves & Brown, 1987). Even the protocols mandated for routine health care are dreaded and avoided by many individuals (Liddell, Ackerman, & Locker, 1990; Locker, Liddell, & Burman, 1991). As a consequence, needed preventive care is not received, serious conditions are diagnosed too late for optimal treatment, and the experience of acute and chronic illness is rendered even more difficult than would otherwise be the case. All health professionals face a serious challenge in recognizing and managing the anxiety associated with the conditions they diagnose, treat, and attempt to prevent.

This chapter describes and evaluates the ways in which clinical hypnosis has been used to manage the anxiety associated with a variety of medical conditions and their treatment. It describes the nature of the hypnotic interventions that have been employed in the management of anxiety in medical settings and reviews the most recent systematically gathered data concerning these applications. Because the application of hypnosis in medicine and surgery has recently been reviewed by Frankel (1987) and Brown (1992), the focus here will be largely on developments since these reviews, with an emphasis on medical conditions and treatments that characteristically evoke

significant anxiety. To provide an appropriate context for the nonspecialist, I begin with a brief overview of clinical hypnosis and describe some of the more important considerations involved in its use.

AN OVERVIEW OF CLINICAL HYPNOSIS

Hypnosis has a serious claim to being one of the oldest forms of psychological treatment (Crabtree, 1993; Spanos & Chaves, 1991). Anecdotal reports indicate that hypnotic procedures were being used to control the pain and anxiety associated with major surgery, including mastectomies and limb amputations as well as dental extractions, in the early nineteenth century (Deane, 1844; Delatour, 1826; Ward & Topham, 1842; West, 1836). These accounts appeared prior to the discovery of inhalation anesthetics during the late 1840s, a time when there were no satisfactory pharmacological means of achieving pain control in surgery. Not surprisingly, surgery was normally approached reluctantly and with considerable anxiety, when approached at all (Fülöp-Miller, 1938; Rey, 1993). Accordingly, reports of surgery accomplished successfully with hypnosis were dramatic and captured the attention of laypeople as well as health professionals (Chaves & Dworkin, 1997). The profound insensitivity to pain reported in some surgical patients treated with hypnosis gave rise to the enduring notion that hypnosis could only be understood as a mysterious altered state of consciousness (Chaves, 1997). This thesis played an enormous role in shaping theoretical, clinical, and experimental work on hypnosis and, combined with the involvement of lay hypnotists, probably helped to locate the topic outside the mainstream of psychology and health care for much of its history (Spanos & Chaves, 1989, 1991). Rigorous research on experimental and clinical hypnosis during the last half-century, as well as recent theoretical shifts within the field that have emphasized the role of social and cognitive factors in hypnosis, may be helping to bring hypnosis back within the mainstream (e.g. Barber, 1969; Barber, Spanos, & Chaves, 1974; Rhue, Lynn, & Kirsch, 1993; Sarbin & Coe, 1972; Spanos & Chaves, 1989).

While close examination of early clinical reports does not provide compelling evidence that surgeries and other medical and dental procedures were routinely accomplished painlessly with hypnosis, it does seem to indicate that these patients responded to the surgical procedures with less than the expected anxiety (Chaves, 1989; Chaves & Dworkin, 1997). Observers frequently remarked on the calmness of the patients throughout the procedure (Deane, 1844; Ward & Topham, 1842). In addition, these patients would sometimes even deny knowledge that the clinical procedure had been done. These were startling reports that, not surprisingly, led to controversy, especially after the discovery of inhalation anesthetics provided meaningful treatment alternatives (Smith, 1847; Winter, 1991). Advocates of hypnosis, including some from academic medicine, remained committed to it, especially in the early days of inhalation anesthesia when techniques and dosages had not been worked out and operative mortality was high. The details of this interesting period are reviewed elsewhere (Chaves & Dworkin, 1997).

Medical and dental professionals revived interest in hypnosis near the end of the nineteenth century and again during World War I and II and during other military conflicts when injuries on the battlefield often necessitated surgery without benefit of chemical analgesics and anesthetics (Kunzelmann, Dunninger, & Hurka, 1989; Levy & Neumann, 1984). Until recent years, however, these reports remained mostly anecdotal (Bonilla, Quigley, & Bowers, 1961; Manusov & Murray, 1992; Todorovic, 1959). Beginning with Hull's (1933) classic work on experimental hypnosis, scientific interest in the topic flourished, especially during the last 50 years. Moreover, within the last

decade systematic studies have appeared that are beginning to establish an evidence-based foundation for the clinical application of hypnosis in medicine and dentistry. Before we consider these studies, we must first spell out more precisely what we mean by a hypnotic intervention.

THE NATURE OF HYPNOTIC INTERVENTIONS

A wide variety of treatment interventions is subsumed under the label *hypnotic*. Indeed, at times it can be difficult to decide on operational grounds whether an intervention is properly labeled hypnotic or not (Benson, Arns, & Hoffman, 1981). For purposes of our discussion, it is useful to distinguish between formal and informal hypnotic interventions.

Formal Hypnotic Interventions

Formal hypnotic interventions are characterized by an explicit definition of the therapeutic transaction as one involving the use of hypnosis. The simple definition of the situation as hypnosis, without any additional elements of the traditional hypnotic interventions, has long been known to increase response to suggestion and to play an important role in eliciting many of the subjective alterations in experience that have come to be associated with hypnosis (Barber & Calverley, 1964a). Adding other elements of the traditional process, such as eye closure and the adoption of a soothing tone of voice, brings additional subjective alterations into play (Barber & Calverley, 1964b,c, 1965). Defining a therapeutic intervention as hypnotic engages a wide variety of attitudes, expectations, and beliefs that can exert potent effects on the therapeutic relationship and influence treatment outcomes (Kirsch, 1990; Kirsch & Council, 1989). Indeed, at least one meta-analysis of 18 studies (Kirsch, Montgomery, & Sapirstein, 1995) led to the conclusion that augmenting cognitive-behavioral interventions with hypnosis significantly enhances treatment outcomes. Nevertheless, factors ranging from patient acceptance to institutional tolerance can shape the specific ways in which these procedures are used with patients, the selection of patients with whom they are used, and the decision to label these procedures as hypnotic.

The use of clinical hypnosis characteristically begins with a consideration of the patient's pretreatment attitudes, beliefs, and expectations (Chaves, 1989). Misconceptions about hypnosis are corrected while common metaphors and analogies help shape positive attitudes about the hypnotic experience and assist the patient in developing an understanding of how he or she can advance the process as active participants. Movie going and book reading analogies, for example, can help convey an understanding of the simultaneous narrowing of attentional field associated with hypnosis and the suspension of a critical attitude toward the literal content of hypnotic suggestions, illustrated by the experience of being required to look beyond the printed symbols on a page or the two-dimensional images of movie actors engaged in dialogues while standing in front of plywood sets (Barber, Spanos, & Chaves, 1974).

Pretreatment assessment also provides an important opportunity to elicit important elements of the patient's symptom phenomenology that can help to shape the therapeutic suggestions that are subsequently administered (Chaves, 1981). Clinicians pay careful attention to how patients describe their symptoms, and the kinds of spontaneous cognitive strategies they may employ to cope with anxiety-provoking treatments. Such explorations also frequently disclose catastrophizing thoughts and images that amplify the fearful, worrisome aspects of treatment or a disease process that may become the target for later intervention (Brown, Chaves, & Leonoff, 1981; Chaves & Brown, 1978, 1987).

Formal hypnotic inductions are quite diverse (Edmonston, 1986). Common elements include suggestions for eye closure and relaxation, focusing of attention, use of relaxing imagery designed to enhance response to later suggestion, refocusing of attention within the body or to rhythmic events or processes such as breathing, and so forth, although none of these elements is essential (Barber, & De-Moor, 1972). The flexibility of hypnosis as an intervention also enables a wide variety of therapeutic issues to be addressed within the same procedure. Thus, it is possible to simultaneously address the management of uncontrolled pain, depression, increased motivation for exercise, increased appetite, enhanced sense of self-efficacy, desire for increased socialization, and improved ability to sleep (e.g. Chaves, 1985). Idiosyncratically appropriate imagery or self-talk might be employed in administering such suggestions. The beneficial effects of the procedure are often enhanced through the use of self-hypnotic procedures or the use of audiotapes of hypnotic sessions.

Formal hypnotic interventions commonly conclude with the use of posthypnotic suggestions, designed to generalize the response to the therapeutic suggestions outside of the therapeutic setting. Finally, a ritualistic termination procedure is normally employed, followed by a brief posthypnotic interview to learn about the patient's experience during the process and to assess whether there have been any undesirable sequelae associated with the process (Coe, Paterson, & Gwynn, 1995; Crawford, Hilgard, & Macdonald, 1982; Orne, 1965).

Informal Hypnotic Procedures

Informal hypnotic interventions closely resemble their formal counterparts, with the critical exception that the situation is not formally defined as hypnotic (Bartlett, 1970; Owens, 1966). There may be an assessment and preparation process. There may be some elements of an induction process, although not necessarily as ritualized as some hypnotic procedures. Usually there will be extensive use of therapeutically targeted suggestions, and there may be some use of posthypnotic suggestion (Lang & Hamilton, 1994). Sometimes these procedures become difficult to distinguish from other kinds of imaginative or relaxation procedures, although the emphasis on suggestions (designed to elicit experiences that are described as involuntary) rather than instructions may be helpful in making the distinction at times (Spanos & de-Groh, 1983). Informal hypnotic procedures have special appeal when trying to help patients avail themselves of the benefit of these procedures who might otherwise might be skeptical about, frightened of, or hostile to such approaches. They can also be attractive when the institutional climate does not support the use of more formal hypnotic procedures.

The Role of Hypnotizability

Historically, hypnotic ability has been viewed as a relatively unmodifiable trait with anchors in both genetics and early life experience (Hilgard, 1970).

Research in experimental hypnosis, however, has established that hypnotic responsivity can be dramatically altered through interventions designed to influence cognitive processes during the hypnotic experience as well as attitudes and expectations about the process (Spanos, 1986). This finding has implications for the range of individuals with whom hypnotic procedures can be beneficially employed in the clinical setting. The variability of the relationship between hypnotizability and clinical outcomes complicates this conclusion (Brown, 1992; Wadden & Anderton, 1982). Another reason that hypnotizability merits attention is that it may be a risk factor for such disorders as phobias and bulimia (Covino et al., 1994; Frankel & Orne, 1976; Gershman, Burrows, & Reade, 1987) and for heightened stress and catastrophizing in response to somatic symptoms. Wickramasekera (1986) found an interaction between hypnotic ability and negative affectivity in a series of 118 chronic pain patients. Larger increases in skin conductance levels (SCL) were associated with higher levels of hypnotizability. Furthermore, the higher SCLs persisted longer for high than for low hypnotizable, suggesting a delayed recovery from threat. In addition, absorption, which has sometimes been associated with hypnotizability, has been correlated with somatization and global distress indices in a behavioral medicine clinic population and also predicted how bothered patients were by their primary symptoms (Gick, McLeod, & Hulihan, 1997). The issue of hypnotizability will be considered further as we review recent systematic studies on the use of hypnosis to reduce anxiety in medical conditions. We begin with the use of hypnosis in conjunction with various treatment procedures and then consider its use in chronic disease management.

ATTENUATING ANXIETY RELATED TO MEDICAL AND DENTAL PROCEDURES

Medical procedures associated with diagnosis and treatment frequently give rise to high levels of anxiety as well as pain, discomfort, and other unintended and undesirable consequences. It has become increasingly clear that the way procedures are done and the nature and quality of the relationship between the caregiver and the patient play a central role in determining how much anxiety is experienced (Zeltzer, Jay, & Fisher, 1989; Lang & Laser, 1996). In turn, these factors influence the nature and intensity of the adverse experiences associated with the procedures. Let us now examine some of the recent ways that hypnosis has been applied in managing the anxiety accompanying medical diagnostic and treatment procedures.

Hypnosis in Dentistry

Hypnosis was among the first of a variety of psychological and pharmacological techniques that have been used to manage dental anxiety (e.g., de Jongh et al., 1995; Kleinhauz, Eli, & Rubinstein, 1985; Milgrom et al., 1985; Rodolfa, Kraft, & Reilley, 1990). Although there have been a large number of tutorial and clinical papers published on the topic (e.g., Shaw & Niven, 1996), there have been comparatively few systematic investigations. Furthermore, in many of these, hypnosis was employed as one element in a complex treatment protocol that involved other interventions.

Certainly the anxiety accompanying dental treatment has been well documented (Bernstein, Kleinknecht, & Alexander, 1979; Kleinknecht, Klepac, & Alexander, 1973; Locker & Liddell, 1991; Locker, Shapiro, & Liddell, 1996b). Locker, Shapiro, and Liddell (1996a) found that the source of the anxiety can frequently be traced to adverse treatment experiences that involve pain, fear, and embarrassment. Not surprisingly, dental anxiety is associated with avoidance of treatment, decreased satisfaction with treatment, and generally poorer oral health (Klingberg, 1995; Liddell & Locker, 1992; Liddell et al., 1994; Pavi, Kay, & Stephen, 1995; Vassend, 1993; Wisloff, Vassend, & Asmyhr, 1995). Moreover, Aartman, de Jongh, and van der Meulen (1997) found that dentally anxious patients seeking treatment displayed significant elevations on a number of scales on the SCL-90 (Derogatis, Rickles, & Rock, 1976), suggesting that their problem in seeking dental treatment may not be an isolated issue.

McAmmond, Davidson, and Kovitz (1971) compared hypnosis and relaxation training on stress reactions in the dental operatory. Twenty-seven adults showing a high skin conductance (SC) in response to anesthetic injection and who needed dental work were selected for the main study. Pain tolerance was measured with a pressure algometer. Insertion of a needle for a mandibular block injection—but without the anesthetic—served as a second pain stimulus. Subjects were assigned to one of three groups: hypnosis, relaxation, and control. The relaxation procedure was administered by audiotape, while the hypnotic procedure was done "live" with the hypnotic procedure terminated before testing. Subsequently, the subjects were exposed to a hypnotic procedure or relaxation procedure and retested. Following testing, the subjects rated the "success" of their participation on a 7-point scale. No dental care was provided. Five months later, the subjects were contacted to see if they had made an appointment with their dentist. The results were stratified by baseline SC levels. No treatment main effect was observed for either injectional or pressure algometer pain. However, hypnosis was more effective than relaxation or control for subjects with high baseline SC levels. In addition, more hypnosis subjects than controls returned for dental treatment during the 5-month follow-up.

The application of hypnosis in dentistry received a significant infusion of enthusiasm following Joseph Barber's (1977) report of the successful use of the technique in 99 out of 100 dental patients. Unfortunately this investigation was not well controlled and this success rate has not been confirmed in any more recent investigations. For example, Gillett and Coe (1984) examined (1) the effectiveness of Barber's hypnotic procedure for producing "rapid induction analgesia" (RIA) in its usual form (which is not particularly brief, the label notwithstanding) and in a shortened form (SI), (2) the relationship of hypnotic susceptibility to analgesic responsiveness, and (3) the effect of dental procedure discomfort level on hypnotic analgesia. They administered the RIA or SI to 60 adult dental patients before their dental treatment. Measures of hypnotic susceptibility and dentists' ratings of the discomfort levels involved in the various dental procedures were obtained. They found that hypnotic analgesia had an overall effectiveness rate of 52%, which failed to replicate Barber's 99% success rate. RIA and SI were equally effective. Hypnotic susceptibility level did not relate significantly to success with hypnotic analgesia. The level of dental procedure discomfort was the clearest predictor of success with hypnotic analgesia; greater discomfort ratings were less likely to be associated with successful hypnotic analgesia.

Lu, Lu, and Hersh (1995) added hypnosis to a complex intervention for 18 drug-dependent patients who were highly anxious about dental treatment. All of the patients had previously failed to be successfully treated with sedation alone. Hypnotic intervention occurred either before sedation, when IV was employed (midazolam or diazepam plus methohexital) or following sedation, when an intramuscular (IM) sedative was employed (meperidine plus promethazine). Treatment outcome was judged to be good or excellent in 11 of the 18 patients. It was noted that tolerance or cross-tolerance between a drug being abused may have accounted for many of the treatment failures. In another series of 17 cases (Lu & Lu, 1996), hypnosis was reportedly used successfully for reducing the amount of pharmacological sedation for dentally fearful and medically compromised patients who were at increased risk due to their underlying conditions.

Moore, Abrahamsen, and Brodsgaard (1996) compared the effects of hypnotherapy (HT) with group psychotherapy (GT) and individual desensitization (SD) for dentally anxious adults. All treated patients improved compared to an untreated control group. The HT and SD patients required more treatment hours than the GT patients. After 1 year the number of dropouts was greater in the HT group than the SD group, although the largest number of dropouts was from the GT group. Some of the attrition in the HT group was thought to be related to changes in treatment providers.

Gershman, Burrows, and Reade (1987) studied 130 patients who represented a 50% random sample of consecutive patients seen in an orofacial pain clinic for unmanageable dental phobic disorder over an 8-year period. They found a weak relationship between hypnotizability and dental anxiety. Patients with multiple phobic disorders were more hypnotizable than those with single phobias. There was a moderate relationship between hypnotizability and treatment outcome. The results were interpreted as supporting use of hypnosis in dentistry for treatment of dental phobias.

Hammarstrand, Berggren, and Hakeberg (1995) compared psychophysiological and hypnotherapeutic approaches to the treatment of dental anxiety. The 22 female subjects were chosen from the waiting list of the Dental Fears Research and Treatment Clinic. The median time of avoidance of dental care was 9.5 years. One group received HT, while the other group underwent a behavioral treatment based on psychophysiological principles (PP). Both therapies took eight sessions and were followed by standardized conventional dental test treatments. Nine patients were not able to conclude the treatment sessions (6 HT and 3 PP). These patients did not differ significantly from the remaining patients before treatment. The PP group reported a decrease in dental fear as well as an improvement in mood during dental situations, as compared to the HT group. General fear levels decreased but not significantly. Eleven patients completed conventional dental treatment according to a dentist's behavioral rating scale, indicating that they were relaxed and no problems occurred during the treatments. These patients were referred to general practitioners within the community dental service. The study indicated that a majority of the patients, who had completed the behavioral therapy and the dental test treatments, became less fearful of dental care and were able to manage conventional dental care, including acceptance of referral to a new dentist.

Gokli et al. (1994) studied the use of hypnosis as an adjunct to local anesthesia in a series of 29 pediatric dental patients. Pulse rate was significantly lowered under hypnosis. There was also less crying with hypnosis. Other disruptive behaviors (leg movement, hands raised, orophysical resistence) were also reduced, but not significantly. Lu (1994) noted that hypnosis combined with pharmacological sedation is still not popular because so few practitioners are trained in both techniques. He described a series of 13 patients 4 to 11 years old who needed operative dental work and were selected on the bases of previous use of ketamine and a history of violent crying and struggling before sedation and during recovery. All were crying upon entering the dental office. The hypnotic procedure was initiated by an assistant who began by playing a game of "pretend you are asleep." When the children were "under," the dentist entered and gave the patients an injection in their thighs. Informal behavioral observations indicated the patients responded favorably; however, there was no control group.

Enqvist and Fischer (1997) investigated the effects of a preoperative hypnotic intervention for patients undergoing extraction of third mandibular molars. Hypnosis patients listened to an audiotape that included posthypnotic suggestions for healing and recovery as well as coping strategies for dealing with pain and stress. One surgeon who was blind to group assignment performed all of the surgeries. Presurgical anxiety, measured on a visual analog scale increased significantly in the control group but remained at baseline levels in the experimental group. Postoperative analgesic consumption was significantly reduced in the hypnosis group compared to the control group.

Enqvist, von Konow, and Bystedt (1995) studied the effects of pre- and perioperative hypnotic suggestions on the psychophysiological response of patients to maxillofacial surgery involving repositioning of the maxilla or the mandible. This surgery is normally performed under general anesthesia and is accompanied by blood losses approaching 1000 cc or more, as well as highly variable amounts of postoperative edema. Sixty patients were randomly assigned to one of three groups: A, preoperative hypnosis; B, preoperative hypnosis plus suggestions given during general anesthesia; and C, suggestions given during anesthesia alone. A group of surgical patients undergoing comparable procedures with the same surgeon served as a control.

Patients receiving preoperative suggestions showed a 30% reduction in blood loss, while those receiving pre- and perioperative suggestions showed a 26% reduction. Those receiving perioperative suggestions alone showed a 9% reduction in blood loss. Significantly lowered systolic blood pressure was found in groups B and C only. Although patients in group C left the hospital significantly sooner than patients in the other groups, differences in age and gender for patients in this group were thought to render the finding difficult to interpret.

Although application of hypnosis in dentistry has focused primarily on its use in operative dental procedures, it has also been used in the management of parafunctional habits, such as bruxing and clenching, as well as chronic pain related to temporomandibular disorder (TMD). Most of the reports pertaining to these applications are uncontrolled case studies (e.g., Clarke & Reynolds, 1991; LaCrosse, 1994; Somer, 1991; Wardlaw, 1994). Some experimental studies have also suggested the complex effects of hypnotic interventions on the orofacial musculature during stress. For example, Manns et al. (1990) explored the effect of hypnosis on the relationship between tonic elevator mandibular activity and the vertical dimension during states of vigilance. In 12 subjects, hypnosis reduced tonic EMG activity and led to a great increase of interocclusal space.

Stam provided both a case report and a study pertaining to the use of hypnosis in the management of TMD (Stam, McGrath, & Brooke, 1984a,b). In the study, 41 TMD patients were assigned to one of three treatment groups: (1) hypnosis and cognitive coping skills, (2) relaxation and cognitive coping skills, or (3) no-treatment control. The mean duration of pain was 23 months. Hypnotizability was assessed prior to treatment. The treatment groups received their assigned treatments for four weekly sessions. Patients in the hypnosis and relaxation groups reported equivalent responses in the three primary TMD symptoms: reductions in pain and in abnormal sounds in the temporomandibular joint, and improved jaw mobility. Hypnotic susceptibility was significantly correlated with reductions in reported pain for the treatment groups. Age and symptom duration were not related to treatment outcome. Facial pain patients scored higher on measures of suggestibility than the college norms, and their scores seemed to predict the outcome of psychologically based treatments for TMD (Stam, 1986). It would be interesting to explore whether hypnotizability also predicts the outcome of nonpsychological treatments of this complex disorder.

When hypnosis is associated with anxiety reduction in the dental setting, it may be because anxiety is reduced directly. Some studies, however, support the notion that hypnotic procedures may reduce anxiety by reducing pain. Sharav and Tal (1987), for example, found that hypnosis reduced pain of electric tooth pulp stimulation more than a saline placebo. Hypnosis could abolish pain at currents up to 150 μA. Changes in facial expression were also noted, with more calmness under hypnosis.

Joubert and Van-Os (1989) examined the effect of hypnosis, placebo, paracetamol, and naloxone on the response to dental pulp stimulation. Eight healthy volunteers with varying degrees of hypnotic susceptibility participated in a trial to evaluate analgesia induced by RIA. RIA produced increases in the pain threshold in the majority of subjects. The magnitude of the response was unrelated to hypnotizability. Neither placebo nor paracetamol capsules affected pain threshold. The effect of RIA on pain threshold was not reversed by naloxone, casting doubt on the possible involvement of endorphins in this phenomenon.

Interventional Radiology

Lang and associates (Lang & Berbaum, 1997; Lang & Hamilton, 1994; Lang et al., 1996) have reported an interesting series of investigations involving the use of hypnosis in interventional radiology. Anxiety has been documented in up to 78% of patients undergoing these procedures (Lang & Laser, 1996). Although anxiety is normally managed by intravenous conscious sedation, undertreatment can result in cardiovascular strain and restlessness that can compromise the success of the procedure. Pharmacological oversedation, on the other hand, can lead to respiratory and cardiovascular depression, increasing procedural risk (Lang & Hamilton, 1994). Accordingly, Lang and her colleagues (Lang & Hamilton, 1994) evaluated a nonpharmacological alternative for anxiety reduction that they call "anodyne imagery." This procedure consisted of "conditioned relaxation, induction of a trance state, and guided processing of the patient's internal imagery." Baseline levels of IV sedation were established for 100 consecutive patients who had undergone procedures that had involved 1 hour or more on the procedural table. Twenty-one patients underwent the anodyne imagery condition (16 were compared with matched controls, while 5 had previously undergone an equivalent procedure without anodyne imagery and thus served as their own controls). All patients were informed that they could receive as much IV sedation as they wished within limits of safety. Anodyne imagery patients requested significantly less IV sedation in both intra- and intergroup comparisons.

In a related investigation, Lang and Berbaum (1997) obtained pain ratings from 96 patients undergoing lower extremity arteriography or percutaneous nephrostomy. Ratings were obtained during one of two baseline periods before or two periods after the radiology staff (nurses and technologists) had been trained in the use of nonpharmacological analgesia (which included rapport building, use of suggestion, provision of control, and encouragement, as well as relaxation training, imagery, and self-hypnosis). A unique feature of this study is that the collection of pain ratings was initiated by a hospital-wide quality assurance committee so that neither the staff nor the authors were aware that the data were being collected. Pain was significantly reduced for those patients undergoing the procedures with the "trained" staff. There was a trend for these patients to request less pharmacological sedation as well.

Lang et al. (1996) provided an additional evaluation of whether self-hypnotic relaxation can reduce the need for intravenous conscious sedation during interventional radiological procedures. Sixteen patients were randomized to an experimental group, and 14 patients were randomized to a control group. All had patient-controlled analgesia. Experimental patients additionally had self-hypnotic relaxation with hypnotizability assessed with the Hypnotic Induction Profile (HIP) (Spiegel, 1973). Self-hypnosis patients used less drugs and reported less pain. More control patients exhibited oxygen desaturation and/or needed interruptions of their procedures for hemodynamic instability. The benefits of self-hypnosis did not correlate with hypnotizability. Taken together, these studies provide strong support for the conclusion that a complex treatment protocol that includes self-hypnosis can reduce the pain and anxiety that accompany a range of interventional radiologic procedures and reduce reliance on IV sedation for these procedures.

Surgical and Postsurgical Applications

The use of hypnosis as a preparatory strategy for anesthesia and surgery has recently been reviewed by Kessler and Dane (1996). Its use before and during medical procedures has also been addressed by Bejenke (1996). Clinical reports have also suggested its value as an adjunct to local anesthetics in the management of high-risk and fearful patients (Schultz-Stübner, 1996). Ashton et al. (1997) assessed the impact of preoperative self-hypnotic training on patients scheduled to undergo first-time elective coronary artery bypass surgery. Thirty-two patients were randomized into a study group and a nontreated control group. Self-hypnosis included relaxation suggestions and eye closure coupled with specific therapeutic suggestions pertaining to aspects of the operative procedure and recovery period (e.g., relaxing muscles of the throat for intubation, keeping the incision free from infection, minimizing bleeding, reducing pain).

Hypnotizability was assessed using the HIP. Patients were asked to practice the procedure hourly the night before surgery and as often as possible postoperatively. Compliance, assessed by interview on the fifth postoperative day, was estimated at 100% for the preoperative practice and 65% for the postoperative practice. Intraoperative parameters, as well as length of stay in intensive care and morbidity, were similar for both groups. Hypnosis patients had significantly greater reductions on the tension subscale of the Profile of Mood States (Lorr & McNair, 1971) than controls. The hypnosis patients required more postoperative pain medication (acetaminophen plus oxycodone) than controls, although this was due almost entirely to the noncompliant patients. The authors did not assess the effects of hypnotizability on the observed reduction in tension. Unfortunately training was restricted to a single preoperative visit. In addition, the reliance on a self-hypnotic procedure rather than tape-recorded procedures postoperatively may have been less than optimal. It also would have been helpful to track measures of anxiety and pain over the postoperative period. An additional limitation of this study was that some of the control patients interpreted the HIP as a relaxation technique and continued to use it as a relaxation procedure. It is not uncommon for control subjects to employ adaptive coping strategies spontaneously in clinical settings as well as experimental studies involving pain (Chaves & Barber, 1974; Chaves & Brown, 1987).

Blankfield et al. (1995), on the other hand, were unable to demonstrate an effect of taped therapeutic suggestions and taped music in coronary artery bypass patients. They conducted a randomized, single-blinded, placebo-controlled trial in which 66 patients listened either to suggestion or musical tapes interoperatively or postoperatively. Twenty-nine patients listened to blank tapes interoperatively and no tapes postoperatively. Half of the patients who listened to a tape reported that they found it helpful, but there were no differences in length of stay in intensive care, duration of postoperative stay, narcotic usage, nurse ratings of anxiety and progress, depression, activities of daily living, or cardiac symptoms, regardless of whether or not the patients reported being helped by the tape. Unlike the Ashton et al. (1997) study, Blankfield et al., (1995) did not provide a preoperative intervention, which may account for their inability to demonstrate an effect of the tapes on many of their outcome measures. Moreover, recent evidence casts serious doubt on the value of intrasurgical suggestions when patients are unconscious (Block et al., 1991; Melzack et al., 1996; Russell & Wang, 1997).

A more intensive treatment intervention was used by Enqvist et al. (1997), who examined the role of anxiety, stress, and expectations in the control of postoperative nausea and vomiting (PONV). After general anesthesia and surgery, PONV may have an incidence as high as 70%, regardless of antiemetic drug therapy. Enqvist et al. employed preoperative hypnosis and mental preparation by means of an audiotape to reduce nausea and vomiting before elective breast reduction surgery. Fifty women were randomized to a control group or a hypnosis group. Patients in the hypnosis group listened to a 20-minute audiotape daily for 4 to 6 days prior to surgery. A hypnotic induction was followed by suggestions as to how to relax, to dissociate any experienced pain, and to experience states incompatible with nausea and vomiting postoperatively (e.g., thirst and hunger). A training portion of the tape asked patients to rehearse their own strategies for stress reduction. Premedication and anesthetic procedures were standardized. Patients in the hypnosis group had significantly less vomiting, 39% compared to 68% in the control group; less nausea; and diminished need for postoperative analgesics.

Faymonville and associates at the University Hospital of Liège, Belgium, report using hypnosis with over 1,300 surgical patients since 1992. In a retrospective study, they found that the use of hypnosis as an adjunct to conscious sedation led to improved intraoperative patient comfort, reduced anxiety and pain, and diminished need for anxiolytic and analgesic agents (Faymonville et al., 1995). As a consequence, they conducted a prospective investigation (Faymonville et al., 1997). Sixty patients undergoing elective plastic surgery (e.g., rhinoplasties, face lifts, breast augmentation) were randomly allocated to either a stress-reducing control treatment (CON) or hypnosis (HYP) treatment. Both treatments were administered by the same anesthesiologist. Patient anxiety, pain, and perceived control were monitored by the patient using visual analog scales (VASs) before, during, and after surgery. In addition, patient behavior during surgery was monitored by a psychologist and

PONV was assessed. The CON treatment included emotional support through continuous information, reassurance, and distraction. It included encouragement to employ cognitive strategies to assist in coping. The HYP state was described to patients as a "state of mental focalization on a pleasant life experience" (p. 362); however, the word *hypnosis* was deliberately not employed. The hypnotic procedure involved eye fixation, muscle relaxation, and permissive and indirect suggestions that varied from patient to patient. Neither group received explicit suggestions for analgesia. The two psychological treatments were augmented with midazolam and alfentinol to provide conscious sedation. Criteria for administration of analgesic and anxiolytic drugs included verbal and nonverbal patient complaints, tachypnea, tachycardia, and/or hypertension and were the same in both groups.

The main findings included a reduction in the intraoperative dosages of midazolam and alfentinol in the HYP group. In spite of this reduction in pharmacological sedation, peri- and postoperative pain and anxiety were also lower in the HYP group. The HYP treatment was also associated with reduced objective evidence of pain during surgery, enhanced feelings of control, diminished levels of PONV, and higher levels of patient satisfaction. As the authors acknowledge, a major limitation of this investigation is that the same anesthesiologist administered both treatments. Moreover, it proved impractical to have the anesthesiologist responsible for IV sedation to be blinded to the patient psychological treatment condition.

In a related study this same group of investigators (Meurisse et al., 1996) reported on a series of 108 thyroidectomies and 13 cervical explorations for hyperparathyroidism performed under hypnosedation (HYP), which they defined as a technique combining hypnosis and light conscious sedation. Hypnotizability was not assessed and no preparatory training sessions were provided. The operative data and postoperative courses were compared to that of a matched population ($n = 70$) of patients operated on for thyroid diseases under general anesthesia (GA). The surgeons all reported better operating conditions for cervicotomy under HYP than GA, estimated by VAS. The authors attributed this to reduced bleeding in the operative field. Reductions in bleeding have frequently been reported in conjunction with surgical applications of hypnosis (Chaves, 1993; Chaves & Barber, 1976). HYP patients also used less pain medication postoperatively and reported a higher level of satisfaction with the surgical experience compared to the GA patients. Other significant benefits associated with the use of hypnosis in this study included briefer hospital stays, less postoperative fatigue, and a more rapid resumption of social and professional activities.

The advantages associated with the use of hypnosis in surgery and other medical interventions do not seem to be restricted to adults. Lambert (1996) investigated the effects of a hypnosis/guided imagery intervention on the postoperative course of 52 children (matched for age, sex, and diagnosis) who were randomly assigned to an experimental or a control group. Children in the experimental group (HYP) were taught hypnosis/guided imagery during a preadmission visit of 30 minutes' duration 1 week before elective surgery. Children in the control condition (CON) spent a comparable amount of time with a research assistant discussing the surgery and other topics of interest to the children. The surgeries included spinal fusions and other orthopedic procedures, cardiac and thoracic surgery, and general surgery. The dependent variables in this study included numerical pain ratings by the children collected hourly in the immediate postoperative period and intermittently, at the nurses' discretion, until discharge. Children in the HYP group had shorter hospital stays and reported less pain than children in the CON group, even though there was no difference in the amount of pain medication received. Anxiety was reduced (pre- to postsurgically) in the HYP group while it increased in the CON condition, but differences between the groups postoperatively were not significant. Although the author concluded that anxiety was decreased postoperatively, that conclusion is not statistically justified by the data presented. The small number of subjects in this study and the lack of convergent measures of anxiety make it impossible to reach any firm conclusion about the effects of the intervention on anxiety.

Lumbar Punctures and Bone Marrow Aspiration

Zeltzer and colleagues have systematically investigated the use of hypnosis in reducing the anxiety and pain associated with lumbar puncture (LP) and bone marrow aspiration (BMA), as well as its use in reducing

disease-related distressing symptoms in children being treated for cancer (Hilgard & LeBaron, 1984; Zeltzer & LeBaron, 1983, 1986). Zeltzer and LaBaron (1982) compared hypnosis with a nonhypnotic behavioral intervention used to reduce pain and anxiety in 27 children and adolescents undergoing BMAs and 22 undergoing LPs. Patients and observers rated pain and anxiety during one of three procedures prior to and then following the intervention. BMA was rated as more painful than LP prior to the intervention for both groups. While pain was reduced by both hypnotic and nonhypnotic techniques, anxiety was reduced by hypnosis alone. During LP, only hypnosis reduced pain. The behavioral intervention specifically excluded any use of imagery or fantasy and may have been less effective for that reason alone. Similar findings were obtained in a related investigation (Kellerman et al., 1983) in which hypnotic interventions were introduced for 16 adolescents to ameliorate distress associated with BMA, LP, and chemotherapeutic injections. Significant reductions in pain and anxiety were found following treatment.

In a larger study (Ben-Zvi et al., 1982), 51 children from 6 to 17 years of age rated the severity of nausea, vomiting, and the extent to which chemotherapy bothered them during each course of chemotherapy. Sixteen patients reported no symptoms, while the doses administered to 16 others were not constant. After baseline measurement of two matched courses of treatment the remaining 19 patients were randomized to receive hypnosis or supportive counseling during two more matched courses. An additional course with no intervention was assessed in half of the patients. Interventions with both hypnosis and supportive counseling were associated with significant reductions in nausea, vomiting, and the extent to which these symptoms bothered patients. Following termination of the intervention, symptom ratings remained significantly lower than baseline. The authors concluded that chemotherapy-related nausea and emesis in children can be reduced with behavioral interventions, as well as hypnosis, and that reductions are maintained after intervention has been discontinued.

Chronic Musculoskeletal Pain

Hypnosis has at times been integrated into comprehensive treatment programs for patients with chronic low back pain. In one of the first controlled studies

(McCauley et al., 1983), 17 outpatients with low back pain were treated with either self-hypnosis or relaxation treatments. Patients in both groups showed comparable reductions in pain ratings and depression. Self-hypnosis subjects reported less time to sleep onset, and physicians rated their use of medication as less problematic after treatment.

Haanen et al. (1991), conducted a well-controlled study of 40 patients with refractory fibromyalgia (mean duration was 8.5 years) assigned either to hypnotherapy or physical therapy for 12 weeks with follow-up at 24 weeks. Hypnotherapy included eight 1-hour sessions over 3 months augmented with an audiotaped procedure introduced in the third session for daily use thereafter. Patients in the hypnotherapy group showed better outcomes in terms of pain ratings, fatigue on awakening, sleep pattern, and a global assessment (all assessed on VASs) at both 12 and 24 weeks. Similarly, hypnotherapy patients showed a significant decrease in psychological discomfort as measured by the Hopkins Symptom Checklist (Derogatis et al., 1974). The clinical advantage for hypnosis did not extend to more objective measures, such as magnitude production of tenderness with a dolorimeter and counts of the number of tender points. Nevertheless, the authors concluded that hypnosis was useful in relieving symptoms in this population.

Edelson and Fitzpatrick (1989) compared cognitive-behavioral and hypnotic interventions in chronic pain patients. They studied 27 male patients assigned to one of three treatment groups: hypnosis (HYP), cognitive-behavioral (CB), and attention control (AC). The HYP and CB treatments were identical, with the exception of the hypnotic induction procedure. While increases in activity and decreases in pain intensity as well as subjective changes measured by the Melzack-McGill Pain Questionnaire (MPQ) were found for the CB group, only subjective changes were found for the HYP group. The same pattern of results was obtained at time of treatment as well as at 1-month follow-up. The authors interpreted these findings as supporting the superiority of CB in chronic pain management.

Crawford and associates have attempted to elucidate the psychophysiological mechanisms underlying hypnotic analgesia in chronic back pain patients (Crawford et al., 1998). They studied 15 adults with chronic low back pain (mean duration = 4 years), ages 18 to 43 years. All but one proved to be moderately to highly hypnotizable. Subjects were trained to reduce cold pressor pain during the first part of the study. Subsequently, scalp-recorded somatosensory event–related potentials were recorded in response to painful electrical stimulation of the median nerve. Responses were collected under waking and hypnotic attend conditions as well as hypnotic analgesia conditions in an ABA design with subjects serving as their own controls. Pain ratings were significantly reduced under hypnotic analgesia conditions compared to waking-attend and hypnotic-attend conditions. Moreover, the evoked responses during hypnotic analgesia showed an enhanced response at N140 in the anterior frontal electrode placements and a diminished amplitude at P200 and P300 and at several midfrontal and central sites. The results were interpreted as supporting the existence of an inhibitory dissociative process underlying hypnotic analgesia. Patients were encouraged to apply their newly acquired skills in managing experimentally produced pain to their clinical pain and showed improvement over the course of the three experimental sessions. Although interesting, these results need to be interpreted cautiously, as the magnitude of sensory evoked potentials has long been known to be altered by cognitive activity that is under the control of the subjects (e.g., Davis et al., 1968; Donald & Goff, 1971; Zerlin & Davis, 1967). Studies attempting to relate changes in evoked responses specifically to hypnosis must control for these effects as well as for well-known methodological artifacts introduced when hypnotic subjects serve as their own controls (Spanos & Chaves, 1970; Spanos et al., 1984).

Headache and Vaso-Occlusive Pain

Ter Kuile and associates (1996) were interested in assessing the relative roles of relaxation and cognitive change in the response of patients with chronic headaches to psychological treatments. One hundred forty-four patients were randomly assigned for a 7-week treatment period to a cognitive self-hypnosis (CSH) or an autogenic relaxation training (AT) treatment condition. CSH was more effective than AT in changing the cognitive coping strategies that were the target of the intervention. There was only a limited relationship between changes in the use of coping strategies and the pain appraisal (a combined measure of frequency and intensity). Changes in expectation of treatment efficacy were significantly predictive of long-term (6 month) pain reductions. This finding was interpreted as supporting the importance of expectation of pain reduction in psychological methods for pain control (Kirsch & Council, 1989).

Spanos et al. (1993), however, found that expectation could not account for the pain reductions they observed in a study of 136 university student volunteers who reported chronic headaches. They received one or four sessions of either an imagery-based hypnotic treatment or a placebo treatment (described as "subliminal reconditioning") and were compared with a control monitoring group. Hypnotic and placebo groups showed equivalent and significant reductions in headache activity posttreatment and for an 8-week follow-up. The magnitude of headache reduction was unrelated to expectation for treatment success.

Hypnotizability may also play an important role in treatment efficacy for both hypnotic and nonhypnotic treatments for headache. Ter Kuile et al. (1994) compared the efficacy of AT and CSH for the treatment of chronic headache in comparison with a waiting list control. A total of 146 patients were included in the study. There was a significant reduction in the Headache Index scores of both treated groups compared to controls. Treatment gains were greater for the higher than the lower hypnotizable patients, and these gains, as well as the differential, were maintained through follow-up.

Similarly, Nolan, et al. (1994) investigated the use of hypnotic and nonhypnotic response-based imagery training for recurrent headache. In one study, 42 subjects with chronic migraine headache or chronic mixed migraine/tension headaches were randomly assigned to either a hypnotic (HI) or a nonhypnotic imagery treatment (NI) or to a monitoring control condition (MC). Treatment efficacy was assessed at 2-week intervals, beginning with baseline, posttreatment, and at three successive follow-up periods. In a second study, 47 subjects with chronic tension headaches were assigned to one of four conditions (HI/NI/placebo/MC). The results of both studies showed that response-based imagery treatments (HI/NI) produced significant, comparable, and sustained reductions in headache activity.

Whether or not a procedure is labeled hypnotic may be important in the treatment of headache. Zitman et al. (1992) assigned 79 tension headache patients to an abbreviated form of AT, a form of hypnotherapy called future-oriented hypnotic imagery (FOI) that was not characterized as a form of hypnosis, or another FOI-H group in which the procedure was explicitly labeled as hypnotic. Although the three treatments were equally effective at posttreatment, at 6-month follow-up the FOI-H group was superior to the AT group. Unlike the AT and FOI groups, there were no dropouts from follow-up in the FOI-H group.

Dinges et al. (1997) investigated the use of self-hypnosis in the management of vaso-occlusive ischemic pain associated with sickle-cell disease. A cohort of patients who reported three or more episodes of vaso-occlusive pain the preceding year was enrolled in a prospective two-period treatment protocol. After a 4-month conventional treatment phase a self-hypnosis–centered cognitive-behavioral pain management program was implemented over the following 18 months. Weekly group self-hypnosis training sessions continued for the first 6 months, followed by bi-weekly (for 6 months) and triweekly sessions (for the next 6 months). The self-hypnosis intervention was associated with a significant reduction in pain days. The proportion of "bad sleep" nights as well as the use of pain medications decreased significantly during the self-hypnosis treatment phase. Nevertheless, participants continued to report disturbed sleep and required medications on those days during which they did experience pain. The reduction in pain frequency was primarily attributable to the elimination of the less severe episodes of pain. While the authors acknowledge that nonspecific factors may have contributed to these outcomes, self-hypnosis appeared to be a useful adjunct to other approaches for reducing recurrent and unpredictable pain in this population, for whom few treatment alternatives exist.

Cancer

Reports involving the use of hypnosis in the management of cancer began to appear in the 1950s. Its primary use has been as a strategy to control symptoms and as one component in multifaceted supportive therapies (Hilgard & Hilgard, 1983; Hilgard & LeBaron, 1984; Stam & Steggles, 1987; Syrjala & Chapko, 1995). Annotated bibliographies have appeared covering the literature on the use of hypnosis in adult cancer and in children and adolescents (Steggles et al., 1987; Steggles, Damore-Petingola, et al., 1997;

Steggles, Maxwell, et al., 1997). Critical reviews of the role of hypnosis and cancer (e.g., Genuis, 1995; Trijsburg, van Knippenberg, & Rijpma, 1992; Levitan 1992; Stamm, 1989) have generally concluded that hypnosis can be a useful clinical tool in managing the anxiety and other negative symptoms associated with cancer and its treatment.

Syrjala et al. (1987) studied 50 patients receiving chemotherapy and irradiation prior to bone marrow transplantation. Bone marrow transplantation is frequently accompanied by desquamation, inflammation, and ulceration in oropharyngeal mucosa associated with severe pain for 2–3 weeks, often requiring the use of narcotics. Patients were assigned to a hypnosis group, a cognitive training group, and a therapist contact control group for management of pain associated with treatment. Hypnosis patients showed significant reductions in pain compared to the other groups.

In another investigation (Syrjala, Cummings, & Donaldson, 1992), 67 bone marrow transplant patients with hematological malignancies were assigned to one of four treatment groups prior to treatment: hypnosis (HYP), cognitive-behavioral coping skills training (CB), therapist contact control (TC), or treatment as usual (TAU). Hypnosis was effective in reducing reported oral pain for patients undergoing marrow transplantation. Nausea, emesis, and opioid use did not differ significantly between the treatment groups. The cognitive-behavioral intervention employed in this study was not effective in reducing the symptoms measured. Interestingly, imagery was not used with this group.

In a related study, Syrjala et al. (1995) compared oral mucositis pain levels in four groups of cancer patients receiving bone marrow transplants (BMT): (1) TAU, (2) TC, (3) relaxation and imagery training, and (4) training in a package of cognitive-behavioral coping skills including relaxation and imagery. Ninety-four patients completed the study, which involved two training sessions prior to treatment and twice-a-week "booster" sessions during the first 5 weeks of treatment. Patients who received either relaxation and imagery alone or patients who received the package of cognitive-behavioral coping skills reported less pain than patients in the other two groups. The cognitive-behavioral skills package failed to have an additive effect beyond relaxation and imagery alone.

Spiegel and associates (Spiegel, 1990; Spiegel & Bloom, 1983; Spiegel et al., 1989) have completed a 10-year follow-up of 86 women with metastatic breast cancer who were randomized to either a year of weekly psychosocial support groups or routine ontologic care. The psychosocial intervention was complex and included self-hypnosis. Survival duration for the women receiving psychosocial support was significantly longer (36.6 months vs. 18.9 months), although the intervention was focused on quality rather than duration of life. Moreover, in other phases of the investigation the intervention was also associated with reduced mood disturbance and phobic preoccupation, improved coping, and reduced pain.

It is unclear what mechanisms might be mediating these effects. Social isolation itself seems to be a risk factor for cancer (House, Landis, & Umberson, 1988; Reynolds & Kaplan, 1990). Psychosocial factors may serve as a buffer that attenuates the psychophysiological effects of stress. One possibility is that these effects are mediated by the immune system. For example, Kennedy, Kiecolt-Glaser, & Glaser (1988) found reductions in the percentage of T-helper lymphocytes as well as the number and activity of natural killer cells in medical students during examination periods, except for those with strong social support. Moreover, stress has been associated with reduced levels of killer cell activity among breast cancer patients (Levy et al., 1987). Because of the importance of the Spiegel et al. (1989) findings, an effort is underway to replicate them in a multicenter randomized trial being conducted in Canada (Brown et al., 1993).

Hawkins et al. (1995) conducted a randomized, controlled-design study to assess the therapeutic use of hypnosis to control anticipatory and postchemotherapy nausea and vomiting in 30 pediatric oncology patients while controlling for gains that may be derived from nonspecific therapeutic factors. Patients were randomly assigned to one of three groups during chemotherapy: "treatment as usual" control group, therapist-contact group, and a hypnosis training group. Both hypnosis and therapist contact reduced anticipatory nausea, although the authors concluded that the effect of the therapist contact was "statistical" rather than "clinical."

Jacknow et al. (1994) conducted a prospective, randomized, and controlled single-blind trial in 20 patients receiving chemotherapy for treatment of cancer.

Patients were randomized to either hypnosis or standard treatment. Hypnosis was used as primary treatment for nausea and vomiting, with antiemetic medication employed on a supplemental (p.r.n.) basis only, whereas the control group received a standardized antiemetic medication regimen. Patients in the hypnosis group used less p.r.n antiemetic medication than control subjects. The groups did not differ in severity of nausea and vomiting. The hypnosis group experienced less anticipatory nausea than the control group at 1 to 2 months postdiagnosis. The results suggested that self-hypnosis is effective for decreasing antiemetic medication usage and for reducing anticipatory nausea during chemotherapy.

Burn Pain

Hypnosis has been used to alleviate pain as well as reduce anxiety and depression in patients who have experienced severe burns. These patients face significant pain associated with their condition as well as acute exacerbations of their pain associated with treatment, which can include repeated surgeries and wound debridement (Van der Does & Van Dyck, 1989). The successful use of hypnosis can improve comfort, decrease reliance on medication, and contribute to a sense of personal control. Although hypnosis has long been advocated as a valuable tool in this application (e.g., Crasilneck et al., 1955; Ewin, 1986; Schafer, 1975), little systematic evidence has been put forward to support its effectiveness. Van der Does, Van Dyck, and Spijker (1988) conducted a pilot study using hypnosis to reduce pain associated with dressing changes in eight burn patients, all of whom evaluated the intervention as beneficial. Four of these patients were monitored more closely, with pain and anxiety rating collected on a daily basis. These patients showed about a 30% reduction in both mean pain and anxiety ratings.

The effect of hypnosis on burn patients seems much more pronounced in the psychological than in the physiological domain. May and DeClement (1983) monitored 10 physiological parameters related to fluid volume and hemodynamics in 16 patients with burns covering 4% to 83% of their body surface area (BSA) who had been treated with a single hypnotic intervention within several hours of their burn. Compared with 16 matched controls, the only distinguishing variable was an elevated urine output in the hypnosis group during the first 48 hours postburn. The difference was inversely related to burn size up to 35% BSA. Patients with BSAs equal to or greater than 50% who presented with significant physiological stress and hypovolemia were found to be unresponsive to hypnotic interventions. A significant limitation of this study is the relatively modest intensity of the hypnotic intervention.

Patterson and colleagues (Patterson, 1989, 1995; Patterson, Adcock, & Bombardier, 1997; Patterson et al., 1992; Patterson, Goldberg, & Ehde, 1996; Patterson & Ptacek, 1997) have provided a series of important investigations looking at the use of hypnosis with burn patients. In the most recent investigation of 61 patients hospitalized for severe burns (Patterson & Ptacek, 1997), hypnosis was found to be more effective than a nonhypnotic psychological intervention only for patients reporting higher initial pain levels. At lower levels, both treatments were equally effective in reducing pain. These results were consistent with those of an earlier study (Everett et al. 1993) in which 32 burn patients were assigned to the following treatments as adjuncts to opioids for control of pain during dressing changes: hypnosis, lorazipam, hypnosis plus lorazapam, or placebo control. Pain, measured on a VAS, decreased to a comparable degree over consecutive days for all groups. The results support the analgesic advantages of early, aggressive opioid use via patient-controlled analgesia. Taken together, the data suggest that if hypnosis offers a unique advantage for burn patients as compared to other interventions, it may require a substantial treatment intervention with patients who are experiencing comparatively high levels of pain.

Gastrointestinal Disorders

Linkages between psychological distress and gastrointestinal disorders have been recognized for more than 100 years (Goldberg & Davidson, 1997; Francis & Houghton, 1996; Langeluddecke, 1985). Moreover, symptoms referable to the gastrointestinal system are quite common. Irritable bowel syndrome (IBS) affects up to 17% of the general population, although a substantially smaller percentage seek medical care for their condition (Goldberg & Davidson, 1997). Up to 75% of treated patients respond to standard medical treatments, including bulking to relieve con-stipation, spasmolytics to alleviate pain, and anti-diarrheals to help control urgency and diarrhea. For the 25% who do not respond, alternative therapies such as stress management, psychotherapy, or hyp-notherapy have been advocated (Prior & Whorwell, 1986). Although there is general agreement that con-clusions about the beneficial effects of hypnosis are limited by reliance on case reports, the number and consistency of those reports offer encouragement to those reviewing the topic (Whitehead, 1992; Francis & Houghton, 1996).

There are several controlled studies of patients with IBS who did not respond to traditional treat-ments and were treated with hypnosis. One controlled trial of hypnotherapy (Whorwell, Prior, & Faragher, 1984) randomized patients to two groups: a hypnosis group and a supportive therapy control group. Treat-ment effects were measured with visual analog scales and showed significantly greater improvements for the hypnosis group in abdominal pain, bowel habits, distension, and general well-being. Moreover, follow-up revealed that all but two of the hypnosis pa-tients remained in remission, with both relapsing patients responding well to a booster session of hyp-notherapy (Whorwell, Prior, & Colgan, 1987). These investigators also reported on an additional 35 pa-tients added to the series with patients further subdi-vided into classical cases, atypical cases, and cases exhibiting significant psychopathology. The response rates for the groups were 95%, 43%, and 60%, re-spectively. Interestingly, patients over the age of 50 displayed a much lower favorable response rate (25%) than those below age 50 who had classical IBS (100%).

Subsequent studies suggest that the effects of the hypnotic intervention may be mediated by changes in gastrointestinal sensitivity. Prior, Colgan, and Whor-well (1990) compared rectal sensitivity in 15 hypnotic patients and 15 controls with IBS. They found a sig-nificant decrease in rectal sensitivity in patients with diarrhea-predominant IBS both after a course of hyp-notherapy and during a session of hypnosis. No changes in rectal compliance or distension-induced motor activity were found in either group. Nor were there any changes in somatic pain thresholds. The au-thors concluded that changes in visceral sensitivity accounted for the observed treatment effect.

In a related study, Whorwell et al. (1992) examined the effect of hypnotically induced emotional states (excitement, anger, and happiness) on distal colonic motility in 18 patients with IBS. Hypnosis was asso-ciated with decreases in colonic motility as well as decreases in pulse and respiration. When emotions of anger and excitement were suggested, these parame-ters increased. Happiness reduced colonic motility but not significantly lower than the reduction observed during hypnosis alone. Thus, the beneficial effects of hypnosis on gastrointestinal function may be to atten-uate the increases in gastrointestinal motility that may accompany unpleasant emotional states.

Finally, Houghton, Heyman, and Whorwell (1996) assessed the global impact of hypnotherapeutic treat-ment in IBS. They assessed quality of life as well as employment and health-seeking behavior in 25 IBS patients treated with hypnotherapy and 25 control IBS patients matched for disease severity. Visual analog scales were used to assess the patients' symptoms and satisfaction with various aspects of life. Patients treated with hypnotherapy reported less abdominal pain, bloat-ing, flatulence, urinary symptoms, lethargy, backache, and dyspareunia. Quality-of-life measures, such as well-being, mood, locus of control, physical well-being, and work attitude, also favored the hypnotic subjects. Alternatively, the controls were likely to take time off work and visit their physician. The authors concluded that although hypnosis can be expensive to provide, its broad-ranging benefits may justify the expense.

Talley et al. (1996) offered a detailed critique of all of the controlled treatment trials that have been conducted to evaluate the use of a variety of psycho-logical treatments for IBS. They developed a quality algorithm for evaluating the 14 studies they were able to locate that met their selection criteria. Only the Whorwell study of hypnotherapy (Whorwell, Prior, & Faragher, 1984) was judged to have exceeded their quality cut-off score, although concern was expressed about the generalizability of the findings due to the fact that patients were nonconsecutive volunteers from the investigator's private practice.

Respiratory Disorders and Tinnitis

Recent reviews have pointed to the wide array of evi-dence suggesting that hypnosis may play a helpful role in the treatment of respiratory disorders, especially asthma (Covino & Frankel, 1993; Lewith & Watkins, 1996; Wadden & Anderton, 1982). At the same time, these authors acknowledge the absence of randomized controlled trials in this area. While it is important to acknowledge the methodological limitations of studies in this area, it may be useful to consider some studies that are suggestive.

Kohen and associates (Kohen, 1987; Kohen et al., 1984; Kohen & Wynne, 1997) have been studying the use of hypnosis in pediatric populations with asthma as well as other disorders. In an early study (Kohen et al., 1984), they assessed the outcome of hypnotherapeutic interventions for 505 children and adolescents seen by four pediatricians over a period of 1 year and followed for periods ranging from 4 months to 2 years. These patients presented with a variety of problems including enuresis, acute pain, chronic pain, asthma, habit disorders, obesity, encopresis, and anxiety. Employing strict criteria for problem resolution (e.g., all beds dry) and recognizing that some conditions were intrinsically chronic, the authors concluded that 51% of these children and adolescents achieved complete resolution of the presenting problem; an additional 32% achieved significant improvement, 9% showed initial or some improvement, and 7% demonstrated no apparent change or improvement. They employed hypnosis with children as young as 3 years of age, although they concluded that facility with self-hypnosis increased with age in this pediatric population.

In a more recent investigation, focused on asthma, Kohen and Wynne (1997) developed a preschool asthma program that incorporated a hypnotic treatment component. Twenty-five children and their parents participated in the seven-session program. At 1-year follow-up, physician visits for asthma were reduced and symptom severity scores were improved significantly. However, there were no changes in frequency of asthma episodes or in performance on pulmonary function tests before and after the program.

Studies suggesting an improvement of asthmatic symptoms with hypnosis naturally lead to the question of whether there is a fundamental change in physiological function or whether the observed improvements represent only a change in the perception of symptom severity. A recent study by Isenberg, Lehrer, and Hochron (1992) shed some light on this question. They told 33 asthmatic subjects that they were receiving, alternately, an inhaled bronchoconstrictor and inhaled bronchodilator, although they actually were only breathing room air. They found that 35–40% of asthmatics may bronchoconstrict in response to suggestions or stress. Suggestion was found to have a significant effect on perception of bronchial changes, but the correlation between actual and perceived changes was minimal. Correlations among self-report variables indicated that three variables were related to suggestions and asthma: response to suggestion of bronchial change, feelings of physical vulnerability, and anxiety. However, there was no relationship between airway response and hypnotic suggestibility as measured by the Harvard Group Scale.

In a similar vein, Mason, Rogerson, and Butler (1996) found that greater subjective magnitude of improvement was the only outcome that could distinguish hypnosis from counseling in the treatment of tinnitis. Their study looked at subjective outcomes as well as outcomes thought to be more objective, such as tinnitus loudness matches, in 96 patients randomly assigned to either a one-session counseling session or a three-session hypnosis treatment. Forty-five percent of the hypnosis group reported symptomatic improvement at the conclusion of treatment compared to only 14% for the counseling group. This difference was maintained at a 3-month follow-up.

SUMMARY AND CONCLUSIONS

An evidence-based foundation for the use of hypnosis in the management of anxiety associated with medical and dental conditions and their treatment is beginning to be established. It is supported with a number of reasonably well-controlled studies, including prospective randomized trials, that are beginning to replace the uncontrolled case study as the primary source of support in the hypnosis literature. Although the difficulties in conducting and interpreting these investigations are substantial, they will play an increasingly important role in gaining acceptance for hypnosis in clinical settings and sharpening our appreciation of the circumstances in which hypnosis may offer a strategic therapeutic advantage. More studies, with improved methodological rigor, are needed to further advance these applications. The role of hypnotizability, both as a risk factor that may enhance maladaptive responses to stressors and as a skill that facilitates response to clinical hypnotic procedures, needs further investigation, as do the advantages and disadvantages associated with the explicit labeling of these procedures as hypnotic.

Although strategies for enhancing hypnotizability have been studied in the experimental setting, we have little information about enhancing hypnotizability in clinical settings, where more complex motivational and expectational issues may come into play. The intensity of the hypnotic intervention also needs further assessment. Studies that have employed intensive preparation for hypnotic interventions and have monitored compliance and provided reinforcement for ongoing practice with hypnotic procedures seem to achieve more impressive outcomes than those that do not. The range of conditions to which hypnotic procedures can be applied also requires better delineation. At present the number and quality of the studies in some areas, such as cancer and headache treatment, are much better than in other areas.

The pathways through which hypnotic procedures produce clinical gains also need further investigation (Gonsalkorale, 1996). To what extent do hypnotic procedures reduce anxiety directly, or indirectly through the reduction of other symptoms such as pain? Is anxiety reduced through an enhanced sense of personal control and self-efficacy derived from experience with hypnotic skills? What role does expectancy play in mediating the clinical gains achieved with hypnotic procedures? The answers to these questions have theoretical relevance and may be of practical importance as we attempt to optimize treatment efficacy. The available data only hint at the possible answers to these questions. Nevertheless, at present, hypnosis is taking its place along with related cognitive-behavioral and relaxation-oriented techniques as a valuable adjunct and sometimes as a primary tool in the reduction of anxiety associated with medical conditions and their treatment.

REFERENCES

Aartman, I. H., de Jongh, A., & van der Meulen, M. J. (1997). Psychological characteristics of patients applying for treatment in a dental fear clinic. *European Journal of Oral Sciences, 105,* 384–388.

Ashton, C., Jr., Whitworth, G. C., Seldomridge, J. A., Shapiro, P. A., Weinberg, A. D., Michler, R. E., Smith, C. R., Rose, E. A., Fisher, S., & Oz, M. C. (1997). Self-hypnosis reduces anxiety following coronary artery bypass surgery: A prospective, randomized trial. *Journal of Cardiovascular Surgery, 38,* 69–75.

Barber, J. (1977). Rapid induction analgesia: A clinical report. *American Journal of Clinical Hypnosis, 19,* 138–149.

Barber, T. X. (1969). *Hypnosis: A scientific approach.* New York: Van Nostrand Reinhold.

Barber, T. X., & Calverley, D. S. (1964a). The definition of the situation as a variable affecting "hypnotic-like" suggestibility. *Journal of Clinical Psychology, 20,* 438–440.

Barber, T. X., & Calverley, D. S. (1964b). Effect of E's tone of voice on "hypnotic-like" suggestibility. *Psychological Reports, 15,* 139–144.

Barber, T. X., & Calverley, D. S. (1964c). Toward a theory of hypnotic behavior: Effects on suggestibility of defining the situation as hypnosis and defining response to suggestions as easy. *Journal of Abnormal and Social Psychology, 68*(6), 583–592.

Barber, T. X., & Calverley, D. S. (1965). Empirical evidence for a theory of "hypnotic" behavior: The suggestibility enhancing effects of motivational suggestions, relaxation, sleep suggestions, and suggestions that the S will be effectively "hypnotized." *Journal of Personality, 33*(2), 256–270.

Barber, T. X., & De-Moor, W. (1972). A theory of hypnotic induction procedures. *American Journal of Clinical Hypnosis, 15,* 112–135.

Barber, T. X., Spanos, N. P., & Chaves, J. F. (1974). *Hypnotism: Imagination and human potentialities.* New York: Pergamon Press.

Bartlett, K. A. (1970). Knowledge gained from hypnosis. *Journal of the American Dental Association, 80,* 125–132.

Bejenke, C. J. (1996). Painful medical procedures. In J. Barber (Ed.), *Hypnosis and suggestion in the treatment of pain: A clinical guide* (pp. 209–266). New York: Norton.

Benson, H., Arns, P. A., & Hoffman, J. W. (1981). The relaxation response and hypnosis. *International Journal of Clinical and Experimental Hypnosis, 29,* 259–270.

Ben-Zvi, Z., Lam, C., Hoffman, J., Teets-Grimm, K. C., & Kattan, M. (1982). An evaluation of the initial treatment of acute asthma. *Pediatrics, 70,* 348–353.

Bernstein, D. A., Kleinknecht, R. A., & Alexander, L. D. (1979). Antecedents of dental fear. *Journal of Public Health Dentistry, 39,* 113–124.

Blankfield, R. P., Zyzanski, S. J., Flocke, S. A., Alemagno, S., & Scheurman, K. (1995). Taped therapeutic suggestions and taped music as adjuncts in the care of coronary-artery-bypass patients. *American Journal of Clinical Hypnosis, 37,* 32–42.

Block, R. I., Ghoneim, M. M., Sum Ping, S. T., & Ali, M. A. (1991). Efficacy of therapeutic suggestions for improved postoperative recovery presented during general anesthesia. *Anesthesiology, 75*, 746–755.

Bonilla, K. B., Quigley, W. F., & Bowers, W. F. (1961). Experience with hypnosis on a surgical service. *Military Medicine, 126*, 364–366.

Brown, D. P. (1992). Clinical hypnosis research since 1986. In E. Fromm & M. R. Nash (Eds.), *Contemporary hypnosis research* (pp. 427–458). New York: Guilford Press.

Brown, J., Chaves, J. F., & Leonoff, A. (1981). Spontaneous cognitive strategies in two groups of chronic pain patients. Presented to the American Psychological Association, Los Angeles, 1981.

Brown, P., Pritchard, K. I., Koopmans, J., Chochinov, H. M., Navarro, M., Linn, G., Steggles, S., Bellissimo, A., & Goodwin, P. J. (1993). The BEST randomized trial of group psychosocial support in metastatic breast cancer: Pilot results. International Association for Breast Cancer Research, Biennial Meeting. April 25–28, Calgary, Alberta, Canada.

Chaves, J. F. (1981). *Tactics and strategies in clinical hypnosis*. Audiotape series. San Francisco: Proseminar.

Chaves, J. F. (1985). Hypnosis in the management of phantom limb pain. In E. T. Dowd & J. M. Healy (Eds.), *Case studies in hypnotherapy* (pp. 198–209). New York: Guilford Press.

Chaves, J. F. (1989). Hypnotic control of clinical pain. In N. P. Spanos & J. F. Chaves (Eds.), *Hypnosis: The cognitive-behavioral perspective* (pp. 242–272). Buffalo, NY: Prometheus Books.

Chaves, J. F. (1993). Hypnosis in pain management. In J. W. Rhue, S. J. Lynn, & I. Kirsch (Eds.), *Handbook of clinical hypnosis* (pp. 511–532). Washington, DC: American Psychological Association.

Chaves, J. F. (1997). The state of the "state" debate in hypnosis: A view from the cognitive-behavioral perspective. *International Journal of Clinical and Experimental Hypnosis, 45*(3), 251–265.

Chaves, J. F., & Barber, T. X. (1974). Cognitive strategies, experimenter modeling, and expectation in the attenuation of pain. *Journal of Abnormal Psychology, 83*, 356–363.

Chaves, J. F., & Barber, T. X. (1976). Hypnotic procedures and surgery: A critical analysis with applications to "acupuncture analgesia." *American Journal of Clinical Hypnosis, 18*, 217–236.

Chaves, J. F., & Brown, J. F. (1978). Self-generated strategies for the control of clinical pain and stress. Presented at the annual meeting of the American Psychological Association, Toronto, Canada.

Chaves, J. F., & Brown, J. M. (1987). Spontaneous coping strategies for pain. *Journal of Behavioral Medicine, 10*, 263–276.

Chaves, J. F., & Dworkin, S. F. (1997). Hypnotic control of pain: Historical perspectives and future prospects. *International Journal of Clinical and Experimental Hypnosis, 45*(4), 356–376.

Clarke, J. H., & Reynolds, P. J. (1991). Suggestive hypnotherapy for nocturnal bruxism. *American Journal of Clinical Hypnosis, 33*, 248–253.

Coe, W. C., Paterson, P., & Gwynn, M. (1995). Expectation and sequelae to hypnosis: Initial findings. *American Journal of Clinical Hypnosis, 38*, 3–12.

Covino, N. A., & Frankel, F. H. (1993). Hypnosis and relaxation in the medically ill. *Psychotherapy and Psychosomatics, 60*(2), 75–90.

Covino, N. A., Jimerson, D. C., Wolfe, B. E., Franko, D. L., & Frankel, F. H. (1994). Hypnotizability, dissociation, and bulimia nervosa. *Journal of Abnormal Psychology, 103*, 455–459.

Crabtree, A. (1993). From Mesmer to Freud: Magnetic sleep and the roots of psychological healing. New Haven, CT: Yale University Press.

Crasilneck, H. B., Stirman, J. A., Wilson, B. J., McCranie, E. J., & Fogelman, M. J. (1955). Use of hypnosis in the management of patients with burns. *JAMA, 158*, 103–106.

Crawford, H. J., Hilgard, J. R., & Macdonald, H. (1982). Transient experiences following hypnotic testing and special termination procedures. *International Journal of Clinical and Experimental Hypnosis, 30*, 117–126.

Crawford, H. J., Knebel, T., Kaplan, L., Vendemia, J. M., Xie, M., Jamison, S., & Pribram, K. H. (1998). Hypnotic analgesia: 1. Somatosensory event-related potential changes to noxious stimuli and 2. Transfer learning to reduce chronic low back pain. *International Journal of Clinical and Experimental Hypnosis, 46*, 92–132.

Davis, H., Zerlin, S., Bowers, C., & Spoor, A. (1968). Some interactions of the vertex potentials. *Electroencephalography and Clinical Neurophysiology, 24*, 285.

Deane, J. (1844). Amputation of the leg in the mesmeric state. *Boston Medical and Surgical Journal, 32*, 194–197.

de Jongh, A., Muris, P., ter Horst, G., van Zuuren, F., Schoenmakers, N., & Makkes, P. (1995). One-session cognitive treatment of dental phobia: Preparing dental phobics for treatment by restructuring negative cognitions. *Behaviour Research and Therapy, 33*, 947–954.

Delatour, M. (1826). Untitled report. *L'Hermès, 25*, 144–146.

Derogatis, L. R., Lipman, R. S., Richels, K., Uhlenhuth, E. H., & Covi, L. (1974). The Hopkins Symptom Checklist. *Pharmacopsychiatry, 7*, 79–100.

Derogatis, L. R., Rickles, K., & Rock, A. F. (1976). The SCL-90 and the MMPI: A step in the validation of a new self-report scale. *British Journal of Psychiatry, 128,* 280–290.

Dinges, D. F., Whitehouse, W. G., Orne, E. C., Bloom, P. B., Carlin, M. M., Bauer, N. K., Gillen, K. A., Shapiro, B. S., Ohene-Frempong, K., Dampier, C., & Orne, M. T. (1997). Self-hypnosis training as an adjunctive treatment in the management of pain associated with sickle cell disease. *International Journal of Clinical and Experimental Hypnosis, 45,* 417–432.

Donald, M. W., Jr., & Goff, W. R. (1971). Attention-related increases in cortical responsivity dissociated from the contingent negative variation. *Science, 172,* 1163–1166.

Edelson, J., & Fitzpatrick, J. L. (1989). A comparison of cognitive-behavioral and hypnotic treatments of chronic pain. *Journal of Clinical Psychology, 45,* 316–323.

Edmonston, E. E., Jr. (1986). *The induction of hypnosis.* New York: Wiley.

Enqvist, B., Bjorklund, C., Engman, M., & Jakobsson, J. (1997). Preoperative hypnosis reduces postoperative vomiting after surgery of the breasts: A prospective, randomized and blinded study. *Acta Anaesthesiologica Scandinavica, 41,* 1028–1032.

Enqvist, B., & Fischer, K. (1997). Preoperative hypnotic techniques reduce consumption of analgesics after surgical removal of third mandibular molars: A brief communication. *International Journal of Clinical and Experimental Hypnosis, 45,* 102–108.

Enqvist, B., von Konow, L., & Bystedt, H. (1995). Pre- and perioperative suggestion in maxillofacial surgery: Effects on blood loss and recovery. *International Journal of Clinical and Experimental Hypnosis, 43,* 284–294.

Everett, J. J., Patterson, D. R, Burns, G. L., Montgomery, B., & Heimbach, D. (1993). Adjunctive interventions for burn pain control: Comparison of hypnosis and ativan. *Journal of Burn Care and Rehabilitation 14* (6, Nov.–Dec.), 676–683.

Ewin, D. M. (1986). Emergency room hypnosis for the burned patient. *American Journal of Clinical Hypnosis, 29,* 7–12.

Faymonville, M. E., Fissette, J., Mambourg, P. H., Roediger, L., Joris, J., & Lamy, M. (1995). Hypnosis as adjunct therapy in conscious sedation for plastic surgery. *Regional Anesthesia, 20,* 145–151.

Faymonville, M. E., Mambourg, P. H., Joris, J., Vrijens, B., Fissette, J., Albert, A., & Lamy, M. (1997). Psychological approaches during conscious sedation: Hypnosis versus stress reducing strategies: A prospective randomized study. *Pain, 73,* 361–367.

Francis, C. Y., & Houghton, L. A. (1996). Use of hypnotherapy in gastrointestinal disorders. *European Journal of Gastroenterology and Hepatology, 8,* 525–529.

Frankel, F. H. (1987). Significant developments in medical hypnosis during the past 25 years. *International Journal of Clinical and Experimental Hypnosis, 35,* 231–247.

Frankel, F. M., & Orne, M. T. (1976). Hypnotizability and phobic behavior. *Archives of General Psychiatry, 33,* 1259–1261.

Fülöp-Miller, R. (1938). *Triumph over pain.* New York: Bobbs-Merrill.

Genuis, M. L. (1995). The use of hypnosis in helping cancer patients control anxiety, pain, and emesis: A review of recent empirical studies. *American Journal of Clinical Hypnosis, 37*(4), 316–325.

Gershman, J. A., Burrows, G. D., & Reade, P. C. (1987). Hypnotizability and dental phobic disorder. *International Journal of Psychosomatics, 33,* 42–47.

Gick, M., McLeod, C., & Hulihan, D. (1997). Absorption, social desirability, and symptoms in a behavioral medicine population. *Journal of Nervous and Mental Disease, 185,* 454–458.

Gillett, P. L., & Coe, W. C. (1984). The effects of rapid induction analgesia (RIA), hypnotic susceptibility and the severity of discomfort on reducing dental pain. *American Journal of Clinical Hypnosis, 27,* 81–90.

Gokli, M. A., Wood, A. J., Mourino, A. P., Farrington, F. H., & Best, A. M. (1994). Hypnosis as an adjunct to the administration of local anesthetic in pediatric patients. *Journal of Dentistry for Children* (July/August), 272–275.

Goldberg, J., & Davidson, P. (1997). A biopsychosocial understanding of the irritable bowel syndrome: A review. *Canadian Journal of Psychiatry—Revue Canadienne de Psychiatrie, 42,* 835–840.

Gonsalkorale, W. M. (1996). The use of hypnosis in medicine: The possible pathways involved. *European Journal of Gastroenterology and Hepatology, 8*(6), 520–524.

Haanen, H. C. M., Hoenderdos, H. T. W., van Romunde, L. K. J., Hop, W. C. J., Mallee, C., Terwiel, J. P., & Hekster, G. (1991). Controlled trial of hypnotherapy in the treatment of refractory fibromyalgia. *Journal of Rheumatology, 18,* 72–75.

Hammarstrand, G., Berggren, U., & Hakeberg, M. (1995). Psychophysiological therapy vs. hypnotherapy in the treatment of patients with dental phobia. *European Journal of Oral Sciences, 103,* 399–404.

Hawkins, P. J., Liossi, C., Ewart, B. W., Hatira, P., Kosmidis, V. H. & Varvutsi, M. (1995). Hypnotherapy for control of anticipatory nausea and vomiting in children with cancer: Preliminary findings. *Psycho-Oncology, 4*(2), 101–106.

Hilgard, E. R., & Hilgard, J. R. (1983). *Hypnosis in the relief of pain* (2d ed.). Los Altos, CA: Kaufmann.

Hilgard, J. R. (1970). *Personality and hypnosis: A study of imaginative involvement.* Chicago: University of Chicago.

Hilgard, J. R., & LeBaron, S. (1984). *Hypnotherapy of children with pain.* Los Altos, CA: Kaufmann.

Houghton, L. A., Heyman, D. J., & Whorwell, P. J. (1996). Symptomatology, quality of life and economic features of irritable bowel syndrome—the effect of hypnotherapy. *Alimentary Pharmacology and Therapeutics, 10,* 91–95.

House, J. S., Landis, K. R., & Umberson, D. (1988). Social relationships and health. *Science, 241,* 540–545.

Hull, C. L. (1933). *Hypnosis and suggestibility.* New York: Appleton Century.

Isenberg, S. A., Lehrer, P. M., & Hochron, S. (1992). The effects of suggestion on airways of asthmatic subjects breathing room air as a suggested bronchoconstrictor and bronchodilator. *Journal of Psychosomatic Research, 36,* 769–776.

Jacknow, D. S., Tschann, J. M., Link, M. P., & Boyce, W. T. (1994). Hypnosis in the prevention of chemotherapy-related nausea and vomiting in children: A prospective study. *Journal of Developmental and Behavioral Pediatrics, 15,* 258–264.

Joubert, P. H., & Van-Os, B. E. (1989). The effect of hypnosis, placebo, paracetamol, and naloxone on the response to dental pulp stimulation. *Current Therapeutic Research, 46,* 774–781.

Kellerman, J., Zeltzer, L., Ellenberg, L., & Dash, J. (1983). Adolescents with cancer: Hypnosis for the reduction of the acute pain and anxiety associated with medical procedures. *Journal of Adolescent Health Care, 4,* 85–90.

Kennedy, S., Kiecolt-Glaser, J. K., & Glaser, R. (1988). Immunological consequences of acute and chronic stressors: Mediating role of interpersonal relationships. *British Journal of Medical Psychology, 61*(pt. 1), 77–85.

Kessler, R., & Dane, J. R. (1996). Psychological and hypnotic preparation for anesthesia and surgery: An individual difference perspective. *International Journal of Clinical and Experimental Hypnosis, 44,* 189–207.

Kirsch, I. (1990). *Changing expectations: A key to effective psychotherapy.* Pacific Grove, CA: Brooks/Cole.

Kirsch, I., & Council, J. R. (1989). Response expectancy as a determinant of hypnotic behavior. In N. P. Spanos & J. F. Chaves (Eds.), *Hypnosis: The cognitive-behavioral perspective* (pp. 360–379). Buffalo, NY: Prometheus Books.

Kirsch, I., Montgomery, G., & Sapirstein, G. (1995). Hypnosis as an adjunct to cognitive-behavioral psychotherapy: A meta-analysis. *Journal of Consulting and Clinical Psychology, 63,* 214–220.

Kleinhauz, M., Eli, I., & Rubinstein, Z. (1985). Treatment of dental and dental-related behavioral dysfunctions in a consultative outpatient clinic: A preliminary report. *American Journal of Clinical Hypnosis, 28,* 3–9.

Kleinknecht, R. A., Klepac, R. K., & Alexander, L. D. (1973). Origins and characteristics of fear of dentistry. *Journal of the American Dental Association, 86,* 842–848.

Klingberg, G. (1995). Dental fear and behavior management problems in children: A study of measurement, prevalence, concomitant factors, and clinical effects. *Swedish Dental Journal, 103* (suppl.), 1–78.

Kohen, D. P. (1987). A biobehavioral approach to managing childhood asthma. *Children Today, 16,* 6–10.

Kohen, D. P., Olness, K. N., Colwell, S. O., & Heimel, A. (1984). The use of relaxation-mental imagery (self-hypnosis) in the management of 505 pediatric behavioral encounters. *Journal of Developmental and Behavioral Pediatrics, 5,* 21–25.

Kohen, D. P., & Wynne, E. (1997). Applying hypnosis in a preschool family asthma education program: Uses of storytelling, imagery, and relaxation. *American Journal of Clinical Hypnosis, 39,* 169–181.

Kunzelmann, K. H., Dunninger, P., & Hurka, G. (1989). Suggestive Schmerzkontrolle: Fallbeschreibung und Ubersicht. [Suggestive pain control: Case history and review.] *Experimentelle und Klinische Hypnose, 5,* 91–101.

LaCrosse, M. B. (1994). Understanding change: Five-year follow-up of brief hypnotic treatment of chronic bruxism. *American Journal of Clinical Hypnosis, 36,* 276–281.

Lambert, S. A. (1996). The effects of hypnosis/guided imagery on the postoperative course of children. *Journal of Developmental and Behavioral Pediatrics, 17,* 307–310.

Lang, E. V., & Berbaum, K. S. (1997). Educating interventional radiology personnel in nonpharmacologic analgesia: Effect on patients' pain perception. *Academic Radiology, 4,* 753–757.

Lang, E. V., & Hamilton, D. (1994). Anodyne imagery: An alternative to i.v. sedation in interventional radiology. *American Journal of Roentgenology, 162,* 1221–1226.

Lang, E. V., Joyce, J. S., Spiegel, D., Hamilton, D., & Lee, K. K. (1996). Self-hypnotic relaxation during interventional radiological procedures: Effects on pain perception and intravenous drug use. *International Journal of Clinical and Experimental Hypnosis, 44,* 106–119.

Lang, E. V., & Laser, E. (1996). Communicating with the patient: Luxury or necessity? *Academic Radiology, 3,* 786–788.

Langeluddecke, P. M. (1985). Psychological aspects of irritable bowel syndrome. *Australian and New Zealand Journal of Psychiatry, 19,* 218–226.

Levitan, A. A. (1992). The use of hypnosis with cancer patients. *Psychiatric Medicine, 10*(4), 119–131.

Levy, A., & Neumann, M. (1984). The role of suggestion in the treatment of combat reactions within a specific military installation during the war in Lebanon. *Israel Journal of Psychiatry and Related Sciences, 21*(2), 85–91.

Levy, S., Herberman, R., Lippman, M., & d'Angelo, T. (1987). Correlation of stress factors with sustained depression of natural killer cell activity and predicted prognosis in patients with breast cancer. *Journal of Clinical Oncology, 5*(3), 348–353.

Lewith, G. T., & Watkins, A. D. (1996). Unconventional therapies in asthma: An overview. *Allergy, 51,* 761–769.

Liddell, A., Ackerman, C., & Locker, D. (1990). What dental phobics say about their dental experiences. *Journal of the Canadian Dental Association—Journal de l'Association Dentaire Canadienne, 56,* 863–866.

Liddell, A., Di Fazio, L., Blackwood, J., & Ackerman, C. (1994). Long-term follow-up of treated dental phobics. *Behaviour Research and Therapy, 32,* 605–610.

Liddell, A., & Locker, D. (1992). Dental visit satisfaction in a group of adults aged 50 years and over. *Journal of Behavioral Medicine, 15,* 415–427.

Locker, D., & Liddell, A. M. (1991). Correlates of dental anxiety among older adults. *Journal of Dental Research, 70,* 198–203.

Locker, D., Liddell, A., & Burman, D. (1991). Dental fear and anxiety in an older adult population. *Community Dentistry and Oral Epidemiology, 19,* 120–124.

Locker, D., Shapiro, D., & Liddell, A. (1996a). Negative dental experiences and their relationship to dental anxiety. *Community Dental Health, 13,* 86–92.

Locker, D., Shapiro, D., & Liddell, A. (1996b). Who is dentally anxious? Concordance between measures of dental anxiety. *Community Dentistry and Oral Epidemiology, 24,* 346–350.

Lorr, M., & McNair, D. M. (1971). *Manual for the Profile of Mood States.* San Diego, CA: Educational and Industrial Testing Service.

Lu, D. (1994). The use of hypnosis for smooth sedation induction and reduction of postoperative violent emergencies from anesthesia in pediatric dental patients. *Journal of Dentistry for Children* (May/June), 182–185.

Lu, D. P., & Lu, G. P. (1996). Hypnosis and pharmacological sedation for medically compromised patients. *Compendium of Continuing Education in Dentistry, 17,* 32, 34–36, 38–40.

Lu, D. P., Lu, G. P., & Hersh, E. V. (1995). Augmenting sedation with hypnosis in drug-dependent patients. *Anesthesia Progress, 42,* 3–4.

Manns, A., Zuazola, R. V., Sirhan, R., Quiroz, M., & Rocabado, M. (1990). Relationship between the tonic elevator mandibular activity and the vertical dimension during states of vigilance. *Journal of Craniomandibular Practice, 8,* 163–170.

Manusov, E. G., & Murray, G. (1992). Acute trauma and hypnosis. *Military Medicine, 157,* 504–505.

Mason, J. D., Rogerson, D. R., & Butler, J. D. (1996). Client centered hypnotherapy in the management of tinnitus—is it better than counselling? *Journal of Laryngology and Otology, 110*(2), 117–120.

May, S. R., & DeClement, F. A. (1983). Effects of early hypnosis on the cardiovascular and renal physiology of burn patients. *Burns, Including Thermal Injury, 9,* 257–266.

McAmmond, D. M., Davidson, P. O., & Kovitz, D. M. (1971). A comparison of the effects of hypnosis and relaxation training on stress reactions in a dental situation. *American Journal of Clinical Hypnosis, 13,* 233–242.

McCauley, J. D., Thelen, M. H., Frank, R. G., Willard, R. R., & Callen, K. E. (1983). Hypnosis compared to relaxation in the outpatient management of chronic low back pain. *Archives of Physical Medicine and Rehabilitation, 64,* 548–552.

Melzack, R., Germain, M., Belanger, E., Fuchs, P. N., & Swick, R. (1996). Positive intrasurgical suggestion fails to affect postsurgical pain. *Journal of Pain and Symptom Management, 11,* 103–107.

Melzack, R., & Wall, P. (1965). Pain mechanisms: A new theory. *Science, 150,* 971–979.

Meurisse, M., Faymonville, M. E., Joris, J., Nguyen Dang, D., Defechereux, T., & Hamoir, E. (1996). Chirurgie endocrinienne sous hypnose: De la fiction a l'application clinique quotidienne. [Endocrine surgery by hypnosis: From fiction to daily clinical application.] *Annales d'Endocrinologie, 57*(6), 494–501.

Milgrom, P., Weinstein, P., Kleinknecht, R., & Getz, T. (1985). *Treating fearful dental patients.* Reston, VA: Reston Publishing.

Moore, R., Abrahamsen, R., & Brodsgaard, I. (1996). Hypnosis compared with group therapy and individual desensitization for dental anxiety. *European Journal of Oral Sciences 104*(5–6), 612–618.

Nolan, R. P., Spanos, N. P., Hayward, A. A., & Scott, H. A. (1994). The efficacy of hypnotic and nonhypnotic response-based imagery for self-managing recurrent headache. *Imagination, Cognition and Personality, 14,* 183–201.

Orne, M. T. (1965). Undesirable effects of hypnosis: The determinants and management. *International Journal of Clinical and Experimental Hypnosis, 4,* 226–237.

Owens, H. E. (1966). Hypnosis in dentistry. *Journal of the California Dental Association, 42,* 525–531.

Patterson, D. R. (1989). Hypnotherapy as an adjunct to narcotic analgesia for the treatment of pain for burn debridement. *American Journal of Clinical Hypnosis, 31,* 156–163.

Patterson, D. R. (1995). Non–opioid-based approaches to burn pain. *Journal of Burn Care and Rehabilitation, 16*(3), 372–376.

Patterson, D. R., Adcock, R. J., & Bombardier, C. H. (1997). Factors predicting hypnotic analgesia in clinical burn pain. *International Journal of Clinical and Experimental Hypnosis, 45,* 377–395.

Patterson, D. R., Everett, J. J., Burns, G. L., & Marvin, J. A. (1992). Hypnosis for the treatment of burn pain. *Journal of Consulting and Clinical Psychology, 60,* 713–717.

Patterson, D. R., Goldberg, M. L., & Ehde, D. M. (1996). Hypnosis in the treatment of patients with severe burns. *American Journal of Clinical Hypnosis, 38,* 200–212.

Patterson, D. R., & Ptacek, J. T. (1997). Baseline pain as a moderator of hypnotic analgesia for burn injury treatment. *Journal of Consulting and Clinical Psychology, 65,* 60–67.

Pavi, E., Kay, E. J., & Stephen, K. W. (1995). The effect of social and personal factors on the utilisation of dental services in Glasgow, Scotland. *Community Dental Health, 12,* 208–215.

Prior, A., Colgan, S. M., & Whorwell, P. J. (1990). Changes in rectal sensitivity after hypnotherapy in patients with irritable bowel syndrome. *Gut, 31,* 896–898.

Prior, A., & Whorwell, P. J. (1986). Management of irritable bowel syndrome. *Biomedicine and Pharmacotherapy, 40*(1), 4–5.

Rey, T. (1993). *The history of pain.* Cambridge, MA: Harvard University Press.

Reynolds, P., & Kaplan, G. A. (1990). Social connection and the risk for cancer: Prospective evidence from the Alameda County study. *Behavioral Medicine, 16*(3), 101–110.

Rhue, J. W., Lynn, S. J., & Kirsch, I. (Eds.). (1993). *Handbook of clinical hypnosis.* Washington, DC: American Psychological Association.

Rodolfa, E. R., Kraft, W., & Reilley, R. R. (1990). Etiology and treatment of dental anxiety and phobia. *American Journal of Clinical Hypnosis, 33,* 22–28.

Russell, I. F., & Wang, M. (1997). Absence of memory for intraoperative information during surgery under adequate general anaesthesia. *British Journal of Anaesthesia, 78*(1), 3–9.

Sarbin, T. R., & Coe, W. C. (1972). *Hypnosis: A social-psychological analysis of influence communication.* New York: Holt, Reinhart & Winston.

Schafer, D. W. (1975). Hypnosis use on a burn unit. *International Journal of Clinical and Experimental Hypnosis, 23,* 1–14.

Schultz-Stübner, S. (1996). Hypnose—eine nebenwirkungsfreie Alternative zur medikamentösen Sedierung bei Regionalanästhesien. [Hypnosis—an alternative to sedatives without side effects during regional anesthesia.] *Anaesthesist, 45,* 965–969.

Sharav, Y., & Tal, M. (1987). Hypnotic anesthesia to electric tooth-pulp stimulation: Sensation, reflex activity and placebo effect. *Pain,* (suppl. 4), S271.

Shaw, A. J., & Niven, N. (1996). Theoretical concepts and practical applications of hypnosis in the treatment of children and adolescents with dental fear and anxiety. *British Dental Journal, 180,* 11–16.

Smith, J. V. C. (1847). Mesmeric examinations. *Boston Medical and Surgical Journal, 37,* 85.

Somer, E. (1991). Hypnotherapy in the treatment of the chronic nocturnal use of a dental splint prescribed for bruxism. *International Journal of Clinical and Experimental Hypnosis, 39,* 145–154.

Spanos, N. P. (1986). Hypnosis and the modification of hypnotic susceptibility. In P. L. N. Naish (Ed.), *What is hypnosis?* (pp. 85–120). Philadelphia: Open University Press.

Spanos, N. P., & Chaves, J. F. (1970). Hypnosis research: A methodological critique of experiments generated by two alternative paradigms. *American Journal of Clinical Hypnosis, 13,* 108–127.

Spanos, N. P., & Chaves, J. F. (1991). History and historiography of hypnosis. In S. J. Lynn & J. W. Rhue (Eds.), Theories of hypnosis (pp. 43–78). New York: Guilford Press.

Spanos, N. P., & Chaves, J. F. (Eds.). (1989). *Hypnosis: The cognitive-behavioral perspective.* Buffalo, NY: Prometheus.

Spanos, N. P., & de-Groh, M. (1983). Structure of communication and reports of involuntariness by hypnotic and nonhypnotic subjects. *Perceptual and Motor Skills, 57*(3), 1179–1186.

Spanos, N. P., Hodgins, D. C., Stam, H. J., & Gwynn, M. I. (1984). Suffering for science: The effects of implicit social demands on response to experimentally induced pain. *Journal of Personality and Social Psychology, 46*(5), 1162–1172.

Spanos, N. P., Liddy, S. J., Scott, H., Garrard, C., Sine, J., Tirabasso, A., & Hayward, A. (1993). Hypnotic suggestion and placebo for the treatment of chronic headache in a university volunteer sample. *Cognitive Therapy and Research, 17,* 191–205.

Spiegel, D. (1990). Facilitating emotional coping during treatment. *Cancer, 66* (suppl. 6), 1422–1426.

Spiegel, D., & Bloom, J. R. (1983). Group therapy and hypnosis reduce metastatic breast carcinoma pain. *Psychosomatic Medicine, 45,* 333–339.

Spiegel, D., Bloom, J. R., Kraemer, H. C., & Gottheil, E. (1989). Effect of psychosocial treatment on survival of patients with metastatic breast cancer. *Lancet, 2,* 888–891.

Spiegel, H. (1973). *Manual for the Hypnotic Induction Profile* (rev.). New York: Soni Medica.

Stam, H. J. (1986). Hypnotizability and the treatment of chronic facial pain. *International Journal of Clinical and Experimental Hypnosis, 34,* 182–191.

Stam, H. J., McGrath, P. A., & Brooke, R. I. (1984a). The effects of a cognitive-behavioral treatment program on temporo-mandibular pain and dysfunction syndrome. *Psychosomatic Medicine, 46,* 534–545.

Stam, H. J., McGrath, P. A., & Brooke, R. I. (1984b). The treatment of temporomandibular joint syndrome through control of anxiety. *Journal of Behavior Therapy and Experimental Psychiatry, 15,* 41–45.

Stam, H., & Steggles, S. (1987). Predicting the onset of progression of cancer from psychological characteristics. *Journal of Psychosocial Oncology, 5*(2), 35–46.

Stamm, H. J. (1989). From symptom relief to cure: Hypnotic interventions in cancer. In N. P. Spanos & J. F. Chaves (Eds.), *Hypnosis: The cognitive-behavioral perspective* (pp. 313–339). Buffalo, NY: Prometheus Books.

Steggles, S., Damore-Petingola, S., Maxwell, J., & Lightfoot, N. (1997). Hypnosis for children and adolescents with cancer: An annotated bibliography, 1985–1995. *Journal of Pediatric Oncology Nursing, 14,* 27–32.

Steggles, S., Maxwell, J., Lightfoot, N. E., Damore-Petingola, S., & Mayer, C. (1997). Hypnosis and cancer: An annotated bibliography 1985–1995. *American Journal of Clinical Hypnosis, 39,* 187–200.

Steggles, S., Stam, H. J., Fehr, R., & Aucoin, P. (1987). Hypnosis and cancer: An annotated bibliography 1960–1985. *American Journal of Clinical Hypnosis, 29,* 281–290.

Syrjala, K. L., & Chapko, M. E. (1995). Evidence for a biopsychosocial model of cancer treatment–related pain. *Pain, 61,* 69–79.

Syrjala, K. L., Cummings, C., & Donaldson, G. W. (1992). Hypnosis or cognitive behavioral training for the reduction of pain and nausea during cancer treatment: A controlled clinical trial. *Pain, 48,* 137–146.

Syrjala, K. L., Cummings, C., Donaldson, G., & Chapman, C. R. (1987). Hypnosis for oral pain following chemotherapy and radiation. *Pain* (suppl. 4), S171.

Syrjala, K. L., Donaldson, G. W., Davis, M. W., Kippes, M. E., & Carr, J. E. (1995). Relaxation and imagery and cognitive-behavioral training reduce pain during cancer treatment: A controlled clinical trial. *Pain, 63,* 189–198.

Talley, N. J., Owen, B. K., Boyce, P., & Paterson, K. (1996). Psychological treatments for irritable bowel syndrome: A critique of controlled treatment trials. *American Journal of Gastroenterology, 91,* 277–283.

ter Kuile, M. M., Spinhoven, P., Linssen, A. C., & van Houwelingen, H. C. (1996). Cognitive coping and appraisal processes in the treatment of chronic headaches. *Pain, 64,* 257–264.

ter Kuile, M. M., Spinhoven, P., Linssen, A. C., Zitman, F. G., Van Dyck, R., & Rooijmans, H. G. (1994). Autogenic training and cognitive self-hypnosis for the treatment of recurrent headaches in three different subject groups. *Pain, 58,* 331–340.

Todorovic, D. D. (1959). Hypnosis in military medical practice. *Military Medicine, 34,* 121–125.

Trijsburg, R. W., van Knippenberg, F. C., & Rijpma, S. E. (1992). Effects of psychological treatment on cancer patients: A critical review. *Psychosomatic Medicine, 54,* 489–517.

Turk, D., Meichenbaum, D. H., & Genest, M. (1983). *Pain and behavioral medicine.* New York: Guilford Press.

Van der Does, A. J., & Van Dyck, R. (1989). Does hypnosis contribute to the care of burn patients? Review of the evidence. *General Hospital Psychiatry, 11,* 119–124.

Van der Does, A. J., Van Dyck, R., & Spijker, R. E. (1988). Hypnosis and pain in patients with severe burns: A pilot study. *Burns, Including Thermal Injury, 14,* 399–404.

Vassend, O. (1993). Anxiety, pain and discomfort associated with dental treatment. *Behavior Research and Therapy, 31,* 659–666.

Wadden, T. A., & Anderton, C. H. (1982). The clinical use of hypnosis. *Psychological Bulletin, 91,* 215–243.

Ward, W., & Topham, W. (1842). *Account of a case of successful amputation of the thigh during the mesmeric state, without knowledge of the patient.* London: Bailliere.

Wardlaw, F. (1994). Hypnosis in the treatment of bruxism. *Australian Journal of Clinical and Experimental Hypnosis, 22,* 97–107.

West, B. H. (1836). Experiments in animal magnetism. *Boston Medical and Surgical Journal, 14,* 349–351.

Whitehead, W. E. (1992). Behavioral medicine approaches to gastrointestinal disorders. Special Issue: Behavioral medicine: An update for the 1990s. *Journal of Consulting and Clinical Psychology, 60,* 605–612.

Whorwell, P. J., Houghton, L. A., Taylor, E. E., & Maxton, D. G. (1992). Physiological effects of emotion: Assessment via hypnosis. *Lancet, 340,* 69–72.

Whorwell, P. J., Prior, A., & Colgan, S. M. (1987). Controlled trial of hypnotherapy in the treatment of refractory irritable bowel syndrome. *Gut, 28,* 423–425.

Whorwell, P. J., Prior, A., & Faragher, E. B. (1984). Controlled trial of hypnotherapy in the treatment of severe refractory irritable-bowel syndrome. *Lancet, 2,* 1232–1234.

Wickramasekera, I. (1986). A model of people at high risk to develop chronic stress-related somatic symptoms: Some predictions. *Professional Psychology, 17,* 437–447.

Winter, A. (1991). Ethereal epidemic: Mesmerism and the introduction of inhalation anesthesia to early Victorian London. *Social History of Medicine, 4,* 1–27.

Wisloff, T. F., Vassend, O., & Asmyhr, O. (1995). Dental anxiety, utilisation of dental services, and DMFS status in Norwegian military recruits. *Community Dental Health, 12,* 100–103.

Zeltzer, L. K., Jay, S. M., & Fisher, D. M. (1989). The management of pain associated with pediatric procedures. *Pediatric Clinics of North America, 36,* 941–964.

Zeltzer, L., & LaBaron, S. (1982). Hypnotic and nonhypnotic techniques for reduction of pain and anxiety during painful procedures in children and adolescents with cancer. *Journal of Pediatrics, 101,* 1032–1035.

Zeltzer, L., & LeBaron, S. (1983). Behavioral intervention for children and adolescents with cancer. *Behavioral Medicine Update, 5,* 17–22.

Zeltzer, L., & LeBaron, S. (1986). The hypnotic treatment of children in pain. *Advances in Developmental and Behavioral Pediatrics, 7,* 197–234.

Zerlin, S., & Davis, H. (1967). The variability of single evoked vertex potentials in man. *Electroencephalography and Clinical Neurophysiology, 23,* 468–472.

Zitman, F. G., Van-Dyck, R., Spinhoven, P., & Linssen, A. C. (1992). Hypnosis and autogenic training in the treatment of tension headaches: A two-phase constructive design study with follow-up. *Journal of Psychosomatic Research, 36,* 219–228.

CHAPTER 8

THE MANY FACES OF INSOMNIA

Peter J. Hauri

Insomnia literally means "no sleep." Obviously this is an exaggeration. Except for the very few cases of fatal familial insomnia (Lugaresi & Montagna, 1994), all insomniacs do get some sleep. *DSM-IV* (American Psychiatric Association, 1994) defines insomnia as a complaint of difficulty initiating or maintaining sleep or of nonrestorative sleep that lasts for at least 1 month (criterion A) and causes clinically significant distress or impairment in social, occupational, or other important areas of functioning (criterion B). Criterion B is needed because normal sleep varies from about 4 hours per night to about 9 hours per night. If you sleep very little at night but feel well during the day, you may not be an insomniac but a person with a very low need to sleep.

Traditionally we have subdivided insomnia into four categories: difficulties falling asleep, mid-sleep awakenings, early morning awakenings, and non-restorative sleep. This subdivision is unsatisfactory. Not only is there a vast overlap among the four categories with most insomniacs fitting into more than one (Hohagen et al., 1994); the behavioral and pharmacological treatments for these different kinds of insomnias are very similar, often identical. Furthermore, these insomnia subtypes are age-related: Difficulties falling asleep are typical of the young; early morning awakenings are the norm in the elderly.

A better way to subdivide insomnia would be to distinguish transient insomnia (lasting a few days), short-term insomnia (lasting weeks), and chronic insomnia (lasting months and years). Distinguishing insomnia into these three categories has significant implications, not only for the diagnostic tools that need to be applied but also for behavioral and pharmacological treatment (Spielman & Glovinsky, 1991).

Recent polls suggest that about one-third of the U.S. adult population reports occasional difficulties with sleeping. About 10–12% rate their sleep problems as chronic and serious (Roth, 1996). Females are somewhat more likely to complain about insomnia than males, and insomnia complaints increase with age (Mellinger, Balter, & Uhlenhuth, 1985). While there is evidence that we sleep less now than in previous centuries, there is no solid evidence that insomnia has become more prevalent in recent years. We understand our current age as being very stressful, but earlier ages had their own stressors, such as potential starvation or death by the plague.

While insomnia has immediate and dramatic subjective effects (e.g., on ability to concentrate, mood, and daytime functioning), it is much harder to find objective, laboratory-documented impairment. A few minor differences have been established: The performance of insomniacs is more variable and slightly slower than that of good sleepers on reaction time tests (Pedrosi et al., 1995; Hauri, 1997a), and there is an impairment in the Romberg test (Mendelson, Garnett, & Linnoila, 1984). While rote memory is not affected, more complex memory may be (Mendelson et al., 1984). Edinger et al. (1997) suggest that the lack of significant performance decrements in insomniacs may, in part, be an artifact of our testing procedure: In most performance assessments of insomniacs, both the patients and the normal controls sleep in the laboratory on the night before the test. It has been shown that the first night in the laboratory is quite detrimental to the sleep of normals, much less so (or even beneficial) to the sleep of insomniacs (Hauri & Olmstead, 1989).

Sound sleep is associated with improved immune function (Moldofsky et al., 1986). This often poses a dilemma for the behavioral therapist: It is true that good sleep may be important for health, but desperately seeking sleep is counterproductive, as will be discussed later. While sleep is best when one does not care and when one acts as if sleep were of no concern, telling insomniacs that sleep is irrelevant may help them sleep better, but it is not compatible with the scientific evidence (Benca & Quintas, 1997).

Insomnia is related to other life issues. In a study on navy Seals, those who complained about insomnia were more likely to drop out of the program and they received fewer promotions than good sleepers (Johnson & Spinweber, 1983). In depression-prone individuals, insomnia is clearly a risk factor and the reoccurrence of poor sleep often heralds a depressive episode (Ford & Kamerow, 1989). Many try to self-medicate for their insomnia through alcohol or other drugs (40% have tried OTCs or alcohol for their insomnia) (Gallup, 1991; Johnson et al., 1998). Obviously, in some of these issues, cause–effect relationships are not established: For example, you may be likely to drop out of a difficult program and, at the same time, be an insomniac because of third factors such as neuroticism.

COMMONALITIES AMONG INSOMNIACS

There are some areas in which insomniacs are different from normals. However, statistically established differences do not imply that all insomniacs showed a difference. There is considerable overlap between insomniacs and normals.

On the MMPI, insomnia patients consistently show more deviations than normals (Coursey, Buchsbaum, & Frankel, 1975; Kales et al., 1976). Many insomnia patients report increased depression and anxiety as well as increased somatization. Also typical for insomnia is repression—i.e., the denial of psychological or emotional factors and the emphasis of somatic explanations.

Hyperarousal

There is considerable evidence that insomnia patients are generally and chronically hyperaroused. They score high on scales measuring hyperarousal (Regestein et al., 1993) and they are sensation avoiders when compared with normal sleepers (Coursey, Buchsbaum, & Frankel, 1975). This suggests that they are chronically overstimulated. They show an increased metabolic rate, both during wakefulness and sleep (Bonnet & Arand, 1992). They also show increased body temperature and increased fast activity on the EEG. These EEG in-

TABLE 8.1. Hyperarousal in Insomnia

	INSOMNIA PATIENTS	NORMALS WHO ARE SLEEP-DEPRIVED
Metabolic rate	High	Low
Body temperature	High	Low
EEG waves	Fast	Slow

creases in fast waves are found during wakefulness, at sleep onset, and during sleep (Freedman, 1986; Lamarche & Ogilvie, 1997). The general hyperarousal in insomnia patients is counterintuitive because normals who are sleep-deprived show exactly the opposite, a general decrease in arousal (Table 8.1). These findings are of crucial importance to the behavioral therapy of insomnia. It seems that sleep loss is much less relevant in insomnia than the fact that such patients are chronically hyperaroused both night and day. If one deals with an insomnia patient, one is not dealing with a normal person who unfortunately has lost some sleep, but with someone who is chronically "hyper," as if that person were undergoing a constant caffeine "drunk" (Bonnet & Arand, 1992). Bonnet and Arand (1995b) would even suggest that the lack of sleep is the organism's own attempt to cure the "hyper" physiology by sleep deprivation, which typically slows a person down. Although not all researchers have accepted this view and there is an occasional piece of evidence to the contrary (Lack & Lushington, 1997), it helps in thinking about insomnia. Our task is to effect a general slowdown in both physiological and psychological processes throughout both night and day. It is unknown to what extent this hyperarousal is innate and to what extent it is acquired by life circumstances and behaviors. It probably depends on the individual case.

Sleep State Misperception

It has been documented repeatedly that many insomnia patients underestimate the amount of sleep they actually get according to the polysomnogram. In some cases this underestimation is extreme: A patient may claim that he has not slept for days and weeks, when the polysomnogram shows considerable sleep. Such patients are said to suffer from a sleep state misperception syndrome (they perceive that they are awake when they are actually sleeping). To diagnose such a syndrome requires that a patient sleep in a laboratory where the "true" amount of sleep can be assessed. However, in many aspects, persons with a sleep state misperception syndrome are very similar to patients with "true" insomnia: They show similar abnormalities on the MMPI and they are both hyperaroused (Bonnet & Arand, 1995a). More importantly, they respond to the same treatment modalities (behavioral, pharmacological) as do true insomnia patients. This was dramatically demonstrated to me when, in 1973, after a college student spent 3 nights in our laboratory, I diagnosed him as having sleep state misperception. The patient then sought help from Dr. Richard Bootzin, who at that time was developing stimulus control therapy and did not know of this student's sleep evaluation. A few months later the patient returned to my lab, claiming that he had been cured by Bootzin's technique. Incredulous, I had him sleep in the lab again. The EEG showed no improvement, yet the patient felt cured. Unfortunately I was not measuring hyperarousal at that time, but only sleep as defined by EEG. I speculate that Bootzin's technique decreased hyperarousal in this patient, even though it did not affect EEG-defined sleep.

Because patients with sleep state misperception have similar hyperarousal and similar MMPI psychopathology as those with true insomnia and because both appear to respond to the same behavioral and pharmacological techniques, the distinction between the two categories is academic in most cases. Therefore, it is not necessary to make a referral of the insomnia patient to a sleep disorders center to rule out sleep state misperception, although on occasion a sleep evaluation may be beneficial, if only to keep the patient from receiving higher and higher doses of hypnotics in a desperate attempt to get sleep. Indeed, many specialists wonder whether the diagnostic category of sleep state misperception makes sense or whether it should be abolished (Borkovec, 1979; Trinder, 1988).

ETIOLOGY

Nosologic Issues

Currently there are three viable classification systems for insomnia: (1) The International Classification of Sleep Disorders (ICSD, 1990) is a detailed classifica-

tion system developed by sleep specialists. There are over 80 individual diagnostic categories, about 25 of which are associated with insomnia. (2) *DSM-IV*, the psychiatric classification system (APA, 1994) has room for four different insomnia categories: primary (no other medical or psychiatric diagnosis), related to another mental disorder, due to a general medical condition, and substance-induced. (3) Of practical importance to the sleep clinician is the International Classification of Diseases, 9th revision, because most insurance companies abide by that classification. ICD-9 first classifies all sleep disorders into organic and nonorganic categories, a distinction that is often difficult to make and not always relevant. There are four distinct insomnia classes in ICD-9: acute and persistent nonorganic insomnia, organic insomnia associated with sleep apnea, and other organic insomnia (including idiopathic, periodic limb movements, stimulant dependent, etc.).

No matter which classification system is used, insomnia may also be a sign of another sleep problem such as a delayed sleep phase, a circadian sleep disorder, or periodic limb movements of sleep. For example, a student who has extreme difficulty falling asleep at night and then sleeps until the next afternoon may well complain about his sleep-onset insomnia, but the correct classification would be delayed sleep phase, a circadian rhythm disturbance.

Main Causes of Insomnia

Clinical judgment as well as two cluster analyses (Edinger et al., 1996; Hauri, 1983) have established eight areas as important in the diagnosis and etiology of insomnia: psychiatric/psychological, medical, drug-related, psychophysiological, lifestyle and sleep hygiene–related, circadian, environmental, and idiopathic. When interviewing a patient with an insomnia complaint, it is important to review these areas, because the more in detail one understands the cause of insomnia, the more detailed the treatment can become. Buysse et al. (1997) have shown that in the hand of the beginning clinician most insomnia is undifferentiated and most patients receive the same combination of relaxation therapy and medication. In the hands of the more experienced specialist much finer distinctions are made and more and different treatment modalities are used.

1. *Psychiatric/psychological:* This is the most common cause of insomnia (Silva et al., 1996). It is the primary reason for insomnia in over half of patients. Anxiety in all its various forms often relates to insomnia. In others, there is a specific, almost phobic, fear of insomnia. Depression is often present but frequently denied. Stress is often a more easily accepted explanation for insomniacs who deny emotional problems, and stress management is often the only treatment a strongly repressing insomniac is willing to accept. Other patients have PDSD, obsessive-compulsive disorder, somatoform disorder, various adjustment disorders, or axis II issues. However, in my experience, even more common in insomnia are various issues not diagnosable by *DSM-IV*, such as boredom after retirement, financial issues, poor self-esteem, poor marriage, and so forth.

2. *Medical:* Although medical issues are less often the cause of insomnia than psychiatric/psychological ones, it is important to be aware that many biological abnormalities can cause poor sleep. This would include hypothyroidism, pain, neurologic degenerative issues, and allergies. While not every insomnia patient needs a general medical evaluation before treatment, such an evaluation is clearly needed when our behavioral approaches seem to be marginally or not at all effective. A clinician also needs to be aware that both the restless legs syndrome (RLS) and sleep-onset central apneas may present in the office as insomnia.

In RLS, patients feel uncomfortable aches in their legs when trying to fall asleep, often described as "creepy crawly" or "heebie jeebie." (It is almost diagnostic for RLS when patients state that while their feelings are awful, they cannot be described.) The feelings disappear when the legs are moved (e.g., when walking). There is a clear circadian rhythm to them (worst at night). Although a subclass of restless legs may be associated with circulatory problems and may be treatable with temperature biofeedback (Ancoli-Israel, Seifert, & Lemon, 1986), in general, restless legs are a medical problem that needs to be referred to a sleep specialist (Fredrickson & Krueger, 1994).

Sleep-onset central apneas are often seen in anxious patients who hyperventilate while awake. In falling asleep, automatic regulatory mechanisms take over. Breathing may stop for a few seconds because

the patient's O_2 saturation is too high, the CO_2 saturation too low. This stopped breathing awakens the patient, who anxiously overbreathes again. These oscillations may occasionally go on for 20 to 40 minutes and be described as sleep-onset insomnia. These sleep-onset central apneas are not related to the much better known obstructive sleep apneas, which need attention in a sleep disorders center. Also, they are not related to central apneas occurring during sleep, a condition that has serious medical implications. Relaxation training and management of the anxiety are often successful in central sleep-onset apneas.

3. *Drug-related:* Many medications affect sleep. These include stimulants and anorectics, prednisone, opioids, theophylline, and some selective serotonin reuptake inhibitors (SSRI), among others. In other cases, it is the withdrawal from a sedating agent that causes insomnia (i.e., withdrawal from anxiolytic medications, antihistamines). Some drugs are sleep toxins. For example, insomnia has been reported decades after carbon monoxide poisoning or up to 2 years after severe alcoholism.

4. *Psychophysiological (learned):* In its pure form, patients with learned insomnia initially had insomnia for another reason, such as stress. After a few days or weeks of sleeping very poorly because of this other reason, patients become concerned about sleep and make strong attempts to sleep better. The harder they try to sleep, the worse sleep gets, in a vicious cycle. Such patients are easily identified. They are falling asleep quite easily when relatively motionless but trying to stay awake (such as watching television or listening to lectures). When they then go to bed, they are unable to fall asleep for hours, apparently because they are now trying too hard to sleep. In addition, the stimuli surrounding bedtime, such as the bed itself, the time, the behaviors such as brushing teeth, all may become conditioned stimuli for arousal and frustration just as surely as Pavlovian dogs salivate to the bell. Such conditioned patients find that they sleep much better away from their own bedroom (e.g., in a hotel, on the living room couch) (Hauri & Fisher, 1986).

While the pure form of psychophysiological insomnia is relatively rare, the two learned factors of trying too hard to sleep and conditioning play a significant role in almost all chronic insomnias. They are hard to extinguish, especially in patients who have had occasional nights of poor sleep even before the conditioning occurred. If the learned maladaptive pattern is occasionally reinforced by these naturally occurring poor nights, extinction cannot occur.

5. *Lifestyle and sleep hygiene:* Sleep is imbedded in the 24-hour rhythm. Some patients become insomniac because they attempt to sleep at very irregular times. Other patients attempt to work at highly stressful jobs until shortly before the desired sleep onset, not leaving time for relaxation. In still others, poor sleep hygiene develops as a response to chronic insomnia and then aggravates the problem: Patients may drink more coffee to remain awake or more alcohol to fall asleep, they may give up exercise because they are too tired, or they may stay in bed longer in a desperate attempt to capture at least some more sleep.

6. *Circadian:* Most bodily functions follow an internal, circadian "clock." Sleep and wakefulness are no exception. Unfortunately this circadian clock is not exactly 24 hours. If your clock is markedly slower than 24 hours, then you will become a night owl. When the clock on the wall says it is 11 p.m., your body might feel it is only 8 p.m.; when it says 7 a.m., your body will feel that it is 4 a.m. This causes difficulties going to bed at night and difficulties getting up in the morning. Such a pattern is frequently seen in young humans, from the age of about 15 to 25. Alternatively, if your clock is faster than 24 hours, then you will be a "lark," getting up early and going to bed early. Insomnia associated with circadian issues is also found in shift work and jet lag or in patients who have lost much of their rhythm (e.g., because they have been confined to bed rest for a long time because of illness).

7. *Environmental factors:* Humans can adapt to many different sleeping environments. However, there is a limit to such habituation. Globus et al. (1974) have shown that humans sleeping close to a busy airport are awakened frequently by the loud noise, even if they are no longer aware that they awaken. Kageyama et al. (1997) report that sleeping close to a road with high nighttime traffic affects sleep on a chronic basis, with little evidence of habituation. Clearly, environmental factors such as safety, noise, temperature, and light can affect our sleep. They are often overlooked by sleep specialists.

8. *Idiopathic Insomnia:* Whether a person is asleep or awake depends on the balance between those neuronal mechanisms that push arousals and those that push sleep. This sleep/wake push-pull system is very complex. It stands to reason that some may be better endowed in this area than others or that either the wakefulness or the sleep side of the equation is overemphasized. Some patients with insomnia may simply be at the extreme waking tail of the normal curve or there may be some lesion or abnormality. Idiopathic insomnia often manifests itself in early childhood (Hauri & Olmstead, 1980), but not all early childhood insomnia is idiopathic. Severe abuse, stress, or maladaptive conditioning may also cause insomnia in children as young as 2 or 3 years of age.

The eight etiologies described here are not mutually exclusive. Most severe insomnias are multidetermined. Also, demarcations between the different factors are often unclear. For example, patients with a severe neurologic imbalance in the sleep/wake system may become insomniacs without any psychiatric component (idiopathic insomnia). When the neurologic imbalance is not as extreme, it may take some conditioning to trigger the insomnia (psychophysiological insomnia). If the psychiatric factor is severe, it may cause insomnia without any neurologic predisposition. Choosing where to draw the line is often arbitrary.

Acute versus Chronic Insomnia

Treatment considerations change depending on how long insomnia has lasted (see Figure 8.1). If the insomnia had an abrupt onset and has lasted for only days, there is almost always a cause to be detected and treated. Behavioral techniques are probably inappropriate in this case except for a short review of sleep hygiene, mainly because behavioral techniques are too slow to effect the needed change. Pharmacological methods seem more appropriate. If the insomnia has lasted for weeks, it is likely that, besides the precipitating events, there have been changes in the patient's thinking and behaving that contribute to the maintenance of the insomnia. If the insomnia has been chronic (years and decades), these perpetuating factors are usually the ones that maintain the insomnia, while the precipitating factors have become almost irrelevant.

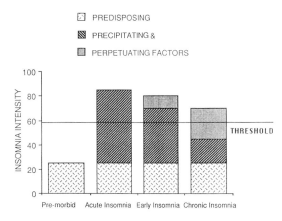

FIGURE 8.1. Factors in the Development of Insomnia

Source: Reprinted by permission from A. J. Spielman and P. B. Glovinsky (1991), "The Varied Nature of Insomnia," in P. J. Hauri (Ed.), *Case Studies in Insomnia* (New York: Plenum Medical Book Company).

THE ASSESSMENT OF INSOMNIA

The Interview

A thorough clinical interview is the main tool when assessing insomnia (Hauri, 1993). Typically (because insomnia patients are often repressors) one first asks about the current state of the insomnia complaint and about its history. One then reviews medical issues (e.g., restless legs, medications). Only when some rapport has been built does one approach psychiatric issues such as anxiety, depression, and stress. At the end of the interview it is important for the clinician to communicate what factors appear to be paramount in this insomnia and how treatment should proceed. Unless both clinician and patient have the same understanding on what needs to be addressed, behavioral treatment is unlikely to work. For example, as long as the patient is convinced that his insomnia is based on a biochemical imbalance in the brain and that only drugs will help, behavioral treatment is likely to be unsuccessful.

Questionnaires

It is often useful to have patients fill out some questionnaires before the interview. A 1- to 2-week sleep log is usually requested, indicating not only the patients' time to go to bed, sleep latency, total number of awakenings, and the like, but also subjective ratings of the quality of each night. However, this has some inherent problems: The more patients focus on the clock to report their sleep accurately on the log, the worse insomnia often gets. Screening questionnaires, both for sleep issues and for psychopathology, often expedite the interview. Depending on the clinician's preference, one might consider the MMPI, Beck Depression and Anxiety Scales, or the HCL90. Other tools assess specific dimensions of insomnia, such as Regestein et al.'s (1993) Hyperarousal Scale or Morin's (1993) Belief and Attitude about Sleep Scale.

Psychophysiological Evaluation

If a patient seems agitated and tense, it is often difficult to assess whether this reflects anxiety or excessive muscle tension or sympathetic arousal. Although "tension" is often treated as a single concept, in most studies the subcomponents of tension correlate only poorly with each other. It is often useful to measure frontalis muscle tension and finger temperature over 10 or 20 minutes while the patient is lying down. Initially the patient is told that the technician is calibrating the machine and to simply lie still. After recording a 5- to 10-minute baseline, the technician then tells the patient that now is the time to relax as deeply as possible. One observes what happens to muscle tension and to hand temperature (a measure of sympathetic arousal). Of interest are not only absolute levels but differences in trends before and after the relaxation instructions are given. Many insomnia patients can relax when not asked to do so but then become tense when the command to relax is given. Others can relax acceptably for 3 or 4 minutes but become increasingly tense as the test goes on. The psychophysiological evaluation may give important suggestions for how to approach relaxation training if needed.

Actigraphy

Actigraphy uses a watch-size gadget worn at the nondominant wrist for a week (taking it off only for showers and bathing). The gadget contains a motion detector and considerable memory, recording for each minute or half minute throughout the 7 days how many movements are carried out. Movements are much more frequent when the patient is alert, less frequent when the patient is sleeping. Periods of non-activity are interpreted as sleep. There are considerable problems using this procedure with insomniacs, who often lie in bed motionless but awake or who may have periodic limb movements and appear awake even when sleeping. Nevertheless, the procedure often gives a good account of overall rhythmicity of sleeping and waking, daytime naps, wakefulness during the night, and so forth (Hauri & Wisbey, 1992).

Polysomnography

In this procedure a patient sleeps a night in the sleep disorders center while some EEG channels, eye movements, muscle tension of the chin, various respiratory parameters, leg twitches, and so on are recorded. Often a videotape is synchronized to these recordings. This procedure is excellent for determining the cause of excessive daytime somnolence (such as apnea or periodic leg movements) or for diagnosing the subtypes of parasomnia, such as what kind of sleep terrors a patient has. It is rarely indicated in cases of insomnia unless one suspects periodic limb movements or sleep-onset central apneas. This is so because the variables of interest in insomnia (e.g., time to sleep onset, number of awakenings, total bed time) are poorly assessed by one night in the laboratory. Adaptation effects disturb the first night in unpredictable ways (Hauri & Olmstead, 1989), and insomniacs are notoriously variable sleepers, alternating some good nights with some much worse ones (Karacan et al., 1973). Thus, one would have to keep an insomnia patient in the laboratory for a minimum of three, if not five, nights to get a feeling of how he sleeps, and even that may be unreliable. For example, the patient's bedtimes may be much more regular in the sleep laboratory where there are no distractions suggesting he stay up late one night, go early to bed on another night. A recent position paper by the American Sleep Disorders Association (Reite et al., 1995) does not recommend the routine use of polysomnography in insomnia.

TREATMENT OF INSOMNIA

If the investigation of insomnia has yielded some specific factors, one treats them first. If restless legs seem to cause insomnia, medication is available (usually starting with Sinemet 25/100 at bedtime). If marital discord is an important factor, marital therapy is the treatment of choice. If there is depression, treating that with cognitive therapy or medications is more efficient than treating insomnia. However, when these factors are treated, there often remains a large residue of insomnia that is usually associated with poor sleep hygiene or with maladaptive learning that has occurred. The rest of this discussion assumes that the specific factors have already been addressed but that a remnant of insomnia has remained.

Pharmacological Treatment of Insomnia

A detailed discussion of medications for insomnia is not indicated here. Nevertheless, a few issues need to be mentioned.

Hypnotics

The main problem with hypnotics is said to be their habituation over time and the rebound in insomnia when the drug is withdrawn. This used to be a serious issue with barbiturates, which habituated in 2 weeks or less in most cases and gave severe insomnia rebound. It is a much lesser problem with the benzodiazepines. They can often be taken for months before habituation occurs. Indeed, there seems to be a small number of insomnia patients who never habituate to benzodiazepines. Another problem with benzodiazepines may be that they distort sleep, mainly by suppressing delta (deep) sleep and decreasing REM sleep. It is debatable whether this suppression of delta sleep and decrease of REM is of clinical relevance. Newer nonbenzodiazepine hypnotics are now available (e.g., Ambien) or will be available shortly. They are said to be even less habit-forming and to disturb sleep architecture less.

Half-life is an important issue when selecting sleeping pills. If the half-life is long, there may be daytime sedation; if it is short, the hypnotic may not cover the entire night. For example, Ambien, with a half-life of about 2 hours, is useless in early morning awakenings when it is given at bedtime.

Whether one can mix hypnotics and behavioral therapy is a difficult issue. Some advocate this mixture, suggesting that one might give hypnotics to help patients immediately, until such time as behavioral therapy can be learned (Morin & Kwentus, 1988; Milby et al., 1993). However, Hauri (1997b) found that a combination of drugs and behavior therapy may not be indicated. Insomniacs who learned sleep hygiene and relaxation therapy without having access to hypnotics showed better sleep improvement on a 1-year follow-up than those who were also given hypnotics while learning the behavioral techniques.

Acute versus Chronic Treatment

If insomnia is serious but has lasted only a few days, medication is often the treatment of choice. It is important to extinguish the insomnia as soon as possible in order to keep the patient from learning maladaptive sleep habits. Medication may even be used in a prophylactic way, say in cases in which patients sleep very poorly before a big exam or giving an important talk. Other cases of acute insomnia need only treatment of the precipitating factor. For example, in the case of a severe grief reaction following the loss of a loved one, one deals only with the grief. It may not be adaptive to extinguish the insomnia with hypnotics if this prevents part of the natural mourning. On the other hand, behavioral therapies are the treatments of choice for chronic insomnia. In such insomnias the learned, perpetuating factors are usually paramount and need to be addressed. Also, there are issues with habituation and rebound if hypnotics are used chronically.

"Natural" Potions

Patients often ask about melatonin or vitamins or minerals or herbal preparations. It appears that, in general, these preparations do little for most insomnia patients. However, there are bona fide case reports suggesting that, in rare patients, such preparations have helped markedly or even cured the insomnia. If patients are interested in such preparations, it might be wise to let them try these potions in a careful experiment. Patients might use the preparation for 1 or 2 weeks and every morning rate their sleep (1 = serious insomnia, 5 = an average night, 10 = excellent sleep), then compare it with sleep when off these potions.

Improving Sleep Hygiene

It is impossible to work with insomnia without giving patients some advice on how to improve sleep hygiene. Considering the frequency with which such advice

has been given, remarkably little actual research has been carried out. When sleep hygiene has been studied, it was often used as a control condition against which to measure the efficacy of other behavioral treatments. In such situations, sleep hygiene advice seems to produce only limited improvement and lower satisfaction (Schoicket, Bertelson, & Lacks, 1988). However, one may wonder about the quality of the sleep hygiene advice in such a situation.

There is no sleep hygiene advice that seems to work uniformly for all patients. For example, the large majority of insomnia patients sleep better if they avoid daytime naps. However, there is a sizable minority who sleep better if a short nap is allowed, maybe 30 minutes. Because of the large variability of responses to individual sleep hygiene measures, it is often best to use the "co-scientist" model that was just described for the evaluation of melatonin and other potions. That is, each sleep hygiene rule is used for a 1- or 2-week trial period, then abandoned for 1 or 2 weeks. Each morning the patient rates his or her sleep on a scale from 1 to 10. Based on these numbers, one determines whether a certain rule is helpful for the patient's sleep. If the results are ambiguous, one might retry the experiment. Obviously, however, this co-scientist approach only uncovers short-term effects; effects that might develop over weeks or months will not be found using this method.

Often one does well to let the patient take the lead in what factors should be investigated. However, sooner or later, the following issues might be brought up for evaluation by the co-scientist method.

Curtailing Time in Bed

Normal sleeping adults often artificially curtail their sleep. We now sleep about 90 minutes less than we did before the invention of electricity. However, insomniacs often stay in bed excessively long. Excessive times in bed lead to shallower sleep, with more awakenings, less stage 3 and 4, and excessive stage 1.

One would expect that people who stay in bed longer than needed would first satisfy their sleep need and then awaken, leading to early morning wakefulness. For unknown reasons, this rarely happens. Rather, people who stay in bed longer than needed typically sleep well during the first few hours, then experience long and disturbing mid-sleep awakenings, only to fall asleep soundly again toward morning, close to getting-up time. Clinical experience suggests that if such patients curtail their time in bed to the time needed to sleep prior to the development of insomnia, sleep often becomes deeper, the mid-night awakenings disappear, and the patient feels more alert during the day.

Exercise

Exercise has a profound effect on sleep (Youngstedt, O'Connor, & Dishman, 1997). It clearly improves sleep quality in depressed elderly insomniacs (Singh, Clements, & Fiatoroni, 1997). People who keep fit by exercising typically fall asleep more easily, awaken less during the night, and show less stage 1 (light sleep) and more stage 3 and 4 (deep sleep) (Baekeland & Lasky, 1966). The main benefits do not occur after one evening of intense exercise (Hauri, 1968). Rather, fitness has to be developed over a period of some weeks before marked changes in sleep develop.

As discussed earlier, insomnia patients are hyperaroused. Exercise increases metabolism and body temperature initially, but after a few hours, metabolism and body temperature plummet to lower levels than they would have reached had no exercise occurred. This may be the reason why exercise in the morning rarely seems to affect sleep, because the decrease in metabolism has washed out. Similarly, exercise too close to bedtime may be detrimental to sleep. It appears, at least from clinical experience, that exercise 5 or 6 hours before going to bed may be ideal.

Bedroom Clock

Looking at the clock during the night may cause arousal and frustration in most insomniacs. It is always the wrong time! Therefore, it is best for many to set the alarm clock and then hide it. This may be one of the reasons why some insomniacs sleep much better in the sleep laboratory: Most patient bedrooms in the laboratory do not have a clock. Hiding all clocks is more than a simple "trick" for many insomniacs. Attitudes toward insomnia often change drastically if one is no longer a slave to how many minutes one has slept last night.

Distracting Activity

Trying hard to sleep and becoming frustrated is a major problem in chronic insomnia. The harder one

tries, the less one sleeps. This is especially true in patients who have observed that they fall asleep easily when not trying (e.g., when watching television, listening to a lecture, or when driving). In those situations they are relatively motionless while trying to stay awake, a situation that is more conducive to sleep than desperately trying to sleep. The old technique of "counting sheep" is based on this. Anyone who has ever tried to count an actual herd of over 100 sheep while they are constantly moving around knows how this task absorbs all attention. The technique no longer works because most of us have not had any experience with that task. Rather, we distract our attention best when watching television or reading.

Considerable discussion has centered on whether the distracting activity should be in bed or in a different room (Sloan et al., 1993). Both methods have their advocates, both among sleep researchers and patients. Those who have their patients read in a different room are concerned about stimulus associations. Reading in bed, in their opinion, leads to an association between the bed and arousal. This is a legitimate concern. However, reading in bed has the advantage that when one is finally sleepy, one can simply turn off the light and fall asleep. Reading in another room brings the problem that one then has to return to the bedroom when sleepy, and walking to the bedroom often arouses the patient again. Most likely this question, too, should be resolved for each patient with the co-scientist model, unless Bootzin's stimulus control technique is employed in its entirety. Certainly, lying in bed unable to sleep and becoming more and more frustrated is counterproductive and needs to be avoided.

Patients who are told to read in bed do best with a paradoxical technique: Read in bed as long as you possibly can, fighting sleep. Turn off the light only when you really can read no longer. Two associations are developed: one, between reading in bed and becoming severely sleepy; the other, between turning off the bedroom light and then falling asleep quickly (patients initially report reading "for hours," although they have no clock to verify this). Over a period of days or weeks the amount of reading that is necessary becomes shorter and shorter, until just reading a few pages leads to drowsiness and easy sleep onset. A Gallup poll (1991) reports that about one-third of the adult U.S. population read themselves to sleep in bed.

Avoiding Alcohol, Nicotine, and Caffeine

Alcohol makes many people feel relaxed and may help them fall asleep. However, alcohol leads to increased and long arousals during the night. By morning, most have slept more poorly after an alcohol-induced night than after a sober night.

Nicotine, too, is a stimulant. However, nicotine withdrawal is also a stressor. Therefore, heavy smokers find that they often need to smoke immediately before going to bed or during the night to avoid nicotine withdrawal. However, in a few weeks, after a heavy smoker has passed through the time of nicotine withdrawal, sleep becomes better (Wolter et al., 1996).

Caffeine is a stimulant that is often overlooked. In addition, many patients are exquisitely sensitive to caffeine in coffee or even chocolate or black tea. A co-scientist study, using multiple doses of caffeine, might indicate how much of it and at what time it is tolerable in a specific insomniac. Usually one advises against such stimulants from lunch on.

Bedtime Snack

Ever since Kleitman et al.'s exhaustive 1937 study, it was known that some food just before bedtime helped with sleep. This is not only true in humans, but in animals as well: Hungry lions, for example, sleep very little, but they may sleep for up to 24 hours after they have had their fill. It is unclear whether this effect is caused by a digestive hormone such as Fara et al. (1969) suggest or whether it may be associated with some food stuffs that were ingested (e.g., tryptophan). In any case, in our weight-conscious society in which the desired weight is often below the "ideal" weight, it makes sense to reserve a few calories for a bedtime snack if one sleeps poorly.

Regular Sleep Habits

Sleep and waking are regulated by the circadian rhythm. It makes sense to go to bed and get up at about the same time to help with this rhythm. A sleep log or wrist actigraph easily indicates how regular an insomniac patient is with this. However, in my experience, this is rarely a serious problem with severe insomniacs. They often err much more on the side of

compulsive adherence to exact clock times. This prevents them from enjoying some evening activities that would be helpful for sleep or lifestyle.

Moving bed and arousal times can be a factor in improving insomnia. For example, patients with difficulties falling asleep might be asked to get up an hour earlier, while those who have early morning awakenings might be asked to remain alert for an hour longer in the evening. These manipulations, however, take a few weeks before they are beneficial.

Scheduling Worry Time

Many insomnia patients complain that their minds are racing during the night. Often this suggests psychopathology (e.g., when a severely anxious patient is able to keep his thoughts under control while highly active during the day but then needs to avoid them at night by racing "mumbo jumbo" thoughts). At other times, however, racing thoughts or worrying at night simply mean that not enough time has been allocated during the day to settle issues. In that case it is often useful to have insomnia patients reserve 30 minutes in the early evening "to do the work of worrying."

In one worry method, patients are asked to sit quietly, letting their mind wander, with a number of 3×5 cards in their hands. When their thoughts hit on a worrisome thought, they are asked to write it down. There are two types of such thoughts: First, there are all the minute issues of life that need to be remembered, such as contacting a friend tomorrow, carrying out the garbage, checking up on deadlines, and so forth. These issues should all be noted on a "to do" list. Second, there are larger issues to be noted individually, one per card. Once most concerns are collected, usually within about 10 minutes, the patient sorts the larger issues into piles such as family, job, financial. Each card is then individually considered. One decides what can actually be done about each issue tomorrow. It is rarely possible to solve the entire problem. Rather, one determines what could be done tomorrow to "get off the dime." Maybe more information needs to be collected tomorrow before one can make a decision, or one might contact a sick friend and give some moral support, even though one cannot resolve that person's medical problem, and the like. Many insomnia patients report that after writing these temporary solutions on the card that states the problem, they can more easily let go of the problem during the night. Many insomniacs use this "worry time" only during periods of increased insomnia or stress, not during periods of good functioning.

Lifestyle

This is often an overlooked issue if the therapist is excessively focused on sleep. It is difficult to sleep well when one is overstressed and overcommitted or when one works until shortly before retiring to bed, against impossible odds, or in a hopeless situation. In some cases these stressors are externally imposed (e.g., by work demands that the patient simply cannot meet). In many more cases, however, these stressors are internally driven—say, by feelings of insecurity or inferiority. Patients who are feeling inferior might hope that they will do an adequate job if they work much harder than anyone else. These feelings need to be addressed (e.g., by cognitive therapy) before one can give advice to the patient on how to structure the day, how to relax more and work less. Insomnia may also be caused by excessive boredom, such as is often experienced when a very busy executive retires without having developed any hobby or when a patient's usual life is disrupted by some medical problem.

Behavioral Therapy

Behavioral therapy is clearly the treatment of choice in chronic insomnia. This is especially true for psychophysiological insomnia, idiopathic insomnia, and patients with inadequate sleep hygiene. However, even in other chronic insomnias such as those associated with psychiatric or medical illness, behavioral therapy is often crucial because, as discussed earlier, it is hard to have chronic insomnia without developing secondary, perpetuating factors that need to be addressed with behavioral therapy.

Surprisingly, behavioral therapies seem to work about equally well when used with sleep onset insomnia as when used with frequent nocturnal awakenings or early morning insomnia. Even normal sleepers awaken quite frequently throughout the night (e.g., five to seven times each hour when studied in the laboratory). In normal sleepers these awakenings are very short, often lasting no more than a few seconds and being promptly forgotten. The issue in insomnia

is not why the patients awaken but why they then have such a hard time returning to sleep.

Two meta-analyses summarized the current evidence on nonpharmacological therapies (Morin, Culbert, Schwartz, 1994; Murtagh & Greenwood, 1995). Both are based on self-reported data. These data suggest that, on average, patients with sleep-onset problems who are treated with behavioral therapy fall asleep faster than 81% of the untreated controls. Those with sleep maintenance problems sleep better after behavioral therapy than 74% of the untreated controls. Sleep latency typically decreases from a reported 60 minutes pre treatment to about 35 minutes post treatment, when averaged over all behavioral techniques. Morin, Culbert, and Schwartz (1994) found that stimulus control therapy and sleep restriction therapy are the most effective behavioral treatments, while sleep hygiene was least effective. Murtagh and Greenwood (1995) found no difference in efficacy among the various behavioral therapies.

Stimulus Control Therapy

Many of our behaviors are under the control of stimuli in our environment. When good sleepers brush their teeth at night and get into bed, the stimuli around them are associated with relaxation and rapid sleep onset in a process called classical conditioning. However, because these stimuli in insomnia patients have been paired with their inability to sleep, with frustration, and with arousal, they will trigger insomnia. Stimulus control therapy tries to break these maladaptive associations.

The following six steps are discussed in detail with the patient (Bootzin, Epstein, & Wood, 1991):

1. Lie down, intending to go to sleep, only when you are sleepy.
2. Do not use your bed for anything but sleep. Sexual activity is the only exception. On such occasions, follow these instructions afterward, when you intend to go to sleep.
3. If you find yourself unable to fall asleep easily, get up and go to another room. Stay up as long as needed and return to the bedroom only when you feel like you really can fall asleep. Remember, the goal is to associate your bed with falling asleep quickly. Although clock watching should

be avoided, if you are in bed more than about 10 minutes without falling asleep and you have not gotten up, you are not following this instruction.

4. Repeat step #3 as often as necessary.
5. Set the alarm and get up at the same time each morning, no matter how you slept. That helps maintain circadian cycling.
6. No naps during the day.

It is critical to note that in Bootzin's stimulus control instructions the injunction to avoid reading or watching television in bed is part of an entire package, which includes getting out of bed whenever one cannot sleep. This cannot be taken out of context. Simply forbidding insomnia patients to read or watch television in bed but then letting them lie there frustrated for hours reinforces the maladaptive associations rather than breaking them.

Stimulus control training can be carried out in groups or with individuals. Of all the techniques that are available for the treatment of insomnia today, the Bootzin technique is by far the best researched. In all studies comparing that technique with any other behavioral treatment of insomnia, stimulus control has always been found either equal or superior to the other techniques.

It is important that patients understand the rationale for the rules that are given and how they apply to them. For example, a patient who feels that her insomnia is based on a chemical imbalance in the brain rather than on any behavioral issue will have great difficulties following these instructions unless that preconception is first dealt with using cognitive therapy.

Cognitive Therapy

Most patients with insomnia subscribe to various erroneous beliefs and attitudes about their sleep. These beliefs often aggravate or even cause the insomnia. At the very least, they make the treatment of insomnia very difficult unless they are first addressed (Morin, 1993).

Examples of cognitive errors found in insomnia are described below.

Unrealistic Expectations

Patients may believe that they need a minimum of 8 hours of sleep and that the more sleep they get, the healthier and more refreshed they will be. They may worry that not getting enough sleep will lead to nervous breakdowns or serious medical disorders. Such expectations need to be evaluated using both the patients' own experiences but also the research evidence on the role of sleep and the (minimal) consequences of partial sleep deprivation.

Cognitive Distortions

When insomniacs are asked how they typically sleep and later are asked to record night-by-night sleep in a log, the two responses are often markedly discrepant. Insomniacs are prone to remember only the very bad nights or the very bad consequences that have occurred on some occasions when they did not sleep. They are not likely to remember the fact that they have functioned quite well despite poor sleep on some other occasions. Similarly, "black and white" thinking causes problems, with all nights being classified as either awful or excellent. This makes it difficult to appreciate small improvements in sleep. Catastrophizing is also a problem. It is often countered by studying people who were serious insomniacs and yet achieved greatness in life.

Misattribution

Mainly because patients with insomnia are typically repressors, they prefer to attribute any personal problem to their inability to sleep. This causes excessive concern about sleep that often aggravates insomnia. It is helpful to sort out those problems that may be associated with poor sleep and to distinguish them from those (e.g., social shyness) that one would have even if one slept well. For those other problems, one can then teach different coping skills, with the result that the patients' lives get better and their sleep improves.

Cognitive therapy is a carefully researched skill. It requires training. Simply telling patients that their thoughts and attributes are wrong yields nothing but resistance. Helping patients to evaluate their misconceptions and misattributions in the light of their own and others' experience and in the light of research often helps to question these assumptions. In this way, one tries to replace maladaptive thoughts with more functional ones, decatastrophize poor sleep, and reattribute problems that are not caused by insomnia.

Relaxation Therapy

One would expect relaxation therapy to be the most effective treatment of insomnia if Bonnet's hyperarousal theory is correct. While relaxation is useful in many cases, it is typically less effective than that (Hauri, 1981). It seems possible that we simply have not given relaxation an adequate chance. If a person is hyperaroused for 24 hours a day, one 30-minute relaxation session a day is unlikely to take care of the entire problem.

There is no clear consensus on how specific this relaxation therapy should be. Previously in this paper, three different kinds of tension and arousal were suggested: anxiety or psychological tension, muscular tension, and sympathetic arousal. It would seem likely that each type of tension may need a different relaxation method. Some relaxation trainers do try to distinguish the different types of arousal and train accordingly. No careful matching study has yet been carried out. However, it has been shown (Hauri et al., 1982) that those insomnia patients who are not muscularly tense do not benefit from EMG biofeedback training. They may even be harmed by it.

Sleep Curtailment

Research has shown that insomniacs sleep much better after sleep deprivation (Webb & Agnew, 1974). They fall asleep faster, and show fewer awakenings, more stage 3 and 4 sleep, and longer total sleep after a night of no sleep at all. Unfortunately the improvement is short-lived, no more than one or two nights. Sleep restriction therapy is designed to exploit these temporary improvements in sleep after sleep loss, while temporarily accepting daytime sleepiness as a side effect (Glovinsky & Spielman, 1991).

As practiced by Spielman, Saskin, and Thorpy (1987), one first has the patient fill out sleep logs. One then restricts bedtime hours to the total hours of actual sleep that are reported on these logs (although never less than 4.5 hours in bed). Typically one keeps the wake-up time constant, while the time to go to bed is delayed. For example, if a patient is allotted 5 hours of time in bed and wants to get up at 7 a.m., that patient would have to remain out of bed until 2 a.m. Helping the patient to do so requires some social engineering. It is unlikely that patients can stay up until 2 a.m. if they watch television, sitting alone. Rather, they might have to organize others to help (e.g., by playing cards, walking, or talking).

Each morning the patient reports the pertinent data to the therapist's answering machine. This would involve information about when the patient went to bed, how many hours were actually slept, the get-up time, and so on. If, according to these telephone calls, sleep efficiency for the past five nights has been higher than 90%, an additional 15 or 30 minutes of bed time is allocated. (Initially it was suggested to curtail sleep even more if sleep efficiency on the moving 5-day average dropped below 85%, but this procedure was experienced as being too punitive and therapeutically ineffective.) In the elderly, Spielman typically lowers his sleep efficiency criteria by 5% and, if indicated, allows a short afternoon nap (Glovinsky & Spielman, 1991).

Patients who are able to carry out this procedure show considerable improvement in sleep efficiency. Often, relatively normal sleep is achieved in less than 2 months. However, this procedure is not easy to follow, and frequent therapist contacts seem necessary to avoid a high dropout rate.

Bright Light Therapy

It has been shown in numerous studies that bright light changes the timing of the sleep/wake rhythm. The neurologic substrate of this is known: The circadian "clock" resides in the suprachiasmatic nucleus, and the retino-hypothalamic tract leads directly from the retina to that nucleus.

To treat disordered sleep, one needs intense bright light, at least 2,500 lux. There seems to be a stimulus/response curve—the brighter the light, the less exposure time seems necessary. Therefore, most clinicians prefer about 10,000 lux when trying to shift the circadian rhythm.

Initially bright light was used mainly to treat delayed and advanced sleep phase (Terman, 1994). For example, if a patient reports being excessively somnolent during the evening but then awakens much too early in the morning, he is classified as having an advanced sleep phase syndrome and bright light is applied in the evening, a few hours before the patient goes to bed. If a patient cannot fall asleep in the evening but then sleeps late in the morning, this is a delayed sleep phase syndrome and bright light is applied in the early morning. Typically a "nudging" procedure is used: For example, the patient who falls asleep no earlier than 4 a.m. and then sleeps until noon is first asked to get up at 11 a.m. and expose his eyes to bright light for 30 to 60 minutes; later, he gets up at 10 a.m., and so on. The time that he can fall asleep gradually advances as the morning exposure is done earlier and earlier.

It has been shown that bright light affects the timing of the circadian rhythm (the "hands" of the clock), not the inherent periodicity (the "mechanism" of the clock). Therefore, such bright light therapy has to be incorporated into the lifestyle of the patient. An elderly person with an advanced sleep phase might have to make it a habit to go outside for a walk after dinner. A high school student with a seriously delayed sleep phase might be asked to ride a bicycle to school (exposing his eyes to bright light) rather than taking the bus.

In northern latitudes it is often not possible to do bright light therapy with outdoor light only, especially in the winter. A specially designed bright light box may be needed. A useful rule of thumb is that light is bright enough for this therapy from about 30 minutes after sunrise to about 30 minutes before sunset. Another rule of thumb is that light is bright enough for treatment if a simple camera does not automatically flash when a picture is taken in that position. Thus, overcast outdoor light is still acceptable; most indoor light is not.

Recently it has been shown that the same procedures for advanced and delayed sleep phase can also be used for patients with difficulties falling asleep and those with early morning awakenings, even if the circadian rhythm is not seen as the primary reason for the insomnia (Campbell, Dawson, & Anderson, 1993; Rosenberg, 1991).

Concerning side effects of this therapy, patients with eye problems other than needing corrective glasses should first check with their ophthalmologist. Also, there occasionally are complaints of irritability, eye strain, or headaches. Bright light is discontinued or exposure time shortened if these complaints last for longer than a few minutes after light exposure. A theoretical possibility is that bright light might trigger a hypomanic episode, especially in someone who is predisposed in that direction. It rarely happens.

Side effects can often be managed by decreasing the time or the intensity of the light exposure. Care is indicated in patients who take photosensitizing drugs such as hydrochlorothiazide, some diuretic agents, amiodarone, or long-term lithium (Roberts et al., 1992).

CONCLUSIONS

It is clear that the treatment for insomnia has come a long way in the last 30 years. It is considerably more complex than had initially been assumed. However, once one has acquired the skills needed to diagnose and treat this problem, dealing with insomnia is a very rewarding activity.

REFERENCES

American Psychiatric Association (1994). *Diagnostic and statistical manual of mental disorders* (4th ed.). Washington, DC: Author.

Ancoli-Israel, S., Seifert, A. R., Lemon, M. (1986). Thermal biofeedback and periodic movements in sleep: Patients' subjective reports and a case study. *Biofeedback and Self-Regulation, 11*(3), 177–188.

Baekeland, F., & Lasky. R. (1966). Exercise and sleep patterns in college athletes. *Perceptual Motor Skills, 23,* 1203.

Benca, R. M., & Quintas, J. (1997). Sleep and host defenses: A review. *Sleep, 20*(11), 1027–1037.

Bonnet, M. H., & Arand, D. L. (1992). Caffeine use as a model of acute and chronic insomnia. *Sleep, 15,* 526–536.

Bonnet, M. H., & Arand, D. L. (1995a). Sleep state misperception: Misperception by clinicians? *Sleep Research, 24* [abstract], 200.

Bonnet, M. H., & Arand, D. L. (1995b). Twenty-four-hour metabolic rate in insomniacs and matched normal sleepers. *Sleep, 18,* 581–588.

Bootzin, R. R., Epstein, D., & Wood, J. M. (1991). Stimulus control instructions. In P. J. Hauri (Ed.), *Case studies in insomnia* (pp. 19–28). New York: Plenum Medical.

Borkovec, T. D. (1979). Pseudo (experiential) insomnia and idiopathic (objective) insomnia: Theoretical and therapeutic issues. *Advances in Behavioral Research and Therapy, 2,* 27–55.

Buysse, D. J., Reynolds, C. F., III, Kupfer, D. J., Thorpy, M. J., Bixler, E., Kales, A., Manfredi, R., Vgontzas, A., Stepanski, E., Roth, T., Hauri, P., & Stapf, D. (1997). Effects of diagnosis on treatment recommendations in chronic insomnia—a report from the APA/NIMH DSM-IV Field Trial. *Sleep, 20*(7), 542–552.

Campbell, S. S., Dawson, D., & Anderson, M. W. (1993). Alleviation of sleep maintenance insomnia with timed exposure to bright light. *Journal of American Geriatric Society, 41,* 829–836.

Coursey, R. D., Buchsbaum, M., & Frankel, B. L. (1975). Personality measures and evoked responses in chronic insomniacs. *Journal of Abnormal Psychology, 84,* 239–249.

Edinger, J. D., Fins, A. I., Goeke, J. M., McMillan, D. K., Gersh, T. L., Krystal, A. D., & McCall, W. V. (1996). Insomnia. The empirical identification of insomnia subtypes: A cluster analytic approach. *Sleep, 19*(5), 398–411.

Edinger, J. D., Fins, A. I., Sullivan, R. J., Jr., Marsh, G. R., Dailey, D. S., Hope, T. V., Young, M., Shaw, E., Carlson, D., & Vasilas, D. (1997). Do our methods lead to insomniacs' madness?: Daytime testing after laboratory and home-based polysomnographic studies. *Sleep, 20*(12), 1127–1134.

Edinger, J. D., Morey, M. C., Sullivan, R. J., et al. (1993). Aerobic fitness, acute exercise and sleep in older men. *Sleep, 16,* 351–359.

Fara, J. W., Rubinstein, E. N., Sonnenschein, R. R. (1969). Visceral and behavioral responses to intraduodenal fat. *Science, 166,* 110–111.

Ford, D., & Kamerow, D. (1989). Epidemiologic study of sleep disturbances and psychiatric disorders: An opportunity for prevention? *JAMA, 262,* 1479–1484.

Fredrickson, P. A., & Krueger, B. R. (1994). Fatal familial insomnia: A new prion disease. In M. H. Kryger, T. Roth, & W. C. Dement (Eds.), *Principles and practice of sleep medicine* (2d ed.) (pp. 523–534). Philadelphia: Saunders.

Freedman, R. R. (1986). EEG power spectra in sleep-onset insomnia. *Electroencephalography Clinical Neurophysiology, 63,* 408–413.

Gallup Organization. (1991). *Sleep in America: A national survey of U.S. adults.* Princeton, NJ: National Sleep Foundation.

Globus, G., Friedmann, J., Cohen H., et al. (1974). The effects of aircraft noise on sleep electrophysiology as recorded in the home. In W. D. Ward (Ed.), *Proceedings of the International Congress on Noise as a Public Health Problem* (pp. 587–591). Washington, DC: U.S. Environmental Protection Agency.

Glovinsky, P. B., & Spielman, A. J. (1991). Sleep restriction therapy. In P. J. Hauri (Ed.), *Case studies in insomnia* (pp. 49–63). New York: Plenum Medical.

Hauri, P. (1968). Effects of evening activity on early night sleep. *Psychophysiology, 4*(3), 267–277.

Hauri, P. (1981). Treating psychophysiologic insomnia with biofeedback. *Archives of General Psychiatry, 38,* 752–758.

Hauri, P. J. (1983). A cluster analysis of insomnia. *Sleep, 6,* 326–338.

Hauri, P. J. (1991). Sleep hygiene, relaxation therapy, and cognitive interventions. In P. J. Hauri (Ed.), *Case studies in insomnia* (pp. 65–84). New York and London: Plenum.

Hauri, P. J. (1993). Clinical sleep research: Consulting about insomnia: A method and some preliminary data. *Sleep, 16*(4), 344–350.

Hauri, P. J. (1997a). Cognitive deficits in insomnia patients. *Acta Neurologica Belgica, 97,* 113–117.

Hauri, P. J. (1997b). Insomnia: Can we mix behavioral therapy with hypnotics when treating insomniacs? *Sleep, 20*(12), 1111–1118.

Hauri, P., & Fisher, J. (1986). Persistent psychophysiologic (learned) insomnia. *Sleep, 9*(1), 38–53.

Hauri, P., & Olmstead, E. (1980). Childhood-onset insomnia. *Sleep, 3*(1), 59–65.

Hauri, P. J., & Olmstead, E. M. (1989). Reverse first night effect in insomnia. *Sleep, 12*(2), 97–105.

Hauri, P. J., Percy, L., Hellekson, C., Hartmann, E., & Russ, D. (1982). The treatment of psychophysiologic insomnia with biofeedback: A replication study. *Biofeedback and Self-Regulation, 7*(2), 223–235.

Hauri, P. J., & Wisbey, J. (1992). Wrist actigraphy in insomnia. *Sleep, 15*(4), 293–301.

Hohagen, F., Kappler, C., Schramm, E., Riemann, D., Weyerer, S., & Berger, M. (1994). Short notes: Sleep onset insomnia, sleep maintaining insomnia and insomnia with early morning awakening—temporal stability of subtypes in a longitudinal study on general practice attenders. *Sleep, 17*(6), 551–554.

ICD-9-CM. (1980). *Manual of the international classification of diseases* (9th rev.) (clinical modification). Washington, DC: U.S. Government Printing Office.

ICSD. (1990). *International classification of sleep disorders: Diagnostic and coding manual.* Diagnostic Classification Steering Committee (M. J. Thorpy, Chairman). Rochester, MN: American Sleep Disorders Association.

Johnson, E. O., Roehrs, T., Roth, T., & Breslau, N. (1998). Epidemiology of alcohol and medication as aids to sleep in early adulthood. *Sleep, 21*(2), 178–186.

Johnson, L. C., & Spinweber, C. L. (1983). Good and poor sleepers differ in navy performance. *Military Medicine, 148,* 727–731.

Kageyama, T., Kabuto, M., Nitta, H., Kurokawa, Y., Taira, K., Suzuki, S., & Takemoto, T. (1997). Insomnia: A population study on risk factors for insomnia among adult Japanese women: A possible effect of road traffic volume. *Sleep, 20*(11), 963–971.

Kales, A., Caldwell, A. B., Preston, T. A., et al. (1976). Personality patterns in insomnia. *Archives of General Psychiatry, 33,* 1128–1134.

Karacan, I., Williams, R. L., Littell, R. C., et al. (1973). Insomniacs: Unpredictable and idiosyncratic sleepers. *Proceedings of the First European Congress on Sleep Research* (pp. 120–132), Basel, Switzerland, 1972. Basel: Karger.

Kleitman, N., Mullin, F. J., Cooperman, N. R., & Titelbaum, S. (1937). *Sleep characteristics*. Chicago: University of Chicago Press.

Lack, L., & Lushington, K. (1997). The endogenous temperature rhythms of sleep maintenance [Abstract no. 565]. Eleventh meeting of the association of professional sleep societies, San Francisco, June 10–15, 1997. *APSS Abstract Book*, ASDA/SRS, p. 283.

Lamarche, C. H., & Ogilvie, R. D. (1997). Electrophysiological changes during the sleep onset period of psychophysiologic insomniacs, psychiatric insomniacs, and normal sleepers. *Sleep, 20*(9), 724–733.

Lugaresi, E., & Montagna, P. (1994). Fatal familial insomnia: A new prion disease. In M. H. Kryger, T. Roth, & W. C. Dement (Eds.), *Principles and practice of sleep medicine* (2d ed.) (pp. 547–548). Philadelphia: Saunders.

Mellinger, G., Balter, M., & Uhlenhuth, E. (1985). Insomnia and its treatment: Prevalence and correlates. *Archives of General Psychiatry, 42*, 225–232.

Mendelson, W. B., Garnett, D., & Linnoila, M. (1984). Do insomniacs have impaired daytime functioning? *Biological Psychiatry, 19*, 1261–1264.

Milby, J. B., Williams, V., Hall, J. N., Khuder, S., McGill, T., & Wooten, V. (1993). Effectiveness of combined triazolam–behavioral therapy for primary insomnia. *American Journal of Psychiatry, 150*, 1259–1260.

Moldofsky, H., Lue F. A., Eisen, J., Keystone, E., & Gorczynski, R. M. (1986). The relationship of interleukin-1 and immune functions to sleep in humans. *Psychosomatic Medicine, 48*, 309–317.

Morin, C. M. (1993). Insomnia: Psychological assessment and management. In D. M. Barlow (Ed.), *Treatment manuals for practitioners* (vol. 1). New York: Guilford Press.

Morin, C. M., Culbert, J. P., & Schwartz, S. M. (1994). Nonpharmacological interventions for insomnia: A meta-analysis of treatment efficacy. *American Journal of Psychiatry, 151*, 1172–1180.

Morin, C. M., & Kwentus, J. A. (1988). Area review: Sleep disorders, behavioral and pharmacological treatments for insomnia. *Annals of Behavioral Medicine, 10*, 91–100.

Morin, C. M., Stone, J., Trinkle, D., et al. (1993). Dysfunctional beliefs and attitudes about sleep among older adults with and without insomnia complaints. *Psychology of Aging, 8*, 463–467.

Murtagh, D. R., & Greenwood, K. M. (1995). Identifying effective psychological treatments for insomnia: A meta-analysis. *Journal of Consulting Clinical Psychology, 63*, 79–89.

Pedrosi, B., Roehrs, T. A., Rosenthal, L., et al. (1995). Daytime functioning and benzodiazepine effects in insomniacs compared to normals. In M. H. Chase, L. D. Rosenthal, & C. O'Connor (Eds.), *Sleep research.* [Abstract 24:48.] Los Angeles: Brain Information Service.

Regestein, Q. R., Dambrosia, J., Hallett, M., et al. (1993). Daytime alertness in patients with primary insomnia. *American Journal of Psychiatry, 150*, 1529–1534.

Reite, M., Buysse, D., Reynolds, C., et al. (1995). An American Sleep Disorders Association review: The use of polysomnography in the evaluation of insomnia. *Sleep, 18*, 58–70.

Roberts, J. E., Reme, C. E., Dillion, J., et al. (1992). Exposure to bright light and the concurrent use of photosensitizing drugs. *New England Journal of Medicine, 326*, 1500–1501.

Rosenberg, R. (1991). Assessment and treatment of delayed sleep phase syndrome. In P. J. Hauri (Ed.), *Case studies in insomnia* (pp. 193–205). New York: Plenum Medical.

Roth, T. (1996). Social and economic consequences of sleep disorders. *Sleep, 19*(8), S46–S47.

Schoicket, S. L., Bertelson, A. D., & Lacks, P. (1988). Is sleep hygiene a sufficient treatment for sleep maintenance insomnia? *Behavior Therapy, 19*, 183–190.

Silva, J., Chase, M., Sartorius, N., et al. (1996). Fast track report: Special report from a symposium held by the world health organization and the world federation of sleep research societies: An overview of insomnias and related disorders—recognition, epidemiology, and rational management. *Sleep, 19*, 412–416.

Singh, N. A., Clements, K. M., & Fiatarone, M. A. (1997). Sleep, sleep deprivation, and daytime activities: A randomized controlled trial of the effect of exercise on sleep. *Sleep, 20*(2), 95–101.

Sloan, E. P., Hauri, P., Bootzin, R., Morin, C., Stevenson, M., & Shapiro, C. M. (1993). The nuts and bolts of behavioral therapy for insomnia. *Journal of Psychosomatic Research, 37*, (suppl. 1), 19–37.

Spielman, A. J., & Glovinsky, P. B. (1991). Introduction: The varied nature of insomnia. In P. J. Hauri (Ed.), *Case studies in insomnia* (pp. 1–16). New York: Plenum Medical.

Spielman, A. J., Saskin, P., & Thorpy, M. J. (1987). Treatment of chronic insomnia by restriction of time in bed. *Sleep, 10*, 45–56.

Terman, M. (1994). Light treatment. In M. H. Kryger, T. Roth, & W. C. Dement (Eds.), *Principles and practice of sleep medicine* (2d ed.) (pp. 1012–1029). Philadelphia: Saunders.

Trinder, J. (1988). Subjective insomnia without objective findings: A pseudodiagnostic classification? *Psychology Bulletin, 103*, 94–197.

Webb, W., & Agnew, H. (1974). The effects of a chronic limitation of sleep length. *Psychophysiology, 11*, 265–274.

Wolter, T. D., Hauri, P. J., Schroeder, D. R., Wisbey, J. A., Croghan, I. T., Offord, K. P., Dale, L. C., & Hurt, R. D. (1996). Effects of 24-hr nicotine replacement on sleep and daytime activity during smoking cessation. *Preventive Medicine, 25*, 601–610.

Youngstedt, S. D., O'Connor, P. J., & Dishman, R. K. (1997). The effects of acute exercise on sleep: A quantitative synthesis. *Sleep, 20*, 203–214.

CHAPTER 9

THE MANAGEMENT OF STRESS AND ANXIETY IN CHRONIC FATIGUE SYNDROME

Trudie Chalder
Anthony Cleare
Simon Wessely

The main purpose of this chapter is to describe the management of stress and anxiety in patients with chronic fatigue syndrome (CFS). However, given the controversial nature of CFS, particularly in relation to etiology, it is necessary to give an overview of the subject, highlighting some of the areas of contention. The relationship between fatigue and anxiety will then be examined. We will describe both the process and the content of cognitive-behavioral treatment.

OVERVIEW

Fatigue as a subjective symptom is difficult to define. The problem has vexed writers for years, and at one time it led to the suggestion that the term be abandoned altogether (Muscio, 1921). Although the history of fatigue probably goes back far longer, it came into prominence in the middle of the nineteenth century as a consequence of a number of cultural and social factors, in particular the idea that inactivity was immoral (Rabinbach, 1990). Industrialization demanded that workers perform for long hours, and the quest was on to understand fatigue and conquer it. In 1869 Beard established the concept of neurasthenia (McEvedy & Beard, 1973), which he ascribed to social conditions such as exhaustion in the middle classes and the changing status of women. Soon after, "fatigue laboratories" were opened. However, by the advent of World War II the interest in fatigue waned, laboratories closed and the subject did not surface again until the late 1980s, again probably as a result of social and cultural factors not dissimilar to those

previously associated with neurasthenia, only this time with a different label, that of "myalgic encephalomyelitis" (ME).

The striking feature of both neurasthenia in the late nineteenth century and CFS today is their ability to cause dissent. The dissent revolves around differing interpretations of the relative contributions of physical and psychological factors. The passions aroused are essentially because of what was and is at stake: the issue of what constitutes legitimate suffering (Wessely, Hotopf, & Sharpe, 1998). CFS seen as a physical disease implies legitimacy whereas CFS seen as a psychological illness implies malingering. At the heart of the debate is an outmoded dualistic view of illness that assumes that the mind and body operate separately.

As with neurasthenia, suggested etiologies have reflected this dualistic view and have included possible neuromuscular dysfunction, viral infection, immune dysfunction, and psychiatric disorder such as depression. However, the symptom of fatigue is likely to be related to a combination of factors that contribute to both the onset and the perpetuation of the symptom or disorder. Given the circumstances in which fatigue arises, it is also difficult to believe that "stress" does not have a role.

The Nature of Fatigue

Fatigue is a problematic concept, which has many synonyms, including *weakness, fatiguability, sleepiness, tiredness, desire for rest, lassitude*, and *boredom*. The sensory quality of fatigue is associated with emotional states of irritability, depression, pain, frustration, and anxiety (Bartley, 1943; Berrios, 1990; Cameron, 1973; McFarland, 1971). Although there is little systematic research into the cognitions associated with fatigue, clinical experience suggests that it is typically accompanied by negative self-statements such as, "I must stop what I am doing, or the symptoms will get worse." Behaviorally fatigue is often a signal to stop or reduce activity, despite the wealth of evidence that inactivity produces chronic fatigue (Kottke, 1966; Zorbas & Matveyev, 1986). We will return to these factors later in this chapter.

Scope of the Problem

Fatigue is a ubiquitous symptom that is best viewed on a continuum with the fatigue that we all sometimes experience at one end of the spectrum and CFS and all its associated disability at the more severe end of the spectrum (David et al., 1990; Lewis & Wessely, 1992; Pawlikowska et al., 1994). Prevalence rates vary according to the population and setting in which it is studied. In one British community survey, 38% of respondents reported substantial fatigue (Cox et al., 1987). In another, 18% reported fatigue of at least 6 months' duration (Pawlikowska et al., 1994). In primary care between 10% and 20% of respondents report substantial fatigue (Buchwald, Sullivan, & Komaroff, 1987; David et al., 1990; Kroenke et al., 1988).

With regard to CFS, prevalence rates appear similar across settings. In a UK community sample, although between 0.5% and 1% of subjects fulfilled criteria for CFS, only 0.2% believed they were suffering from CFS or ME (Pawlikowska et al., 1994). Not surprisingly, more people fulfill criteria for CFS than seek help or are diagnosed. In a UK primary care setting a 0.5% prevalence rate was found (Wessely et al., 1997), while slightly variable rates, ranging between 0.3% and 1%, were found in an American primary care study, depending on the criteria used (Bates et al., 1993).

Definitions of CFS

Patients with CFS have been referred to by a variety of labels; *myalgic encephalomyelitis* (ME) remains in common use but the etiologically neutral term *chronic fatigue syndrome* is preferred (Royal College of Physicians, 1996). Operational criteria from the United Kingdom, United States, and Australia all require a main complaint of disabling fatigue, as well as other symptoms such as sleep disturbance, mood disorder, and muscle pain, with no identifiable organic disease and marked disability (Fukuda et al., 1994; Holmes et al., 1988; Lloyd et al., 1990; Schluederberg et al., 1992; Sharpe et al., 1991).

In the first American case definition (Holmes et al., 1988) eight somatic symptoms or six symptoms and two signs were required, in addition to a main complaint of medically unexplained disabling fatigue. However, the criteria were revised first by Schluederberg et al., (1992), who suggested that patients with fibromyalgia and certain psychiatric disorders be included, and then by Fukuda et al. (1994), who reduced the minimum number of symptoms required to four. These revisions were made in response to accumulating evidence suggesting that CFS may represent the more severe end of a spectrum of fatiguing illnesses (David et al., 1990; Pawlikowska et al., 1994), with little justification for assuming that certain symptoms are characteristic of the syndrome. In addition, given that somatic symptoms are associated with psychiatric disorders, including numerous specific somatic symptoms in the criteria may have actually biased the selection of cases toward patients with well-defined psychiatric illness (Hickie et al., 1995; Katon & Russo 1992; Lane, Manu, & Matthews, 1991; Wessely et al., 1996).

The UK criteria are the only criteria that include mental as well as physical fatigue (Sharpe et al., 1991). The symptoms should be present for 6 months, and patients suffering from physical diseases known to produce fatigue should be excluded. Patients with depression and anxiety are not excluded but the presence of a major mental illness such as schizophrenia or anorexia would be considered an exclusion criterion. The Australian criteria do not require fatigue to be of definite onset (Lloyd et al., 1990), but it seems likely that patients with long illness durations will fulfil criteria for somatization disorder.

Clinical Description

Patients complain of exhaustion. They say that this subjective state is unfamiliar and unlike the sort of tiredness they used to feel when well. Many CFS patients, who by definition have a wide range of symptoms, believe their illness will last a long time, have a profound impact on their lives (Moss-Morris, 1997), is out of control (Chalder, Power, & Wessely, 1996; Moss-Morris, Petrie, & Weinman, 1996; Ray, Jeffries, & Weir, 1997), and feel particularly negative about possibilities for cure (Heijmans, 1998; Moss-Morris, Petrie, & Weinman, 1996). The fatigue is usually exacerbated by activity and even minor exertions can leave the patient feeling unwell for days. Many patients complain of additional symptoms such as headache, pain, and flu-like symptoms.

Disability varies considerably. At the more severe end of the spectrum an inability to work is common with some confined to a wheelchair or bedridden. Activities are often avoided for fear of bringing about a worsening of symptoms. Most patients will complain of abnormal sleep patterns, particularly onset or sleep maintenance insomnia, hypersomnia, and daytime sleepiness (Morriss, Wearden, & Battersby, 1997). Of particular interest are patients' beliefs about the cause of their problem. Many, at least in specialist settings, hold strong physical illness attributions (Chalder, Power, & Wessely, 1996; Hickie et al., 1990; Lane, Manu, & Matthews, 1991; Ray et al., 1992; Sharpe et al., 1992; Trigwell et al., 1995; Vercoulen et al., 1994; Wessely & Powell, 1989). Some worry they have a chronic viral infection, while others believe they have some sort of immune dysfunction.

From the doctor's perspective views tend to be divided. Some believe the problem to be psychiatric—that is, a form of depression or anxiety—while others view it as an organic disease of uncertain etiology. Others believe it doesn't exist at all. This mind–body split that prevails in our society can be unhelpful at the best of times but is particularly so when considering a heterogeneous condition such as CFS.

Comorbidity

There is no doubt that fatigue can be associated with almost any illness or disease you care to imagine; an overlap between psychological distress, psychiatric disorder, and fatigue is taken as read. Up to 75% of patients with CFS in both primary and secondary care also have a psychiatric disorder (David, 1991). What is questioned is the nature of the relationship.

Does fatigue cause psychiatric disorder, or do people become distressed as a result of the fatigue? A number of studies provide evidence for fatigue being a precursor to later depression (Cadoret, Wilmer, & Troughton, 1980; Dryman & Eaton, 1991; Hemphill, Hall, & Crookes, 1952; Lindberg, 1965; Widmer & Cadoret, 1978; Wilson et al., 1983). However, although fatigue may precede depression, it does not necessarily cause it.

Depression

It has been suggested that depression is an understandable consequence of a physical illness. However, the rate of psychiatric disorder is higher in CFS than in other medical conditions with a similar degree of associated disability (Fischler et al., 1997; Gold et al., 1990; Hickie et al., 1990; Johnson, DeLuca, & Natelson, 1996; Katon et al., 1991; Taerk et al., 1987; Wessely & Powell, 1989). The idea that CFS is a form of depression has also been suggested. However, at least a quarter have no psychiatric disorder at all. The association between CFS and psychiatric disorder is part of an inevitable consequence of the overlap in concepts and criteria (Wessely et al., 1996), although some researchers believe that the rates of psychiatric disorder in CFS have been overemphasized and overestimated (Farmer et al., 1995; Hickie et al., 1990).

Fatigue and Anxiety

A high proportion of patients with anxiety disorders complain of fatigue (Angst & Dobler Mikola, 1985; Winokur & Holeman, 1963). In primary care more than 50% of individuals with fatigue were also cases of anxiety (Kroenke et al., 1988). Other research that has examined the prevalence of anxiety disorders in CFS found relatively low rates (Buchwald et al., 1994; Farmer et al., 1995; Hickie et al., 1990; Kruesi, Dale, & Straus, 1989; Lane, Manu, & Matthews, 1991; Lindal et al., 1997; Taerk et al., 1987; Wessely & Powell, 1989; Wood et al., 1991). However, this could be attributable to their reliance on diagnostic sytems such as the *DSM-111*, RDC, and CATEGO, which use a hierarchical system of diagnosing that excludes anxiety disorders in the presence of mood disorders (Fischler et al., 1997).

A recent study that used an interview technique, intended to reduce the minimization of psychopathology, reported much higher rates (Fischler et al., 1997). It found that 56.6% of CFS patients had generalized anxiety disorder, 30.2% agoraphobia, 20.8% social phobia, 37.7% simple phobia, 13.2% panic disorder, and only 3.8% obsessive-compulsive disorder.

In phobic disorders one of the main defining characteristics is avoidance. The avoidance is directly related to fearful cognitions, usually about the meaning or consequences of symptoms. An example is a patient who avoids going into supermarkets for fear of having a heart attack or collapsing. The fears are directly related to misattribution of bodily symptoms. This is very similar to a patient with CFS who avoids exercise or activity for fear of making symptoms of fatigue worse (Deale, Chalder, & Wessely, 1998). Shands and Finesinger (1952) described this similarity after reviewing 100 patients with chronic fatigue. They wrote that fatigue is a danger signal closely related to anxiety and that the behavior indicated by the signal, fatigue, is that of desisting. In clinical practice it can be very difficult to distinguish between avoidant behavior secondary to phobias and avoidant behavior as a result of exhaustion.

Hyperventilation

As hyperventilation is associated with anxiety and panic, and fatigue is one of the symptoms of anxiety (Folgering & Snik, 1988), it seems likely that some patients with CFS may hyperventilate when anxious. Some researchers have claimed that all patients with CFS hyperventilate (Rosen et al., 1990). Although this figure is a gross overestimation, resting pCO_2, suggestive of mild hyperventilation, was higher in CFS subjects compared to controls in an American study (Lavietes et al., 1996). In a study carried out in the United Kingdom, between 13 and 16% of patients with CFS fulfilled criteria for hyperventilation (Saisch et al., 1994). Hyperventilation when present tended to be related to asthma or panic. The relatively low rates of hyperventilation appear to match the rates of anxiety disorders in CFS patients. While it is important to recognize anxiety and panic in order to treat the problem appropriately, the role of anxiety should not be overemphasized at this stage.

Autonomic Arousal

Most patients with CFS will complain of a variety of physical and mental symptoms including fatigue. It has been suggested that some of these symptoms such as dizziness, or fainting in response to standing, could be explained by autonomic arousal and that a predisposition to neurally mediated hypotension or vasovagal syncope may underlie some of the symptoms of CFS (Bou-Holaigah et al., 1995; Rowe et al., 1995). Sympathetic dysfunction in response to stress has been found in CFS (Pagani et al., 1994) as has an increased heart rate in response to moderate exercise (Riley et al., 1990). Given that autonomic arousal is commonly part of anxiety, fainting is common in blood and injury phobias, and inactivity is a well-known cause of postural hypotension, the most likely explanations for autonomic arousal in CFS are the presence of anxiety and/or deconditioning or lack of fitness.

Hypochondriasis

By definition, *hypochondriasis* means an abnormal anxiety about one's health (Fowler & Fowler, 1991). Undoubtedly patients are concerned about their health, specifically symptoms that affect their quality of life. A study carried out by an American group found that quality of life in CFS patients correlated with severity of physical symptoms and intensity of hypochondriacal beliefs and preoccupations (Manu et al., 1996). It appears that CFS patients have high expectations with regard to their health as well as other areas of their life. A common belief is that good health is synonymous with the absence of symptoms, and patients often associate the presence of symptoms with sickness (Manu et al., 1996). Although it is true that these patients are ill, the characteristic pattern of reducing activities as a way of coping has been shown to be strongly associated with perpetuation of the problem (Antoni et al., 1994; Chalder, Power, & Wessely, 1996; Sharpe et al., 1992).

In our specialist clinic for adolescents with CFS we have noted a similar process. The parent (usually the mother) worry intensively about the meaning of symptoms in their children, and consequently encourage behavior that in the long term worsens the symptoms of fatigue and disability.

ETIOLOGY OF CFS

Biological Theories

Viruses

Patients with CFS usually date the onset of their symptoms to a viral infection, "a dose of flu I just couldn't shake off." But is this correct, or could selective recall, chance, and a search for an explanation for their illness underlie this link? This question was answered by a controlled prospective study involving 2,000 subjects: Half presented to their GP with a symptomatic viral infection and half attended for another reason (Wessely et al., 1995). Six months later there was no difference in the rates of chronic fatigue or CFS. On the other hand, those who ended up with chronic fatigue or chronic fatigue syndrome were more likely to have suffered prior fatigue or psychological distress before they presented with the viral infection.

There is, however, consistent evidence that certain viral agents causing severe illness, such as the Epstein-Barr virus (EBV), viral hepatitis, Q fever, or viral meningitis, are associated with prolonged fatigue reactions (Benjamin & Hoyt, 1945; Berelowitz et al., 1995; Hotopf, Noah, & Wessely, 1996; Lepow et al., 1962; Marmion et al., 1996; Muller et al., 1958). An EBV study (Hotopf, Noah, & Wessely, 1996) showed that approximately 16% of subjects reported fatigue of at least 6 months' duration, but that the median length was only 10 weeks. This suggested that some patients were more vulnerable to the effects of these viruses. Further study clarified this: Previous psychiatric disorder and a prolonged convalescence from illness, involving bed rest and/or time off work, both increase the likelihood of fatigue chronicity after severe viral infection. The response of the doctor may be important too: Provision of a sick note and an unclear diagnosis were both associated with the development of CFS (Cope, David, & Mann, 1994).

Immunological Dysfunction

Patients with chronic fatigue and CFS report experiencing symptoms associated with colds and flu such as sore throats, swollen glands, and irregular thermoregulation. It has been suggested that this may reflect abnormalities of natural killer cell activity and

T cell subsets (Masuda et al., 1994; Straus et al., 1993). However, immunological changes are not unexpected or peculiar to CFS. Similar findings are reported in patients with major depression (Maes, Bosmans, Suy, Vandervorst, et al., 1991; Maes, Bosmans, Suy, Minner, et al., 1991; Maes, Jacobs, & Lambreckhts, 1992), and it seems unlikely that immunological abnormalities are primary etiological factors in the majority, but they may be related to factors such as well-being, behavior, and cognitions.

Muscle Dysfunction

Because of the presence of muscle pain and exercise-related fatigue, muscle dysfunction was initially proposed as a possible cause. These ideas were then superseded by concepts of fatigue resulting from central nervous system dysfunction. With regard to muscle structure, studies appear to conflict in their findings and conclusions, with some authors finding type II atrophy (anaerobic, fast-twitch, white muscle fibers) in subjects with CFS (Behan, More, & Behan, 1991; Byrne, Trounce, & Dennett, 1985; Byrne & Trounce, 1987), while others do not (Connolly et al., 1993; Grau et al., 1992; Preedy et al., 1993). In an important study by Edwards et al., (1993) a range of abnormalities was found in both CFS patients and normals. It is possible that most abnormalities found are due to lack of fitness or deconditioning.

A number of studies have examined muscle strength and performance. There does not appear to be compelling evidence of peripheral neuromuscular dysfunction (Kent-Braun et al., 1993; Lloyd, Gandevia, & Hales, 1991; Miller, Allen, & Gandevia, 1996; Riley et al., 1990; Stokes, Cooper, & Edwards, 1988), or of abnormal postexertional fatiguability (Gibson et al., 1993; Lloyd, Hales, & Gandevia, 1988; Sisto et al., 1996). To date, studies have failed to reveal evidence that exercise is associated with either a deterioration in performance or with relapse (McCully, Sisto, & Natelson, 1996), despite many subjective reports to the contrary. It appears that adults, and parents of children with CFS, tend to overrate their premorbid exercise tolerance (Fry & Martin, 1996; Riley et al., 1990), a factor probably related to high self-expectations and symptom monitoring.

The most likely causes of fatigue and muscle pain in patients with CFS are inactivity, bed rest, lack of fitness, symptom monitoring, and fearfulness—in essence, similar factors to those that perpetuate the physiological arousal in anxiety. The deleterious effects of bed rest are numerous and have long been recognized and documented. They include muscle wasting, changes in the cardiovascular response to exertion, intolerance of activity, sleepiness, exhaustion, poor sleep and appetite, postural hypotension, increased autonomic arousal, and a decreased desire for activity (Booth, 1987; Greenleaf & Kozlowski, 1982; Haines, 1974; Lamb, Stevens, & Johnson, 1965; Zuber & Wilgosh, 1963).

Undoubtedly some patients with CFS are unfit (Riley et al., 1990), as are patients with depression and anxiety (Hemphill, Hall, & Crookes, 1952; Jones & Mellersh, 1946). The authors recently found breathlessness on exertion (a proxy for being unfit) to be one of the main predictors of fatigue in primary care 18–45-year-olds, even when controlling for possible confounders such as asthma (Chalder, 1998).

Neuroendocrine Factors

The HPA axis is the primary long-term mediator of the body's stress response. Initial interest in this axis was generated by the observation that Addison's disease and CFS share fatigue, myalgia, arthralgia, and sleep and mood disturbance prominently among their symptoms. Recent research has revealed consistent findings of mild hypocortisolism in CFS sufferers. Findings include reduced basal morning (Cleare et al., 1995; Poteliakhoff, 1981) and evening (Demitrack et al., 1991) plasma cortisol levels, reduced 24-hour urinary free cortisol (UFC) output (Demitrack et al., 1991; Dinan et al., 1997) and reduced salivary cortisol levels (Strickland et al., 1998), albeit with two failures to replicate the data (Wood et al., 1997; Young et al., 1998). The exact site of disturbance in the axis is not yet clear: while some data point toward a hypothalamic dysfunction (Demitrack et al., 1991; Scott, Medbak, & Dinan, 1998a), other data are compatible with reduced adrenal gland function (Scott, Medback, & Dinan, 1998b).

Many factors influence cortisol secretion; for example, night shift working may produce similar changes to those seen in CFS, suggesting that these changes may be secondary to the observed sleep disruption in CFS. However, low doses of cortisol (hydrocortisone), sufficient to replace any hypothesized deficiency without suppressing endogenous cortisol release, can alleviate fatigue in a minority of nondepressed CFS patients (Cleare et al., 1999; McKenzie et al., 1998). This suggests that low cortisol, whether of primary or secondary origin, may be another perpetuating factor. What is not known is whether succesful treatment of CFS leads to a normalization of these HPA axis disturbances.

Neurochemical Factors

Serotonin (5-HT) has been the most studied of the central neurotransmitters. Early studies suggested that the fatigue felt after exercise was associated with a rise in plasma levels of tryptophan relative to other amino acids. By extension, it was hypothesized that increased brain 5-HT levels could be at least partly responsible for the subjective feeling of fatigue (Blomstrand, Celsing, & Newsholme, 1988).

In CFS a number of intriguing findings have emerged. Increased levels of levels of 5-HIAA have been found in cerebrospinal fluid (CSF) and plasma (Demitrack et al., 1992) of CFS patients compared to healthy controls, suggesting increased turnover of 5-HT in the brain. More recently several studies have directly investigated central 5-HT function in CFS patients using the neuropharmacological challenge paradigm. Our group published a study using d-fenfluramine, a drug that selectively causes release of 5-HT from the raphe nuclei neurones and inhibits the reuptake of released 5-HT. We measured the endocrine responses in patients with CFS and compared them to both healthy controls and a group of depressed subjects (Cleare et al., 1995). CFS subjects showed a markedly higher prolactin response than controls, in contrast to depressed patients, who had a reduced response. Three further studies have replicated this finding with d-fenfluramine and buspirone (Bakheit et al., 1992; Sharpe, Clements, et al., 1996; Sharpe et al., 1997), while another paper has not (Yatham et al., 1995).

Thus, most studies point to an increase in 5-HT function, and possibly specifically of 5-HT$_{1A}$ receptor function. Further refinement of the methods of studying 5-HT function are now underway. The importance of these changes is not yet understood. It is possible they are of physiological significance, as

5-HT is known to be important in the physiological control of sleep, appetite, and mood. In parallel with the opposite 5-HT changes, these features are disturbed in opposite directions in classic endogenous depression (insomnia, anorexia, agitation) and CFS (hypersomnia, hyperphagia, and retardation). Given what we know about brain physiology, it is also conceivable that these changes could be secondary to low cortisol levels (Cleare et al., 1995; Demitrack et al., 1991; Scott & Dinan, 1998) or the effects of inactivity, sleep disturbance or disruption, of circadian rhythms.

Other findings, as yet unreplicated and of uncertain significance, have also emerged. The main metabolite of noradrenaline, MHPG, is reduced in CFS (Demitrack et al., 1992), while fatigued athletes differ from nonfatigued athletes in having lower plasma noradrenaline (Odagiri et al., 1996). Another study has suggested upregulated cholinergic receptors (Chaudhuri et al., 1997).

Neuroimaging

There have been several studies using modern neuroimaging techniques to study cerebral blood flow in CFS. While a number of abnormalities have been found, including lowered perfusion of the brain stem and frontal lobes, other studies have suggested that alternative illnesses were diagnosable in those with abnormalities, while the relationship with depression remains unclear (Cope & David, 1996).

APPLYING A COGNITIVE-BEHAVIORAL FORMULATION

Given the multidimensional and heterogeneous nature of fatigue, it seems that continuing to search for a single specific organic cause would be misguided. Although research carried out to this end has achieved much in terms of our understanding of what is and what is not important in CFS, it now seems clear that a multitude of factors contribute to the onset, while different factors are responsible for perpetuating the condition. A cognitive-behavioral formulation of CFS takes into account such factors and assumes that physiological, cognitive, and behavioral responses are important in maintaining the condition. Interventions aim to modify both behavioral and cognitive responses in order to bring about a change in the individual's physiological response (fatigue). This model is widely accepted and has proven validity in the field of anxiety disorders.

Generic Cognitive-Behavioral Model

Beck's cognitive theory of emotional disorders (Beck, 1989) posits that emotional disorders are maintained by distortions in thinking. On a superficial or surface level, information processing is characterized by negative automatic thoughts. However, the negative thoughts are a reflection of the deeper, underlying dysfunctional assumptions and core beliefs, also known as schemata, which are stored in the persons memory and may not be consciously accessible. These schemata shape how an individual behaves in general and responds to specific situations (Wells, 1997). Schemata are formed in childhood and probably result from a complex interaction of the individual's responses to external experiences.

Cognitive Theory of Anxiety Disorders

In anxiety disorders the main worry or preoccupation appears to be related to danger and an inability to cope (Beck, Emergy, & Greenberg, 1985; Beck, Laude, & Bohnert, 1974; Rachman, Lopatka, & Levitt, 1988) and reflects the activation of underlying schemata such as, "The world is a dangerous place and I cannot cope." Once danger schemata have been activated by an external stressor, the physical manifestations of anxiety such as palpitations become a threat. In illness phobias, physical symptoms are often interpreted as a sign of a physical illness. When a danger appraisal is elicited, the person experiences self-doubts, negative evaluations, and negative predictions. The somatic manifestation of this consists of symptoms such as unsteadiness and weakness (Wells, 1997). The behavioral response such as avoidance or reassurance seeking is intended to protect against danger. However it is well recognized that the very action that is meant to reduce fear, both cognitively and physiologically, actually perpetuates it.

COGNITIVE-BEHAVIORAL MODEL OF CFS

Symptoms of fatigue can be understood using the same paradigm as described for anxiety. We have already noted the overlap between anxiety and fatigue and CFS. In CFS the predominant symptom is that of fatigue, but a wide range of other physical symptoms is usually reported by patients. Once fatigue has been triggered, the problem is both maintained and made worse by cognitive and behavioral factors such as fear and avoidance.

Illness Attributions and Cognitions

Many patients with somatic complaints, regardless of their exact nature, have a tendency to persistently misinterpret innocuous physical symptoms as evidence of something more serious. In CFS, specific attributions and beliefs are likely to influence fear and avoidance behavior (Wessely et al., 1991) . These include beliefs about the nature of the illness, beliefs about the meaning of symptoms, fears about the consequences of activity, and fear that activity or exercise will make symptoms worse (Chalder, Power, & Wessely, 1996; Deale, Chalder, & Wessely, 1998). In chronic illness generally, such beliefs are associated with perpetuation of disability and symptoms (Sensky, 1990). Longitudinal studies have demonstrated that making physical illness attributions for fatigue predicts the degree of disability in patients with CFS (Chalder, Power, & Wessely, 1996; Sharpe, Hawton, et al., 1996; Wilson et al., 1994). In an effort to control and reduce symptoms, patients become hypervigilant and oversensitized to bodily sensations. This symptom focusing may exacerbate unpleasant sensations and has been shown to be associated with fatigue in patients with CFS (Ray, Jeffries, & Weir, 1995).

Behavior

Believing that activity and exercise will make symptoms worse or cause organic damage naturally leads the individual to reduce activities. However, prolonged rest and avoidance of activity are central in sustaining the cycle of symptoms and disability in CFS (Chalder, Butler, & Wessely, 1996). Sharpe and colleagues (1992) found that avoiding exercise predicted disability, while Ray and colleagues (1995) found an association between functional impairment and accommodating to the illness in patients with CFS.

Factors That Contribute to the Development of Fatigue

Examining the role of predisposing and precipitating factors in the development of CFS is complicated and costly; consequently, research in this area is preliminary.

Predisposing Factors

Some authors have suggested and there is some evidence that premorbid personalities of patients with CFS are characterized by a marked hyperactivity or "workaholism" and achievement orientation and high standards for work performance (Salit, 1997; Surawy et al., 1995; Van Houdenhove et al., 1995; Ware & Kleinman, 1992). Although it was thought that a Type A personality may predispose individuals to developing CFS, there has been little evidence for the type A construct in patients with CFS compared to patients with irritable bowel syndrome (IBS) or to healthy controls (Lewis, Cooper, & Bennett, 1994).

Surawy et al., (1995) suggested that patients with CFS strive hard to achieve in order to preserve self-esteem and to maintain a particular schemata, or core belief. The two most common underlying assumptions were, "If I don't meet all my responsibilities to others all the time, I am a failure" and "I must never admit to difficulties and it's stupid to have miserable thoughts." It makes sense therefore that when compensatory coping behaviors such as working very hard are no longer helpful and physical and mental symptoms of fatigue are experienced, the individual wonders whether he or she is suffering from a physical illness, that of CFS. The prevailing culture also has to be taken into account. As CFS, referred to in the media as ME, is being promoted as a disease with an as yet undiscovered physical cause, it is likely that this will influence individual beliefs about symptoms and illness.

It has been suggested that perfectionism plays an important role in the development of CFS. There is some evidence for a relationship in female nurses between physical and mental fatigue and negative components of perfectionism, including doubts about actions, parental expectations, parental criticism, and concern over mistakes (Magnusson, Nias, & White, 1996). More specifically, physical fatigue was reported by those who perceived their parents as having high expectations. This result is in keeping with other studies that have found an association between negative components of perfectionism and neuroticism (Flett et al., 1991) and fatigue and emotionality (Blakely et al., 1991), raising the issue of confounding. However, in Magnusson, Nias, and White's study (1996), neuroticism was controlled for, ruling out this possibility. One study examined perfectionism in CFS compared to a control group with rheumatoid arthritis (Wood & Wessely, in press). No differences were found.

In addition to individual personality characteristics that contribute to the development of CFS, a number of other specific precipitating factors are important in the development of fatigue.

Precipitating Factors

Role of Stress. There is general agreement that stress has a significant direct effect on a wide range of psychological and physical problems (Henderson, Byrne, & Duncan-Jones, 1981). Chronic fatigue is no exception. In addition, the assessment of the perceived adequacy of social support has proved to be a major predictor of mental health (Henderson, Byrne, & Duncan-Jones, 1981; Kessler, 1983).

Retrospectively, patients with CFS report both infection and life stress as being associated with the onset of their illness (Sharpe et al., 1992). A number of cross-sectional case control studies carried out in hospital populations have examined the role of stress in the development of CFS (Dobbins et al., 1995; Reyes et al., 1996; Wood et al., 1991). In one series (Dobbins et al., 1995), one-third of patients reported a stressful event prior to onset, while in another this rose to 95% (Wood et al., 1991). Among CFS subjects with a gradual onset of their illness the occurrence of three or more stressful events was significantly associated with the illness, and the risk increased proportionally to the number of events (Reyes et al., 1996). An as yet unpublished case control study, which used the Life Events and Difficulties Schedule (LEDS), found that about 60% of subjects with CFS compared to 20% of community controls had experienced a severe event or difficulty before the onset of their illness (Hatcher, 1997).

In 1994, Lewis and colleagues (1994) compared CFS and IBS patients, seen in an outpatient clinic of a general hospital, with respect to the number of significant life events experienced prior to the onset of the illness, compared with normal controls (GP attenders). Life events were recorded for the 2 years prior to the onset of the illness, although duration of illness was not recorded, so patients may have been ill for several years before entering the study. All three groups were asked to indicate how much support they received in coping with problems prior to the onset of and during their illness. The CFS group did not experience any more life events than the other two groups. However they perceived less overall support both before and after the onset of their illness (Lewis, Cooper, & Bennett, 1994).

A more recent study inquired about the occurrence of stressful events prior to the onset of fatigue (Salit, 1997). Eighty-five percent of CFS subjects compared to 6% of the controls reported a stressful event prior to the onset of their fatigue. However, the CFS subjects had been ill for nearly 5 years, so, as with other studies, it is possible that problems of recall bias or reverse causality may have accounted for the association.

In the only published primary care longitudinal study to examine the role of life events on fatigue, a much stronger association was found between social adversity and depression than between adversity and the postviral fatigue syndrome (Bruce-Jones et al., 1994). This result concurs with the work of the first author. In a primary care study, although there was an association between negative life events and acute severe and chronic fatigue, the association between life events and psychological distress, as measured by the general health questionnaire, was greater (Chalder, 1998).

SUMMARY

Symptoms of fatigue can therefore be precipitated by a stressor such as an infection, a negative life event, or chronic stress and are perpetuated by physical illness

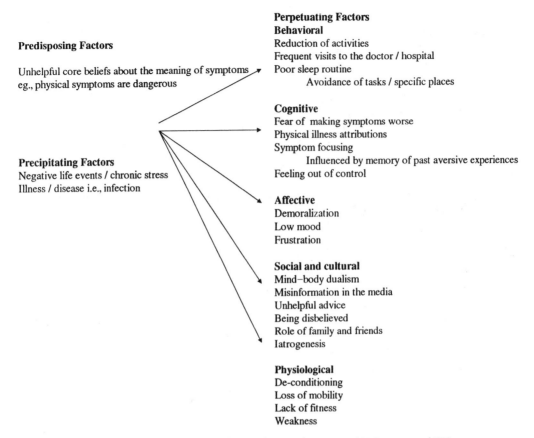

FIGURE 9.1. Factors that Contribute to the Development and Maintenance of CFS

attributions, fearful cognitions, and avoidant coping strategies. The model described here was adapted from models that have achieved acceptance in understanding and treating other conditions such as chronic pain (Philips, 1987) and lead to a number of possible interventions. In accordance with the model, success should result from reducing avoidance behavior and addressing unhelpful thoughts and fears about the effects of activity and exercise.

In both anxiety disorders and chronic fatigue, treatment is based on a model of understanding the condition. A three-systems model (Lang, 1970), in which cognitive, behavioral, and physiological responses are seen to be largely synchronous but which become desynchronous in unhealthy individuals, is used to guide which behavioral and/or cognitive interventions are used. In other words, the way people act and think is modified in order to bring about a change in their physiological response.

In CFS the dominant symptom is more often than not fatigue, but other symptoms associated with autonomic arousal are common. (See Figure 9.1 for summary of model.)

A REHABILITATION PROGRAM BASED ON COGNITIVE-BEHAVIORAL THERAPY

The main aim of treatment is to enable patients to carry out their own rehabilitation with some support and guidance from their therapist. The long-term aims of treatment will vary from patient to patient, but usually individuals are able to specify clearly what they would like to achieve at the end of treatment. Targets will be defined quite clearly and often include returning to work, part or full time, and resuming activities that they previously felt unable to carry out.

The treatment will involve the introduction of a consistent, graded approach to activity, establishing a sleep routine and using cognitive strategies to help combat unhelpful thoughts that interefere with the rehabilitative process.

Success, however, depends upon several things. A thorough assessment should be carried out that will form the basis of a formulation of the patient's problem. This formulation will be shared with the patient before treatment starts. It should help the process of engagement and will form part of the rationale for treatment. Engaging patients with CFS poses a particular challenge to health professionals, and this will be discussed in more detail later. Throughout treatment, progress is constantly reviewed and goals adjusted in collaboration with the patient. The process is not dissimilar to any process of short- to medium-term psychotherapy. However in the authors' experience, it can take longer to overcome problems of CFS than of anxiety disorders, which are usually more circumscribed. It often takes several months and sometimes a year or more for patients to reach their long-term goals. It is important therefore for the therapist to be patient, as patients' confidence in the approach grows slowly over time.

Assessment

The assessment should include not only a detailed description of symptoms but also, more importantly, a detailed behavioral analysis of what the patient is able to do in relation to work, home, private, and social aspects of his or her life. The quality and quantity of sleep should be inquired after. A detailed account of activity, rest, and sleep patterns should be obtained by asking the patient to keep a diary for 2 weeks. This will be used as a guide for setting the initial behavioral goals and can be used throughout treatment to monitor progress. Specific fears about the consequences of activity and exercise should be elicited, as should more general ideas about the nature of the illness. Circumstances surrounding the onset should be discussed, as this information may be useful when giving the patient a rationale for treatment and why lifestyle factors may need to be addressed during treatment. It is important at this stage to inquire about the presence of depression and/or anxiety. If severe, such disorders may require

treatment in their own right, either before CBT or concurrently.

Engagement

Patients have often had to fight to have their problems recognized and diagnosed. This is bound to lead to difficulties in the relationship between the health professional and the patient if the issue isn't acknowledged.

Engaging the patient and forming a therapeutic alliance is a continual process. While the doctor is carrying out the assessment, the patient, who may be sensitive to being disbelieved, may be looking for evidence that the doctor thinks the problem is "all in the mind." During this early stage of treatment the therapist should be explicit in conveying belief in the reality of the symptoms and should pay careful attention to the language that is used. The term *psychological* should be avoided, first because it is a broad term that means different things to different people and also because it may set the scene for disagreement between patient and doctor. The patient's symptoms are real, and it helps to state and restate this. Rather than debating whether the problem is physical or psychological—a mind–body split that is unhelpful in any illness—it is far more useful to direct the discussion toward how the problem can best be managed, taking into account physiological, behavioral, and cognitive factors.

Rationale for Treatment

Offering the patient a rationale for treatment should be a prerequisite to any intervention. It stands to reason that having an understanding of how and why treatment works will aid compliance. It can be helpful to offer patients a formulation of their problems, using a cognitive-behavioral framework. Information gathered during the assessment will be utilized during this process. A distinction is made between precipitating and perpetuating factors.

The rationale will vary depending on the individual's circumstances but essentially the patient should be told that the emphasis will be on establishing a consistent level of activity every day regardless of symptoms. The amount of activity is then gradually increased and rest decreased as the patient becomes more confident. It can helpful to point out that rest is useful in an acute illness but is rarely restorative in the longer term. A sleep routine should also be established as quickly as possible.

The rationale should be repeated several times during the course of treatment. It can be useful to ask the patient to explain the rationale to the doctor in order to check out whether it has been clearly understood and to discuss any concerns. Before commencing treatment, it is important that the patient is clear about what it entails and that he or she agrees to at least try what is being offered. The aims of treatment should be explicitly negotiated and agreed upon with the patient. These aims are best defined in terms of specific and realistic achievements, such as swimming a certain number of lengths every day and socializing again.

It is important to address the role of continuing investigations and other treatments, as they may detract from the rehabilitation process. It is better to call a halt to further investigations and treatments and to give the patient a positive diagnosis of CFS before commencing cognitive behavioral therapy (CBT).

Structure

Patients are usually seen every 2 weeks for up to 15 sessions of face-to-face treatment. Follow-ups are carried out at 3 and 6 months and then 1 year to monitor progress and tackle any residual problems. Questionnaires are given to assess fatigue, disability, and psychological distress before and after treatment and at follow-up. At the beginning of treatment, long-term targets are negotiated with the patient to ensure that both the therapist and the patient are working toward similar goals. At every subsequent session, short-term goals are agreed upon. Patients keep hourly records of their activity and rest throughout treatment so that progress can be monitored and problems discussed. Problems are anticipated and problem-solving strategies are used to elicit effective coping. Discussion during sessions often revolves around exploring issues that may be preventing the patient from making changes.

Activity Scheduling

Goals are initially negotiated using the baseline diaries and typically involve a variety of specific tasks, but usually include a mixture of social-, work-, and leisure-related activities. Short walks or tasks carried out in even "chunks" throughout the day are ideal and are interspersed with rests. The emphasis is on consistency and breaking the association between experiencing symptoms and stopping activity. The goals, for example, walking for 10 minutes three times daily, are gradually built up as tolerance to symptoms increases, until the longer-term targets are reached. This usually takes several months. Fatigue levels do not decrease very much initially, but between discharge and follow-up, marked reductions in fatigue would be expected. Tasks such as reading, which require concentration, can be included, but mental functioning seems to improve in synchrony with physical functioning.

Establishing a Sleep Routine

Early on in treatment, patients are asked to keep a diary of bed time, sleep time, wake-up time, and get-up time. The total number of hours spent asleep is calculated, and a variety of strategies should then be used to improve both quality and quantity of sleep. A routine of going to bed and getting up at a preplanned time, while simultaneously cutting out daytime catnaps, helps to prevent insomnia. Change in sleep routine can be accomplished slowly depending on the severity of the problem. For those who sleep too much the amount of time they spend asleep can be reduced gradually. For a detailed description of sleep management see Morin (1993).

Modifying Negative and Unhelpful Thinking

It is important to prevent unhelpful thoughts from blocking progressive increases in activity. Information about the nature of CFS and the process of rehabilitation should be shared with the patient throughout treatment, as many patients will have been given incorrect or misleading information about their illness. Explanations of the physiological effects of inactivity can help patients comply with activity scheduling and can decrease catastrophizing. Patients should be reassured about the safety of exercise; written self-help information reinforcing these messages can be helpful (Chalder, 1995). In reality, unhelpful beliefs about the harmful effects of exercise will diminish as patients become more active and confident. However, some will need more structured cognitive therapy using traditional methods (Beck, 1989). Specific negative thoughts such as, "My muscles will be damaged by exercising too much" should be recorded in a diary. Patients should be encouraged to summon alternative, less catastrophic interpretations of events. These too should be recorded in a diary and discussed during consultations. With some patients, core beliefs and dysfunctional assumptions relating to perfectionism or self-worth can be addressed in the conventional way.

Tackling Other Problems

When there is a clear-cut phobic disorder, it should be treated in the conventional way, that is, with graded exposure. During the process of treatment, patients with CFS will gradually build up their repertoire of activities, but it may be some time before their fatigue reduces. This is clearly different in phobic disorders. During prolonged exposure the therapist would expect significant anxiety reduction to occur within sessions. At times it can be difficult to decide which problems should be tackled first. As a general rule we would advocate always starting with the goal that is most easily achieved and which is likely to bring about rapid change in symptom experience.

Related social or psychological difficulties will often emerge during treatment. It is important that these are tackled in a problem-solving way; otherwise, they may prevent further progress. It is important, however, to keep the focus on rehabilitation. Being distracted from the main task at hand may lead to treatment failure. Improvements in one particular area of a patient's life will usually generalize to other areas.

Pharmacological Interventions

Antidepressants

Two placebo-controlled studies of fluoxetine in CFS have provided inconsistent results. The first gave a 3-month course of treatment to both depressed and nondepressed CFS patients. Neither placebo nor fluoxetine produced changes in fatigue or depression, even in the depressed group (Vercoulen, Swanink, Zitman, et al., 1996). However, it was suggested that this was a particularly chronic group of patients treated

for an insufficient length of time (Cleare & Wessely, 1996). The second study, again using 20 mg daily of fluoxetine, found modest benefits on both fatigue and depression after a 6-month course (Wearden et al., 1998). However, patients were also taking part in an exercise trial that may have affected results.

Little other controlled evidence exists in CFS, although there are suggestions that phenelzine (Natelson et al., 1996) or low-dose tricyclics may be helpful, the latter particularly so if pain or insomnia predominate (Goodnick & Sandoval, 1993). In particular, patients in whom primary fibromyalgia can be diagnosed may respond in terms of pain, sleep disturbance, and depression to low dose tricyclics (Goldenberg et al., 1986; Goldenberg et al., 1996). However, the benefits of these treatments are generally modest for most patients, with perhaps 20% showing very significant clinical gains (Wessely, Hotopf, & Sharpe, 1998).

Low-Dose Hydrocortisone

Because of the finding of reduced cortisol levels, two studies have investigated a replacement strategy. A full replacement dose (30 mg daily) produced mild benefit, but also endogenous adrenal suppression (McKenzie et al., 1998). Smaller doses (5–10 mg daily) produced large reductions in fatigue in about 28% compared to 9% in the placebo group, without adrenal suppression (Cleare et al., 1999). Potential side effects probably preclude such strategies as routine treatments, but the results do suggest that low cortisol levels may be a significant perpetuating factor in fatigue chronicity.

Other Agents

A recent evidence-based review of this area concluded that the evidence for the efficacy and safety of treatments such as antiviral agents, immunotherapy, or dietary supplements is still lacking, with reports of successes in early trials not replicated (Wessely, Hotopf, & Sharpe, 1998). They cannot as yet be recommended.

Evidence for the Efficacy of CBT

An uncontrolled pilot study carried out at the National Hospital for Neurology in London (Butler et al., 1991) resulted in a 70% improvement rate in those who started treatment. A 4-year follow-up reassuringly confirmed that patients who had initially improved retained their gains (Bonner et al., 1994). Since then two randomized controlled trials have demonstrated that the 70% improvement rate in the pilot study was a robust finding. The first trial carried out in Oxford randomized 60 patients to either CBT or treatment as usual. Seventy-three percent of the patients in the CBT group improved in terms of fatigue disability and illness beliefs (Sharpe, Hawton, et al., 1996). The second trial, carried out by the authors at King's College Hospital, controlled for nonspecific treatment factors by comparing CBT with a relaxation control. At 6-month follow-up, 70% of the CBT group and 19% of the control group were improved (Deale et al., 1997).

An exercise trial carried out by Fulcher and White (1997) at St. Bartholomews Hospital, London, in which 66 CFS patients, with no psychiatric disorder or sleep disturbance, were randomized to either aerobic exercise or flexibility exercises, demonstrated about a 55% improvement rate in the exercise group, compared with 26% of the control group. This provides evidence for using exercise as part of the rehabilitation program even though some patients may be fearful of attempting aerobic exercise at the beginning of treatment. Given that walking is an important component of CBT, it appears that the two approaches have much in common.

Predictors of Outcome

Various studies show that poor outcome in untreated groups is associated with older age, greater functional impairment, multiple somatic complaints, comorbid psychiatric disorder, and holding a belief that the illness is due solely to physical causes (Clark et al., 1995; Sharpe et al., 1992; Vercoulen, Swanink, Fennis, et al., 1996). Little is known about outcome predictors in patients treated with CBT. Physical illness attributions do not appear to be associated with poor outcome in patients who have received CBT (Bonner et al., 1994; Deale et al., 1997). In one randomized controlled trial, poor outcome appeared to be related to patients negotiating medical retirement (Deale et al., 1997). In the authors' experience, severe depression can also lead to treatment failure.

REFERENCES

Angst, J., & Dobler Mikola, A. (1985). The Zurich Story. V. Anxiety and phobia in young adults. *European Archives of Psychiatry and Clinical Neurosciences 235*, 171–178.

Antoni, M., Brickman, A., Lutgendorf, S., et al. (1994). Psychosocial correlates of illness burden in chronic fatigue syndrome. *Clinical Infectious Diseases, 18* (suppl 1); S73–S78.

Bakheit, A., Behan, P., Dinan, T., Gray, C., & O'Keane, V. (1992). Possible upregulation of hypothalamic 5-hydroxy-tryptamine receptors in patients with post-viral fatigue syndrome. *British Medical Journal, 304*, 1010–1012.

Bartley, S. H. (1943). Conflict, frustration and fatigue. *Psychosomatic Medicine, 5*, 160–162.

Bates, D., Schmitt, W., Lee, J., Kornish, R., & Komaroff, A. (1993). Prevalence of fatigue and chronic fatigue syndrome in a primary care practice. *Archives of Internal Medicine, 153*, 2759–2765.

Beck, A. T. (1989). *Cognitive therapy and the emotional disorders.* London: Penguin.

Beck, A. T., Emery, G., & Greenberg, R. L. (1985). *Anxiety disorders and phobias: A cognitive perspective.* New York: Basic Books.

Beck, A. T., Laude, R., & Bohnert, M. (1974). Ideational components of anxiety neurosis. *Archives of General Psychiatry 31*, 319–325.

Behan, W., More, I., & Behan, P. (1991). Mitochondrial abnormalities in the post-viral fatigue syndrome. *Acta Neuropathology, 83*, 61–65.

Benjamin, J., & Hoyt, R. (1945). Disability following post-vaccinal (yellow fever) hepatitis: A study of 200 patients manifesting delayed convalescence. *JAMA, 128*, 319–324.

Berelowitz, G., Burgess, A., Thanabalasingham, T., Murray-Lyon, I., & Wright, D. (1995). Post-hepatitis syndrome revisited. *Journal of Viral Hepatitis, 2*, 133–138.

Berrios, G. (1990). Feelings of fatigue and psychopathology. *Comprehensive Psychiatry, 31*, 140–151.

Blakely, A., Howard, R., Sosich, R., Murdoch, J., Menkes, D., & Spears, G. (1991). Psychological symptoms, personality and ways of coping in chronic fatigue syndrome. *Psychological Medicine, 21*, 347–362.

Blomstrand, E., Celsing, F., & Newsholme, E. A. (1988). Changes in plasma concentrations of aromatic and branched-chain amino acids during sustained exercise in man and their possible role in fatigue. *Acta Physiological Scandinavica, 133*, 115–121.

Bonner, D., Butler, S., Chalder, T., Ron, M., & Wessely, S. (1994). A follow up study of chronic fatigue syndrome.

Journal of Neurology, Neurosurgery and Psychiatry, 57, 617–621.

Booth, F. (1987). Physiologic and biochemical effects of immobilization on muscle. *Clinical Orthopaedics, 10*, 15–20.

Bou-Holaigah, I., Rowe, P., Kan, J., & Calkins, H. (1995). The relationship between neurally mediated hypotension and the chronic fatigue syndrome. *JAMA, 274*, 961–967.

Bruce-Jones, W., White, P., Thomas, J., & Clare, A. (1994). The effect of social adversity on the fatigue syndrome, psychiatric disorders and physical recovery, following glandular fever. *Psychological Medicine, 24*, 651–659.

Buchwald, D., Pearlman, T., Kith, P., & Schmaling, K. (1994). Gender differences in patients with chronic fatigue syndrome. *Journal of General Internal Medicine, 9*, 397–401.

Buchwald, D., Sullivan, J., & Komaroff, A. (1987). Frequency of "chronic active Epstein-Barr virus infection" in a general medical practice. *JAMA, 257*, 2303–2307.

Butler, S., Chalder, T., Ron, M., & Wessely, S. (1991). Cognitive behaviour therapy in chronic fatigue syndrome. *Journal of Neurology, Neurosurgery and Psychiatry, 54*, 153–158.

Byrne, E., & Trounce, I. (1987). Chronic fatigue and myalgia syndrome: Mitochrondrial and glycolytic studies in skeletal muscle. *Journal of Neurology, Neurosurgery and Psychiatry, 50*, 743–746.

Byrne, E., Trounce, I., & Dennett, X. (1985). Chronic relapsing myalgia (Post viral?): Clinical, histological, and biochemical studies. *Australia New Zealand Journal of Medicine, 15*, 305–308.

Cadoret, R., Wilmer, R., & Troughton, E. (1980). Somatic complaints: harbinger of depression in primary care. *Journal of Affective Disorders, 2*, 61–70.

Cameron, C. (1973). A theory of fatigue. *Ergonomics, 16*, 633–648.

Chalder, T. (1995). *Coping with chronic fatigue*. London: Sheldon Press.

Chalder, T. (1998). Factors contributing to the development and maintenance of fatigue in primary care. *Institute of Psychiatry*, London, p. 250.

Chalder, T., Butler, S., & Wessely, S. (1996). In patient treatment of chronic fatigue syndrome. *Behavioural Psychotherapy, 24*, 351–365.

Chalder, T., Power, M., & Wessely, S. (1996). Chronic fatigue in the community: "A question of attribution." *Psychological Medicine, 26*, 791–800.

Chaudhuri, A., Majeed, T., Dinan, T., & Behan, P. O. (1997). Chronic fatigue syndrome: A disorder of central cholinergic neurotransmission. *Journal of Chronic Fatigue Syndrome, 3*, 3–16.

Clark, M., Katon, W., Russo, J., Kith, P., Sintay, M., & Buchwald, D. (1995). Chronic fatigue: Risk factors for symptom persistence in a 2.5-year follow up study. *American Journal of Medicine, 98*, 187–195.

Cleare, A. J., Bearn, J., Allain, T., et al. (1995). Contrasting neuroendocrine responses in depression and chronic fatigue syndrome. *Journal of Affective Disorders, 35*, 283–289.

Cleare, A. J., Heap, E., Malhi, G. S., Wessely, S., O'Keane, V., & Miell, J. (1999). Low-dose hydrocortisone in chronic fatigue syndrome: A randomised crossover trial. *Lancet, 353*, 455–458.

Cleare, A. J., & Wessely, S. C. (1996). Fluoxetine and chronic fatigue syndrome. *Lancet, 347*, 1770–1772.

Connolly, S., Smith, D., Doyle, D., & Fowler, C. (1993). Chronic fatigue: Electromyographic and neuropathological evaluation. *Journal of Neurology, 240*, 435–438.

Cope, H., & David, A. (1996). Neuroimaging in chronic fatigue syndrome. *Journal of Neurology, Neurosurgery and Psychiatry, 60*, 471–473.

Cope, H., David, A., & Mann, A. (1994). "Maybe it's a virus?" Beliefs about viruses, symptom attributional style and psychological health. *Journal of Psychosomatic Research, 38*, 89–98.

Cox, B., Blaxter, M., Buckle, A., et al. (1987). *The Health and Lifestyle Survey*. London: Health Promotion Research Trust.

David, A. S. (1991). Postviral fatigue syndrome and psychiatry. *British Medical Bulletin, 47*, 966–988.

David, A., Pelosi, A., McDonald, E., et al. (1990). Tired, weak or in need of rest: Fatigue among general practice attenders. *British Medical Journal, 301*, 1199–1202.

Deale, A., Chalder, T., Marks, I., & Wessely, S. (1997). A randomised controlled trial of cognitive behaviour versus relaxation therapy for chronic fatigue syndrome. *American Journal of Psychiatry, 154*, 408–414.

Deale, A., Chalder, T., & Wessely, S. (1998). Illness beliefs and outcome in chronic fatigue syndrome: Is change in causal attribution necessary for clinical improvement? *Journal of Psychosomatic Research, 45*, 77–83.

Demitrack, M., Dale, J., Straus, S., et al. (1991). Evidence for impaired activation of the hypothalamic-pituitary-adrenal axis in patients with chronic fatigue syndrome. *Journal of Clinical Endocrinology and Metabolism, 73*, 1224–1234.

Demitrack, M., Gold, P., Dale, J., Krahan, D., Kling, M., & Straus, S. (1992). Plasma and cerebrospinal fluid monoamine metabolism in patients with chronic fatigue syndrome: Preliminary findings. *Biological Psychiatry, 32*, 1065–1077.

Dinan, T. G., Majeed, T., Lavelle, E., Scott, L. V., Berti, C., & Behan, P. (1997). Blunted serotonin-mediated activation of the hypothalamic-pituitary-adrenal axis in chronic fatigue syndrome. *Psychoneuroendocrinology, 22*, 261–267.

Dobbins, J., Natelson, B., Brassloff, I., Drastal, S., & Sisto, S. (1995). Physical, behavioral and psychological risk factors for chronic fatigue syndrome: A central role for stress? *Journal of Chronic Fatigue Syndrome, 1*, 43–58.

Dryman, A., & Eaton, W. (1991). Affective symptoms associated with the onset of major depression in the community: Findings from the U.S. National Institute of Mental Health Epidemiologic Catchment Area Program. *Acta Psychiatrica Scandinavica, 84*, 1–5.

Edwards, R., Gibson, H., Clague, J., & Helliwell, T. (1993). Muscle physiology and histopathology in chronic fatigue syndrome. In A. Kleinman & S. Straus (Eds), *Chronic fatigue syndrome* (vol. 173) (pp. 101–131). Chichester, England: Wiley.

Farmer, A., Jones, I., Hillier, J., Llewelyn, M., Borysiewicz, L., & Smith, A. (1995). Neuraesthenia revisited: ICD-10 and DSM-III-R psychiatric syndromes in chronic fatigue patients and comparison subjects. *British Journal of Psychiatry, 167*, 503–506.

Fischler, B., Cluydts, R., De Gucht, V., Kaufman, L., & DeMeirleir, K. (1997). Generalised anxiety disorder in chronic fatigue syndrome. *Acta Psychiatrica Scandinavica, 95*, 405–413.

Flett, G., Hewitt, P., Blankstein, K., & O'Brien, S. (1991). Perfectionism and learned resourcefulness in depression and self-esteem. *Personality and Individual Differences, 12*, 61–68.

Folgering, H., & Snik, A. (1988). Hyperventilation syndrome and muscle fatigue. *Journal of Psychosomatic Research, 32*, 165–171.

Fowler, H. W., & Fowler, F. G. (1991). The concise Oxford Dictionary. Oxford, England: Clarendon Press.

Fry, A., & Martin, M. (1996). Cognitive idiosyncrasies among children with the chronic fatigue syndrome: Anomalies in self-reported activity levels. *Journal of Psychosomatic Research, 41*, 213–223.

Fukuda, K., Straus, S., Hickie, I., Sharpe, M., Dobbins, J., & Komaroff, A. (1994). The chronic fatigue syndrome: A comprehensive approach to its definition and study. *Annals of Internal Medicine, 121*, 953–959.

Fulcher, K., & White, P. (1997). Randomised controlled trial of graded exercise in patients with chronic fatigue syndrome. *British Medical Journal, 314*, 1647–1652.

Gibson, H., Carroll, N., Clague, J., & Edwards, R. (1993). Exercise performance and fatiguability in patients with chronic fatigue syndrome. *Journal of Neurology, Neurosurgery and Psychiatry, 156*, 993–998.

Gold, D., Bowden, R., Sixbey, J., et al. (1990). Chronic fatigue: A prospective clinical and virologic study. *JAMA, 264*, 48–53.

Goldenberg, D., Felson, D., & Dinerman, H. (1986). Randomised, controlled trial of amitriptyline and naproxen in treatment of patients with fibrositis. *Arthritis and Rheumatism, 29*, 1371–1377.

Goldenberg, D., Mayskiy, M., Mossey, C., Ruthazer, R., & Schmid, C. (1996). A randomized, double-blind crossover trial of fluoxetine and amitriptyline in the treatment of fibromyalgia. *Arthritis and Rheumatism, 39*, 1852–1859.

Goodnick, P., & Sandoval, R. (1993). Psychotropic treatment of chronic fatigue syndrome and related disorders. *Journal of Clinical Psychiatry, 54*, 13–20.

Grau, J., Casademont, J., Pedrol, E., et al. (1992). Chronic fatigue syndrome: Studies on skeletal muscle. *Clinical Neuropathology, 11*, 329–332.

Greenleaf, J., & Kozlowski, S. (1982). Physiological consequences of reduced physical activity during bed rest. *Exercise and Sport Sciences Reviews, 10*, 84–119.

Haines, R. (1974). Effect of bed rest and exercise on body balance. *Journal of Applied Physiology, 36*, 323–327.

Hatcher, S. A. (1997). A case controlled study of CFS and life events.

Heijmans, M. (1998). Coping and adaptive outcome in chronic fatigue syndrome: Importance of illness cognitions. *Journal of Psychosomatic Research, 45*, 39–51.

Hemphill, R., Hall, K., & Crookes, T. (1952). A preliminary report on fatigue and pain tolerance in depressive and psychoneurotic patients. *Journal of Mental Science*, 433–440.

Henderson, S., Byrne, D. G., & Duncan-Jones, P. (1981). *Neurosis and the social environment*. New York: Academic Press.

Hickie, I., Lloyd, A., Hadzi-Pavlovic, D., Parker, G., Bird, K., & Wakefield, D. (1995). Can the chronic fatigue syndrome be defined by distinct clinical features? *Psychological Medicine, 25*, 925–935.

Hickie, I., Lloyd, A., Wakefield, D., & Parker, G. (1990). The psychiatric status of patients with chronic fatigue syndrome. *British Journal of Psychiatry, 156*, 534–540.

Holmes, G., Kaplan, J., Gantz, N., et al. (1988). Chronic fatigue syndrome: A working case definition. *Annals of Internal Medicine, 108*, 387–389.

Hotopf, M., Noah, N., & Wessely, S. (1996). Chronic fatigue and minor psychiatric morbidity after viral meningitis: A controlled study. *Journal of Neurology, Neurosurgery and Psychiatry, 60*, 504–509.

Johnson, S., DeLuca, J., & Natelson, B. (1996). Depression in fatiguing illness: Comparing patients with chronic fatigue syndrome, multiple sclerosis and depression. *Journal of Affective Disorders, 38*, 21–30.

Jones, M., & Mellersh, V. (1946). Comparison of exercise response in anxiety states and normal controls. *Psychosomatic Medicine, 8*, 180–187.

Katon, W., Buchwald, D., Simon, G., Russo, J., & Mease, P. (1991). Psychiatric illness in patients with chronic fatigue and rheumatoid arthritis. *Journal of General Internal Medicine, 6*, 277–285.

Katon, W., & Russo, J. (1992). Chronic fatigue syndrome criteria: A critique of the requirement for multiple physical complaints. *Archives of Internal Medicine, 152*, 1604–1609.

Kent-Braun, J., Sharma, K., Weiner, M., Massie, B., Miller, R. (1993). Central basis of muscle fatigue in chronic fatigue syndrome. *Neurology, 43*, 125–131.

Kessler, R. C. (1983). Methodological issues in stress research: Design and analysis. In H. B. Kaplan (Ed), *Psychosocial stress: Recent developments in theory and method*. New York: Academic Press.

Kottke, F. (1966). The effects of limitation of activity upon the human body. *JAMA, 196*, 117–122.

Kroenke, K., Wood, D., Mangelsdorff, D., Meier, N., & Powell, J. (1988). Chronic fatigue in primary care: Prevalence, patient characteristics and outcome. *JAMA, 260*, 929–934.

Kruesi, M., Dale, J., & Straus, S. (1989). Psychiatric diagnoses in patients who have chronic fatigue syndrome. *Journal of Clinical Psychiatry, 50*, 53–56.

Lamb, L., Stevens, P., & Johnson, R. (1965). Hypokinesia secondary to chair rest from 4 to 10 days. *Aerospace Medicine, 36*, 755–763.

Lane, T., Manu, P., & Matthews, D. (1991). Depression and somatization in the chronic fatigue syndrome. *American Journal of Medicine, 91*, 335–344.

Lang, P. (1970). Stimulus control and the desensitisation of fear. In D. Lewis (Ed), *Learning approaches to therapeutic behaviour* (pp. 148–173). Chicago: Aldine Press.

Lavietes, M., Natelson, B., Cordero, D., Ellis, S., & Tapp, W. (1996). Does the stressed patient with chronic fatigue syndrome hyperventilate? *International Journal of Behavioural Medicine, 3*, 70–83.

Lepow, M., Coyne, N., Thompson, L., Carver, D., & Robbins, F. (1962). A clinical, epidemiological and laboratory investigation of aseptic meningitis during the four-year period, 1955–1958. II. The clinical disease and its sequelae. *New England Journal of Medicine, 266*, 1188–1193.

Lewis, G., & Wessely, S. (1992). The epidemiology of fatigue: More questions than answers. *Journal of Epidemiology and Community Health, 46*, 92–97.

Lewis, S., Cooper, C., & Bennett, D. (1994). Psychosocial factors and chronic fatigue syndrome. *Psychological Medicine, 24*, 661–671.

Lindal, E., Berhmann, S., Thorlacius, S., & Stefansson, J. (1997). Anxiety disorders: A result of long-term chronic fatigue—the psychiatric characteristics of sufferers from Iceland disease. *Acta Neurologica Scandinavica, 96*, 158–162.

Lindberg, B. (1965). Somatic complaints in the depressive symptomatology. *Acta Psychiatrica Scandinavica, 41*, 419.

Lloyd, A., Gandevia, S., & Hales, J. (1991). Muscle performance, voluntary activation, twitch properties and perceived effort in normal subjects and patients with the chronic fatigue syndrome. *Brain, 114*, 85–98.

Lloyd, A., Hales, J., & Gandevia, S. (1988). Muscle strength, endurance and recovery in the postinfection fatigue syndrome. *Journal of Neurology, Neurosurgery and Psychiatry, 51*, 1316–1322.

Lloyd, A., Hickie, I., Boughton, R., Spencer, O., & Wakefield, D. (1990). Prevalence of chronic fatigue syndrome in an Australian population. *Medical Journal of Australia, 153*, 522–528.

Maes, M., Bosmans, E., Suy, E., Minner, B., & Raus, J. (1991). A further exploration of the relationships between immune parameters and the HPA-axis activity in depressed patients. *Psychological Medicine, 21*, 313–320.

Maes, M., Bosmans, E., Suy, E., Vandervorst, C., DeJonckheere, C., & Raus, J. (1991). Depression-related disturbances in mitogen-induced lymphocyte responses and interleukin-1 beta and soluble interleukin-2 receptor production. *Acta Psychiatrica Scandinavica, 84*, 379–386.

Maes, M., Jacobs, J., & Lambreckhts, J. (1992). Evidence for a systemic immune activation during depression: Results of leucocyte enumeration by flow cytometry in conjunction with antibody staining. *Psychological Medicine, 22*, 45–53.

Magnusson, A., Nias, D., & White, P. (1996). Is perfectionism associated with fatigue? *Journal of Psychosomatic Research, 41*, 377–384.

Manu, P., Affleck, G., Tennen, H., Morse, P., & Escobar, J. (1996). Hypochondriasis influences quality of life outcomes in patients with chronic fatigue. *Psychotherapy and Psychosomatics, 65*, 76–81.

Marmion, B., Shannon, M., Maddocks, I., Strom, P., & Penttila, I. (1996). Protracted fatigue and debility after acute Q fever. *Lancet, 347*, 977–978.

Masuda, A., Nozoe, S., Matsuyama, T., & Tanaka, H. (1994). Psychobehavioral and immunological characteristics of adult people with chronic fatigue and patients with chronic fatigue syndrome. *Psychosomatic Medicine, 56*, 512–518.

McCully, K., Sisto, S., & Natelson, B. (1996). Use of exercise for treatment of chronic fatigue syndrome. *Sports Medicine, 21*, 35–48.

McEvedy, C., & Beard, A. (1973). A controlled study follow up of cases involved in an epidemic of "benign myalgic encephalomyelitis." *British Journal of Psychiatry, 122*, 141–150.

McFarland, R. A. (1971). Understanding fatigue in modern life. *Ergonomics, 14*, 1–10.

McKenzie, R., O'Fallon, A., Dale, J., et al. (1998). Low-dose hydrocortisone treatment of chronic fatigue syndrome: Results of a placebo controlled study of its efficacy and safety. *JAMA, 280*, 1061–1066.

Miller, T., Allen, G., & Gandevia, S. (1996). Muscle force, perceived effort, and voluntary activation of the elbow flexors assessed with sensitive twitch interpolation in fibromyalgia. *Journal of Rheumatology, 23*, 1621–1627.

Morin, C. M., Culbert, J. P., & Schwartz, S. M. (1994). Non-pharmacological interventions for insomnia: A meta-analysis of treatment. *American Journal of Psychiatry, 151*, 1172–1180.

Morriss, R., Wearden, A., & Battersby, L. (1997). The relation of sleep difficulties to fatigue, mood and disability in chronic fatigue syndrome. *Journal of Psychosomatic Research, 42*, 597–605.

Moss-Morris, R. (1997). The role of illness cognitions and coping in the aetiology and maintenance of the chronic fatigue syndrome (CFS). In J. Weinman & K. Petrie (Eds.), *Perceptions of health and illness: Current research and applications* (pp. 411–439). Reading, MA: Harwood Academic Publishers.

Moss-Morris, R., Petrie, K., & Weinman, J. (1996). Functioning in chronic fatigue syndrome: Do illness perceptions play a role? *British Journal of Health Psychology, 1*, 15–25.

Muller, R., Nylander, I., Larsson, L., Widen, L., & Frankenhauser, M. (1958). Sequelae of primary aseptic meningo-encephalitis: A clinical, sociomedical, electroencephalographic and psychological study. *Acta Psychiatrica Neurologica Scandinavica, 33* (suppl. 126), 1–115.

Muscio, B. (1921). Is a fatigue test possible? *British Journal of Psychology, 12*, 31–46.

Natelson, B., Cheu, J., Pareja, J., Ellis, S., Policastro, T., & Findley, T. (1996). Randomized double-blind, controlled placebo-phase in trial of low dose phenelzine in the chronic fatigue syndrome. *Psychopharmacology, 124*, 226–230.

Odagiri, Y., Shimomitsu, T., Iwane, H., & Katsumura, T. (1996). Relationships between exhaustive mood state and changes in stress hormones following an ultra-endurance race. *International Journal of Sports Medicine, 17*, 325–331.

Pagani, M., Lucini, D., Mela, G., Langewitz, W., & Malliani, A. (1994). Sympathetic overactivity in subjects complaining of unexplained fatigue. *Clinical Science, 87*, 655–661.

Pawlikowska, T., Chalder, T., Hirsch, S., Wallace, P., Wright, D., & Wessely, S. (1994). A population based study of fatigue and psychological distress. *British Medical Journal, 308*, 743–746.

Philips. C. (1987). Avoidance behaviour and its role in sustaining chronic pain. *Behaviour Research and Therapy, 25*, 273–279.

Poteliakhoff, A. (1981). Adrenocortical activity and some clinical findings in chronic fatigue. *Journal of Psychosomatic Research, 25*, 91–95.

Preedy, V., Smith, D., Salisbury, J., & Peters, T. (1993). Biochemical and muscle studies in patients with acute onset post-viral fatigue syndrome. *Journal of Clinical Pathology, 46*, 722–726.

Rabinbach, A. (1990). *The human motor: Energy, fatigue and the origins of modernity*. New York: Basic Books.

Rachman, S. J., Lopatka, K., & Levitt, L. (1988). Experimental analysis of panic. II. Panic patients. *Behaviour Research and Therapy, 26*, 33–44.

Ray, C., Jeffries, S., & Weir, W. (1995). Coping with chronic fatigue syndrome: Illness responses and their relationship with fatigue, functional impairment and emotional status. *Psychological Medicine, 25*, 937–945.

Ray, C., Jefferies, S., Weir, W. (1997). Coping and other predictors of outcome in chronic fatigue syndrome: A 1-year follow-up. *Journal of Psychosomatic Research, 43*, 405–415.

Ray, C., Weir, W., Cullen, S., & Phillips, S. (1992). Illness perception and symptom components in chronic fatigue syndrome. *Journal of Psychosomatic Research, 36*, 246–256.

Reyes, M., Dobbins, J. G., Mawle, A. C., et al. (1996). Risk factors for chronic fatigue syndrome: A case control study. *Journal of Chronic Fatigue Syndrome, 2*, 17–32.

Riley, M., O'Brien, C., McCluskey, D., Bell, N., & Nicholls, D. (1990). Aerobic work capacity in patients with chronic fatigue syndrome. *British Medical Journal, 301*, 953–956.

Rosen, S. D., King, J. C., Wilkinson, J. B., & Nixon, P. G. F. (1990). Is chronic fatigue syndrome synonymous with effort syndrome. *Journal of the Royal Society of Medicine, 83*, 761–764.

Rowe, P., Bou-Holaigah, I., Kan, J., & Calkins, H. (1995). Is neurally mediated hypotension an unrecognised cause of chronic fatigue? *Lancet, 345*, 623–624.

Royal Colleges of Physicians. (1996). *Chronic fatigue syndrome: Report of a Committee of the Royal Colleges of Physicians, Psychiatrists and General Practitioners*. London: Author.

Saisch, S., Deale, A., Gardner, W., & Wessely, S. (1994). Hyperventilation and chronic fatigue syndrome. *Quarterly Journal of Medicine, 87*, 63–67.

Salit, I. (1997). Precipitating factors for the chronic fatigue syndrome. *Journal of Psychiatric Research, 31*, 59–65.

Schluederberg, A., Straus, S., Peterson, P., et al. (1992). Chronic fatigue syndrome research: Definition and medical outcome assessment. *Annals of Internal Medicine, 117*, 325–331.

Scott, L. V., & Dinan, T. G. (1998). Urinary free cortisol excretion in chronic fatigue syndrome, major depression and in healthy volunteers. *Journal of Affective Disorders, 47*, 49–54.

Scott, L. V., Medbak, S., & Dinan, T. G. (1998a). Blunted adrenocorticotropin and cortisol responses to corticotropin-releasing hormone stimulation in chronic fatigue syndrome. *Acta Psychiatrica Scandinavica, 97*, 450–457.

Scott, L. V., Medbak, S., & Dinan, T. G. (1998b). The low dose adrenocorticotropin test in chronic fatigue syndrome and in health. *Clinical Endocrinology, 48*, 733–737.

Sensky, T. (1990). Patients' reaction to illness. *British Medical Journal, 300*, 622–623.

Shands, H., & Finesinger, J. (1952). A note on the significance of fatigue. *Psychosomatic Medicine, 14*, 309–314.

Sharpe, M., Archard, L., Banatvala, J., et al. (1991). Chronic fatigue syndrome: Guidelines for research. *Journal of the Royal Society of Medicine, 84*, 118–121.

Sharpe, M., Clements, A., Hawton, K., Young, A., Sargent, P., & Cowen, P. (1996). Increased prolactin response to buspirone in chronic fatigue syndrome. *Journal of Affective Disorders, 41*, 71–76.

Sharpe, M., Hawton, K., Clements, A., & Cowen, P. J. (1997). Increased brain serotonin function in men with chronic fatigue syndrome. *British Medical Journal, 315*, 164–165.

Sharpe, M., Hawton, K., Seagroatt, V., & Pasvol, G. (1992). Follow up of patients with fatigue presenting to an infectious diseases clinic. *British Medical Journal, 302*, 347–352.

Sharpe, M., Hawton, K., Simkin, S., et al. (1996). Cognitive behaviour therapy for chronic fatigue syndrome: A randomized controlled trial. *British Medical Journal, 312*, 22–26.

Sisto, S., MaManca, J., Cordero, D., et al. (1996). Metabolic and cardiovascular effects of a progressive exercise test in patients with chronic fatigue syndrome. *American Journal of Medicine, 100*, 634–640.

Stokes, M., Cooper, R., & Edwards, R. (1988). Normal strength and fatigability in patients with effort syndrome. *British Medical Journal, 297*, 1014–1018.

Straus, S., Fritz, S., Dale, J., Gould, B., & Strober, W. (1993). Lymphocyte phenotype and function in the chronic fatigue syndrome. *Journal of Clinical Immunology, 13*, 30–40.

Strickland, P., Morriss, R., Wearden, A., & Deakin, W. (1998). A comparison of salivary cortisol in chronic fatigue syndrome, community depression and healthy controls. *Journal of Affective Disorders, 47*, 191–194.

Surawy, C., Hackmann, A., Hawton, K., & Sharpe, M. (1995). Chronic fatigue syndrome: A cognitive approach. *Behavior Research and Therapy, 33*, 535–544.

Taerk, G., Toner, B., Salit, I., Garfinkel, P., & Ozersky, S. (1987). Depression in patients with neuromyasthenia (benign myalgic encephalomyelitis). *International Journal of Psychiatry in Medicine, 17*, 49–56.

Trigwell, P., Hatcher, S., Johnson, M., Stanley, P., & House, A. (1995). Abnormal illness behaviour in chronic fatigue syndrome and multiple sclerosis. *British Medical Journal, 311*, 15–18.

Van Houdenhove, B., Onghena, P., Neerinckx, E., & Hellin, J. (1995). Does high "action-proneness" make people more vulnerable to chronic fatigue syndrome? A controlled psychometric study. *Journal of Psychosomatic Research, 39*, 633–640.

Vercoulen, J., Swanink, C., Fennis, J., Galama, J., van der Meer, J., & Bleijenberg, G. (1994). Dimensional assessment of chronic fatigue syndrome. *Journal of Psychosomatic Research, 38*, 383–392.

Vercoulen, J., Swanink, C., Fennis, J., Galama, J., van der Meer, J., & Bleijenberg, G. (1996). Prognosis in chronic fatigue syndrome: A prospective study on the natural course. *Journal of Neurology, Neurosurgery and Psychiatry, 60*, 489–494.

Vercoulen, J., Swanink, C., Zitman, F., et al. (1996). Fluoxetine in chronic fatigue syndrome: A randomized, double-blind, placebo-controlled study. *Lancet, 347*, 858–861.

Ware, N., & Kleinman, A. (1992). Culture and somatic experience—the social course of illness in neurasthenia and chronic fatigue syndrome. *Psychosomatic Medicine, 54*, 546–560.

Wearden, A., Morriss, R., Mulliss, R., et al. (1998). Randomised, double-blind, placebo controlled treatment trial of fluoxetine and graded exercise for chronic fatigue syndrome. *British Journal of Psychiatry, 172*, 485–490.

Wells, A. (1997). *Cognitive therapy of anxiety disorders: A practice manual and conceptual guide*. Chichester, England: Wiley.

Wessely, S., Butler, S., Chalder, T., & David, A. (1991). The cognitive behavioural management of the post-viral fatigue syndrome. In R. Jenkins & J. Mowbray (Eds.), *Postviral fatigue syndrome* (pp. 305–334). Chichester, England: Wiley.

Wessely, S., Chalder, T., Hirsch, S., Pawlikowska, T., Wallace, P., & Wright, D. (1995). Post infectious fatigue:

A prospective study in primary care. *Lancet, 345,* 1333–1338.

Wessely, S., Chalder, T., Hirsch, S., Wallace, P., & Wright, D. (1996). Psychological symptoms, somatic symptoms and psychiatric disorder in chronic fatigue and chronic fatigue syndrome: A prospective study in primary care. *American Journal of Psychiatry, 153,* 1050–1059.

Wessely, S., Chalder, T., Hirsch, S., Wallace, P., & Wright, D. (1997). The prevalence and morbidity of chronic fatigue and chronic fatigue syndrome: A prospective primary care study. *American Journal of Public Health, 87,* 1449–1455.

Wessely, S., Hotopf, M., & Sharpe, M. (1998). *Chronic fatigue and its syndromes.* Oxford, England: Oxford University Press.

Wessely, S., & Powell, R. (1989). Fatigue syndromes: A comparison of chronic "postviral" fatigue with neuromuscular and affective disorder. *Journal of Neurology, Neurosurgery and Psychiatry, 52,* 940–948.

Widmer, R., & Cadoret, R. (1978). Depression in primary care—changes in pattern of patient visits and complaints during a developing depression. *Journal of Family Practice, 7,* 293–302.

Wilson, A., Hickie, I., Lloyd, A., et al. (1994). Longitudinal study of the outcome of chronic fatigue syndrome. *British Medical Journal, 308,* 756–760.

Wilson, D., Widmer, R., Cadoret, R., & Judiesch, K. (1983). Somatic symptoms: A major feature of depression in a family practice. *Journal of Affective Disorders, 5,* 199–207.

Winokur, G., & Holeman, E. (1963). Chronic anxiety neurosis: Clinical and sexual aspects. *Acta Psychiatrica Scandinavica, 39,* 384.

Wood, B., & Wessely, S. (in press). Personality characteristics in chronic fatigue syndrome and rheumatoid arthritis. *Journal of Psychosomatic Research.*

Wood, B., Wessely, S., Papadopoulos, A., Poon, L., & Checkley, S. (1997). Salivary cortisol profiles in chronic fatigue syndrome. *Neuropsychobiology, 37,* 1–4.

Wood, G., Bentall, R., Gopfert, M., & Edwards, R. (1991). A comparative psychiatric assessment of patients with chronic fatigue syndrome and muscle disease. *Psychological Medicine, 21,* 619–628.

Yatham, L. N., Morehouse, R. L., Chisholm, B. T., Haase, D. A., MacDonald, D. D., & Marrie, T. J. (1995). Neuroendocrine assessment of serotonin (5-HT) function in chronic fatigue syndrome. *Canadian Journal of Psychiatry, 40,* 93–96.

Young, A. H., Sharpe, M., Clements, A., Dowling, B., Hawton, K. E., & Cowen, P. J. (1998). Basal activity of the hypothalamic-pituitary-adrenal axis in patients with the chronic fatigue syndrome (neurasthenia). *Biological Psychiatry, 43,* 236–237.

Zorbas, Y., Matveyev, I. (1986). Man's desirability in performing physical exercises under hypokinesia. *International Journal of Rehabilitation, 9,* 170–174.

Zuber, J., & Wilgosh, L. (1963). Prolonged immobilization of the body: Changes in performance and the electroencephalogram. *Science, 140,* 306–308.

CHAPTER 10

THE GERIATRIC PATIENT

Cynthia T. M. H. Nguyen
Jennifer Hoffman Goldberg
Javaid I. Sheikh

Feelings of stress or anxiety are normal human emotions and can be an adaptive way of anticipating and responding to danger or stressful life events. At excessive levels, however, anxiety can manifest itself as a clinical syndrome that causes significant distress and interferes with occupational, social, and other areas of functioning. Patients with anxiety may present with a variety of symptoms in cognitive (e.g., worry, fearfulness, nervousness), behavioral (e.g., agitation, exaggerated startle response), and physiological (e.g., palpitations, tachycardia, urinary frequency) domains.

In managing anxiety in the geriatric medical patient, there are two broad categories to consider: (1) preexisting anxiety disorders that develop as a primary disorder in late life or persist from younger years and may complicate medical treatment, and (2) symptoms of anxiety that develop during the course of medical illnesses and their treatment.

For geriatric patients in both categories, anxiety can have profound effects on quality of life, health care utilization, morbidity, and mortality. A detailed description of the late-life phenomenology of primary anxiety disorders listed in the *DSM-IV* (American Psychiatric Association, 1994), with diagnostic criteria, is beyond the scope of this chapter and is discussed elsewhere (Sheikh, 1996). We will, however, address the clinical presentation of geriatric anxiety in medical settings. Our management strategies cover all types of clinically significant anxiety in late-life primary anxiety disorders as well as anxiety secondary to medical illness and substance use.

PREVALENCE, RISK FACTORS, AND CLINICAL PRESENTATIONS

Prevalence and Risk Factors

Patients with chronic medical disorders are especially vulnerable to psychiatric disorders. In a community survey based on data from the NIMH ECA Program, people with a chronic medical illness were found to have a 41% increased risk of a recent psychiatric disorder; specifically, more than 11% of those with chronic medical conditions had a recent anxiety disorder (Wells, Golding, & Burnham, 1988). Several studies suggest that anxiety disorders as a group are the most common psychiatric disorders in older adult populations (Hocking & Koenig, 1995; Sheikh & Salzman, 1995). In addition, because more than 80% of Americans older than 65 report at least one chronic medical condition and most have multiple chronic problems (National Center for Health Statistics, 1987), geriatric patients are at increased risk for anxiety in medical disorders.

Many additional psychosocial and physiological factors render older medical patients more susceptible to anxiety than other patients. These can include cultural differences, financial changes, loss of physical functioning and mobility, loss of independence, living situation changes, and role changes (e.g., retirement or becoming a caregiver to a spouse) (Hocking & Koenig, 1995). Two additional stressors, terminal illness and bereavement, are especially difficult and may also cause anxiety and depression. In the terminally ill geriatric patient, anxiety, depression and cognitive disorder appear to be the most common psychiatric symptoms to develop (Breitbart & Jacobsen, 1996). In the dying patient, anxiety may foreshadow an impending medical crisis such as cardiac arrest, pulmonary embolism, dehydration, or an electrolyte imbalance (Strain, Liebowitz, & Klein, 1981). In terminally ill patients who are alert and cognitively intact, anxiety may stem from psychological reasons rather than purely medical ones (Holland, 1989). Existential issues of death may be highly anxiety-provoking. Bereaved older adults can exhibit clinically significant symptoms of depression or anxiety (Frank et al., 1997; Prigerson et al., 1996).

Numerous physiological changes occur with aging that both increase susceptibility to stress and anxiety and mimic syndromal anxiety symptoms. For example, sleep architecture changes as a result of the aging process. In an epidemiological study of older adults, over half of those surveyed reported sleep problems (especially insomnia) most of the time (Foley et al., 1995). Insomnia may interact with or obscure other psychiatric disorders, including anxiety and depression (Beck & Stanley, 1997; Folks & Fuller, 1997). The body's ability to respond to stress diminishes with age (Sunderland et al., 1991). After being warmed or chilled, older adults take longer to return to normal body temperature. Resting levels of stress hormones, like epinephrine, norepinephrine, and glucocorticoids, are elevated in older rats and humans (Sapolsky, 1994). Other physiological changes alter older adults' response to pharmacological interventions. As these are particularly important in the pharmacological treatment of anxiety in the geriatric patient, they will be discussed in that section.

Clinical Presentations

Older patients experiencing anxiety often present with medical complaints rather than psychiatric concerns. Anxiety is usually accompanied by somatic symptoms, and physical illnesses may be easier to accept than mental disorders. As a result, geriatric patients are frequently seen in medical as opposed to mental health settings. Anxiety is thus often underdiagnosed and undertreated in older patients (Lindesay, 1991). For example, patients presenting with atypical angina and no evidence of cardiovascular disease may

have panic disorder (Beitman et al., 1990; Carter, Servan-Schreiber, & Perlstein, 1997).

Conversely, anxiety is often the chief complaint in an older patient with an acute medical disorder. Anxiety can mimic and be difficult to distinguish from clinical manifestations of some medical disorders. Anxiety accompanies numerous medical disorders such as those described in greater detail in other chapters of this volume, including disorders like Parkinson's, pulmonary disease, cardiovascular disease, and dementia that occur frequently in older patients. For example, Stein and colleagues found that 33% of patients with Parkinson's met criteria for an anxiety disorder (Stein et al., 1990). Panic disorder was diagnosed in 8% of outpatients with chronic obstructive pulmonary disease (COPD) in one study (Karajgi et al., 1990) while 40% of mostly geriatric COPD patients reported significant anxiety in another study (White et al., 1997). Cardiovascular disorders such as pulmonary embolus, arrhythmia, and angina can be associated with anxiety (Stoudemire, 1996). Wands and colleagues (1990) reported that 38% of patients with early dementia were found to have anxiety. Sudden onset of anxiety can signal a rapidly deteriorating medical condition in patients with or without a chronic medical illness (Wise & Griffies, 1995).

The psychosocial stress of an acute or chronic medical illness and medical treatment procedures may also create or exacerbate already existing anxiety. Patients may develop PTSD after traumatic medical procedures or interventions, such as resuscitation after a cardiac arrest (Davis & Breslau, 1994; Kutz et al., 1994). Claustrophobia has been reported after magnetic resonance imaging scanning (Kilborn & Labbe, 1990). Chronic specific phobias of things like seeing blood or receiving an injection can make medical procedures extremely anxiety-provoking.

FACTORS COMPLICATING PROPER ASSESSMENT

Failure to take into account both medical and psychiatric etiologies of anxiety can lead to diagnostic confusion. In addition, higher prevalence of medical conditions and cognitive decline that can accompany old age can contribute to making diagnosis difficult. Factors to consider in evaluating anxiety in medical disorders in older patients include polypharmacy, substance use, and comorbid depression.

Polypharmacy

A complete assessment of all currently used substances is especially important because most medically ill geriatric patients are taking several medications concurrently. The average older person typically takes six to eight different medications per day. One survey revealed that the average older patient fills 13 prescriptions a year. Although people 65 and over constitute 12% of the population, they are prescribed 30% of all medications and 25% of prescriptions for psychotropic medications, and they are the largest consumers of over-the-counter drugs (National Center for Health Statistics, 1987; Stewart et al., 1989). Polypharmacy can lead to unexpected and undesirable anxiety symptoms due to drug interactions. Moreover, drug interactions can also enhance or reduce the effectiveness of any pharmacological treatment of anxiety symptoms. A host of drugs can mimic or produce anxiety. These include over-the-counter compounds containing pseudoephedrine hydrochloride (e.g., Claritin-D, Sudafed) or phenylpropanolamine (e.g., Afrin, Drixoral), caffeine, diet pills (Acutrim, Dexatrim), antidepressants with stimulating properties (including selective serotonin reuptake inhibitors [SSRIs] and over-the-counter compounds like St. John's Wort), thyroid replacement therapies, steroids, aerosolized beta agonists, and other bronchodilators. Additionally, withdrawal from benzodiazepines or other sedatives may cause symptoms of anxiety. A detailed history of current prescribed and over-the-counter medications (including analgesics, herbals, and vitamin supplements) needs to be obtained from the patient and/or collateral sources.

Substance Use

Substance use (e.g., alcohol or drug dependence) can be both a consequence and a cause of anxiety and must be adequately ruled out as a primary diagnosis. Alcoholism is often overlooked in all patients, but especially in geriatric patients. Patients may have a life-long pattern of drinking small amounts daily. When these older patients are hospitalized, withdrawal can be problematic and present as anxiety. Diagnosis may be difficult because of comorbidity of alcoholism with both psychiatric and medical illness. Careful history of alcohol use from collateral sources (friends, family, caregivers) is therefore essential in the management of anxiety in older patients.

Comorbid Depression

Comorbid depression and anxiety appear to be extremely common in older adults (Flint, 1994). The relationship between depression and anxiety is complex. High rates of comorbidity have been found among groups diagnosed with depression and groups diagnosed with an anxiety disorder. In a small sample of geriatric psychiatry outpatients, Alexopoulos (1991) reported that while only 2% had an anxiety disorder exclusively, 38% of depressed patients also met criteria for an anxiety disorder according to *DSM-III*. The Guy's/Age Concern Survey reported that 39% of phobic subjects had comorbid depression compared to only 11% of nonphobic subjects (Lindesay, Briggs, & Murphy, 1989). The presence and severity levels of generalized anxiety disorder and depression were especially associated. Studying geriatric adults in South Africa who had been diagnosed with depression, Ben-Arie and colleagues found that 26% also had generalized anxiety and 5% had panic attacks (Ben-Arie, Swartz, & Dickman, 1987). Comorbidity is common even in geriatric medical patients. For example, in a study of geriatric cancer patients, Derogatis and colleagues (1983) reported that 13% evidenced mixed anxiety-depressive syndromes, while 8% evidenced an anxiety disorder exclusively.

Mixed anxiety-depression (MAD) syndrome is included in the *DSM-IV* appendix as a research category. While not an official diagnostic category, it is one of the most frequently encountered presentations in medical settings and in geropsychiatry. Just as anxiety and depressive disorders often co-occur, subsyndromal symptoms of anxiety and depression frequently co-exist. MAD is marked by symptoms of both anxiety and depression that cause significant distress or functional impairment even though they fail to meet criteria for an established disorder.

ASSESSMENT AND DIFFERENTIAL DIAGNOSIS IN CLINICAL SETTINGS

Clinical Assessment

Assessment and diagnosis are critical steps in the treatment process. The choice of what to assess reflects where one believes it will be important to intervene, with direct implications for what diagnoses can be made and for the focus of treatment. A thorough medical and psychiatric history, an assessment of functional status, a comprehensive medical examination, as well as the diagnostic considerations discussed previously should be made before beginning treatment.

Several self-rated and observer-rated anxiety scales are available that help in the assessment of specific anxiety symptoms and can be used to mark treatment progress over time, with several caveats. Commonly used anxiety scales, reviewed in greater detail elsewhere (e.g., Sheikh, 1991), are discussed briefly here.

The Hamilton Anxiety Rating Scale (HARS) (Hamilton, 1959) is one of the most commonly used observer-rated instruments. The HARS has been shown to differentiate older generalized anxiety disorder patients from controls (Beck, Stanley, & Zebb, 1996). Because the HARS items emphasize somatic symptoms, its validity in an older, medically ill population has been questioned (Sheikh, 1991).

Self-rated scales frequently used in the evaluation of anxiety include the Hopkins Symptom Check List (SCL-90-R) (Derogatis, 1983), a general symptom inventory, and several anxiety-specific scales: the Beck Anxiety Inventory (BAI) (Beck et al., 1988), the Fear Questionnaire (FQ) (Marks & Mathews, 1979), the Penn-State Worry Questionnaire (PSWQ) (Meyer et al., 1990), and the State-Trait Anxiety Inventory (STAI) (Spielberger, Gorsuch, & Lushene, 1970). One additional self-report measure, the Worry Scale (WS) (Wisocki, Handen, & Morse, 1986), has been developed to assess worries unique to an older adult population. The psychometric properties of these scales in older adults still need examination, but recent studies have begun to report on the validity of these scales with several older adult populations (e.g. Kabacoff et al., 1997; Steer et al., 1994; Wetherell & Arean, 1997), including older adults with generalized anxiety disorder (Beck, Stanley, & Zebb, 1995, 1996; Stanley, Beck, & Zebb, 1996). The BAI looks especially promising for use with older patients.

Laboratory tests are an important part of this assessment, both to identify medical disorders and to objectively assess substance use. A complete blood count, blood glucose, an electrocardiogram, folate levels, thyroid function screen, vitamin B12, and a complete toxicology screen aid in the identification of medical causes of anxiety. Acute psychiatric symptoms warrant a head-imaging procedure.

Differential Diagnosis

Determining the etiology of both medical illnesses and psychiatric symptoms is critical in diagnosing a patient with anxiety due to a general medical disorder versus a primary anxiety disorder or adjustment disorder. Diagnosis of any mental disorder "due to a general medical condition" relies on three criteria: (1) evidence from the history, physical examination, or laboratory findings that the disturbance is the direct physiological consequence of a general medical condition; (2) the disturbance is not better accounted for by another mental disorder; and (3) the disturbance does not occur exclusively during the course of delirium (American Psychiatric Association, 1994). A causal, physiological sequence between the medical condition and anxiety symptoms must be implied.

Other associations are often seen. As discussed previously, the medical illness and medical treatment procedures can act as significant psychosocial stressors themselves and lead to considerable stress and anxiety. When the medical condition is thought to act primarily by means of a psychosocial mechanism, the appropriate anxiety disorder, or an adjustment disorder, should be diagnosed and treated. Patient history is especially important here. A patient with a personal and family history of an anxiety disorder may be more appropriately diagnosed with a primary anxiety disorder rather than due to a medical condition, as may a patient with persisting anxiety after the medical disorder has been treated.

TREATMENT OF STRESS AND ANXIETY

While anxiety in the medically ill is related to worse outcome, treating anxiety symptoms has been shown to result in better medical outcomes. A review by Mumford and colleagues of 34 studies found that general psychological intervention predicted shorter length of stays following surgery for patients of all ages (Mumford, Schlesinger, & Glass, 1982). Most of what we know empirically about the treatment of anxiety is based on studies with younger patients rather than empirical data from treatment studies with older adults. Given this caveat, here we briefly review the efficacy of both psychosocial and pharmacological interventions. For many disorders the optimal treatment of anxiety involves a combined approach using both psychosocial and pharmacological interventions. Clinically these treatments that have been developed for younger populations are used in the management of anxiety for the geriatric population, sometimes with adaptations to make them more appropriate for work with older adults.

Psychosocial Treatment

Despite the volume of systematic studies documenting effective treatments for younger adults, there is a dearth of studies investigating the psychosocial treatment of anxiety disorders in the elderly. Even less is known about the management of anxiety in specific groups of older adults, like those who are also medically ill. The efficacy of numerous therapies for older adults is often extrapolated from evidence with younger populations (Sheikh & Salzman, 1995). Sometimes modifications are made to treatment protocols in an effort to make them more suitable for a geriatric population, yet these modifications have not been systematically investigated (Beck & Stanley, 1997). Future research studies should continue to empirically address the application of these treatments, in both individual and group formats, with geriatric patients.

As discussed in the previous section, accurate assessment and diagnosis are essential in the identification of appropriate treatment. Treatments should be tailored to specific anxiety symptoms or disorders and to individual patient variables such as course and intensity of symptoms, anxiety scale scores, medical and psychiatric comorbidities, history, past therapy experience, internal resources (e.g., motivation, cognitive functioning), external resources (e.g., social support, feasibility), and patient treatment preferences (Sheikh & Cassidy, in press). Although pharmacotherapy is frequently the first line of anxiety treatment with older adults in medical settings, psychosocial treatments are often preferred due to their success and to issues of prescribing additional medications in an older medical population, considering their vulnerability to adverse drug reactions, polypharmacy, and medical comorbidities.

A recent review of empirically supported treatments for adult mental disorders by DeRubeis and Crits-Christoph (1998) confirmed three primary types of efficacious treatment across anxiety disorders: applied relaxation, exposure therapy, and cognitive therapy. These and other therapeutic techniques are described in greater detail in other chapters in this volume. Briefly, behavioral approaches include techniques like relaxation, exposure, reinforcement, and real-world behavioral experimentation. *Applied relaxation* often consists of breathing exercises (e.g., Clark, Salkovskis, & Chalkley, 1985) and tension-relaxation of different muscle groups within the body designed to produce relaxation (e.g., Bernstein & Borkovec, 1973). *Exposure therapy* (e.g., Bandura, 1969; Marks, 1997; Sherman, 1972) typically involves introducing the individual to a feared object or situation, often in combination with applied relaxation, until the fear response abates. Exposure can occur both in real-life situations (in vivo) and through the use of fantasy or imagery (in vitro). Exposure can be graded over time so that the individual starts with less fearful encounters and works up to more threatening scenarios (systematic desensitization) or can begin with the presentation of a highly feared stimuli (flooding). Exposure continues until anxiety levels diminish. *Cognitive therapy* (e.g., Barlow & Cerny, 1988; Beck, Emery, & Greenberg, 1985) is based on the premise that anxiety is due to cognitions that produce fearful feelings. Therapy usually involves individuals monitoring their thoughts in fearful situations and documenting these cognitions. Individuals are then taught to replace these thoughts with alternatives that will result in less distress. Monitoring and practice assignments are completed between sessions.

Cognitive techniques are usually used in combination with the development of additional coping strategies (e.g., social skills training), other behavioral techniques, and psychoeducation. The term *cognitive-behavioral therapy (CBT)* denotes therapies that integrate both cognitive and behavioral approaches. Treatment plans often involve using these and other approaches in combination with pharmacotherapy.

DeRubeis and Crits-Christoph's (1998) list of efficacious treatments for adult anxiety disorders is summarized in Table 10.1. These include several treatments developed specifically for a given disorder, like Barlow and Cerny's (1988) treatment for panic disorder. A treatment is considered empirically supported only if it "compares favorably with an empirically-supported treatment in a well-conducted study involving a large sample size" (DeRubeis & Crits-Christoph, 1998, p. 38).

Although we again emphasize that controlled clinical trials comparing psychosocial treatments for older adult subjects are lacking, a few research studies and case reports support the efficacy of using these therapies, especially CBT, with geriatric individuals. For panic disorder, case studies support the use of CBT among older adults specifically (Rathus & Sanderson, 1996). A recent study by Swales and colleagues (Swales, Solfvin, & Sheikh, 1996) reported significant improvement among older adults with panic disorder using CBT and applied relaxation, and these gains were maintained at 3-month follow-up.

Despite the number of reports of older adults and older veterans with PTSD, little research has addressed this group. One recent study suggests that group psychotherapy may be an effective treatment for older veterans (Snell & Padin-Rivera, 1997). Current treatment strategies usually involve the use of CBT and pharmacotherapy. We know of no treatment studies for specific phobias, social phobia, or obsessive-compulsive disorder in older adults. Specific phobias often go untreated in the general population, although treatment with behavior therapy results in significant improvement in about 75–85% of cases (Öst, 1989). Social phobia is usually treated with cognitive-behavioral techniques including social skills training, applied relaxation, exposure, and cognitive therapy with strong evidence for their effectiveness (Heimberg, 1989; Heimberg & Barlow, 1991).

One controlled study has compared CBT and nondirective supportive psychotherapy for older adults with generalized anxiety disorder (GAD) (Stanley, Beck, & Glassco, 1997). In this study both treatments were carried out in small-group formats. The CBT followed a standardized individual protocol with modifications only for a group format. Participants in both conditions had significantly lower worry, anxiety, and depression scores post-treatment and at 6-month follow-up.

As mentioned before, little treatment data are available for older adults with MAD. Treatment studies of adults with comorbid depression and anxiety (panic or GAD) suggest that GAD patients respond to both depression-targeted psychotherapy and pharmacotherapy, although at a slower rate. Patients with depression and panic, however, had poor recovery (Brown et al., 1996). A complementary group therapy program for geriatric inpatients with depression and

TABLE 10.1. Empirically Supported Treatments for Adult Anxiety Disorders (Individual and Group)

ANXIETY DISORDER	TREATMENT
Generalized anxiety disorder	Cognitive therapy Applied relaxation
Social phobia	Exposure (alone or in combination with cognitive-behavioral therapy)
Obsessive-compulsive disorder	Exposure and response prevention
Agoraphobia	Exposure therapy
Panic disorder	Cognitive therapy Exposure therapy Applied relaxation

anxiety emphasizing psychoeducation and participation has reported some benefits (Moffatt, Mohr, & Ames, 1995). CBT has also been successful for treating depression and anxiety in younger medically ill patients. Studies are currently underway by our research group to examine the efficacy of pharmacotherapy and CBT for MAD.

In addition to these treatments for specific anxiety disorders, general stress and anxiety symptoms in medically ill older adults can be attenuated with information about medical procedures, psychoeducation, and relaxation techniques. Several studies have supported the usefulness of relaxation training for reducing anxiety in elderly community volunteers (DeBerry, 1982; DeBerry, Davis, & Reinhard, 1989; Sallis et al., 1983; Scogin et al., 1992). Especially for elders with dementia, anxiety symptoms can be helped by environmental and behavioral changes like the introduction of time schedules; memory aids; familiar home objects; and orienting objects like clocks, radios, and calendars.

Pharmacological Treatment

The pharmacological management of anxiety in older medical patients is more complicated than treatment of young healthy patients not only because of concomitant illnesses and polypharmacy but also because of age-related physiological changes. Some age-related vulnerabilities have been addressed previously in this chapter. Age-related changes in pharmacodynamics, the effects produced by certain concentrations of a drug, and pharmacokinetics, the bioavailability of a given dose of a medication, also influence the management of anxiety in older patients.

For a given concentration of a medication, the risk of adverse effects is greater in older adults than in younger patients. Moreover, the adverse side effects of drug–drug interactions increase substantially with polypharmacy. One medication may alter the absorption, metabolism, or clearance of another. In addition, an adverse side effect of a medication may have greater impact on a geriatric patient's medical status than on that of a younger patient. For example, orthostatic hypotension, a common side effect of some psychotropic medications, may merely cause lightheadedness in younger patients but may predispose older patients to falls and hip fractures.

The bioavailability of a drug is based on absorption, distribution, metabolism, and clearance. In older patients, gastric acid secretion is decreased, resulting in reduced drug absorption. An increased ratio of fat-to-lean body mass with aging affects the distribution of lipid-soluble medications, such as many antidepressants, antipsychotics, and sedatives. Thus, with the increased volume of lipophilic drugs, the physiological effects, both therapeutic and toxic, may be prolonged. In older patients, hepatic (liver) metabolism is decreased. Fewer plasma proteins are synthesized and as a consequence older patients have decreased protein binding. As some medications are bound to plasma proteins, drug concentrations of these unbound agents are increased in the serum. With decreased hepatic function, renal function, and cardiac output, clearance may be further delayed in geriatric medical patients. The overall effect of these pharmacokinetic changes is that many drugs are eliminated slowly and metabolized less efficiently in older patients than in younger ones (von Moltke et al., 1995).

Several general principles should be followed in treating anxiety in geriatric medical patients. As previously discussed, thorough medical evaluation and psychiatric assessment should be done. This includes gathering collateral data and obtaining baseline laboratory tests. With all medications in this population, it is wise to "start low and go slow" to account for the previously described physiological vulnerabilities. Drugs may be given in divided doses throughout the day to minimize possible adverse side effects. However, with divided doses, noncompliance may be an issue of concern, especially in medically ill older patients taking multiple medications. Liquid medications may be easier for some patients to take. When making medication adjustments, only one change should be attempted at a time. Close monitoring is essential in managing anxiety in older patients with medical disorders.

ANTIANXIETY MEDICATIONS USED IN LATE LIFE

Several classes of compounds are used as anxiolytics. Their descriptions and indications are presented in detail elsewhere in this text. Here we briefly describe the different classes of medications used to treat anxiety in medically ill geriatric patients. We will only focus on considerations for use that have specific relevance to this geriatric population. Some medications, such as barbiturates and chloral hydrate, that were used in the past as anxiolytics had higher risks of adverse effects in older patients (e.g., central nervous system depression and paradoxical agitation with barbiturates) and are not discussed here.

Benzodiazepines

Benzodiazepines have been the most frequently prescribed anxiolytics for both young and older patients (Beardsley et al., 1989). They are also commonly used as hypnotics for complaints of insomnia. Because older patients are more sensitive to both the therapeutic and the toxic effects of benzodiazepines, low doses are recommended; higher doses that are therapeutic in younger patients may actually be toxic in geriatric patients (Meyer, 1982).

These medications are beneficial in older medical patients with anxiety because they have a rapid onset and little effect on cardiovascular status. However, there are many potential complications of benzodiazepine use in older patients. These include excessive daytime drowsiness, cognitive impairment and confusion, ataxia, risk of falls, depression, paradoxical reactions, amnestic syndromes, respiratory problems, abuse and dependence potential, and breakthrough withdrawal reactions. Patients may develop a withdrawal syndrome characterized by confusion, delirium, and seizures. In general, because of these complications, long-term use of benzodiazepines should be avoided in geriatric medical patients.

Benzodiazepines with a long half-life (e.g., diazepam, flurazepam, and quazepam) are metabolized via oxidative pathways in the liver into active metabolites. Because oxidation (Phase I reactions) becomes less efficient with age, accumulation of these drugs occurs in geriatric patients. Phase II (conjugative metabolism) reactions, however, are minimally affected by age. Short- to medium-half-life benzodiazepines (e.g., lorazepam, oxazepam, and temazepam) are preferred in older medical patients because they require only Phase II metabolism, are cleared more rapidly, and accumulate less. Older patients with hepatic disease should be treated with one of these shorter-acting benzodiazepines. Benzodiazepines can also induce ventilatory suppression in patients with pulmonary

disease. Again, the medium- to short-half-life agents that are conjugated are preferred in these patients, who are more often than not, the elderly.

Buspirone

Unlike the benzodiazepines, which can cause respiratory depression, the anxiolytic buspirone, an azapirone derivative and a 5-HT$_{1A}$ partial agonist, may be helpful for patients with pulmonary disease. Animal studies have shown that buspirone stimulates respiratory drive (Garner et al., 1989). Buspirone is well tolerated and is devoid of side effects like sedation, psychomotor impairment, and the potential for abuse seen with the benzodiazepines. There also seem to be no significant pharmacokinetic differences between young and older patients (Gammans et al., 1989). Nevertheless, although buspirone's side effect profile is suitable for use in geriatric medical patients, in clinical situations its effectiveness remains somewhat inconsistent and requires further study.

Antidepressants

In recent years, the role of antidepressants in the treatment of anxiety disorders, especially in older patients, has become more prominent. Because of the potentially problematic side effect profile of the benzodiazepines, antidepressants (especially the SSRIs) are often the first choice for the treatment of anxiety in geriatric patients.

Tricyclic Antidepressants (TCAs)

Use of all TCAs has been declining in the older medical patient population because of the risk of detrimental side effects and because of the rise in the use of SSRIs, with their relatively safer side effect profiles. Some of the side effects of the TCAs include orthostatic hypotension, cardiac toxicity, memory impairment, delirium, seizures, and anticholinergic toxicity. Anticholinergic side effects can be manifested by blurred vision, dry mouth, urinary retention, constipation, and tachycardia. Anticholinergic medications like the TCAs may produce an acute delirium, especially in older patients with brain injury. Extreme caution and careful monitoring should be used for patients with preexisting intraventricular conduction delays, sick sinus syndrome, second-degree heart block, bifascicular heart block, and prolonged QT intervals; they are at higher risk for arrhythmias. (Roose et al., 1987). Patients with preexisting hypotension, impaired left ventricular functioning, or bundle branch block are at risk for orthostatic hypotension with tricyclic use (Rizos, Sargenti, & Jeste, 1988). Tricyclics may also exacerbate congestive heart failure in patients with very low cardiac output (Stoudemire & Moran, 1998). Older medical patients with glaucoma or prostatic hypertrophy should be monitored carefully while on anticholinergic tricyclics.

Increased age correlates with elevated serum levels of a given dose of the tertiary TCAs amitriptyline and imipramine. On the other hand, metabolism of the secondary TCAs demethylated nortriptyline and desipramine are less affected by age than the TCAs discussed here (Nies et al., 1977). Therefore, nortriptyline and desipramine are preferred because of their lower propensity to cause adverse side effects.

Monoamine Oxidase Inhibitors (MAOIs)

MAOIs are effective in anxiety disorders like panic and agoraphobia. However, the side effects and dietary restrictions that accompany MAOIs make use of these medications more problematic in older medical patients. MAOIs should be used with caution in this population because of their effects on blood pressure. Sudden hypotensive episodes observed in patients on MAOIs can be particularly dangerous in geriatric patients due to the risk of falls. Hypertensive crises may be precipitated by interactions with other drugs such as phenylpropanolamine, pseudoephedrine, and certain foods like aged cheese, cured meat, wine or beer, and soy sauce. Meperidine (demerol) is an absolute contraindication with MAOIs as it can cause a fatal reaction. In diabetic older patients, there is an increased risk of weight gain and carbohydrate craving. Bleeding problems may occur in patients on MAOIs and anticoagulants like warfarin.

Selective Sertotonin-Reuptake Inhibitors (SSRIs)

Given their efficacy and favorable side effect profile, the SSRIs are a preferred choice in treating anxiety in older patients with medical disorders. There is usually no significant withdrawal or dependence with SSRIs. These medications may be given in a single daily dose to maximize compliance. However, SSRIs, especially fluoxetine, may be activating and may cause increased anxiety. Some anxious geriatric patients who already tend to overendorse somatic symptoms may find the gastrointestinal distress commonly associated with SSRI use intolerable. Therefore, older patients should be started on these medications at minuscule daily doses.

There are various drug interactions with SSRIs that must be taken into account before prescribing to older medical patients. For example, fluvoxamine was found to increase warfarin concentrations by 60% and increase propranolol (a commonly used beta blocker) levels fivefold (Benfield & Ward, 1986). Gidal and colleagues reported an increase in carbamazepine (an anticonvulsant often used as a mood stabilizer) levels with fluoxetine (Gidal et al., 1993). Extrapyramidal (Parkinsonian-like) side effects are most likely to occur in older patients, especially those with preclinical Parkinson's disease (Dave, 1994). Similarly, SSRIs may exacerbate symptoms of preexisting Parkinson's (Steur, 1993).

Atypical Antidepressants

Fewer studies have been conducted on the newer atypical antidepressants. Bupropion appears to have minimal effects on the cardiovascular system and does not normally cause orthostatic hypotension. However, it may cause hypertension (Cooper, 1988). It also lowers the threshold for seizures and should be avoided in patients with epilepsy or a history of head trauma. Nefazodone causes some mild orthostatic hypotension (Taylor et al., 1995). In older patients the sedative qualities of mirtazapine may be useful for the treatment of anxiety. However, in older patients, mirtazapine shows reduced clearance and was associated with dry mouth and dizziness (Halikas, 1995; Stoudemire, 1996). Venlafaxine looks promising in the treatment of some forms of anxiety (Feighner, Entsuah, & McPherson, 1998). In general Venlafaxine is well tolerated by older patients, although there is a risk of hypertension especially in patients with preexisting problems and who are taking higher dosages (Feighner, 1995).

Miscellaneous Drugs

Neuroleptics. Clinical experience suggests that low-dose, high-potency traditional neuroleptics like haloperidol can be modestly effective in anxiety and agitation associated with dementia in older patients. These types of medications may be more appropriate for psychotic symptoms than behavioral problems. These neuroleptics can cause anticholinergic effects, orthostatic hypotension, sedation, further cognitive decline, and extrapyramidal reactions including late-developing adverse effects like tardive dyskinesia. Atypical neuroleptics, such as olanzapine or risperidone, have a lower incidence of extrapyramidal reactions, sedation, and anticholinergic symptoms and may be preferable in the older patient population. Risperidone, however, should be used cautiously in older people as it can cause hypotension even at low doses. Neuroleptics for anxiety and agitation associated with dementia should be used for brief periods, with frequent evaluations and documentation of need. In general, because older and medically ill patients are more sensitive than younger patients to a given oral dose of these drugs, neuroleptics should be used in low doses and with extreme caution.

Anticonvulsants. Valproate and carbamazapine show a moderate degree of effectiveness in the treatment of anxiety and agitation associated with dementia in older patients. However, carbamazepine has a high risk of potential toxicity (ataxia, sedation, diplopia) and may not be desirable for use in older patients. In medically ill geriatric patients even greater caution should be used because of possible hematological and cardiac toxicity. For patients with preexisting liver disease, both valproate and carbamazepine would be relatively contraindicated. However, valproate in older patients (without liver disease) appears to be safe (Puryear, Kunik, & Workman, 1995).

Beta Blockers. Reports suggest that beta blockers may be efficacious for some geriatric patients with anxiety and agitation. Propranolol showed a moderate degree of success in several studies, but the risk of hypotension, sedation, and decreased cardiac output is high in older patients. These medications should not be given to older patients with cardiovascular disorder or chronic obstructive pulmonary disease (especially asthma) (Salzman, Satlin & Burrows, 1998).

Antihistamines. Antihistamines like hydroxyzine and diphenhydramine hydrochloride are sometimes used in clinical settings to manage mild anxiety in spite of the lack of studies demonstrating efficacy or safety. Prolonged use of these medications in older patients, however, is fraught with potential problems such as anticholinergic effects, excessive sedation, confusion, and disorientation.

ISSUES FOR FUTURE RESEARCH

Despite the extensive needs for managing anxiety in older medically ill patients, there remains a dearth of controlled studies examining the treatment of anxiety in this population. Conducting controlled clinical trials of both psychosocial and pharmacological treatments in older adults is the first priority. In conjunction with this goal, systematic examination of several components of psychosocial treatment is needed, including modifications helpful for older adults, individual and group formats, the treatment of specific anxiety disorders, and short-term interventions for acute anxiety symptoms in medical settings. On the pharmacological front, research studies need to establish not only the efficacy of different drugs in older adult populations, but also safe and standardized guidelines for the use of anti-anxiety drugs in older patients and their use in medically ill patients taking numerous other drugs. The efficacy of treatments that combine psychotherapy and pharmacotherapy also deserves investigation. Only after consideration of these issues can we empirically address the management of anxiety in medically ill geriatric patients and the specific concerns inherent in this group.

REFERENCES

Alexopoulos, G. S. (1991). Anxiety and depression in the elderly. In C. Salzman & B. D. Lebowitz (Eds.), *Anxiety in the elderly: Treatment and research* (pp. 131–150). New York: Springer.

American Psychiatric Association. (1994). *Diagnostic and statistical manual of mental disorders* (4th ed.). Washington, DC: Author.

Bandura, A. (1969). *Principles of behavior modification.* New York: Holt, Rinehart and Winston.

Barlow, D. H., & Cerny, J. A. (1988). *Psychological treatment of panic.* [Treatment Manuals for Practitioners Series.] New York: Guilford Press.

Beardsley, R. S., Larson, D. B., Burns, B. J., Thompson, J. W., & Kamerow, D. B. (1989). Prescribing of psychotropics in elderly nursing home patients. *Journal of the American Geriatric Society, 37*(4), 327–330.

Beck, A. T., Emery, G., & Greenberg, R. L. (1985). *Anxiety disorders and phobias: A cognitive perspective.* New York: Basic Books.

Beck, A. T., Epstein, N., Brown, G., & Steer, R. (1988). An inventory for measuring clinical anxiety: Psychometric properties. *Journal of Consulting and Clinical Psychology, 56*(6), 893–897.

Beck, J. G., & Stanley, M. A. (1997). Anxiety disorders in the elderly: The emerging role of behavior therapy. *Behavior Therapy, 28*(1), 83–100.

Beck, J. G., Stanley, M. A., & Zebb, B. J. (1995). Psychometric properties of the Penn State Worry Questionnaire in older adults. *Journal of Clinical Geropsychology, 1*(1) 33–42.

Beck, J. G., Stanley, M. A., & Zebb, B. J. (1996). Characteristics of generalized anxiety disorder in older adults: A descriptive study. *Behavior Research and Therapy, 34*(3), 225–234.

Beitman, B. D., Mukerji, V., Alpert, M., & Peters, J. C. (1990). Panic disorder in cardiology patients. *Psychiatric Medicine, 8*(2), 67–81.

Ben-Arie, O., Swartz, L., & Dickman, B. J. (1987). Depression in the elderly living in the community: Its presentation and features. *British Journal of Psychiatry, 150,* 169–174.

Benfield, P., & Ward, A. (1986). Fluvoxamine: A review of its pharmacodynamic and pharmacokinetic properties, and therapeutic efficacy in depressive illness. *Drugs, 32*(4), 313–334.

Bernstein, D. A., & Borkovec, T. D. (1973). *Progressive relaxation: A manual for the helping professions.* Champaign, IL: Research Press.

Breitbart, W., & Jacobsen, P. B. (1996). Psychiatric symptom management in terminal care. *Clinics in Geriatric Medicine, 12*(2), 329–347.

Brown, C., Schulberg, H. C., Madonia, M. J., Shear, M. K., & Houck, P. R. (1996). Treatment outcomes for primary care patients with major depression and lifetime anxiety disorders. *American Journal of Psychiatry, 153*(10), 1293–1300.

Carter, C. S., Servan-Schreiber, D., & Perlstein, W. M. (1997). Anxiety disorders and the syndrome of chest pain with normal coronary arteries: Prevalence and pathophysiology. *Journal of Clinical Psychiatry, 58* (suppl. 3), 70–75.

Clark, D. M., Salkovskis, P. M., Chalkley, A. J. (1985). Respiratory control as a treatment for panic attacks. *Journal of Behavior Therapy and Experimental Psychiatry, 16,* 23–30.

Cooper, E. S. (1988). Effective control of hypertension. *Mayo Clinic Proceedings, 63*(7), 732–735.

Dave, M. (1994). Fluoxetine-associated dystonia [letter]. *American Journal of Psychiatry, 151*(1), 149.

Davis, G. C., & Breslau, N. (1994). Post-traumatic stress disorder in victims of civilian trauma and criminal violence. *Psychiatric Clinics of North America, 17*(2), 289–299.

DeBerry, S. (1982). The effects of meditation-relaxation on anxiety and depression in a geriatric population. *Psychotherapy: Theory, Research, and Practice, 19,* 512–521.

DeBerry, S., Davis, S., & Reinhard, K. E. (1989). A comparison of meditation-relaxation and cognitive-behavioral techniques for reducing anxiety and depression in a geriatric population. *Journal of Geriatric Psychiatry, 22,* 231–247.

Derogatis, L. R. (1983). *SCL-90-R. Administration, scoring and procedures manual-II.* Baltimore, MD: Clinical Psychometric Research.

Derogatis, L. R., Morrow, G. R., Fetting, J., Penman, D., Piasetsky, S., Schmale, A. M., Henrichs, M., & Carnicke, C. L., Jr. (1983). The prevalence of psychiatric disorders among cancer patients. *JAMA, 249*(6), 751–757.

DeRubeis, R. J., & Crits-Christoph, P. (1998). Empirically supported individual and group psychological treatments for adult mental disorders. *Journal of Consulting Clinical Psychology, 66*(1), 37–52.

Feighner, J. P. (1995). Cardiovascular safety in depressed patients: Focus on venlafaxine. *Journal of Clinical Psychiatry, 56*(12), 574–579.

Feighner, J. P., Entsuah, A. R., & McPherson, M. K. (1998). Efficacy of once-daily venlafaxine extended release (XR) for symptoms of anxiety in depressed outpatients. *Journal of Affective Disorders, 47,* 55–62.

Flint, A. J. (1994). Epidemiology and comorbidity of anxiety disorders in the elderly. *American Journal of Psychiatry, 151*(5), 640–649.

Foley, D. J., Monjan, A. A., Brown, S. L., Simonsick, E. M., Wallace, R. B., & Blazer, D. G. (1995). Sleep complaints among elderly persons: An epidemiologic study of three communities. *Sleep, 18*(6), 425–432.

Folks, D. G., & Fuller, W. C. (1997). Anxiety disorders and insomnia in geriatric patients. *Psychiatric Clinics of North America, 20*(1), 137–164.

Frank, E., Prigerson, H. G., Shear, M. K., & Reynolds, C. F., III. (1997). Phenomenology and treatment of bereavement related distress in the elderly. *International Clinical Psychopharmacology, 12* (suppl. 7), S25–S29.

Gammans, R. E., Westrick, M. L., Shea, J. P., Mayol, R. F., & LaBudde, J. A. (1989). Pharmacokinetics of buspirone in elderly subjects. *Journal of Clinical Pharmacology, 29*(1), 72–78.

Garner, S. J., Eldridge, F. L., Wagner, P. G., & Dowell, R. T. (1989). Buspirone, an anxiolytic drug that stimulates respiration. *American Review of Respiratory Diseases, 139*(4), 946–950.

Gidal, B. E., Anderson, G. D., Seaton, T. L., Miyoshi, H. R., & Wilenksy, A. J. (1993). Evaluation of the effect of fluoxetine on the formation of carbamazepine epoxide. *Therapeutic Drug Monitoring, 15*(5), 405–409.

Halikas, J. A. (1995). Org 3770 (mirtazapine) versus trazodone: A placebo controlled trial in depressed elderly patients. *Human Psychopharmacology, 10*, S125–S133.

Hamilton, M. (1959). The assessment of anxiety scales by rating. *British Journal of Medical Psychology, 32*, 50–55.

Heimberg, R. G. (1989). Cognitive and behavioral treatments for social phobia: A critical analysis. *Clinical Psychology Review, 9*, 107–128.

Heimberg, R., & Barlow, D. (1991). New developments in cognitive-behavioral therapy for social phobia. *Journal of Clinical Psychiatry, 52*(11), 21–30.

Hocking, L. B., & Koenig, H. G. (1995). Anxiety in medically ill older patients: A review and update. *International Journal of Psychiatry in Medicine, 25*(3), 221–238.

Holland, J. C. (1989). Anxiety and cancer: The patient and family. *Journal of Clinical Psychiatry, 50*, 20–25.

Kabacoff, R. I., Segal, D. L., Hersen, M., & Van Hasselt, V. B. (1997). Psychometric properties and diagnostic utility of the Beck Anxiety Inventory and the State-Trait Anxiety Inventory with older adult psychiatric outpatients. *Journal of Anxiety Disorders, 11*(1), 33–47.

Karajgi, B., Rifkin, A., Doddi, S., & Kolli, R. (1990). The prevalence of anxiety disorders in patients with chronic obstructive pulmonary disease. *American Journal of Psychiatry, 147*(2), 200–201.

Kilborn, L. C., & Labbe, E. E. (1990). Magnetic resonance imaging scanning procedures: Development of phobic response during scan and at one-month follow-up. *Journal of Behavioral Medicine, 13*(4), 391–401.

Kutz, I., Shabtai, H., Solomon, Z., Neumann, M., & David, D. (1994). Post-traumatic stress disorder in myocardial infarction patients: Prevalence study. *Israel Journal of Psychiatry and Related Sciences, 31*(1), 48–56.

Lindesay, J. (1991). Phobic disorders in the elderly. *British Journal of Psychiatry, 159*, 531–541.

Lindesay, J., Briggs, K., & Murphy, E. (1989). The Guy's/Age Concern survey. Prevalence rates of cognitive impairment, depression and anxiety in an urban elderly community. *British Journal of Psychiatry, 155*, 317–329.

Marks, I. (1997). Behaviour therapy for obsessive-compulsive disorder: A decade of progress. *Canadian Journal of Psychiatry, 42*(10), 1021–1027.

Marks, I. M., & Mathews, A. M. (1979). Brief standard self-rating for phobic patients. *Behaviour Research and Therapy, 17*(3) 263–267.

Meyer, B. R. (1982). Benzodiazepines in the elderly. *Medical Clinics of North America, 66*(5), 1017–1035.

Meyer, T. J., Miller, M. L., Metzger, R. L., & Borkovec, T. D. (1990). Development and validation of the Penn State Worry Questionnaire. *Behaviour Research and Therapy, 28*(6), 487–495.

Moffatt, F., Mohr, C., & Ames, D. (1995). A group therapy programme for depressed and anxious elderly inpatients. *International Journal of Geriatric Psychiatry, 10*(1), 37–40.

Mumford, E., Schlesinger, H. J., & Glass, G. V. (1982). The effect of psychological intervention on recovery from surgery and heart attacks: An analysis of the literature. *American Journal of Public Health, 72*(2), 141–151.

National Center for Health Statistics. (1987). Current estimates from the National Health Interview Survey: *Vital and Health Statistics 1987*, No. 10, in *Aging America: Trends and Projections, 1986–1987* (p. 164). Washington, DC: U.S. Government Printing Office.

Nies, A., Robinson, D. S., Friedman, M. J., Green, R., Cooper, T. B., Ravaris, C. L., & Ives, J. O. (1977). Relationship between age and tricyclic antidepressant plasma levels. *American Journal of Psychiatry, 134*(7), 790–793.

Öst, L. G. (1989). One-session treatment for specific phobias. *Behaviour Research and Therapy, 27*(1), 1–7.

Prigerson, H. G., Shear, M. K., Newsom, J. T., Frank, E., Reynolds, C. F., III, Maciejewski, P. K., Houck, P. R., Bierhals, A. J., & Kupfer, D. J. (1996). Anxiety among widowed elders: Is it distinct from depression and grief? *Anxiety, 2*(1), 1–12.

Puryear, L. J., Kunik, M. E., & Workman, R., Jr. (1995). Tolerability of divalproex sodium in elderly psychiatric patients with mixed diagnoses. *Journal of Geriatric Psychiatry and Neurology, 8*(4), 234–237.

Rathus, J. H., & Sanderson, W. C. (1996). Cognitive behavioral treatment of panic disorder in elderly adults: Two case studies. *Journal of Cognitive Psychotherapy, 10*(4), 271–280.

Rizos, A. L., Sargenti, C. J., & Jeste, D. V. (1988). Psychotropic drug interactions in the patient with late-onset depression or psychosis. Part 2. *Psychiatric Clinics of North America, 11*(1), 253–277.

Roose, S. P., Glassman, A. H., Giardina, E. G., Walsh, B. T., Woodring, S., & Bigger, J. T. (1987). Tricyclic antidepressants in depressed patients with cardiac conduction disease. *Archives of General Psychiatry, 44*(3), 273–275.

Sallis, J. F., Lichstein, K. L., Clarson, A. D., Staligaitis, S., & Campbell, M. (1983). Anxiety and depression management for the elderly. *International Journal of Behavioral Geriatrics, 1*, 3–12.

Salzman, C., Satlin, A., & Burrows, A. B. (1998). Geriatric psychopharmacology. In A. F. Schatzberg & C. B. Nemeroff (Eds), *Textbook of psychopharmacology* (2d ed.) (pp. 961–977). Washington, DC: American Psychiatric Press.

Sapolsky, R. M. (1994). *Why zebras don't get ulcers.* New York: Freeman.

Scogin, F., Rickard, H. C., Keith, S., Wilson, J., & McElreath, L. (1992). Progressive and imaginal relation training for elderly persons with subjective anxiety. *Psychology and Aging, 7*, 418–424.

Sheikh, J. I. (1991). Anxiety rating scales for the elderly. In C. Salzman & B. D. Lebowitz (Eds.), *Anxiety in the elderly: Treatment and research* (pp. 251–265). New York: Springer.

Sheikh, J. I. (1996). Anxiety disorders. In J. Sadavoy, L. W. Lazarus, L. F. Jarvik, & G. T. Grossberg (Eds.), *Comprehensive review of geriatric psychiatry—II* (2d ed.) (pp. 615–636). Washington, DC: American Psychiatric Press.

Sheikh, J. I., & Cassidy, E. L. (in press). Treatment of anxiety disorders in the elderly: Issues and strategies. *Journal of Anxiety Disorders.*

Sheikh, J., & Salzman, C. (1995). Anxiety in the elderly: Course and treatment. *Psychiatric Clinics of North America, 18*(4), 871–883.

Sherman, P. W. (1972). Real life exposure as a primary therapeutic factor in desensitization treatment of fear. *Journal of Abnormal Psychology, 79*, 19–28.

Snell, F. I., & Padin-Rivera, E. (1997). Post-traumatic stress disorder and the elderly combat veteran. *Journal of Gerontological Nursing, 23*(10), 13–19.

Spielberger, C. D., Gorsuch, R. C., & Lushene, R. E. (1970). *Manual for the State-Trait Anxiety Inventory.* Palo Alto, CA: Consulting Psychologists Press.

Stanley, M. A., Beck, J. G., & Glassco, J. D. (1996). Treatment of generalized anxiety in older adults: A preliminary comparison of cognitive-behavioral and supportive approaches. *Behavior Therapy, 27*(4), 565–581.

Stanley, M. A., Beck, J. G., & Zebb, B. J. (1996). Psychometric properties of four anxiety measures in older adults. *Behaviour Research and Therapy, 34*(10), 827–838.

Steer, R. A., Willman, M., Kay, P. A. J., & Beck, A. T. (1994). Differentiating elderly medical and psychiatric outpatients with the Beck Anxiety Inventory. *Assessment, 1*(4), 345–351.

Stein, M. B., Heuser, I. J., Juncos, J. L., & Uhde, T. W. (1990). Anxiety disorders in patients with Parkinson's disease. *American Journal of Psychiatry, 147,* 200–201.

Steur, E. N. (1993). Increase of Parkinson disability after fluoxetine medication. *Neurology, 43*(1), 211–213.

Stewart, R. B., May, F. E, Moore M. T., & Hale W. E. (1989). Changing patterns of psychotropic drug use in the elderly: A five-year update. *Annual Pharmacotherapy, 23*(7–8), 610–613.

Stoudemire, A. (1996). Epidemiology and psychopharmacology of anxiety in medical patients. *Journal of Clinical Psychiatry, 57* (suppl. 7), 64–72, 73–75.

Stoudemire, A., & Moran, M. G. (1998). Psychopharmacology in the medically ill patient. In A. F. Schatzberg & C. B. Nemeroff (Eds.), *Textbook of psychopharmacology* (2d ed.) (pp. 931–959). Washington, DC: American Psychiatric Press.

Strain, J. J., Liebowitz, M. R., & Klein, D. F. (1981). Anxiety and panic attacks in the medically ill. *Psychiatric Clinics of North America, 4*, 333–348.

Sunderland, T., Lawlor, B. A., Martinez, R. A., & Mochan, S. E. (1991). Anxiety in the elderly: Neurobiological and clinical interface. In C. Salzman & B. D. Lebowitz (Eds.), *Anxiety in the elderly: Treatment and research* (pp. 105–129). New York: Springer.

Swales, P. J., Solfvin, J. F., & Sheikh, J. I. (1996). Cognitive-behavioral therapy in older panic disorder patients. *American Journal of Geriatric Psychiatry, 4*, 46–60.

Taylor, D. P., Carter, R. B., Eison, A. S., Mullins, U. L., Smith, H. L., Torrente, J. R., Wright, R. N., & Yocca, F. D. (1995). Pharmacology and neurochemistry of nefazodone, a novel antidepressant drug. *Journal of Clinical Psychiatry, 56* (suppl. 6), 3–11.

von Moltke, L. L., Greenblatt, D. J., Schmider, J., Harmatz, J. S., & Shader, R. I. (1995). Metabolism of drugs by cytochrome P450 3A isoforms: Implications for drug interactions in psychopharmacology. *Clinical Pharmacokinetics, 29* (suppl. 1), 33–43.

Wands, K., Merskey, H., Hachinski, V. C., Fisman, M., Fox, H., & Boniferro, M. (1990). A questionnaire investigation of anxiety and depression in early dementia. *Journal of the American Geriatric Society, 38*(5), 535–538.

Wells, K. B., Golding, J. M., & Burnam, M. A. (1988). Psychiatric disorder and limitations in physical functioning in a sample of the Los Angeles general population. *American Journal of Psychiatry, 145*(6), 712–717.

Wetherell, J. L., & Arean, P. A. (1997). Psychometric evaluation of the Beck Anxiety Inventory with older medical patients. *Psychological Assessment, 9*(2), 136–144.

White, R. J., Rudkin, S. T., Ashley, J., Stevens, V. A., Burrows, S., Pounsford, J. C., Cratchley, G., & Ambler, N. R. (1997). Outpatient pulmonary rehabilitation in severe chronic obstructive pulmonary disease. *Journal of the Royal College of Physicians of London, 31*(5), 541–545.

Wise, M. G., & Griffies, W. S. (1995). A combined treatment approach to anxiety in the medically ill. *Journal of Clinical Psychiatry, 56* (suppl. 2), 14–19.

Wisocki, P. A., Handen, B., & Morse, C. K. (1986). The Worry Scale as a measure of anxiety among the elderly: A clinical comment. *Clinical Gerontologist, 4*(3), 50–52.

CHAPTER 11

PSYCHOLOGICAL FACTORS AND IMMUNITY IN HIV INFECTION: Stress, Coping, Social Support, and Intervention Outcomes

Susan Kennedy

The relationships among psychological variables, changes in immune and endocrine function, and possible health outcomes have long been of interest to researchers and practitioners. It has been only recently, however, that these complex relationships have begun to be more clearly understood. There is now substantial evidence that cells of the immune system interact with the nervous and endocrine systems (e.g., Ader, Felten, & Cohen, 1991). For example, lymphocytes possess receptor sites for a number of neurotransmitters and neuroendocrine substances, respond to signals from the brain, and relay information back to the nervous and endocrine systems (Ader, Felten, & Cohen, 1991; Blalock, 1989; Blalock, Bost, & Smith, 1985; Carr & Blalock, 1989; Felten et al., 1985). It is believed that psychological factors may have effects on immune function through these neuroimmune-endocrine pathways.

To explore the possible immune effects of psychological factors in humans, early work in psychoneuroimmunology examined changes in immune responses in healthy individuals experiencing stressful life events. A number of stressful events, including marital disruption, bereavement, and care giving, were shown to have negative effects on several immune measures (Bartrop et al., 1977; Kiecolt-Glaser, Fisher, et al., 1987; Kiecolt-Glaser, Glaser, et al., 1987; Kiecolt-Glaser et al., 1988; Schleifer et al., 1983).

In more recent studies investigating possible health consequences of stressful experiences, healthy medical students who reported higher stress levels during academic examinations were slower to produce antibody to a hepatitis B vaccine (Glaser et al., 1992). In addition, elderly adults providing care for a spouse with Alzheimer's disease were impaired in their antibody response to an influenza virus vaccine relative to a well-matched group of comparison subjects (Kiecolt-Glaser et al., 1996). Moreover, the stress associated with care giving has been found to significantly impair the healing of an experimentally induced wound in a group of 13 elderly women (Kiecolt-Glaser et al., 1995). Collectively these studies suggest that in otherwise healthy individuals, stressful life events may have health-related outcomes, including increased susceptibility to infectious disease or more prolonged recovery times from injury or surgical procedures (Glaser et al., 1992; Kiecolt-Glaser et al., 1995, 1996).

Further support for possible stress-associated health effects was shown in a series of studies by Cohen and colleagues (Cohen, Tyrrell, & Smith, 1991, 1993). Subjects in these studies who reported higher levels of stress or who were experiencing more stressful events were more likely to develop cold symptoms than individuals reporting lower stress levels. In a later study (Cohen et al., 1997), persons with more social ties (including ties to family and friends, job, and community) were most resistant to developing colds. The importance of healthy social relationships to immune competence and disease progression

Acknowledgments: I wish to express gratitude to Dr. Rob Bonneau for his insightful suggestions and helpful comments on an earlier draft of this manuscript, and to Drs. Ronald Glaser and Janice Kiecolt-Glaser for their continued collegiality, encouragement, and support.

has been widely studied, with social support generally found to be associated with better prognosis of disease outcome in cancer patients (e.g., Levy et al., 1985), healthier immune outcomes in divorced or separated women (Kiecolt-Glaser, Fisher, et al., 1987), and stronger immune responses in a group of current and former elderly caregivers (Esterling, Kiecolt-Glaser, & Glaser, 1996).

The growing evidence that stress might impact on immune function has raised the important question of whether behavioral interventions might be effective in strengthening immune responses in populations with chronic illness. Work with cancer patients by Fawzy and colleagues (Fawzy et al., 1990, 1993) found enhanced immune function in a group of malignant melanoma patients randomly assigned to an intervention program consisting of stress management techniques and coping strategies. The benefits of the intervention were apparent at a 6-year follow-up which indicated lower mortality and lower disease recurrence in the intervention subjects (Fawzy et al., 1993).

Spiegel and colleagues also found beneficial effects of intervention in a group of breast cancer patients. Women in this study who were randomly assigned to the year-long weekly intervention sessions had significantly longer survival times than women in the no-intervention group, and at a 10-year follow-up the only survivors from the study were women who had been members of the intervention group (Spiegel et al., 1989).

The acquired immune deficiency syndrome (AIDS) was first brought to the attention of the public in the early 1980s, as descriptions of rare and debilitating infections and cancers surfaced in a sample of homosexual men. Since that time the human immunodeficiency virus (HIV) has been identified as the etiologic agent of AIDS, and a constellation of symptoms has been described that characterize the illness, including neuronal damage and subsequent dementia, significant weight loss ("wasting"), opportunistic infections, lymphoma, and Kaposi's sarcoma. These symptoms are the result of the profound immunosuppression associated with HIV infection.

Importantly, however, many individuals infected with HIV often remain asymptomatic for a number of years, while others develop symptoms of AIDS more quickly following initial infection (Curran et al.,

1988; Kaplan, Wofsky, & Volberding, 1987; Munoz et al., 1988). The variability in disease progression has prompted a number of researchers to examine the relationships between psychological factors, subsequent immune changes, and health status in HIV-infected individuals. This question is of utmost importance as psychological variables may have the most significant health outcomes in individuals whose immune systems are already compromised, such as HIV-infected persons or persons with AIDS (Kiecolt-Glaser & Glaser, 1987).

This chapter will begin with a brief overview of the immunology of HIV and AIDS. Studies will then be presented that examine the impact of stressful events and coping on immune changes and health status in HIV-infected individuals. The importance of social relationships will then be discussed followed by a discussion of studies that examine the outcomes of behavioral or cognitive interventions in HIV-infected individuals.

IMMUNOPATHOLOGY OF HIV INFECTION/AIDS

The distinguishing immunological parameter associated with the time course of HIV infection is a progressive decline in the number of helper/inducer T-lymphocytes (CD4 cells) (Detels et al., 1987; Fahey et al., 1990). CD4 lymphocytes are critical for a number of important immune functions, including assisting in antibody production from B lymphocytes and stimulating replication of cytotoxic T-lymphocytes and helper/inducer T-lymphocytes by the production of interleukin 2. In addition, CD4 lymphocytes release interferon-gamma, a glycoprotein that facilitates the ability of natural killer (NK) cells to destroy cancer cells and cells that have become infected with virus (Herberman et al., 1982; Whiteside & Herberman, 1994). Significant loss of these cells by HIV infection, therefore, renders the immune system ineffective in protecting against infectious agents and viruses.

In the laboratory, numbers of CD4 cells in a blood sample can be quantified by the use of monoclonal antibodies, which bind to particular molecules on the cell surface, thereby identifying a cell from a population of lymphocytes as a helper/inducer T-lymphocyte, an NK cell, and so on. Numbers of helper/inducer T-lymphocytes in a blood sample are often compared to numbers of suppressor/cytotoxic T-lymphocytes (CD8 cells), cells that regulate the function of helper/inducers and B lymphocytes when their activity is no longer necessary. The ratio of helper to suppressor lymphocytes is sometimes used as an index of overall immune competence (e.g., Herbert & Cohen, 1993; Kennedy, Kiecolt-Glaser, & Glaser, 1988), with low ratios observed in AIDS patients, chemotherapy patients, and others who are immunocompromised and high ratios typical in patients with certain autoimmune diseases.

In addition to quantification of T-lymphocytes, it is also possible to assess the function of these cells by stimulating their proliferation with mitogens, substances thought to stimulate bacteria and viruses found in the environment. Decreased proliferative responses may indicate poorer lymphocyte function (Kennedy, Kiecolt-Glaser, & Glaser, 1988).

Although there are other immune changes that accompany the progression of HIV, the loss of CD4 lymphocytes is generally used as the primary marker of disease status in infected individuals. In fact, the relationship between CD4 cell loss and the appearance of AIDS-related symptoms is well established (e.g., Detels et al, 1987; Fahey et al., 1987; Patarca et al., 1996).

PSYCHOLOGICAL AND PSYCHOSOCIAL INFLUENCES ON HIV PROGRESSION

Stressful Events and Coping Style

The relationships between stressful life events, coping style, immune responses, and HIV progression have been explored by a number of investigators. Although there is some suggestion that psychological factors might have an impact on HIV progression, other studies find little evidence of these relationships.

Learning that one is positive for HIV is likely to be a significant stressor for any individual, and how one copes with HIV infection and probable subsequent development of AIDS may be critical for the rate of progression of the infection. Ironson et al. (1990) found increased anxiety and intrusive thoughts in a sample of homosexual men following notification of their HIV-positive serostatus. However, no differences were found in lymphocyte proliferative responses to mitogens, relative to prenotification baseline, suggesting a "dissociation" between psychological and immune events.

In a subsequent study, plasma cortisol levels were measured in addition to mitogen responses in a larger sample of homosexual men learning of their HIV serostatus (Antoni et al., 1991). Cortisol is an adrenal hormone that is typically elevated in times of distress, emergency, or threat. As expected, seronegative men were less distressed and anxious, had decreased cortisol levels, and increased mitogen responses following notification of antibody status. However, men who learned that they tested positive for HIV also had decreased cortisol levels after notification and showed no changes in mitogen responses from baseline, despite increases in anxiety and distress.

Because HIV-positive individuals show smaller catecholamine responses to stressors relative to HIV-negative individuals (e.g., Kumar et al., 1991), these paradoxical findings may be attributed to an impaired feedback loop from the adrenal gland to the pituitary and hypothalamus that results in lower pituitary-adrenal activity and lower levels of cortisol (Kumar et al., 1991).

The relationship between cognitive processing style and immune function in asymptomatic homosexual men awaiting notification of HIV serostatus was examined by Lutgendorf and colleagues (Lutgendorf, Antoni, Ironson, Klimas, Kumar, et al., 1997). Higher scores on the avoidance scale of the Impact of Events Scale were associated with poorer mitogen responses as well as lower percentages of CD4 lymphocytes. In addition, higher intrusion subscale scores were also predictive of lower CD4 counts. These data suggest that one's particular style of cognitive processing may be an important predictor of subsequent immune changes in individuals with a recent diagnosis of HIV and suggest the need for future efforts aimed at cognitive interventions with these individuals.

One aspect of cognitive processing that has received considerable attention in the literature is attributional style, which refers to how one perceives and designates the causes of events in his or her environment. To explore the possibility that attributional style might be related to immune function and the onset of AIDS in HIV-positive individuals, Segerstrom et al. (1996) obtained CD4 counts from a group of gay men at an initial interview time point and a time point 18 months later. Men who engaged in more internal negative attributions (i.e., those who attributed more negative events to themselves) had a faster decline of CD4 lymphocytes at the 18-month follow-up; there was no effect, however, of attributional style on the subsequent diagnosis of AIDS.

A number of studies have examined the importance of coping style to immune changes in HIV-positive individuals. Goodkin and colleagues (Goodkin, Fuchs, et al., 1992) found that passive coping style was associated with lower total lymphocyte counts and lower CD4 counts. Recognizing the limitations of this study due to the small sample size ($n = 11$), the investigators performed a subsequent study using a larger sample of 62 asymptomatic HIV-positive gay men (Goodkin, Blaney, et al., 1992). Coping strategies were assessed using the Coping Orientations to Problems Experienced (COPE) scale, and blood samples were obtained for quantification of HIV antibody and NK cell function. Greater NK cell cytotoxicity was associated with more active styles of coping. Thus, how one adapts to the stress of a life-threatening illness may be critical for certain aspects of immune function.

Taylor, Kemeny, and colleagues have conducted a series of well-designed studies with large sample sizes examining coping style and adaptation in HIV-positive men and individuals with AIDS (Reed et al., 1994; Taylor et al., 1992). In one study, 550 homosexual men who were aware of their HIV serostatus were given a series of psychological questionnaires that assessed optimism about AIDS, coping, distress levels, and perceived control over AIDS (Taylor et al., 1992). Seropositive men had more AIDS-related optimism than seronegative men; in addition, this optimism was related to active coping style and higher levels of perceived control over AIDS in the HIV-positive group. Although it is surprising that men with a positive serostatus would be more optimistic about AIDS and perceive themselves as having control over AIDS, the researchers note that the "illusion" of optimism in HIV-positive men may serve as a way of coping (Taylor et al., 1992). Although immune measures were not taken in this study, previous work has supported a relationship between active coping style and better NK cell function in HIV-positive men (Goodkin, Fuchs, et al., 1992), and between self-esteem instability and avoidance coping in gay men (Martin & Knox, 1997).

A critical question is the extent to which coping style and adaptation might predict survival time in individuals who have developed full-blown AIDS. This question was explored in a study by Reed et al. (1994). In persons with life-threatening illnesses such as AIDS, the process of accepting one's illness and likely death is typically viewed as both adaptive and necessary (e.g., Kubler-Ross, 1987, as cited in Reed et al., 1994). Curiously, however, realistic acceptance in this study was related to *shorter* survival times and could not be accounted for by other factors, such as CD4 cell count, age, distress level, or drug use. Although speculative, the authors suggest that the effect of realistic acceptance on decreased survival time in this sample may have immunologic correlates involving virus progression. In contrast to these findings, however, Ironson et al. (1994) found that denial of HIV infection was associated with lower mitogenic responses of lymphocytes and greater loss of CD4 cells as well as increased reports of symptoms at a 1-year follow-up.

Not all studies have found associations between psychological factors and immune system changes, however. Kessler et al. (1991) obtained self-reports of stressful events from a sample of HIV-positive gay men and found no relationship between these events and the onset of AIDS-related symptoms, or to numbers of CD4 lymphocytes in the 6 months previous to the time that initial data were obtained.

Similarly, a longitudinal study conducted by Perry et al. (1992) examined the relationships between CD4 cell counts and a number of psychological variables, including anxiety, stressful events, and avoidant/intrusive thoughts about AIDS, in a sample of HIV-seropositive individuals. No relationships were obtained between psychological variables and CD4 counts at the initial time point or at 6- and 12-month follow-up. Finally, Vassend, Eskild, and Halvorsen (1997) found no association between passive coping, anxiety, and CD4 counts in HIV-infected persons.

Interpersonal Relationships: Social Support, Bereavement, and Depression

The importance of interpersonal relationships to health is well recognized. Social support has been found to be predictive of mortality in a group of elderly individuals (Blazer, 1982) as well as being linked to self-reports of physical symptoms in elderly persons (Cohen, Teresi, & Holmes, 1985). Cohen and Wills (1985) describe the effects of social support in terms of providing a "buffer" that might protect an individual from the potentially harmful effects of stress.

Recently the relationship between social support and immune function has been examined. Men and women who were recently divorced or separated and students who reported that they were lonely showed decreased NK cell function, lower percentages of helper T-lymphocytes, decreased mitogen responses of lymphocytes, and a greater incidence of upper respiratory tract infections that limited their daily activities (Kiecolt-Glaser et al., 1984; Kiecolt-Glaser, Fisher, et al., 1987; Kiecolt-Glaser et al., 1988).

However, the mere presence of an individual is not sufficient; rather, the quality of one's relationship with others has been found to be critical. For example, social relationships that are positive are correlated with attenuated endocrine and autonomic indices of stress (Kamarck, Manuck, & Jennings, 1990), while hostile or unstable social relationships are associated with physiological disturbances, including endocrine and immune changes (e.g., Kiecolt-Glaser et al., 1993). Moreover, in a study of divorced and married women, poorer-quality marriages were associated with more impaired immune measures (Kiecolt-Glaser, Fisher, et al., 1987).

Individuals with HIV infection are faced with a number of illness-related stressors that involve coping with the likelihood of their impending death, as well as losing close friends or partners to AIDS. In fact, it is not uncommon for individuals in the gay community to experience numerous losses over time (Dean, Hall, & Martin, 1988). Thus, the question of the relationship of social relationships to immune status, HIV progression, and possible disease outcome is an important one that has been investigated by a number of researchers. Specifically, these studies have focused on the effects of social support, loss, and intimacy.

Evidence of the importance of social support in HIV-infected individuals was provided by Hays, Turner, and Coates (1992). A sample of gay men was studied longitudinally for depression levels and symptoms related to HIV infection. Higher social support satisfaction levels were found to be predictive of lower depression scores 1 year later. Furthermore, a specific type of social support, informational support,

was the best predictor of lower depression scores at the 1-year time point. Informational support may provide the individual with a realistic perspective on the nature of the illness as well as with more practical information, including available medical and personal resources.

Straits-Troster et al. (1994) gathered psychological data from a sample of HIV-positive homosexual men and a group of healthy controls. Blood samples were also obtained for quantification of CD4 lymphocytes. Seropositive men who described themselves as lonely perceived themselves as less competent in initiating social interaction and less competent in providing support to others. In addition, there were differences in CD4 counts between "low lonely" and "high lonely" individuals, with the lonelier HIV-infected men having significantly fewer numbers of CD4 lymphocytes, an effect that was independent of the stage of HIV infection.

Similarly, the beneficial immune consequences of social support were studied in a longitudinal investigation of HIV-infected hemophilic men (Theorell et al., 1995). Subjects in this study were given "availability of attachment" scores (AVAT; Theorell et al., 1995) based on completed questionnaires that assessed sources of emotional support. It was found that subjects with low AVAT scores had faster CD4 cell count declines but only at the 5-year time sample point. At earlier sample points no differences in CD4 counts between low- and high-AVAT subjects were found.

Social support may therefore be an important mediator of immunity in individuals with HIV. In further support of this, the effects of bereavement in HIV-infected individuals who have lost a friend or partner to AIDS have been studied by a number of investigators. Losing a loved one is described as one of the most stressful events that an individual can experience (Holmes & Rahe, 1967). In early studies of immune consequences associated with bereavement, bereaved men whose wives died of an extended bout with breast cancer had significant decreases in mitogen responses of lymphocytes after her death, as compared with prebereavement levels, even though the wife's death was anticipated (Bartrop et al., 1977). Similarly, NK cell activity was found to be impaired in a sample of men during bereavement relative to prebereavement levels (Irwin et al., 1987).

Kemeny et al. (1994) examined the immune correlates in a group of HIV-seropositive and HIV-seronegative homosexual men who had recently lost a close friend to AIDS. No immune differences between the bereaved and nonbereaved men were reported; however, there was a relationship between depressed mood, lower CD4 numbers, and decreased mitogen responses of lymphocytes in the *non*bereaved group, suggesting that depressed mood and grief may be manifested differently in terms of the immune response.

Subsequently, Kemeny and Dean (1995) assessed CD4 cell loss and symptom onset over the course of 3 to 4 years in a group of asymptomatic HIV-positive men who had recently lost a friend to AIDS. Compared to a nonbereaved group of seropositive men, the bereaved individuals were more depressed and had significantly more somatic complaints and cognitive disturbances than nonbereaved men. In addition, bereaved individuals showed a faster decline of CD4 cell numbers, even when a number of potential confounding variables were controlled for (age, drug use, health status at the start of the study). As previously reported by Kemeny (Kemeny et al., 1994), a distinction was found between grief and depression, with depression related to the loss of CD4 lymphocytes,

and grief unrelated to cell loss in the second study (Kemeny & Dean, 1995). Importantly, the differences in CD4 cell decline were not apparent until 2 years following bereavement and remained significantly different between the groups at the 3- to 4-year follow-up (Kemeny & Dean, 1995). These data are shown in Figure 11.1.

A number of researchers have suggested that the level of intimacy within a social relationship may be critical for an individual's psychological well-being (e.g., Gove, Hughes, & Style, 1983; Hobfoll & Lerman, 1988). For instance, spousal relationships characterized by high intimacy levels have been associated with less psychological distress during a period of time when a son or daughter was experiencing a medical problem (Hobfoll & Lerman, 1988), possibly by offering protection against stressor effects (Cohen & Wills, 1985; Miller & Lefcourt, 1983).

The immune effects of losing an intimate partner to AIDS were examined in a group of HIV-positive men by Kemeny and colleagues (Kemeny et al., 1995). Compared to nonbereaved men, bereaved men were found to have significantly higher levels of neopterin in serum samples (an indicator of subsequent AIDS development) as well as lower mitogen responses of lymphocytes. Contrary to what was

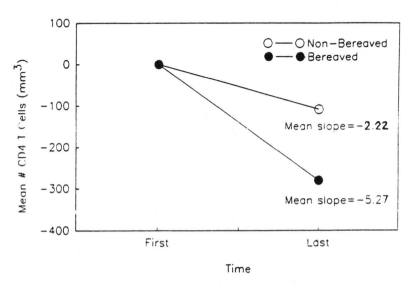

FIGURE 11.1. Mean Slopes of CD4 T Cells over a 3- to 4-Year Follow-up Period in Bereaved and Nonbereaved Men

Source: Kemeny and Dean (1995). Reprinted with permission of Guilford Publications, Inc.

hypothesized, there was no relationship between neopterin levels or decreased mitogenesis and depressed mood. Depressed mood was related to lower CD4 number, however, but only in the nonbereaved group.

Collectively the studies on interpersonal relationships and immune function in HIV-infected individuals are important for several reasons. First, they provide further evidence for the effect of bereavement on immune function found in previous work (Bartrop et al., 1977; Irwin et al., 1987; Schleifer et al., 1983). Secondly, they underscore the importance of obtaining longitudinal data from HIV-infected individuals over relatively long periods of time and at multiple sample points to provide a clearer understanding of time-sensitive immune changes related to bereavement (e.g., Kennedy, Glaser, & Kiecolt-Glaser, 1990; Theorell et al., 1995). Finally, they suggest the need for studies that further investigate the immune correlates and possible health consequences of depression versus grief (Kemeny et al., 1994, 1995).

The reports of relationships between social support, bereavement, and immune function in HIV-infected individuals have not been consistent, however. For example, Kessler et al. (1991) examined symptom onset in HIV-positive men who had been bereaved and found no relationship of bereavement to CD4 count or onset of symptoms. Work by Goodkin and colleagues (Goodkin, Blaney, et al., 1992; Goodkin, Fuchs, et al., 1992) suggested only possible relationships between social support and NK cell activity in an HIV-positive sample but stronger associations between coping style and NK cell function.

INTERVENTION AND STRESS MANAGEMENT IN HIV INFECTION

One of the most exciting and potentially useful areas of psychoneuroimmunology research is that of the immune outcomes associated with behavioral interventions (e.g., Kiecolt-Glaser & Glaser, 1992).

For individuals with chronic illness such as HIV, interventions that might modify immune function with possible outcomes related to the progression of HIV or to symptom onset are of monumental importance. Two interventions that have been investigated in this regard are cognitive-behavioral stress management (CBSM) and aerobic exercise training.

Antoni et al. (1991) randomly assigned asymptomatic gay men to either a CBSM group or to a control group. All men in the study were initially unaware of their HIV serostatus but were notified of their serostatus 5 weeks after the intervention began. Two blood samples, as well as psychological data, were obtained 72 hours prior to notification and 1 week following notification. Men who were in the CBSM group and who were found to be HIV positive had significantly higher numbers of CD4 lymphocytes and NK cells, as well as higher mitogen responses of lymphocytes; no increases in depression scores were found for these men from the first to second sample points. In contrast, men in the control group who were HIV positive were more depressed following serostatus notification, but only slightly impaired in terms of mitogenesis and CD4 cell counts.

More recently, Lutgendorf et al. (1998) randomly assigned symptomatic HIV-positive men to either a 10-week CBSM condition or a no-intervention condition. Men in the CBSM group showed increases in coping strategies and in a number of social support measures after intervention. Of particular importance was the finding that members of the intervention group learned coping strategies that facilitated acceptance of their HIV infection. A previous study by this group (Lutgendorf, Antoni, Ironson, Klimas, Kumar, et al., 1997) found that CBSM was effective in reducing levels of distress and anxiety and in decreasing antibody titers to a human herpes virus, herpes simplex virus-2 (HSV-2). No effect of CBSM on number of CD4 lymphocytes or on other immune measures was found in this study, however.

Thus, CBSM appears to be beneficial in modulating a number of psychological and immune parameters in HIV-infected individuals. Not all studies have reported positive effects of stress management, however. Coates et al. (1989) assessed lymphocyte subset numbers, NK cell activity, and mitogen responsiveness in a sample of HIV-positive men randomly assigned to either 8 weeks of stress reduction training or a control group. Pre- and posttreatment assessments were made with no significant differences found between intervention members and controls on any immune measures.

In addition to CBSM, aerobic exercise training has been investigated as a useful intervention in HIV-infected individuals. LaPerriere et al. (1990) randomly assigned a group of 50 asymptomatic gay men to either an aerobic exercise training group or a control group for 5 weeks prior to notification of HIV serostatus. Immune measures, as well as self-reports of distress and anxiety, were gathered 72 hours prior and 1 week following notification. Men who were HIV positive and who had been given aerobic exercise training were indistinguishable from seronegative men, both on measures of depression and anxiety and in terms of numbers of NK cells at the postnotification sample point. Seropositive men in the control condition, however, were more depressed and anxious and had significant decreases in NK cell numbers following notification of serostatus.

As reviewed by LaPerriere and colleague, however, studies on the effects of exercise intervention and immune changes in HIV infection must be carefully examined in terms of the stage of infection of participants, as studies that report beneficial effects of exercise have typically used subjects in the earlier stages of the infection (LaPerriere et al., 1997).

CONCLUDING COMMENTS

Individuals with HIV infection are faced with a number of potentially stressful events that might influence immunity and, ultimately, disease progression. These include learning of one's seropositive status (e.g., Ironson et al., 1990) and losing friends or partners to AIDS (Kemeny et al., 1994, 1995; Kemeny & Dean, 1995). This chapter has presented findings from a number of studies suggesting that coping style and social relationships may be important modulators of stress-associated immune changes in HIV-positive individuals (e.g., Goodkin, Blaney, et al., 1992; Goodkin, Fuchs, et al., 1992; Hays et al., 1992; Lutgendorf, Antoni, Ironson, Klimas, Fletcher, et al., 1997; Straits-Troster et al., 1994).

However, evidence for these relationships has not been consistently reported in the literature (e.g., Kessler et al., 1991; Perry et al., 1992; Vassend, Eskild, & Halvorsen, 1997). These discrepant findings may be due, at least in part, to important differences in methodology between the studies, including differences in stage of infection at the time of study and the length of time subjects are studied, as well as differences in subject populations used (Kemeny, 1994; Uchino, Cacioppo, & Kiecolt-Glaser, 1996).

The stage of HIV infection must be considered in studies of psychosocial modulation of HIV. This may be most critical when evaluating the effects of interventions (LaPerriere et al., 1997). For example, many studies that have reported beneficial intervention effects in HIV-positive persons have been done during the asymptomatic stage of the illness (e.g., Antoni et al., 1991; LaPerriere et al., 1990). Clearly there is a need for studies similar to that of Lutgendorf et al. (1998) that examine cognitive and behavioral interventions at later stages of HIV infection, particularly once symptoms have begun to appear (Schneiderman et al., 1994).

Not unrelated to this is the inherent value of longitudinal studies. Prospective research designs that follow a cohort of HIV-positive individuals over relatively long time periods may be particularly important in studies of progressive illnesses, including HIV/AIDS (Kemeny, 1994; Theorell et al., 1995; Uchino, Cacioppo, & Kiecolt-Glaser, 1996), especially when one considers that meaningful changes in immunity may occur only over long periods of time in HIV-infected individuals (Kemeny, 1994). The value of longitudinal studies is seen in the study by Theorell et al. (1995), in which immune correlates of social support in HIV-positive men were only seen during the fourth and fifth years of the study, but not in the first 2 years. Studies such as this, therefore, underscore the need to follow subjects with HIV for extended time periods.

Although this chapter has focused primarily on studies that use homosexual men as subjects, HIV infection is certainly not limited to this population. Studies that include a diverse representation of age groups (including children with HIV) and ethnic backgrounds and that examine gender differences are crucial in investigations of psychological influences on HIV, as these factors may be related to differences in rates of HIV progression (e.g., Kemeny, 1994; Schneiderman et al., 1994).

Finally, an important methodological concern in any psychoimmunology study using human subjects is the importance of gathering data from subjects on a number of health-related behaviors, including nutritional status, sleep patterns, and drug use, as all of these may affect immunity and therefore might confound the effects of stress (e.g., Ironson et al., 1994; Kiecolt-Glaser & Glaser, 1988).

The research examining psychological contributions to HIV progression is important and promises to aid in our understanding of the ways in which coping strategies and social support might alter immune function and disease outcome. Future work in this exciting area will continue to elucidate the complex interactions among psychological variables and neuroimmune-endocrine systems, with possible outcomes to pathogenesis and health.

REFERENCES

Ader, R., Felten, D. L., & Cohen, N. (Eds.). (1991). *Psychoneuroimmunology* (2d ed.). San Diego, CA: Academic Press.

Antoni, M. H., Baggett, L., Ironson, G., LaPerriere, A., August, S., Klimas, N., Schneiderman, N., & Fletcher, M. A. (1991). Cognitive-behavioral stress management intervention buffers distress responses and immunologic changes following notification of HIV-1 seropositivity. *Journal of Consulting and Clinical Psychology, 59,* 906–915.

Bartrop, R. W., Lazarus, L., Luckhurst, E., Kiloh, L. G., & Penny, R. (1977). Depressed lymphocyte function after bereavement. *Lancet, 1,* 834–836.

Blalock, J. E. (1989). A molecular basis for bidirectional communication between the immune and neuroendocrine systems. *Physiological Reviews, 69,* 1–32.

Blalock, J. E., Bost, K. L., & Smith, E. M. (1985). Neuroendocrine peptide hormones and their receptors in the immune system: Production, processing and action. *Journal of Neuroimmunology, 10,* 31–40.

Blazer, D. (1982). Social support and mortality in an elderly community population. *American Journal of Epidemiology, 115,* 684–694.

Carr, D. J., & Blalock, J. E. (1989). From the neuroendocrinology of lymphocytes toward a molecular basis of the network theory. *Hormone Research, 31,* 76–80.

Coates, T., McKusick, L., Kuno, R., & Stites, D. P. (1989). Stress reduction training changed number of sexual partners but not immune function in men infected with HIV. *American Journal of Public Health, 79,* 885–887.

Cohen, S., Doyle, W. J., Skoner, D. P., Rabin, B. S., & Gwaltney, J. M. (1997). Social ties and susceptibility to the common cold. *Journal of the American Medical Association, 277,* 1940–1944.

Cohen, S., Teresi, J., & Holmes, D. (1985). Social networks, stress, and physical health: A longitudinal study of an inner-city elderly population. *Journal of Gerontology, 40,* 478–486.

Cohen, S., Tyrrell, D. A. J., & Smith, A. P. (1991). Psychological stress and susceptibility to the common cold. *New England Journal of Medicine, 325,* 606–612.

Cohen, S., Tyrrell, D. A. J., & Smith, A. P. (1993). Negative life events, perceived stress, negative affect, and susceptibility to the common cold. *Journal of Personality and Social Psychology, 64,* 131–140.

Cohen, S., & Wills, T. A. (1985). Stress, social support, and the buffering hypothesis. *Psychological Bulletin, 109,* 5–24.

Curran, J. W., Jaffe, H. W., Hardy, A. M., Morgan, W. M., Selk, R. M., & Dondero, T. J. (1988). Epidemiology of HIV infection and AIDS in the United States. *Science, 239,* 610–616.

Dean, L., Hall, W. E., & Martin, J. L. (1988). Chronic and intermittent AIDS related bereavement in a panel of homosexual men in New York City. *Journal of Palliative Care, 4,* 54–57.

Detels, R., Visscher, B. R., Fahey, J. L., Sever, J. L., Gravell, M., Madden, D. L., Schwartz, K., Dudley, J. P., English, P. A., & Powers, H. (1987). Predictors of clinical AIDS in young homosexual men in a high risk area. *International Journal of Epidemiology, 16,* 271–276.

Esterling, B. A., Kiecolt-Glaser, J. K., & Glaser, R. (1996). Psychosocial modulation of cytokine-induced natural killer cell activity in older adults. *Psychosomatic Medicine, 58,* 264–272.

Fahey, J. L., Giorgi, J. V., Martinez-Maza, O., Detels, R., & Taylor, J. M. G. (1987). Immune pathogenesis of AIDS and related syndromes. *Annals of the Institute Pasteur/Immunology, 138,* 245–252.

Fahey, J. L., Taylor, J. M., Detels, R., Hofmann, B., Melmed, R., Nishanian, P., & Giorgi, J. (1990). The prognostic value of cellular and serologic markers in infection with human immunodeficiency virus Type 1. *New England Journal of Medicine. 322,* 166–172.

Fawzy, F. I., Fawzy, N. W., Hyun, C. S., Elashoff, R., Guthrie, D., Fahey, J., & Morton, D. (1993). Malignant melanoma: Effects of an early structured psychiatric intervention, coping, and affective state on recurrence and survival six years later. *Archives of General Psychiatry, 50,* 681–689.

Fawzy, F. I., Kemeny, M. E., Fawzy, N. W., Elashoff, R., Morton, D., Cousins, N., & Fahey, J. L. (1990). A structured psychiatric intervention for cancer patients: I. Changes over time in immunological measures. *Archives of General Psychiatry, 47,* 729–735.

Felten, D. L., Felten, S. Y., Carlson, S. L., Olschowka, J. A. & Livnat, S. (1985). Noradrenergic sympathetic innervation of lymphoid tissue. *Journal of Immunology, 135,* 755S–765S.

Glaser, R., Kiecolt-Glaser, J. K., Bonneau, R. H., Malarkey, W., Kennedy, S., & Hughes, J. (1992). Stress-induced modulation of the immune response to recombinant hepatitis B vaccine. *Psychosomatic Medicine, 54*, 22–29.

Goodkin, K., Blaney, N. T., Feaster, D., Fletcher, M. A., Baum, M. K., Mantero-Atienza, E., Klimas, N. G., Millon, C., Szapocznik, J., & Eisdorfer, C. (1992). Active coping style is associated with natural killer cell cytotoxicity in asymptomatic HIV-1 seropositive homosexual men. *Journal of Psychosomatic Research, 36*, 635–650.

Goodkin, K., Fuchs, I., Feaster, D., Leeka, J., & Rishel, D. D. (1992). Life stressors and coping style are associated with immune measures in HIV-1 infection: A preliminary report. *International Journal of Psychiatry in Medicine, 22*, 155–172.

Gove, W., Hughes, M., & Style, C. B. (1983). Does marriage have positive effects on the psychological well-being of the individual? *Journal of Health and Social Behavior, 24*, 122–131.

Hays, R. B., Turner, H., & Coates, T. J. (1992). Social support, AIDS-related symptoms, and depression among gay men. *Journal of Consulting and Clinical Psychology, 60*, 463–469.

Herberman, R. B., Ortaldo, J. R., Riccardi, C., Timonen, T., Schmidt, A., Maluish, A., & Djeu, J. (1982). Interferon and NK cells. In T. C. Merigan & R. M. Friedman (Eds.), *Interferons*. London: Academic Press.

Herbert, T. B., & Cohen, S. (1993). Stress and immunity in humans: A meta-analytic review. *Psychosomatic Medicine, 55*, 364–379.

Hobfoll, S. E., & Lerman, M. (1988). Personal relationships, personal attitudes, and stress resistance: Mothers' reactions to their child's illness. *American Journal of Community Psychology, 16*, 565–589.

Holmes, T., & Rahe, R. (1967). The Social Readjustment Rating Scale. *Journal of Psychosomatic Research, 11*, 213–218.

Ironson, G., Friedman, A., Klimas, N., Antoni, M., Fletcher, M. A., LaPerriere, A., Simoneau, J., & Schneiderman, N. (1994). Distress, denial, and low adherence to behavioral interventions predict faster disease progression in gay men infected with human immunodeficiency virus. *International Journal of Behavioral Medicine, 1*, 90–105.

Ironson, G., LaPerriere, A. R., Antoni, M. H., O'Hearn, P., Schneiderman, N., Klimas, N., & Fletcher, M. A. (1990). Changes in immune and psychosocial measures as a function of anticipation and reaction to news of HIV-1 antibody status. *Psychosomatic Medicine, 52*, 247–270.

Irwin, M., Daniels, M., Bloom, E., Smith, T. L., & Weiner, H. (1987). Impaired natural killer cell activity during bereavement. *Brain, Behavior and Immunity, 1*, 98–104.

Kamarck, T. W., Manuck, S. B., & Jennings, J. R. (1990). Social support reduces cardiovascular reactivity to psychological challenge: A laboratory model. *Psychosomatic Medicine, 52*, 42–58.

Kaplan, L. D., Wofsky, C. B., & Volberding, P. A. (1987). Treatment of patients with acquired immunodeficiency syndrome and associated manifestations. *Journal of the American Medical Association, 257*, 1367–1376.

Kemeny, M. E. (1994). Stressful events, psychological responses, and progression of HIV infection. In R. Glaser & J. K. Kiecolt-Glaser (Eds.), *Handbook of human stress and immunity*. San Diego, CA: Academic Press.

Kemeny, M. E., & Dean, L. (1995). Effects of AIDS-related bereavement on HIV progression among New York City gay men. *AIDS Education and Prevention, 7*, 36–47.

Kemeny, M. E., Weiner, H., Duran, R., Taylor, S. E., Visscher, B., & Fahey, J. L. (1995). Immune system changes after the death of a partner in HIV-positive gay men. *Psychosomatic Medicine, 57*, 547–554.

Kemeny, M. E., Weiner, H., Taylor, S. E., Schneider, S., Visscher, B., & Fahey, J. L. (1994). Repeated bereavement, depressed mood, and immune parameters in HIV seropositive and seronegative gay men. *Health Psychology, 13*, 14–24.

Kennedy, S., Glaser, R., & Kiecolt-Glaser, J. K. (1990). Psychoneuroimmunology. In J. T. Cacioppo & L. G. Tassinary (Eds.), *Principles of psychophysiology: Physical, social and inferential elements*. New York: Cambridge University Press.

Kennedy, S., Kiecolt-Glaser, J. K., & Glaser, R. (1988). Social support, stress, and the immune system. In B. R. Sarason, I. G. Sarason, & G. R. Pierce (Eds.), *Social support: An interactional view*. New York: Wiley.

Kessler, R. C., Foster, C., Ostrow, D., Wortman, C., Phair, J., & Chmiel, J. (1991). Stressful life events and symptom onset in HIV infection. *American Journal of Psychiatry, 148*, 733–738.

Kiecolt-Glaser, J. K., Fisher, L., Ogrocki, P., Stout, J. C., Speicher, C. E., & Glaser, R. (1987). Marital quality, marital disruption, and immune function. *Psychosomatic Medicine, 49*, 13–34.

Kiecolt-Glaser, J. K., Garner, W., Speicher, C. E., Penn, G., & Glaser, R. (1984). Psychosocial modifiers of immunocompetence in medical students. *Psychosomatic Medicine, 46*, 7–14.

Kiecolt-Glaser, J. K., & Glaser, R. (1988). Methodological issues in behavioral immunology research with humans. *Brain, Behavior and Immunity, 2*, 67–78.

Kiecolt-Glaser, J. K., & Glaser, R. (1992). Psychoneuroimmunology: Can psychological interventions modulate immunity? *Journal of Consulting and Clinical Psychology, 60,* 569–575.

Kiecolt-Glaser, J. K., Glaser, R., Gravenstein, S., Malarkey, W. B., & Sheridan, J. (1996). Chronic stress alters the immune response to influenza virus vaccine in older adults. *Proceedings of the National Academy of Sciences, 93,* 3043–3047.

Kiecolt-Glaser, J. K., Glaser, R., Shuttleworth, E. C., Dyer, C. S., Ogrocki, P., & Speicher, C. E. (1987). Chronic stress and immunity in family caregivers of Alzheimer's disease victims. *Psychosomatic Medicine, 49,* 523–535.

Kiecolt-Glaser, J. K., Kennedy, S., Malkoff, S., Fisher, L., Speicher, C. E., & Glaser, R. (1988). Marital discord and immunity in males. *Psychosomatic Medicine, 50,* 213–229.

Kiecolt-Glaser, J. K., Malarkey, W. B., Chee, M., Newton, T., Cacioppo, J. T., Mao, H., & Glaser, R. (1993). Negative behavior during marital conflict is associated with immunological down-regulation. *Psychosomatic Medicine, 55,* 395–409.

Kiecolt-Glaser, J. K., Marucha, P. T., Malarkey, W. B., Mercado, A. M., & Glaser, R. (1995). Slowing of wound healing by psychological stress. *Lancet, 346,* 1194–1196.

Kumar, M., Morgan, R., Szapocznik, J., & Eisdorfer, C. (1991). Norepinephrine response in HIV+ subjects. *Journal of AIDS, 4,* 782–785.

LaPerriere, A., Antoni, M. H., Schneiderman, N., Ironson, G., Klimas, N., Caralis, P., & Fletcher, M. A. (1990). Exercise intervention attenuates emotional distress and natural killer cell decrements following notification of positive serologic status for HIV-1. *Biofeedback and Self-Regulation, 15,* 125–131.

LaPerriere, A., Klimas, N., Fletcher, M. A., Perry, A., Ironson, G., Perna, F., & Schneiderman, N. (1997). Changes in CD4+ cell enumeration following aerobic exercise training in HIV-1 disease: Possible mechanisms and practical applications. *International Journal of Sports Medicine, 18,* S56–S61.

Levy, S., Herberman, R., Maluish, A., Schliew, B., & Lippman, M. (1985). Prognostic risk assessment in primary breast cancer by behavioral and immunological parameters. *Health Psychology, 4,* 99–113.

Lutgendorf, S. K., Antoni, M. H., Ironson, G., Klimas, N., Fletcher, M. A., & Schneiderman, N. (1997). Cognitive processing style, mood, and immune function following HIV seropositivity notification. *Cognitive Therapy and Research, 21,* 157–184.

Lutgendorf, S. K., Antoni, M. H., Ironson, G., Klimas, N., Kumar, M., Starr, K., McCabe, P., Cleven, K., Fletcher, M. A., & Schneiderman, N. (1997). Cognitive-behavioral stress management decreases dysphoric mood and herpes simplex virus–type 2 antibody titers in symptomatic HIV-seropositive gay men. *Journal of Consulting and Clinical Psychology, 65,* 31–43.

Lutgendorf, S. K., Antoni, M. H., Ironson, G., Starr, K., Costello, N., Zuckerman, M., Klimas, N., Fletcher, M. A., & Schneiderman, N. (1998). Changes in cognitive coping skills and social support during cognitive behavioral stress management intervention and distress outcomes in symptomatic human immunodeficiency virus (HIV) seropositive gay men. *Psychosomatic Medicine, 60,* 204.

Martin, J. I., & Knox, J. (1997). Self-esteem instability and its implications for HIV prevention among gay men. *Health and Social Work, 22,* 264–273.

Miller, L. C., & Lefcourt, H. M. (1983). The stress buffering function of social intimacy. *American Journal of Community Psychology, 11,* 127–139.

Munoz, A., Carey, V., Saah, A. J., Phair, J. P., Kingsley, L. A., Fahey, J. L., Ginzburg, H. M., & Polk, B. F. (1988). Predictors of decline in CD4 lymphocytes in a cohort of homosexual men infected with human immunodeficiency virus. *Journal of Acquired Immune Deficiency Syndromes, 1,* 396–404.

Patarca, R., Friedlander, A., Harrington, W. J., Cabral, L., Byrnes, J. J., & Fletcher, M. A. (1996). Peripheral blood T cell subsets as prognostic indicators of chemotherapy outcome in AIDS patients with large cell lymphoma. *AIDS Research and Human Retroviruses, 12,* 645–649.

Perry, S., Fishman, B., Jacobsberg, L., & Frances, A. (1992). Relationships over 1 year between lymphocyte subsets and psychosocial variables among adults with infection by human immunodeficiency virus. *Archives of General Psychiatry, 49,* 396–401.

Reed, G. M., Kemeny, M. E., Taylor, S. E., Wang, H-Y., & Visscher, B. (1994). Realistic acceptance as a predictor of decreased survival time in gay men with AIDS. *Health Psychology, 13,* 299–307.

Schleifer, S. J., Keller, S. E., Camerino, M., Thornton, J. C., & Stein, M. (1983). Suppression of lymphocyte stimulation following bereavement. *Journal of the American Medical Association, 250,* 374–377.

Schneiderman, N., Antoni, M., Ironson, G., Klimas, N., LaPerriere, A., Kumar, M., Esterling, B., & Fletcher, M. A. (1994). HIV-1, immunity, and behavior. In R. Glaser & J. K. Kiecolt-Glaser (Eds.), *Handbook of human stress and immunity.* San Diego, CA: Academic Press.

Segerstrom, S. C., Taylor, S. E., Kemeny, M. E., Reed, G. M., & Visscher, B. R. (1996). Causal attributions predict rate of immune decline in HIV-1 seropositive gay men. *Health Psychology, 15,* 485–493.

Spiegel, D., Bloom, J., Kraemer, H., & Gottheil, E. (1989). Effect of psychosocial treatment on survival of patients with metastatic breast cancer. *Lancet, 2,* 888–901.

Straits-Troster, K. A., Patterson, T. L., Semple, S. J., Temoshok, L., Roth, P. G., McCutchan, J. A., Chandler, J. L., Grant, I., and the HIV Neurobehavioral Research Center Group. (1994). The relationship between loneliness, interpersonal competence, and immunologic status in HIV-infected men. *Psychology and Health, 9,* 205–219.

Taylor, S. E., Kemeny, M. E., Aspinwall, L. G., Schneider, S. G., Rodriguez, R., & Herbert, M. (1992). Optimism, coping, psychological distress, and high-risk sexual behavior among men at risk for acquired immunodeficiency syndrome (AIDS). *Journal of Personality and Social Psychology, 63,* 460–473.

Theorell, T., Blomkvist, V., Jonsson, H., Schulman, S., Berntorp, E., & Stigendel, L. (1995). Social support and the development of immune function in human immunodeficiency virus infection. *Psychosomatic Medicine, 57,* 32–36.

Uchino, B. N., Cacioppo, J. T., & Kiecolt-Glaser, J. K. (1996). The relationship between social support and physiological processes: A review with emphasis on underlying mechanisms and implications for health. *Psychological Bulletin, 119,* 488–531.

Vassend, O., Eskild, A., & Halvorsen, R. (1997). Negative affectivity, coping, immune status, and disease progression in HIV infected individuals. *Psychology and Health, 12,* 375–388.

Whiteside, T. L., & Herberman, R. B. (1994). Role of human natural killer cells in health and disease. *Clinical and Diagnostic Laboratory Immunology, 1,* 125–133.

CHAPTER 12

ANXIETY AND CORONARY HEART DISEASE

Ray W. Winters
Neil Schneiderman

The relative contributions of biomedical and psychosocial factors in the etiology and clinical expression of heart disease have long been an issue in behavioral medicine. Studies that have sought to assess the role of psychosocial factors in the disease process have emphasized the importance of risk-augmenting behaviors such as smoking, alcohol consumption, and the Type A behavior pattern, or they have stressed the importance of affective states linked to emotional distress. As pointed out by a number of investigators, these two sets of variables are by no means independent and in fact would be expected to be linked. It is not uncommon, for example, for individuals experiencing high levels of affective distress to engage in behaviors that are dangerous to their health, such as overeating, alcohol consumption, and smoking, all of which have been implicated in myocardial infarction (MI) and cardiac arrhythmias (e.g., Myers & Dewar, 1975). Thus, insights into the links between affective states and behavior patterns can advance our understanding of disease mechanisms.

The aim of this chapter is to clarify the role of anxiety in the etiology of coronary heart disease (CHD) and post-MI morbidity and mortality. Accomplishing this goal depends in large measure upon our understanding of the adaptive functions of anxiety. Anxiety will be viewed from a biobehavioral control systems perspective in which the human organism is considered to be a composite of interrelated feedback-regulated control systems designed to maintain physical and emotional health (Schwartz, 1983; Suls & Fletcher, 1985). According to this perspective, a negative affective state such as anxiety is an element of a negative feedback process.

As an emotional response to person–environment transactions involving threat and uncertainty, anxiety has motivational characteristics in that it engenders coping behaviors. Threat and uncertainty also lead to increases in cardiovascular and neuroendocrine activity that mobilize energy resources required for coping; however, if effective coping does not occur, these cardiovascular/neuroendocrine responses may contribute to atherogenesis and post-MI morbidity and mortality.

Compromised physical and/or emotional health results from disregulation within a biobehavioral control system. When negative emotions such as anxiety are viewed from a control systems perspective, there are two major reasons why disregulation may occur: (1) There is attenuation or distortion of feedback information from the external environment or internal milieu (i.e., the subjective feelings linked to anxiety are suppressed), or (2) there are constraints placed upon the coping behaviors motivated by anxiety. Accordingly, a major thesis of this chapter is that anxiety becomes a risk factor in CHD when an individual is not cognizant of subjective feelings during life situations involving threat and uncertainty or when coping behaviors motivated by anxiety are constrained by life circumstances. The cardiovascular and neuroendocrine responses elicited when this control system is disregulated are thought to contribute to atherogenesis. Similarly, the cardiovascular/neuroendocrine response pattern associated with the threat and uncertainty evoked by acute MI would be particularly detrimental to a compromised myocardium that is vulnerable to insult. Thus, effective management of anxiety following an acute MI is particularly important to post-MI morbidity and mortality.

DEFINING ANXIETY AND CHARACTERIZING ITS FUNCTIONS

Anxiety can be characterized as a state of the central nervous system (CNS) associated with the anticipation of harm or vulnerability in response to perceived threat (Winters, Ironson, & Schneiderman, 1990). Although anxiety is usually considered to be an affective state, it has motivational properties in that it leads to behavioral changes that serve to remove the aversive stimuli that were assessed as posing a threat (Miller, 1951; Mowrer, 1947; Rosen & Schulkin, 1998). There are a variety of coping responses that are motivated by anxiety, including defensive behaviors (the fight/flight response), behavioral inhibition (passive avoidance), goal-directed behavior in which the reinforcer is safety (i.e., active avoidance), and cognitive coping. As an emotional response to perceived threat, anxiety usually leads to changes in subjective feelings, which will be referred to here as the *subjective affective component of anxiety*, and changes in activity in the autonomic nervous system coupled with activation of the hypothamic-pituitary-adrenocortical (HPAC) system—the autonomic and neuroendocrine response to threat—will be referred to as the *peripheral physiological component of anxiety*. The subjective affective component of anxiety, as an emotional experience, varies from one of tension and discomfort in situations in which effective coping responses are available to a sense of helplessness, uncertainty and distress when no clear coping response is available (Winters et al., 1990). The emphasis of most research on the peripheral physiological component of anxiety has been on the cardiovascular and neuroendocrine changes that result from the activation of the sympathetic division of the autonomic nervous system. This response is referred to as *sympathetic arousal,* and it is characterized by increases in heart rate, cardiac output, and blood pressure and the secretion of the catecholamines, norepinephrine and epinephrine, by the medulla of the adrenal gland. The neuroendocrine pathway that mediates the secretion of norepinephrine and epinephrine by the adrenal medulla during sympathetic arousal is referred to as the *sympathoadrenomedullary system (SAM system)*. Activation of the HPAC system, which leads to the secretion of cortisol, is also an important

element of the peripheral physiological component of anxiety (Rosen & Schulkin, 1998).

When the stimuli that pose a threat to an individual can be identified, they usually fall into one of three categories (Gray, 1987): a signal for an impending aversive stimulus (e.g., criticism or other forms of negative feedback), a signal for the withholding of a stimulus that had previously served as a positive reinforcer (e.g., failure at work or loss of a loved one), or a novel stimulus. A key process involved with the perceived threat associated with psychosocial stressors is cognitive appraisal (Lazarus, 1991). The process of cognitive appraisal confers emotional meaning to a particular event or set of circumstances based upon the goals, values, and beliefs of the individual doing the appraising (Lazarus, 1991). Often the terms *ego threat* or *threat to self-esteem* are used by cognitively oriented behavioral scientists (e.g., Lazarus, 1991) to refer to a threat linked to psychosocial stressors.

Engel (1985) points out that it is paramount to delineate coping behaviors when discussing hypothetical constructs, such as anxiety, when those constructs are linked to environmental stressors. As pointed out by Lazarus (1991), this becomes particularly important when discussing anxiety because coping behaviors may not be available. Lazarus uses the term *secondary appraisal* to refer to the cognitive process by which the individual determines coping potential when a negative emotion is evoked. In fact, his definition of anxiety, which is narrower than the one provided in the present chapter, refers to an affective state characterized by uncertainty about the future, ego-threat, and a situation in which no clear coping response is available. These situations require cognitive changes, such as cognitive reappraisal, to mitigate anxiety. Indeed, cognitive coping can be an effective coping response motivated by anxiety.

Anxiety can be a normal reaction to perceived threat and serve as a positive motivating force for adaptive coping responses that allow the individual to escape or avoid noxious stimuli. The increased nonspecific arousal associated with anxiety may also facilitate goal-directed behaviors involving positive reinforcement. Although there are a variety of behaviors (or the inhibition of behaviors) that may be coupled with anxiety, situations involving threat typically lead to sympathetic arousal and the adrenal secretions that result from activation of the HPAC and SAM systems. It is the cardiovascular and/or the neuroendocrine responses to threat that are proposed to have an important role in atherogenesis, morbidity, and mortality following myocardial infarction. It is important to be cognizant of the fact that these responses, which constitute the peripheral physiological component of anxiety, may occur in the absence of the subjective affective component of anxiety. The subjective experience of anxiety is proposed to have a health-promoting function in that it engages cognitive and behavioral coping mechanisms that mitigate affective distress. As a case in point, individuals who show the Type A behavior pattern and who are keenly aware of their own negative affective states, such as anxiety, are thought to be at lower risk for CHD than their less aware Type A counterparts (Suls & Sanders, 1988). Anxiety can only motivate health-promoting behaviors if threatening situations that evoke deleterious cardiovascular/neuroendocrine responses also elicit a subjective (phenomenal) affective state that is negative.

ANXIETY, SYMPATHETIC AROUSAL, AND CARDIOVASCULAR REACTIVITY

Schneiderman (1977) proposed that recurrent activation of the sympathetic nervous system may contribute to atherogenesis because of the hemodynamic disturbances that occur when there are abrupt increases in blood pressure and heart rate. Following this line of thinking, it was suggested (Schneiderman, 1987) that heightened cardiovascular responsivity to psychosocial stressors may be a marker for subsequent development of CHD. This view receives support from research using an animal model for atherogenesis (e.g., Manuck et al., 1989) and studies in humans that have used cardiovascular reactivity to predict the development of atherosclerosis (e.g., Everson et al., 1997).

A number of studies provide evidence for a relationship between anxiety and cardiovascular responsivity for individuals who show situation-specific anxiety. As examples, Glass et al. (1983) observed that individuals who were found to have test anxiety showed increases in heart rate, systolic blood pressure,

and diastolic blood pressure to a Stroop task and a mental arithmetic task. Subjects testing high for social anxiety show significantly higher systolic blood pressure than controls during an impromptu speech (Turner, Beidel, & Larkin, 1986; Beidel, Turner, & Dancu, 1985) and higher heart rate and systolic blood pressure in an opposite-sex social interaction (Beidel, et al., 1985). Situation-specific anxiety is not a necessary requirement for increased cardiovascular reactivity to threat. Matthews, Manuck, and Saab (1986) found that high-anxiety adolescents, as measured by the State-Trait Anxiety Inventory (STAI), showed higher levels of systolic blood pressure prior to public speaking and higher levels of heart rate prior to and after giving the speech than low-anxiety subjects.

If the heightened cardiovascular response to threat contributes to heart disease or the recovery from MI, it should have deleterious effects upon a myocardium that has been compromised by CHD. Indeed, there is evidence that sympathetic arousal affects cardiac functioning in patients with MI. Stressful situations such as public speaking have been found to induce ST-segment depression in patients with CHD (Taggart, Carruthers, & Sommerville, 1973), and even a mild stressor such as a mental arithmetic task can produce ST-segment depression in many (6 of 16) angina and CHD patients (Deanfield et al., 1984). Twelve of the 16 patients in the Deanfield et al. study showed tomographic evidence of ischemia during the mental arithmetic task. Based upon an analysis of evoked hemodynamic changes, these authors suggest that there is a greater reduction in myocardial blood flow during a mild mental stressor than during supine bicycle exercise. Studies using a mental quiz as the psychosocial stressor in patients with angina pectoris (Schiffer et al., 1980) also provide evidence for stress-induced myocardial ischemia.

In general, the heightened sympathetic arousal in response to psychosocial stress involving threat renders the patient with compromised cardiac functioning vulnerable to ischemic and arrhythmic complications (Rozanski, Krantz, & Bairey, 1991; Priori, Zuanetti, & Schwartz, 1988; Naiura & Goldstein, 1992; Verrier & Mittelman, 1997), and it is certainly reasonable to hypothesize that a healthy individual with a heightened sensitivity to threat and/or sympathetic reactivity may be at increased risk for CHD. Several mechanisms for the pernicious effects of heightened sympathetic arousal upon a compromised myocardium have been proposed, including increased platelet aggregation without proportional increases in fibrinolytic activity (e.g., Brezinski et al., 1988), a lower threshold for fibrillation (e.g., Kamarck & Jennings, 1991), increased vascular tone in the coronary arteries (Panza, Epstein, & Quyyumi, 1991), and increased shearing forces within the coronary arteries due to turbulence (e.g., Kamarck & Jennings, 1991).

ANIMAL MODEL OF THREAT AND ATHEROSCLEROSIS

Male cynomolgus monkeys form dominance or status hierarchies when they live in groups, and an animal's rank is based upon his abilities to defeat other group members in fights. There is rather convincing evidence from a series of studies (e.g., Kaplan et al., 1982; Kaplan et al., 1987) that posing a threat to the social standing of dominant animals in this environmental setting contributes to coronary artery atherosclerosis. In a representative study (Kaplan et al., 1982), two groups of 15 monkeys were each subdivided into three 5-member groups; all 30 animals were fed a moderately atherosclerotic diet. The 15 animals in the high-threat condition, referred to as the unstable social condition, were periodically redistributed among the three subgroups over 22 months. Group membership in the stable social condition remained constant for the duration of the experiment. Every time the animals in the unstable social condition were redistributed, there was a threat to the social standing of the more dominant animals; fights occurred, and new status hierarchies were established. The animals were ranked by the experimenters according to the outcome of fights. The results revealed that dominant animals in the unstable social condition (high threat to social status) showed significantly greater coronary artery atherosclerosis than the dominant animals in the stable social group. Their level of coronary atherosclerosis was also significantly higher than that of subordinate animals who were also in the unstable social condition and had experienced roughly the same number of fights and changes in group membership. The atherosclerotic

plaques that developed in the high-threat dominant animals could not be accounted for by total serum cholesterol levels, high-density lipoprotein concentrations, blood pressures, ponderosity, or fasting glucose concentrations.

A subsequent study from the same laboratory (Kaplan et al., 1987) replicated earlier findings and also demonstrated that long-term administration of the beta-adrenergic blocking agent propranolol had an antiatherogenic effect among the high-risk animals (i.e., dominant animals in the unstable social condition). This observation provides support for the view that the development of atherosclerosis was due, at least in part, to the activation of the sympathetic nervous system that occurs when an animal is exposed to psychosocial stressors involving threat. More specifically, the authors suggested that propranolol was protecting against sympathetically mediated hemodynamic disturbances and/or neuroendocrine changes that were contributing to arterial lesions and subsequent plaque formation. Changes in cardiovascular activity that occur during sympathetic arousal lead to arterial flow disturbances, such as sheering stress and turbulence, that may cause injury to the arterial endothelium. Additionally, sympathetic arousal elevates circulating catecholamines, which may also contribute to arterial lesions by influencing the mobilization of lipids and platelet aggregation.

A laboratory stressor, threat of capture, has also been shown to accelerate atherogenesis in cynomolgus monkeys (Manuck et al., 1989). In these studies the experimenter displayed a large "monkey glove" for 15 minutes and made stylized gestures that mimicked the encounters that normally precede capture and physical handling of the animals. Heart rate responsivity to the threat of capture was found to be an excellent predictor for subsequent development of coronary atherosclerosis. Necropsy following this procedure revealed that both male (Manuck, Kaplan, & Clarkson, 1983) and female (Manuck et al., 1989) monkeys that showed the largest increments in heart rate to the laboratory challenge manifested significantly greater coronary artery atherosclerosis (roughly twice the level) than their low heart rate reactor counterparts. High heart rate reactivity was observed among the more aggressive males and less aggressive females, respectively.

ANXIETY AND THE TYPE A BEHAVIOR PATTERN

The Type A behavior pattern is characterized by an extremely high level of competitiveness, an enhanced sense of time urgency, impatience, high achievement motivation, and hostility; individuals showing a relative absence of these behavioral characteristics are classified as Type B. Type A is often assessed by self-report scales such as the Framingham Scale and the Jenkins Activity Scale, but the Structured Interview (SI) is the most widely accepted measure of this behavior pattern (Byrne et al., 1985; Miller et al., 1991). Prospective studies provide evidence that the Type A pattern when coupled with potential for hostility, one of the subcomponents of Type A measured by the SI, is a significant predictor of CHD (Manuck, Kaplan, & Matthews, 1986; Matthews et al., 1977; Williams, Barefoot, & Shekelle, 1985). Potential for hostility is defined in the SI as the disposition to respond to frustration with expressed emotions signifying anger, disgust, resentment, or irritation (Manuck, Kaplan, & Matthews, 1986). The behaviors in the SI considered to reflect a potential for hostility include challenges to the interviewer, argumentative exchanges, rudeness, and making condescending remarks to the interviewer.

The Type A individual places a high premium on achievement and competition, so he or she would be exposed to many situations in life that pose a threat—the potential for failure is always present in a competitive environment. Yet, Type A scores on a self-report measure of anxiety, the STAI, are often not substantially different from scores of normative samples (e.g., Jenni & Wollersheim, 1979; Lobitz & Brammel, 1981). There is, however, some indirect evidence for self-reported anxiety in Type A's. As examples, Dimsdale et al. (1978) found that Type A patients awaiting cardiac catheterization reported a high level of subjective tension which can be taken to mean that they were anxious. Similarly, significant relationships have been found between the Type A behavioral pattern and measures of emotional distress in a sample of healthy Type A's who were free of CHD (e.g., Byrne & Rosenman, 1986; Francis, 1981).

There are a variety of self-report measures of psychosocial distress that can be taken as valid and reliable indices of chronic dysphoria, and it seems reasonable to assume that these measures, to varying degrees, tell us something about how anxious an individual tends to be, at least when assessed by self-report. It is difficult to conceive of many stressful situations in which there is no element of threat and uncertainty about the future. Suls and Wan (1989) performed a meta-analysis of studies that assessed the relationship between the Type A pattern and dysphoria. The measures of Type A examined were the SI and a variety of self-report measures including the Jenkins Activity Scale, the Framingham Scale, the Bortner Scale, and the Adjective Checklist. The results revealed that the Type A pattern is associated with reported feelings of chronic distress when Type A behavior is assessed by self-report measures such as the Jenkins Activity Scale, but not when measured by the SI, on which classification is based on overt behaviors. This is a provocative finding in view of the observation that the SI is a better predictor of CHD than any of the self-report measures (Byrne et al., 1985; Friedman & Booth-Kewley, 1987; Miller et al., 1991).

As pointed out by Suls (1990), the most salient difference between the self-report measures of Type A and the SI is that the self-report measures require that the individual be aware of his or her own competitiveness, hostility, sense of time urgency, and impatience, whereas these characteristics are assessed by nonverbal gestures and speech patterns in the SI. Moreover, the Type A pattern is not a particularly strong predictor of CHD unless the score on the potential for hostility subcomponent of the SI is high (Dembroski et al., 1989). The potential for hostility measure tells us something about interpersonal style, but it does not require that the individual showing the style be aware of it, as would be the case for the self-report measures. More specifically, potential for hostility is an emotional expressive style (Dembroski & Costa, 1987; Friedman & Booth-Kewley, 1987); it says nothing about the feelings that might be coupled with these behaviors.

Suls (1990) infers from the results of his meta-analysis that Type A's who are at the greatest risk for CHD are the ones who are less aware of their own behavior or its causes, and they are less likely to experience the subjective component of negative affective states such as anxiety. Other investigators have made a similar proposal (Herman et al., 1981; Keltikangas-

Järvinen, & Jokinen, 1989). Viewed from a biobehavioral control systems perspective (Schwartz, 1983; Suls & Fletcher, 1985), a negative affective state such as anxiety or anger is a component of a negative feedback mechanism that serves as a monitor of person–environment transactions. If the emotion is intense enough, it motivates health-promoting coping responses. Altering feedback information severely compromises the integrity and effectiveness of a control system. Anxiety serves as a warning signal in situations involving disease-promoting, dysfunctional person–environment transactions, and the attenuation or distortion of this information has long-term negative consequences for health.

As pointed out by Suls (1990), in order to understand the role of negative affective states in the etiology of CHD, it is important to make a distinction between two types of hostility (Costa, McCrae, & Dembroski, 1989). Neurotic hostility is related to anxiety, feelings of resentment, annoyance, and depression, whereas the SI-measured potential for hostility or expressive hostility is a reflection of interpersonal style. Although many people show both types of hostility, an individual's score on one dimension is not a particularly good predictor of his or her score on the other (Costa, McCrae, & Dembroski, 1989). In fact, Musante et al. (1989) reported that in a sample of healthy men, individuals who showed a high score on the measure of potential for hostility did not show the angry feelings that one would expect to be associated with the behaviors displayed. Similar results were reported by Siegman (1989) in angiography patients. Patients showing high levels of expressive hostility showed low levels of negative affect. Moreover, the degree of coronary occlusion in these patients was positively correlated with expressive hostility but negatively correlated with neurotic hostility. The implication of these findings with respect to the Type A behavior pattern as a risk factor for CHD is: Behavior does not predict affect. The fact that a Type A shows a high level of expressive hostility does not mean that he or she feels angry or is experiencing a high level of negative affect. Dissociation between affect and behavior would be a consequence of a control system that is compromised due to attenuation of negative feedback (i.e., a suppression of the subjective experience associated with negative affective emotions such as anger and

anxiety) (Spoont, 1992). According to Suls (1990), Type A's who distort or attenuate this feedback information are at a greater risk for CHD than their more self-aware Type A counterparts, although self-aware Type A's are still at a greater risk for CHD than Type B's (Suls & Sanders, 1988).

A number of studies show that Type A's show exaggerated (relative to Type B's) cardiovascular reactivity to laboratory stressors (Contrada & Krantz, 1988; Harbin, 1989; Houston, 1988; Howard et al., 1990; Sundin et al., 1995); enhanced neuroendocrine responses to psychosocial stressors have also been reported (Harbin, 1989; Williams et al., 1982). The relationship between Type A personality and enhanced cardiovascular/neuroendocrine reactivity is dependent upon the instrument used to assess Type A and is more evident in some cognitive tasks than in others (Harbin, 1989); nevertheless, it appears that Type A's are showing the peripheral physiological component of the emotional response to situations involving threat. Thus, it seems reasonable to hypothesize that there is a dissociation between the subjective affective component and the peripheral physiological component of anxiety in many Type A's, at least when this behavior pattern is measured by an SI.

Findings from several sources support the view that the two components of the anxiety response are dissociated, at least in some Type A's. In an experiment in which Type A's and Type B's were threatened with shock if they made errors on a task, Type A's denied being afraid, although their physiological arousal was higher than that of the Type B's (Pitney & Houston, 1980). In addition, Type A's are known to deny early symptoms of CHD such as chest pains (Matthews et al., 1983; Weidner & Matthews, 1978), and a substantial number of Type A's in coronary care units deny that they have had a heart attack even though there is clear evidence to the contrary (Hackett, Cassem, & Wishnie, 1968).

To summarize, Type A's who show a peripheral physiological response to threat but not the subjective affective component of anxiety (as measured by self-report) are proposed to be at higher risk for CHD than self-aware Type A's. Viewed from a biobehavioral control systems perspective, there is distortion and/or attenuation of feedback information and thus disregulation. Evidence for disregulation is provided by the finding reported by numerous investigators that

Type A's have a proclivity for placing themselves in situations in which they are likely to encounter stressful life events (Byrne, 1981; Dimsdale et al., 1978; Falger, Bressors, & Dijkstra, 1980; Smith & Anderson, 1986). Without the subjective affective component of anxiety there is no motivation for Type A's to engage in coping behaviors that would serve to minimize the threat-evoked cardiovascular/ neuroendocrine hyperactivity that contributes to atherogenesis.

ANXIETY AND RECOVERY FROM MYOCARDIAL INFARCTION

Anxiety is probably the most common immediate affective response to acute MI. Lloyd and Cawley (1982) found that, for patients who reported affective symptoms, 55% of first-time survivors of an MI and 42% of the patients who experienced more than one infarction reported anxiety as their predominant emotional response. Moser and Dracup (1996) report that two-thirds of the acute MI patients they studied showed anxiety levels that were above normal, and the anxiety levels of 26% of this group were equivalent to or higher than those observed in psychiatric inpatients. These types of observations regarding the relationship between acute MI and anxiety have been reported by a number of investigators (e.g., Ben-Sira & Eliezer, 1990; Byrne, 1990a; Crowe et al., 1996; Malan, 1992). Patients suffering from MI are faced with the threat of death, protracted disability, unavoidable dependency upon others, and the possibility that they may never engage in the pleasurable activities to which they are accustomed. An individual's anxiety state subsequent to hospitalization is an important predictor of post-MI mortality (Thomas et al., 1997), in-hospital cardiac complications (Moser & Dracup, 1996), and self-reported physical functioning after catheterization for CHD (Sullivan et al., 1997).

There are a number of physiological changes associated with heightened anxiety that would be expected to impact recovery from MI. Threat leads to the cardiovascular and neuroendocrine changes that occur during sympathetic arousal and activation of the HPAC system. These changes would be particularly deleterious to a compromised myocardium that is vulnerable to insult. In view of the pernicious effects of the peripheral physiological component of

anxiety, one would expect that MI patients would be at a high risk for cardiac complications during recovery. Moser and Dracup (1996) report that patients with high post-MI anxiety levels were 4.9 times more likely to have in-hospital MI complications than their less anxious counterparts. They defined MI complications as reinfarction, new onset ischemia, ventricular fibrillation, sustained ventricular tachycardia, or in-hospital death.

Effective management of anxiety seems to be particularly important after acute MI, and systematic programs that utilize psychological counseling and promote emotional support are routinely offered in a number of hospitals. As pointed out by Schneiderman and Saab (1996), psychosocial interventions are particularly important for acute MI patients because anxiolytic agents often produce sedation without allaying the MI patient's anxiety. Furthermore, anti-anxiety medications frequently lead to physiological complications that may interfere with recovery.

Several outcome studies that have assessed the effectiveness of post-MI treatment programs have been encouraging (e.g., Gruen, 1975; Julian, 1987; Oldenburg & Perkins, 1984). As discussed elsewhere (Byrne, 1990b; Moser & Dracup, 1996), the focus of these programs should be upon the elements of the patient's situation that evoke the peripheral physiological component of the anxiety response. Thus, in addition to providing increased social support, psychosocial interventions should emphasize a reduction in uncertainty and promote coping responses on the part of the patient. Enhancing a patient's feelings of perceived control is particularly important to recovery from a cardiac event such as an MI or coronary bypass surgery (Moser & Dracup, 1995).

ANXIETY AS A RISK FACTOR IN CORONARY HEART DISEASE

Level of anxiety following an MI predicts subsequent arrhythmic and ischemic complications, but unequivocal support for a causal role for anxiety in the pathogenesis of CHD has not been established. Several studies have provided evidence for a relationship between anxiety and CHD, but some have not. Byrne (1979) used Eysenck's Neuroticism Scale to assess state anxiety in patients admitted to a coronary care unit because they reported acute chest pains.

Trait anxiety was found to be significantly higher for patients in which tests established an MI than in those patients for whom an MI could not be confirmed. Similarly, Spielberger and Rickman (1990), in their analysis of studies examining the relationship between anxiety and CHD, conclude that STAI scores of individuals with a history of MI are slightly higher than those of healthy individuals with a similar socioeconomic status. If it is assumed that anxiety is a component of most emotional responses to psychosocial stressors (Byrne & Byrne, 1990), there are findings reported by several investigators that are consistent with the view that anxiety contributes to CHD. A number of studies show a significant correlation between CHD and acute emotional distress (Bianchi, Fergusson, & Walshe, 1978; Spittle & James, 1977) and with chronic signs of emotional distress or anxiety (Eaker, Pinsky, & Castelli, 1992; Friedman & Booth-Kewley, 1987; Gupta & Verma, 1983; Kubzansky et al., 1997; Thiel, Parker, & Bruce, 1973). These observations coupled with those showing a relationship between CHD and state measures of anxiety, including the Byrne (1979) and Spielberger and Rickman (1990) papers discussed here, provide support for the view that anxiety and CHD are causally linked. In contrast, a number of investigators report that coronary atherosclerosis is infrequent in subjects prone to high anxiety states (e.g., Blumenthal et al., 1979; Costa, 1981; DeMaria et al., 1980). Negative findings in these types of studies have led some investigators such as Rosenman (1990) to assert that it is unlikely that anxiety is a risk factor in the pathogenesis of coronary atherosclerosis.

Assertions like Rosenman's make sense if we consider how anxiety and its functions have been characterized in the present chapter. Viewed from our perspective, there are a number of reasons why it will be difficult to establish a relationship between CHD and self-reported anxiety. The peripheral physiological component of anxiety can be extremely pernicious to cardiovascular structures, but, as a negative affective state, anxiety can have a protective function against disease because it motivates coping responses. Suppose, for example, an individual displays a high sensitivity to threat as a disposition. Situations involving threat could evoke sympathetic arousal and neuroendocrine activity that, if frequent and intense enough, would increase the risk for CHD. Yet, if this individual is very self-aware and heeds the message of danger provided by the subjective affective component of anxiety, he or she may engage in health-promoting coping behaviors such as structuring his or her life to minimize threat or by taking medication (e.g., beta-adrenergic blockers) to minimize the harmful effects of the cardiovascular/neuroendocrine response. It is also possible that individuals may show unhealthy coping responses that serve to reduce anxiety, such as alcohol consumption, and in this way, anxiety may influence CHD indirectly through established risk factors. Even though there is very little experimental evidence for this avenue to CHD (Byrne, 1990a), it cannot be discounted entirely.

In our view, anxiety will only be revealed as a risk factor for CHD when: (1) the individual's ability to cope with subjectively experienced anxiety is situationally constrained, or (2) the individual faced with threat reveals evidence of sympathetic arousal but does not show the subjective component of anxiety and thus is not motivated to engage in health-promoting coping behaviors (as was suggested for the Type A individual at highest risk for CHD). In regard to situational constraints, recall the studies involving an animal model for atherogenesis. The results of those experiments provided evidence that the threat of loss of social status contributed to the atherosclerosis in cynamolgous monkeys who were high in the dominance hierarchy. It is also important to be cognizant of the fact that there were no coping resources available in those experiments because the experimenter had control over the structure of the social environment of the animals; that is, the animals did not have the option of withdrawing from the experiment, thereby reducing their exposure to threat. Many people find themselves in a life situation that is analogous to the one experienced by the cynamolgous monkeys. For example, many people are engaged in occupations that evoke high levels of anxiety, but, due to factors such as low education level or limited job experience, these individuals are not afforded the realistic option of coping with the anxiety by leaving the job and finding one that is better for their health. Individuals in these anxiety-provoking occupations would be expected to be at a higher risk for CHD. Indeed, there is evidence that individuals whose occupations are characterized by high levels of uncertainty and threat such as air traffic controllers and pilots have a higher incidence of CHD than the general population (e.g., Bolm-Audorff & Siegrist, 1983). Similarly, self-employed individuals show twice the risk of CHD compared to workers who are not self-employed (Magnus, Matroos, & Strackee, 1983).

Many individuals find themselves in life situations in which anxiety is high but coping resources are limited. A life stressor such as a loss of a loved one would be expected to evoke high levels of anxiety among the other emotions elicited. There is substantial evidence that seeking and receiving social support in this situation would be a health-promoting coping response (e.g., Andrews et al., 1978). But suppose the individual experiencing this type of emotional distress does not have a social support system to turn to in times of need. It is this type of individual that we propose is at higher risk for CHD because effective coping behaviors are situationally constrained. In our view, the relationship between anxiety and CHD can only be understood by a careful analysis of people in this and similar types of situations in which coping options are limited.

Controllability is a term used in the anxiety literature to refer to the availability of effective coping responses in situations involving threat. If effective coping responses are not available to individuals faced with threat and uncertainty about future outcomes, the peripheral physiological component of anxiety has a longer duration and/or is evoked more frequently than in situations in which control is high. Stated differently, control reduces uncertainty and threat and thereby the peripheral physiological component of anxiety. Controllability has been found to be an important concept in understanding the relationship between occupational stress and CHD. Work demands, per se, cannot be considered to be linked to CHD (Byrne & Byrne, 1990), but when coupled with level of perceived control by the worker have been shown to predict CHD. Alfredson, Karasek, and Theorell (1982) studied the relationship between occupational stress and CHD in a representative sample of workers employed in a wide variety of occupations in Sweden and found a significantly higher prevalence of CHD among workers who had both heavy workloads and a low level of control over work practices. A similar relationship between job demands, controllability, and CHD has been reported by other investigators (Bosma et al., 1997; Karasek et al.,1981;

Steenland, Johnson, & Nowlin, 1997; Theorell et al., 1998)

In general, one would expect an inverse relationship between status in the workplace hierarchy and controllability. Thus, if coping response availability is a factor in CHD, people low in the hierarchy should be at the greatest risk for CHD. Indeed, there is abundant evidence that blue-collar workers are significantly overrepresented among MI patients (Bennet, 1996; Bolm-Audorff & Siegrist, 1983; French & Caplan, 1970; Leigh & Miller, 1998; Steenland, Johnson, & Nowlin, 1997), and this cannot be accounted for simply by the level of physical activity (Steenland, Johnson, & Nowlin, 1997). Certainly controllability is not the only reason (or even the most important one) for the relationship between status in the workplace and CHD, but there is evidence that increased controllability among blue-collar workers is protective against CHD (Steenland, Johnson, & Nowlin, 1997; Theorell et al., 1998).

In our discussion of the relationship among anxiety, the Type A behavior pattern, and CHD, it was pointed out that the subjective affective component and the peripheral physiological component of the anxiety response may become dissociated. Thus, there may be sympathetic arousal and a neuroendocrine response to threat without a subjective negative affective experience. One implication of this assertion is that individuals who are less self-aware would not be expected to endorse items scored for anxiety on self-report measures such as the STAI. Thus, the component of the anxiety response that is proposed to contribute to CHD will, for many individuals tested, go undetected. We believe that this inherent flaw in self-report measures of anxiety accounts, at least in part, for the contradictory findings in studies that have sought to assess the relationship between anxiety and CHD.

Individuals who show the physiological component of anxiety but report that they do not feel anxious are referred to as "repressors," or people who show a repressive coping style (Asendorpf & Scherer, 1983; Weinberger, Schwartz, & Davidson, 1979). Viewed from a biobehavioral control systems perspective, negative feedback has been distorted and attenuated in the control system that regulates person–environment transactions. Thus, repressors do not cope with anxiety because there is no motivational imperative to do so; they are ignoring a danger signal. Repressors would be at a particularly high risk for CHD if they show the Type A behavior pattern because Type A individuals have a proclivity for placing themselves in situations in which they are likely to encounter stressful life events (Byrne, 1981; Dimsdale et al., 1978; Falger, Bressors, & Dijkstra, 1980; Smith & Anderson, 1986). Repressors can be identified by using a measure of defensiveness along with self-report anxiety measures (Asendorpf & Scherer, 1983). When identified in this way, subjects who report low anxiety but high defensiveness show heart rate reactivity to a laboratory challenge that cannot be distinguished from the high heart rate observed in subjects who report high anxiety on a self-report measure.

SUMMARY AND CONCLUSIONS

Anxiety is an emotional response to threat and uncertainty that is characterized by a subjective affective experience, cardiovascular changes that are coupled with an aroused sympathetic nervous system, and increases in neuroendocrine activity. Results from studies using an animal model of atherogenesis are consistent with the view that the sympathetic arousal and/or neuroendocrine changes elicited by threat contribute to the development of coronary artery atherosclerosis. There is also evidence that the sympathetic arousal and neuroendocrine changes that constitute the peripheral physiological component of anxiety have a significant impact upon morbidity and mortality following acute MI.

The subjective affective experience elicited by threat has motivational properties in that it may lead to health-promoting coping behaviors that serve to diminish the peripheral physiological component of anxiety. We believe that anxiety becomes a risk factor in the pathogenesis of CHD when the subjective affective component of the emotional response to threat is suppressed. Accordingly, Type A individuals who suppress this component of anxiety and other negative affective experiences are thought to be at a greater risk for CHD than their more self-aware Type A counterparts. Awareness of negative affective states such as anxiety is more likely to lead to coping behaviors that minimize exposure to threat, whereas Type A's showing low self-awareness appear to seek out stressful situations. Low self-awareness may also

lead an individual to engage in health practices, such as excessive alcohol consumption, that have been established as traditional risk factors in CHD.

In our view, anxiety is also a risk factor in CHD when coping resources are constrained by life circumstances. Social support has a protective function in atherogenesis, and many individuals who experience high levels of anxiety and emotional distress do not have adequate social support systems to turn to in times of need. Similarly, many people who have limited options with respect to their choice of occupation and find themselves in jobs associated with the threat and uncertainty that are linked to low levels of controllability.

Our observations regarding the functions of anxiety have several implications with respect to health care. First, enhanced self-awareness of subjective emotional states should be one goal of programs that seek to assist individuals, such as those showing the Type A pattern, who engage in behavior practices that place them at higher risk for CHD. Secondly, anxiety is one of the earliest and most intense emotional responses to acute MI. If this affective response is not managed effectively, the heightened cardiovascular and neuroendocrine activity may lead to serious cardiac complications including reinfarction, ventricular fibrillation, sustained ventricular tachycardia, or death. Finally, occupational stress is a risk factor in CHD when high work demands are coupled with low levels of personal control. Increased controllability in the workplace has a protective function with respect to CHD, so managerial programs that increase worker decision latitude and promote a general sense of personal control in the work environment should be encouraged.

REFERENCES

Alfredson, L., Karasek, R., & Theorell, T. (1982). Myocardial infarction risk and psychosocial work environment: An analysis of the male Swedish working force. *Social Science and Medicine, 16,* 463–467.

Andrews, G., Tennant, C., Hewson, D., & Vaillant, G. (1978). Life event stress, social support, coping style, and risk of psychological impairment. *Journal of Nervous and Mental Disease, 16,* 307–316.

Asendorpf, J. B., & Scherer, K. R. (1983). The discrepant repressor: Differentiation between low anxiety, high anxiety, and repression of anxiety by autonomic-facial-verbal patterns of behavior. *Journal of Personality and Social Psychology, 45,* 1334–1346.

Beidel, D. C., Turner, S. M., & Dancu, C. V. (1985). Physiological, cognitive and behavioral aspects of social anxiety. *Behavior Research and Therapy, 23,* 109–117.

Bennett, S. (1996). Socioeconomic inequalities in coronary heart disease and stroke mortality among Australian men, 1979–1993. *International Journal of Epidemiology, 25,* 266–275.

Ben-Sira, Z., & Eliezer, R. (1990). The structure of readjustment after heart attack. *Social Science and Medicine, 30,* 523–536.

Bianchi, G., Fergusson, D., & Walshe, J. (1978). Psychiatric antecedents of myocardial infarction. *Medical Journal of Australia, 16,* 297–301.

Blumenthal, J. A., Thompson, L. W., Williams, R. B., & Kong, Y. (1979). Association of anxiety proneness and coronary heart disease. *Journal of Psychosomatic Research, 23,* 17–21.

Bolm-Audorff, U., & Siegrist, J. (1983). Occupational morbidity data in myocardial infarction. *Journal of Occupational Medicine, 25,* 367–371.

Bosma, H., Marmot, M. G., Hemingway, H., Nicholson, A. C., Brunner, E., & Stansfeld, S. A. (1997). Low job control and risk of coronary heart disease in Whitehall II (prospective cohort) study. *British Medical Journal, 314,* 558–565.

Brezinski, D. A., Tofler, G. H., Muller, J. E., Pohjola-Sintonen, S., Willich, S. N., Schafer, A. I., Czeisler, C. A., & Williams, G. H. (1988). Morning increase in platelet aggregability: Association with assumption of the upright position. *Circulation, 78,* 35–40.

Byrne, D. G. (1979). Anxiety as state and trait following survived myocardial infarction. *British Journal of Social and Clinical Psychology, 18,* 417–423.

Byrne, D. G. (1981). Type A behavior, life events and myocardial infarction: Independent or related risk factors? *British Journal of Medical Psychology, 54,* 371–377.

Byrne, D. G. (1990a). Anxiety and the heart: A psychological perspective. In D. G. Byrne & R. H. Rosenman (Eds.), *Anxiety and the heart.* New York: Hemisphere.

Byrne, D. G. (1990b). Psychological aspects of outcomes and interventions following heart attack. In D. G. Byrne & R. H. Rosenman (Eds.), *Anxiety and the heart.* New York: Hemisphere.

Byrne, D. G., & Byrne, A. E. (1990). Anxiety and coronary heart disease. In D. G. Byrne & R. H. Rosenman (Eds.), *Anxiety and the heart.* New York: Hemisphere.

Byrne, D. G., & Rosenman, R. H. (1986). The Type A behavior pattern as a precursor to stressful events: A confluence of coronary risks. *British Journal of Medical Psychology, 58,* 75–82.

Byrne, D. G., Rosenman, R. H., Schiller, E., & Chesney, M. A. (1985). Consistency and variation among instruments purporting to measure the Type A behavior pattern. *Psychosomatic Medicine, 47,* 242–261.

Contrada, R. J., & Krantz, D. S. (1988). Stress, reactivity, and Type A behavior: Current status and future directions. *Annals of Behavioral Medicine, 10,* 64–70.

Costa, P. T. (1981). Neuroticism as a factor in the diagnosis of angina pectoris. *Behavioral Medicine Update, 3,* 18–20.

Costa, P. T., Jr., McCrae, R. R., & Dembroski, T. (1989). Agreeableness versus antagonism: Explication of a potential risk factor for CHD. In A. Siegman & T. Dembroski (Eds.), *In search of coronary-prone behavior: Beyond Type A* (pp. 41–63). Hillsdale, NJ: Erlbaum.

Crowe, J. M., Runions, J., Ebbesen, L. S., Oldridge, N. B., & Steiner, D. L. (1996). Anxiety and depression after acute myocardial infarction. *Heart Lung, 25,* 98–107.

Deanfield, J. E., Shea, M. J., Kensett, M., Horlock, P., Wilson, R. A., DeLandsheere, C. M., & Selwyn, A. P. (1984). Silent myocardial ischemia due to mental stress. *Lancet, 2,* 1001–1005.

DeMaria, A. N., Lee, G., Amsterdam, E. A., Low, R., & Mason, D. T. (1980). The anginal syndrome with normal coronary arteries: Etiologic and prognostic considerations. *Journal of the American Medical Association, 244,* 826–828.

Dembroski, T. M., & Costa, P. T. (1987). Coronary-prone behavior: Components of the Type A pattern and hostility. *Journal of Personality, 55,* 211–236.

Dembroski, T. M., MacDougall, J. M., Costa, P. T. Jr., & Grandits, G. A. (1989). Components of hostility as predictors of sudden death and myocardial infarction in the Multiple Risk Factor Intervention Trial. *Psychosomatic Medicine, 51,* 514–522.

Dimsdale, J. E., Hackett, T. P., Block, P. C., & Hutter, A. M. (1978). Emotional correlates of Type A behavior pattern. *Psychosomatic Medicine, 40,* 580–583.

Eaker, E. D., Pinsky, J., & Castelli, W. P. (1992). Myocardial infarction and coronary death among women: Psychosocial predictors from a 20-year follow-up of women in the Framingham study. *American Journal of Epidemiology, 135,* 854–864.

Engel, B. T. (1985). Stress is a noun! No, a verb, no, an adjective! In T. M. Field, P. M. McCabe, & N. Schneiderman (Eds.), *Stress and coping.* London: Earlbaum.

Everson, S. A., Lynch, J. W., Chesney, M. A., Kaplan, G. A., Goldberg, D. E., Shade, S. B., Cohen, R. D., Salonen, R., & Salonen, J. T. (1997). Interaction of workplace demands and cardiovascular reactivity in progression of carotid atherosclerosis: Population based study. *British Medical Journal, 314,* 553–558.

Falger, P., Bressors, I., & Dijkstra, P. (1980). Levensloop patronen van hartinfarct patienten en van controlegroegen: Enkele overeenkomsten en verschillen. *Gerontologie, 11,* 240–257.

Francis, K. T. (1981). Perceptions of anxiety, hostility and depression in subjects exhibiting the coronary-prone behavior pattern. *Journal of Psychiatric Research, 16,* 183–190.

French, J. R. P., & Caplan, R. D. (1970). Psychosocial factors in coronary heart disease: Critique of some of the research. *Industrial Medicine and Surgery, 39,* 31–45.

Friedman, H. S., & Booth-Kewley, S. (1987). Personality, Type A behavior, and coronary heart disease: The role of emotional expression. *Journal of Personality and Social Psychology, 53,* 783–792.

Glass, D. C., Lake, C. R., Contrada, R. J., Kehoe, K., & Erlanger, L. R. (1983). Stability of individual differences in physiological responses to stress. *Health Psychology, 2,* 317–341.

Gray, J. A. (1987). *The psychology of fear and stress* (2d ed.). Cambridge, England: Cambridge University Press.

Gruen, W. (1975). Effects of brief psychotherapy during the hospitalization period on the recovery process in heart attacks. *Journal of Consulting and Clinical Psychology, 43,* 223–232.

Gupta, L. N., & Verma, R. K. (1983). Psychosocial antecedents of myocardial infarction. *Indian Journal of Medical Research, 77,* 697–701.

Hackett, T., Cassem, N., & Wishnie, H. (1968). The coronary care unit: An appraisal of its psychological hazards. *New England Journal of Medicine, 279,* 1365–1370.

Harbin, T. J. (1989). The relationship between the Type A behavior pattern and physiological responsivity: A quantitative review. *Psychophysiology, 26,* 110–119.

Herman, S., Blumenthal, J. A., Black, G. M., & Chesney, M. A. (1981). Self-ratings of Type A (coronary prone) adults: Do Type A's know they are Type A's: *Psychosomatic Medicine, 43,* 405–413.

Houston, B. K. (1988). Cardiovascular and neuroendocrine reactivity, global Type A, and components of Type A behavior. In B. K. Houston & C. R. Snyder (Eds.), *Type A behavior pattern* (pp. 212–252). New York: Wiley.

Howard, J. H., Rechnitzer, P. A., Cunningham, D. A., Wong, D., & Brown, H. A. (1990). Type A behavior, personality, and sympathetic response. *Behavioral Medicine, 16,* 149–160.

Jenni, M., & Wollersheim, J. (1979). Cognitive therapy, stress management training and Type A behavior pattern. *Cognitive Therapy and Research, 3,* 61–73.

Julian, D. G. (1987). Quality of life after myocardial infarction. *American Heart Journal, 114,* 241–244.

Kamarck, T., & Jennings, J. R. (1991). Biobehavioral factors in sudden cardiac death. *Psychological Bulletin, 109,* 42–75.

Kaplan, J. R., Manuck, S. B., Adams, M. R., Weingand, K. W., & Clarkson, T. B. (1987). Inhibition of coronary atherosclerosis by propranolol in behaviorally predisposed monkeys fed an atherogenic diet. *Circulation, 76,* 1364–1372.

Kaplan, J. R., Manuck, S. B., Clarkson, T. B., Lusso, F. M., & Taub, D. M. (1982). Social status, environment, and atherosclerosis in cynomolgus monkeys. *Arteriosclerosis, 2,* 359–368.

Karasek, R., Baker, D., Marxer, F., Ahlbom, A., & Theorell, T. (1981). Job decision latitude, job demands, and cardiovascular disease. *American Journal of Public Health, 71,* 694–705.

Keltikangas-Järvinen, L., & Jokinen, J. (1989). Type A behavior, coping mechanisms and emotions related to somatic risk factors of coronary heart disease in adolescents. *Journal of Psychosomatic Research, 33,* 17–27.

Kubzansky, L. D., Kawachi, I., Spiro, A., III, Weiss, S. T., Vokonas, P. S., & Sparrow, D. (1997). Is worrying bad for your heart? A prospective study of worry and coronary heart disease in the Normative Aging Study. *Circulation, 95,* 818–824.

Lazarus, R. S. (1991). *Emotion and adaption.* Oxford, England: Oxford University Press.

Leigh, J. P., & Miller, T. R. (1998). Occupational illness within two national data sets. *International Journal of Occupational and Environmental Health, 4(2),* pp. 99–113.

Lloyd, G. G., & Cawley, R. H. (1982). Psychiatric morbidity after myocardial infarction. *Quarterly Journal of Medicine, 51,* 33–42.

Lobitz, W., & Brammel, H. (1981). Anxiety management training versus aerobic conditioning for cardiac stress management. Paper presented at the annual meeting of the American Psychological Association, Los Angeles.

Magnus, K., Matroos, A. W., & Strackee, J. (1983). The self-employed and the self-driven: Two coronary prone sub-populations from the Zeist study. *American Journal of Epidemiology, 118,* 799–805.

Malan, S. S. (1992). Psychosocial adjustment following MI: Current views and nursing implications. *Journal of Cardiovascular Nursing, 6,* 57–70.

Manuck, S. B., Kaplan, J. R., Adams, M. R., & Clarkson, T. B. (1989). Behaviorally elicited heart rate reactivity and atherosclerosis in female cynomolgus monkeys (*macaca fascicularis*). *Psychosomatic Medicine, 51,* 306–318.

Manuck, S. B., Kaplan, J. R., & Clarkson, T. B. (1983). Behaviorally induced heart rate reactivity and atherosclerosis in cynomolgus monkeys. *Psychosomatic Medicine, 45,* 95–108.

Manuck, S. B., Kaplan, J. R., & Matthews, K. A. (1986). Behavioral antecedents of coronary heart disease and atherosclerosis. *Arteriosclerosis, 6,* 2–14.

Matthews, K. A., Glass, D. C., Rosenman, R. H., & Bortner, R. (1977). Competitive drive, pattern A, and coronary heart disease: A further analysis of some data from the Western Collaborative Group Study. *Journal of Chronic Diseases, 30,* 489–498.

Matthews, K. A., Manuck, S. B., & Saab, P. G. (1986). Cardiovascular responses of adolescents during a naturally occurring stressor and their behavioral and psychophysiological predictors. *Psychophysiology, 23,* 198–209.

Matthews, K. A., Siegel, J. M., Kuller, L., Thompson, M., & Varat, M. (1983). Determinants of decisions to seek medical treatment by patients with acute myocardial infarction symptoms. *Journal of Personality and Social Psychology, 44,* 1144–1156.

Miller, N. E. (1951). Learnable drives and rewards. In S. S. Stevens (Ed.), *Handbook of experimental psychology* (pp. 435–472). New York: Wiley.

Miller, T. Q., Turner, C. W., Tindale, R. S., Posavac, E. J., & Dugoni, B. L. (1991). Reasons for the trend toward null findings in research on Type A behavior. *Psychological Bulletin, 110,* 469–485.

Moser, D. K., & Dracup, K. (1995). Psychosocial recovery from a cardiac event: The influence of perceived control. *Heart Lung, 24,* 273–280.

Moser, D. K., & Dracup, K. (1996). Is anxiety early after myocardial infarction associated with subsequent ischemic and arrhythmic events? *Psychosomatic Medicine, 58,* 395–403.

Mowrer, O. H. (1947). On the dual nature of learning: Reinterpretation of conditioning and problem solving. *Harvard Educational Review, 17,* 102–148.

Musante, L., MacDougall, J. M., Dembroski, T., & Costa, P. T., Jr. (1989). Potential for hostility and dimensions of anger. *Health Psychology, 8,* 343–354.

Myers, A., & Dewar, A. H. (1975). Circumstances attending 10 sudden deaths from coronary artery disease with coroner's necropsies. *British Heart Journal, 37,* 1133–1143.

Naiura, R., & Goldstein, M. G. (1992). Psychological factors affecting physical condition: Cardiovascular disease literature review. *Psychosomatic Medicine, 33,* 146–155.

Oldenburg, B., & Perkins, R. (1984). *Psychological intervention in myocardial infarction.* Unpublished manuscript. Prince Henry Hospital, Department of Psychiatry, Sydney, Australia.

Panza, J. A., Epstein, S. E., & Quyyumi, A. A. (1991). Circadian variation in vascular tone and its relation to a-sympathetic vasoconstrictor activity. *New England Journal of Medicine, 325,* 986–990.

Pittner, M. S., & Houston, B. K. (1980). Response to stress, cognitive coping strategies, and the Type A behavior pattern. *Journal of Personality and Social Psychology, 36,* 147–157.

Priori, S. G., Zuanetti, G., & Schwartz, P. J. (1988). Ventricular fibrillation induced by the interaction between acute myocardial ischemia and sympathetic hyperactivity: Effect of nifedipine. *American Heart Journal, 116,* 37–43.

Rosen, R. B., & Schulkin, J. (1998). From normal fear to pathological anxiety. *Psychological Review, 105,* 325–350.

Rosenman, R. H. (1990). Anxiety and the heart: A cardiological perspective. In D. G. Byrne & R. H. Rosenman (Eds.), *Anxiety and the heart.* New York: Hemisphere.

Rozanski, A., Krantz, D. S., & Bairey, C. N. (1991). Ventricular response to mental stress testing in patients with coronary artery disease: Pathophysiologic implications. *Circulation, 83* (suppl. 2), 137–144.

Schiffer, R., Hartley, L. H., Schulman, C. L., & Abelmann, W. H. (1980). Evidence for emotionally-induced coronary arterial spasm in patients with angina pectoris. *British Heart Journal, 44,* 62–66.

Schneiderman, N. (1977). Animal models relating behavioral stress and cardiovascular pathology. In T. M. Dembroski, S. M. Weiss, J. L. Shields, S. G. Haynes, & M. Feinleib (Eds.), *Coronary-prone behavior.* New York: Springer-Verlag.

Schneiderman, N. (1987). Psychophysiologic factors in atherogenesis and coronary artery disease. *Circulation* (suppl. 76), 41–47.

Schneiderman, N., & Saab, P. G. (1996). Anxiety afer myocardial infarction predicts in-hospital complications: Important association highlights need for research on rapid psychosocial intervention after infarction. *Psychosomatic Medicine, 58,* 402–403.

Schwartz, G. E. (1983). Disregulation theory and disease: Application to the repression/cerebral disconnection/cardiovascular disorder hypothesis. *International Review of Applied Psychology, 32,* 95–118.

Siegman, A.W. (1989). The role of hostility, neuroticism, and speech style in coronary artery disease. In A. W. Siegman & T. Dembroski (Eds.), *In search of coronary-prone behavior: Type A* (pp. 65–89). Hillsdale, NJ: Erlbaum.

Smith, T. W., & Anderson, N. B. (1986). Models of personality and disease: An interactional approach to Type A behavior and cardiovascular risk. *Journal of Personality and Social Psychology, 50,* 1166–1173.

Spielberger, C. D., & Rickman, R. L. (1990). Assessment of state and trait anxiety in cardiovascular disorders. In D. G. Byrne & R. H. Rosenman (Eds.), *Anxiety and the heart.* New York: Hemisphere.

Spittle, B., & James, B. (1977). Psychosocial factors and myocardial infarction. *Australian, New Zealand Journal of Psychiatry, 11,* 37–43.

Spoont, M. R. (1992). Modulatory role of serotonin in neural information processing: Implications for human psychopathology. *Psychological Bulletin, 112,* 330–350.

Steenland, K., Johnson, J., & Nowlin, S. (1997). A follow-up study of job strain and heart disease among males in the NHANES1 population. *American Journal of Industrial Medicine, 31,* 256–260.

Sullivan, M. D., LaCroix, A. Z., Baum, C., Grothaus, L. C. & Katon, W. J. (1997). Functional status in coronary artery disease: A one-year prospective study of the role of anxiety and depression. *American Journal of Medicine, 103*(5), 348–356.

Suls, J. (1990). Type A behavior pattern: The role of anxiety, self-awareness, and denial. In D. G. Byrne & R. H. Rosenman (Eds.), *Anxiety and the heart.* New York: Hemisphere.

Suls, J., & Fletcher, B. (1985). The relative efficacy of avoidant and nonavoidant coping strategies: A meta-analysis. *Health Psychology, 4,* 249–288.

Suls, J., & Sanders, G. S. (1988). Type A behavior as a risk factor for physical disorder. *Journal of Behavioral Medicine, 11,* 201–226.

Suls, J., & Wan, C. K. (1989). The relationship between Type A behavior pattern and chronic emotional distress: A meta-analysis. *Journal of Personality and Social Psychology, 57,* 503–512.

Sundin, O., Ohman, A., Palm, T., & Ström, G. (1995). Cardiovascular reactivity, Type A behavior, and coronary heart disease: Comparisons between myocardial infarction patients and controls during laboratory-induced stress. *Psychophysiology, 32,* 28–35.

Taggart, P., Carruthers, M., & Sommerville, W. (1973). Electrocardiograms, plasmas catecholamines, and lipids, and their modification by oxprenolol when speaking before an audience. *Lancet, 2,* 341–346.

Theorell, T., Tsutsumi, A., Hallquist, J., Reuterwall, C., Hogstedt, C., Fredlund, P., Emlund, N., & Johnson, J. V. (1998). Decision latitude, job strain, and myocardial infarction: A study of working men in Stockholm. The SHEEP Study Group. Stockholm Heart Epidemiology Program. *American Journal of Public Health, 88,* 382–388.

Thiel, H. G., Parker, D., & Bruce, T. A. (1973). Stress factors and the risk of myocardial infarction. *Journal of Psychosomatic Research, 17,* 43.

Thomas, S. A., Friedmann, E., Wimbush, F., & Schron, E. (1997). Psychological factors and survival in the cardiac arrhythmia suppression trial (CAST): A reexamination. *American Journal of Critical Care, 6,* 116–126.

Turner, S. M., Beidel, D. C., & Larkin, K. T. (1986). Situational determinants of social anxiety in clinic and nonclinic samples: Physiological and cognitive correlates. *Journal of Consulting and Clinical Psychology, 54,* 523–527.

Verrier, R. L., & Mittelman, M. A. (1997). Cardiovascular consequences of anger and other stress states. *Bailliers Clinical Neurology, 6,* 245–259.

Weidner, G., & Matthews, K. A. (1978). Reported physical symptoms elicited by unpredictable events and the Type A coronary-prone behavior pattern. *Journal of Personality and Social Psychology, 36,* 1213–1220.

Weinberger, D. A., Schwartz, G. E., & Davidson, R. J. (1979). Low-anxious, high-anxious, and repressive coping styles: Psychometric patterns and behavioral and physiological responses to stress. *Journal of Abnormal Psychology, 88,* 369–380.

Williams, R. B., Barefoot, J., & Shekelle, R. B. (1985). The health consequences of hostility. In M. Chesney & R. H. Rosenman (Eds.), *Anger and hostility in cardiovascular and behavioral disorders* (pp. 173–186). Washington, DC: Hemisphere.

Williams, R. B., Lane, J. D., Kuhn, C. M., Melosh, W., White A. D., & Schanberg, S. M. (1982). Type A behavior and elevated physiological and neuroendocrine responses to cognitive tasks. *Science, 218,* 483–485.

Winters, R. W., Ironson, G. H., & Schneiderman, N. (1990). The neurobiology of anxiety. In D. G. Byrne & R. H. Rosenman, *Anxiety and the heart.* New York: Hemisphere.

CHAPTER 13

ASTHMA AND PANIC DISORDER

Jonathan M. Feldman
Nicholas D. Giardino
Paul M. Lehrer

Asthma and panic disorder (PD) co-occur in individuals much more often than would be expected by chance. Perhaps this is not surprising, because the symptoms of the two disorders are so similar. However, the functional relationship between the two is not clear. Asthma and PD may be linked by a common pathophysiology, or the connection may be more psychological. Furthermore, special care must be given when treating those with both disorders, because what may be therapeutic for one condition can, under some circumstances, be unhelpful, or even dangerous, for the other.

In this chapter we will discuss the possible causes of the high co-occurrence of PD and asthma, review current psychoeducational and pharmacological treatments for both, and discuss the ways that single-disorder treatments may interact for comorbid individuals. Finally, we will outline a proposed protocol for the treatment of patients with asthma-panic comorbidity.

ASTHMA AND PANIC DISORDER: CO-OCCURRENCE AND ANXIETY

Asthma

Asthma is a chronic respiratory disease of unknown etiology. The most recent Expert Panel Report on the Guidelines for the Diagnosis and Management of Asthma (National Heart, Lung, and Blood Institute, 1997) defines asthma as a chronic inflammatory disorder causing recurrent respiratory symptoms, such as wheezing, breathlessness, and cough. Inflammation also results in an exacerbation of existing bronchial hyperresponsiveness to several stimuli.

Agreement on a precise definition of asthma has been difficult to attain. This may be partly due to the diverse frames of reference of those studying the disease (Busse & Reed, 1988). Also, while the current guideline focuses almost exclusively on immunologic processes, there is considerable evidence that complex interactions among many physiological and psychological processes play a role in the development, maintenance, and treatment of asthma.

Asthma affects between approximately 6 and 9% of the U.S. population (Turkeltaub & Gergen, 1991). About one-third of the roughly 15 million Americans with asthma are children (Adams & Marano, 1995; Centers for Disease Control and Prevention, 1996). Sex differences in the prevalence of asthma change across the life span. As children, boys are more likely to have asthma than girls. From ages 15 to 45, the prevalence is higher among women. In later years, rates are again higher in men. The prevalence, morbidity, and mortality of asthma in industrialized countries have increased since the 1970s (Kussin & Fulkerson, 1995; Shirakawa et al., 1997). The increase in mortality is particularly alarming because asthma is a potentially reversible condition for which new and better treatments have become available.

Panic Disorder

The lifetime prevalence rate of PD in the United States[1] is between 1.5 and 3.7%, with 1-year preva-

Acknowledgments: The authors wish to thank Stuart Hochron, Benjamin Liberatore, and Barbara Palmeri for their helpful comments on previous versions of this manuscript.

1. Epidemiological studies used *DSM-III-R* (American Psychiatric Association, 1987) diagnostic criteria to assess PD. Rates and patterns of PD from countries around the world, particularly Western countries, are fairly consistent with U.S. figures (Weissman et al., 1997).

lence rates between 1 and 2% (Eaton, Dryman, & Weissman, 1991; Eaton et al., 1994; Horwath, Johnson, & Hornig, 1993; Kessler et al., 1994). More than twice this number have experienced panic attacks but do not meet criteria for PD (Eaton et al., 1994). PD is two to three times more common in women than in men. There is also some evidence that the rates of PD may be increasing in the United States (Weissman et al., 1997). The occurrence of PD onset in childhood has recently been described (Moreau & Weissman, 1992; VonKorff, Eaton, & Keyl, 1985) and may represent a subtype of PD associated with increased risk of familial transmission (Goldstein et al., 1997).

It is still a matter of debate whether the occurrence of panic attacks is biological or psychological in origin, although it seems likely that they stem from an interaction between both. For example, in biological provocation procedures (e.g., inhalation of CO_2-enriched air), psychological manipulations (e.g., perceived control over the delivery of CO_2) have been shown to have very strong triggering effects (Sanderson, Rapee, & Barlow, 1989).

A *DSM-IV* diagnosis of PD requires not only that an individual has recurrent panic attacks, but that the person develops anxious apprehension over their reoccurrence (American Psychiatric Association, 1994). A relatively high percentage of the population reports experiencing panic attacks, although most never develop PD (Brown & Cash, 1990; Norton et al., 1985; Rapee, Ancis, & Barlow, 1987; Salge, Beck, & Logan, 1988). Most people who experience or have experienced panic are not overly concerned about the attacks or the possibility of having another in the future. Thus, it appears that the propensity to have panic attacks may be separate from the propensity to develop fear over having panic attacks, to perceive them as uncontrollable, and to become highly vigilant to somatic cues that might signal the onset of the next attack (Barlow, 1997).

Asthma with Panic Disorder

While no population studies have been published to our knowledge, the prevalence of PD with asthma can be estimated from several studies that used small, selected patient samples. These studies have shown that there is an increased prevalence of PD (range: 6.5–24%) among those with asthma (Carr, Lehrer,

& Hochron, 1992; Carr et al., 1994; Karajgi et al., 1990; Shavitt, Gentil, & Mandetta, 1992; Yellowlees et al., 1987, 1988). Variability in results can be explained by differences between studies in diagnostic procedures and asthma patient samples.

Studies have also found that certain chronic respiratory diseases, including asthma, are three times more common in those with PD than in those with other psychiatric disorders or in the general population (Spinhoven et al., 1994; Zandbergen et al., 1991). PD may be preferentially associated with intermittent respiratory disease, such as asthma, while depression is found more often in those with continuous respiratory problems (Kinsman et al., 1983, 1973; Spinhoven et al., 1994). The prevalence of comorbid PD/asthma is greater than the product of their individual prevalence rates; thus, it is likely that either one disorder facilitates the other, or that there is some vulnerability common to both disorders.

Asthma and PD share strikingly similar phenomenology. Respiratory-related symptoms, such as sensations of dyspnea, dizziness, chest tightness, choking, and smothering, are common in both disorders. Panic and fear are also common features of asthma (Carr, Lehrer, & Hochron, 1995; Kinsman et al., 1973; van der Schoot & Kapstein, 1990). Phobic avoidance of situations related to acute attacks is seen in both conditions (Barlow, 1988; Yellowlees & Kalucy, 1990). Both asthma and PD are characterized by hyperventilation and elevated thoracic muscle tone (Beck & Scott, 1988; Martin et al., 1980). There is also some evidence of immune dysfunction in PD (Yeragani, Balon, & Pohl, 1991).

It is tempting to speculate that the two disorders share some common pathophysiology. For example, hyperventilation and dyspnea are symptoms common to both. Many regard hyperventilation as synonymous with anxiety, although anxiety is often absent (Bass & Gardner, 1985) or secondary to hyperventilation (Lum, 1976). Also, hyperventilation has been shown to produce airway obstruction in those with asthma (Kilham, Tooley, & Silverman, 1979), probably due to increased airway cooling effects (Gilbert, Fouke, & McFadden, 1988). Airway obstruction may also lead to hyperventilation. Individuals with asthma tend to show an exaggerated increase in respiratory drive in response to experimentally induced respiratory resistance (Kelsen, Fleegler, & Altose, 1979). Because this response occurs during the first 100 milliseconds of the occluded breath (i.e., before any observable cortical response), it is believed to be mediated solely by brain stem reflexes (Chapman, Santiago, & Edelman, 1980).

Dyspnea can be a direct effect of airway narrowing in asthma, but it is also often a trigger for hyperventilation in panic attacks (Papp, Klein, & Gorman, 1993). Hyperventilation can produce unpleasant body sensations, the fear of which may contribute to PD (Chambless, 1984). Panic-fear is often associated with dyspnea in patients with asthma, and there is some evidence that the sequelae of dyspnea may contribute to panic attacks in at least a subset of PD patients (Carr, Lehrer, & Hochron, 1992). Also, patients with PD may have abnormal proprioception of respiratory stimuli, such as those associated with respiratory resistive loads (Tiller, Pain, & Biddle, 1987), similar to that found in asthma. Thus, shared respiratory dysregulation may contribute to the pathophysiology of PD as well as asthma (Smoller et al., 1996). The experience of dyspnea in both disorders may also be linked by CO_2 sensitivity. Medullary chemoreceptors and/or the locus coeruleus may be stimulated as a result of bronchoconstriction in asthma, inducing the expression of an underlying vulnerability to panic (Perna et al., 1997; Svensson, 1987). Repeated stimulation of chemoreceptors may lead to "derangement of the suffocation alarm monitor," posited by Klein (1993) to underlie the development of PD.

The relationship between PD and asthma is neither exclusive nor direct. There is a higher prevalence rate of several nonrespiratory diseases, such as cardiovascular and cerebrovascular disease, among those with PD, compared with those with other psychiatric disorders or those with no psychiatric disorder (Weissman et al., 1990). In fact, PD is the most frequently diagnosed anxiety disorder associated with medical illnesses (Cassem, 1990). In addition, PD and asthma seem to be independently transmitted in families of those with asthma (Perna et al., 1997).

Finally, there is evidence that, among asthmatics, cognitive variables such as fear of bodily sensations or irrational beliefs about the consequences of anxiety (but not pulmonary function) are significantly related to PD (Carr, Lehrer, & Hochron, 1992; 1994; Porzelius, Vest, & Nochomovitz, 1992). Similarly, asthma severity is unrelated to presence of PD (Carr et al., 1996). Rather, asthma may simply produce the

threatening bodily sensations (i.e., the asthma attack) or an uncontrollable event to which chronic anxiety develops or is conditioned among susceptible individuals. Cognitive variables may play a role in this susceptibility. Repeated asthma attacks may lead to reciprocal reactions of stress, autonomic, immune, and cognitive-emotional factors. Subsequently, other cognitive processes may promote specific associations among asthma symptoms, panic, and situations (Schmidt-Traub & Bamler, 1997). Thus, asthma may not be related in any biologically specific way to the etiology or maintenance of PD, but rather would be equivalent to cardiac or vestibular problems as a source of fear-provoking somatic cues.

Panic-Fear in Asthma

Panic-fear is a factor-analytically derived construct from a questionnaire designed to assess symptoms of asthma, the Asthma Symptom Checklist (ASC) (Kinsman et al., 1973). The Panic-Fear subscale has been used to assess *illness-specific* panic-fear, elicited specifically in response to asthma symptoms. An asthmatic patient with high levels of illness-specific panic-fear will tend to be vigilant concerning breathing difficulties and to respond to asthma exacerbation at the beginning stages of an attack.

Generalized panic-fear refers to anxiety that extends beyond asthma symptoms and thus reflects global and stable aspects of a personality style. To measure generalized panic-fear, the same group of researchers again used a factor-analytically derived scale, utilizing items from the Minnesota Multiphasic Personality Inventory (MMPI) (Dirks et al., 1977). Generalized panic-fear is highly correlated ($r = .83$) with the Taylor Manifest Anxiety Scale, which is often employed as a measure of trait anxiety (Kinsman et al., 1980).

Illness-specific and generalized panic-fear have different effects on asthma morbidity and response to treatment. Staudenmayer et al. (1979) demonstrated that asthmatics with high illness-specific panic-fear were rehospitalized for asthma half as frequently within 6 months after discharge, compared with asthmatics having low illness-specific panic-fear. No between-group differences were found on objective measures of pulmonary function. Thus, symptom-focused panic-fear may be particularly adaptive for patients with asthma.

Both high and low levels of generalized panic-fear appear to be generally maladaptive for asthma. Asthmatics with high generalized panic-fear tend to be prescribed the most intensive medication regimens (Dirks, Horton, et al., 1978) have the longest periods of hospitalization (Dirks et al., 1977) and highest rates of rehospitalization (Dirks et al., 1980). Very low levels of generalized panic-fear have also been associated with poor medical outcome, possibly due to neglect of treatment. These patients tend to report underutilization of medication (Kleiger & Dirks, 1979) and to have high rates of rehospitalization (Dirks, Kinsman, et al., 1978). All of these above findings are independent of any differences in pulmonary function.

Generalized panic-fear is a better predictor of asthma morbidity than illness-specific panic-fear (Dirks, Fross, & Evans, 1977). However, illness-specific panic-fear has been shown to predict medical outcome within the group of asthmatic patients with moderate generalized panic-fear (Dirks, Fross, & Paley, 1978). Asthmatics who score high on both measures are most likely to panic during asthma attacks. They are also prone to overmedication (Kinsman, Dirks, & Dahlem, 1980), hyperventilation (Kinsman, Dirks, & Jones, 1980), and poor self-management skills. The group characterized by moderate generalized panic-fear and high illness-specific panic-fear is most likely to show a favorable outcome (Kinsman, Dirks, & Jones, 1982). These asthmatics manifest the lowest rates of rehospitalization among the various groups (Dirks, Fross, & Paley, 1978). In general, this group utilizes illness-specific panic-fear as a warning signal, without high levels of trait anxiety interfering with appropriate self-management behavior. Low scores on both measures of panic-fear may predict disregard of symptoms and avoidance of medical assistance—a dangerous combination (Kinsman, Dirks, & Jones, 1982). These studies demonstrate the need to assess both illness-specific and generalized panic-fear to effectively determine the role of panic-fear in asthma.

The pathway by which high levels of panic worsen asthma may, at least in part, be through greater perceptual sensitivity and overinterpretation of respiratory sensations. Van Peski-Oosterbaan et al. (1996) found that patients with comorbid asthma and PD tended to report greater levels of dyspnea during a histamine challenge test than asthmatics without PD, although there were no differences between the two groups on objective pulmonary function measures. Similarly, asthmatics with high generalized panic-fear mislabeled various nonrespiratory sensations (e.g., fatigue, worry, panic) as symptoms of asthma (Dirks, Schraa, & Robinson, 1982).

Parental behaviors may create additional problems for children with asthma. Parents' fearful reactions to asthma attacks may exacerbate the child's condition by leading to overmedication with beta agonists for attacks that are marked by panic (Baron & Marcotte, 1994; Creer & Reynolds, 1990). Psychoeducational interventions for parents that explain the differences between asthma and PD may alleviate these problems.

Implications for Asthmatics with Panic Disorder

The research on generalized panic-fear suggests that similar risks may apply to patients with clinical PD, but there is little research on this relationship. Data from our laboratory indicate that asthmatics with PD score higher on the MMPI-Panic Fear and the ASC-Panic Fear scales than asthmatics without PD (see Table 13.1). In addition, case studies have reported findings in anxiety patients with asthma that are consistent with the literature on elevated scores on the MMPI-Panic Fear and ASC-Panic Fear scales. Bernstein, Sheridan, and Patterson (1991) presented three examples of asthmatics with PD who displayed overmedication, extreme symptom vigilance, and excessive utilization of medical resources.

TABLE 13.1. Panic-Fear in Asthma and PD

MEASURE	ASTHMA ONLY (n = 89)		ASTHMA AND PD (n = 11)			
	M	SD	M	SD	t	p
Age	25.97	6.62	27.17	7.78		
MMPI-PF	3.99	2.34	5.27	2.87	1.67	<.10
ASC-PF	1.63	.52	2.06	.68	2.54	<.02

Source: Data are taken from a study of panic and asthma that was reported previously (Carr et al., 1994, 1995, 1996; Carr, Lehrer, & Hochron, 1992).

MMPI-PF = Minnesota Multiphasic Personality Inventory Panic-Fear scale

ASC-PF = Asthma Symptom Checklist Panic-Fear scale

Tietz, Kahlstrom, and Cardiff (1975) reported three asthma-related deaths in patients who manifested extreme generalized and illness-specific panic-fear, which interfered with medical treatment. Clearly more empirical research is required in patients with asthma and PD in order to gain a better understanding of which risk factors to target in treatment.

Differentiating Asthma from Panic

Misdiagnosis of asthma or PD and treatment for the wrong condition may explain cases of treatment failure for both disorders and may even lead to exacerbation of the disease. This may be particularly problematic for comorbid individuals. Objective measures of pulmonary function provide the best means of differentiating panic from asthma symptoms. However, the pattern of symptoms also may be helpful, particularly when symptoms arise suddenly and no equipment is available to measure pulmonary function. Schmaling and Bell (1997) administered the ASC to a group of PD patients and a matched sample of asthmatics. Wheezing, mucus production, and coughing were the symptoms that provided the best discrimination between the two groups and predicted asthma membership. Panic-fear and hyperventilation symptoms were better predictors of PD. Panic attacks can also generally be distinguished from asthma attacks by a more rapid onset (i.e., peak of symptoms within 10 minutes) and shorter overall duration. In addition, it would be prudent to investigate the possibility of PD in asthmatics who report a family history of anxiety disorders or depression (Goldstein et al., 1994).

Assessment of PD may be more difficult in pediatric asthma because of a limited vocabulary for describing panic symptoms. Baron and Marcotte (1994) reported a case of a 3-year-old with asthma who described a giant approaching him before attacks. Further assessment revealed the presence of PD, with the giant representing feelings of imminent doom. The authors suggest that poor descriptions of panic symptoms may be one reason for the limited data on PD in children. Thus, rates of comorbid asthma and PD may be high in children as well. Physicians must be particularly cognizant of ambiguous descriptions of events surrounding asthma attacks in children that may represent underlying panic.

PROBLEMATIC DRUG INTERACTIONS IN COMORBID ASTHMA AND PANIC DISORDER

Despite the similarity of symptoms, pharmacological treatment of asthma and PD operate through different and sometimes opposing mechanisms. In some cases, pharmacological agents commonly used to treat one disorder may exacerbate or induce symptoms in patients with both conditions. The next two sections will review the potential adverse consequences of pharmacological treatments that pertain to people with both disorders.

Anxiogenic Side Effects of Asthma Medications

Beta-Adrenergic Agonists

The primary side effects of the β_2-agonists are associated with sympathetic activation. Moderate doses of inhaled medication produce fewer of these adverse effects than standard oral administration. Nevertheless, the inhaled route can also produce systemic effects by stimulating β_2 receptors located in striated muscle, vascular smooth muscle tissue, or cardiac muscle, thus leading to tremor, peripheral vasodilation, and tachycardia (Kelly, 1992). Albuterol is a β_2-agonist commonly prescribed on a p.r.n. basis for the treatment of acute exacerbation of asthma. Inhalation of albuterol has been shown to produce minimal systemic side effects at conventional doses (Bagnato et al., 1996; Lenney & Evans, 1986; Rodrigo & Rodrigo, 1996). However, adverse effects, such as tremors and tachycardia, do appear in a dose-dependent manner quickly after inhalation (Bennett & Tattersfield, 1997; Lenney & Evans, 1986; Scalabrin, Sole, & Naspitz, 1996).

The quick-acting sympathetic effects of β_2-agonist medication may exacerbate anxiety and panic among comorbid or misdiagnosed individuals, sometimes leading to further overmedication, when additional medication is taken to reduce respiratory panic symptoms mistaken as asthma. The dose-dependent nature of β_2-agonist side effects may aggravate this maladaptive cycle. Shavitt, Gentil, and Croce (1993) reported a case of such an occurrence in an asthmatic patient with undiagnosed PD. During a panic episode the patient attempted to treat the symptoms with repeated inhalation of albuterol, which ultimately resulted in loss of consciousness and a need for hospitalization and mechanical ventilation. Similarly, Rihmer (1997) described a patient who experienced panic attacks that had been misdiagnosed as asthma. The administration of albuterol increased the frequency and severity of panic attacks and precipitated the development of full-blown PD.

Controlled studies have shown that, among PD patients, isoproterenol, a nonselective beta-adrenergic agonist, can provoke panic attacks that are described as similar to previous panic episodes (Pohl et al., 1988). PD patients who consume nonselective over-the-counter beta agonists may also experience exacerbated anxiety or panic due to sympathomimetic actions of these agents.

Confusion between asthma and panic symptoms may have catastrophic consequences, particularly if the patient attributes an asthma attack to panic and fails to take beta agonist medication. Thus, knowledge of the differences between symptoms and the side effects of beta agonist medication is a crucial component of treatment in this population. Over the long term an adequate medication regimen for asthma may improve PD by decreasing the frequency or intensity of panicogenic body sensations and may improve asthma by reduction of generalized panic, with its deleterious behavioral effects on asthma.

Theophylline

Theophylline-based medications are sometimes used for treating asthma and can also mimic panic sensations due to stimulatory effects in the cardiovascular, gastrointestinal, and central nervous systems. Side effects of theophylline can include tachycardia, nausea, vomiting, tremors, nervousness, and agitation (see Minton & Henry, 1996, for review; Rall, 1985). In addition, co-administration of fluvoxamine with theophylline can lead to a toxic reaction (Sperber, 1991; van den Brekel & Harrington, 1994) by reducing theophylline clearance (Rasmussen et al., 1995). Thus, serum theophylline concentrations should be closely monitored when asthmatics with PD are prescribed theophylline and fluvoxamine for their comorbid condition.

Corticosteroids

The administration of oral corticosteroids is associated with psychiatric symptoms in a dose-dependent manner (Boston Collaborative Drug Surveillance Program, 1972). Hall et al. (1979) reported that emotional lability and anxiety were the most frequent symptoms to occur among medical patients taking daily doses of 40 mg or more of prednisone. Short-term increases in the dose of prednisone among children with asthma have also been associated with increases in anxiety and depression (Bender, Lerner, & Poland, 1991). Thus, exacerbation of PD may occur at high doses of oral corticosteroid treatment. Although less is known about the effects of inhaled corticosteroids, patients should be monitored for the possibility of anxiety symptoms at higher doses (Wamboldt, Yancey, & Roesler, 1997). Asthmatics with PD who consume combinations of beta agonists, theophylline, and corticosteroids are likely to be at greater risk for experiencing anxiety or panic-like sensations.

Respiratory Side Effects of PD Medications

Benzodiazepines

The respiratory effects of benzodiazepines in high doses may have direct implications for patients with PD accompanied with severe persistent asthma. The administration of benzodiazepines has been shown to lead to respiratory depression, with associated decreased respiratory drive and reduced oxygen blood levels, in both healthy and pulmonary patients (Casali et al., 1977; Delpierre et al., 1981; Flogel et al., 1993; Nozaki-Taguchi et al., 1995). In patients with milder forms of asthma the adverse effects of benzodiazepines may be sufficiently small to allow their safe use; however, precaution should be taken when arterial oxygen tension is reduced.

Monoamine Oxidase Inhibitors (MAOIs)

The administration of MAOIs may interact with asthma medications, such as theophylline and beta-adrenergic agonists, leading to dangerous or even fatal consequences. The combination of these medications may result in exaggerated sympathetic activity and hypertensive crisis. A recent review of MAOIs concluded that even the newer, more reversible agents should not be prescribed in conjunction with drugs that have sympathomimetic effects (Livingston & Livingston, 1996).

Tricyclic Antidepressants and Selective Serotonin Reuptake Inhibitors (SSRIs)

Precautions should also be taken with the administration of tricyclic antidepressants and SSRIs in asthmatics with PD. Wamboldt et al. (1997) found that the combination of tricyclic antidepressants and multiple asthma medications led to small increases in systolic blood pressure in children with asthma. As noted previously, the combination of fluvoxamine and theophylline may result in a toxic interaction. Furthermore, Humble and Wistedt (1992) reported exacerbation of cardiac and respiratory panic symptoms in PD patients during the first week of citalopram treatment, despite a low starting dose of 5 mg/day. Asthmatics with PD should be closely monitored and adequately instructed about these sensations due to their potential confusion with asthma symptoms.

Beta-Adrenergic Antagonists

Beta blockers are sometimes used to treat autonomic symptoms of panic. Beta-adrenergic antagonists are contraindicated in patients with asthma because the pharmacological effects are precisely the opposite of the beta-adrenergic agonist medication used to treat asthma. Propanolol, a nonselective beta-blocker, has been shown to induce bronchoconstriction in patients with asthma, but not in control subjects (Okayama et al., 1987). The use of beta blockers as eye drops to treat glaucoma may also precipitate asthma attacks (Le Jeunne et al., 1989).

Other Medications Used to Treat PD

Clonidine, an α_2-adrenoceptor agonist, is sometimes used to treat PD, although it is not considered a first-line drug. The effects of clonidine on asthma may be beneficial or detrimental, depending on the type of administration (Dinh Xuan et al., 1988; Foxworth et al., 1995; Lindgren, Ekstrom, & Andersson, 1986).

Venlafaxine, a selective norepinephrine and serotonin reuptake inhibitor, has recently been employed for PD treatment (Pollack et al., 1996) and appears to have minimal respiratory effects.

Relapse in PD

Relapse is a notable problem across all pharmacological treatments for PD (Pollack & Otto, 1997). There is little evidence of lingering antipanic effects after medication has been stopped (Rickels & Schweizer, 1994). Asthmatics with PD may be at especially high risk for relapse due to the anxiogenic nature of asthma medications and recurrent asthma episodes that may produce fearful bodily sensations (e.g., dyspnea). Clearly, asthmatic patients with PD would benefit from skills training and educational interventions in order to self-manage these two overlapping, chronic conditions.

BEHAVIORAL TREATMENT COMPONENTS AND RATIONALE

The treatment of comorbid patients with asthma and PD is an area that has received little attention in the literature. In an uncontrolled study, Park, Sawyer, and Glaun (1996) applied principles of cognitive-behavioral therapy (CBT) for PD to asthmatic children who displayed pulmonary function deficits that were less severe than their high levels of medication consumption and symptom report would indicate. After completion of the intervention, the rate of hospital admissions for asthma decreased. Other indices of asthma morbidity were not available for analysis.

To the best of our knowledge, there have been no published treatment-outcome studies of clinical PD in adult patients with asthma. The treatment we will outline here incorporates components of Panic Control Treatment (Barlow & Craske, 1994) and asthma self-management programs (National Heart, Lung, and Blood Institute, 1997; Reynolds et al., 1989). The proposed protocol has been adapted for the comorbid group and supplemented with a biofeedback treatment specially suited for this population.

Psychoeducational Programs

Devine (1996) conducted a meta-analysis of 31 studies of psychoeducational treatments for adults with asthma and concluded that these programs, particularly education and relaxation-based behavioral therapies, offer multiple benefits. Asthma education programs have been shown to be cost-effective as well. Taitel et al. (1995) reported a cost–benefit ratio of 1:2.28, with the greatest savings attributed to declines in hospital admissions and amount of lost income due to asthma.

Progressive Muscle Relaxation

The similarities between high MMPI—Panic Fear and PD patients (e.g., excessive utilization of medical resources, hyperventilation) suggest the importance of applying treatment strategies to reduce generalized panic-fear. The recommendation of Kinsman, Dirks, Jones, et al. (1980) to reduce high levels of trait panic-fear in patients with asthma is incorporated into the proposed treatment through progressive muscle relaxation (PMR).

PMR has potential benefits for both asthma and PD. The rationale for relaxation therapy in asthma is to achieve reductions in bronchoconstriction via decreases in parasympathetic reactivity (Lehrer, 1998). In studies from our laboratory, PMR has been found to significantly reduce airway reactivity and improve pulmonary function (Lehrer et al., 1986; Lehrer et al., 1994). In both of these studies, however, deterioration in pulmonary function was noted *within* sessions, although improvement occurred *across* sessions. Decreases in pulmonary function measures correlated with decreases in heart rate, which may reflect parasympathetic rebound within sessions (Lehrer, Hochron, et al., 1997). Thus, we propose that relaxation *not* be used *during* an asthma attack. PMR may, however, be helpful in preventing asthma attacks by decreasing autonomic responsivity, which may also be adaptive for PD by facilitating habituation and exposure to panic triggers (Michelson & Marchione, 1991).

Peak Flow Monitoring

Regular monitoring of peak flow upon arising in the morning and during symptom exacerbation is a standard component of asthma care. It can provide early warning of an asthma attack, thus leading to early medical intervention. Although the Expert Panel recommends peak flow monitoring only for patients with moderate to severe persistent asthma (National Heart, Lung, and Blood Institute, 1997), we propose that all comorbid patients with asthma and PD can benefit from using the peak flow meter to help distinguish between asthma and panic sensations by comparing obtained values to those recorded during an asthma attack. Peak flow monitoring will also function to maintain illness-specific panic-fear in patients, as symptom vigilance is beneficial in asthma (Kinsman, Dirks, Jones, et al., 1980). Home peak flow monitoring with an action plan for asthma treatment has been shown to reduce the frequency of emergency room visits (Cowie et al., 1997). However, Giannini et al. (1997) found low sensitivity in the ability of peak flow meters to detect mild bronchoconstriction. Thus, attention to other signs and symptoms of asthma (e.g., presence of mucus, coughing) should be considered, in addition to peak flow measures, to determine proper action plans for treatment.

Heart Rate Variability Biofeedback

We and others have previously theorized that normal homeostatic regulation of both psychological and physiological states is characterized by complex patterns of overlapping periodicities and that the action of homeostatic mechanisms is reflected in the occurrence and coupling of oscillations at various frequencies (Garfinkel, 1983; Giardino, Lehrer, & Feldman, in press; Glass & Mackey, 1979, 1988; Goldberger & Rigney, 1990; Hyndman, 1973; Weiner, 1975, 1989, 1991; Weiss, 1969; West, 1990). One such oscillation, the periodic variability in heart rate, has been studied to understand the normal interplay of regulatory processes that maintain physiological stability, as well as the autonomic underpinnings of many clinical disorders. Components of heart rate variability (HRV) are associated with autonomic regulatory processes and have been shown to deviate from normal in both asthma (Davis et al., 1986; Kallenbach et al., 1985; Lehrer et al., 1996) and PD (Friedman et al., 1993; Klein et al., 1995; Middleton, Ashby, & Robbins, 1994; Tucker et al., 1997; Yeragani et al., 1993). Furthermore, in PD, restoration of normal cardiac rhythms has been shown to accompany clinical improvement following psychological or pharmacological therapy (Middleton & Ashby, 1995; Tucker et al., 1997; Yeragani et al., 1994). Thus, it is possible that an intervention aimed directly at the induction of healthy cardiac rhythms may benefit both disorders.

In our laboratory, we recently conducted a study in which a small number of patients with asthma were given biofeedback to assist in increasing short-term HRV (Lehrer, Carr, et al., 1997). Compared to EMG biofeedback and a waiting list control, those given training in HRV biofeedback showed significant improvement in pulmonary function and a reduction in the report of asthma symptoms. These improvements were associated with increases in low-frequency HRV during treatment sessions. It is unclear whether improvements were due to the strengthening of autonomic regulatory mechanisms (Vaschillo, 1984) or to the mechanical airway effects of slow deep breathing that accompany voluntary increases in HRV. In either case, this method is particularly well suited to treating those with both asthma and PD. Also, if our preliminary findings are replicated, this method may be found useful during asthma attacks, as well as preventatively. HRV biofeedback has been used in Russia for treating both asthma (Smetankin, 1997) and anxiety disorders (Chernigovskaya et al., 1990).

Other studies using slow breathing techniques as part of yoga have similarly shown beneficial effects in asthma (Fluge et al., 1994; Jain & Talukdar, 1993; Singh, 1987; Singh et al., 1990). Cappo and Holmes (1984) reported that rapid inhalation and slow exhalation breathing at six breaths per minute led to reductions in subjective report and physiological levels of arousal in response to a laboratory stressor. This is the rate at which people tend to breathe during HRV biofeedback (Lehrer, Carr, et al., 1997).

CBT for PD Adapted for Asthmatics

Traditional CBT for PD consists of cognitive restructuring, breathing retraining, and interoceptive and situational exposure (Barlow, 1997). This section outlines the major components that we have adapted for use with asthma.

Cognitive restructuring for PD attempts to identify and correct catastrophic misinterpretations of bodily sensations. For patients with asthma, this task is complicated by the frightening and sometimes life-threatening nature of their physical symptoms, which can overlap with panic sensations (e.g., dyspnea). The key to cognitive restructuring in asthmatics with PD is to teach patients to discriminate between asthma and panic symptoms in order to

correctly address bodily sensations. It is extremely important that this process be accurately executed due to the potentially catastrophic consequences that can occur by mislabeling asthma symptoms as strictly panic-related. Carr et al. (1994) concluded that asthmatic patients with PD would be appropriate candidates for cognitive restructuring based upon their higher levels of anxiety sensitivity and fear of bodily sensations in comparison to asthmatic patients without PD.

Exposure to interoceptive stimuli associated with panic, in combination with cognitive restructuring, is also an effective component of PD treatment (Craske et al., 1997; Gould, Otto, & Pollack, 1995). This type of exposure is employed in the treatment of PD for the purposes of extinguishing anxious feelings associated with feared bodily sensations. Breathing retraining in PD treatment involves an explanation of stress-induced hyperventilation, instruction in slow breathing, and voluntary hyperventilation (Clark, Salkovskis, & Chalkley, 1985). Education about hyperventilation would be particularly useful to patients with asthma. This explanation is expanded in our protocol to include differentiation between hyperventilation and wheezing. Slow breathing is also incorporated into the treatment through HRV biofeedback, as previously described. Voluntary hyperventilation, though, may trigger bronchospasm in asthma and is therefore not included in our treatment.

Other respiratory-related interoceptive exposure exercises are excluded from the protocol, pending further evaluation, because of possible risks associated with asthma. Thus, adjustments to the protocol from Panic Control Treatment have been made, as follows:

1. The production of chest tightness by holding a breath may be particularly risky for patients with asthma due to the possibility of bronchoconstriction following a deep inhalation (Gayrard et al., 1979). It is therefore not included in our protocol.

2. Inhaling through a thin straw to produce sensations of breathing difficulty may actually be a particularly useful exercise for asthma, but its effects and risks have not been systematically studied in an asthmatic population. Inspiratory resistive load training, over a duration of 6 months, has been shown to increase inspiratory muscle strength and endurance in patients with asthma (Weiner et al.,

1992). However, our protocol does not include this exercise due to the need for further research on its safety and efficacy in asthmatics.

3. Implementing physical activity to produce tachycardia should be coordinated with the patient's physician due to the possibility of exercise-induced bronchoconstriction or other health risks. However, exercise is rarely contraindicated for asthma. In some cases, pretreatment with β_2-agonist medication before exercise may be necessary (National Heart, Lung, and Blood Institute, 1997).

4. Our protocol substitutes "pursed lips breathing" for exercises that may trigger bronchospasm. Although pursed lips breathing may not be as beneficial for the purpose of creating feared bodily sensations as holding a breath, it is a proven safe alternative to other respiratory-related exercises and may also improve ventilation in pulmonary patients (Breslin, 1992; van der Schans et al., 1997).

CBT also includes in vivo exposure for PD patients who exhibit agoraphobic avoidance. Asthmatic patients with PD may be particularly prone to phobic avoidance of situations in which there is a risk of breathing difficulties (Yellowlees & Kalucy, 1990). This avoidance behavior is based upon appropriate attempts to eliminate asthma triggers or allergens. However, excessive avoidance may result from a cycle of fear, hyperventilation, and panic. Thus, situational exposure may be added to the treatment for patients with agoraphobia once asthma and panic triggers have been clearly differentiated.

TREATMENT FOR COMORBID ASTHMA AND PANIC DISORDER

The following protocol is proposed primarily for use with adult patients with comorbid asthma and PD. It has not yet been subject to empirical evaluation. The method is derived from well-validated manuals for separate treatments of PD (Craske, Brown, & Barlow, 1991) and asthma (Kotses et al., 1995; Taitel et al., 1995) and has been updated according to the recent consensus guidelines for management of asthma (National Heart, Lung, and Blood Institute, 1997). The treatment is intended to be administered in close

consultation with the patient's physician in order to ensure proper medication regimens and to allow for review of medical records. This type of team approach may also increase patient compliance with the protocol. The patient is encouraged to be an active participant in all aspects of treatment and to work closely with his or her physician. A complete medical examination is strongly recommended before the commencement of therapy. The proposed treatment protocol consists of 10 sessions, each lasting approximately 60 minutes. This section provides brief summaries of the protocol. A patient workbook is also being developed.

Sessions 1–2: Treatment Rationale and Education

A major aim of the initial session is to present the treatment rationale. The goal of treatment is for the patient to gain control over asthma and panic through self-management. The treatment helps patients identify the predictable aspects of asthma and panic and counteract feelings of helplessness. The patient learns to distinguish between asthma and panic attacks in order to apply appropriate treatment and prevention strategies. The therapist explains that improvement in one condition can also lead to benefits for the other. Active participation and home practice on the part of the patient are necessary to achieve these positive gains.

Educational information about asthma and PD is a major component of the treatment. The therapist explains the basic physiology of respiration and describes the changes that occur during an asthma attack. The similarities between asthma and panic attacks are then described. For example, both panic and asthma demonstrate reversibility and can occur on an irregular basis. Asthma and panic attacks can both be triggered by stress. The list of overlapping symptoms includes shortness of breath or smothering, hyperventilation, feelings of choking or chest tightness, rapid pulse, sweating, fear of losing control, and fear of dying. In both asthma and panic attacks, the physical sensations experienced are real bodily symptoms.

During the initial sessions, the therapist stresses the importance of distinguishing between asthma and panic attacks and events that trigger each. Asthma attacks can be triggered by a range of stimuli, including allergens, irritants, pollutants, smoke, exercise, cold air, respiratory infections, food additives, and even laughing. Asthma is generally distinguished by airway obstruction, and symptoms commonly include wheezing, mucus production, and coughing. Panic attacks are more frequently characterized by symptoms of hyperventilation, without mucous congestion or coughing. Panic attacks may result from experiencing a feared bodily sensation, anxious anticipation of a feared object, or even entering a stuffy room.

The concept of self-monitoring of symptoms, behaviors, and thoughts is introduced as an aid to help the patient differentiate between asthma and panic triggers and symptoms and to learn when these attacks occur. The patient is instructed on how to record the details of asthma attacks (e.g., location, time, early warning signs, peak flow reading) and how to complete the Panic Sequences Form (Barlow & Craske, 1994) and the Panic Attack Record (Barlow & Craske, 1994) in the event of attacks. Patients also monitor anxiety, depression, and anticipation about panic in the Daily Mood Record (Barlow & Craske, 1994).

The therapist also provides training in accurate use of a peak flow meter. The patient is instructed to use the device upon arising in the morning, before taking bronchodilator medication, and when symptoms exacerbate. Patients are trained to take their asthma medication based upon the zone system of symptom assessment and peak flow values (see National Heart, Lung, and Blood Institute, 1997). The therapist differentiates between preventive treatment (daily anti-inflammatory medicine) and rescue bronchodilators (short-acting β_2-agonists). Specific guidelines and decision trees are constructed for consumption of additional medication when peak flow falls 20% or more below personal best values. The patient is to use non-pharmacological treatments for smaller decreases.[2] The patient keeps daily records of morning peak flow, medication consumption, asthma symptoms, and interference with activities. Proper technique for using

inhalers to deliver asthma medication is also taught (see National, Heart, Lung, and Blood Institute, 1997).

The therapist introduces the patient to the concepts of PMR (see Lehrer & Carr, 1997, for protocol) and HRV biofeedback (see Lehrer, Carr, et al., 1997). Relaxation is an important component of self-management, as muscle tension exists in both asthma and panic. Relaxation training will teach the patient to recognize and control muscle tension. Through biofeedback training, the patient will learn more effective breathing techniques to control and prevent asthma. Both relaxation and biofeedback allow the patient to effectively utilize problem-solving skills and reduce levels of anxiety. These techniques should be practiced on a daily basis and, once adequately learned, applied during anticipation or exposure to psychological stress. Slow breathing and HRV biofeedback may be useful during asthma or panic attacks. Relaxation techniques are advised during panic episodes, but not in response to asthma attacks.

Homework: Self-Monitoring Assignments

If attack occurs:	Asthma attack records (time, location, early warning signs, peak flow)
	Panic Attack Record
	Panic Sequences Form
Daily assignments:	Daily Mood Record
	Asthma diary (morning peak flow, medication, symptoms, restrictions)

Sessions 3–4: Asthma Self-Management

Each session from this point forward begins with a check-in period to review self-monitoring and assignments from the previous session. The therapist introduces the topic of asthma self-management strategies with a review and explanation of common myths that are associated with asthma (see Table 13.2). The therapist also discusses the importance of the patient's ability to understand and ask his or her physician questions about medications.

Asthma prevention strategies focus on medication adherence and identification of common asthma

---

2. The criteria for consumption of additional asthma medication may be changed to a more stringent peak flow value (e.g., at least 10% below personal best) for patients with asthma that deteriorates rapidly. The frequency of peak flow monitoring may also be increased when morning values are more than 20% below personal best.

TABLE 13.2. Common Myths about Asthma

1. Asthma is in the head.
2. Feelings cause asthma.
3. Everyone outgrows asthma.
4. Asthma can be cured.
5. Asthma causes breathing to get progressively worse.
6. Individuals with asthma should not exercise.

Source: Taken from *Living with Asthma: Help for Adults with Asthma* (pp. 18–19) by R. V. Reynolds, H. Kotses, T. L. Creer, G. Bruss, & C. A. Joyner (1989), unpublished manual, Ohio University, Department of Psychology, Athens. Copyright 1989 by authors.

TABLE 13.3. Common Misinterpretations Associated with Panic Attacks

1. I am going crazy.
2. I am losing control.
3. My nerves might become exhausted and I may collapse.
4. I am having a heart attack.
5. I am going to faint.

Source: Taken from *Mastery of Your Anxiety and Panic II: Client Workbook* (pp. 49–52) by D. H. Barlow and M. G. Craske (1994), Albany, NY: Graywind. Copyright © 1994 by Graywind Publications.

triggers. Reactions to provoking stimuli may occur in one or both of two phases, an immediate (within minutes of exposure) and a late or delayed (hours after exposure) response. The therapist reviews techniques to minimize asthma triggers (e.g., avoidance of allergens). Physical and emotional signs that may warn of an oncoming attack are discussed (e.g., chronic cough, fatigue). The patient is asked to determine his or her early warning signs as an assignment.

It is important for the patient to understand strategies to manage an asthma attack. The therapist presents an attack management decision tree consisting of signs, symptoms, peak flow values, and appropriate patient responses at various levels of asthma severity, which correspond to the colors of a traffic light (see National Heart, Lung, and Blood Institute, 1997). The patient develops (with consultation from the medical team) an individual action plan, which includes the following: names of all medications and how to administer each; dose and frequency of all medications; time until medication takes effect and what each does; what to do if a dose is missed; side effects and what to do about them; when to call the physician; and, finally, when to seek emergency treatment. Session 3 concludes with instruction in slow, abdominal breathing and HRV biofeedback. PMR training of the arms and legs is provided at the end of Session 4.

Homework

Self-monitoring and home practice of PMR and
    HRV biofeedback
Identify early warning signs of asthma attacks
Construct action plan

Sessions 5–6: Panic Attack Management

The therapist explains the physiology of panic, the fight-flight response, and the various physical, behavioral, and cognitive effects of panic. A major focus is to provide the patient with a detailed explanation of the physiology of hyperventilation and how misinterpretation of symptoms can trigger a vicious cycle of panic. The therapist explains how confusing anxiety with asthma symptoms can maintain this cycle via maladaptive thoughts and behaviors. For example, panic symptoms may mistakenly lead the patient to take asthma medication that may lead to further increases in anxiety.

An explanation of the panic cycle is followed by cognitive restructuring techniques. The therapist begins by clarifying common misinterpretations associated with panic attacks (see Table 13.3), particularly emphasizing the fear of losing control or dying. Traditional CBT techniques are employed to identify, evaluate, and challenge maladaptive self-statements, such as overestimation errors and catastrophic thoughts. The therapist explains the concept of prediction testing as a method of determining the accuracy of predictions that were made when the patient was feeling anxious. The patient is also prompted to identify subtle physical sensations, thoughts, and general stressors that may trigger panic. Session 5 concludes with HRV biofeedback; Session 6 comes to a close with PMR of the trunk.

Homework

Self-monitoring and home practice of PMR and HRV
    biofeedback

Modifying Self-Statements Worksheet:
    Overestimating and Catastrophizing
Prediction Testing Form
List of probable panic triggers

Sessions 7–8: Differentiating between Asthma and Panic Attacks

The patient is prompted for a review of the similarities and differences between asthma and PD. The therapist discusses the various ways that the two conditions can adversely impact upon each other. Conversely, panic may also be useful during actual asthma flares

by serving as a signal to use the peak flow meter. A main focus of this discussion is the relationship between anxiety and asthma-related decisions. The distinction between illness-specific and generalized panic-fear is linked with the importance of differentiating between asthma and panic symptoms. The therapist incorporates specific examples pertaining to the patient in the discussion of these areas.

The next stage of treatment is the construction of decision trees for the purpose of making a differential identification of an asthma attack versus a panic attack (see Figure 13.1). The first step is to label the patient's asthma and panic triggers. In cases in which the trigger may be the same (e.g., stress) or is not clear,

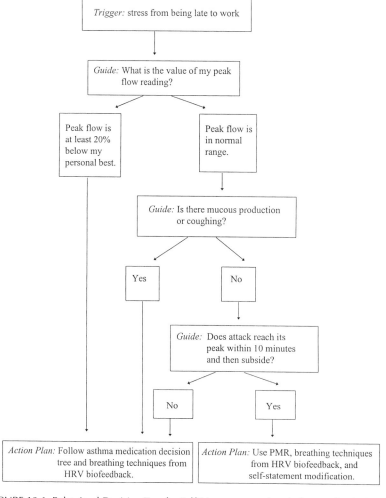

FIGURE 13.1. Behavioral Decision Tree for Self-Management of an Asthma or Panic Attack

the patient utilizes guides to aid in the decision process. Each potential trigger is then linked to appropriate action plans, and the therapist reiterates the rationale for each intervention. This process is intended to increase the patient's sense of control over both asthma and PD. The patient practices HRV biofeedback at the end of Session 7; PMR of the neck and eye muscles completes Session 8.

Homework

Self-monitoring and home practice of PMR and HRV biofeedback

Modifying Self-Statements Worksheets

Differentiating asthma from panic attacks:
Label triggers and symptoms of asthma versus panic attacks
Construct decision trees

Sessions 9–10: Imagery Exposure, Problem Solving, and Relapse Prevention

The therapist introduces interoceptive exposure as a method of confronting feared bodily sensations. Interoceptive exposure exercises from Panic Control Treatment (e.g., spinning, quick head lifts) are applied if nonrespiratory panic symptoms (e.g., dizziness, nausea) are present.

Respiratory-related exposure is limited to pursed lips breathing or conducted through the use of guided imagery. For example, the therapist instructs the patient to imagine what it would feel like to hyperventilate, including images of shortness of breath, dizziness, headache, and tingling. Physical exercises designed to increase heart rate and induce shortness of breath (e.g., step-ups) may be applied in consultation with the patient's physician. The patient incorporates the respiratory-related exposure with traditional interoceptive exposure and practices the exercises that produce his or her most feared sensations. The therapist emphasizes that exposure to panic-related cues is in contrast to the avoidance of asthma triggers.

The topic of problem solving is also presented to the patient as a technique to help cope with the lingering problems of asthma and PD. The therapist guides the client through the following series of steps:

1. Define the problem.
2. Gather information about the problem.
3. Brainstorm possible solutions.
4. Evaluate solutions.
5. Pick the highest-ranked solution and implement it.
6. Evaluate the outcome.

The final session addresses the topic of lapses in self-management. The therapist discusses the importance of continuing asthma medication adherence, and the patient identifies potential obstacles that may interfere with this goal (e.g., confusion with panic symptoms, intermittent nature of symptoms, side effects). Symptoms of panic are more likely to recur during periods of stress. The patient is instructed that these symptoms are not a sign of relapse and that interruption of the panic cycle is still required. The therapist reviews appropriate treatment techniques through the use of the decision trees. HRV biofeedback and PMR of the speech region are employed at the end of sessions 9 and 10, respectively.

Homework

Self-monitoring and home practice of PMR and HRV biofeedback

Modifying Self-Statements Worksheets

Practice of interoceptive exposure exercises, rating anxiety level (0 = none; 8 = extreme) for each trial

Applying problem-solving skills to specific issues

REFERENCES

Adams, P. F., & Marano, M. A. (1995). Current estimates from the National Health Interview Survey, 1994. *Vital Health Statistics, 10,* 193.

American Psychiatric Association. (1987). *Diagnostic and statistical manual of mental disorders* (3d ed.). Washington, DC: Author.

American Psychiatric Association. (1994). *Diagnostic and statistical manual of mental disorders* (4th ed.). Washington, DC: Author.

Bagnato, G. F., Mileto, A., Gulli, S., Oriti, S., DiCesare, E., Cinquegrani, M., Bonaiuto, M., Saitta, A., & Purello D'Ambrosio, F. (1996). Acute cardiovascular effects of salmeterol in subjects with stable bronchial asthma. *Monaldi Archives for Chest Disease, 51,* 275–278.

Barlow, D. H. (1988). *Anxiety and its disorders: The nature and treatment of anxiety and panic.* New York: Guilford Press.

Barlow, D. H. (1997). Cognitive-behavioral therapy for panic disorder: Current status. *Journal of Clinical Psychiatry, 58* (suppl. 2), 32–36.

Barlow, D. H., & Craske, M. G. (1994). *Mastery of your anxiety and panic II.* Albany, NY: Graywind.

Baron, C., & Marcotte, J. É. (1994). Role of panic attacks in the intractability of asthma in children. *Pediatrics, 94,* 108–110.

Bass, C., & Gardner, W. N. (1985). Respiratory and psychiatric abnormalities in chronic symptomatic hyperventilation. *British Medical Journal, 290,* 1387–1390.

Beck, J. G., & Scott, S. K. (1988). Physiological and symptoms responses to hyperventilation: A comparison of frequent and infrequent panickers. *Journal of Psychopathology and Behavioral Assessment, 10,* 117–127.

Bender, B. G., Lerner, J. A., & Poland, J. E. (1991). Association between corticosteroids and psychologic change in hospitalized asthmatic children. *Annals of Allergy, 66,* 414–419.

Bennett, J. A., & Tattersfield, A. E. (1997). Time course and relative dose potency of systemic effects from salmeterol and salbutamol in healthy subjects. *Thorax, 52,* 458–464.

Bernstein, J. A., Sheridan, E., & Patterson, R. (1991). Asthmatic patients with panic disorders: Report of three cases with management and outcome. *Annals of Allergy, 66,* 311–314.

Boston Collaborative Drug Surveillance Program. (1972). Acute adverse reactions to prednisone in relation to dosage. *Clinical Pharmacology and Therapeutics, 13,* 694–698.

Breslin, E. H. (1992). The pattern of respiratory muscle recruitment during pursed-lip breathing. *Chest, 101,* 75, 78.

Brown, T. A., & Cash, T. F. (1990). The phenomenon of nonclinical panic: Parameters of panic, fear and avoidance. *Journal of Anxiety Disorders, 4,* 15–29.

Busse, W. W., & Reed, C. E. (1988). Asthma: Definitions and pathogenesis. In E. Middleton, Jr., C. E. Reed, E. F. Ellis, N. F. Adkinson, Jr., & J. W. Yunginer (Eds.), *Allergy: Principles and practice* (pp. 969–998). St. Louis, MO: Mosby.

Cappo, B. M., & Holmes, D. S. (1984). The utility of prolonged respiratory exhalation for reducing physiological and psychological arousal in non-threatening and threatening situations. *Journal of Psychosomatic Research, 28,* 265–273.

Carr, R. E., Lehrer, P. M., & Hochron, S. M. (1992). Panic symptoms in asthma and panic disorder: A preliminary test of the dyspnea-fear theory. *Behaviour Research and Therapy, 30,* 251–261.

Carr, R. E., Lehrer, P. M., & Hochron, S. M. (1995). Predictors of panic-fear in asthma. *Health Psychology, 14,* 421–426.

Carr, R. E., Lehrer, P. M., Hochron, S. M., & Jackson, A. (1996). Effect of psychological stress on airway impedance in individuals with asthma and panic disorder. *Journal of Abnormal Psychology, 105,* 137–141.

Carr, R. E., Lehrer, P. M., Rausch, L. L., & Hochron, S. M. (1994). Anxiety sensitivity and panic attacks in an asthmatic population. *Behavior Research and Therapy, 32,* 411–418.

Casali, L., Pozzi, E., Rampulla, C., & Serra, R. (1977). Psychotropic drugs: Influence on respiratory function. *International Journal of Clinical Pharmacology, 15,* 480–484.

Cassem, E. H. (1990). Depression and anxiety secondary to medical illness. *Psychiatric Clinics of North America, 13,* 597–612.

Centers for Disease Control and Prevention. (1996). Asthma mortality and hospitalization among children and young adults—United States, 1980–1993. *Morbidity and Mortality Weekly Report, 45,* 350–353.

Chambless, D. (1984). The assessment of fear of fear in agoraphobics: The Body Sensations Questionnaire and the Agoraphobic Cognitions Questionnaire. *Journal of Consulting and Clinical Psychology, 52,* 1090–1097.

Chapman, R. W., Santiago, T. V., & Edelman, N. H. (1980). Brain hypoxia and control of breathing: Neuromechanical control. *Journal of Applied Physiology, 49,* 497–505.

Chernigovskaya, N. V., Vaschillo, E. G., Petrash, V. V., & Rusanovskii, V. V. (1990). Voluntary control of the heart rate as a method of correcting the functional state in neurosis. *Human Physiology, 16,* 105–111.

Clark, D. M., Salkovskis, P. M., & Chalkley, A. J. (1985). Respiratory control as a treatment for panic attacks. *Journal of Behavior Therapy and Experimental Psychiatry, 16,* 23–30.

Cowie, R. L., Revitt, S. G., Underwood, M. F., & Field, S. K. (1997). The effect of a peak flow-based action plan in the prevention of exacerbations of asthma. *Chest, 112,* 1534–1538.

Craske, M. G., Brown, T. A., & Barlow, D. H. (1991). Behavioral treatment of panic disorder: A two-year follow-up. *Behavior Therapy, 22,* 289–304.

Craske, M. G., Rowe, M., Lewin, M., & Noriega-Dimitri, R. (1997). Interoceptive exposure versus breathing retraining within cognitive-behavioural therapy for panic disorder with agoraphobia. *British Journal of Clinical Psychology, 36,* 85–99.

Creer, T. L., & Reynolds, R. V. (1990). Asthma. In M. Hersen & V. B. VanHasselt (Eds.), *Psychological aspects of developmental and physical disabilities* (pp. 57–72). Newbury Park, CA: Sage.

Davis, P. B., Simpson, D. M., Paget, G. L., & Turi, V. (1986). Beta-adrenergic responses in drug-free subjects with asthma. *Journal of Allergy and Clinical Immunology, 77,* 871–879.

Delpierre, S., Jammes, Y., Grimaud, C., Dugue, P., Arnaud, A., & Charpin, J. (1981). Influence of anxiolytic drugs (prazepam and diazepam) on respiratory center output and CO_2 chemosensitivity in patients with lung diseases. *Respiration, 42,* 15–20.

Devine, E. C. (1996). Meta-analysis of the effects of psychoeducational care in adults with asthma. *Research in Nursing and Health, 19,* 367–376.

Dinh Xuan, A. T., Matran, R., Regnard, J., Vitou, P., Advenier, C., & Lockhart, A. (1988). Comparative effects of rilmenidine and clonidine on bronchial responses to histamine in asthmatic subjects. *British Journal of Clinical Pharmacology, 26,* 703–708.

Dirks, J. F., Fross, K. H., & Evans, N. W. (1977). Panic-fear in asthma: Generalized personality trait vs. specific situational state. *Journal of Asthma, 14,* 161–167.

Dirks, J. F., Fross, K. H., & Paley, A. (1978). Panic-fear in asthma—state-trait relationship and rehospitalization. *Journal of Chronic Disease, 31,* 605–609.

Dirks, J. F., Horton, D. J., Kinsman, R. A., Fross, K. H., & Jones, N. F. (1978). Patient and physician characteristics influencing medical decisions in asthma. *Journal of Asthma, 15,* 171–178.

Dirks, J. F., Kinsman, R. A., Horton, D. J., Fross, K. H., & Jones, N. F. (1978). Panic-fear in asthma: Rehospitalization following intensive long-term treatment. *Psychosomatic Medicine, 40,* 5–13.

Dirks, J. F., Kinsman, R. A., Jones, N. F., Spector, S. L., Davidson, P. T., & Evans, N. W. (1977). Panic-fear: A personality dimensions related to length of hospitalization in respiratory illness. *Journal of Asthma Research, 14,* 61–71.

Dirks, J. F., Schraa, J. C., Brown, E. L., & Kinsman, R. A. (1980). Psycho-maintenance in asthma: Hospitalization rates and financial impact. *British Journal of Medical Psychology, 53,* 349–354.

Dirks, J. F., Schraa, J. C., & Robinson, S. K. (1982). Patient mislabeling of symptoms: Implications for patient–physician communication and medical outcome. *International Journal of Psychiatry in Medicine, 12,* 15–27.

Eaton, W. W., Dryman, A., & Weissman, M. M. (1991). Panic and phobias. In L. N. Robins & D. A. Reigier (Eds.), *Psychiatric disorders in America: The Epidemiologic Catchment Area Study* (pp. 159–179). New York: Free Press.

Eaton, W. W., Kessler, R. C., Wittchen, H. U., & Magee, W. J. (1994). Panic and panic disorder in the United States. *American Journal of Psychiatry, 151,* 413–420.

Flogel, C. M., Ward, D. S., Wada, D. R., & Ritter, J. W. (1993). The effects of large-dose flumazenil on midazolam-induced ventilatory depression. *Anesthesia and Analgesia, 77,* 1207–1214.

Fluge, T., Richter, J., Fabel, H., Zysno, E., Weller, E., & Wagner, T. O. (1994). Long-term effects of breathing exercises and yoga in patients with bronchial asthma. *Pneumologie, 48,* 484–490.

Foxworth, J. W., Reisz, G. R., Pyszczynski, D. R., & Knudson, S. M. (1995). Oral clonidine in patients with asthma: No significant effect on airway reactivity. *European Journal of Clinical Pharmacology, 48,* 19–22.

Friedman, B. H., Thayer, J. F., Borkovec, T. D., Tyrrell, R. A., Johnsen, B. H., & Colombo, R. (1993). Autonomic characteristics of nonclinical panic and blood phobia. *Biological Psychiatry, 34,* 298–310.

Garfinkel, A. (1983). A mathematics for physiology. *American Journal of Physiology, 245,* R455–R466.

Gayrard, P., Orehek, J., Grimaud, C. H., & Charpin, J. (1979). Mechanisms of the bronchoconstrictor effects of deep inspiration in asthmatic patients. *Thorax, 34,* 234–240.

Giannini, D., Paggiaro, P. L., Moscato, G., Gherson, G., Bacci, E., Bancalari, L., Dente, F. L., DiFranco, A., Vagaggini, B., & Giuntini, C. (1997). Comparison between peak expiratory flow and forced expiratory volume in one second (FEV_1) during bronchoconstriction induced by different stimuli. *Journal of Asthma, 34,* 105–111.

Giardino, N. D., Lehrer, P. M., & Feldman, J. M. (in press). The role of oscillations in self-regulation. In D. Kenny & F. J. McGuigan (Eds.), *Stress and health: Research and clinical applications.* Chur, Switzerland: Harwood Academic Publishers.

Gilbert, I. A., Fouke, J. M., & McFadden, E. R., Jr. (1988). Intra-airway thermodynamics during exercise and hyperventilation in asthmatics. *Journal of Applied Physiology, 64,* 2167–2174.

Glass, L., & Mackey, M. C. (1979). Pathological conditions resulting from instabilities in physiological control systems. *Annals of the New York Academy of Sciences, 316,* 214–235.

Glass, L., & Mackey, M. C. (1988). *From clocks to chaos: The rhythms of life.* Princeton, NJ: Princeton University Press.

Goldberger, A. L. & Rigney, D. R. (1990). Sudden death is not chaos. In S. Krasner (Ed.), *The ubiquity of chaos.* Washington, DC: American Association for the Advancement of Science.

Goldstein, R. B., Weissman, M. W., Adams, P. B., Horwath, E., Lish, J. D., Charney, D., Woods, S. W., Sobin, C., & Wickramaratne, P. J. (1994). Psychiatric disorders in relatives of probands with panic disorder and/or major depression. *Archives of General Psychiatry, 51,* 383–394.

Goldstein, R. B., Wickramaratne, P. J., Horwath, E., & Weissman, M. M. (1997). Familial aggregation and phenomenology of "early"-onset (at or before age 20 years) panic disorder. *Archives of General Psychiatry, 54,* 271–279.

Gould, R. A., Otto, M. W., & Pollack, M. H. (1995). A meta-analysis of treatment outcome for panic disorder. *Clinical Psychology Review, 15,* 819–844.

Hall, R. C. W., Popkin, M. K., Stickney, S. K., & Gardner, E. R. (1979). Presentation of the steroid psychoses. *Journal of Nervous and Mental Disease, 167,* 229–236.

Horwath, E., Johnson, J., & Hornig, C. D. (1993). Epidemiology of panic disorder in African-Americans. *American Journal of Psychiatry, 150,* 465–469.

Humble, M., & Wistedt, B. (1992). Serotonin, panic disorder and agoraphobia: Short-term and long-term efficacy of citalopram in panic disorders. *International Clinical Psychopharmacology, 6* (suppl. 5), 21–39.

Hyndman, B. W. (1973). The role of rhythms in homeostasis. *Kybernetics, 15,* 227–236.

Jain, S. C., & Talukdar, B. (1993). Evaluation of yoga therapy programme for patients with bronchial asthma. *Singapore Medical Journal, 34,* 306–308.

Kallenbach, J. M., Webster, T., Dowdeswell, R., Reinach, S. G., Millar, R. N., & Zwi, S. (1985). Reflex heart rate control in asthma: Evidence of parasympathetic overactivity. *Chest, 87,* 644–648.

Karajgi, B., Rifkin, A., Doddi, S., & Kolli, R. (1990). The prevalence of anxiety disorders in patients with chronic obstructive pulmonary disease. *American Journal of Psychiatry, 147,* 200–201.

Kelly, H. W. (1992). Asthma. In M. A. Koda-Kimble & L. Y. Young (Eds.), *Applied therapeutics: The clinical use of drugs* (5th ed.) (pp. 15–24). Vancouver, WA: Applied Therapeutics.

Kelsen, S. G., Fleegler, B., & Altose, M. D. (1979). The respiratory neuromuscular response to hypoxia, hypercapnia, and obstruction in airflow in asthma. *American Review of Respiratory Disease, 120,* 517–527.

Kessler, R. C., McGonable, K. A., Zhao, S., Nelson, C. B., Hughes, M., Eshleman, S., Wittchen, H. U., & Kendler, K. S. (1994). Lifetime and 12-month prevalence of *DSM-III-R* psychiatric disorders in the United States: Results from the national comorbidity survey. *Archives of General Psychiatry, 51,* 8–19.

Kilham, H., Tooley, M., & Silverman, M. (1979). Running, walking and hyperventilation causing asthma in children. *Thorax, 34,* 582–586.

Kinsman, R. A., Dirks, J. F., & Dahlem, N. W. (1980). Noncompliance to prescribed-as-needed (PRN) medication use in asthma: Usage patterns and patient characteristics. *Journal of Psychosomatic Research, 24,* 97–107.

Kinsman, R. A., Dirks, J. F., Dahlem, N. W., & Heller, A. S. (1980). Anxiety in asthma: Panic-fear symptomatology and personality in relation to manifest anxiety. *Psychological Reports, 46,* 196–198.

Kinsman, R. A., Dirks, J. F., & Jones, N. F. (1980). Levels of psychological experience in asthma: General and illness-specific concomitants of panic-fear personality. *Journal of Clinical Psychology, 36,* 552–561.

Kinsman, R. A., Dirks, J. F., & Jones, N. F. (1982). Psychomaintenance of chronic physical illness: Clinical assessment of personal styles affecting medical management. In T. Millon, C. Green, & R. Meagher (Eds.), *Handbook of clinical health psychology* (pp. 435–466). New York: Plenum.

Kinsman, R. A., Dirks, J. F., Jones, N. F., & Dahlem, N. W. (1980). Anxiety reduction in asthma: Four catches to general application. *Psychosomatic Medicine, 42,* 397–405.

Kinsman, R. A., Fernandez, E., Schocket, M., Dirks, J. F., & Covino, N. A. (1983). Multidimensional analysis of the symptoms of chronic bronchitis and emphysema. *Journal of Behavioral Medicine, 6,* 339–357.

Kinsman, R. A., Luparello, T. J., O'Banion, K., & Spector, S. (1973). Multidimensional analysis of the subjective symptomatology of asthma. *Psychosomatic Medicine, 35,* 250–267.

Kleiger, J. H., & Dirks, J. F. (1979). Medication compliance in chronic asthmatic patients. *Journal of Asthma Research, 16,* 93–96.

Klein, D. F. (1993). False suffocation alarms, spontaneous panics, and related conditions: An integrative hypothesis. *Archives of General Psychiatry, 50,* 306–317.

Klein, E., Cnaani, E., Harel, T., Braun, S., & Ben-Haim, S. A. (1995). Altered heart rate variability in panic disorder. *Biological Psychiatry, 37,* 18–24.

Kotses, H., Bernstein, I. L., Bernstein, D. I., Reynolds, R. V. C., Korbee, L., Wigal, J. K., Ganson, E., Stout, C., & Creer, T. L. (1995). A self-management program for adult asthma. Part I: Development and evaluation. *Journal of Allergy and Clinical Immunology, 95,* 529–540.

Kussin, P. S., & Fulkerson, W. J. (1995). The rising tide of asthma: Trends in the epidemiology of morbidity and mortality from asthma. *Respiratory Care Clinics of North America, 1,* 163–175.

Lehrer, P. M. (1998). Emotionally triggered asthma: A review of research literature and some hypotheses for self-regulation therapies. *Applied Psychophysiology and Biofeedback, 23,* 13–41.

Lehrer, P., & Carr, R. (1997). Progressive relaxation. In W. T. Roth & I. D. Yalom (Eds.), *Treating anxiety disorders* (pp. 83–116). San Francisco: Jossey-Bass.

Lehrer, P., Carr, R. E., Smetankine, A., Vaschillo, E., Peper, E., Porges, S., Edelberg, R., Hamer, R., & Hochron, S. (1997). Respiratory sinus arrhythmia versus neck/trapezius EMG and incentive inspirometry biofeedback for asthma: A pilot study. *Applied Psychophysiology and Biofeedback, 22,* 95–109.

Lehrer, P. M., Hochron, S., Carr, R., Edelberg, R., Hamer, R., Jackson, A., & Porges, S. W. (1996). Behavioral task-induced bronchodilation in asthma during active and passive tasks: A possible cholinergic link to psychologically induced airway change. *Psychosomatic Medicine, 58,* 413–422.

Lehrer, P. M., Hochron, S., Mayne, T., Isenberg, S., Carlson, V., Lasoski, A. M., Gilchrist, J., Morales, D., & Rausch, L. (1994). Relaxation and music therapies for asthma among patients prestabilized on asthma medication. *Journal of Behavioral Medicine, 17,* 1–24.

Lehrer, P. M., Hochron, S. M., Mayne, T., Isenberg, S., Lasoski, A. M., Carlson, V., Gilchrist, J., & Porges, S. (1997). Relationship between changes in EMG and respiratory sinus arrhythmia in a study of relaxation therapy for asthma. *Applied Psychophysiology and Biofeedback, 22,* 183–191.

Lehrer, P. M., Hochron, S. M., McCann, B., Swartzman, L., & Reba, P. (1986). Relaxation decreases large-airway but not small-airway asthma. *Journal of Psychosomatic Research, 30,* 13–25.

Le Jeunne, C. L., Hugues, F. C., Dufier, J. L., Munera, Y., & Bringer, L. (1989). Bronchial and cardiovascular effects of ocular topical β-antagonists in asthmatic subjects: Comparison of timolol, carteolol, and metipranolol. *Journal of Clinical Pharmacology, 29,* 97–101.

Lenney, W., & Evans, N. A. P. (1986). Nebulized salbutamol and ipratropium bromide in asthmatic children. *British Journal of Diseases of the Chest, 80,* 59–65.

Lindgren, B. R., Ekstrom, T., & Andersson, R. G. (1986). The effect of inhaled clonidine in patients with asthma. *American Review of Respiratory Disease, 134,* 266–269.

Livingston, M. G., & Livingston, H. M. (1996). Monoamine oxidase inhibitors: An update on drug interactions. *Drug Safety, 14,* 219–227.

Lum, L. C. (1976). The syndrome of habitual chronic hyperventilation. *Recent Advances in Psychosomatic Medicine, 3,* 196–229.

Martin, J., Powell, E., Shore, S., Emrich, J., & Engel, L. A. (1980). The role of respiratory muscles in the hyperinflation of bronchial asthma. *American Review of Respiratory Disease, 121,* 441–447.

Michelson, L. K., & Marchione, K. (1991). Behavioral, cognitive, and pharmacological treatments of panic disorder with agoraphobia: critique and synthesis. *Journal of Consulting and Clinical Psychology, 59,* 100–114.

Middleton, H. C., & Ashby, M. (1995). Clinical recovery from panic disorder is associated with evidence of changes in cardiovascular regulation. *Acta Psychiatrica Scandinavica, 91,* 108–113.

Middleton, H. C., Ashby, M., & Robbins, T. W. (1994). Reduced plasma noradrenaline and abnormal heart rate variability in resting panic disorder patients. *Biological Psychiatry, 36,* 847–849.

Minton, N. A., & Henry, J. A. (1996). Acute and chronic human toxicity of theophylline. *Human and Experimental Toxicology, 15,* 471–481.

Moreau, D., & Weissman, M. M. (1992). Panic disorder in children and adolescents: A review. *American Journal of Psychiatry, 149,* 1306–1314.

National Heart, Lung, and Blood Institute. (1997). *Expert panel report 2: Guidelines for the diagnosis and management of asthma.* National Asthma Education and Prevention Program. Washington, DC: U.S. Department of Health and Human Services.

Norton, G. R., Harrison, B., Hauch, J., & Rhodes, L. (1985). Characteristics of people with infrequent panic attacks. *Journal of Abnormal Psychology, 94,* 216–221.

Nozaki-Taguchi, N., Isono, S., Nishino, T., Numai, T., & Taguchi, N. (1995). Upper airway obstruction during midazolam sedation: Modification by nasal CPAP. *Canadian Journal of Anaesthesia, 42,* 685–690.

Okayama, M., Yafuso, N., Nogami, H., Lin, Y. N., Horio, S., Hida, W., Inoue, H., & Takishima, T. (1987). A new method of inhalation challenge with propanolol: Comparison with methacholine-induced bronchoconstriction and role of vagal nerve activity. *Journal of Allergy and Immunology, 80,* 291–299.

Papp, L. A., Klein, D. F., & Gorman, J. M. (1993). Carbon dioxide hypersensitivity, hyperventilation, and panic disorder. *American Journal of Psychiatry, 150,* 1149–1157.

Park, S. J., Sawyer, S. M., & Glaun, D. E. (1996). Childhood asthma complicated by anxiety: An application of cognitive behavioural therapy. *Journal of Paediatrics and Child Health, 32,* 183–187.

Perna, G., Bertani, A., Politi, E., Colombo, G., & Bellodi, L. (1997). Asthma and panic attacks. *Biological Psychiatry, 42,* 625–630.

Pohl, R., Yeragani, V. K., Balon, R., Rainey, J. M., Lycaki, H., Ortiz, A., Berchou, R., & Weinberg, P. (1988). Isoproterenol-induced panic attacks. *Biological Psychiatry, 24,* 891–902.

Pollack, M. H., & Otto, M. W. (1997). Long-term course and outcome of panic disorder. *Journal of Clinical Psychiatry, 58* (suppl. 2), 57–60.

Pollack, M. H., Worthington, J. J., Otto, M. W., Maki, K. M., Smoller, J. W., Manfro, G. G., Rudolph, R., & Rosenbaum, J. F. (1996). Clinical trials—anxiety disorders. *Psychopharmacology Bulletin, 32,* 667–670.

Porzelius, J., Vest, M., & Nochomovitz, M. (1992). Respiratory function, cognitions and panic in chronic obstructive pulmonary patients. *Behaviour Research and Therapy, 30,* 75–77.

Rall, T. W. (1985). Central nervous system stimulants: The methylxanthines. In A. G. Gilman, L. S. Goodman, T. W. Rall, & F. Murad (Eds.), *Goodman and Gilman's the pharmacological basis of therapeutics* (7th ed.) (pp. 589–603). New York: Macmillan.

Rapee, R., Ancis, J., & Barlow, D. H. (1987). Emotional reactions to physiological sensations: Comparison of panic disorder and nonclinical subjects. *Behaviour Research and Therapy, 26,* 265–269.

Rasmussen, B. B., Mäenpää, J., Pelkonen, O., Loft, S., Poulsen, H. E., Lykkesfeldt, J., & Brøsen, K. (1995). Selective serotonin reuptake inhibitors and theophylline metabolism in human liver microsomes: Potent inhibition by fluvoxamine. *British Journal of Clinical Pharmacology, 39,* 151–159.

Reynolds, R. V., Kotses, H., Creer, T. L., Bruss, G., & Joyner, C. A. (1989). *Living with asthma: Help for adults with asthma.* Unpublished manual, Ohio University, Department of Psychology, Athens.

Rickels, K., & Schweizer, E. (1994). Risk-benefit issues in pharmacological treatment of panic disorder. In B. E. Wolfe & J. D. Maser (Eds.), *Treatment of panic disorder: A consensus development conference* (pp. 207–217). Washington, DC: American Psychiatric Press.

Rihmer, Z. (1997). Successful treatment of salbutamol-induced panic disorder with citalopram. *European Neuropsychopharmacology, 7,* 241–242.

Rodrigo, G., & Rodrigo, C. (1996). Metered dose inhaler salbutamol treatment of asthma in the ED: Comparison of two doses with plasma levels. *American Journal of Emergency Medicine, 14,* 144–150.

Salge, R. A., Beck, J. G., & Logan, A. C. (1988). A community survey of panic. *Journal of Anxiety Disorders, 2,* 157–167.

Sanderson, W. C., Rapee, R. M., & Barlow, D. H. (1989). The influence of an illusion of control on panic attacks induced via inhalation of 5.5% carbon dioxide–enriched air. *Archives of General Psychiatry, 46,* 157–164.

Scalabrin, D. M. F., Sole, D., & Naspitz, C. K. (1996). Efficacy and side effects of beta$_2$-agonists by inhaled route in acute asthma in children: Comparison of salbutamol, terbutaline, and fenoterol. *Journal of Asthma, 33,* 407–415.

Schmaling, K. B., & Bell, J. (1997). Asthma and panic disorder. *Archives of Family Medicine, 6,* 20–23.

Schmidt-Traub, S., & Bamler, K. J. (1997). The psycho-immunological association of panic disorder and allergic reaction. *British Journal of Health Psychology, 36,* 51–62.

Shavitt, R. G., Gentil, V., & Croce, J. (1993). Panic and asthma: A dangerous mislabeling. *European Psychiatry, 8,* 41–43.

Shavitt, R. G., Gentil, V., & Mandetta, R. (1992). The association of panic/agoraphobia and asthma: Contributing factors and clinical implications. *General Hospital Psychiatry, 14,* 420–423.

Shirakawa, T., Enomoto, T., Shimazu, S., & Hopkin, J. M. (1997). The inverse association between tuberculin responses and atopic disorder. *Science, 275,* 77–79.

Singh, V. (1987). Effect of respiratory exercises on asthma: The pink city lung exerciser. *Journal of Asthma, 24,* 355–359.

Singh, V., Wisniewski, A., Britton, J., & Tattersfield, A. (1990). Effect of yoga breathing exercises (pranayama) on airway reactivity in subjects with asthma. *Lancet, 335,* 1381–1383.

Smetankin, A. (1997). Developments in Russia: Progress in the biofeedback treatment of childhood asthma. *Biofeedback Newsmagazine, 25,* 8–11.

Smoller, J. W., Pollack, M. H., Otto, M. W., Rosenbaum, J. F., & Kradin, R. L. (1996). Panic anxiety, dyspnea, and respiratory disease: Theoretical and clinical considerations. *American Journal of Respiratory and Critical Care Medicine, 154,* 6–17.

Sperber, A. D. (1991). Toxic interaction between fluvoxamine and sustained release theophylline in an 11-year-old boy. *Drug Safety, 6,* 460–462.

Spinhoven, P., Ros, M., Westgeest, A., & van der Does, A. J. W. (1994). The prevalence of respiratory disorders in panic disorder, major depressive disorder and V-code patients. *Behaviour Research and Therapy, 32,* 647–649.

Staudenmayer, H., Kinsman, R. A., Dirks, J. F., Spector, S. L., & Wangaard, C. (1979). Medical outcome in asthmatic patients: Effects of airways hyperreactivity and symptom-focused anxiety. *Psychosomatic Medicine, 41,* 109–118.

Svensson, T. H. (1987). Peripheral, autonomic regulation of locus coeruleus noradrenergic neuron in brain: Putative implications for psychiatry and psychopharmacology. *Psychopharmacology, 92,* 1–7.

Taitel, M. S., Kotses, H., Bernstein, I. L., Bernstein, D. I., & Creer, T. L. (1995). A self-management program for adult asthma. Part II: Cost–benefit analysis. *Journal of Clinical Immunology, 95,* 672–676.

Tietz, W., Kahlstrom, E., & Cardiff, M. (1975). Relationship of psychopathology to death in asthmatic adolescents. *Journal of Asthma Research, 12,* 199–206.

Tiller, J., Pain, M., & Biddle, N. (1987). Anxiety disorder and perception of inspiratory resistive loads. *Chest, 91,* 547–551.

Tucker, P., Adamson, P., Miranda, R., Scarborough, A., Williams, D., Groff, J., & McLean, H. (1997). Paroxetine increases heart rate variability in panic disorder. *Journal of Clinical Psychopharmacology, 17,* 370–376.

Turkeltaub, P. C., & Gergen, P. J. (1991). Prevalence of upper and lower respiratory conditions in the U.S. population by social and environmental factors: Data from the second National Health and Nutrition Examination Survey, 1976 to 1980. *Annals of Allergy, 67,* 147–154.

van den Brekel, A. M. & Harrington, L. (1994). Toxic effects of theophylline caused by fluvoxamine. *Canadian Medical Association Journal, 151,* 1289–1290.

van der Schans, C. P., de Jong, W., de Vries, G., Postma, D. S., Koeter, G. H., & van der Mark, T. W. (1997). Respiratory muscle activity and pulmonary function during acutely induced airways obstruction. *Physiotherapy Research International, 2,* 167–177.

van der Schoot, T. A. W., & Kapstein, A. A. (1990). Pulmonary rehabilitation in an asthma clinic. *Lung, 168,* 495–501.

van Peski-Oosterbaan, A. S., Spinhoven, P., van der Does, A. J. W., Willems, L. N. A., & Sterk, P. J. (1996). Is there a specific relationship between asthma and panic disorder? *Behaviour Research and Therapy, 34,* 333–340.

Vaschillo, E. G. (1984). The dynamics of slow-wave cardiac rhythm structure as an index of the functional state of an operator. Unpublished doctoral dissertation, Leningrad State University.

VonKorff, M. R., Eaton, W. W., & Keyl, P. M. (1985). The epidemiology of panic attacks and panic disorder: Results of three community surveys. *American Journal of Epidemiology, 122,* 970–981.

Wamboldt, M. Z., Yancey, A. G., Jr., & Roesler, T. A. (1997). Cardiovascular effects of tricyclic antidepressants in childhood asthma: A case series and review. *Journal of Child and Adolescent Psychopharmacology, 7,* 45–64.

Weiner, H. (1975). Are psychosomatic diseases, diseases of regulation? *Psychosomatic Medicine, 37,* 289–291.

Weiner, H. (1989). The dynamics of the organism. *Psychosomatic Medicine, 51,* 608–635.

Weiner, H. (1991). The revolution in stress theory and research. In R. Liberman & J. Yager (Eds.), *Stress in psychiatry and medicine.* New York: Plenum.

Weiner, P., Azgad, Y., Ganam, R., & Weiner, M. (1992). Inspiratory muscle training in patients with bronchial asthma. *Chest, 102,* 1357–1361.

Weiss, P. (1969). The living system: Determinism stratified. In A. Koestler & J. R. Smythies (Eds.), *Beyond reductionism.* Boston: Beacon.

Weissman, M. M., Bland, R. C., Canino, G. J., Faraveli, C., Greenwald, S., Hwu, H. G., Joyce, P. R., Karam. E. G., Lee, C. K., Lellouch, J., Lépine, J. P., Newman, S. C., Oakley-Brown, M. A., Rubio-Stipec, M., Wells, J. E., Wickramarante, P. J., Wittchen, H. U., & Yeh, E. K. (1997). The cross-national epidemiology of panic disorder. *Archives of General Psychiatry, 54,* 305–309.

Weissman, M. M., Markowitz, J. S., Ouellette, R., Greenwald, S., & Kahn, J. P. (1990). Panic disorder and cardiovascular/cerebrovascular problems: Results from a community survey. *American Journal of Psychiatry, 147,* 1504–1508.

West, B. J. (1990). Fractal physiology and chaos in medicine. Teaneck, NJ: World Scientific.

Yellowlees, P. M., Alpers, J. H., Bowden, J. J., Bryant, G. D., & Ruffin, R. E. (1987). Psychiatric morbidity in patients with chronic airflow obstruction. *Medical Journal of Australia, 146,* 305–307.

Yellowlees, P. M., Haynes, S., Potts, S., & Ruffin, R. E. (1988). Psychiatric morbidity in patients with life-threatening asthma. *Medical Journal of Australia, 149,* 246–249.

Yellowlees, P. M., & Kalucy, R. S. (1990). Psychobiological aspects of asthma and the consequent research implications. *Chest, 97,* 628–634.

Yeragani, V. K., Balon, R., & Pohl, R. (1991). A comparative study of immune status in panic disorder patients and controls. *Acta Psychiatrica Scandinavica, 84,* 396–397.

Yeragani, V. K., Pohl, R., Berger, R., Balon, R., Ramesh, C., Glitz, D., Srinivasan, K., & Weinberg, P. (1993). Decreased heart rate variability in panic disorder patients: A study of power-spectral analysis of heart rate. *Psychiatry Research, 46,* 89–103.

Yeragani, V. K., Srinivasan, K., Pohl, R., Berger, R., Balon, R., & Ramesh, C. (1994). Effects of nortriptyline on heart rate variability in panic disorder patients: A preliminary study using power spectral analysis. *Neuropsychobiology, 29,* 1–7.

Zandbergen, J., Bright, M., Pols, H., Fernandez, I., de Loof, C., & Greiz, E. J. L. (1991). Higher lifetime prevalence of respiratory diseases in panic disorder? *American Journal of Psychiatry, 148,* 1583–1585.

CHAPTER 14

EPILEPSY AND NONEPILEPTIC SEIZURES

Daniel T. Williams
Marcia P. Bergtraum

Stress and anxiety can impact both on epilepsy and on nonepileptic seizures in a variety of ways. First, as with most chronic medical conditions reviewed in this text, there is much data indicating that stress and anxiety can physiologically activate bona fide epileptic seizures in vulnerable individuals. Second, it is well established that stress and anxiety can activate nonepileptic seizures of both physiological and psychogenic origin. Probably the most challenging initial task facing the clinician in the management of a patient with uncontrolled seizures is the clarification of the nature of the seizure episodes as the prerequisite for informed treatment intervention. Consequently, we will address first, in some detail, the diversity of seizure phenomena and the process of differential diagnosis. The challenge of appropriate therapeutic intervention can then be considered, once appropriate differential diagnosis and associated clinical assessment have been completed.

Quite apart from the issue of seizures themselves, there are many other areas involving both psychopathology and quality of life in which the management of stress and anxiety has great relevance for patients with epilepsy and/or nonepileptic seizures. These issues are well addressed in the excellent review by McConnell and Duncan (1998) and will not be detailed here.

DEFINITIONS AND CLASSIFICATIONS

Epilepsy

Epilepsy can be defined as "a chronic brain disorder of various etiologies, characterized by recurrent seizures due to excessive discharge of cerebral neurons . . ." (Gastaut, 1973). Such seizures may occur in many conditions other than epilepsy, such as alcohol withdrawal, drug intoxication, electrolyte imbalance, vitamin deficiencies, and eclampsia. However, these seizures tend to remit by treatment of the underlying disturbance. The term *epilepsy* refers to a chronic condition during which seizures tend to recur if not treated, reflecting an underlying state of vulnerability or hyperexcitability within the central nervous system (Duffy, 1998).

In the International Classification of the Epilepsies and Epileptic Syndromes (Commission on Classification, 1989), syndromes are determined by several factors: the age of onset of seizures; seizure type(s); precipitating factors; severity; chronicity; prognosis; circadian cycling; genetic predisposition; interictal EEG findings; the presence of localized or diffuse cerebral pathology; and underlying neurological, neurophysiological, and neuropsychological abnormalities. While the details of this classification are beyond the scope of this chapter, the reader is referred to the discussion of this subject by Alarcon (1998).

Before considering the role that stress and anxiety may have in activating epileptic seizures, it is worth noting that epileptic seizures themselves may simulate anxiety and other psychiatric symptoms. Thus, epileptic seizures presenting with fear or panic are common in focal or partial seizures in children. If occurring at night, they may be misdiagnosed as night terrors or nightmares, which do not have epileptiform EEG abnormalities during the episodes. Similarly, absence seizures in childhood may be subtle and unrecognized, leading to misdiagnosis as attention deficit disorder, oppositional daydreaming, or dissociative disorder.

Approximately 30% of patients with moderate to severe developmental disabilities have epilepsy (Tuchman, Rapin, & Shimmas, 1991). Seizures in these patients may take unusual forms and may be difficult to differentiate from nonepileptic events, such as stereotypies. Nonconvulsive status epilepticus is easily missed in patients with developmental disabilities because it may present only as changes in affect, behavior, or subtle cognitive deterioration (Staufenberg & Brown, 1994). Associated symptoms, such as incontinence, aggression, and various forms of self-stimulation, may present further problems of differential diagnosis from epilepsy.

Epileptic auras in adults, particularly in temporal and occipital focal/partial epilepsies, may have features suggesting psychotic symptoms. Thus, visual hallucinations and/or illusions may occur in patients with occipital epilepsy or with temporal or parietal seizures propagating to the occipital cortex. Auditory hallucinations may occur as an ictal phenomenon in temporal lobe seizures. Abnormal psychic or somato-sensory experiences as well as affective symptoms, including fear or terror, may be common manifestations of focal/partial seizures. The ictal phenomena, however, tend to be more brief and circumscribed, usually lasting a few seconds to 1–2 minutes, in contrast to the primary psychiatric symptoms with which they may sometimes be confused. This contrasts with psychotic hallucinations that are interpreted by the patient as actual perceptions in the context of a generalized, delusionally distorted interpretation of the environment. (Of course, one must consider that in some individuals, epilepsy and psychosis may co-exist.)

Finally, the clinical manifestations of nonconvulsive status epilepticus, including simple-partial status, complex-partial status, and absence status epilepticus, may resemble various forms of psychiatric illness. Affective symptoms, dissociative symptoms, and anxiety symptoms are part of a broad spectrum of psychiatric presentations of these disorders (Shorvon, 1994). Such complexity at the neurology-psychiatry interface necessitates vigilance by clinicians in both domains.

Nonepileptic Seizures

A nonepileptic seizure can be defined as a paroxysmal clinical seizure that is not associated with a seizure discharge during concomitant electroencephalogram (EEG) recording (Gates, 1998). Nonepileptic seizures can, in turn, be divided into physiological and psychogenic nonepileptic events.

Physiological nonepileptic seizures include a broad spectrum of clinical conditions. Syncope is the most common in this category, with stress and anxiety being common precipitants of syncope in vulnerable individuals. The mechanisms generating syncope can be diverse, ranging from cardiac arrhythmia to autonomic failure associated with a simple vasovagal event. In young children, breath-holding spells may generate isolated clonic activity, or even a brief clonic phase, lasting 2–3 seconds. Often the precipitating stress or anxiety or the prodrome of lightheadedness, clamminess, and sweatiness in adolescents or adults will help distinguish syncope from epilepsy. The distinction may be more difficult, however, in a cognitively impaired, aged patient, who may be confused after the event. The possibilities of cardiologic, metabolic, endocrinologic, or other nonepileptic organic etiologies clearly must be considered in such a case.

Paroxysmal toxicity, such as that induced by amphetamines or cocaine, may not only stimulate panic attacks, psychotic episodes, or epileptic seizures acutely, but may actually predispose to development of epilepsy when used chronically, through a well-documented kindling effect. Similarly, alcohol intoxication may generate alcoholic hallucinosis and/or delirium tremens 24 to 72 hours after cessation, but also withdrawal seizures around the same time.

Other categories of physiological nonepileptic seizures include paroxysmal sleep disorders (Snyder, 1998), paroxysmal movement disorders, migraine and other forms of transient cerebrovascular ischemic attacks, as well as paroxysmal endocrine disturbances such as pheochromocytoma (Gates, 1998). It should be noted that many of these conditions can be activated by stress and anxiety.

Psychogenic nonepileptic seizures similarly encompass a broad spectrum of components, each with distinct phenomenologic features as well as diagnostic and treatment considerations (Williams et al., 1993).

Conversion seizures are the most commonly encountered type of psychogenic nonepileptic seizure. A conversion disorder is characterized by a loss or alteration of motor or sensory functioning that suggests physical disorder, but that instead is apparently an expression of a psychological conflict or a need

(American Psychiatric Association, 1994). After appropriate investigation the disturbance cannot be explained by any physical disorder or known pathophysiological mechanism. Psychological factors are judged to play a primary etiological role. Thus, a temporal relationship may exist between the onset or worsening of the symptom and the presence of an environmental stress that activates a psychological conflict or a need. Alternatively, the symptom may be noted to free the patient from a noxious activity or encounter. The symptom is not intentionally produced or feigned. Finally, the symptom causes clinically significant distress or impairment of functioning or warrants medical evaluation. There tends to be a female-to-male preponderance from 2:1 to 10:1 in adulthood.

Somatization disorder and undifferentiated somatoform disorder are more chronic and polysymptomatic variants of conversion disorder, with the associated requirement that the symptoms not be intentionally produced or feigned (American Psychiatric Association, 1994). In the case of somatization disorder there is a history of many physical complaints of several years' duration, beginning before age 30, which result in treatment being sought and/or significant impairment in important areas of functioning. Additional diagnostic criteria for somatization disorder include: four pain symptoms, two gastrointestinal symptoms, one sexual symptom, and one pseudoneurological symptom (commonly psychogenic nonepileptic seizures). After appropriate medical evaluation these symptoms either cannot be fully explained by a known medical condition (or substance abuse), or, when there is a related medical condition, the physical complaints or resulting impairment are in excess of what would be expected from objective clinical data.

Undifferentiated somatoform disorder has a more modest number and type of symptomatic requirements and a requisite duration of at least 6 months, positioning it in both severity and requisite chronicity between conversion disorder and somatization disorder.

It has been estimated that approximately 1% of the adult female population has one of the more chronic forms of somatoform disorders noted here (Ford, 1983; Smith, 1990), while it is rarely diagnosed in males. There is a higher incidence of antisocial personality disorder among those with a somatoform disorder

than in the general population. The clinical course tends to be chronic but fluctuating, and with rare incidence of spontaneous remission. A clinically important issue is the possibility that untreated protracted or recurrent episodes of conversion disorder in childhood or adolescence may predispose to subsequent development of somatization disorder (Williams & Hirsch, 1988). This points to the merits of early diagnostic and treatment intervention to diminish prospective chronicity.

Factitious disorders are characterized by physical or psychological symptoms that are intentionally produced or feigned, hence being by definition under voluntary control (American Psychiatric Association, 1994). The sense of voluntary control is subjective and can only be inferred by an outside observer, giving rise to ready diagnostic confusion with somatoform disorders. The judgment that symptoms are voluntarily produced is based on observations of behavior suggesting dissimulation or concealment, after excluding all other possible causes of the behavior. However, it should be noted that this behavior has a compulsive quality and hence is voluntary in the sense of being deliberate and purposeful, while implying a lack of full control that is an inherent feature of a compulsive behavior. Another essential feature is the psychological need to assume the sick role, as evidenced by the absence of external incentives for the behavior, such as economic gain, avoidance of onerous responsibilities, or attaining more comfortable circumstances via the sick role. This is important in distinguishing factitious disorders from malingering.

In its more chronic forms, factitious disorder may be associated with either physical symptoms (Munchausen syndrome) or psychological symptoms (Ganser's syndrome, pseudopsychosis, or pseudodementia). These manifestations are generally associated with severe dependent, masochistic, or antisocial personality disorders. Here again, these chronic forms of maladaptation are thought to derive from uncorrected patterns of using factitious symptoms as expressions of distress that frequently date from childhood. Iatrogenic problems may ensue from misguided medical and surgical interventions. A variant of this syndrome is Munchausen syndrome by proxy, first reported by Meadow (1982), in which children are presented by their parent(s) for medical evaluation and treatment for medically unfounded illnesses, resulting in repeated unwarranted and frequently harmful interventions.

Malingering, which is not classified as a psychiatric disorder, is characterized by the voluntary production and presentation of false or grossly exaggerated physical or psychological symptoms. In contrast to factitious disorder, the symptoms in malingering are produced in pursuit of a goal that is readily recognizable with an understanding of the individual's circumstances rather than his or her individual psychology (Kellner, 1991; Yudofsky, 1985). Examples of such readily understandable goals include the avoidance of school or work, the securing of financial compensation, the evasion of punishment, or the acquisition of drugs. An example of parentally induced malingering in a school-age child would be parents' encouraging their child, directly or indirectly, to persevere in reporting symptoms in the wake of an accident, for purposes of enhancing financial claims.

As with somatoform disorders and factitious disorders, the determination of a patient's volitional intent is often not possible with certainty by the clinician, especially at the outset of the clinical assessment. The particular characteristic of the malingerer, namely that of deceiving and manipulating the physician into unwitting compliance with a goal of the malingerer's choosing, is particularly likely to elicit strong countertransference feelings on the part of the physician when this diagnosis is suspected. Because the confrontational presentation of such suspicion to a patient will likely sabotage any prospects of a therapeutic relationship and transform it into a hostile, adversarial one, it is particularly important to refrain from such confrontation until all other differential diagnostic possibilities have been adequately considered and explored. It is important to note that somatoform disorders may include "secondary gains," which may falsely lead to the presumption of malingering. It is therefore best in ambiguous cases to give the patient, at least initially, the benefit of the doubt, so as to preserve the clinician's therapeutic leverage with a view to symptom alleviation. Failure of the patient (and/or parents in the case of child patients) to respond cooperatively to exhaustive supportive measures at appropriate psychotherapeutic intervention would become a reasonable basis for more critically revising one's initial diagnostic premise.

Additional psychiatric syndromes that may present with nonepileptic events of psychogenic origin include hypochondriasis, panic disorder, various forms of dissociative disorder, posttraumatic stress disorder, and various forms of psychotic disorder (Gates, 1998). Clearly an adequate assessment of a patient in whom the possible presence of psychogenic nonepileptic seizures has been considered requires a thorough psychiatric assessment to clarify the presence or absence of many potentially contributory psychiatric disorders.

Comorbidity of Seizure Types

To illustrate the differential diagnostic complexity that may pertain, consider a patient with uncontrolled seizures who is referred by a neurologist for psychiatric consultation because of apparent emotional precipitant of at least some seizures. The referring and consulting clinicians must discern what proportion of the seizures represent uncontrolled epileptic seizures, physiological or psychogenic nonepileptic seizures, or stress-induced epileptic seizures. Furthermore, they must consider whether some undiagnosed physical condition (e.g., central nervous system infection, tumor, or degenerative disease) may be contributory. They must also be aware that two or more of these conditions can co-exist in the same patient. Finally, quite apart from clarification of the nature of the seizure problem, there may be considerable psychopathology that may or may not impact on the seizures, but may clinically merit independent diagnostic assessment and treatment. The result can be and often is a diagnostic and therapeutic challenge that taxes the resources of even the most seasoned neurologists and psychiatrists (Williams & Mostofsky, 1982; Williams et al., 1993).

DIFFERENTIAL DIAGNOSIS

The crucial task of differential diagnosis of epileptic and nonepileptic seizures can be aided by history, physical examination, EEG recordings, neuroimaging, and various laboratory tests. Most often the evaluating physician is unable to observe the patient's seizures, so a careful and detailed medical history from a reliable observer in addition to the patient is often of primary importance in defining the initial diagnostic premise. A careful physical examination, delineating the presence of a previously unappreciated neurological or other medical abnormality, may further help define a previously unrecognized cause of seizures.

Even in patients with documented epilepsy, as most seizures are brief and infrequent, the majority of EEG recordings are interictal. Yet these interictal recordings often show abnormalities that can help diagnose and classify epileptic seizures. On the other hand, a single EEG in an awake individual will show epileptiform abnormalities in only 50% of patients with epilepsy.

Long-Term EEG Monitoring

In modern epilepsy monitoring units, which are progressively more widely available, telemetry permits ongoing and simultaneous recording of both the EEG and a video picture of the patient's clinical symptoms during extended periods, from several hours to days (Gates & Hemmes, 1990). The playback and review of events during this recording allows correlations between clinical and EEG events that allow a definitive diagnosis of epilepsy and/or nonepileptic seizures to be made in cases in which seizure history and standard EEG records were inconclusive. It is important to be certain that the recorded events are typical examples of the events the patient suffers. Review of the videotape with family members or other observers can help confirm this.

The experience of epilepsy centers with inpatient long-term monitoring (LTM) units is that the yield of seizures can be increased if the patient is withdrawn from anticonvulsants. While this has both diagnostic and therapeutic value for both epileptic and psychogenic nonepileptic seizure patients, it is important to note that this should be done in the hospital under the supervision of experienced personnel because of the potential danger involved.

Aside from its value in delineating epileptic seizure subtypes that have been difficult to record during EEG sessions, LTM has particular value in the assessment of nonepileptic seizures. The experience of Gates's group with psychogenic nonepileptic seizures identified a coincidence of epilepsy and psychogenic events in 58% of the patients with psychogenic events. It should be noted, however, that there is considerable variability in this proportion among various monitoring centers. Roughly 25% of patients admitted to the epilepsy monitoring unit at Columbia-Presbyterian

Medical Center are found to have psychogenic nonepileptic seizures. However, of these patients, only 10% had co-existing epileptiform seizures as well (unpublished data).

A problem arises periodically when a patient fails to have spontaneous seizure events in the LTM unit. A variety of suggestive techniques have been reported for precipitating psychogenic seizures in such circumstances (Cohen & Suter, 1982; Guberman, 1982; Linder, 1973; Peterson et al., 1950; Riley & Berndt, 1980).

The use of saline infusion as a suggestive technique (Cohen & Suter, 1982) has the advantage of being readily standardized and administered without the necessary presence of a mental health professional. It has the additional advantage of appealing to patients who would be highly resistant to the directly presented notion of a psychological etiology of their seizure events. The major disadvantage of this procedure is that it involves some degree of dissimulation, which could potentially complicate engagement of the patient in subsequent psychotherapeutic endeavor, unless the preparation of the patient, the diagnostic procedure, and the debriefing of the patient are done most judiciously.

The use of hypnosis to induce psychogenic seizures (Williams et al., 1993) has the advantage of directly demonstrating to the patient the phenomenon of psychogenic precipitation of seizure events, thereby establishing clearly and promptly both the rationale for psychotherapeutic intervention and the mental health professional who can initiate the process. The disadvantages include the greater difficulty in standardizing a hypnotic induction process, which is most effective when individualized, and the high likelihood of resistance and/or nonhypnotizability in some patients (e.g., those with factitious disorder, malingering, or psychosis). At this point, our preference is to defer the use of suggestive techniques to precipitate seizures until after an initial psychiatric consultation. At that juncture a more informed clinical judgment can be made about the preferred course of further diagnostic intervention.

Clinician's Approach to the Patient

One's tactical approach to the patient and family is important in establishing an appropriate rapport that is crucial for effective diagnostic assessment and treatment for all patients, but especially so with those having suspected stress-induced seizures. The patient with a somatoform disorder, for example, is by definition unaware of the relationship between environmental stress or intrapsychic conflict and the consequent appearance of the presenting symptoms. With such a patient a confrontational approach during the initial assessment is clearly counterproductive. Any inquiries that are perceived by the patient as seeking to establish such etiological connections in an accusatory tone are likely to be met with disbelief, denial, and resentment. A preferable approach, in general, is to begin by having the neurologist supportively explain to the patient that psychological/psychiatric consultation is being sought because of the possibility that stress factors may be playing some role in the patient's presenting symptoms, as they do in many commonly encountered medical problems. Most patients can accept the postulate that stress may intensify seizure frequency in analogy to the widely recognized observation that stress can increase heart rate and blood pressure.

The psychotherapist reemphasizes this point on initial contact with the patient. This opens the way for a collaborative dialog in which the patient (and family) can help the psychotherapist with two difficult tasks: first, understanding potential "stress" contributors to the seizures and then, one hopes, enabling the patient to attenuate these. If available medical information at the time of initial referral is not conclusive regarding the presence or absence of epilepsy, it is important to clarify that issue with the patient and family. It should also be explained that ongoing contact will be maintained with the neurologist, as both assessments proceed concurrently. An effective "team approach" minimizes the prospects of patients splitting the staff as a maladaptive defensive maneuver.

Psychological/psychiatric assessment should yield a detailed picture of the patient's individual strengths and weaknesses, social relationships, school or work functioning, and pattern of family interaction. The process of exploring these areas will often yield additional clues as to whether there exists a combination of intrinsic vulnerabilities in the patient and cumulative stressors in his or her environment that would predispose to the development of stress-induced seizures. Both patients and relatives should be specifically asked about any possible history of physical or sexual abuse, because the reported incidence of such abuse in patients with psychogenic seizures is high (Lowman

& Richardson, 1987). Every effort should be made to establish as fully as possible not only a clearly defined psychiatric diagnosis (American Psychiatric Association, 1994), but also a tentative formulation of potential psychodynamic and/or behavioral contingencies that might contribute specifically to stress-induced seizures. Formal psychological testing may be a valuable adjunct in the assessment of these patients (Batzel et al., 1991; Lowman & Richardson, 1987), but often cannot be arranged under the time constraints of an inpatient diagnostic assessment focused on seizure etiology.

After the completion of neurological and psychological/psychiatric evaluations, it is frequently helpful to have a joint meeting if possible with the patient, the neurologist, and the psychotherapist, particularly if the evaluation has been done in an inpatient setting. Such a meeting helps clarify the diagnosis to the patient and avoid misunderstandings or triangularizations between the patient and different clinicians.

PATHOGENESIS OF STRESS-INDUCED SEIZURES

It has long been recognized that a significant proportion of individuals with well-documented epilepsy report that some of their seizures seem to be precipitated by emotional stress (Fenwick, 1991; Gowers, 1885; Mattson, 1991). Indeed, the phenomenon of stress-induced epileptic seizures has been demonstrated electroencephalographically by many workers both in experimental animals (Lockard, 1980; Martinek & Hork, 1970; Swinyard et al., 1963) and in clinical populations (Antebi & Bird, 1992; Guey et al., 1969; Stevens, 1962).

It may be clinically advantageous when communicating with patients and their families to use the terms *stress-induced epileptic seizures* and *stress-induced nonepileptic seizures* to distinguish between these two categories. This may help avoid the negative connotation perceived by some patients in the term *psychogenic seizures* or in the even more pejorative and unfortunate term *pseudoseizures.*

Fenwick (1991) and Antebi and Bird (1992) outline the multifactorial determinants of the genesis of epileptic seizures in any individual. The term *seizure threshold,* viewed as relatively stable for the individual, has come to designate a general level of vulnerability to seizures based on genetic and constitutional factors. Independent of this intrinsic attribute of the individual, more transient influences, such as biochemical, metabolic, or psychological changes, may impact on the seizure threshold. Facilitating influences on this threshold may increase the likelihood of seizures during the time of our impact. Alternatively, some stimuli may evoke seizures directly, with a high degree of chronologic proximity and predictability. Antebi and Bird classify the facilitating and evocative stimuli as either physical (motor, sensory, or visceral) or psychological (cognitive or affective).

If uncomplicated by significant independent psychopathology, stress-induced epileptic seizures may be approached therapeutically with a variety of symptom-focused psychological and/or behavioral interventions (Mostofsky, 1993). If significant psychopathology coexists, this clearly needs to be addressed as well (McConnell & Duncan, 1998).

With respect to the broad domain of stress-induced nonepileptic seizures, the psychiatric categories of somatoform disorders, factitious disorders, and malingering are each complex and multidetermined, precluding any simple schema of etiology and pathogenesis. For any one of these categories an adequate assessment would have to consider the possible etiologic roles of psychodynamically based psychosexual conflicts, gratification of dependency needs, reaction to environmental stress, the phenomenon of dissociation, and neurophysiological predisposition, as well as anxiety and depression (Williams et al., 1993). Clinical formulations in this domain often involve hypothesis building based on historical information elicited from the patient and/or family or others with a view to garnering the most comprehensive possible understanding of pathogenesis as the soundest basis for treatment intervention. This approach avoids having the psychotherapist fixate prematurely on a plausible hypothesis that appeals to the psychotherapist, but which may be inaccurate and alienate the patient, thus undermining the prospects for successful treatment.

In this spirit, a preliminary hypothesis that is presented tentatively to the patient, seeking clarification or validation, has a better prospect of gaining thoughtful consideration than an interpretation presented with an authoritarian, judgmental tone.

TREATMENT OF STRESS-INDUCED SEIZURES

A variety of treatment approaches have been used with patients having stress-induced seizures. As with most psychotherapeutic interventions, controlled studies are extremely difficult to implement (Goldstein, 1990; Karasu, Conte, & Plutchik, 1984). Those therapeutic approaches that eclectic clinical experience has found useful will be considered here. Each of these treatment approaches has some potential value for some patients. Often, different treatment approaches can be effectively combined in the management of a given patient. It is consequently advantageous for the clinician to be well informed about as many of these approaches as possible, to be able to innovatively structure a treatment plan that most effectively meets the unique needs of each patient.

Implicit in this discussion is the observation that there does not yet exist a direct correlation between the specific type of stress-induced seizure and the specific type of treatment intervention clinically indicated. While a variety of modalities are outlined, some common underlying features may be delineated. These include the following:

1. Psychotherapeutic and behavioral intervention provides a framework, through careful, thoughtful review of the history, whereby the patient (and family) can discern and articulate postulated stress contributors to the uncontrolled seizures.

2. Once postulated stress contributants are identified, a strategy for their attenuation or control can be delineated. This engenders a sense of hope in the patient and family that a new level of understanding and a new treatment intervention can be brought to bear. An intrinsic calming effect on the patient is inherent in this process, if successfully applied.

3. Concomitant with the new treatment intervention there is an implicit or explicit dealing with secondary gain features that may have significantly contributed to the development and/or perpetuation of the symptoms.

4. The patient's self-esteem is protected by judicious handling of the above considerations. This frequently involves an emphasis on self-mastery, crediting the patient for active, collaborative participation in the treatment.

Reassurance, Placebo, and Suggestion

Variations on the theme of suggestion have been used throughout history, sometimes quite successfully, by religious healers, physicians, and others, as a way of relieving the symptoms of the various somatizing disorders that may give rise to seizures (Williams, 1997b). This approach involves the use of reassurance, placebo, and/or suggestion to foster symptom relinquishment without generating sophisticated grasp, by contemporary psychiatric standards, of the symptom's psychogenic determinants. Historically the use of prayer or an associated religious ceremony is often involved, for which the patient and/or family makes some monetary or other contribution as part of a process of expiation of sin or appeasement of the deity. In a more contemporary secular context the use of placebo can serve a comparable function in mobilizing the positive expectation and belief of the patient that relief of illness will be forthcoming thanks to the powerful forces of pharmacological intervention that the scientific revolution has generated. Recent studies have clarified the capacity of placebo to affect neurophysiological functioning by activating the release of endorphins within the central nervous system, so that dismissing this process as "merely suggestion" is unwarranted (Spiegel & Albert, 1983). The use of these nonspecific modalities employed by medical practitioners prior to referral for psychological or psychiatric consultation may be effective for the relief of acute conversion symptoms that arise in response to a short-term and self-limited environmental stress. When used supportively and sensitively in such a setting, this approach may be effective in achieving sustained symptom relief. Further, it should be noted, the nonspecific effects of reassurance, placebo, and suggestion exert a powerful auxiliary influence in combination with any of the more specific treatments that will be outlined here.

Complications may arise, however, when a physician prescribes anticonvulsant medication with or without the knowledge that a stress-induced nonepileptic seizure disorder exists. Here one may initiate a long-standing medication regimen for the patient with considerable untoward side effects that may vitiate and outweigh initial placebo benefits (Dodrill, 1991; Smith, 1991).

Additional complications may arise when a treatment approach based exclusively on reassurance, placebo, or suggestion is used indiscriminately for such seizures, including those with complex, sustained intrapsychic determinants and/or in the presence of continuing, unmanageable environmental stress. In such situations this approach is counterproductive: It will be either totally ineffective or of only short-term benefit, with subsequent emergence of symptom recurrence or substitution. Furthermore, there is a loss of confidence by the patient and family in the clinician who takes such an approach. This is so because an attempt has been made to remove a symptom that has been serving a defensive function, albeit maladaptively, without an effort to alleviate the patient's underlying sources of distress.

Individual and Family Therapies

Only brief discussion of individual and family therapies can be outlined here. Because a myriad of intermingling etiological factors may pertain, it behooves the clinician to address as many of the pertinent issues as possible in the course of history taking. Based on a thorough exploration of relevant factors in this context, a working hypothesis regarding the evolution of the psychogenic seizure disorder is likely to emerge. With this working hypothesis in mind, the clinician's next task is to explore possible ways to alleviate pathogenic environmental influences impinging on the patient and/or to augment the patient's capacity for mastering ongoing sources of distress.

Alleviating environmental stress often involves working with the patient's immediate family and significant others. If marital conflict with an adult patient's spouse or between a child patient's parents is apparently contributing to a patient's psychogenic seizures, for example, direct counseling of the family member as well as the patient should be considered. Similarly, if a "valedictorian syndrome" exists in a school-age child, whereby parents, teachers, and/or even the patient have generated excessive demands for academic achievement relative to the youngster's actual intellectual capacity, then direct, supportive counseling of both the patient and the family as well as communication with teachers may be needed in order to alleviate this frequent contributant to somatization. As another example, if sexual abuse or seduction has been a precipitating factor, clearly the protection of the patient from the perpetrator as well as supportive alleviation of the patient's associated feelings of guilt and/or violation are essential ingredients in the treatment plan.

Dealing with the apparent dynamics of intrapsychic and family conflict in patients with psychogenic seizures requires tact and sensitivity. It is useful to view the somatizing symptom as a makeshift refuge to which the patient has intuitively and sometimes unconsciously retreated under duress. The clinician is challenged to formulate for the patient and family a safe and honorable route by which the symptom can be understood as a maladaptive defense encumbrance that can be relinquished with dignity in favor of a more effective coping method. There are many ways to do this, but the clinician commonly presents some version of a working hypothesis to the patient (and family, when appropriate) to aid the process of cognitive, emotional, and behavioral reorientation. The extent to which this process can be "worked through" with the patient and family members in terms of conscious understanding of the relevant dynamics is variable.

In the pursuit of the therapeutic goals noted here, several specialized treatment approaches are often helpful in the context of individual and/or family therapy. Some of these will be briefly discussed.

Psychodynamic Psychotherapy

From the time of Freud's initial exploration of the dynamics of hysteria until recently it was believed by many that psychoanalysis or intensive long-term dynamic psychotherapy was the specific treatment of choice for somatoform disorders (Kellner, 1989). It is now apparent that only a minority of the total number of patients with these disorders are candidates for such therapy. This is true in part because of the combined demands of time, money, and intellectual investment that most patients and families simply do not have. Equally important, however, is the fact that, for many patients, other approaches can achieve therapeutic results more rapidly and with much less expense.

Clearly psychiatrists who work with patients having psychogenic seizures must have a sophisticated grasp of the subtle and complex factors involved in the diverse intrapsychic, interpersonal, and environmental fields that impinge on these patients. It is not nec-

essary, however, for each patient to attain a full level of insight in order to achieve effective and sustained symptom relief. Extended psychodynamic work can certainly add new dimensions of self-understanding for those with the resources to use this approach. Yet, for the many who for various reasons cannot or do not wish to do so, more supportive and directive methods of treatment are more appropriate.

Hypnosis

Freud's interest in developing the technique of psychoanalysis was heavily influenced by the limitations he observed both in Charcot's authoritarian use of hypnosis to treat stress-induced nonepileptic seizures and by Freud's own use of hypnosis to treat various forms of hysteria (Freud, 1955a). These limitations included the narrow use of abreaction and suggestion without benefit of the dynamic understanding of symptom formation that Freud was subsequently to develop. Freud himself in later years foresaw how public health needs would rekindle a need for hypnosis to enable more widespread, expeditious therapeutic application of psychodynamic insights (Freud, 1955b).

Further considerations about the use of hypnosis with patients having seizures and other somatizing disorders are outlined elsewhere (Williams, 1997a,b). Admonitions sometimes expressed against the use of hypnosis with such patients are based on the erroneous assumption that hypnosis necessarily involves the simplistic and authoritarian use of direct suggestion. Furthermore, there are some positive benefits to enabling a patient and family to learn that the patient's capacity for dissociation can be elicited under controlled therapeutic conditions. In this context, the dissociation that is an essential ingredient in the symptom formation of somatoform disorders can be clearly understood by the patient and family as a manageable psychological attribute that can be channeled, under therapeutic auspices, in the service of symptom alleviation. Teaching the patient a self-hypnosis exercise can help shift the patient's (and family's) attention away from preoccupation with the sick role and toward the mastery experience of returning to normal functioning.

The basis for advocating the use of hypnosis as a therapeutic adjunct for patients with psychogenically precipitated epileptic seizures is less clearly established. However, Spiegel (1991) has reviewed the growing body of evidence pointing to the capacity of hypnosis to impact on a variety of neurophysiological processes, providing suggestive support for this clinical intervention. Thus, highly hypnotizable subjects are capable of producing bidirectional changes in cortical event-related potential amplitude to sensory stimuli, depending on the cognitive task employed during hypnosis. By contrast, subjects not easily hypnotized, studied under identical, controlled conditions, showed no such changes. The demonstrated capacity of hypnotic trance states to influence gastric acid secretion (Klein & Spiegel, 1989), pain perception (Spiegel, Bierre, & Rootenberg, 1989), and blood pressure (Benson & Klipper, 1976) provides a plausible rationale for the therapeutic application of hypnosis for stress-induced epileptic seizures.

In the format used by our group, measurement of hypnotic capacity using the Hypnotic Induction Profile (Spiegel & Spiegel, 1978) is part of the initial assessment of all patients being evaluated for possible psychogenic seizures. If combined neurological and psychiatric assessment supports the impression of stress-induced seizures, hypnotizable patients are taught a self-hypnosis exercise as part of the treatment program. The content of this exercise is individualized, based on the history, cognitive capacity, and psychodynamic picture presented by the patient. Furthermore, other aspects of the treatment are also individualized, including the frequency and format of individual and family therapy; associated behavior modification strategies; and, in some cases, psychopharmacological intervention. It is thus evident that while the use of self-hypnosis as a treatment intervention for stress-induced seizures incorporates many of the features of relaxation and desensitization outlined by Fenwick (1989, 1991), delineation of the specific impact of hypnosis under such varied clinical conditions is not currently feasible.

Behavior Modification

Therapeutic strategies geared to symptom alleviation in the somatizing disorders must deal with the secondary gain features of the symptoms. (In the case of malingering, these are equivalent to the primary gain features.) Especially with children, adolescents, and retarded patients, but also with many nonretarded

adults, the long-range benefits of a therapeutic endeavor may be difficult for the patient to appreciate if the immediate benefits of the symptom constitute a substantial deterrent to symptom relinquishment. It is therefore essential that any ongoing secondary gain features of a symptom be diminished or eliminated. Indeed, this is crucial if the symptom's removal is to be sustained.

Mostofsky and Balaschak (1977) and Mostofsky (1993) illustrate a number of ways in which behavior modification strategies can be formulated with seizure patients, taking into account the existing contingencies of reinforcement that impinge on the patient. A number of subsequent reviews (Fenwick, 1989, 1991; Goldstein, 1990) have updated the status of the behavioral treatments of epilepsy. Because these reviews are detailed and comprehensive, they will not be re-outlined here. Suffice it to say that a growing number of behavioral studies with improved methodologies provide abundant evidence of the close relationship between epileptic seizure activity and the psychological state of the patient. It follows that seizure control in many patients can be significantly influenced by altering the patient's outlook and behavior. A variety of behavioral strategies are addressed by these reviews, with no clear delineation yet feasible of the specific correlation between the optimal behavioral intervention for specific seizure type.

Psychotropic Medication

Insofar as stress-induced epileptic and nonepileptic seizures frequently co-exist with other psychiatric disorders responding to medication, the psychiatrist should be prepared to consider the potential value of psychotropic medications in treating patients with stress-induced seizures. In our experience, depression is a particularly common comorbidity in these patients and appropriate use of antidepressant medication is frequently helpful (McConnell & Duncan, 1998). The additional therapeutic value of such medication for many of these patients (aside from psychopharmacological benefit) is that it permits more ready acceptance of a treatment program when there is a "biological" component on the part of patients resistant to accepting a primary psychological explanation of their disorder. The obvious caveat here is that with patients who have both nonepileptic and epileptic seizures, one must evaluate the potential impact of psychotropic medication both on the epileptic seizure threshold and on the level of co-existing anticonvulsant medication. Clinical experience suggests that selective serotonin reuptake inhibitors are the antidepressants best tolerated in this population. Similar considerations of benefits, side effects, and potential drug interactions apply to the use of other anti-anxiety and antipsychotic medications.

Special Considerations with Children, Adolescents, and Retarded Patients

The importance of effectively engaging the family or other caregivers of children, adolescents, and retarded patients cannot be overemphasized. While this principle would apply to any psychotherapeutic intervention with such patients, the additional features of dependency and disability engendered by uncontrolled seizures reinforces this. Parents and/or other caregivers should be interviewed early in the diagnostic process as important sources of relevant information that may not be available from the patient or the medical chart. Similarly, these caregivers will most often be crucial in formulating treatment plans that involve rearranging contingencies of reinforcement for ongoing behavior, supportively reviewing therapeutic communications with the patient, and administering medication.

Supportive Reality Testing

Even the most experienced of clinicians will encounter some patients and families with whom extensive combined neurological, psychotherapeutic, and behavioral endeavor geared toward symptom alleviation is unsuccessful in establishing clinically adequate improvement in seizure control. Sometimes this may be related to the intractable nature of the epileptic disorder that resists available options of pharmacological and/or surgical intervention. In such circumstances, psychotherapeutic support is often needed for the patient and family struggling to cope with the patient's impaired level of functioning.

In other situations, however, efforts at clinical intervention with patients having uncontrolled nonepileptic seizures are defeated by the tenacious conscious or unconscious psychological investment that the patient and/or family has made in the incurability of the presenting seizure symptoms. Clinical experience suggests that this latter form of failure is more common when a somatizing disorder (with or without associated epilepsy) has become chronic and has gone through a succession of failed medical and psychotherapeutic interventions. In these cases the somatizing disorder often appears to be interwoven with associated personality disorder in the patient and/or family, variably involving dependent, histrionic, antisocial, masochistic, or borderline features. In such situations the degree of individual and/or family psychopathology frequently constitutes a substantial source of resistance to appropriate treatment. These circumstances are particularly common in patients with somatization disorder, factitious disorder, and malingering. In such circumstances, referral to a psychiatric inpatient service familiar with treatment of patients having stress-induced seizures may be appropriate. Such patients and/or families, initially unwilling to explore somatizing aspects of their illness, may be willing to address features of the patient's anxiety, depression, or other dysphoric symptoms that can be the starting point for therapeutic work. Some patients and families will, however, be unengageable in treatment despite the most flexible and extended efforts. If frank abuse or neglect of the patient is documented and efforts at engagement of the patient and family in treatment are unsuccessful, the involvement of appropriate legal and welfare agencies may be necessary.

CONCLUSION

A neuropsychiatrically sophisticated assessment of patients with uncontrolled seizures may be helpful in delineating stress-inducing contributors to the seizures and hence may allow formulation of a more effective treatment program. Differential diagnosis is clearly the first task, requiring an appreciation of potential multifactorial contributors to both epileptic and nonepileptic seizures, as well as of the many different phenomenologic manifestations of both types of seizures. Once a reasonably informed working hypothesis regarding diagnosis is established, the therapist's task involves helping the patient reformulate his or her strategy of coping with ongoing life stresses and thus achieve improved seizure control. Accumulated clinical experience points to a number of specific therapeutic techniques that may be helpful. The therapist who approaches this task will expand the potential for effective intervention by being able to integrate those techniques that seem most pertinent to the needs of the individual patient, while effectively conveying an empathic sensitivity for the patient's struggle to improve his or her level of functioning.

REFERENCES

Alarcon, G. (1998). Diagnosis and classification of the epilepsies: Pathophysiological and psychiatric aspects. In H. W. McConnell & P. J. Snyder (Eds.), *Psychiatric comorbidity in epilepsy: Basic mechanisms, diagnosis and treatment* (pp. 37–84). Washington, DC: American Psychiatric Press.

American Psychiatric Association. (1994). *Diagnostic and statistical manual of mental disorders* (4th ed.). Washington, DC: American Psychiatric Association.

Antebi, D., & Bird, J. (1992). The facilitation and evocation of seizures. *British Journal of Psychiatry, 160,* 154–164.

Batzel, L. W., Dodrill, C. B., Dubinsky, B. L., et al. (1991). An objective method for the assessment of psychosocial problems in adolescents with epilepsy. *Epilepsia, 32,* 202–211.

Benson, H., & Klipper, M. Z. (1976). *The relaxation response.* New York: Morrow.

Cohen, R. J., & Suter, C. (1982). Hysterical seizures: Suggestion as a provocative EEG test. *Annals of Neurology, 11,* 391–395.

Commission on Classification and Terminology of the International League against Epilepsy. (1989). Proposal for revised classification of epilepsies and epileptic syndromes. *Epilepsia, 30,* 389–399.

Dodrill, C. B. (1991). Behavioral effects of antiepileptic drugs. In D. B. Smith, D. M. Treiman, & M. R. Trimble (Eds.), *Neurobehavioral problems in epilepsy* (pp. 213–214). New York: Raven Press.

Duffy, J. D. (1998). The shifting paradigm of epilepsy: A review of historical trends and current perspectives. In H. W. McConnell & P. J. Snyder (Eds.), *Psychiatric comorbidity in epilepsy: Basic mechanisms, diagnosis, and treatment* (pp. 1–14). Washington, DC: American Psychiatric Press.

Fenwick, P. (1989). Behavioral treatment of epilepsy. *International Review of Psychiatry, 1,* 297–306.

Fenwick, P. (1991). Evocation and inhibition of seizures: Behavioral treatment. In D. B. Smith, D. M. Treiman, & M. R. Trimble (Eds.), *Neurobehavioral problems in epilepsy* (pp. 163–184). New York: Raven Press.

Ford, C. V. (1983). *The somatizing disorders: Illness as a way of life:* New York: Elsevier Biomedical.

Freud, S. (1955a). An autobiographical study. In J. Strachey (Ed.), *The standard edition of the complete psychological works of Sigmund Freud* (vol. 20) (pp. 3–74). London: Hogarth Press.

Freud, S. (1955b). Lines of advance in psychoanalytic therapy. In J. Strachey (Ed.), *The standard edition of the complete psychological works of Sigmund Freud* (vol. 17) (pp. 195–168). London: Hogarth Press.

Gastaut, H. (1973). *Dictionary of epilepsy.* Geneva, Switzerland: World Health Organization.

Gates, J. R. (1998). Diagnosis and treatment of nonepileptic seizures. In H. W. McConnell & P. J. Snyder (Eds.), *Psychiatric comorbidity in epilepsy: Basic mechanisms, diagnosis, and treatment* (pp. 187–204). Washington, DC: American Psychiatric Press.

Gates, J. R., & Hemmes, R. (1990). Role and implementation of long-term monitoring for epilepsy. *Seminars in Neurology, 10,* 357–365.

Goldstein, L. H. (1990). Behavioral and cognitive-behavioral treatments for epilepsy: A progress review. *British Journal of Clinical Psychology, 29,* 257–269.

Gowers, W. R. (1885). *Epilepsy and other chronic convulsive diseases.* New York: Wood.

Guberman, A. (1982). Psychogenic seizures in nonepileptic patients. *Canadian Journal of Psychiatry, 27,* 401–404.

Guey, J., Bureau, M., Dravet, C., et al. (1969). Study of the rhythm of petit-mal absences in children in relation to prevailing situations. *Epilepsia, 10,* 441–451.

Karasu, T. B., Conte, H. R., & Plutchik, R. (1984). Psychotherapy outcome research. In T. B. Karasu (Ed.), *The psychosocial therapies* (pp. 831–872). Washington, DC: American Psychiatric Association.

Kellner, R. (1989). Somatoform and factitious disorders. In American Psychiatric Association (Ed.), *Treatments of psychiatric disorders* (vol. 3) (pp. 2119–2184). Washington, DC: American Psychiatric Association.

Kellner, R. (1991). *Psychosomatic symptoms and somatic syndromes.* Washington, DC: American Psychiatric Press.

Klein, K. B., & Spiegel, D. (1989). Modulation of gastric acid secretion by hypnosis. *Gastroenterology, 96,* 1383–1387.

Lesser, R. P. (1985). Psychogenic seizures. In T. A. Pedley & B. S. Meldrum (Eds.), *Recent advances in epilepsy* (no. 2). Edinburgh: Churchill Livingston.

Linder, H. (1973). Psychogenic seizure states: A psychodynamic study. *International Journal of Clinical and Experimental Hypnosis, 21,* 261–271.

Lockard, J. S. (1980). A primate model of clinical epilepsy: Mechanisms of action through quantification of therapeutic effects. In J. S. Lockard & A. A. Ward (Eds.),

Epilepsy: A window to brain mechanisms (pp. 11–49). New York: Raven Press.

Lowman, R. L., & Richardson, L. M. (1987). Pseudo-epileptic seizures of psychogenic origin: A review of the literature. *Clinical Psychology Review, 7,* 363–389.

Martinek, Z., & Hork, F. (1970). Development of so called "genuine" epileptic seizures in dogs during emotional excitement. *Physiologia Bohemoslovaca, 19,* 185–195.

Mattson, R. H. (1991). Emotional effects on seizure occurrence. In D. B. Smith, D. M. Treiman, & M. R. Trimble (Eds.), *Neurobiological problems in epilepsy* (pp. 453–460). New York: Raven Press.

McConnell, H. W., & Duncan, D. (1998). Treatment of psychiatric comorbidity in epilepsy. In H. W. McConnell & P. J. Snyder (Eds.), *Psychiatric comorbidity in epilepsy: Basic mechanisms, diagnosis, and treatment* (pp. 245–362). Washington, DC: American Psychiatric Press.

Meadow, R. (1982). Munchausen syndrome by proxy. *Archives Diseases of Children, 57,* 92–98.

Mostofsky, D. I. (1993). Behavior modification and therapy in the management of epileptic disorders. In D. I. Mostofsky & Y. Loyning (Eds.), *The neurobehavioral treatment of epilepsy* (pp. 67–82). Hillsdale, NJ: Erlbaum.

Mostofsky, D. I., & Balaschak, B. A. (1977). Psychobiological control of seizures. *Psychological Bulletin, 84,* 723–750.

Peterson, D. B., Sumner, J. W., & Jones, G. A. (1950). Role of hypnosis in differentiation of epileptic from convulsive-like seizures. *American Journal of Psychiatry, 107,* 428–433.

Riley, T. L., & Berndt, T. (1980). The role of the EEG technologist in delineating pseudoseizures. *American Journal of EEG Technology, 20,* 89–96.

Shorvon, S. D. (1994). *Status epilepticus: Its clinical features and treatment in children and adults.* Cambridge, MA: Cambridge University Press.

Smith, D. B. (1991). Cognitive effects of antiepileptic drugs. In D. B. Smith, D. M. Treiman, & M. R. Trimble (Eds.), *Neurobehavioral problems in epilepsy* (pp. 197–212). New York: Raven Press.

Smith, G. R., Jr. (1990). *Somatization disorder in the medical setting.* Washington, DC: National Institute of Mental Health, U.S. Government Printing Office.

Snyder, P. J. (1998). Sleep and seizures: A selective review. In H. W. McConnell & P. J. Snyder (Eds.), *Psychiatric comorbidity in epilepsy: Basic mechanisms, diagnosis, and treatment* (pp. 115–132). Washington, DC: American Psychiatric Press.

Spiegel, D. (1991). Neurophysiological correlates of hypnosis and dissociation. *Journal of Neuropsychiatry and Clinical Neurosciences, 3,* 440–445.

Spiegel, D., & Albert, L. (1983). Naloxone fails to reverse hypnotic alleviation of chronic pain. *Psychopharmacology, 81,* 140–143.

Spiegel, D., Bierre, P., & Rootenberg, J. (1989). Hypnotic alteration of somatosensory perception. *American Journal of Psychiatry, 146,* 749–754.

Spiegel, H., & Spiegel, D. (1978). *Trance and treatment: Clinical uses of hypnosis.* New York: Basic Books.

Staufenberg, E. F., & Brown, S. W. (1994). Some issues in nonconvulsive status epilepticus in children and adolescents with learning difficulties. *Seizure, 3,* 95–105.

Stevens, J. (1962). Endogenous conditioning to abnormal cerebral electrical transients in man. *Science, 137,* 974–976.

Swinyard, E. A., Mijahara, J. T., Clark, L. D., et al. (1963). The effect of experimentally-induced stress on pentylenetetrazol threshold in mice. *Psychopharmacologia, 4,* 343–353.

Tuchman, R. F., Rapin, I., & Shimmas, S. (1991). Autistic and dysphasic children, II: Epilepsy. *Pediatrics, 88,* 1219–1225.

Williams, D. T. (1997a). Hypnosis. In J. M. Weiner (Ed.), *Textbook of child and adolescent psychiatry* (2d ed.) (pp. 893–904). Washington, DC: American Psychiatric Press.

Williams, D. T. (1997b). Somatoform disorders, factitious disorders and malingering. In J. D. Noshpitz (Ed.), *Handbook of child and adolescent psychiatry* (vol. 2) (pp. 563–578). New York: Wiley.

Williams, D. T., & Hirsch, G. (1988). The somatizing disorders: Somatoform disorders, factitious disorders and malingering. In C. J. Kestenbaum & D. T. Williams (Eds.), *Handbook of clinical assessment of children and adolescents* (vol. 2) (pp. 734–768). New York: New York University Press.

Williams, D. T., & Mostofsky, D. (1982). Psychogenic seizures in childhood and adolescence. In T. Riley & A. Roy (Eds.), *Pseudoseizures* (pp. 169–184). Baltimore, MD: Williams & Wilkins.

Williams, D. T., Walezak, T., Berten, W., Nordli, D., & Bergtraum, M. (1993). Psychogenic seizures. In D. I. Mostofsky & Y. Loyning (Eds.), *The neurobehavioral treatment of epilepsy* (pp. 83–106). Hillsdale, NJ: Erlbaum.

Yudofsky, S. (1985). Malingering. In H. I. Kaplan & B. J. Sadock (Eds.), *Comprehensive textbook of psychiatry* (vol. 2) (4th ed.) (pp. 1862–1864). Baltimore, MD: Williams & Wilkins.

CHAPTER 15

ANXIETY AND ITS MANAGEMENT IN IRRITABLE BOWEL SYNDROME

Edward B. Blanchard
Shannon M. Turner

WHAT IS IRRITABLE BOWEL SYNDROME?

Irritable bowel syndrome (IBS) is a widespread functional disorder of the lower gastrointestinal (GI) tract. Although it has historically been conceptualized as a GI disorder, we will attempt to show in this chapter that anxiety plays a large role in many cases of IBS and that it is at least useful, if not correct, to conceptualize IBS as an anxiety disorder variant.

We readily acknowledge that we are not the first to conceptualize IBS this way. Latimer (1983) made the point 15 years ago that IBS sufferers could be thought of as neurotics (the predecessor of our current day anxiety disorders) who happened to focus heavily on GI symptoms. Despite his pioneering empirical and conceptual work on this topic, it has failed to have a major impact in the field.

Clinical Criteria for Diagnosis

Until recently the diagnosis of IBS both on a clinical basis and for research used the so-called clinical criteria, which made IBS a residual diagnosis, or a

TABLE 15.1. Clinical Criteria for Diagnosis of IBS

1. Cramping abdominal pain and/or severe abdominal tenderness.
2. Altered bowel habit, either frequent diarrhea or constipation or alternating diarrhea and constipation.
3. Symptoms have been present most days for at least 3 months.
4. Rule out other possible causes of symptom picture by appropriate tests:
   a. Inflammatory bowel disease
   b. Lactose intolerance
   c. Parasites
   d. Other GI diseases

Source: Adapted from Latimer (1983).

diagnosis based on exclusion. In Table 15.1 are listed the clinical criteria for diagnosis. From the criteria listed in Table 15.1, it is apparent that one needed to exclude all of the other medical conditions that could lead to a similar symptom picture. Once the tests for these other diseases had been done and found to be negative, the residual diagnosis was IBS. One difficulty with this residual diagnosis approach (which was similar to the approach taken by *DSM-III* [American Psychiatric Association, 1980] for generalized anxiety disorder [GAD]) is that the majority of patients with this symptom picture were, in fact, suffering from IBS.

The Rome Criteria—toward a Positive Diagnosis

The last 10 to 12 years have seen a growing research interest in IBS and other functional GI disorders. Within this research community there was dissatisfaction with clinical diagnostic criteria. A team of gastroenterologists and behavioral scientists has published a new set of diagnostic criteria for IBS that lends itself to making a positive diagnosis of IBS rather than an exclusionary diagnosis. The agreement on these criteria grew out of a meeting in Rome; hence they have been called the Rome criteria. They are presented in Table 15.2.

These criteria still require the conduct of medical tests to exclude other GI diseases but are much more a diagnosis of inclusion. The intellectual roots of the criteria are a paper by Manning et al. (1978) that examined 109 unselected patients with abdominal pain and change in bowel habit by use of a 15-item (symptoms) questionnaire. About 18 months later the authors felt extremely confident of the diagnosis of 32 IBS

TABLE 15.2. Rome Criteria for Diagnosis of IBS

Continuous or recurrent symptoms for at least 3 months of:
1. Abdominal pain or discomfort, relieved with defecation, or associated with a change in frequency or consistency of stool and
2. An irregular (varying) pattern of defecation at least 25% of the time (2 or more of):
   a. Altered stool frequency
   b. Altered stool form (hard or loose/watery stool)
   c. Altered stool passage (straining or urgency, feeling of incomplete evacuation)
   d. Passage of mucus
   e. Bloating or feeling of abdominal distension

Source: Adapted from Drossman et al. (1990), *Gastroenterology International, 3,* 159–172.

patients and 33 patients with organic GI disease. Comparison of the two samples revealed four symptoms that discriminated between the two samples at the .01 level or better: looser stools at onset of pain, more frequent bowel movements at onset of pain, pain often eased after bowel movement, and visible distension. Three other symptoms approached this level (.05 $<p<$.10): feeling of distension, mucus per rectum, and frequent feeling of incomplete emptying. No single symptom completed separated these two samples. In fact, the highest level of diagnostic efficiency for any single symptom was 77%. These symptoms became known as the "Manning criteria" and heavily influenced the Rome criteria. Most research over the last 5 years has used the Rome criteria.

Epidemiology—the Potential Size of the Problem

There may be as many as 20 to 40 million adults in the United States who have suffered from IBS in their lifetime. Somewhat dated epidemiological data suggest that the U.S. lifetime prevalence of IBS ranges from 8% (Whitehead et al., 1982) to 17% (Drossman et al., 1982) of adults.

Two high-quality epidemiological studies have recently been reported. In the first, Talley et al. (1991) surveyed an age- and sex-stratified sample of 1,021 residents of a midwestern county with a well-validated self-report questionnaire to identify GI symptoms and functional GI disorders. The response rate was 82% for this largely Caucasian sample age 30 to 65. Using the Manning criteria, they found a 1-year prevalence of 17.0 per 100 for IBS. Interestingly, only about

half of those who met the criteria, including six or more episodes of abdominal pain, had sought medical attention.

In the second, larger study, Drossman et al. (1993) sent questionnaires on functional GI symptoms to 8,250 households, randomly selected to match the U.S. adult population demographically and geographically. Their response rate was 66%. They found a prevalence of 11.2% for IBS, diagnosed by the Rome criteria, with females outnumbering males 14.5% to 7.7%. Fewer than half (46%) had ever seen a physician because of the problem.

There is thus some discrepancy in prevalence rate—11% versus 17%; however, even the lower value means 20 million American adults suffer from this problem. Interestingly, both studies found roughly half of the identified cases had ever sought medical attention for the problem, a point to be addressed in a later section of this chapter. Finally, this problem appears to need a more precise survey utilizing trained telephone interviewers to gather data of higher quality.

Psychological Distress in IBS Patients

One of the consistent findings in psychosocial studies of IBS patients is that, as a group, they show a relatively high level of psychological distress, both as measured by standardized psychological tests and as indicated by structured psychiatric diagnostic interviews. The latter topic will be discussed in more detail in a later section of this paper.

In Table 15.3 are summarized data from several reports from the CSAD (Center for Stress and Anxiety Disorders, University at Albany). In Table 15.4 are summarized similar data from studies from other laboratories. From the results in Table 15.3, one can see that the IBS samples seen in Albany at the CSAD are, on average, mildly depressed and mildly anxious. The mean Beck Depression Inventory (BDI) (Beck et al., 1961) score is between 11 and 12, indicating a noticeable but mild level of depression. This is confirmed by the average Minnesota Multiphasic Personality Inventory (MMPI) Depression scale score of 70.2.

State Anxiety scores are more variable, with a mean of about 47. According to published norms (Spielberger, 1983), this score is at the 45th percentile for psychiatric patients, the 61st percentile for general

TABLE 15.3. Summary of Psychological Test Scores from IBS Patients Seen at CSAD

STUDY CHARACTERISTICS AND PSYCHOLOGICAL MEASURES	BLANCHARD (1993)	SCHWARZ ET AL. (1993)	GREENE & BLANCHARD (1994)	PAYNE & BLANCHARD (1995)	VOLLMER & BLANCHARD (1998)
Sample size	121	121	20	34	29
Diagnostic criteria	Clinical	Clinical	Clinical	Rome	Rome
STAI-State	48 median	50.7	40.1	44.3	60.0
STAI-Trait	46 median	47.2	47.1	48.5	59.2
Beck Depression Inventory	10 median	11.3	11.2	12.5	12.3
Psychosomatic Symptoms Checklist—total		41.3			
MMPI 1. Hypochondriasis		68.4			
2. Depression		70.1			
3. Hysteria		65.8			
4. Psychopathic dev.		63.7			
6. Paranoia		60.7			
7. Psychasthenia		66.7			
8. Schizophrenia		63.4			
9. Hypomania		55.0			

Notes: STAI is Spielberger et al.'s State-Trait Anxiety Inventory.
Blanchard (1993) and Schwarz et al. (1993) are the same sample.
In Blanchard (1993) the distribution of scores was given, hence the median. All other values are means.

medical patients, and the 84th percentile for normal middle-age females. The Trait Anxiety scores are more stable, averaging between 47 and 48. According to the norms, this score is at the 54th percentile for psychiatric patients, the 72nd percentile for general medical patients, and the 90th percentile for normal middle-age females.

Clearly, based upon the State-Trait Anxiety Inventory (STAI), our IBS patients are, on average, noticeably anxious, especially when compared to normal adults. Their average scores place them at about the median of the distribution for psychiatric patients.

Examining Table 15.4, one finds psychological test scores similar to those in Table 15.3; that is, anxiety and depression scores that indicate on average mild to moderate levels. Interestingly, a comparison of the two relatively large samples (Schwarz et al.,

1993 and Drossman et al., 1988) on the MMPI reveals relatively more depression, anxiety, and somatization among an IBS patient sample seeking psychological treatment than among an IBS patient sample seeking medical care from gastroenterologists.

In all of the studies that compared IBS patients to normal, non-ill controls (Schwarz et al., 1993; Drossman et al., 1988; Whitehead et al., 1988), one finds significantly greater levels of anxiety, depression, and somatization among those IBS patients seeking medical or psychological care.

IBS Patients and IBS Nonpatients

In the preceding section, we demonstrated that most samples of IBS patients have consistently shown, as a group, elevations into the clinical range on standard

TABLE 15.4. Summary of Psychological Test Scores from IBS Patients Seen by Various Authors

STUDY CHARACTERISTICS AND MEASURES	BENNETT & WILKINSON (1985)	LYNCH & ZAMBLE (1989)	DROSSMAN ET AL. (1988)		WHITEHEAD ET AL. (1988)
Sample size	33	21	72		10
Diagnostic criteria	Clinical	Clinical	Manning		Manning
STAI-State					
STAI-Trait	42.7	44.4			
Beck Depression Inventory		10.5			
Psychosomatic Symptoms Checklist—total		47.8			
MMPI			(a)	(b)	
1. Hypochondriasis			33%	62	
2. Depression			21%	59	
3. Hysteria			20%	61	
4. Psychopathic dev.			23%	60	
6. Paranoia			17%	59	
7. Psychasthenia			23%	61	
8. Schizophrenia			25%	63	
9. Hypomania			19%	64	
McGill Pain Quest.			9.1		
Hopkins Symptom Checklist					
Somatization					1.34
Obsessive-compulsive					1.32
Interpersonal sensitivity					0.93
Depression					1.15
Anxiety					0.95
Hostility					1.05
Phobia					0.51
Paranoia					0.83
Psychoticism					0.32
Eysenck Personality Inventory—Neuroticism		13.6			

Notes: (a) Percent of sample with T-score greater than 70.
      (b) Interpolated means from figure 2, Drossman et al., 1988

psychological tests of anxiety, depression, and somatization. Two studies published about 10 years ago give a different perspective on the idea that all IBS patients are also psychologically distressed. In both studies, patients attending gastroenterology clinics and who were diagnosed with IBS were compared to community samples who met the GI symptomatic criteria for IBS but who had not sought medical attention for their GI symptoms.

In the first study, Drossman et al. (1988) examined 72 IBS patients, 82 individuals who met the criteria for IBS but who never sought treatment for it (from among 3,000 students and University of North Carolina hospital employees undergoing routine physical exams), and 84 normal, non-ill controls. Average age was 28; 89% were female. On the MMPI the IBS patients scored higher than the IBS nonpatients on Hypochondriasis and Depression and lower on Ego Strength. On Psychasthenia, the measure most related to chronic anxiety, 23% of the IBS patients had T-scores above 70, while 9% of the IBS nonpatients had such elevations. In a pain diary the IBS patients reported pain on 8.2 out of 14 days, whereas the IBS nonpatients reported it only 3.0 days.

In the second study, Whitehead et al. (1988) examined 149 middle-class women of average age 47 to diagnose either IBS, functional bowel (a group who meet clinical criteria for IBS) disorders, lactose malabsorption, or non-ill controls. None of the groups had sought medical treatment for GI problems. They were also given the Hopkins Symptom Checklist. From the Johns Hopkins University GI Clinics, 121 women with diagnoses of IBS, lactose malabsorption, or functional bowel disorder were assessed. Analyses showed consistently higher levels of psychological distress, including the Global Severity Index, for clinic attendees versus those with diagnosable disorders who were not seeking care. Of particular relevance were comparisons of IBS patients ($n = 10$) to IBS nonpatients ($n = 16$). There were much higher scores for the IBS patients on somatization, depression, hostility, and anxiety.

It thus seems clear that those individuals with IBS who seek medical care for their GI problems are consistently more psychologically distressed than individuals with IBS who do not seek medical care (a sizable proportion, almost half, according to Talley et al.'s [1991] survey). It is not clear which comes first, the care-seeking tendency or the psychological distress. It does seem to be the case, however, that IBS patients have more pain-related symptoms. Thus, it may be that it is abdominal pain that leads a patient to seek medical care rather than "neuroticism." However, it could also be that living with a chronic pain problem leads to the psychological distress seen on the tests.

CHANGES FOR IBS PATIENTS IN PSYCHOLOGICAL TEST SCORES AS A RESULT OF PSYCHOLOGICAL TREATMENT

As demonstrated in the preceding section, IBS patients show a noticeable degree of psychological distress as measured by standardized psychological tests. Moreover, as elegantly demonstrated by Drossman et al. (1988) and Whitehead et al. (1988), individuals with diagnosable IBS based upon GI symptoms but who are not seeking medical or psychological services show significantly lower levels of elevation on the psychological tests than do treatment-seeking IBS sufferers.

In this section we examine whether psychological treatment for the IBS leads to changes in the psychological distress. In Table 15.5 are summarized the psychological treatment studies that have also reported either psychological test scores before and after treatment or psychiatric ratings before and after treatment.

Examining the results in Table 15.5, one finds generally that active treatment, regardless of the type (even active attention placebo), usually leads to pre–post reductions in anxiety and depression, whereas symptom monitoring and/or routine medical care does not lead to change. Guthrie et al. (1991), with brief psychodynamic psychotherapy; Bennett and Wilkinson (1985), with a combination of cognitive and behavioral procedures; Whorwell, Prior, and Faragher (1984) with hypnotherapy; and Payne and Blanchard (1995), with cognitive therapy, each showed greater change in anxiety and/or depression for the treated cases than was found in comparison conditions. The level of change in BDI scores is typically from mildly depressed to the normal range, for example, so that these are clinically meaningful as well as statistically significant changes.

TABLE 15.5. Changes in Psychological Distress among IBS Patients Receiving Psychological Treatment

AUTHORS	TREATMENT CONDITIONS	SAMPLE SIZE	WITHIN-GROUP CHANGE IN PSYCHOLOGICAL DISTRESS				BETWEEN-GROUP DIFFERENCES IN CHANGE. PRE-POST SIG.
			MEASURE	PRE-TX	POST-TX	SIG. PRE-POST	
Svedlund et al. (1983)	E. 10 sessions psychodynamic psychotherapy over 3 mo.	50	Anxiety Rating	E 5.1 C 6.1	3.9 5.6	ns ns	Anxiety—ns Depression—ns
	C. Routine medical care with drugs	51	Depression Rating	E 3.7 C 4.6	2.2 3.8	ns ns	
Guthrie et al. (1991)	E. 7 sessions psychodynamic psychotherapy + relax. tape over 3 mo.	53	HRSD	E 13.5 C 10.0	3.5 6.0	N/R	HRDS E changed more than C, $p < .001$ Anxiety changed more than C, $p < .01$
	C. Routine medical care + GI diary checks	49	Clinical Anxiety Scale rating	E 6.2 C 7.5	3.6 6.2	N/R	
Bennett & Wilkinson (1985)	E. Multicomponent CBT	12	STAI-Trait	E C>42.7	N/R	$p < .01$	E changed greater than C, $p = .02$
	C. Three-drug regimen	12					
Lynch & Zamble (1989)	E. Multicomponent CBT	11	BDI	E 13.6 C 8.2	4.6 7.1	ns ns	No differential change
	C. GI symptom monitoring for 8 weeks	10	STAI-Trait	E 50.5 C 37.8	40.0 34.7	ns ns	
Blanchard et al. (1992) Study 1	E. Multicomponent CBT 10 sessions	10	BDI	E 14.0 C-1 15.0 C-2 12.2	8.4 7.9 11.7	.01 .05 ns	No differential change
	C-1 Attn. placebo 10 sessions	10	STAI-State	E 44.4 C-1 43.2 C-2 47.5	33.3 36.3 42.2	.025 ns ns	
	C-2 GI symptom monitoring 8 weeks	10	STAI-Trait	E 46.4 C-1 44.9 C-2 53.3	37.9 40.8 48.5	.001 ns .05	
Study 2	E. Multicomponent CBT 10 sessions	31	BDI	E 11.1 C-1 11.1 C-2 10.6	6.6 6.7 10.5	<.001 <.001 ns	No differential change
	C-1 Attn. placebo 10 sessions	30	STAI-State	E 52.4 C-1 50.5 C-2 51.6	35.9 36.2 44.5	<.001 <.001 .01	
	C-2 GI symptom monitoring 8 weeks	31	STAI-Trait	E 48.1 C-1 45.3 C-2 47.3	43.8 39.6 46.5	.01 <.001 ns	

Study	Condition	n	Measure	Group			p	Results
Greene & Blanchard (1994)	E. Cognitive therapy	10	BDI	E	10.6	5.1	<.01	No differential change
	C. Symptom monitoring 8 weeks	10		C	11.8	9.5	ns	
			STAI-State	E	41.1	38.4	ns	
				C	39.1	38.5	ns	
			STAI-Trait	E	49.9	43.7	ns	
				C	44.1	42.5	ns	
Payne & Blanchard (1995)	E. Cognitive therapy	12	BDI	E	14.6	8.3	.01	E changed more than C-1 or C-2, p = .01
	C-1 Support groups	12		C-1	11.2	10.8	ns	
				C-2	11.7	11.3	ns	
	C-2 Symptom monitoring 8 weeks	10	STAI-State	E	49.1	43.8	ns	
				C-1	41.5	41.6	ns	
				C-2	41.8	40.9	ns	
			STAI-Trait	E	53.0	44.9	.01	E changed more than C-1 or C-2, p = .01
				C-1	46.8	47.2	ns	
				C-2	45.1	46.2	ns	
Whorwell, Prior, & Faragher (1984)	E. Hypnotherapy 8 sessions	15	Rating of general well-being	E.	0.0	3.0	.001	E > C, p < .001
	C. Supportive psychotherapy + drug placebo	15		C.	0.1	0.6	ns	
Whorwell, Prior, & Colgan (1987)	E. Hypnotherapy 10 sessions	50	Rating of general well-being	E.	0.1	2.5	N/R	
Houghton, Jeyman, & Whorwell (1996)	E. Hypnotherapy 12 sessions	25	Quality of life, psychic well-being, mood	E		65	.001	E > C
				C		35	ns	
				E		65	.01	
				C		42	ns	
Harvey et al. (1989)	E-1 Individual hypnotherapy	16	GHQ score > 5 at post-tx.	E-1 and E-2		8/33		No difference between E-1 and E-2
	E-2 Group hypnotherapy	17						

Note: E refers to experimental treatments
C refers to control condition

As reference to Table 15.5 clearly shows, there are numerous instances in which, as a group, treated IBS patients have shown greater changes in psychological measures of anxiety, depression, and somatization than found in control or comparison conditions. Because most treatments do not work for everyone in the treatment condition, one might wonder whether there are differential effects on the psychological distress mirroring differential GI symptom relief found within a group of patients receiving a particular treatment. Put another way, one wonders if there is a dose–response relationship between GI symptom relief and relief of accompanying psychological distress.

One paper from our center has addressed this topic by combining the data from three small treatment studies (Blanchard et al., 1987) in which all treated patients received a combination of relaxation, biofeedback, and cognitive therapy. Of the 30 treated patients on whom psychological test data were available, 18 were judged to be successes based on a 50% or greater reduction in primary GI symptoms of abdominal pain and tenderness, diarrhea, and constipation based on daily GI symptom diary entries from 2 weeks before treatment and 2 weeks afterward. Twelve patients were judged to be failures because of less than 50% reduction in GI symptoms. Nine other patients had monitored symptoms for 8 weeks and completed the psychological tests before and after that monitoring phase. In Table 15.6 are the results from the BDI and STAI for these 39 IBS patients.

For depression and state-anxiety, successfully treated patients showed more psychological change than the treatment failures and those IBS patients who only monitored symptoms. The differential change was not significant for trait-anxiety. It thus seems clear that successful reduction of GI symptoms is accompanied by noticeable psychological symptom relief. In fact, for the treatment successes the post-treatment scores are within the normal range on depression (BDI) and state-anxiety; there is also a notable reduction in trait-anxiety scores. An examination of possible dose–response effect found a nearly significant ($r = .28$, $p = .07$) correlation between the composite GI symptom reduction score and changes in state-anxiety. The relations were much less (and nonsignificant) for depression and trait-anxiety. It thus might be the case that IBS is a *somatopsychic* disorder: that the psychological distress is secondary to the somatic symptoms and that alleviation of GI symptoms is accompanied by similar alleviation of anxiety and depression.

However, evidence for this hypothesis is not strong. For example, in most published reports (Corney & Stanton, 1990; Liss, Alpers, & Woodruff, 1973; Masand et al., 1995; McKegney, 1977; Turner et al., 1988), symptoms of psychological distress antedated the onset of IBS symptoms. In addition, both Blanchard et al. (1990) and Walker et al. (1990) reported that when compared with sufferers of inflammatory bowel disease (IBD), a chronic, disabling, and med-

TABLE 15.6. Pretreatment and Posttreatment Psychological Test Scores for
Successfully and Unsuccessfully Treated IBS Patients and Symptom-Monitoring Controls

TEST	GROUP	PRETREATMENT	POSTTREATMENT	WITHIN-GROUP CHANGE	
				t	p
Beck Depression Inventory	Tx. Success	14.3	7.1	2.93	.009
	Tx. Failure	13.6	12.8	.38	ns
	Symp. Monitoring	14.3	13.2	.97	ns
STAI-State	Tx. Success	41.7	31.3	2.92	.009
	Tx. Failure	48.3	49.2	−.16	ns
	Symp. Monitoring	42.8	48.7	−1.96	.086
STAI-Trait	Tx. Success	45.4	38.7	3.24	.005
	Tx. Failure	52.9	46.6	2.64	.027
	Symp. Monitoring	53.8	51.6	1.40	ns

Source: Adapted from table 1 (p. 36), E. Blanchard, C. Radnitz, S. Schwarz, D. Neff, and M. Gerardi, "Psychological Changes Associated with Self-Regulatory Treatment of Irritable Bowel Syndrome" (1987) *Biofeedback and Self-Regulation, 12,* 31–37.

ically dangerous disease of the lower bowel similar in presentation to the IBS, IBS patients report significantly more psychological distress and/or diagnosable psychopathology.

PSYCHIATRIC COMORBIDITY IN IBS

It is well established that psychological distress—that is, symptoms of anxiety, depression, and somatization—is a common feature of individuals with IBS. However, this could arise because psychiatric disorders are comorbid with IBS. The presence of psychiatric disorder is generally assessed by structured and/or semi-structured psychiatric interviews such as the Anxiety Disorders Interview Schedule (ADIS-IV; DiNardo, Brown, & Barlow, 1994), the Diagnostic Interview Schedule (DIS; Robins, Helzer, & Croughan, 1981), or the Composite International Diagnostic Interview (CIDI; Robins, Wing, & Wittchen, 1988), which are based upon and reflect internationally accepted systems of classification of mental disorder. When assessed in this manner, prevalence of psychiatric disorder in individuals with IBS has been estimated at between 54% and 100% (Walker, Roy-Byrne, & Katon, 1990). The disorders most commonly observed in this population include depression, dysthymia, hypochondriasis, somatization disorder, panic disorder, and GAD. Results of an early study conducted by Liss et al. (1973) indicated that 92% of their sample of patients diagnosed with the "irritable colon" (otherwise known as IBS) suffered from some form of psychiatric illness. Diagnostic breakdown of their sample was as follows: seven patients were diagnosed with "hysteria" and six with "anxiety neurosis"; two experienced "primary affective disorder, [depression]," and eight experienced nonspecific psychiatric disturbance (Liss et al., 1973, p. 155). Similarly, Walker et al. (1990) reported that significantly more IBS patients reported lifetime and/or present diagnoses of major depression, GAD, somatization disorder, panic disorder, simple phobia, and somatization disorder than did their IBD control group.

The majority of the psychiatric disorders recognized in IBS patients are disorders of the affective spectrum, especially the mood and anxiety disorders. Lydiard et al. (1993) reported that 94% of their sample had had lifetime Axis I diagnoses, with 46% reporting major depression, 31% reporting panic disorder, and 34% GAD. Blewett et al. (1996) excluded individuals with somatoform disorders and still found that 56% of their sample had experienced a mood or anxiety disorder at some point in their lives. When current diagnoses were considered, 33% had major depression, 19% had panic disorder, and 14% of the sample experienced GAD at the time of assessment. Moreover, Sullivan, Jenkins, and Blewett (1995) found that in a well-controlled study of a potential link between IBS and mood disorders a significantly higher prevalence of mood and anxiety disorders was found in the family histories of IBS patients and patients with major depression than were evident in the histories of the control group (a group of relatives of individuals with organic brain diseases). Lyketsos et al. (1987) reported that dysthymia was more common in IBS sufferers than in somatically ill controls. Blanchard et al. (1990) found that 37% of their treatment-seeking IBS patients met *DSM-III-R* criteria for GAD. Lastly, in a recent reanalysis of structured interview data, 87% of treatment-seeking IBS patients were found to have an anxiety disorder (Turner et al., 1988).

Indeed, mood and/or anxiety disorders are found not only in samples of treatment-seeking IBS sufferers, but also in community samples of individuals with medically unexplained gastrointestinal symptoms (Walker et al., 1992). Similarly, in psychiatric samples, IBS has also been frequently documented. For example, in an interview study of 87 inpatients with diagnoses of affective disorders, Dewsnap et al. (1996) reported that 40% met diagnostic criteria for IBS. Similarly, Masand et al. (1995) found that in a controlled investigation of IBS prevalence in psychiatric outpatients, 27% met criteria for IBS, versus 1% of the control group. Lydiard et al. (1986) reported that 44% of 41 patients seeking treatment for panic disorder at an anxiety disorders clinic volunteered gastrointestinal complaints (especially diarrhea and cramping) as prominent symptoms. Tollefson et al. (1991) found that in a sample of psychiatric outpatients diagnosed with *DSM-III-R* major depression or GAD, 33% of the total sample met criteria for IBS, with 29% of the subjects with major depression and 37% of the GAD sample receiving an IBS diagnosis. Finally, in a more recent report of two cases of successful cognitive-behavioral treatment of "bowel obsessions," Hatch (1997) found that both individuals carried diagnoses of IBS. Clearly the literature suggests significant comorbidity of the mood and anxiety disorders with IBS.

IS IBS, AT ITS CORE, A DISORDER OF THE AFFECTIVE SPECTRUM?

High diagnostic comorbidity and the frequent finding that onset of the mood/anxiety disorder generally precedes IBS symptom onset have led some researchers to suggest that IBS may well represent a somatic manifestation of psychiatric illness (Hislop, 1971; Latimer, 1983; Lydiard, 1992; Turner et al., manuscript under review).

Based on the prevalence of depression (73%), and the 80% treatment success rate with tricyclics and phenothiazines, in his sample of 67 IBS patients, Hislop (1971) suggested that IBS is caused by depression. In his report, Lydiard (1992) makes a similar conceptual statement, in that he attributes the successful treatment with benzodiazepines of individuals with panic disorder and comorbid IBS (the improvement in IBS symptoms closely paralleled improvement in panic) as signal of a common etiology. Lydiard also alludes to a body of neurobiological research that has revealed a possible "brain-gut" link between anxiety and IBS. Lydiard (1992), Walker et al. (1990), Svensson (1987), and Clouse (1988) report on the potential involvement of the enteric nervous system (ENS), often considered the "third division" of the autonomic nervous system (ANS), but structurally resembling the central nervous system (CNS) rather than the peripheral nervous system (PNS). In short, high levels of activity in the locus coeruleus, a pontine noradrenergic nucleus, have been "correlated with vigilance and attention to novel or fear-provoking stimuli, . . . [and] less activation with . . . behaviors such as sleep, grooming and feeding" (Walker et al., 1990, p. 569). The locus coeruleus receives afferent input from the viscera (Lydiard, 1992), and is innervated directly by the medullary nucleus solitarius, known to communicate with the GI system. Walker, Roy-Byrne, and Katon (1990) and Clouse (1988) suggest that the locus coeruleus, with both afferent and efferent connections with the GI system, may provide the "missing link" between anxiety and IBS.

Finally, Turner et al. (1998) have also suggested that IBS may be etiologically related to GAD, due to the abovementioned neurobiological evidence, high comorbidity between the IBS and GAD, similarity in symptomatic presentation, and relative (in)effectiveness of selected pharmacological and psychological interventions with IBS patients. This specific hypothesis will now be discussed in greater detail.

IBS AND GAD

In an analysis of structured psychiatric interview data collected from 53 treatment-seeking individuals with IBS, Turner et al. (1988) attempted to investigate the prevalence of anxiety disorders (particularly GAD) using *DSM-III-R* diagnostic criteria, and then *DSM-IV* criteria. If the prevalence of GAD remained the same utilizing the differing diagnostic criteria (e.g., based upon empirical evidence of the nondiscriminability of the autonomic symptom cluster, which was removed from the GAD criteria in *DSM-IV*), we hypothesized that this would suggest (1) the validity of the change and (2) that GAD and IBS were indeed related, if not the same diagnostic entity. Results indicated that 62% of the sample met diagnostic criteria for GAD *at both times,* suggesting that the change in GAD criteria was valid. However, the findings that 38% of the sample did not meet diagnostic criteria for GAD, and that 23% did not apparently suffer from an anxiety disorder makes the second hypothesis less likely.

If IBS and GAD did indeed represent the same diagnostic entity, it would theoretically follow that treatments effective for one would also be effective for the other. Based upon reviews of both the pharmacological and psychological treatment literatures for IBS (Blanchard, 1993; Klein, 1988), one might conclude that no treatment is significantly effective for IBS. However, one well-controlled study suggested that desipramine may effectively manage IBS symptoms, compared to anxiolytic treatment (Greenbaum, 1984); and three more recent investigations by Blanchard and colleagues (Greene & Blanchard, 1994; Payne & Blanchard, 1995; Vollmer & Blanchard, 1998) support the efficacy of cognitive therapy for IBS. For GAD, benzodiazepines are the most commonly prescribed (albeit not most effective) treatments (Davison & Neale, 1997), although recent successes with intensive relaxation training (Borkovec & Whisman, 1996) and CBT (Borkovec & Costello, 1993) have been documented.

The efficacy of both relaxation training (Blanchard et al., 1993) and CBT (as mentioned above) has been demonstrated with individuals with IBS (efficacy both on GI and affective/anxiety symptoms), and tricyclic antidepressants have enjoyed limited effectiveness in individuals with GAD (Davison & Neale, 1997). It should be noted, however, that in the majority of published, placebo-controlled trials of pharmacological/psychological interventions, few active agents/interventions perform significantly better than placebo (Turner, Hermann, & Blanchard, 1998). This suggests a psychological component to IBS, but the precise nature of this is as yet unknown.

In short, interventions with demonstrated efficacy for IBS have been occasionally utilized successfully with GAD, and vice versa, suggesting that GAD and IBS may share common etiological features, although, as the following discussion will reveal, this interpretation is not without its problems.

LONG-TERM FOLLOW-UP RESULTS FROM PSYCHOLOGICAL TREATMENT OF IBS

A question of considerable clinical and practical importance is how well the results of the various psychological treatments hold up over time. Many of the studies report only 1- to 5-month follow-up results. In Table 15.7 are summarized the seven controlled trials for which follow-ups of 1 year or more have been reported. Fortunately, these reports span the entire gamut of psychological treatments that have been reported for the treatment of IBS.

Examining the table, several things stand out. First, most treatment trials comparing a specific active psychological treatment to symptom monitoring with a wait-list control cross the patients in the control condition over to the active treatment within weeks of completing the initial trial. While this seems necessary from an ethical point of view and is advantageous from the point of view of having a large cohort of similarly treated patients, it dilutes our ability to make long-term between-group comparisons. The

two exceptions, Svedlund et al. (1983) and Shaw et al. (1991), maintained patients in the comparison conditions, routine medical care, and a new antispasmodic medication, respectively, for the entire year. Most research teams were able to hold 90% or better of the treated patients in a 1-year follow-up and 70 to 80% in 2- to 4-year follow-ups.

Very importantly, there was very good maintenance of significant improvement in GI symptoms, especially pain reduction, at the follow-up assessment. It appears that once patients improve on GI symptoms, they are able to maintain that improvement, regardless of the form of therapy. Thus, the results hold up for brief psychodynamic psychotherapy (Guthrie et al., 1991; Svedlund et al., 1983), hypnotherapy (Whorwell et al., 1987), bowel sound biofeedback (Radnitz & Blanchard, 1989) and various combinations of cognitive and behavioral therapeutic techniques (Schwarz et al., 1990; Shaw et al., 1991; van Dulmen et al., 1996).

If one examines long-term changes in psychological state, however, very little data are available. Svedlund et al. (1983) reported continued improvement in reduced anxiety and depression based on physician ratings, and Whorwell, Prior, and Colgan (1987) reported good maintenance of improvement in ratings of general well-being. Van Dulmen, Fennis, and Bleijenberg (1996) found no significant initial or follow-up improvement in patient ratings of general well-being. This latter finding does indicate stability of results, however.

In conclusion, the accumulated research gives reason for optimism: Many brief psychological treatments appear to lead to significant short-term improvement in GI symptoms (and psychological state [see Table 15.5]). These improvements seem well-maintained over 1 to 4 years with little intervening or booster therapy. These kinds of results bode well for the long-term cost-effectiveness of psychological therapies for IBS.

SUMMARY AND CONCLUSIONS

Little direct evidence exists for any of the etiological hypotheses discussed for IBS, although all remain present in the literature. Indeed, as Sammons and

TABLE 15.7. End of Treatment and Long-Term Follow-up Results from Controlled Trials with IBS

AUTHORS	TREATMENT CONDITIONS	LENGTH OF FOLLOW-UP	NO. OF PATIENTS WHO COMPLETED TREATMENT	NO. OF PATIENTS WHO COMPLETED FOLLOW-UP	PERCENT	END OF TREATMENT RESULTS	FOLLOW-UP RESULTS	
							GI SYMPTOMS	PSYCHOLOGICAL SYMPTOMS
Svedlund et al. (1983)	Brief dynamic psychotherapy vs. (C) routine medical care	12 mo.	E 50 C 50	E 49 C 50	98 100	E > C physician rating of abdominal pain, overall somatic symptoms	E > C physician rating of abdominal pain, bowel dysfunction, overall somatic symptoms	Both groups improved on physician rating of anxiety and depression
Guthrie et al. (1991)	Brief dynamic psychotherapy + relaxation vs. (C) symptom monitoring for 3 mo., then treated	12 mo.	E 46 C 43	43 40	93 93	E > C physician rating. Patient rating of abdominal pain and overall severity of symptoms E > C HRSD and Clinical Anxiety Scale	All treated patients. Improved on total bowel symptoms by patient questionnaire	N/R
Whorwell Prior, & Colgan (1987)	Hypnotherapy + home practice of autohypnosis vs. (C) supportive psychotherapy	18 mo. (14–21)	50 Controls not followed	48	96	E > C patient diary ratings abdominal pain, bowel dysfunction, general well-being	84% of treated patients were improved on bowel symptoms	Significant improvement in ratings of well-being
Schwarz et al. (1986)	CBT (relaxation, biofeedback, cognitive therapy) vs. symptom monitoring. Symptom monitoring then treated (Neff et al. 1987)	12 mo.	17	16	94	E > C CPSR score of 50% or greater (avg. GI Sx.)	8/14 clinically improved on diary CPSR, 15/16 global ratings improved (x – 73%)	N/R

Karoly (1987) point out in their literature review, etiological assumptions cannot be made based solely upon prevalence rates, comorbidity, and "therapeutic dissection" (e.g., etiological postulation based upon treatment success with a particular compound or intervention). A significant number of IBS patients do not meet current criteria for psychiatric disorders, and methodological issues (e.g., retrospective reporting biases, inconsistent classification systems/diagnostic criteria for IBS and psychopathology, etc.) often cloud interpretation of study results. In addition, given that IBS is a relatively heterogeneous disorder, it is possible that there is no single, unitary cause and therefore no single effective treatment.

In fact, the identification of a specific psychiatric disorder as "pathognomonic" for IBS may be irrelevant, given the ongoing debate about classification of anxiety and mood disorders (Barlow, 1988). Similarly, equating IBS with clinical anxiety might be premature because, as mentioned here, a subset of IBS patients does not complain of predominant psychological symptomatology. This, however, may be accounted for by the common observation that IBS patients often report multiple, vague, organically inexplicable physical complaints. This situation may indicate that these individuals may or may not be experiencing somatization or mood and/or anxiety problems, but are "somatic amplifiers," as noted in Barsky et al. (1988) and are focusing on and reporting somatic symptoms to the exclusion of psychological ones, as the former are more culturally acceptable.

Clearly, further research is necessary. While high levels of comorbidity of anxiety disorders and IBS have been repeatedly demonstrated, to our knowledge few investigators have examined *change* in comorbidity. Most researchers interested in psychological factors in IBS have documented change in dimensional mood and anxiety symptoms, which is encouraging; however, it is still unclear whether treatment of a "comorbid" disorder may in fact lead to improvement in the GI symptom complex. We speculate that in some individuals this may indeed be the case; however, this remains an empirical question. In particular, longitudinal investigations would be useful in clarifying onset and course of both problems, and further knowledge of the psychophysiological and/or biopsychosocial interactions in the etiology of both the affective spectrum disorders and the functional gastrointestinal illnesses would be educative.

REFERENCES

American Psychiatric Association. (1980). *Diagnostic and statistical manual of mental disorders* (3d ed.). Washington, DC: Author.

Barlow, D. H. (1988). *Anxiety and its disorder: The nature and treatment of anxiety and panic.* New York: Guilford Press.

Barsky, A. J., Goodson, J. D., Lane, R. S., & Cleary, P. D. (1988). The amplification of somatic symptoms. *Psychosomatic Medicine, 50,* 510–519.

Beck, A. T., Ward, C. H., Mendelson, M., Mock, J., & Erbaugh, J. (1961). An inventory for measuring depression. *Archives of General Psychiatry, 5,* 561–571.

Bennett, P., & Wilkinson, S. (1985). Comparison of psychological and medical treatment of the irritable bowel syndrome. *British Journal of Clinical Psychology, 24,* 215–216.

Blanchard, E. B. (1993). Irritable bowel syndrome. In R. J. Gatchel & E. B. Blanchard (Eds.), *Psychophysiological disorders* (pp. 23–62). Washington, DC: American Psychological Association.

Blanchard, E. B., Greene, B., Scharff, L., & Schwarz-McMorris, S. P. (1993). Relaxation training as a treatment for irritable bowel syndrome. *Biofeedback and Self-Regulation, 18,* 125–132.

Blanchard, E. B., Radnitz, C., Schwarz, S. P., Neff, D. F., & Gerardi, M. A. (1987). Psychological changes associated with self-regulatory treatments of irritable bowel syndrome. *Biofeedback and Self-Regulation, 12,* 31–38.

Blanchard, E. B., Scharff, L., Schwarz, S. P., Suls, J. M., & Barlow, D. H. (1990). The role of anxiety and depression in the irritable bowel syndrome. *Behaviour Research and Therapy, 28,* 401–405.

Blanchard, E. B., Schwarz, S. P., Suls, J. M., Gerardi, M. A., Scharff, L., Greene, B., Taylor, A. E., Berreman, C., & Malamood, H. S. (1992). Two controlled evaluations of multicomponent psychological treatment of irritable bowel syndrome. *Behaviour Research and Therapy, 30,* 175–189.

Blewett, A., Allison, M., Calcraft, B., Moore, R., Jenkins, P., & Sullivan, G. (1996). Psychiatric disorder and outcome in irritable bowel syndrome. *Psychosomatics, 37,* 155–160.

Borkovec, T. D., & Costello, E. (1993). Efficacy of applied relaxation and cognitive-behavioral therapy in the treatment of generalized anxiety disorder. *Journal of Consulting and Clinical Psychology, 61,* 611–619.

Borkovec, T. D., & Whisman, M. A. (1996). Psychosocial treatment for generalized anxiety disorder. In M. Mavissakalian & R. E. Prien (Eds.), *Long-term treatment of anxiety disorders* (pp. 171–199). Washington, DC: American Psychiatric Association.

Clouse, R. E. (1988). Anxiety and gastrointestinal illness. *Psychiatric Clinics of North America, 11,* 399–417.

Corney, R. H., & Stanton, R. (1990). Physical symptom severity, psychological and social dysfunction in a series of outpatients with irritable bowel syndrome. *Journal of Psychosomatic Research, 34,* 483–491.

Davison, G. C., & Neale, J. M. (1997). *Abnormal psychology* (7th ed.) (rev.). New York: Wiley.

Dewsnap, P., Gomborone, J., Libby, G., & Farthing, M. (1996). The prevalence of symptoms of irritable bowel syndrome among acute psychiatric inpatients with an affective diagnosis. *Psychosomatics, 37,* 385–389.

DiNardo, P. A., Brown, T. A., & Barlow, D. H. (1994). *The anxiety disorders interview schedule (ADIS-IV)* (4th ed.). Albany, NY: Phobia and Anxiety Disorders Clinic, Center for Stress and Anxiety Disorders, SUNY-Albany.

Drossman, D. A., Li, Z., Andruzzi, E., Temple, R. D., Talley, N. J., Thompson, W. G., Whitehead, W. E., Janssens, J., Funch-Jensen, P., Corazziari, E., Richter, J. E., & Koch, G. G. (1993). U.S. Householder Survey of Functional Gastrointestinal Disorders: Prevalence, sociodemography and health impact. *Digestive Diseases and Sciences, 38,* 1569–1580.

Drossman, D. A., McKee, D. C., Sandler, R. S., Mitchell, C. M., Cramer, E. M., Lowman, B. C., & Burger, A. L. (1988). Psychosocial factors in the irritable bowel syndrome: A multivariate study of patients and non-patients with irritable bowel syndrome. *Gastroenterology, 95,* 701–708.

Drossman, D. A., Sandler, R. S., McKee, D. C., & Lovitz, A. J. (1982). Bowel patterns among subjects not seeking health care: Use of a questionnaire to identify a population with bowel dysfunction. *Gastroenterology, 83,* 529–534.

Drossman, D. A., Thompson, W. G., Talley, N. J., Funch-Jensen, P., Janssens, J., & Whitehead, W. E. (1990). Identification of subgroups of functional gastrointestinal disorders. *Gastroenterology International, 3,* 159–172.

Greenbaum, D. S. (1984). Comments on comparison with anxiolytic therapy. *Psychopharmacology Bulletin,* 622–628.

Greene, B., & Blanchard, E. B. (1994). Cognitive therapy for irritable bowel syndrome. *Journal of Consulting and Clinical Psychology, 62,* 576–582.

Guthrie, E., Creed, F., Dawson, D., & Thonenson, B. (1991). A controlled trial of psychological treatment for the irritable bowel syndrome. *Gastroenterology, 100,* 450–457.

Harvey, R. F., Hinton, R. A., Gunary, R. M., & Barry, R. E. (1989). Individual and group hypnotherapy in treatment of refractory irritable bowel syndrome. *Lancet, 1,* 424–425.

Hatch, M. L. (1997). Conceptualization and treatment of bowel obsessions: Two case reports. *Behaviour Research and Therapy, 35,* 253–257.

Hislop, I. G. (1971). Psychological significance of the irritable colon syndrome. *Gut, 12,* 452–457.

Houghton, L. A., Jeyman, D. J., & Whorwell, P. J. (1996). Symptomatology, quality of life and economic features of irritable bowel syndrome: The effect of hypnotherapy. *Alimentary Pharmacology and Therapeutics, 10,* 91–95.

Klein, K. B. (1988). Controlled treatment trials in the irritable bowel syndrome: A critique. *Gastroenterology, 95,* 232–241.

Latimer, P. R. (1983). *Functional gastrointestinal disorders: A behavioral medicine approach.* New York: Springer.

Latimer, P. R. (1983). Irritable bowel syndrome: Psychosomatic illness review: No. 7 in a series. *Psychosomatics, 24,* 205–218.

Liss, J. L., Alpers, D., & Woodruff, Jr., R. A. (1973). The irritable colon syndrome and psychiatric illness. *Diseases of the Nervous System* (April/May), 151–157.

Lydiard, R. B. (1992). Anxiety and the irritable bowel syndrome. *Psychiatric Annals, 22,* 612–618.

Lydiard, R. B., Fossey, M. D., Marsh, W., & Ballenger, J. C. (1993). Prevalence of psychiatric disorders in patients with irritable bowel syndrome. *Psychosomatics, 34,* 229–234.

Lydiard, R. B., Laraia, M. T., Howell, E. F., & Ballenger, J. C. (1986). Can panic disorder present as irritable bowel syndrome? *Journal of Clinical Psychiatry, 47,* 470–473.

Lyketsos, C. G., Lyketsos, G. C., Richardson, S. C., & Beis, A. (1987). Dysthymic states and depressive syndromes in physical conditions of presumably psychogenic origin. *Acta Psychiatrica Scandinavica, 76,* 529–534.

Lynch, P. N., & Zamble, E. (1989). A controlled behavioral treatment study of irritable bowel syndrome. *Behavior Therapy, 20,* 509–523.

Manning, A. P., Thomson, W. G., Heaton, K. W., & Morris, A. F. (1978). Towards positive diagnosis of the irritable bowel. *British Medical Journal, 2,* 653–654.

Masand, P. S., Kaplan, D. S., Gupta, S., Bhandary, A. N., Nasra, G. S., Kline, M. D., & Margo, K. L. (1995). Major depression and irritable bowel syndrome: Is there a relationship? *Clinical Psychiatry, 56,* 363–366.

McKegney, F. P. (1977). Psychiatric syndromes associated with gastrointestinal syndromes. *Clinical Gastroenterology, 6,* 675–688.

Payne, A., & Blanchard, E. B. (1995). A controlled comparison of cognitive therapy and self-help support groups in the treatment of irritable bowel syndrome. *Journal of Consulting and Clinical Psychology, 63,* 779–786.

Radnitz, C. L., & Blanchard, E. B. (1989). A one- and two-year follow-up study of bowel sound biofeedback as a treatment for irritable bowel syndrome. *Biofeedback and Self-Regulation, 14,* 333–338.

Robins, L. N., Helzer, J. E., & Croughan, J. (1981). National Institute of Health Diagnostic Interview Schedule. *Archives of General Psychiatry, 38,* 381–389.

Robins, L., Wing, J. K., & Wittchen, H. V. (1988). The Composite International Diagnostic Interview. *Archives of General Psychiatry, 45,* 1069–1078.

Sammons, M. T., & Karoly, P. (1987). Psychosocial variables in irritable bowel syndrome: A review and proposal. *Clinical Psychology Review, 7,* 187–204.

Schwarz, S. P., Blanchard, E. B., Berreman, C. F., Scharff, L., Taylor, A. E., Greene, B. R., Suls, J. M., & Malamood, H. S. (1993). Psychological aspects of irritable bowel syndrome: Comparisons with inflammatory bowel disease and non-patient controls. *Behaviour Research and Therapy, 31,* 297–304.

Shaw, G., Srivastava, E. D., Sadlier, M., Swann, P., James, J. Y., & Rhodes, J. (1991). Stress management for irritable bowel syndrome: A controlled trial. *Digestion, 50,* 36–42.

Spielberger, C. D. (1983). *Manual for the State-Trait Anxiety Inventory—STAI (Form Y).* Palo Alto, CA: Consulting Psychologists Press.

Sullivan, G., Jenkins, P. J., & Blewett, A. E. (1995). Irritable bowel syndrome and family history of psychiatric disorder: A preliminary study. *General Hospital Psychiatry, 17,* 43–46.

Svedlund, J., Sjodin, I., Ottosson, J-O., & Dotevall, G. (1983). Controlled study of psychotherapy in irritable bowel syndrome. *Lancet,* 589–592.

Svensson, T. H. E. (1987). Peripheral, autonomic regulation of locus coeruleus noradrenergic neurons in brain: Putative implications for psychiatry and psychopharmacology. *Psychopharmacology, 92,* 1–5.

Talley, N. J., Zinsmeister, A. R., VanDyke, C., & Melton, L. J. (1991). Epidemiology of colonic symptoms and the irritable bowel syndrome. *Gastroenterology, 101,* 927–934.

Tollefson, G. D., Tollefson, S. L., Pederson, M., Luxenberg, M., & Dunsmore, G. (1991). Comorbid irritable bowel syndrome in patients with generalized anxiety and major depression. *Annals of Clinical Psychiatry, 3*(3), 215–222.

Turner, S. M., Blanchard, E. B., Greene, B., & Payne, A. (1988). Conceptual issues in classification: Generalized anxiety disorder (GAD) and irritable bowel syndrome (IBS). Unpublished manuscript under editorial review. Logan: Utah State University.

Turner, S. M., Hermann, C. U., & Blanchard, E. B. (1998). A preliminary meta-analytic review of the pharmacological, dietary, and psychological treatment literatures for the irritable bowel syndrome (IBS). Unpublished manuscript under editorial review. Logan: Utah State University.

van Dulmen, A. M., Fennis, J. F. M., & Bleijenberg, G. (1996). Cognitive-behavioral group therapy for irritable bowel syndrome: Effects and long-term follow-up. *Psychosomatic Medicine, 58,* 508–514.

Vollmer, A., & Blanchard, E. B. (1998). Controlled comparison of individual versus group cognitive therapy for irritable bowel syndrome. *Behavior Therapy, 29,* 19–33.

Walker, E. A., Katon, W. J., Jemelka, R. P., & Roy-Byrne, P. P. (1992). Comorbidity of gastrointestinal complaints, depression, and anxiety in the Epidemiologic Catchment Area (ECA) study. *American Journal of Medicine, 92,* 1A-26S–1A-30S.

Walker, E. A., Roy-Byrne, P. P., & Katon, W. J. (1990). Irritable bowel syndrome and psychiatric illness. *American Journal of Psychiatry, 147,* 565–572.

Walker, E. A., Roy-Byrne, P. P., Katon, W. J., Li, L., Amos, D., & Jiranek, G. (1990). Psychiatric illness and irritable bowel syndrome: A comparison with inflammatory bowel disease. *American Journal of Psychiatry, 147,* 1656–1661.

Whitehead, W. E., Bosmajian, L., Zonderman, A. B., Costa, P. T., & Schuster, M. M. (1988). Symptoms of psychological distress associated with irritable bowel syndrome: Comparison of community and medical clinic samples. *Gastroenterology, 95,* 709–714.

Whitehead, W. E., Winget, C., Fedoravicius, A. S., Wooley, S., & Blackwell, B. (1982). Learned illness behavior in patients with irritable bowel syndrome and peptic ulcer. *Digestive Diseases and Sciences, 27,* 202–208.

Whorwell, P. J., Prior, A., & Colgan, S. M. (1987). Hypnotherapy in severe irritable bowel syndrome: Further experience. *Gut, 28,* 423–425.

Whorwell, P. J., Prior, A., & Faragher, E. B. (1984). Controlled trial of hypnotherapy in the treatment of severe refractory irritable bowel syndrome. *Lancet,* 1232–1234.

CHAPTER 16

THE PSYCHOLOGIST'S ROLE IN THE TREATMENT OF DENTAL PROBLEMS

Barbara G. Melamed

Joshua Fogel

More than 22% of the U.S. civilian population 18 years of age and older are estimated to have experienced pain in the mouth or teeth more than once in the last 6 months (Lipton, Ship, & Larach-Robinson, 1993). In addition, more than 5% avoid dentists because of fear or anxiety. Dental patients sometimes exhibit symptoms associated with anxiety, depression, or pain syndromes. Six percent of the U.S. adult civilian population experience a symptom pattern involving a pain in the jaw joint and/or face. Women report these symptoms 2.1 times more often than men. These pain syndromes can either be psychosomatic or psychogenic, with stress and anxiety often associated with them.

A sampling of syndromes/diseases in dental patients of special interest to psychologists is discussed in this chapter. Dentists see patients with anorexia nervosa, aphthous ulcers, atypical facial pain, atypical odontalgia, body dysmorphic disorder, bruxism, bulimia, burning mouth syndrome, dental phobia, factitious ulceration, monosymptomatic hypochondriac psychosis, myofascial pain dysfunction syndrome, and temporomandibular joint pain dysfunction syndrome (Feinmann & Harrison, 1997; Van Der Bijl, 1995).

Psychologists should market their consultation and liaison services to dentists even though some skepticism exists regarding the need for psychologic treatments for dental patients. Some dentists feel that psychometric assessments are pseudoscience because the assessments are often subjective (Christensen & McKay, 1995). The psychologist should be prepared to refute these claims and demonstrate the scientific basis for a treatment recommendation.

Dental patients often resist mental health referrals, believing that the referral infers that their illness is "in their mind." In fact, there is a large degree of overlap between dental anxiety, social anxiety, and blood injury fears. Many individuals who are multiphobic and have agoraphobic and social interaction fears are also afraid of dentists and dental treatment. These patients often score higher on the Anxiety Sensitivity Index and Spielberger Trait Anxiety Index (Locker, Shapiro, & Liddell, 1997; McNeil et al., 1993). In addition, the comorbidity of panic disorder with agoraphobia and dental anxiety and other specific phobias is over 65% (Starcevic & Bogojevic, 1997). Interestingly, dental phobia often precedes panic disorder with agoraphobia by years and may be etiologically relevant as a predisposition to agoraphobia. Although a joint session with the dentist can help eliminate this mental illness diagnosis stigma, in general, many could benefit from evaluation of their psychosocial needs as well (Feinmann & Harrison, 1997).

Even individuals without psychopathology may experience distress during dental procedures. This is understandable when the dental situation is viewed as a situation similar to experimental neurosis, in which the dental patient must remain in a somewhat noxious situation for a period of time with little or no opportunity to control or even protest the treatment. Thus, the dental setting takes on a unique interest for psychologists. Many patients may be able to tolerate occasional dental treatment by being adequately prepared by instructions, including information about sensations to expect, and modeling of coping styles to manage stress. Or the dentist may suggest psychological treatments incorporating biofeedback, as these treatments are viewed by many dental patients as medical and not psychological (Gevirtz et al., 1995). Sometimes biofeedback should be used in therapy to assuage patient fears about visiting a psychologist.

Filmed modeling has been used to prepare children for routine dental treatments (Melamed, 1998). In addition, fluoridation in drinking water has reduced carious conditions, and many children do not associate pain with dental treatment as they see the dentist for prophylaxis and dental sealants rather than drilling and injections.

Besides psychologists working with dentists regarding dental syndromes, physicians such as neurologists, otorhinolaryngologists (ENTs), and rheumatologists are often involved in treating dental patients (Gevirtz et al., 1995; Lennon et al., 1989). For example, about 50% of patients suffering from temporomandibular disorders first visit a physician and not a dentist (Lennon et al., 1989; Okeson & De Kanter, 1996). Psychologists should market their skills to these health care providers and be prepared to work in a multidisciplinary environment.

This chapter discusses some syndromes associated with stress and anxiety in patients in the dental setting. The epidemiology, etiology, assessment, and treatment of dental anxiety/phobia, temporomandibular disorder, and preparation for oral surgery will be addressed.

DENTAL ANXIETY/PHOBIA

Epidemiology

Some degree of dental fear is found in up to 80% of the population (Pavlov, 1997). Various studies show that 40–50% of people are afraid to visit a dentist, about 20% are highly anxious, and about 5% are so extremely anxious that they avoid dental treatment (De Jongh et al., 1995; Feinmann & Harrison, 1997; Litt, 1996). Dental fear in children has reported ranges from 3 to 21% (Klingberg, 1995; Raadal et al., 1995).

Assessment

Different self-report questionnaires are used to assess dental anxiety. They can be grouped into a few categories. Questionnaires often cited in the current literature will be discussed here.

One category of self-report questionnaires assesses general anxiety. The four-item Dental Anxiety Scale (DAS) is the most popular scale. It is very easy to use but does not distinguish between individuals with high dental anxiety or phobia as none of its four questions addresses the issue of oral injections (Hakeberg & Berggren, 1997). It has been used in many studies with varying populations and outcomes as part of routine assessment (e.g., Berggren et al., 1995; Berggren, Carlsson, Hägglin, et al., 1997; Berggren, Carlsson, Hakeberg, et al., 1997; De Jongh et al., 1995; Eli et al., 1997; Elter, Strauss, & Beck, 1997; Liddell & Locker, 1997; Locker & Liddell, 1995; Milgrom et al., 1997; Robertson, Gatchel, & Fowler, 1991; Wilson & Sinisko, 1997).

The Dental Fear Survey (DFS) contains 20 items. Factor analysis shows that it assesses three areas of fear reactions—avoidance, autonomic arousal, and fear of specific objects or situations (Berggren et al., 1995). Some recent studies have used it (e.g., Berggren, Carlsson, Hägglin, et al., 1997; Berggren, Carlsson, Hakeberg, et al., 1997; Hakeberg & Berggren, 1997; Litt, Nye, & Shafer, 1995; Wilson & Sinisko, 1997).

The Fear Survey Schedule II (FSS-II) contains 51 items. Five items were added to the scale, and factor analysis shows five factors consisting of fear of illness and death, fear of failure and embarrassment, fear of social situations, fear of physical injuries, and fear of animals and natural phenomenon (Berggren et al., 1995). LISREL analysis using the same procedures as in Berggren et al. (1995) determined two additional factors, general fear and a fear of social interaction, for a total of seven factors (Hakeberg et al., 1995). A recent study used the FSS-II with satisfactory results (Berggren, Carlsson, Hägglin, et al., 1997).

The Dental Anxiety Inventory (DAI: Stouthard, Hoogstraten, & Mellenbergh, 1995) contains 36 items. It has items that the DAS and DFS do not fully assess.

The State-Trait Anxiety Inventory (STAI) has two subscales of trait and state anxiety that each contain 20 items. It has been used in many recent studies (e.g., Berggren, Carlsson, Hägglin, et al., 1997; De Jongh et al., 1995; Robertson, Gatchel, & Fowler, 1991).

Another category of self-report questionnaires assesses cognition. Some examples follow. The Dental Beliefs Survey (DBS) contains 15 items that test for the patient's confidence in the dentist–patient interaction (e.g., Berggren, Carlsson, Hägglin, et al., 1997;

Berggren, Carlsson, Hakeberg, et al., 1997). The Dental Cognitions Questionnaire (DCQ: De Jongh et al., 1995) contains 38 items that assess the frequency and believability of negative cognitions related to dental treatment.

In addition to these two categories, the following self-report questionnaires also exist. The Symptom Checklist–90 (Revised) (SCL-90[R]) contains nine subscales, including ones on anxiety and phobic anxiety, and three global scales. It is used to identify psychometric profiles of different groups of dental patients and to predict the success of behavior therapy in treating dental fear and avoidance (Eli et al., 1997). It is often used in studies of dental fear (e.g., Berggren, Carlsson, Hakeberg, 1997).

The Pain Anxiety Symptoms Scale (PASS: McCracken, Zayfert, & Gross, 1992) contains 53 items with subscales of somatic anxiety, cognitive anxiety, fear of pain, and escape/avoidance. This scale assesses fear of pain behaviors in the cognitive, motor, and physiological spheres. It can assist in identifying the type of anxiety (e.g., Liddell & Locker, 1997).

The Iowa Dental Control Index (IDCI: Logan et al., 1991) contains four items with subscales of desire for dental control and felt dental control (e.g., Liddell & Locker, 1997).

The Miller Behavioral Style Scale (MBSS) can also assess control, in more detail. It contains four questions eliciting imagined reactions to stressful situations including one specific to dental treatment. It is useful in determining "monitors" who prefer control versus "blunters" who do not prefer control (Litt et al., 1995).

The Social Attributes of Dental Anxiety Scale (SADAS: Kent et al., 1996) has 12 items with two subscales of psychological reactions related to dentistry. It assesses how dental fears relate to the patient's daily lifestyle and activities outside the dental office.

Besides the adult self-report questionnaires discussed here, there are specific child assessment questionnaires. The Children's Fear Survey Schedule—Short Form (CFFS-SF) is a short form containing 18 items from the 50 items of the regular scale. It assesses general fears in children (Klingberg et al., 1995). The Children's Fear Survey Schedule—Dental Subscale (CFFS-DS) contains 15 items relating to children's fears in dental settings. It is a very popular subscale (e.g., Klingberg et al., 1995; Raadal et al., 1995; Weinstein et al., 1996). The Child Dental Control Assessment (CDCA: Weinstein et al., 1996) contains 20 items. A factor analysis determined that it has five subscales of dentist-mediated control, active coping, cognitive withdrawal, reassurance, and physical escape. The State-Trait Anxiety Inventory for Children (STAI-C) is similar to the adult form explained above.

Children's behavioral assessments are currently not as popular in the recent literature. The Behavior Profile Rating Scale developed by Melamed (Geffken, Rodrique, & Streisand, 1998) has been shown to be valid and reliable in children from 4 through 11. It consists of 27 categories across two dimensions: separation from the mother and office behavior. Examples of categories include "refuses to leave mother," "crying," and "leaves chair." Each category or behavior has a weighted factor indicating degree of disruption, as determined by dentists' ratings. Concurrent validity has been reported in its significant correlations with observational and self-report measures of fear and anxiety.

Though scarce, some work can be found in the current literature. An ecological method for determining dental stress in 2- to 3-year-old children focuses on certain behaviors. However, the method needs more work to qualify this assessment style (Rousset, Lambin, & Manas, 1997). Some suggest that ticklish children are more anxious (Melamed & Williamson, 1991). The popular Child Behavior Checklist (CBC) is a poor predictor of dental anxiety in children (Raadal et al., 1995).

The Children's Dental Fear Picture Test (CDFPT: Klingberg, 1995) is a projective test that contains three subtests using dental setting pictures, pointing pictures, and sentence completion tasks. The dental setting pictures consist of a set of 10 pictures of animals in different dental settings. The pointing pictures consist of a set of 5 pictures with separate tests for boys and girls. The sentence completion tasks consist of a set of 15 sentences.

Treatment

Many psychological treatments have been designed to help avoidant patients obtain dental treatment. These have varied depending upon the degree of anxiety of the patient, concurrent psychiatric problems, and the nature of the impending procedure. In some cases, teaching the patient to tolerate more pain has been helpful, and the use of biofeedback, systematic desensitization, and gradual exposure to the dental setting has encouraged more appropriate responses. With most of the behavioral approaches (Melamed, 1998), success can be achieved in about 10 sessions or less. In more severe cases or when a long procedure must be tolerated, conscious sedation or premedication may be necessary. The basic ingredient of successful treatment is a confident practitioner who pays attention to the patient's desire for information, encourages the patient to participate in controlling some aspect of the treatment, and provides follow-up treatment to ensure that a positive experience was achieved. Specific cognitive behavioral packages have been designed with respect to repeated periodontal and root canal procedures, and these will be discussed in the relevant sections. The use of hypnosis and distraction techniques might be most effectively employed with patients who express little desire for information and tend to exhibit a blunting style of coping.

TEMPOROMANDIBULAR DISORDERS

Temporomandibular disorders (TMDs) are a number of disorders having symptoms of orofacial pain, masticatory dysfunction, or both. Common symptoms are clicking and crepitus (crackling) sounds. Glaros and Glass (1993) provide an excellent review of the anatomy of the temporomandibular area.

The International Association for the Study of Pain's criteria for TMDs are (1) tenderness in one or more muscles of mastication together with (2) clicking or popping noise in the temporomandibular joint (TMJ), and/or (3) limitation of mandibular range (Raphael & Marbach, 1997). Many people offer different classifications for TMD. However, an ideal classification system for TMDs has not yet been developed (Okeson, 1997).

TMDs were previously known with varying names such as Costen's syndrome, craniomandibular disorders, myofascial pain-dysfunction syndrome, temporomandibular joint dysfunction syndrome, temporomandibular pain-dysfunction syndrome, and TMJ. The American Dental Association chose the term *temporomandibular disorders* to ease the confusion regarding the multiple names (Glaros & Glass, 1993).

Epidemiology

Prevalence rates for TMD range widely, as there is yet not one commonly accepted definition for TMD (Le Resche, 1997). Some studies show that 40–75% of adults have at least one sign of TMD, with 33% having at least one pain symptom (Dimitroulis, Dolwick, & Gremillion, 1995; Okeson & De Kanter, 1996).

Ratios for female to male prevalence range from 2:1 to 9:1 (Bush et al., 1993; Le Resche, 1997; Okeson & De Kanter, 1996). About 3–7% of the population seek care for their symptoms (Dimitroulis, Dolwick, & Gremillion, 1995; Dworkin, Von Korff, & Le Resche, 1992; Okeson & De Kanter, 1996).

TMD is not as common among children. Prevalence rates range from 2–4%, with no difference between males and females (Le Resche, 1997). TMD is more frequent from puberty to middle age and is less prevalent among older people (Le Resche, 1997; Stohler, 1997). These rates for TMD are apparently consistent cross-culturally (Stohler, 1997).

Theory

The exact etiology for TMDs is unknown. Different theories are offered to explain the disorder. While bruxism, or the nonfunctional clenching or grinding of teeth, is relatively common in children and adolescents, its treatment is more controversial. The issue of continuity of this disturbance with later temporomandibular joint dysfunction in adults has not been well studied. Since bruxism is often the cause of TMJ, perhaps early treatment would help prevent formation of habits that lead to adult problems. The incidence of bruxism is high and continuous across developmental periods. If nocturnal bruxism is viewed as a sleep disorder, then prevention of TMJ can be a beneficial outcome of early treatment. The incidence of bruxism in children with otitis media or common ear infection due to allergy or other infections of the Eustachian tubes may indicate this as the initiating source of the habit. Apparently both the mandible and the middle ear have nuclei stimulation from the trigeminal nerve. Therefore, the hypothesis of risk factors as precursors of TMJ dysfunction deserves further investigation (Glaros & Melamed, 1992).

The structural model suggests that structural abnormalities lead to abnormal jaw muscle and jaw function with eventual pain (Biondi & Picardi, 1993; Turk, Penzien, & Rains, 1995). These abnormalities include occlusal disharmony, malocclusion, malposition or malformation of the condyle, and abnormal form or position of the glenoid fossa (Mew, 1997).

The functional model suggests that psychological stress (Mew, 1997; Okeson & De Kanter, 1996; Turk, Penzien, & Rains, 1995) or emotional tension (Biondi & Picardi, 1993) causes the TMD pain. Some feel that emotional strain combined with local physical stress causes increased sensitivity (Feinmann & Harrison, 1997).

Various studies support the functional model. One study of TMD patients showed that 82% suffered adverse life events 6 months prior to the pain; perhaps resulting in increased sensitivity to the previously unnoticed pain (Morris et al., 1997).

TMD patients have increased negative affect (e.g., distress, anxiety, and tension) and more bodily complaints. TMD pain strongly correlates with trait anxiety (Vassend, Krogstad, & Dahl, 1995). Type A patients were 3.4 times more likely to report TMD problems as compared to Type B patients (Nellis, Conti, & Hicks, 1992). Patients reported that they felt that stress and anxiety aggravated their symptoms (Kallenberg et al., 1997).

It is important to differentiate phantom tooth pain from the typical neuralgias (trigeminal neuralgia). Cases have been reported (Law & Lilly, 1995) in which individuals misdiagnosed for neuralgias have undertaken endodontic treatment unnecessarily when the pain was of odontolgenic origin. Also confused with this is pain associated with acute herpes zoster, pulpitis, TMJ, or arthritis of the TMJ. The etiology of atypical facial pain is frequently attributed to psychological factors, anxiety, depression, and hysterias, although evidence for this is lacking. Phantom tooth pain occurs when individuals do not adjust to a new crown, or when pain from a removed tooth occurs in other areas (Marbach, 1996).

Neuromatrix theory (Melzack, 1993) posits that the knowledge of every cusp and groove of the individual's dental occlusion resides in the brain as a coherent unit or occlusal neurosignature. Thus, for some individuals, alteration of the dental occlusion results in a neural input that the neuromatrix cannot recognize as one's own bite. Regardless, at the onset the result is often the same: The person engages in a lifelong search for the "correct" bite. It is more likely that this is due to a combination of altered central nervous system (CNS) processing or a combined peripheral-CNS etiology. Some of these patients develop myofascial pain secondary to the phantom bite syndrome. Just as the brain can produce commands for movements to limbs that have been amputated or painful fatigue in a tightly clenched phantom fist of an arm amputee, so, too, can pain be produced in the face by similar neural patterns. There may be a genetic predisposition for phantom pain syndrome. The incidence of the latter will increase as people are living longer and will have more dentures or implants than previously.

However, some disagree with the functional model. Hathaway (1997) states that there is no greater incidence of anxiety, depression, or major mental illness among TMD patients than among general medical patients.

Some suggest that oral behaviors (e.g., chewing of gum, pencils, erasers, ice, cheeks, lips, or fingernails) or work-related behaviors (e.g., raising the shoulder to place the phone receiver on the ear) puts pressure on the temporomandibular area and causes pain (Gevirtz et al., 1995; McGlynn et al., 1990). Some feel that stressful events trigger these maladaptive oral behaviors (Gramling et al., 1996). Other suggested causes for TMD are prior orthodontic treatments, bruxism, a diet of chewing hard foods, muscle parafunction, oral posture, or prior trauma (Mew, 1997).

Different reasons are suggested for the greater prevalence of TMD in women as compared to men. First, women are more sensitive to psychologic stress than men. Second, women have a higher measured level of tension in the masticatory muscles than men. This results in more adaptive morphologic changes. Third, women have estrogen-dependent receptors in the TMJ. Fourth, there are more women than men seeking or being referred for health care. This makes TMD discovery more common among women (Bush et al., 1993).

Some question the first reason because males and females free of TMD symptoms feel no difference in pain sensation (Bush et al., 1993). In addition, a study of TMD patients determined that the anxiety levels of both females and males were equal (Krogstad et al., 1996).

Assessment

Many people struggle with various diagnoses from health care providers before being diagnosed with TMD (Garro, 1994). As the exact etiology of TMD is unknown, a complete assessment should combine both a physical and psychosocial assessment. A common bias with psychosocial self-assessment is that the patient often underreports the TMD symptoms' duration (Raphael & Marbach, 1997).

The dentist's physical assessment usually involves physical palpation, examination, and perhaps X-rays or MRIs (Dimitroulis et al., 1995). The best standard for mandibular movement measurement is millimeter measurement of the width of the open mouth (Binderman & Singer, 1996).

During the physical assessment, symptoms can be grouped into primary and secondary symptoms. Primary symptoms involve facial muscle pain; preauricular pain; TMJ sounds of jaw clicking, popping, catching, and locking; limited mouth opening; and increased pain associated with chewing. Secondary symptoms are referred pains resulting in earaches, headaches, and neck aches (Okeson & De Kanter, 1996).

A physical diagnosis tool is the Facial Tenderness Schematic. It has left and right profiles of a human head and neck. It can be used for the patient to specify the various pain locations (Gramling et al., 1996; Peterson et al., 1993).

A few checklists and questionnaires are commonly used during the physical diagnosis. The Craniomandibular Index has dysfunction indices for TMJ noise during movement and tenderness of the joint. It has a palpation index for measurement of muscle pain by palpation (Peterson et al., 1993). The Orofacial Pain Symptom Checklist has responses dichotomized with either yes or no. It has indices of dysfunction associated with joint movement, parafunction, pain symptoms, and circumoral symptoms (Bush et al., 1993). The Temporomandibular Pain Dysfunction Disorder

Clinical Form is a clinical assessment instrument that measures TMD pain at palpation, joint and muscle symptoms, and location and severity of symptoms (Suvinen, Hanes, & Reade, 1997).

Psychosocial assessment is done by psychologists and focuses on aspects of: (1) parafunctional oral habits, (2) general lifestyle habits (e.g., poor exercise and eating habits resulting in muscle deconditioning), (3) pain management, (4) stress management, (5) compliance, (6) attitude, (7) chemical dependency (especially over-the-counter medications), (8) general health, (9) patient's hypotheses about the causes of pain, and (10) patient hurdles (e.g., time, money, and energy) (Hathaway, 1997).

The IMPATH:TMJ is an assessment tool that can be done on a computer or on a computer-scanned pencil-and-paper instrument. It can supplement a patient's personal history (Glaros & Glass, 1993).

The TMJ Scale is a 97-item self-report questionnaire symptom inventory with 10 subscales for pain, palpation pain, malocclusion, joint dysfunction, range of motion limitation, non-TMD factors, psychological factors, stress, chronicity, and a global summary scale that indicates if TMD is present. These subscales are compared to the sample norms compiled during the scale validation (Wexler & McKinney, 1995). This test has the advantage that it can be done on a computer and takes about 15 minutes to complete. A disadvantage is that the test is proprietary and costs from $14 to $18 to score (Glaros & Glass, 1993).

Pain assessment can be done in various ways. Common methods use visual analog scales (Bush et al., 1993; Glaros & Glass, 1993; Peterson et al., 1993), numerical rating scales (Turner et al., 1995), facial pain diaries (Flor & Birbaumer, 1993; Glaros & Glass, 1993; Gramling et al., 1996), and/or the McGill Pain Questionnaire (Bush et al., 1993; Peterson et al., 1993).

Psychophysiological pain assessment is based upon the premise that pain leads to reflex muscle spasms resulting in sympathetic activation. These muscle spasms may become conditioned to innocuous stimuli and cause pain even when pain-inducing stimuli are absent (Flor & Birbaumer, 1994).

Small portable devices with the ability to store information for a few hours may be used to assess the patient's daily electromyograph (EMG). However, some patients find it uncomfortable (Gevirtz et al., 1995).

A baseline for adults of non-pain, TMD-masseter EMG values is 4.86 microvolts ($SD = .11$). The older the patient, the more elevated the EMG microvolt amount. An average increase of 1 microvolt from age 14 to 70 is normal (Hudzinski & Lawrence, 1992).

A method of grouping pain patients that can be used to tailor treatment relies on the West Haven–Yale Multidimensional Pain Inventory (WHYMPI). It has three sections. The first section has 28 questions about the patient's pain and the impact of that pain on various aspects of the patient's life. The second section is concerned with the frequency with which the patient's significant other engages in each of 14 possible reactions to the patient's pain. The third section is concerned with how often the respondent engages in 14 daily activities (Gramling et al., 1996).

The WHYMPI classifies TMD patients into three groups—dysfunctional (DYS), interpersonally distressed (ID), and adaptive copers (AC). Each group has a different profile (Dahlström, Widmark, & Carlsson, 1997; Rudy et al., 1995). The DYS group has a profile of high pain levels, symptom interference with life activities, affective distress, low levels of activity, and low feelings of life control. The ID group has a profile similar to the DYS group but also has low social support and a high frequency of negative responses from significant others. The AC group has a profile of activity despite the pain, high control, and low psychological distress (Dahlström, Widmark, & Carlsson, 1997; Rudy et al., 1995).

A few different self-report questionnaires exist for cognitive assessment. The Pain-Related Control Scale contains 18 items with two subscales of helplessness and resourcefulness. It assesses beliefs of pain's controllability and predictability (Flor, Behle, & Birbaumer, 1993). The Pain-Related Self-Statements Scale contains 15 items with two subscales of catastrophizing and coping that assess situation-specific cognitions that either promote or hinder attempts to cope with pain (Flor, Behle, & Birbaumer, 1993). The Coping Strategies Questionnaire assesses six cognitive strategies and one behavioral strategy with regard to pain control, the Ways of Coping Checklist assesses appraisals and coping strategies for the stressor that the patient identifies as most significant, and the Vanderbilt Pain Management Inventory contains 27 items and assesses passive and active coping strategies (Suvinen & Reade, 1995). The Temporomandibular Pain Dysfunction Disorder Questionnaire contains four subscales of coping strategies, anamnestic, psychologic profile, and illness behavior (Suvinen, Hanes, & Reade, 1997).

Illness behavior can be assessed through an interview method using the Illness Behavior Assessment Schedule. It can also be assessed with a self-report questionnaire called the Illness Behavior Questionnaire that contains 62 items with seven subscales (Suvinen & Reade, 1995).

The Facial Action Coding System is a method for observing facial expressions and movement to detect pain. The popular UAB Pain Behavior Scale cannot be used with TMD patients because the aching pain felt would not be detected as it is not as severe as in other pain syndromes (Glaros & Glass, 1995).

In addition to these questionnaires, many other factors influence behavior. They are social class, social role, age, gender, learning, stress, interpersonal factors, and even the type of illness. Cultural factors can include family, social, and environmental factors (Suvinen & Reade, 1995).

The affective portion of pain can be assessed with the popular scales of the MMPI-2, State-Trait Anxiety Scale, Beck Depression Inventory, Hamilton Depression Scale, and the Symptom Checklist 90—Revised (Suvinen & Reade, 1995).

A social support assessment is important as many TMD patients feel estranged from and misunderstood by others because of their facial pain. A substantial minority feel that others believe that their condition came from personality problems. These stigma perceptions cause relationship problems with intimate partners. This is especially problematic as most estranged TMD patients tend to rely more on household members for support than do less estranged patients (Lennon et al., 1989).

Treatment

Besides the pain from TMD, there is financial anguish too. Most treatment regimens are expensive, and most insurance companies do not pay for them (Garro, 1994).

The most effective treatment for TMD is not known. Little is known about the superiority of one biomedical treatment over another. No existing studies show that physical pathology variables are better than psychological variables for predicting a positive treatment outcome (Dworkin, 1997). Dental treatment for TMD relates to the practitioner and his or her field of expertise. Prosthodontists and restorative dentists usually do occlusal restorative procedures, orthodontists do orthodontic procedures, and oral and maxillofacial surgeons do surgery (Goldstein, 1998).

As there are varying results for all treatments, a commonsense strategy should be followed. First, treatment should be tailored to the individual. Second, treatment should follow a multidisciplinary approach. Third, treatment should focus on conservative modalities (Dimitroulis et al., 1995; Goldstein, 1998; Turk, Penzien, & Rains, 1995).

Gevirtz et al. (1995) offer a comprehensive, step-by-step system for treating the TMD patient using a multidisciplinary approach. The following paragraphs will discuss the common treatments for TMD as performed by dentists, physical therapists, and psychologists.

Dental treatment ranges from conservative to more risky. Conservative treatment involves placing intraoral splints or bite guards (interocclusal appliance therapy) to prevent clenching or grinding (Gevirtz et al., 1995; Okeson & De Kanter, 1996). More risky treatments are occlusal adjustment involving "equilibration" of the fit between the upper and lower teeth. The teeth are ground to make a better fit. This treatment is irreversible (Dimitroulis et al., 1995; Gevirtz et al., 1995).

The treatment goals of dental procedures are reducing TMJ loading, stabilizing the joint, redistributing forces to the joint, relaxing the neuromusculature affecting the joint, decreasing the effects of parafunctional activity, decreasing the medications needed, and reducing the wear of tooth structure (Binderman & Singer, 1996). Some suggest that interocclusal appliance therapy has mostly a placebo effect as there is only a minimal change in physiological symptoms while there is a great change in psychosocial symptoms (Suvinen, Hanes, & Reade, 1997)

There are many pharmacotherapeutic choices for TMD. These include: analgesics such as nonsteroidal anti-inflammatory drugs or narcotics (Binderman & Singer, 1996; Dimitroulis et al., 1995; Dos Santos, 1995; Okeson & De Kanter, 1996); corticosteroids (Dos Santos, 1995); muscle relaxants such as the ben-

zodiazepenes (Dos Santos, 1995; Dellemijn & Fields, 1994; Dimitroulis et al., 1995; Hathaway, 1997); antidepressants (Dimitroulis et al., 1995); and injections done intramuscularly, extramuscularly, or in the TMJ (Dos Santos, 1995; Wright & Schiffman, 1995).

Physical therapy treatments include alpha stimulation, cold packs, cooling sprays, electrogalvanic stimulation, hot water bottles, massage, microampere or microcurrent electrical neural stimulation, moist heat, neuroprobe, soft lasers, transcutaneous electrical nerve stimulation (TENS), trigger point compression (also known as myotherapy or ischemic compression), and ultrasound. Exercises of the jaw and joint are also used (Binderman & Singer, 1996; Dimitroulis et al., 1995; Dos Santos, 1995; Okeson & De Kanter, 1996; Wright & Schiffman, 1995).

Psychologists treat TMD with patient education, biofeedback, hypnosis, behavior therapy, and cognitive behavior therapy (CBT).

Patient education involves teaching the patient self-management skills. These skills are to (1) use hot or cold packs, (2) eat soft foods, (3) rest the jaw muscles, (4) avoid caffeine, (5) watch oral habits, (6) watch sleep habits, (7) not open the mouth wide, (8) use over-the-counter medications when necessary, (9) avoid stress, and (10) maintain a home oral exercise program (Dimitroulis et al., 1995; Okeson & De Kanter, 1996; Wright & Schiffman, 1995). Biofeedback involves electromyographic feedback from the masseter muscles. This helps relax the tense muscles (Biondi & Picardi, 1993; Dos Santos, 1995; Wright & Schiffman, 1995). Hypnosis involves relaxation to counteract the stress (Golan, 1989). Crasilneck (1995) suggests a bombardment of six hypnotic techniques: (1) relaxation, (2) displacement, (3) age regression, (4) glove anesthesia, (5) hypnoanesthesia, and (6) self-hypnosis.

Behavior therapy has many, varied techniques. Habit reversal therapy has the goal of responding to a parafunctional habit with a competing behavioral response opposite to that of the parafunctional habit. The patient is taught awareness training, use of competing responses, relaxation training, and deep breathing exercises (Gevirtz et al., 1995; Gramling et al., 1996; Peterson et al., 1993).

Nocturnal alarm systems prevent clenching and grinding during sleep. The alarm system monitors EMG activity from the masseter muscle and an alarm sounds when the EMG exceeds a threshold for a time period or when a certain number of suprathreshold EMG events occur within a brief period (Gevirtz et al., 1995; Glaros & Glass, 1993).

Other forms of behavioral therapy focus on lifestyle counseling, stress management, relaxation training, and progressive muscle relaxation (Binderman & Singer, 1996; Dimitroulis et al., 1995; Dworkin, 1997; Hathaway, 1997; McGlynn et al., 1990; Wright & Schiffman, 1995).

One form of behavior therapy that is strongly discouraged is massed negative practice. This technique involves scheduling deliberate and repeated jaw clenching to supposedly reduce subsequent nocturnal EMG measured jaw activity. This technique exposes patients to the risk of broken teeth, increased pain, and more severe TMD. It has only limited evidence for efficacy (Gevirtz et al., 1995).

CBT interventions are cost-effective with regard to overall clinic visits and dollar costs. One study showed a 77% decrease in clinic visits after 12 months of CBT (Dworkin, 1997). CBT offered for two sessions before standard dental treatment has improved treatment results compared with groups without CBT (Dworkin et al., 1994; Turner et al., 1995).

Combination therapies using a few different modalities of intraoral appliance, biofeedback, stress management (consisting of education, cognitive training skills, progressive muscle relaxation), and homework to practice biofeedback were more effective than individual therapies (Greco et al., 1997; Rudy et al., 1995; Turk et al., 1996). However, some studies show that individual biofeedback is more effective than a combination of therapies (Flor & Birbaumer, 1993, 1994).

Future Directions

TMD remains an enigma. More studies are needed to determine which treatments are most effective. Randomly controlled clinical trials are desperately needed, as there is a dearth of them in the literature. For example, a MEDLINE search from 1980–1992 showed over 4,000 references to TMD. However, less than 5% of them were randomized controlled trials (Antczak-Bouckoms, 1995). Perhaps with increased experimentation there will finally be an ideal cure for TMD.

DENTAL SURGERY

Epidemiology

A 1994 Gallup survey (Delfino, 1997) on public attitudes and experience regarding oral surgery was used to address three areas of concern to both dental patients and dental professionals: surgery-related anxiety, anesthesia preferences, and preoperative information or counseling needs. Of the 1,008 adult respondents, 57% had undergone oral surgery at some time, 22% within the last 5 years. Among these patients, more than one in five (22%) had suffered anxiety levels high enough to delay them in seeking prompt treatment. An additional 30% reported moderate anxiety levels, whereas 48% reported no anxiety before oral surgery.

Extractions

The removal of teeth, or extraction, is the most common dental surgical procedure. Most adults with the assistance of conscious sedation have little problems tolerating such procedures. It is the expectation of pain that leads to fear and anxiety about extractions. Research (Miller et al., 1995) has shown that adrenal stress response associated with tooth extraction is greater than that associated with other dental procedures, including root canal. The physiological stress of various dental procedures as measured by salivary cortisol response showed a 55% increase in cortisol production during prophylaxis and a 148% increase with extraction.

In a novel study of patient preparation for third molar extraction or removal of wisdom teeth, Ader et al. (1992) found that simple instructions provided by interactive videodisc on what to expect regarding the procedures for the surgery and recovery sufficed to reduce patient anxiety. Information provided by videotape also imparted knowledge about the impending procedure. Each of these methods of providing information was superior to the dental surgeon alone giving preparation. These findings are consistent with a Gallup poll in which 98% of the respondents valued receiving information about their oral surgery procedure and the type of anesthesia to be used.

Endodontics

The area of endodontics, which requires several sessions to accomplish a root canal, has been a source of greater concern regarding dental preparation and psychological needs. The prevalence of root canal surgery has produced a specialty for this procedure, which is usually necessitated by multiplicative factors including broken teeth, inflamed gingivitis, nonvital root, and/or pulp impaction. Although the procedure itself does not differ dramatically from restorative treatment, the aspect of it which is most difficult involves the flaring of the canals prior to filling to make sure all debris or sources of infection are removed. This involves several visits. During this time the patient is left with a temporary filling and usually mild to severe soreness.

A review of the literature revealed that long-term follow-up of patients after therapy has not been done to ascertain whether patients perceive that they have problems related to their endodontically treated teeth. One important survey (Lobb, Zakariasen, & McGrath, 1996) did find that 22% of patients who had had endodontic treatment, reached by telephone 1 year after completion of endodontic procedures related to a single tooth, and who had filled out occurrence and magnitude of pain reports 3 days after treatment reported problems after root canal; of those, 53% said that the problems were pain-related. Eight percent said they would not have another root canal; 42% of those said it was because of pain or pain and expense. This a relatively high frequency of perceived problems in the year following endodontic therapy. All of these problems are related to pain and restorative concerns. Surprisingly, most of the patients did not seek treatment by revisiting their endodontist. Some may have sought treatment from their general practitioner. In many patients, pain symptoms were minimal, that is, slight sensitivity to masticatory pressures or a response of, "It doesn't really hurt but it feels different from my other teeth."

Treatment

Patients who reported concern about oral surgery value anesthesia in a conscious awake state, insensibility to pain, rapid recovery, and procedure-specific amnesia. Thus, the routine use of conscious sedation in the oral and maxillofacial surgeon's office is the single most effective treatment (Delfino, 1997). Patients overwhelmingly want to know all about the procedure they will have, how it will be done, and what analgesic modalities are available. The provision of dental treatment under both local anesthesia and sedation has an excellent safety record. Meechan and Skelly (1997) provide a review of prevention of anesthesia-related problems, which occur rarely during dental surgery.

In more extensive comparisons of behavior therapy treatments in preparation for oral surgery it is generally shown that the patient's preference for type of information can lead to the selection of the most effective preparatory package. In one study (Litt, Nye, & Shafer, 1995), when third-molar extraction patients were prepared with a coping style preparation that matched their own, the preparation was more likely to reduce their anxiety. Thus, those patients who prefer to distract themselves may benefit from interventions that require the least possible personal investment of attention and effort. Another study found that patients instructed on their sensations (sensory focus) during root canal therapy showed a reduction in pain reports immediately after treatment if they had a high desire for control and felt little control (Logan et al., 1995).

In a comparison of fearful dental patients receiving hypnotherapy, behavioral treatment, and general anesthesia, those receiving eight sessions of cognitive behavioral therapy reported a significant decrease in dental fear as well as a rise in mood during dental situations (Hammarstrand, Berggren, & Hakeberg, 1995).

The best predictors of success in coping with periodontal surgery were the patient's age and pretreatment ratings of pain (Baume, Croog, & Nalbandian, 1995, 1997). Presurgery scores on dental anxiety, fatigue, and depression were positively associated with measures of postsurgery pain after the first surgery and were negatively associated with positive well-being scores. Younger women reported significantly greater impairment of life activities during recovery than did older women after both surgery episodes.

SUMMARY
AND CONCLUSIONS

The role of psychology in dental behavioral science needs to be expanded during this decade. While difficult dental management problems have become an integral part of the dentist's own role over the last two decades, the current review indicated that problems, which have often been difficult to alleviate by dentists alone, can have far greater success when the combined efforts are initiated.

The fact that many dentists have begun to view syndromes such as atypical facial pain, bruxism, myofascial pain dysfunction, and temporomandibular joint pain dysfunction syndrome as problems having both psychiatric and dental routes enhances the possibility that a true working collaboration can be beneficial to both professions. Ultimately the patient will be more satisfied with treatment and dental costs will be reduced.

Among the most effective approaches psychologists have introduced in dental practices are education and behavioral management programs to eliminate fears associated with dental pain caused by treatment itself. The questionnaires which have been developed to identify those patients most at risk for having fear-related problems have been described and offer assistance to those psychologists new to this area.

Treatments currently used with both adults and children include reducing fear by systematic desensitization, biofeedback, or information. The need for the patient to experience a sense of control during treatment can likewise be enhanced by the use of hypnosis, distraction, and imagery techniques discussed in this chapter.

Although there has been a continuing controversy over the cause of temporomandibular joint disorders, major agreements regarding the treatment of choice have been reached. The largest benefits have been derived by treating patients with both dental appliances, such as nocturnal bruxism devices or splints for malocclusions, and the application of psychological treatments including EMG biofeedback and muscle relaxation training. The chapter has provided the clinician with a set of tools to use in evaluating the patient's pain-related surgeries, family history, pain tolerance, and pain sensitivities and fears.

REFERENCES

Ader, D. N., Seibring, A. R., Bhaskar, P., & Melamed, B. G. (1992). Information seeking and interactive videodisc preparation for third molar extraction. *Journal of Oral and Maxillofacial Surgery, 50,* 27–31.

Antczak-Bouckoms, A. A. (1995). Epidemiology of research for temporomandibular disorders. *Journal of Orofacial Pain, 9,* 226–234.

Baume, R. M., Croog, S. H. & Nalbandian, J. (1995). Pain perception, coping strategies and stress management among periodontal patients with repeated surgeries. *Perceptual and Motor Skills, 80,* 307–319.

Berggren, U., Carlsson, S. G., Gustafsson, J. E., & Hakeberg, M. (1995). Factor analysis and reduction of a Fear Survey Schedule among dental phobic patients. *European Journal of Oral Sciences, 103,* 331–338.

Berggren, U., Carlsson, S. G., Hägglin, C., Hakeberg, M., & Samsonowitz, V. (1997). Assessment of patients with direct conditioned and indirect cognitive reported origin of dental fear. *European Journal of Oral Sciences, 105,* 213–220.

Berggren, U., Carlsson, S. G., Hakeberg, M., Hägglin, C., & Samsonowitz, V. (1997). Assessment of patients with phobic dental anxiety. *Acta Odontologica Scandinavica, 55,* 217–222.

Binderman, A. F., & Singer, M. T. (1996). Treatment of orofacial pain and temporomandibular disorders. *Current Opinion in Periodontology, 3,* 184–190.

Biondi, M., & Picardi, A. (1993). Temporomanibular joint pain-dysfunction syndrome and bruxism: Etiopathogenesis and treatment from a pyschosomatic integrative viewpoint. *Psychotherapy and Psychosomatics, 59,* 84–98.

Bush, F. M., Harkins, S. W., Harrington, W. G., & Price, D. D. (1993). Analysis of gender effects on pain perception and symptom presentation in temporomandibular pain. *Pain, 53,* 73–80.

Christensen, L. V., & McKay, D. C. (1995). Biologic vs. psychologic dentistry. *Cranio, 13,* 69–71.

Crasilneck, H. B. (1995). The use of the Crasilneck bombardment technique in problems of intractable organic pain. *American Journal of Clinical Hypnosis, 37,* 255–266.

Dahlström, L., Widmark, G., & Carlsson, S. G. (1997). Cognitive-behavioral profiles among different categories of orofacial pain patients: Diagnostic and treatment implications. *European Journal of Oral Sciences, 105,* 377–383.

De Jongh, A., Muris, P., Schoenmakers, N., & Ter Horst, G. (1995). Negative cognitions of dental phobics: Reliability and validity of the Dental Cognitions Questionnaire. *Behaviour Research and Therapy, 33,* 507–515.

Delfino, J. (1997). Public attitudes toward oral surgery: Results of a Gallup poll. *Journal of Oral & Maxillofacial Surgery, 55,* 564–567.

Dellemijn, P. L. I., & Fields, H. L. (1994). Do benzodiazepines have a role in chronic pain management? *Pain, 57,* 137–152.

Dimitroulis, G., Dolwick, M. F., & Gremillion, H. A. (1995). Temporomandibular disorders. 1. Clinical evaluation. *Australian Dental Journal, 40,* 301–305.

Dimitroulis, G., Gremillion, H. A., Dolwick, M. F., & Walter, J. H. (1995). Temporomandibular disorders. 2. Non-surgical treatment. *Australian Dental Journal, 40,* 372–376.

Dos Santos, J., Jr. (1995). Supportive conservative therapies for temporomandibular disorders. *Dental Clinics of North America, 39,* 459–477.

Dworkin, S. F. (1997). Behavioral and educational modalities. *Oral Surgery, Oral Medicine, Oral Pathology, Oral Radiology and Endontics, 83,* 128–133.

Dworkin, S. F., Turner, J. A., Wilson, L., Massoth, D., Whitney, C., Huggins, K. H., Burgess, J., Sommers, E., & Truelove, E. (1994). Brief group cognitive-behavioral intervention for temporomandibular disorders. *Pain, 59,* 175–187.

Dworkin, S. F., Von Korff, M. R., & Le Resche, L. (1992). Epidemiologic studies of chronic pain: A dynamic-ecologic perspective. *Annals of Behavioral Medicine, 14,* 3–11.

Eli, I., Uziel, N., Baht, R., & Kleinhauz, M. (1997). Antecedents of dental anxiety: Learned responses versus personality traits. *Community Dentistry and Oral Epidemiology, 25,* 233–237.

Elter, J. R., Strauss, R. P., & Beck, J. D. (1997). Assessing dental anxiety, dental care use and oral status in older adults. *Journal of the American Dental Association, 128,* 756–762.

Feinmann, C., & Harrison, S. (1997). Liaison psychiatry and psychology in dentistry. *Journal of Psychosomatic Research, 43,* 467–476.

Flor, H., Behle, D. J., & Birbaumer, N. (1993). Assessment of pain-related cognitions in chronic pain patients. *Behaviour Research and Therapy, 31,* 63–73.

Flor, H., & Birbaumer, N. (1993). Comparison of the efficacy of electromyographic cognitive-behavioral therapy, and conservative medical interventions in the treatment of chronic musculoskeletal pain. *Journal of Consulting and Clinical Psychology, 61,* 653–658.

Flor, H., & Birbaumer, N. (1994). Psychophysiological methods in the assessment and treatment of chronic musculoskeletal pain. In J. G. Carlson, A. R. Seifert, & N. Birbaumer (Eds.), *Clinical applied psychophysiology* (pp. 171–184). New York: Plenum.

Garro, L. C. (1994). Narrative representations of chronic illness experience: Cultural models of illness, mind, and body in stories concerning the temporomandibular joint (TMJ). *Social Science and Medicine, 38,* 775–788.

Geffken, G., Rodrique, J., & Streisand, R. (1998). *Handbook of Child Behavioral Assessment.* New York: Guilford.

Gevirtz, R. N., Glaros, A. G., Hopper, D., & Schwartz, M. S. (1995). Temporomandibular disorders. In M. S. Schwartz (Ed.), *Biofeedback: A practitioner's guide* (2d ed.), (pp. 411–428). New York: Guilford.

Glaros, A. G., & Glass, E. G. (1993). Temporomandibular disorders. In R. J. Gatchel & E. B. Blanchard (Eds.), *Psychophysiological disorders: Research and clinical applications* (pp. 299–356). Washington, DC: American Psychological Association.

Glaros, A. G., & Melamed, B. G. (1992). Bruxism in children: Etiology and treatment. *Applied and Preventive Psychology, 1,* 191–199.

Golan, H. P. (1989). Temporomandibular joint disease treated with hypnosis. *American Journal of Clinical Hypnosis, 31,* 269–274.

Goldstein, B. H. (1998). The TMD controversies. *Journal of the Canadian Dental Association, 64,* 65–66.

Gramling, S. E., Neblett, J., Grayson, R., & Townsend, D. (1996). Temporomandibular disorder: Efficacy of an oral habit reversal treatment program. *Journal of Behavior Therapy and Experimental Psychiatry, 27,* 245–255.

Greco, C. M., Rudy, T. E., Turk, D. C., Herlich, A., & Zaki, H. H. (1997). Traumatic onset of temporamandibular disorders: Positive effects of a standardized conservative treatment program. *Clinical Journal of Pain, 13,* 337–347.

Hakeberg, M., & Berggren, U. (1997). Dimensions of the Dental Fear Survey among patients with dental phobia. *Acta Odontologica Scandinavica, 55,* 314–318.

Hakeberg, M., Gustafsson, J. E., Berggren, U., & Carlsson, S. G. (1995). Multivariate analysis of fears in dental phobic patients according to a reduced FSS-II scale. *European Journal of Oral Sciences, 103,* 339–344.

Hammarstrand, G., Berggren, U., & Carlsson, S. G. (1995). Psychophysiological therapy vs. hypnotherapy in the treatment of dental patients with dental phobia. *European Journal of Oral Sciences, 103,* 399–404.

Hathaway, K. M. (1997). Evaluation and management of maladaptive behaviors and psychological issues in temporomandibular disorder patients. *Dental Clinics of North America, 41,* 341–354.

Hudzinski, L. G., & Lawrence, G. (1992). Normal EMG surface electrode levels for treating myofacial contraction and related headache. *Headache Quarterly, 3,* 415–420.

Kallenberg, A., Wenneberg, B., Carlsson, G. E., & Ahlmen, M. (1997). Reported symptoms from the masticatory system and general well-being in rheumatoid arthritis. *Journal of Oral Rehabilitation, 24,* 342–349.

Kent, G., Rubin, G., Getz, T., & Humphris, G. (1996). Development of a scale to measure the social and psychological effects of severe dental anxiety: Social attributes of the Dental Anxiety Scale. *Community Dentistry and Oral Epidemiology, 24,* 394–397.

Klingberg, G. (1995). Dental fear and behavior management problems in children. *Swedish Dental Journal, 103,* 1–78.

Klingberg, G., Berggren, U., Carlsson, S. G., & Norén, J. G. (1995). Child dental fear: Cause-related factors and clinical effects. *European Journal of Oral Sciences, 103,* 405–412.

Krogstad, B. S., Jokstad, A., Dahl, B. L., & Vassend, O. (1996). The reporting of pain, somatic complaints and anxiety in a group of patients with TMD before and 2 years after treatment: Sex differences. *Journal of Orofacial Pain, 10,* 263–269.

Law, A. S., & Lilly, J. P. (1995). Trigeminal neuralgia mimicking odontogenic pain: A report of two cases. *Oral Surgery, Oral Medicine, Oral Pathology, Oral Radiology and Endodontics, 80,* 96–100.

Le Resche, L. (1997). Epidemiology of temporomandibular disorders: Implications for the investigation of etiologic factors. *Critical Reviews in Oral Biology and Medicine, 8,* 291–305.

Lennon, M. C., Link, B. G., Marbach, J. J., & Dohrenwend, B. P. (1989). The stigma of chronic facial pain and its impact on social relationships. *Social Problems, 36,* 117–134.

Liddell, A., & Locker, D. (1997). Gender and age differences in attitudes to dental pain and dental control. *Community Dentistry and Oral Epidemiology, 25,* 314–318.

Lipton, A. A., Ship, J. A., & Larbach-Robinson, D. (1993). Estimated prevalence and distribution of reported orofacial pain in the United States. *Journal of the American Dental Association, 124,* 115–121.

Litt, M. D. (1996). A model of pain and anxiety associated with acute stressors: Distress in dental procedures. *Behaviour Research and Therapy, 34,* 459–476.

Litt, M. D., Nye, C., & Shafer, D. (1995). Preparation for oral surgery: Evaluating elements of coping. *Journal of Behavioral Medicine, 18,* 435–459.

Lobb, W. K., Zakariasen, K. L., & McGrath, P. J. (1996). Endodontic treatment outcomes: Do patients perceive problems? *Journal of the American Dental Association, 127,* 597–600.

Locker, D., & Liddell, A. (1995). Stability of Dental Anxiety Scale scores: A longitudinal study of older adults. *Community Dentistry and Oral Epidemiology, 23,* 259–261.

Locker, D., Shapiro, D., & Liddell, A. (1997). Overlap between dental anxiety and blood-injury fears: Psychological characteristics and response to dental treatment. *Behaviour Research and Therapy, 35,* 583–590.

Logan, H. L., Baron, R. S., & Kahout, F. (1995). Sensory focus as therapeutic treatments for acute pain. *Psychosomatic Medicine, 57,* 475–484.

Logan, H. L., Baron, R. S., Keeley, K., Law, A., & Stein, S. (1991). Desired control and felt control as mediators of stress in a dental setting. *Health Psychology, 10,* 352–359.

McCracken, L. M., Zayfert, C., & Gross, R. T. (1992). The Pain Anxiety Symptoms Scale: Development and validation of a scale to measure fear of pain. *Pain, 50,* 67–73.

McGlynn, F. D., Glaros, A. G., Le Resche, L., Massoth, D. L., & Weifenbach, J. M. (1990). Biobehavioral research in dentistry: Some directions for the 1990s. *Annals of Behavioral Medicine, 12,* 133–140.

McNeil, D., Vrana, S., Cuthbert, B., Melamed, B. G., & Lang, P. J. (1993). Emotional imagery in simple and social phobia: Fear versus anxiety. *Journal of Abnormal Psychology, 102*(2): 212–225.

Meechan, J. G., & Skelly, A. M. (1997). Problems complicating dental treatment with local anaesthesia or sedation: Prevention and management. *Dental Update, 24,* 278–283.

Melamed, B. G. (1998). Preparation for medical procedures. In R. T. Ammerman & J. V. Campo (Eds.), *Handbook of Pediatric Psychology and Psychiatry.* New York: Guilford.

Melamed, B. G., & Williamson, D. J. (1991). Programs for the treatment of dental disorders: Dental anxiety and temporomandibular disorders. In R. H. Rozensky, J. J. Sweet, & S. Tovian (Eds.), *Handbook of clinical psychology in medical settings* (pp. 539–565). New York: Plenum.

Melzack, R. P. (1993). Pain: Past, present and future. *Canadian Journal of Experimental Psychology, 47,* 615–629.

Mew, J. R. C. (1997). The aetiology of temporomandibular disorders: A philosophical overview. *European Journal of Orthodontics, 19,* 249–258.

Milgrom, P., Coldwell, S. E., Getz, T., Weinstein, P., & Ramsay, D. S. (1997). Four dimensions of fear of dental patients. *Journal of the American Dental Association, 128,* 756–762.

Miller, C. S., Dembo, J. B., Falace, D. A., & Kaplan, A. L. (1995). Salivary cortisol response to dental treatment of varying stress. *Oral Surgery, Oral Medicine, Oral Pathology, Oral Radiology, and Endodontics, 79,* 436–441.

Miller, S. (1987). Monitoring and blunting: Validation of a questionnaire to assess style of information seeking under threat. *Journal of Personality and Social Psychology, 52*(2): 345–353.

Morris, S., Benjamin, S., Gray, R., & Bennett, D. (1997). Physical, psychiatric and social characteristics of the temporomandibular disorder pain dysfunction syndrome: The relationship of mental disorders to presentation. *British Dental Journal, 182,* 255–260.

Nellis, T. A., Conti, P. A., & Hicks, R. A. (1992). Temporomandibular joint dysfunction and Type A-B behavior in college students. *Perceptual and Motor Skills, 74,* 360–362.

Okeson, J. P. (1997). Current diagnostic classification schema and assessment of patients with temporomandibular disorders. *Oral Surgery, Oral Medicine, Oral Pathology, Oral Radiology and Endodontics, 83,* 61–64.

Okeson, J. P., & De Kanter, R. J. A. M. (1996). Temporomandibular disorders in the medical practice. *Journal of Family Practice, 43,* 347–356.

Pavlov, C. (1997). Managing dental phobia. *Ontario Dentist, 74,* 23–27.

Peterson, A. L., Dixon, D. C., Talcott, G. W., & Kelleher, W. J. (1993). Habit reversal treatment of temporomandibular disorders: A pilot investigation. *Journal of Behavior Therapy and Experimental Psychiatry, 27,* 245–255.

Raadal, M., Milgrom, P., Weinstein, P., Mancl, L., & Cauce, A. M. (1995). The prevalence of dental anxiety in children from low-income families and its relationship to personality traits. *Journal of Dental Research, 74,* 1439–1443.

Raphael, K. G., & Marbach, J. J. (1997). When did your pain start? Reliability of self-reported age of onset of facial pain. *Clinical Journal of Pain, 13,* 352–359.

Robertson, C., Gatchel, R. J., & Fowler, C. (1991). Effectiveness of a videotaped behavioral intervention in reducing anxiety in emergency oral surgery patients. *Behavioral Medicine, 17,* 77–85.

Rousset, C., Lambin, M., & Manas, F. (1997). The ethological method as a means for evaluating stress in children two to three years of age during a dental examination. *ASDC Journal of Dentistry for Children, 64,* 99–106.

Rudy, T. E., Turk, D. C., Kubinski, J. A., & Zaki, H. S. (1995). Differential treatment responses of TMD patients as a function of psychological characteristics. *Pain, 61,* 103–112.

Starcevic, V., & Bogojevic, G. (1995). Comorbidity of panic disorder with agoraphobia and specific phobia: Relationship with the subtypes of specific phobia. *Comprehensive Psychiatry, 12,* 143–150.

Stohler, C. S. (1997). Phenomenology, epidemiology, and natural progression of the muscular temporomandibular disorders. *Oral Surgery, Oral Medicine, Oral Pathology, Oral Radiology and Endodontics, 83,* 77–81.

Stouthard, M .E. A., Hoogstraten, J., & Mellenbergh, G. J. (1995). A study on the convergent and discriminant validity of the Dental Anxiety Inventory. *Behaviour Research and Therapy, 33,* 589–595.

Suvinen, T. I., Hanes, K. R., & Reade, P. C. (1997). Outcome of therapy in the conservative management of temporomandibular pain dysfunction disorder. *Journal of Oral Rehabilitation, 24,* 718–724.

Suvinen, T. I., & Reade, P. C. (1995). Temporomandibular disorders: A critical review of the nature of pain and its assessment. *Journal of Orofacial Pain, 9,* 317–339.

Turk, D. C., Penzien, D. B., & Rains, J. C. (1995). Temporomandibular disorders. In A. J. Goreczny (Ed.), *Handbook of health and rehabilitation psychology* (pp. 55–77). New York: Plenum.

Turk, D. C., Rudy, T. E., Kubinski, J. A., Zaki, H. S., & Greco, C. M. (1996). Dysfunctional patients with temporomandibular disorders: Evaluating the efficacy of a tailored treatment protocol. *Journal of Consulting and Clinical Psychology, 64,* 139–146.

Turner, J. A., Whitney, C., Dworkin, S. F., Massoth, D., & Wilson, L. (1995). Do changes in patient beliefs and coping strategies predict temporomandibular disorder treatment outcomes? *Clinical Journal of Pain, 11,* 177–188.

Van Der Bijl, P. (1995). Psychogenic pain in dentistry. *Compendium, 16,* 46–54.

Vassend, O., Krogstad, B. S., & Dahl, B. L. (1995). Negative affectivity, somatic complaints and symptoms of temporomandibular disorders. *Journal of Psychosomatic Research, 39,* 889–899.

Weinstein, P., Milgrom, P., Hoskuldsson, O., Golletz, D., Jeffcott, E., & Koday, M. (1996). Situation-specific child control: A visit to the dentist. *Behaviour Research and Therapy, 34,* 11–21.

Wexler, G. B., & McKinney, M. W. (1995). Assessing treatment outcomes in two temporomandibular disorder diagnostic categories employing a validated psychometric test. *Cranio, 13,* 256–263.

Wilson, J. F., & Sinisko, S. A. (1997). Increased self-reported dental anxiety following completion of a dental history questionnaire. *Psychological Reports, 81,* 59–62.

Wright, E. F., & Schiffman, E. L. (1995). Treatment alternatives for patients with masticatory myofascial pain. *Journal of the American Dental Association, 126,* 1030–1039.

CHAPTER 17

METABOLIC DISEASES: The Hypothalamic Arousal Syndrome

Per Björntorp

Göran Holm

Roland Rosmond

There is considerable evidence that hypertension may arise from frequent or chronic stimulation of the sympathetic nervous system (SNS). Development of novel methods has now made it possible also to measure similar chronic adaptations of the hypothalamic-pituitary-adrenal (HPA) axis in humans. A normal axis with normal secretory rhythm of cortisol and a high suppressibility by dexamethasone is associated with excellent health in measurements of hormones, anthropometry, metabolism, and hemodynamic variables. In sharp contrast are individuals without diurnal rhythm of the HPA axis activity and low suppressibility by dexamethasone, an abnormal "burned-out" axis with high sensitivity for perceived stress. Such subjects have a diminished secretion of sex steroid and growth hormones, abdominal obesity, insulin resistance, dyslipidemia, and elevated blood pressure and heart rate. These associations are strong and consistent (all < 0.001) and found in a considerable fraction of the middle-age Swedish population. These abnormal variables constitute a cluster often called the metabolic syndrome, and are risk factors for cardiovascular disease (CVD), non–insulin-dependent diabetes mellitus (NIDDM), and stroke.

Evidence has been put forward for mechanisms that may explain these statistical associations either via abnormal hyperactivity of the SNS or of the HPA-axis, which are often combined. Among putative pathogenetic factors are social handicaps that probably provide a stressful environment, a supposition strongly supported by controlled studies in nonhuman primates. Traits of depression and anxiety are other robust associates, which may together with smoking and alcohol cluster with social handicaps.

The evidence summarized indicates that pressures in modern, competitive society are followed by generation of most of the established risk factors for CVD, NIDDM, and stroke via overstimulation of hypothalamic centers. Due to the high prevalence of such a "hypothalamic arousal syndrome" and its powerful impact on health, it may be possible that a large fraction of serious, prevalent diseases are mediated via this central pathway.

INTRODUCTION

In spite of impressive advances in biomedical research, the function of the human brain is still almost terra incognita. The complexity of the interactions between various inputs, their processing, and the resulting product in terms of muscular activity, feelings, and logical action modified by cognitive factors is such that we may never reach full understanding of these events. There is always a subconscious survival-level component that is found not only in the primate with the most complex brain cortex, the human, but also through the series of mammals down to primitive organisms.

The power station for the processing of incoming signals is the hypothalamic area. In this region of the brain are centers that through a number of mechanisms strive to counteract threats to homeostasis in several somatic systems. This is accomplished via neuroendocrine events, with adaptations of signals to circulation, body temperature regulation, fluid and salt balance, the immune system, and energy balance. The signals are either mediated through the endocrine or the autonomic nervous system or, most often, both. These events have different time scales, some needing immediate corrections such as maintenance of body temperature regulation and the fluid–salt balance. Others lead to more long-term changes, such as modifications in energy balance, metabolism, the immune system, and hemodynamic functions.

Threat to the homeostasis of these functions comes from various external sources such as toxins, infections, and physical trauma. They may also be mental pressures perceived as threatening, often called stress. This is followed by somatic consequences to adapt the organism to meet such challenges.

Most of the research in this field has been performed in animal models (Henry & Stephens, 1977). Circumstantial evidence suggests that similar events occur in the human being, but solid evidence has not been possible to obtain, mainly because the mechanisms that connect psyche and soma have not been possible to identify with certainty, much less be measured. The difficulties in this area of studies in the human being are due to the complexity of the human cortex, which modifies and compensates for noxious environmental factors. Perception of stress is probably increasing continuously in complex, competitive modern society, particularly in individuals with insufficient coping abilities.

In this review an attempt will be made to summarize the currently available evidence of the somatic consequences of perceived mental stress in the human being. The emphasis will be on two tightly coupled systems, the central SNS and the HPA axis. These are both directly dependent on hypothalamic regulatory centers, and their reactions have been notoriously difficult to separate. This might be due to the fact that the signals from the hypothalamus may have a common pathway. Recent studies have shown that corticotropin-releasing hormone (CRH) acts via two separate receptors, one signaling to the HPA axis and another to the SNS (Richard, 1993). Both types of reactions thus originate from the hypothalamic region and are signs of a hypothalamic arousal.

Chronic SNS activation has previously been discussed as a potential cause of hypertension (Folkow, 1987). Recent research has revealed the possibility that the HPA axis is a major inducer of morbidities in endocrine and metabolic systems. In fact, there is - accumulating evidence that the combined, chronic activation of both the SNS and HPA axis might induce morbidity end-points such as CVD, NIDDM, and stroke. This combined, chronic activation will here be called the *hypothalamic arousal syndrome*. Evidence now suggests that this syndrome may in fact be a major threat to human health in modern society.

Starting from the observation that centralization of body fat stores is a surprisingly powerful independent risk factor for CVD, NIDDM, and stroke, a hypothesis has been put forward that perceived stress and related factors are inducers of a *metabolic syndrome,* in which visceral obesity is an easily visible index of chronic HPA activation. This condition has been labeled a "civilization syndrome" (Björntorp, 1993). Considerable amounts of decisive, new evidence have been obtained, evidence that not only strengthens the hypothesis but widens the scope of this concept. In addition, our understanding of the peripheral mechanisms involved has been broadened. This new information will be integrated into previously available knowledge in this review.

The hypothalamic arousal syndrome is summarized in Figure 17.1. Each part of this syndrome will be systematically discussed in the following sections, based on presently available evidence and with missing information pointed out.

HYPOTHALAMIC AROUSAL

As already mentioned, hypothalamic arousal is followed by activation of both the SNS and HPA axis pathways, perhaps by a common signal that is later divided into activation of both pathways. The selection of signaling pathway might vary. There is a considerable body of evidence from animal experiments that stress reactions leading to hypothalamic arousal differ according to the individual coping with the perceived stressor. The typical consequences are a fight-flight reaction or a depressive, defeat reaction of helplessness. The former is coupled mainly to the SNS pathway and the latter to the HPA axis (Henry &

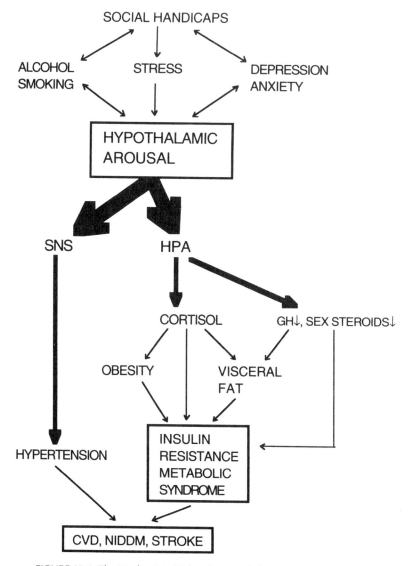

FIGURE 17.1. The Mechanistic Links of a Hypothalamic Arousal Syndrome.

Abbreviations: SNS = central sympathetic nervous system; HPA = the hypothalamic-pituitary-adrenal axis; GH = growth hormone; CVD = cardiovascular disease; NIDDM = non–insulin-dependent diabetes mellitus.

Stephens, 1977). This is difficult to show in humans, which might be due to the complex, overriding, controlling cortex of the human brain or simply because there is no such division of signals in humans.

The apparent differences in reactions to perceived stress in men and women (Frankenhaeuser, 1983) is,

however, an argument in favor of the presence of mechanisms modifying the selection of the SNS and HPA axis pathways in human beings. Furthermore, we have recently observed differences in the consequences of chronic hypothalamic arousal between subjects with different psychosocial and socioeconomic backgrounds (Ljung et al., in preparation). It is currently not known what determines this selection. This is an area of central interest, and work is ongoing to resolve this problem (Richard, personal communication, 1998).

SNS ACTIVATION

Chronic SNS activation seems to lead to the development of hypertension. Essential hypertension in its early phases is characterized by increased heart rate and cardiac output, a hyperkinetic condition caused by SNS activation. In later stages, peripheral resistance is elevated due to pathological regulation of peripheral resistance vessels. Beta-adrenergic blocking agents are now established as an efficient therapy for hypertension, indicating an involvement of the SNS in both early and late phases of essential hypertension (Folkow, 1987; Julius, Esler, & Randall, 1975).

Men with signs of HPA axis activation but without hypertension also clearly display an SNS activation of both heart rate and blood pressure, particularly after stimulation by food ingestion or laboratory stress tests, and excretion of catecholamine metabolites is elevated (Ljung et al., 1998). This might characterize the very early state of the development of hypertension. In young men with borderline hypertension and elevated waist–hip circumference ratio (WHR), a sign of chronic HPA axis activation, there is evidence for peripheral circulatory resistance (Jern et al., 1992). These observations indicate a mixture of reactions in humans along the SNS and HPA axis pathways from hypothalamic arousal.

HPA AXIS ACTIVATION

HPA axis activation results in cortisol secretion, as well as an inhibition of growth and sex steroid hormones (Chrousos & Gold, 1992). Results of experiments in animals suggest that when the HPA axis is frequently or chronically activated, this leads to a loss of normal rhythmicity with low morning values, and the feedback inhibition system is down-regulated (McEwen et al., 1993). This is seen after chronic perceived stress, and the axis is now also adapted to a high sensitivity to stress (Dallman, 1993). This has been considered as a "burnout" of the HPA axis (McEwen et al., 1993).

Such phenomena have been difficult to measure in humans due to the lack of sensitive, discriminative methods that can be applied under nondisturbed conditions. Based on salivary measurements of cortisol, we have recently developed adequate methodology for this purpose (Rosmond, Dallman, & Björntorp, 1998; Rosmond, Holm, & Björntorp, 1998). In brief, the proband collects several saliva samples over an ordinary working day. A standardized lunch is provided to induce a physiological challenge. Perceived stress is reported every hour. A low-dose dexamethasone test is performed. This set of examinations provides information on the variability of cortisol secretion, morning values (which normally are high and pulsative), total cortisol secretion, the status of physiological regulatory mechanisms, the sensitivity to perceived stress, and the feedback regulatory brake provided by glucocorticoid receptors in the brain (Dallman, 1993; McEwen et al., 1993).

This set of several measurements of the various functions of the HPA axis is necessary in order to allow discovery of dysfunctions of the axis of pathogenetic significance. Previously used methods, based on urinary output of free cortisol or blood sampling, do not provide such detailed information.

When these methods are applied on middle-age, randomly selected subjects, we find a frighteningly high prevalence of an HPA axis with low rhythmicity combined with a poor inhibition of cortisol secretion by a low-dose dexamethasone. An exact figure for the prevalence of this abnormality cannot be provided due to the lack of normal values, but an estimation of about 20% in middle-age Swedish men living under urbanized conditions might give an impression of how often more or less pronounced abnormalities are found. This is closely associated with obesity, visceral fat accumulation, low growth and sex steroid hormone secretions, insulin resistance, elevated triglycerides, total and LDL cholesterol (HDL cholesterol correlates negatively), systolic and diastolic blood pressure, and heart rate. These are the characteristics of the metabolic syndrome (Björntorp, 1993). The associations are consistent, dramatically strong ($p < 0.001$ in all measurements), and displayed particularly clearly when perceived stress-related cortisol is measured over the day (Rosmond, Dallman, & Björntorp, 1998).

In contrast, subjects with signs of a healthy HPA axis with maintained diurnal rhythm, high morning cortisol values, and a sensitive dexamethasone suppression test have a favorable health profile with lower body mass index (BMI), higher growth hormone secretion, and lower values of total and LDL cholesterol as well as lower blood pressures than average (Rosmond, Holm, & Björntorp, 1998). This demonstrates the fundamental power of the HPA axis in the regulation of health variables.

There is considerable evidence that these statistical results are cause–effect related. An inhibition of growth and sex steroid hormones by elevated HPA axis activity may be considered established by available, consistent evidence (Chrousos & Gold, 1992). Preferential visceral accumulation of excess body fat is probably due to the high density of glucocorticoid receptors in this region of adipose tissue, mediating the lipid accumulation properties of cortisol. Because the opposing effects of growth and sex steroid hormones are diminished, the cortisol effect is amplified. This is dramatically clear in Cushing's syndrome and vanishes with successful treatment. Furthermore, substitutions with growth hormone and, in men, testosterone lead to improvements (for review of details, see Björntorp, 1996).

Interestingly, obesity, defined as elevated total body fat mass, may also be explained by the sensitization of the HPA axis. Leptin resistance seems to be induced by glucocorticoids and is followed by obesity due to deficient satiety signals (Zahrzewska et al., 1997). Subjects with leptin resistance, defined as elevated BMI and leptin, also have a sensitized HPA axis measured with the methods mentioned above, speaking in favor of such a mechanism. Furthermore, statistical path analyses show that HPA-axis sensitization is directly coupled to BMI (Rosmond & Björntorp, 1998). The tight association between HPA sensitization on the one hand and visceral as well as total fat mass on the other may thus have excess cortisol exposure as a common denominator. This in turn would also explain the consistent, strong statistical couplings among BMI, WHR, and abdominal sagittal diameter, which are estimations of both obesity and central, visceral localization of body fat (Björntorp, 1993; Rosmond, Dallman, & Björntorp, 1998; Rosmond, Holm, & Björntorp, 1998; Rosmond & Björntorp, 1998). Although convincing evidence has

been presented for this mechanism in rats (Zahrzewska et al., 1997), the evidence in the human is so far circumstantial.

This interesting possibility is in concert with several well-established clinical observations. Patients exposed to excess glucocorticoids, such as in Cushing's syndrome or when on chronic treatment with such drugs, usually become obese and report deficient satiation, particularly for carbohydrates. This is also the case with abdominally obese subjects (Strömbom et al., 1996). In contrast, patients with adrenal insufficiency are lean. Most obese animal models have hyperactive adrenals, and obesity disappears after adrenalectomy (York, 1992).

Insulin resistance is probably explained mainly by the elevated cortisol secretion as a consequence of HPA axis sensitization, a well-established phenomenon. The elevated concentrations of free fatty acids (FFA) of that condition adds to this effect and are probably derived from the enlarged central adipose tissue depots, which are sensitive to agents stimulating lipid mobilization such as cortisol and catecholamines. The perturbations of secretion of sex steroid hormones probably add to this abnormality. (For a detailed review, see Björntorp, 1993.)

Reaven (1988) has suggested and provided considerable evidence for the induction of dyslipidemia and hypertension by insulin resistance. Based on what has been discussed here on SNS activation, it seems at least equally likely that the elevated blood pressure and heart rate observed in relation to HPA axis sensitization are mediated via a parallel hypothalamic arousal of the SNS. These considerations seem to make it likely that the HPA axis perturbation may in fact cause other endocrine perturbations, visceral obesity and perhaps obesity in general, and the metabolic abnormalities and that the hemodynamic dysregulations are due to a parallel SNS activation. The anthropometric, metabolic, and hemodynamic abnormalities are established risk factors for CVD, NIDDM, and stroke, with reasonable mechanistic links (Maron, Ridker, & Pearson, 1998). It therefore seems likely that a hypothalamic arousal syndrome is a common underlying risk factor for the mentioned diseases.

We have previously reported the surprising power of the WHR to predict CVD, NIDDM, and stroke independently in both men and women (Björntorp,

1993). BMI, WHR, and abdominal sagittal diameter are, in combination, measurements of abdominal obesity. These indices are consistently, strongly related to the new measurements of perturbed, elevated HPA axis activity, best visible after stimulation either by physiological (lunch) or perceived stress challenges (Rosmond, Dallman, & Björntorp, 1998; Rosmond, Holm, & Björntorp, 1998). As summarized above, there is considerable evidence that abnormalities of HPA axis regulation are followed mechanistically by abdominal obesity. Therefore, elevated BMI, WHR, and abdominal sagittal diameter might be considered as reliable surrogate measurements of perturbations of the HPA axis activity. From this it follows that such perturbations are probably powerful, independent predictors of CVD, NIDDM, and stroke.

The evidence summarized here strongly suggests that a hypothalamic arousal syndrome is the basis and generator of prevalent diseases and their established risk indicators. This conclusion is based on strong, consistent statistical associations, including prospective studies, and reasonably convincing explanatory mechanisms. The prevalence of this syndrome in the middle-age Swedish population is about 20%, suggesting that this pathway is a major inducer of disease in quantitative terms. The hypothalamic arousal syndrome may therefore in fact be considered a major threat of disease in modern society.

PATHOGENESIS OF THE HYPOTHALAMIC AROUSAL SYNDROME

With the background provided here, it becomes of course important to examine potential pathogenetic factors. Some of these are listed in the top of Figure 17.1.

Psychosocial and socioeconomic handicaps have been repeatedly observed to be associated with abdominal obesity, a surrogate measurement of HPA axis sensitivity (Lapidus et al., 1989; Larsson et al., 1989; Rosmond, Lapidus, & Björntorp, 1996; Wing et al., 1991). These are now possible to knit to HPA axis sensitization by direct measurements. Consequently, previously reported as well as now emerging data have demonstrated consistent findings in four different populations of 900 to 1,400 randomly selected

middle-age men or women. Psychosocial handicaps include living alone, divorce, being out of work, and dissatisfaction with work conditions, all of which are more pronounced in men than women. Socioeconomic handicaps found are poor education, physical type of work, poor economy, as indicated by housing conditions, and low social class.

We have previously speculated that these handicaps provide a basis for perceived stress derived from various social problems, resulting in a hypothalamic arousal (Björntorp, 1993). This possibility is difficult to prove in humans by, for example, intervention studies because of obvious ethical problems. Such studies can, however, be performed in nonhuman primates. When monkeys are subjected to a relatively mild psychosocial stress (changes of hierarchy in a colony), they show a submissive, defeat-type of stress reaction. This is followed by a sensitized HPA axis with poor dexamethasone suppression of cortisol secretion, inhibited sex steroid secretion, visceral fat accumulation, insulin resistance, elevated triglyceride and cholesterol and blood pressures, as well as early signs of CVD and NIDDM (Shively et al., 1987). This then is an identical condition to that which we have reported in humans with the hypothalamic arousal syndrome, and therefore it provides convincing evidence that the condition in humans can also be induced by psychosocial and socioeconomic pressure. With the new, sensitive methods we hope to be able to reveal further details of these handicaps' effects.

Depression, or mood changes with depressive traits, and anxiety are other robust associates to the syndrome (Lapidus et al., 1989; Larsson et al., 1989; Rosmond et al., 1996; Rosmond & Björntorp, 1998). In the middle-age male Swedish population the prevalence is about 8%, again a rather surprisingly high figure. These phenomena might well be connected with the social handicaps.

Elevated alcohol intake and a high frequency of smoking are also found. Of these, alcohol particularly is expected to be coupled to social handicaps as a cause or as an effect. The influence of alcohol in quantitative terms has not yet been possible to measure due to the unreliable instruments that we have used, so far, but it is expected to be high and is currently being reinvestigated. It seems likely that other factors are also involved, which are waiting to be defined.

GENETIC ASPECTS

The heritability of obesity, visceral fat accumulation, insulin resistance, hypertension, and dyslipidemia is considerable (Bouchard & Pérusse, 1996). The activity of the HPA axis is almost identical in monozygotic twins (Linkowski et al., 1993). It is therefore likely that the syndrome appears on a genetic basis in susceptible individuals upon sufficient environmental pressure. Information on the detailed phylogenetic expression now available opens up the possibility of focusing on reasonable central candidate genes expressing the syndrome. Results of such studies are currently underway.

SUMMARY AND CONCLUSIONS

Recent observations have provided evidence for a condition of chronic hypothalamic arousal and its consequences in humans. There is convincing previous information available for a pathogenetic pathway of hypertension via SNS activation. HPA axis adaptations have, however, been difficult to measure adequately in humans, but novel techniques have now made this possible. An axis without the normal rhythmicity and a poor suppressibility by a low dose of dexamethasone is, particularly when reacting to perceived stress, closely and consistently associated with other endocrine perturbations, abdominal obesity, insulin resistance, dyslipidemia, and elevated blood pressure and heart rate. This perturbation is found in a large fraction of the middle-age Swedish population and thus is associated with a number of risk factors for CVD, NIDDM, and stroke. In contrast, subjects with a normal HPA axis show a healthy profile in these variables, demonstrating the power of the regulation of the HPA axis for human health.

Reasonable or conclusive evidence has been provided for mechanisms whereby the sensitization of the HPA axis causes other endocrine perturbations than that of cortisol secretion, visceral obesity, insulin resistance, and associated metabolic complications including dyslipidemia as well as hypertension. The hemodynamic perturbations may well be mediated by the SNS via the parallel hypothalamic signals that also activate the HPA axis.

Among putative pathogenetic factors are psychosocial and socioeconomic handicaps, which probably provide a basis for frequent environmental stress. This supposition is strongly supported by results of controlled experiments in nonhuman primates. Depressive and anxiety symptoms are found in about 8% and may well, together with smoking and increased alcohol consumption, be associates to the social handicaps.

Progress in gene mapping has provided the possibility of focusing on central candidate genes, and such studies have commenced.

The evidence summarized indicates that pressures in modern, competitive society cause a hypothalamic arousal syndrome, followed by generation of most established risk factors for CVD, NIDDM, and stroke. Due to the high prevalence of this syndrome, it may be possible that a large fraction of serious, prevalent diseases are generated in this central pathway.

REFERENCES

Björntorp, P. (1993). Visceral obesity: A "civilization syndrome." *Obesity Research, 1,* 206–222.

Björntorp, P. (1996). The regulation of adipose tissue distribution in humans. *International Journal of Obesity-Related Metabolic Disorders, 20,* 291–302.

Bouchard, C., & Pérusse, L. (1996). Current status of the human obesity gene map. *Obesity Research, 4,* 81–90.

Chrousos, G., & Gold, P. W. (1992). The concept of stress and stress system disorders. *JAMA, 267,* 1244–1252.

Dallman, M. F. (1993). Stress update: Adaptation of the hypothalamo-pituitary-adrenal axis to chronic stress. *Trends in Endocrine Metabolism, 4,* 62–69.

Folkow, B. (1987). Stress, hypothalamic function and neuroendocrine consequences. *Acta Medica Scandinavica, 723,* 61–69.

Frankenhaeuser, M. (1983). The sympathetic-adrenal and pituitary-adrenal response to challenge: Comparison between the sexes. In T. M. Dembroski, T. H. Schmidt, & G. Blümchen (Eds.), *Biobehavioral bases of coronary heart disease, human psychophysiology* (pp. 91–105). Basel, Switzerland: Karger.

Henry, J. P., & Stephens, P. M. (1977). *Stress, health, and the social environment. A sociobiological approach to medicine.* New York: Springfield.

Jern, S., Bergbrant, A., Björntorp, P., & Hansson, L. (1992). Relation of central hemodynamics to obesity and body fat distribution. *Hypertension, 19,* 520–527.

Julius, S., Esler, M. D., & Randall, O. S. (1975). Role of autonomic nervous system in mild human hypertension. *Clinical Science and Molecular Medicine, 48,* 243–252.

Lapidus, L., Bengtsson, C., Hällström, T., & Björntorp, P. (1989). Obesity, adipose tissue distribution and health in women—results from a population study in Gothenburg, Sweden. *Appetite, 12,* 25–35.

Larsson, B., Seidell, J., Svärdsudd, K., Wilhelmsen, L., Tibblin, G., & Björntorp, P. (1989). Obesity, adipose tissue distribution and health in men: The study of men born 1913. *Appetite, 13,* 37–44.

Linkowski, P., Van Onderbergen, A., Kerkhofs, M., Bosson, D., Mendlewicz, J., & Van Cauter, E. (1993). Twin study of the 24-h cortisol profile: Evidence for genetic control of the human circadian clock. *American Journal of Physiology, 264,* 173–181.

Ljung, T., Thorén, P., Holm, G., & Björntorp, P. Blood pressure and heart rate reactions, nervous system activity in abdominally obese men. Submitted for publication.

Maron, D. J., Ridker, P. M., & Pearson, T. A. (1998). Risk factors and the prevention of coronary heart disease. In: R. W. Alexander, R. C. Schlant, V. Fuster, R. A. O'Rourke, R. Roberts, & E. H. Sonnenblick (Eds.), *Hurst's the heart, arteries and veins* (pp. 1175–1195). New York: McGraw-Hill.

McEwen, B., Cameron, H., Chao, H., et al. (1993). Adrenal steroids and plasticity of hippocampal neurons: Toward an understanding of underlying cellular and molecular mechanisms. *Cellular and Molecular Neurobiology, 13,* 457–482.

Reaven, G. H. (1988). Role of insulin in human disease. *Diabetes, 37,* 1595–1607.

Richard, D. (1993). Involvement of corticotropin-releasing factor in the control of food intake and energy expenditure. *Annals of the New York Academy of Science, 697,* 155–172.

Rosmond, R., & Björntorp, P. (1998). Endocrine and metabolic aberrations in men with abdominal obesity in relation to anxiodepressive infirmity. *Metabolism, 47,* 1187–1193.

Rosmond, R., & Björntorp, P. (1998). The interactions between hypothalamic-pituitary-adrenal axis activity, testosterone, insulin-like growth factor I and abdominal obesity with metabolism and blood pressure in men.

International Journal of Obesity and Related Disorders, 22, 1184–1196.

Rosmond, R., Dallman, M. F., & Björntorp, P. (1998). Stress-related cortisol secretion in men: Relationships with abdominal obesity and endocrine, metabolic and hemodynamic abnormalities. *Journal of Clinical Endocrinology Metabolism, 83,* 1853–1859.

Rosmond, R., Holm, G., & Björntorp, P. (1998). Salivary cortisol in the diagnosis of the status of the hypothalamic-pituitary-adrenal axis activity. Submitted for publication.

Rosmond, R., Lapidus, L., & Björntorp, P. (1996). The influence of occupational and social factors on obesity and body fat distribution in middle-aged men. *International Journal of Obesity, 20,* 599–607.

Rosmond, R., Lapidus, L., Mårin, P., & Björntorp, P. (1996). Mental distress, obesity and body fat distribution in middle-aged men. *Obesity Research, 4,* 245–252.

Shively, C. A., Clarkson, R. B., Miller, C., & Weingard, K. W. (1987). Body fat distribution as a risk factor for coronary artery atherosclerosis in female Cynomolgus monkeys. *Atherosclerosis, 7,* 226–231.

Strömbom, U., Krotkiewski, K., Blennow, K., Månsson, J.-E., Ekman, T., & Björntorp, P. (1996). The concentrations of monoamine metabolites and neuropeptides in the cerebrospinal fluid of obese women with different body fat distribution. *International Journal of Obesity, 20,* 361–368.

Wing, R. R., Matthews, K. A., Kuller, L. H., Meilahn, E. N., & Plantinga, P. (1991). Waist to hip ratio in middle-aged women: Association with behavioral and psychosocial factors and with changes in cardiovascular risk factors. *Arteriosclerosis Thrombosis, 11,* 1250–1257.

York, D. A. (1992). Genetic models of animal obesity. In P. Björntorp & B. N. Brodoff (Eds.), *Obesity* (pp. 233–240). Philadelphia: Lippincott.

Zahrzewska, K. E., Cusin, J., Sainbury, A., Rohner-Jeanrenaud, F., & Jeanrenaud, B. (1997). Glucocorticoids are counterregulatory hormones of leptin: Towards an understanding of leptin resistance. *Diabetes, 46,* 717–719.

CHAPTER 18

EVALUATION AND TREATMENT OF ANXIETY IN NEUROMUSCULAR REHABILITATION

Philip R. Appel

Joseph Bleiberg

This chapter focuses on clinical practice within a rehabilitation hospital, where the vast majority of clinical work includes assisting patients to manage, productively channel, and overcome anxiety. Treatments for anxiety will be discussed from several points of view, including facilitating attainment of rehabilitation goals, improving adjustment and adaptation to disability, and treating patients with preexisting anxiety disorders who now are in a rehabilitation facility and are experiencing complex, multifactorial anxiety problems.

In keeping with the chapter's emphasis on clinical issues, case examples from the authors' clinical practice are used extensively. Moreover, because managed care and HMOs have dramatically decreased the number of sessions available for treatment; we highlight the use of hypnosis and cognitive behavioral interventions, within an overall sports psychology/performance enhancement model, as an effective yet economical and efficient approach to providing care.

The chapter begins with an examination of anxiety in physical medicine and rehabilitation patients from three main perspectives: the intrapsychic responses of persons faced with physical medicine and rehabilitation diagnoses such as spinal cord injury, stroke, amputation, chronic diseases such as multiple sclerosis, and chronic severe pain; the near universal stresses and precipitants of anxiety intrinsic to the demands and challenges of the physical medicine and rehabilitation setting; and the use of a modified sports psychology model as the basis for effective treatment interventions.

CAUSES AND TYPES OF ANXIETY

Persons with disability have been found to have a greater lifetime incidence of anxiety and depressive disorders (Aoki, Hosaka, & Ishida, 1995; Turner & McLean, 1989). Livneh and Antonak (1994), in an extensive review of research on adjustment to disability, conclude that the majority of individuals who are disabled experience anxiety, denial, and depression before attaining eventual acceptance of and adjustment to disability. Similarly, Hohman (1975) has noted that anxiety and depression are normal responses to abnormal situations in the early stages of rehabilitation. While it is popular to talk about "stages" of adjustment and acceptance, Trieschmann's (1980, 1981) research with spinal cord–injured patients conclusively demonstrated that there is no fixed sequence of stages of adjustment, nor is it typical or necessary for patients to experience all stages. Cook (1979), however, found that the severity of the spinal cord injury was correlated with the presence of anxiety and those patients with quadriplegia tended to be more anxious.

Anxiety and depression are often found together, in an interwoven clinical picture. Starkstein et al. (1990), in a study examining the relationship between anxiety and depression in patients with cerebrovascular injuries, found that almost half of the patients with post stroke major depression also met the criteria for generalized anxiety disorder. Schultz et al. (1997) found that among stroke patients there was a greater likelihood of anxiety being present with increased severity of depressive symptomatology and with a history of greater impairment in function during the acute hospitalization period. Shimoda and Robinson (1998) found that among depressed stroke patients the presence of anxiety significantly interacted with the depression to influence its severity and course. Morton and Wehman (1995), in a review of research examining the psychosocial and emotional sequelae of traumatic brain injury, found that the majority of patients experienced high levels of anxiety and depression for prolonged periods of time. Fann et al. (1995), in a study looking at psychiatric disorders in outpatients with traumatic brain injury, found that 24% of the patients were diagnosed with generalized anxiety disorders. They found that patients who were anxious or depressed were more impaired than those who were neither anxious nor depressed, and that anxious and depressed patients perceived their injuries as more severe and their cognitive functioning as worse. In chronic pain patients, anxiety level is the best predictor of pain-related avoidance behaviors (Asmundson & Taylor, 1996). In a study of 210 adult patients with chronic pain, McCracken, Faber, and Janek (1998) found that physiologic symptoms of anxiety were the strongest predictor of patients' complaining of physical symptoms.

Unlike congenital handicaps, acquired handicaps and disabilities are almost always psychologically traumatic (Castelnuovo-Tedesco, 1981) in that they confront the individual, in perceptually undeniable ways, with the fragility of existence and at least temporarily destroy the illusion of indestructibility. The initial perception of handicap and disability is a traumatic dislocation of the patient's relationship with his or her internal and external world, which, as Janoff-Bulman (1992) notes, is a source of powerful and fundamental anxiety until the patient reestablishes important narcissistic beliefs, including the belief that what happens to him or her is meaningful, that he or she has worth, and that there is continuity in the self, such that there is a coherent overriding concept of self that includes both the pre-injury and the post-injury self. Falvo (1991) describes how disability poses multiple threats to an individual's sense of self and identity by destabilizing the individual's experiences of: physical well-being and sense of body integrity and comfort; sense of independence, privacy, autonomy, and control; ability to fulfill customary roles and

pursue life goals and future plans; and ability to sustain central relationships. The presence of chronic illness or disability can generate anxiety from just the threat of such losses, whether it is of function, independence, love, or security. It is not uncommon for patients to be in a state of anticipatory anxiety about such losses even before they fully comprehend the consequences of their injury or illness and resultant disability.

Normal aging is often accompanied by impairment and disability but generally progresses at a slow enough rate to permit the individual gradually to adjust to the changes over time. Kreuger (1984) views the psychological task associated with aging as "to replace the indignities of physical decay with a sense of unshakable self worth" (p. 3). Kreuger further notes that with an acquired disability the normally gradual process of adaptation to aging and diminished function is traumatically compressed into a few short moments.

Individuals experience reality in light of their own images of reality and then believe these self-created images (Emery & Tracy, 1987). Few individuals have images of themselves as disabled. When an individual is disabled, there are many emotional and intellectual struggles that emerge, including development of an evolving self-image as having a disabled body in an able-bodied world. It is the image of the broken self, the self no longer able to do for oneself and that is dependent upon others, the self that no longer fits into the image of pre-disability life, that engenders suffering and anxiety. There is often a catastrophizing process in which the individual cannot see the possibility of adjustment or accommodation. Fear of the unknown and images of the self as lacking in some basic ability emerge. Such images can act as self-suggestions, and as King (1983) notes, internal images can produce conditioned responses in and of themselves.

THE REHABILITATION ENVIRONMENT

The core purpose of rehabilitation is restoration of the physical and psychological capacities of individuals who, because of traumatic injury or illness, have lost the ability to perform basic daily life functions, ranging from basic survival functions such as eating, personal hygiene, and mobility to higher-order social and vocational role functions such as earning a living and raising a family. These functional limitations include three related but independent factors: impairments, disabilities, and handicaps (Diller & Ben Yishay, 1987). Impairments are deficits in specific motor, sensory, or cognitive abilities, such as the inability to move one's legs. Disabilities represent the effects of impairments on one's capacity to perform specific tasks, such as going to the grocery store. Handicaps are the cumulative effect of disabilities on one's capacity to function effectively in various societal roles such as parenting or employment. Rehabilitation goals are typically described and measured in terms of disability and handicap rather than impairment.

The pursuit of such functional goals is generally ruthlessly practical, with little built-in capacity for diversions caused by the patient's anxiety or other elements of the patient's emotional state. The core process within the rehabilitation hospital is patient education and training, in essence assisting patients to acquire new skills and behaviors in order to ameliorate handicaps. A study examining the types of activities within a rehabilitation hospital found that over 60% of total activities involve the acceleration or deceleration of specific behaviors (Bleiberg & Merbitz, 1982). Anxiety disorders can be major impediments to the rehabilitation process because they interfere with learning new skills and degrade performance of existing skills.

As noted, the rehabilitation process is essentially an educational endeavor in which patients relearn physical and sensory functioning to accomplish basic life activities. Referrals for inpatient rehabilitation, or even outpatient courses of treatment, are predicated on there being functional goals that reasonably can be attained. The length of treatment for a particular patient is often based on a clinical pathway that is also time-driven. Clinical pathways are generic models of care based on the needs of the modal patient with a particular type of disability. Examples of different long-term goals would be independent ambulation in the home, independent mobility with a wheelchair, dressing with minimal assistance, and returning to work. Short-term goals are the intervening

steps to attain the long-term goal. For example, the short-term goals of an individual who sustained a lower limb amputation would include ability to be independent in stump care, fitting of prosthesis, learning how to balance and shift one's weight on the prosthesis, and finally the development of a smooth and well-coordinated gait.

PSYCHOLOGICAL INTERVENTION

Psychological interventions have been directed at: (1) enhancing the patient's attainment of rehabilitation goals, (2) facilitating emotional and cognitive adjustment and adaptation to disability, and (3) treating preexisting psychological conditions exacerbated by the disability (Appel, 1992b). Within these three areas of intervention, we find three different corresponding manifestations of anxiety and sources of stress. Interventions focused on attainment of rehabilitation goals often deal with issues related to anxiety about ability to participate in and achieve rehabilitation goals, in essence being a form of performance anxiety. Interventions related to adjustment and coping focus on existential anxieties related to the various losses and changes in self-image mentioned earlier. Lastly, there is the intersection of preexisting anxiety conditions such as generalized anxiety disorder, panic disorder, or agoraphobia, with the anxieties related to physical disability, with one set of anxieties often exacerbating the other. Livneh and Antonak (1994) have proposed a similar conceptualization of treatment, using a cognitive-behavioral model: (1) assisting the client in dealing with personal meaning of disability; (2) interrupting/disrupting the client's irrational belief systems; (3) teaching coping skills in order to function successfully; and (4) providing client education about condition, status, and functional implications of condition, in order to promote mastery.

Psychological interventions to facilitate patient attainment of rehabilitation goals in many ways mirror sports psychology interventions. The psychologist assesses preperformance mentation, conducts a behavioral analysis of the patient's performance (time and motion studies), trains the patient in mental practice (covert rehearsal) of the desired physical activity, teaches the patient how to set achievable goals, and provides the patient with information/education on how to accomplish the goals. Asken and Goodling (1986) reported the use of sports psychology "psyching up" strategies with an elderly CVA patient to enhance her performance, and Appel (1992a) and Holroyd (1989) described the use of mental practice interventions with rehabilitation patients to improve motor performance.

There are two primary approaches to enhancing psychomotor function: using teaching/learning techniques to enhance underlying skills and abilities, and optimization of the mental state during performance. In the first approach the clinician uses behavioral interventions to shape and expedite the acquisition of target behaviors. In the second approach the patient's state of mind is targeted for shaping or alteration, the goal being to produce mental states that optimize performance, these typically being mental states that emphasize sense of mastery and control, relaxed alertness, and clear vision of the target behavior. In the real-life rehabilitation setting, achieving such optimized states begins with addressing the anxiety that is interfering with achieving or performing the target behaviors. This frequently can be done using simple cognitive-behavioral interventions such as altering negative self-talk, reframing, thought stopping, and challenging and clarifying irrational negative thoughts. For example, Appel (1992a) describes assisting a patient to create an ideal state of mind for performing wheelchair push-ups to avoid pressure sores. The mental state she created allowed her to focus her concentration and bypass her anxiety, which had been manifesting itself as obsessive ruminations and fears about performance.

The techniques described here are similar to the principles and interventions used in sports psychology (Williams & Leffingwell, 1996), which can be readily applied to rehabilitation (Appel, in press). The sports psychology model not only effectively conceptualizes a large part of the rehabilitation process, but it also has the major advantage of couching the psychological components of the intervention in *non*psychopathological terms. The avoidance of a psychopathological framework creates a therapeutic foundation that is more palatable to patients and which conveys the basis for a positive self-image: The patient can identify with the same performance-enhancing techniques used by an Olympic ice skater as opposed to being the victim of an anxiety disorder that must be treated.

Relaxation Training and Hypnosis

Similar to injured athletes, patients often develop habitual movements and postures to compensate for pain or loss of function, and these habits complicate rehabilitation by interfering with the restoration of normal movement patterns. These habits may actually contribute to maintaining or increasing pain because of the biomechanical stresses engendered. Other patients learn to avoid movement in anticipation of discomfort or pain, a phenomenon called kinesophobia. Kinesophobia is similar to a state of anticipatory anxiety, and the bracing and guarding that the individual engages in, in preparation for movement, often restrict the movement and prolong the discomfort because of prolonged muscle tension. Interventions for kinesophobia consist of education about the consequences of bracing and guarding and how increased muscle tone during movement stimulates sensory input, which in turn increases discomfort. The patient also learns that discomfort and pain do not necessarily mean harm.

Relaxation training is a key technique for facilitating natural movement and is done first as a static activity in the traditional way. We find that Gunther's (1968) technique of progressive sensory muscle relaxation, rather than Jacobsen's (1938) relaxation technique, is more effective for this population in general. Gunther's technique is similar to Schultz and Luthe's (1969) autogenic training in that the emphasis is on relaxing to the point that the patient can experience the gravitational pull of the earth on each body segment (portion of the body between the joints) and have a sense of body temperature. This is a very useful technique as it can be taught as a divided attention task in which the patient is encouraged to feel gravity and body temperature no matter what else he or she is doing.

When the patient has paralysis and impaired tactile sensation, relaxation techniques employing either visual or auditory imagery for distraction are often more effective. However, even after careful matching of the patient and technique there is the possibility for problems to develop, as in the case of a 48-year-old spinal cord–injured patient who was quite anxious and when asked to imagine a relaxing and pleasant scene began to get depressed. He had started by imagining a river where he loved to go fishing, but as the image developed, he saw no way that he could get to the river in his wheelchair, and he then began to focus on his disability again. Sometimes the search for an image that will not be a cue for a dysphoric state can be one of trial and error, as neither the therapist nor the patient may know ahead of time the emotions that will be elicited by any given image.

Hypnosis

Kaye and Schindler (1990), in a study of the use of hypnosis as an adjunctive treatment for acute care medical patients, reported that 68% achieved complete or almost complete symptom relief. They concluded that hypnotic treatments along with traditional psychological interventions were an effective tool for professionals working in a consultation-liaison service. Smith (1990) pointed out that the most frequent use of clinical hypnosis is for the purpose of enhancing patients' self-control and that the purpose of training the patient in self-hypnosis is so that the patient can continue to work on the problems in the therapist's absence. Hypnosis is very efficacious for treating anxiety disorders as it facilitates mind–body awareness and self-regulation and gives the patient an experience of self-mastery as well as influencing cognition in a positive manner (Smith, 1990). Spiegel and Spiegel (1988) argue that hypnosis is effective in the treatment of anxiety disorders because of its unique ability to offer differential control over the sensory, emotional, and cognitive aspects of experience. Becker (1963) stated that use of hypnosis to modify the rehabilitation patient's experience of anxiety was very efficacious. Crasilneck and Hall (1985) have written how hypnotically mediated interventions have helped increase patients' tolerance of the emotional sequelae of illness or disability and have increased motivation for participation in the rehabilitation regimen. They have also stated that hypnotic interventions are effective in reducing anxious reactions to the treatment regimen itself. Note that virtually all use of hypnosis, as described in this chapter, refers to using hypnotic interventions within the broader context of a traditional psychological intervention: Hypnosis is part of a psychological intervention, not a complete intervention in and of itself. Holroyd (1987) has written quite persuasively about how hypnosis can potentiate therapeutic interventions regardless of the therapeutic model or paradigm.

Mental Practice and Covert Rehearsal

It is not uncommon for patients to be unable to picture themselves learning what they need to learn. Mental practice and covert rehearsal interventions—defined as the "symbolic rehearsal of a physical activity in the absence of any gross muscular movements" (Richardson, 1967a, p. 95)—can be used to promote images of mastery and efficacy. These interventions are also useful for actually teaching new motor skills, as they have been found to affect primarily the cognitive components of motor tasks (Dennis, 1985; Epstein, 1980; Feltz & Landers, 1983; Ryan & Simons, 1982; Woolfolk et al., 1985. The image of performance can be both a vision of what can be, as well as an inner experience of what has been accomplished.

Mental practice and covert rehearsal are well known in the area of sports psychology (Gould & Damarjian, 1996; Richardson, 1967a, b; Woolfolk et al., 1985), and the use of these interventions in rehabilitation has been described by Appel (1992a), Holroyd (1989), and Asken and Goodling (1986). When mental practice is used in the rehabilitation setting, the patient is asked to covertly rehearse a physical activity using internal or external imagery, experiencing each element of the task in sequence as if he or she were actually engaged in that activity. Epstein (1980) and Suinn (1983) have suggested that internal imagery (feeling oneself do) as opposed to external imagery (seeing oneself do) enhances physical performance. Both techniques when used in combination, starting off with external imagery and then progressing to internal imagery, actually make it easier for the patient to learn the new movement and performance patterns.

An example of the clinical application of these techniques is as follows. A 65-year-old female underwent bilateral below-the-knee amputations secondary to the peripheral vascular disease caused by her insulin-dependent diabetes. She was referred for psychological consultation because she was highly anxious and fearful while learning to ambulate with her prosthetic limbs, and her anxiety was resulting in development of muscle spasms and increased pain. The patient was taught relaxation techniques and then taken through a hierarchy of performance situations. The first consisted of the patient standing with good posture on both of her prostheses. As she was doing this, she was instructed to imagine seeing herself (external imagery) standing in exactly the posture she and her physical therapist would consider ideal. Then she was asked to shift perspective and imagine feeling herself (internal imagery) standing exactly the way she had previously visualized it. While the patient was performing this, it was suggested that she appreciate herself for her efforts to develop these new skills and that she think about the mastery and competence she was obtaining. The next element in the training hierarchy consisted of mental practice sessions in which she was instructed to imagine herself in the physical therapy gym, walking between the parallel bars in the manner prescribed by her physical therapist. She was asked to correct the image until it was just perfect for her. As the patient became proficient with her mental practice skills, her physical therapist was instructed to provide time for the patient to engage in mental practice as a psyching-up strategy prior to the actual physical practice of her ambulation skills. This preperformance intervention served to concentrate her attention and relax her so that any anticipatory anxiety about her physical therapy and performance would be diminished. The hierarchy of situations gradually expanded beyond the physical therapy gym to include the nursing unit, the patient's home, and the patient's neighborhood.

Treatment via Consultation to Physical and Occupational Therapists

When a psychologist is consulted to assist in enhancing a patient's performance, one of the best places to gather data is in the physical therapy gym or occupational therapy area. It is there that the patient can be observed in the performance of rehabilitation goals and the psychologist has the opportunity to talk with the therapists and learn about the performance problems from another perspective. The therapists can provide much information about the performance goals of the patient and what appear to be the impediments to achieving those goals. It is important also to observe the interaction between therapist and patient, as sometimes the performance problems are actually symptoms of interpersonal conflicts (Gans, 1987). An example of interpersonal conflicts interfering with rehabilitation is the case of a 32-year-old female with paraplegia who in physical therapy was being taught to walk with braces and crutches. She had developed a fear of falling that began to generalize to a fear of even going down inclines in her wheelchair. A psychological evaluation revealed that the anxiety that was being expressed as a fear of falling was actually anxiety over unconscious rage directed at her physical therapist. The physical therapist had been frustrated with the patient and told her that she was only going to teach her wheelchair skills. The therapist, who was in a superior and withholding role, threatened the patient's dependency needs. When the dependency issues were made conscious to the patient and she was able to express her rage in psychotherapy, her panic and anxiety disappeared and the rehabilitation regimen was able to continue uneventfully.

When performance difficulties have been observed and assessed, specific performance-enhancing suggestions can be formulated. For example, a patient with debilitating chronic pain had become kinesophobic to the point of claiming that he was unable to engage in physical movements the physical therapist was recommending, and the therapist and patient had reached a therapeutic impasse. The therapist can be encouraged to ask the patient questions designed to stimulate productive discussion about the anxiety, such as: "What do you think would happen if you performed this movement?" "What would you need to know that would allow you to do what I am asking you to do?" "What would help you to feel more confident about your ability to get through what I am asking you to do?" Based on personality variables, guidance can be given to the therapist to provide choices, to provide a structure for the patient to follow, to allow the patient to participate in development of the treatment regimen, and to get interpersonally close or to stay interpersonally distant. Such adjustments to the therapeutic milieu can help the patient's performance anxiety by changing the therapist's stimulus behaviors.

Another approach that we have found to be extremely useful is to co-treat patients, in essence providing psychological treatment simultaneously with the physical therapy treatment. A full range of psychological services can be integrated in this way, including relaxation training, hypnosis, and even exploration of the patient's thoughts and feelings while performing or attempting to perform problematic activities. Here is an example. A patient had fallen 20 feet to the ground from a scaffold at work. She suffered a moderate concussion and fracture of her jaw, hip, and several ribs. One of the main therapy goals, which was necessary for return to employment, was to be able to again climb stairs. However, the patient had become very anxious about stair climbing and had developed an unbalanced gait because she was fearful of placing weight on the leg supporting her broken hip. This fear of weight bearing originated during the 2 weeks following her injury, when there had been substantial pain associated with weight bearing on that leg. The patient's hip surgery had healed quite well and her fear now had no basis, and indeed was resulting in pain to her other leg and back because of her unbalanced gait, in essence having become an unnecessary conditioned habit and a source of new pain. A simple paradoxical intervention (Haley, 1976; Zeig, 1982) was devised to get her to change her behavior. The patient was instructed to practice going up the stairs with only the balls of her feet touching the stair, a maneuver that forces equal weight bearing on both legs and which covertly pushes for speedier movement because of the discomfort of having both heels hanging in the air over the edge of the step. This very rapidly permitted the patient to realize that her anticipatory anxiety and compensatory behaviors were impairing performance unnecessarily.

Facilitating a High Performance State

Another technique for facilitating rehabilitation performance in the face of anxiety is by helping the patient to access cognitive and affective resources that the patient believes would make a difference if only he or she could feel that way while attempting to perform

a given task. An example would be the case of a 35-year-old, single, graduate school–educated woman who was referred for treatment of anxiety related to decreased cognitive performance secondary to a fall in which she struck her head and sustained a severe concussion. Shortly after the fall she was diagnosed with posttraumatic epilepsy. The injury also resulted in moderate hearing loss and the patient was experiencing intermittent vertigo and balance problems. She reported that for at least 20% of her day she was in a fearful and anxious state. Given the patient's need to be able to regulate her emotional experience and feel confident about her ability to perform her job as an educator, it was decided to create a patient-designed high performance state of consciousness that she could elicit by self-cueing.

During the initial interview the patient presented with a deep fascination with Native American beliefs and emphasized how she had a spiritual view of the natural world. It therefore was decided to use Native American rituals for altering consciousness as the vehicle for the intervention. In preparation for the intervention the patient was given a homework exercise to identify the mental and emotional qualities that she felt would enable her to perform optimally given the impairments created by her injury. She returned with a list that included: fluidness of journey, maintaining focus in rough winds, humor, insight, permission to be authentic, an understanding heart, and soaring close to heaven and the sun. The intervention began by having her attend to her breathing as a way of calming herself and focusing her attention and concentration. She then was given the suggestion that she could imagine a "sweat lodge" and that there was a fire with a large cooking pot in the center of the lodge. The qualities that she had listed were treated as ingredients for a recipe in the cooking pot. As each ingredient went into the pot, she was asked to focus on that quality and experience that aspect of herself. While experiencing each quality, she was told to touch the back of her lower teeth with her tongue. This was done until all the qualities were added to the pot. She then was told to imagine drinking a cup of the mixture from the pot and to again touch her tongue against her lower teeth. She was given some time to reflect upon her imaginary sweat lodge and was given suggestions that all of the desired qualities would be available to her whenever she touches her tongue against her lower teeth: She will feel all the sensations that she feels now, think the way she is thinking now, feel the calmness and mastery that she is feeling now, and so on. After some processing of the experience, she was distracted so that the effectiveness of the intervention could be checked. When she was appropriately distracted, she was asked to place her tongue against her lower teeth and report what happened. She reported that she felt an immediate change in her sensory and emotional experience that reminded her of being back in the imagery. Weeks later the patient reported that she was utilizing the technique to great effect to optimize her performance.

ADJUSTMENT TO DISABILITY

Serious injury or illness can shatter an individual's narcissistic sense of omnipotence and invulnerability and the assumption that the world is an orderly and safe place. When these beliefs are shattered, the individual will have great difficulty moving forward with life, and treatment will focus on reparative work to rebuild a set of basic beliefs about the self and the world (Janoff-Bulman, 1992; van der Kolk, & McFarlene, 1996). A major component of this work is assisting the individual to develop cognitive schemes and a model of the world that includes not only adapting to the disability, but also dealing with the perception of being a victim. Treatment may have to deal with the depression over loss and rejection of that which is perceived as self; or the anxiety of not being able to make one's way in the world independently and fear of one's rage about that impotence and dependence (Appel, 1992b). In regard to quality of life, the patient's ability to come to terms with the disability is critical to his or her being able to pursue the life that could be lived in spite of the disability. A whole host of clinically important issues such as treatment compliance, self-care, and integration into the community including return to work are correlated with the mental health of the disabled individual. Individuals who are unable to achieve some kind of mental accommodation not only suffer from the unresolved emotional sequelae, but also typically have poorer physical health and may not achieve the full degree of rehabilitation otherwise possible.

Following is a series of case examples describing a range of ways in which people respond and adapt to disability and the interventions used to help them.

Case One

A 20-year-old female was making a telephone call when a car jumped the curb and crashed into the phone booth she was in. She sustained a compound fracture of the right femur and patella, and most of her quadriceps muscle was sheared off. The patient was in severe pain and was fearful of never being able to walk again, and her emotional response was of mixed anxiety and depression. She developed spontaneous intrusive imagery of being unable to move independently and she became so anxious that she told her psychologist she could not remember ever having walked normally. Her experience of her trauma and resultant disability had become so much a part of her everyday consciousness and sense of self that she was unable to access images of a nondisabled self in her past. Her experience had generalized so that her fear of her present situation had become a filter through which her past was viewed. This intrusive imagery was not the typical posttraumatic phenomenon, in which images of the traumatic event are experienced, but rather focused on her current problems and, most importantly, what she imagined would be her future. She was helped to gain control over her intrusive imagery by treating the images as figures in need of a ground: She was taught to imagine a television set around the intrusive negative imagery, so that the images were symbolically bounded, controlled, and representative of another time.

Once she was taught to have control over her imagery and to reestablish cognitive schemes of a self who was once not disabled, it became easier to build upon the idea that her present experience and ideas of self could change after rehabilitation. Mental practice interventions, using both external and then internal imagery, were utilized to promote better ambulation skills when walking with her brace. This was done hierarchically, beginning with images of herself in the present, in physical therapy, and then working on images of herself ambulating with her assistive equipment easily and skillfully in a variety of future-based settings. At this point the mental rehearsal was also giving her a covert experience of being successful at mastering something that had been making her quite anxious. In order to create a way for the patient to generate her own stimulus control, the sensation of her tongue against her lower teeth was paired with the mental practice state of masterful ambulation. This conditioning was repeated several times within a session so that the sensation of her tongue pressed against her lower teeth produced the cognitive/affective feeling state associated with the mental practice, without having to engage in the mental practice itself.

When the patient had learned that she could have control over her intrusive imagery, a sense of hope, and access to an image of what she needed to master, she was taught hypnoanalgesic techniques for pain management. Follow-up several months later revealed that she was managing her physical and emotional discomfort quite well. She reported that she continued to have a positive outlook, that she had learned how to ambulate even better with her brace, and that she believed that she would be continuing to improve even more in her performance.

Case Two

A 44-year-old, married, high school–educated male was injured at work when he was hit in the head by a falling steel beam. He sustained a severe concussion, fractured cervical vertebrae that required surgical fusion, and left brachial nerve damage. He was referred to the psychologist for assistance with management of persistent shoulder and neck pain. The patient presented as extremely anxious and was easily angered. His anxiety about his condition was so intense that, although his neurologist told him that he would not die from the pain, the patient nonetheless interpreted the statement to mean that he *was* going to die from the pain and he immediately met with his primary care physician, wanting to know why he had not been informed that that he was dying. At the start of treatment his span of attention was quite limited and he was able to concentrate for only 10 to 15 minutes before his attention would wander or anxiety would intrude. The patient was taught self-hypnosis and how to use hypnosis for self-regulation of anxiety and pain. Over the course of 3 years his concentration and attention improved to such an extent

that his self-hypnotic practice could last for 2 to 3 hours at a time. The course of treatment in the beginning dealt with self-regulation strategies and education about pain as well as helping him learn how his emotional states, sleep deprivation, and brain injury would all combine to intensify his pain experience. During the middle phase, much attention was paid to quality-of-life issues and adapting to disability. In the final phase, therapeutic work was directed to refining self-regulation strategies, so that he could feel confident about his ability to respond to any pain and to experience greater quality of life.

At first the patient was taught Gunther's (1968) progressive sensory muscle relaxation exercise, combined with autogenic training and imagery of a safe place utilizing all the senses. He was then taught a variation of Oyle's (1975) technique for pain control, to which he had a good response. He reported that he was able to utilize these techniques at home to reduce his discomfort. The patient was quite kinesophobic and was unable to tolerate his disability and the changes in his body. Accordingly, there were two major target areas for intervention. The first goal consisted of lessening and reducing the anticipatory anxiety surrounding the pain. The second goal was to help him learn to accept if not tolerate his physical condition and physical appearance. (He was quite upset and anxious about an asymmetry to the appearance of his face and head following the injury.) The patient was also taught hypnotically mediated distraction and hypnoanalgesic techniques to assist with his pain. As he often had episodes of pain that were in the severe range (7 out of 10 and higher on a visual analog pain scale), he needed a strategy to respond to an intensity of pain that made it difficult to focus his attention and concentration. He therefore was taught a variant of a mindfulness strategy (Kabat-Zin, 1990) in which he was given the suggestion to observe the pain in his body as movement, to which he could respond as an observer. There was an additional purpose in teaching him this strategy. The hypothesis was that if he could observe his nociception without suffering at severe levels of pain, he could then adopt the same strategy to master his anxiety. He could begin to observe his thoughts and emotions without having to respond to them. The patient attained both goals.

Case Three

A 54-year-old woman had a dislocated clavicle and shoulder pain secondary to a failed intubation while being prepped for a hysterectomy. The patient had gone into respiratory arrest, and in the process of removing the ventilation tube the surgical team inadvertently dislocated her left clavicle from the sternum. As a result, movement of the left shoulder resulted in severe pain. At the initial visit the patient was fixated on talking about how she had "died" and then had been mistreated after being resuscitated. She spoke about the long time spent in the recovery room alone with no one checking on her. It was clear that the patient's pain management problems were being complicated by psychological factors. The attempted surgery had occurred some 12 months prior to her referral to the psychologist. The patient was very anxious and reported being afraid to go to sleep because she feared she might not wake up. She was using alcohol to medicate herself at night for her anxieties.

The first step was to determine what had actually happened. Once this was done, a psychoeducational approach was initiated to have her realize the distinction between cardiac and pulmonary arrest. She was helped to understand that she had not actually died, but that she had been in a critical life-death situation. This brought about a measure of relief. She believed that her physicians had mistreated her because they thought she was worthless: Why else did neither the surgeon nor the anesthesiologist talk with her after the failed surgery? The patient was assisted to describe the event and reprocess the experience in neutral terms. She was taught relaxation techniques for reduction of anxiety. She was helped to switch her identification from that of a helpless patient to an angry consumer. As the patient gained a better understanding of what had happened to her, she ceased making attributions about herself, and her anxiety disappeared. She also stopped abusing alcohol, her sleep improved, and she was able to write a letter to her surgeon and express her feelings appropriately. As her anxiety lessened and sleep improved, her pain became much more manageable and she reported doing much better in physical therapy.

Case Four

A 35-year-old male was the victim of an armed robbery in which he sustained a knife wound to the right axilla. Several weeks later he was a passenger in a car accident in which he sustained a crush injury to his right arm and hand. Over the next 2 years he developed a chronic pain syndrome in that hand, which was diagnosed as neuropathic pain with sympathetic features. The patient was reporting constant pain and he engaged in much bracing and guarding of his right arm and hand to avoid pain. He reported nightmares of the assault. He stated that whenever he saw the scar on his axilla, it brought back feelings of helplessness and of being a victim.

Treatment began by promoting a sense of mastery through teaching him a relaxation and imagery exercise for increasing warmth in the affected hand. He was able to do this successfully, using hand-held thermometers to provide feedback of his hand temperature. He was able to raise temperature in the affected hand by over 8 degrees. He was then taught a hypnotically mediated guided imagery exercise to reduce the intensity of the pain. He responded very well and was able to ablate his awareness of the pain. In addition, he was taught a mindfulness technique for pain reduction and how to use the technique to observe his emotional states without becoming consumed by the emotions themselves. The next task was to address his kinesophobia. This was done through providing information about the need for movement for increased circulation, muscle conditioning, and decreased pain and sensitivity. He then was encouraged to use his arm and hand and was given positive feedback for engaging in activity that required him to use his hand. In addition to acquiring these skills, he was encouraged to talk about the traumatic event. He was seen for a total of seven psychotherapy sessions over a 2-month period, during which he experienced progressive increase in function and diminution of pain, as well as cessation of the posttraumatic nightmares.

Case Five

A 26-year-old military officer had been in a motor vehicle accident. The car he was driving was struck by a drunk driver, who died in the accident. While the patient sustained only relatively mild soft tissue injuries to his shoulders and neck, 2 years later he still was having problems with pain and had been diagnosed with a myofascial pain syndrome, for which he was receiving physical therapy. He also was suffering from posttraumatic symptoms consisting of nightmares of the accident; spontaneous images of approaching headlights; recurrent rumination over what he might have done to prevent the accident; and guilt over having survived when the other person, who was a husband and parent, had not. The intrusive imagery suggested that the patient was unable to assimilate and/or accommodate the psychological material represented by those images. The issue then became one of facilitating the creation of a new cognitive scheme that could accept the information encoded in the intrusive imagery. Using Gestalt therapy principles (Polster & Polster, 1973), the intrusive image was treated as the figure of a gestalt without a ground. A hypnotically mediated guided imagery intervention was used to create a ground for the intrusive images (metaphorically, the unassimilated figure) he was experiencing that could provide meaning and context.

Treatment consisted of assisting the patient to enter a light hypnotic trance in which he was given the suggestion to see the recurring image of the approaching headlights, only this time to alter the image slightly by putting a boundary around it, a TV set. Then he was asked to imagine that the TV set he was looking at was one of hundreds in a wall of television sets, and that all of the television sets were playing images representing all the experiences of his life. He then was asked to imagine moving back from the wall of television sets, gaining perspective and seeing more and more of his life experience, not just the one moment of the accident. He was instructed to practice changing perspective on the images, looking at only one set at a time and many at a time. He then was given the suggestion that whenever he had the intrusive image of the headlights, he could place a TV set around it and see the set among the banks of TV sets that represented all his life experiences, allowing the intrusive image of the headlights to recede in importance when seen in the perspective of his ongoing life. This intervention took place within a single psychotherapy session, and the patient returned 4 weeks later and reported that he had

practiced the technique and become successful in eliminating the intrusive imagery, and his nightmares had stopped.

TREATMENT OF PREEXISTING CONDITIONS

No group of individuals is immune to disability, and individuals with a premorbid psychiatric condition or illness often struggle with an exacerbation of their psychiatric problems when they become ill or disabled. For the chronically depressed person, disability may trigger a recurrence; the paranoid individual may now feel more insecure and threatened because he or she is at the mercy of others; for an individual with schizophrenia the ability to fully process and develop adaptive skills is now additionally compromised. For the anxious person, disability often exacerbates feelings of insecurity and inability. As trauma tends to be associated with regression and the reemergence of primitive coping skills, for some patients the rehabilitation milieu can be very threatening and their responses can actually create problems for the treating team of professionals. In such cases, it is critical for the consulting mental health professional not only to lay out a plan of action for the team to follow in terms of how to behave with the patient, but also to establish a treatment plan for the psychiatric condition that takes into account the patient's medical problems and disability. In many cases, it is important to help the anxious person focus on the present real challenges and to use the injury or illness to teach coping skills that can generalize to the rest of his or her life.

The following is a case example of a premorbidly anxious woman who then developed a series of chronic illnesses. The patient was a 76-year-old woman with a history of pulmonary fibrosis, coronary artery disease, and arthritis and a life-long history of anxiety. For decades she had been a frequent visitor of various emergency rooms, where she would present with difficulty breathing and be diagnosed as having a panic attack. She was referred to the psychologist because her physician felt that the anxiety was exacerbating the pain and disability secondary to her arthritis. The patient told the psychologist that her primary problems were that she had a life-long fear of dying and had always been unable to enjoy life because of this constant worry. Treatment focused on teaching the patient self-regulation techniques so that she could experience a sense of being able to control her physical and psychological reactions. The techniques included a progressive sensory muscle relaxation exercise that incorporated autogenic training plus hypnotic imagery, mindfulness techniques, and deep breathing. Even though the patient had never been in psychotherapy previously, she responded extremely well to the training and reported that she felt less out of control and more hopeful. Over the course of the next six sessions the patient gradually began to talk about her anxieties rather than express them somatically.

SUMMARY AND CONCLUSIONS

The majority of patients presenting with anxiety in the rehabilitation setting are experiencing exogenous states of anxiety (Sheehan & Sheehan, 1982) that arise from dealing in an alternating fashion with loss, disability, and the need to perform. When anxiety impairs attention, concentration, memory, and physical performance, the patient's ability to relearn behaviors, learn compensatory skills, and achieve rehabilitation goals is significantly impacted. As patient complaints of physical problems can often slow the course of treatment, evaluating and treating the patient for anxiety is critical as those patients experiencing physiological symptoms of anxiety are most likely to complain about physical symptoms.

Psychological interventions directed at enhancing attainment of rehabilitation goals are often dealing with the effects of performance anxiety while interventions directed at facilitating adjustment and adaptation to disability are dealing with existential anxieties related to loss. Framing performance issues in rehabilitation as being akin to performance issues in athletics allows the psychologist to use a variety of interventions from the sports psychology literature to facilitate goal attainment. This is even more crucial now that hospital lengths of stays are shortened and third party payers are limiting the number of outpatient visits. Helping patients confront the fragility of existence and the illusion of indestructibility requires them to develop meaning for their situation as well as confront their belief systems. It also requires the attainment of new skills in stress management. Using

hypnosis to potentiate cognitive-behavioral psychotherapy interventions (Holyroyd, 1987) has been shown to facilitate rapid attainment of desired outcomes, and its use should be considered in treatment planning. This is particularly important because of the current zeitgeist in which limited treatment opportunities require that the psychologist accomplish the same treatment goals in a shorter amount of time.

In the end, the goal is to help the patient acquire new coping skills to function successfully as someone with a disability. Providing patients with ways of understanding their condition, prognosis as it were, and the functional implications of their condition will do much to help initiate and promote a sense of mastery.

REFERENCES

Aoki, T., Hosaka, T., and Ishida, A. (1995). Psychiatric evaluation of physical rehabilitation patients. *General Hospital Psychiatry. 17*(6), 440–443.

Appel, P. R. (in press). Hypnosis and suggestion in physical medicine and rehabilitation. In W. Matthews & J. Edgette (Eds.), *Current thinking and research in brief therapy: Solutions, strategies, narratives* (vol. 3). Philadelphia: Taylor & Francis.

Appel, P. R. (1992a). Performance enhancement in physical medicine and rehabilitation. *American Journal of Clinical Hypnosis, 35*(1), 11–19.

Appel, P. R. (1992b). The use of clinical hypnosis in physical medicine and rehabilitation. *Psychiatric Medicine, 10*(1), 133–148.

Asken, M., & Goodling, M. (1986). The use of sports psychology techniques in rehabilitation medicine: A pilot study. *International Journal of Sport Psychology, 17*(2), 156–161.

Asmundson, G. J. G., & Taylor, S. (1996). Role of anxiety sensitivity in pain related fear and avoidance. *Journal of Behavioral Medicine, 19*(6), 577–586.

Becker, F. (1963). Modification of anxiety through the use of hypnosis in physical medicine. *Journal of the American Geriatric Society, 11*, 235–237.

Bleiberg, J., & Merbitz, C. (1982). Learning goals during initial rehabilitation hospitalization. *Archives of Physical Medicine and Rehabilitation, 64*, 448–450.

Castelnuovo-Tedesco, P. (1981). The psychological consequences of physical trauma and defects. *International Review of Psychoanalysis, 8*, 145–154.

Cook, D. W. (1979). Psychological adjustment to spinal cord injury: Incidence of denial, depression and anxiety. *Rehabilitation Psychology, 26*(3), 97–104.

Crasilneck, H. B., & Hall, J. A. (1985). *Clinical hypnosis: Principles and applications* (2d ed.). Orlando, FL: Grune & Stratton.

Dennis, M. (1985). Visual imagery and the use of mental practice in the development of motor skills. *Canadian Journal of Applied Sport Sciences*, 10(4), 4S–16S.

Diller, L., & Ben Yishay, Y. (1987). Outcomes and evidence in neurological rehabilitation in closed head injury. In H. S. Levin, J. Grafman, & H. M. Eisenberg (Eds.), *Neurobehavioral recovery from head injury.* New York: Oxford University Press.

Emery, G., & Tracy N. L. (1987). Theoretical issues in the cognitive-behavioral treatment of anxiety disorders. In L. Michelson & L. M. Ascher (Eds.), *Anxiety and stress disorders.* New York: Guilford.

Epstein, M. L. (1980). The relationship of mental imagery and mental rehearsal to performance of a motor task. *Journal of Sport Psychology*, 2, 211–220.

Falvo, D. R. (1991). *Medical and psychosocial aspects of chronic illness and disability*. Rockville, MD: Aspen.

Fann, J. R., Katon, W. J., Vamoto, J. M., & Esselman, P. C. (1995). Psychiatric disorders and functional disability in outpatients with traumatic brain injuries. *American Journal of Psychiatry*, 152(10), 1493–1499.

Feltz, D. L., & Landers, D. M. (1983). The effects of mental practice on motor skills learning and performance: A meta analysis. *Journal of Sport Psychology*, 5, 25–57.

Gans, J. (1987). Facilitating staff/patient interaction in rehabilitation. In B. Caplan (Ed.), *Rehabilitation psychology desk reference*. Rockville, MD: Aspen.

Gould, D., & Damarjian, N. (1996). Imagery training for peak performance. In J. L. Van Raalte & B. W. Brewer (Eds.), *Exploring sport and exercise psychology*. Washington, DC: American Psychological Association.

Gunther, B. (1968). *Sense relaxation: Below your mind*. New York: Collier.

Haley, J. (1976). *Problem solving therapy.* San Francisco: Jossey-Bass.

Hohman, G. W. (1975). Psychological aspects of treatment and rehabilitation of the spinal cord injured person. *Clinical Orthopaedics and Related Research*, 112, 81–88.

Holroyd, J. (1987). How hypnosis may potentiate psychotherapy. *American Journal of Clinical Hypnosis*, 29, 194–200.

Holroyd, J. (1989). Hypnotherapy with a stroke patient. *International Journal of Clinical and Experimental Hypnosis*, 37, 120–127.

Jannoff-Bulman, R. (1992). *Shattered assumptions: Towards a new psychology of trauma*. New York: Free Press.

Jacobsen, E. (1938). *Progressive relaxation* (2d ed.). Chicago: University of Chicago Press.

Kabat-Zinn, J. (1990). *Full catastrophe living: Using the wisdom of your body and mind to face stress, pain and illness.* New York: Delta.

Kaye, J. M., & Schindler, B. A. (1990). Hypnosis on a consultation-liaison service. *General Hospital Psychiatry*, 12(6), 379–383.

King, D. L. (1983). Image theory of conditioning. In A. S. Sheikh (Ed.), *Imagery: Current theory research, and application*. New York: Wiley.

Kreuger, D. W. (1984). Psychological rehabilitation of physical trauma and disability. In D. W. Kreuger (Ed.), *Rehabilitation psychology*. Rockville, MD: Aspen.

Livneh, H., & Antonak, R. F. (1994). Psychosocial reactions to disability: A review and critique of the literature. *Critical Reviews in Physical and Rehabilitation Medicine*, 6(1), 1–100.

McCracken, L. M., Faber, S. D., & Janek, A. S. (1998). Pain-related anxiety predicts non-specific physical complaints in persons with chronic pain. *Behavior Research and Therapy*, 36(6), 621–630.

Morton, M. V., & Wehman, P. (1995). Psychosocial and emotional sequelae of individuals with traumatic brain injury: A literature review and recommendations. *Brain Injury*, 9(1), 81–92.

Oyle, I. (1975). *The healing mind*. Millbrae, CA: Celestial Arts.

Polster, E., & Polster, M. (1973). *Gestalt therapy integrated*. New York: Vintage.

Richardson, A. (1967a). Mental practice: A review and discussion (part I). *The Research Quarterly*, 38, 95–107.

Richardson, A. (1967b). Mental practice: A review and discussion (part II). *The Research Quarterly*, 38, 263–273.

Ryan, E. D., & Simons, J. (1982). Efficacy of mental imagery in enhancing mental rehearsal of motor skills. *Journal of Sport Psychology*, 4, 41–51.

Schultz, J. H., & Luthe, W. (1969). *Autogenic therapy* (vol. I). New York: Grune & Stratton.

Schultz, S. K., Castillo, C. S., Kosier, J. T., & Robinson, R. G. (1997). Generalized anxiety and depression: Assessment over 2 years after stroke. *American Journal of Geriatric Psychiatry*, 5(3), 229–237.

Sheehan D. V., & Sheehan, K. H. (1982). The classification of anxiety and hysterical states (part 2): Toward a more heuristic classification. *Journal of Clinical Psychopharmacology*, 2, 386–393.

Shimoda, K., & Robinson, R. G. (1998). Effect of anxiety disorder on impairment and recovery from stroke. *Journal of Neuropsychiatry and Clinical Neurosciences*, 10(1), 34–40.

Smith, W. H. (1990). Hypnosis in the treatment of anxiety. *Bulletin of the Menninger Clinic*, 54(2), 209–216.

Spiegel, D., & Spiegel, H. (1988). Assessment and treatment using hypnosis. In C. G. Last & M. Hersen (Eds.), *Handbook of anxiety disorders*. New York: Pergamon.

Starkstein, S. E., Cohen, B. S., Federoff, P., Parikh, R. M., et al. (1990). Relationship between anxiety disorders and depressive disorders in patients with cerebrovascular injury. *Archives of General Psychiatry, 47*(3), 246–251.

Suinn, R. M. (1983). Imagery and sports. In A. A. Sheikh (Ed.), *Imagery: Current theory, research and application*. New York: Wiley.

Trieschmann, R. B. (1980). *Spinal cord injuries: Psychological, social and vocational adjustment*. New York: Pergamon.

Trieschmann, R. B. (1981). Psychosocial issues for persons with spinal cord injuries. *Paraplegia News, 35*(8), 26–31.

Turner, R. J., & McLean, P. D. (1989). Physical disability and psychological distress. *Rehabilitation Psychology, 34*(4), 225–242.

van der Kolk, B. A., & McFarlane, A. C. (1996). The black hole of trauma. In B A. van der Kolk, A. C. McFarlane, & L. Weisaeth (Eds.), *Traumatic stress*. New York: Guilford.

Williams, J. M., & Leffingwell, T. R. (1996). Cognitive strategies in sport and exercise psychology. In J. L. Van Raalte & B. W. Brewer (Eds.), *Exploring sport and exercise psychology*. Washington, DC: American Psychological Association.

Woolfolk, R. L., Murphy, S. M., Gottesfeld, D., & Aitken, D. (1985). Effects of mental rehearsal of task motor activity and mental depiction of task outcome on motor skill performance. *Journal of Sport Psychology, 7*, 191–197.

Zeig, J. (1982). *Ericksonian approaches to hypnosis and psychotherapy*. New York: Brunner Mazel.

CHAPTER 19

STRESS AND ANXIETY IN DERMATOLOGICAL DISORDERS

Ulrich Stangier

Anke Ehlers

The skin is a highly complex structure that fulfills important biological functions as a sense organ and as an immunological barrier. It is common knowledge that the skin has close and manifold relationships with psychological functions. This is reflected in expressions such as "to jump out of one's skin," "to get under one's skin," "it makes my skin crawl," "to be thick (or thin) skinned," and "to be red with rage." Blood vessels and sweat glands react in a highly sensitive manner to changes in the emotional state and the corresponding activation of the autonomic nervous system. The skin is therefore frequently referred to as "the organ of expression" (Koblenzer, 1987). As the most visible organ of the human body the skin also defines the outward appearance and is closely related to the subjective representation of the body, the body image. An abnormal appearance of the skin subtly influences social perceptions and interactions. Finally, the skin is directly accessible and therefore, through scratching or through the application of chemical substances, subject to possible manipulations.

These interactions between the skin and psychological functions are of great importance in dermatological disorders. For instance, negative affect such as anxiety may be a cause and a result of different dermatological problems (Medansky, Handler, & Medansky, 1981):

1. Anxiety may represent a triggering factor for dermatological symptoms or disorders.
2. Anxiety may be a consequence of dermatological disorders because these can be perceived as stigmata that induce social anxiety and cause a negative body image.

3. Anxiety may be caused by irrational beliefs concerning the appearance or health of the skin.
4. Anxiety may be the primary cause of cutaneous symptoms that are presented as a dermatological disease.
5. Anxiety may be relieved by manipulations of the skin.

A large number of dermatological disorders exist in which psychological factors play a major role. Table 19.1 presents a classification of psychological disorders that are related to skin conditions. The present paper will review these disorders, with the exception of psychotic disorders related to dermatological complaints. The latter are reviewed by Koblenzer (1987), to which the interested reader is referred.

PSYCHOLOGICAL FACTORS AFFECTING DERMATOLOGICAL DISORDERS

The Role of Personality in Dermatological Disorders

In his classic psychodynamic account of somatic problems caused by psychological factors, Alexander (1950) included atopic dermatitis among seven prototypical "psychosomatic" disorders. These were each thought to be caused by a specific psychodynamic conflict. The idea that a specific personality structure could explain the exacerbation of dermatological conditions led to numerous studies that aimed to establish specific

TABLE 19.1. Classification of Psychological Problems in Dermatology

PRESENTED PROBLEMS	PSYCHIATRIC DIAGNOSIS ACCORDING TO *DSM-IV*	*DSM-IV* *ICD-10*	OTHER TERMS RELATED TO THE DISORDER
Dermatoses	Psychological factors affecting medical condition	316.00 *F54*	Psychosomatic skin disorders
	Adjustment disorder	309.00/.24 *F43/2*	Emotional reactions to disfiguring diseases
Self-inflicted lesions	Impulse-control disorder	312.30/.39 *F63.3/.8*	Parafactitious disorders; trichotillomania, neurotic excoriations, acne excoriée
	Factitious disease	300.19 *F68.1*	Dermatitis artefacta
Somatoform disorders	Hypochondriasis	300.70	AIDS-phobia, parasitophobia, melanophobia
	Body dysmorphic disorder	*F45.2*	Dysmorphophobia
	Undifferentiated somatoform disorders Conversion disorder	300.81 *F45.1* 300.11 *F45.3*	Pruritus sine materia, cutaneous dysesthesia, cutaneous pain
Psychoses	Delusional disorder, somatic type	297.10 *F22.0*	Delusions of parasitosis Tactile hallucinations

personality factors related to atopic dermatitis and to other dermatological conditions of suspected psychogenic origin, for example, urticaria, psoriasis, or alopecia areata. As first pointed out by Whitlock (1976), the results were largely negative and no specific patterns emerged.

However, there is evidence that patients with dermatological disorders score higher on scales measuring anxiety and depression than the general population. A series of studies found high trait anxiety levels in atopic dermatitis patients (Faulstich Williamson, Duchman, Conerly, & Brantley, 1985; Garrie, Garrie, & Mote, 1974; Ginsburg, Prystowsky, Kornfeld, & Wolland, 1993; Jordan & Whitlock, 1974; White, Horne, & Varigos, 1990; but see Hashiro & Okumura, 1997, for negative findings). High anxiety and depression were also reported for patients with psoriasis (Ginsburg, 1995), urticaria (Hashiro & Okumura, 1994), alopecia areata (Koo, Shellow, Hallman, & Edwards, 1994), vitiligo (Porter, Hill-Beuf, Lerner, & Nordlund, 1987), and scleroderma (Roca, Wigley, & White, 1996) and in severe cases of acne (Wu, Kinder, Trunnell, & Nordlund, 1981) and herpes (Carney, Ross, Ikkos, & Mindel, 1993).

Most of the studies did not examine whether the emotional symptoms occurred before or after the onset of the skin disease. Therefore, the findings cannot be directly interpreted as evidence for the role of anxiety or depression in the etiology of these disorders. It is also plausible to assume that anxiety and depression are a psychological consequence of having a chronic dermatological disorder that may involve disfiguring symptoms (psoriasis, alopecia, vitiligo, or acne), aversive and uncontrollable itching (atopic dermatitis or chronic urticaria), or a progressive and life-threatening course (malignant melanoma, scleroderma, or epidermolysis) (see section on adjustment disorders).

Several findings support this latter interpretation. Rechhardt (1970) examined patients with atopic dermatitis in the acute stage and found abnormal personality traits such as heightened anxiety. In a follow-up study 10 years later, after remission of the skin condition, these characteristics could no longer be observed. Similarly, Rubinow, Peck, Squillace, & Gantt, (1987) found that heightened levels of anxiety and depression in patients with cystic acne were significantly reduced after successful medical treatment with isotretinoin.

Psychological Distress as a Trigger of Dermatological Symptoms

Relationship of Skin Symptoms with the Presence of Stressors

Current research on psychological factors in skin disorders generally uses the diathesis-stress model (Sternbach, 1966) and aims to establish that unspecific psychological factors such as emotional distress exert an influence on the onset or exacerbation of dermatological conditions. In support of this view, many studies found that dermatological patients reported a high number of stressful life events before the onset of illness, compared to control subjects. The studies included patients with atopic dermatitis (Brown, 1972), psoriasis (Al'Abadie, Kent, & Gawkrodger, 1994; Fava, Perini, Santonastaso, & Fornasa, 1980; Lyketsos, Stratigos, Tawil, Psaras, & Lyketsos, 1985), urticaria (Fava et al., 1980; Lyketsos et al., 1985), alopecia areata (Fava et al., 1980; Lyketsos et al., 1985; Perini et al., 1984), and herpes genitalis (Levenson, Hamer, Meyers, Hart, & Kaplowitz, 1987; Silver, Auerbach, Vishniavsky, & Kaplowitz, 1986).

However, the assessment of stressful life events was retrospective in these studies, so the results may be partly due to a bias in reporting a coincidence of psychological factors and illness episodes (Cohen & Lazarus, 1979). To circumvent this bias, researchers have more recently used prospective self-observation of stress and symptoms in standardized diaries. These prospective studies have confirmed the relationship between stressful events and skin symptoms. Moderate correlations were reported for patients with atopic dermatitis (King & Wilson, 1991), psoriasis (Gaston, Lassonde, Bernier-Buzzanga, Hodgins, & Crombez, 1987), acne (Kraus, 1974), and herpes genitalis (Dalkvist, Wahlin, Bartsch, & Forsbeck, 1995). Interestingly, it has been suggested that even the progressive course of severe disorders such as lupus erythemathodes (Wekking, Vingerhoeb, vanDam, Nossent, & Swaak, 1991) and epidermolysis bullosa (Schomer & Vergunst, 1992), a genetic disorder, can be influenced by emotional stressors.

These studies also demonstrated large interindividual differences in the reactivity to stressors, particularly in atopic dermatitis and psoriasis. This indicates that emotional distress is only one of the many factors influencing skin condition in these patient groups. In children, mediating factors such as the family environment and parental behaviors may play a greater role than the stressor itself (Gil et al., 1987). As yet, little is known about factors that predict which patients are responsive to stressors. Gupta, Gupta, and Watteel (1997) found evidence that stress reactivity in atopic dermatitis was associated with intensive itching and increased scratching. A possible biological indicator for stress reactivity in this patient group may be the level of serum IgE, which is correlated with a disposition to exaggerated allergic responses. Scheich, Florin, Rudolph, & Wilhelm (1993) found that an elevated level of serum IgE was associated with increased emotional irritability in atopic dermatitis patients. In psoriasis the results remain inconsistent (Al'Abadie et al., 1994; Baugham & Sobel, 1971; Gupta et al., 1989).

Sources of Stress in Dermatological Patients

When looking at the effects of stressors on dermatological disorders, one has to bear in mind that, as in other chronic disorders, the symptoms and treatment of skin disorders can cause considerable distress (see also section on adjustment disorders). For example, itching can result in tension, lack of concentration, sleeplessness, heightened level of irritation, or limited physical vigor (Marshall, 1993). Fearing scrutiny of others because of visible skin lesions or facing the prospect of never fully recovering from the skin disorder can be very distressing for the patient. Furthermore, treatment of the skin problems is often time-consuming, and anxiety is one of the possible side effects of anti-allergic medications (Pearson, 1988). If the distress caused by the symptoms and the side effects of treatment exceed the patient's coping resources, a vicious cycle may trigger further stress-induced flare-ups.

Another source of stress lies in the potentially negative effects of the disorder on relationships with significant others, including parents or partner. Empirical evidence for negative communication patterns in atopic dermatitis comes from a study by Ehlers, Osen, Wenninger, & Gieler (1994). Patients and their significant others as well as control couples discussed a mutual problem in their relationship. Their verbal and nonverbal behavior was coded with a standardized rating system. The atopic dermatitis couples showed more frequent negative verbal and nonverbal behavior and longer patterns of negative escalation than controls.

Finally, maladaptive coping styles may adversely affect the course of chronic or progressive dermatological disorders. For instance, Temoshok et al., (1984) identified a subgroup of melanoma patients characterized by a "repressive coping style" who had a significantly worse prognosis. In general, however, studies relating coping styles to adaptational outcomes have produced inconsistent results, and the classification of coping styles according to adaptational outcome has been questioned (Zeidner & Saklofske, 1996).

Possible Pathways of Stressor Effects on the Skin

There are several possible pathways that may mediate the effect of emotional distress on the skin. The first hypothesis is that patients with skin disorders show stronger physiological reactions under stressful conditions than controls.

Laboratory studies that induced stress experimentally in dermatologically healthy people found that the duration of itching after histamine provocation (Fjellner, Arnetz, Eneroth, & Kallner, 1985), the intensity of the immediate-type allergic skin reaction (Laidlaw, Booth, & Large, 1994), and the intensity of the delayed-type hypersensitivity skin test (Pariante, Carpiniello, Rudas, Piludu, & Del Giacco, 1994) were positively correlated with negative mood. There was no evidence of increased stress reactivity of electrodermal activity or cutaneous blood flow in patients with atopic dermatitis (Faulstich et al., 1985; Köhler & Weber, 1992), but patients with atopic dermatitis (Buske-Kirschbaum et al., 1997) as well as patients with psoriasis (Arnetz, Fjellner, Eneroth, & Kallner, 1985; Schmid-Ott et al., 1998) were found to be hyporesponsive in their hypothalamus-pituitary-adrenal axis as measured by salivary or plasma cortisol. It is possible that the regulation of the cutaneous immune system (especially of the mast cells) is impaired through interacting T cell subsets (suppressor and helper lymphocytes) (Ring, 1993). Another pathway that might explain the influence of the central nervous system on cutaneous inflammation is the release of neuropeptides from nerve endings in the skin under stress. For example, it has been discussed whether the secretion of neuropeptide substance P is increased under stress, stimulating mast cells and increasing inflammation and itching in psoriasis and atopic dermatitis (Farber & Nall, 1993; Foreman, 1987).

Besides these physiological mechanisms, psychological mechanisms may be involved. Psychological distress may lead to increases in attention to the self and the skin. Itching, a key symptom of many dermatological disorders, is easily influenced by mental and emotional stimuli. For example, mere imagination of itching or similar feelings can act as a trigger (so-called ideosensory itching; Bethune & Kidd, 1961). Thus, increased attention to the skin can serve as a trigger for itching. Furthermore, the general level of tension and negative emotions, particularly depression, seems to lower the itch threshold (Gupta et al., 1989, 1994). (See also the section on adjustment disorders.)

The Effects of Behaviors on the Skin

Scratching

Scratching is one of the major behavioral factors involved in the maintenance of atopic dermatitis. Figure 19.1 illustrates this relationship. Scratching is triggered by itching and reduces the itch sensation. The exact mechanism is not fully understood: Scratching may block a neural circuit in the spinal cord caused by an itch stimulus or it may work by producing pain that substitutes the itch sensation as a counterstimulation (Bernhard, 1994). However, scratching also causes cutaneous injuries that, in turn, through the activation of inflammatory mediators, lead to further itching. Thus, itching and scratching may aggravate each other in a vicious cycle that runs out of control. The patient may persist scratching until the skin bleeds. After the patient has stopped scratching, the perceived loss of control leads to emotional distress and feelings of guilt. These may be increased further by negative reactions of others who are often unable to understand this self-destructive behavior and may assume it shows a lack of self-control or hidden aggression (Bosse & Hünecke, 1981). As a result, excessive scratching may result in resignation, depressive states, and anxiety (Cunliffe & Savin, 1984) and may become the principal problem in atopic dermatitis.

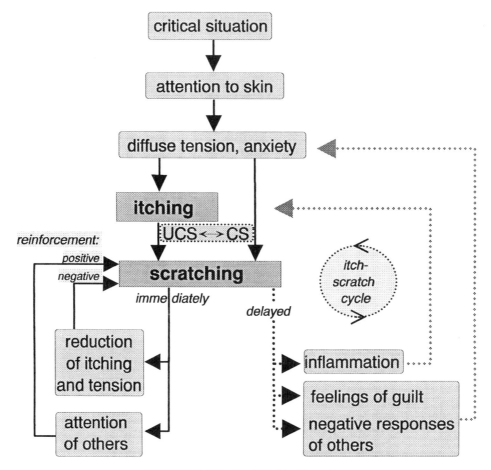

FIGURE 19.1. Behavioral Model of Scratching

From the viewpoint of self-control theory, the loss of control over scratching may be viewed as a problematic habit with conflicting short- and long-term consequences, comparable to addictive behavior (Kanfer & Karoly, 1972). Indeed, patients frequently describe the uncontrollable scratching as an "addiction" or as "compulsion." In the short term the reduction of itching negatively reinforces the scratching behavior. In contrast, the delayed negative consequences on the skin condition do not affect the "compulsive" scratching behavior. In addition, especially in children, attention of significant others may act as positive reinforcement (Allen & Harris, 1966; Gil & Keefe, 1988).

Both classical and operant conditioning mechanisms may contribute to the expansion of scratching behavior beyond that triggered by itch sensations. Jordan and Whitlock (1972) showed that eczema patients, compared to dermatologically healthy controls, more quickly acquired conditioned scratch responses to neutral stimuli that were paired with itching. This explains why atopic dermatitis patients frequently scratch themselves in the absence of itching. Conditioned stimuli include diffuse tension and anger, uncertainty, conflicts in decision making, mental stress, time pressure, boredom, but also available access to the skin (e.g., undressing), the sight of skin changes (e.g., scabs), the awareness of skin sensations (e.g., crawling or tickling sensations), or punishing or limiting measures intended to stop the scratching that produce emotional tension (Ratliff & Stein, 1968). This kind of scratching may be categorized as "habitual" or "automatic" scratching (Azrin, Nunn, & Frantz, 1980). In the short term such habitual scratching remains negatively reinforced by the reduction of tension and possibly positively reinforced by attention of others. In the long term, however, it actually induces itch sensations through irritation of the skin and induces feelings of guilt that increase the patient's level of tension and may thus trigger further itching or scratching.

Other Behaviors

The effects of maladaptive health behaviors on the skin condition are often underestimated. These maladaptive behaviors include poor nutrition, smoking, and the consumption of alcohol. For instance, some investigations found increased alcohol consumption and also a high rate of alcoholism in psoriasis patients (Ginsburg, 1995). A further factor in the course of chronic dermatological disorders is poor skin care and the lack of compliance with the prescriptions for the affected skin. This lack of compliance may increase when stressful life conditions interfere with daily habits, including the regular use of creams and ointments. Insufficient or completely lacking skin care, however, might have detrimental effects on skin disposed to dysregulation.

Clinical Management

Diagnosis and Prevalence

The diagnosis of "Psychological Factors Affecting Medical Condition" (*DSM-IV*, American Psychiatric Association, 1994) is given if psychological factors significantly affect the course of a medical condition. From the results of retrospective studies, one can estimate that this applies to 20–70% of patients with chronic dermatoses, and from prospective studies, 15–30%. It should be noted, however, that the validity of prospective studies is as yet limited because sample sizes have usually been small and observation intervals were often not appropriate.

Clinical Assessment

In dermatological patients the following factors may contribute to the development, exacerbation, or maintenance of the disorder:

1. Psychological symptoms including anxiety and depression
2. Maladaptive styles of coping with stressors
3. Stress-related physiological responses, which may influence the dermatological condition through psychoimmunological mechanisms
4. Scratching and manipulations of the skin
5. Maladaptive health behaviors, such as nutrition, that directly affect the dermatological condition

Standardized diary forms provide useful information for the assessment of these factors in the individual patient. Records of the frequency of skin symptoms (e.g., itching, infections, or hives) and of possible triggering situations (e.g., food intake or stress situations) help in detecting important factors in the exacerbation or maintenance of the skin condition. In addition, the type and intensity of behavioral reactions (e.g., scratching) and emotional reactions should be recorded. Other factors influencing skin condition such as skin care and medication use should be recorded in order to prevent interpretation bias. Stress-inducing beliefs and maladaptive coping behaviors can best be determined in interviews. In addition, a screening for psychological symptoms, for example, with the SCL-90R (Derogatis, 1977), is useful.

A useful basis for further interventions is to develop a multicausal model of the disease with the patient. Frequently information deficits regarding the cause and inadequate attributions (e.g., allergies, danger of contagion) have to be modified before the patient is motivated to engage in psychological interventions.

Treatment

In general, the psychological treatment focuses on the modification of dysfunctional physiological, cognitive, and behavioral reactions to stress situations. Most of the principal intervention methods are not specific to skin disorders, such as relaxation training, cognitive restructuring, problem solving training, and behavioral modification including social skills and communication training aimed at reducing interpersonal distress (Blanchard, 1994). In addition, specific interventions for dermatological conditions include modifications of relaxation, biofeedback training, and self-control techniques to reduce scratching. Treatment studies have often combined several of the treatment components that will be reviewed here, so dismantling studies are needed to establish what the effective and necessary ingredients of the treatment protocols are.

Relaxation Training and Guided Imagery. Several relaxation techniques have proven successful in the behavioral treatment of skin disorders. Progressive muscle relaxation (PMR) is especially useful in pruritic skin diseases. This method has been shown to provide a competing response for scratching as part of the habit-reversal technique (see below). In Öst's (1987) "applied relaxation technique" a complete version of PMR is progressively shortened (from about 20 to 4 min.). When the relaxation response has become automatic, it can be bound to specific cues such as a count-down or certain images (cue-controlled relaxation). The final stage of application is to practice the relaxation response under critical conditions in daily life, for example, in response to the impulse to scratch. Several authors regard guided imagery as a particularly valuable addition to relaxation in the treatment of skin disorders (e.g., Stangier, Ehlers, & Gieler, 1996). Patients are generally guided through imagining or visualizing the healing process. For instance, Gray and Lawlis (1982) used the image of the skin cells as "little, round persons basking on a beautiful warm, peaceful beach . . . totally serene and completely relaxed in a state of utter contentment" (p. 630) for atopic dermatitis patients. Zacchariae, Oster, Bjerring, & Kragballe (1996) instructed patients with psoriasis to imagine bathing in salt water and sun bathing, and Bernard, Kristeller, and Kabat-Zinn (1988) included information about the treatments in the visualization. Autogenic training is a form of relaxation training involving self-suggestions. Luthe and Schultz (1969) suggest extending the standard training with skin-specific formulas for the imagery of coolness, for example, "The skin is quiet and pleasantly cool."

In atopic dermatitis, relaxation techniques have repeatedly been shown to be effective in reducing tension, sympathetic arousal, itching, and scratching. Evidence comes from several case reports (e.g., McMenamy, Katz, & Gipson, 1988), and studies of larger patient groups. In an uncontrolled study, Cole, Roth, and Sachs (1988) evaluated the effectiveness of autogenic training, combined with self-control techniques, in 10 patients. Treatment included 12 weekly group sessions. Compared to baseline, significant reductions in dermatological symptoms and use of topical steroids were observed after treatment as well as at 1-month follow-up. In a randomized controlled trial with 126 patients, Ehlers, Stangier, and Gieler (1995) compared the effectiveness of four group treatments for atopic dermatitis with standard medical care: (1) a cognitive-behavioral treatment including PMR/imagery, self-control techniques to reduce scratching, and stress management; (2) dermatological education to provide information on factors affecting the skin condition and treatment approaches; (3) a combined cognitive-behavioral treatment and dermatological education; and (4) autogenic training including skin-specific formulas. Treatment conditions included 12 weekly group sessions within 3 months. At 1-year follow-up the cognitive-behavioral treatment combined with dermatological education and autogenic training led to larger improvements in skin condition than dermatological education or standard medical care. In addition, the combination of cognitive-behavioral and dermatological treatment was associated with the largest reductions in topical steroids used. These results suggest that relaxation training that is adapted specifically for skin disorders is an effective treatment for atopic dermatitis on its own and in combination with other psychological interventions. A controlled study by Niebel (1995) with 55 patients supported this conclusion using a dismantling design.

Other studies have supported the effectiveness of relaxation training in other dermatological disorders. A multiple baseline study with 4 herpes genitalis patients found PMR to be effective on its own (Koehn, Burnette, & Stark, 1993). Furthermore, PMR was a major component of a group treatment package for herpes genitalis that also included imagery, stress management, social support, and patient education. A controlled trial with 31 patients showed the treatment package to be more effective at 6-month follow-up in reducing frequency, intensity, and duration of herpes genitalis recurrence than social support alone and waiting list control condition (Longo, Clum, & Yaeger, 1988). In a study of 51 *psoriasis* patients, PMR combined with imagery and stress management was more effective than no treatment (the control group condition) (Zacchariae et al., 1996). Unfortunately no follow-up was reported, so it is not clear whether these effects were maintained after treatment.

Biofeedback Training. During the 1980s a series of controlled case studies investigated the use of biofeedback training in the treatment of skin disorders. The physiological target variables were selected depending on the presumed underlying psychophysiological mechanisms; four will be discussed here.

1. *Reduction of skin temperature*: This method was used in case studies with psoriasis patients (Benoit & Harrell, 1981) with the goal of reducing the increased blood flow resulting from inflammation. The results only partially supported the effectiveness of this method. The actual control over the skin temperature did not correlate with the desired change of symptoms. A controlled trial with 26 psoriasis patients compared biofeedback training with relaxation and imagery and waiting list control (Stangier et al., 1988). No group differences were observed in skin condition immediately after treatment, but at 7-month follow-up the group receiving biofeedback training was significantly superior to the control group.

2. *Reduction in skin conductance* (psychogalvanic response, PGR): Biofeedback for skin conductance was based on the hypothesis that a reduction in electrodermal activity would also affect the activity of the sweat glands. In uncontrolled case studies this method significantly reduced the symptoms of dyshidrotic hand eczema (Miller, Conger, & Dymond, 1974; Harris & Sieveking, 1979). However, it is unclear if the results were achieved through a general relaxation effect or through the actual control of the sweat glands. In one chronic case of urticaria, biofeedback training to reduce PGR, combined with autogenic training, also led to a significant remission of symptoms, which was maintained at 8-month follow-up (Moan, 1979).

The following biofeedback methods are explicitly used to achieve a generalized relaxation effect:

3. *Raising skin temperature*: Good results were reported in the treatment of Raynaud´s disease (Freedman, 1987), which is caused by constriction of the blood vessels.

4. *Reducing EMG levels*: Combined with imagery, this method was successfully used in treating atopic dermatitis (Gray & Lawlis, 1982; Haynes, Wilson, Jaffe, & Britton, 1979) and acne (Hughes, Brown, Lawlis, & Fulton, 1983). Significant factors in treatment success included regular practice and the combination with relaxation and imagery techniques.

Despite the positive results obtained with biofeedback training, the mechanisms for its effects remain unexplained (Haynes et al., 1979). It may be that patients learn to reduce their general sympathetic arousal rather than to influence a specific physiological function. A generalized relaxation effect, may be achieved with less effort through relaxation techniques. A specific advantage of biofeedback training might be, however, that the patients improve their perception of specific cutaneous physiological processes. In addition, patients expecting traditional medical treatment may accept this technical treatment better than pure relaxation training.

Interventions to Increase Self-Control of Scratching. In addition to numerous older case studies in this area, more recent and better controlled research on individual (Melin et al., 1986) and group treatment of atopic dermatitis (Cole et al., 1988; Ehlers et al., 1995) has shown that habit-reversal training reduced scratching behavior and led to long-term improvements in the symptoms of atopic dermatitis. In most of these studies the habit-reversal training was given in combination with relaxation methods (Cole et al., 1988; Ehlers et al., 1995), but Melin et al. (1986) demonstrated that habit reversal is effective on its own. In her dismantling study, Niebel (1995) did not find the combination of habit reversal and relaxation to be more effective than relaxation alone, but greater baseline severity of the combined group makes this finding somewhat difficult to interpret.

The habit-reversal technique was first applied by Rosenbaum and Ayllon (1981) in the reduction of habitual scratching. This method includes the following components:

TABLE 19.2. Cognitive-Behavioral Group Program for Atopic Dermatitis Patients
Focusing on Scratching, Interpersonal Behavior, and Relaxation

SESSION	SCRATCHING	INTERPERSONAL BEHAVIOR	RELAXATION
1	Introduction to diary	Role play: assertive behavior	Progressive muscle relaxation: long version
2	Discussion of frequent triggers of scratching	Rehearsal	Rehearsal
3	Triggers and consequences of itch-scratch cycle	Role play: assertive coping with negative reactions to skin lesions	Progressive muscle relaxation: shortened version
4	Simple techniques to control scratching	Rehearsal	Cue-controlled relaxation
5	Introduction to habit-reversal technique	Problem solving training	Rehearsal
6	Identification of negative automatic thoughts	Rehearsal	Differential relaxation
7	Modification of negative automatic thoughts	Direct expression of positive feelings	Exercise: perception of pleasant feelings on skin
8	Triggers of automatic scratching	Direct expression of wishes	Rehearsal
9	Awareness of tension triggering scratching	Rehearsal	Sensory imagery ("cool skin")
10	Self-reinforcement of nonscratching	Direct expression of negative feelings	Rehearsal
11	Factors improving skin condition	Rehearsal	Rehearsal
12	Relapse prevention	Maintenance of training effects	Stabilization of continuing relaxation practice

Source: Stangier, Ehlers, and Gieler (1996). *Neurodermitis bewältigen: Verhaltenstherapie, dermatologische Schulung, autogenes Training (Coping with atopic dermatitis: Behavior therapy, dermatological education, autogenic training).* Berlin, Germany: Springer.

1. *Situation awareness training:* Patients are instructed to describe in detail the situation that triggered the scratching, the act of scratching, and its consequences. They then learn to become aware of their scratching motions toward the skin and to react to this as a signal to break the automatic progression of the scratching action (early warning). Particularly useful in this process are standardized self-observation records that separately record levels of the intensity and frequency of scratching (Ehlers et al., 1995).

2. A *competing response procedure* is subsequently practiced, which can include isometric exercise, tensing of muscles, or other methods (e.g., putting the hand firmly on the itching skin areas) to block the itching sensation.

3. *Symbolic rehearsal:* Finally, a critical situation in which scratching commonly occurs is consciously simulated and all elements of the procedure are performed. Patients are then instructed to use this procedure whenever the urge to scratch occurs in daily life.

The classic habit-reversal techniques are particularly useful in controlling the habitual scratching that occurs in the absence of itching. In more recent studies, several additional methods to increase self-control have been suggested that are designed to influence the itch sensation and the urge to scratch and thus to break the vicious cycle of itching and scratching (Stangier et al., 1996). These methods include imagination techniques to induce sensations of coolness or sensations associated with healing influences on the affected skin, such as bathing in the ocean (e.g., Twerski & Narr, 1974); direct suggestions to achieve a change in the awareness of itching; positive self-instruction (e.g., "I will resist the urge and won't scratch") to replace catastrophic cognitions about itching (e.g., "The itching will never stop"); and distraction techniques to focus concentration on manual or mental activities, pleasant sensations, or other more intensive stimuli. Other strategies for self-control are self-reinforcement for not scratching and stimulus control (situations such as undressing in which scratching is likely are reduced or minimized) (Watson, Tharp, & Krisberg, 1972).

Social Skills and Communication Training. Recent studies suggest that it may be useful to include aspects of social skills and communication training in the treatment of atopic dermatitis (Ehlers et al., 1995; Niebel, 1995). These interventions have the goal of reducing interpersonal stressors that may trigger the skin symptoms. Concurrently they help the patient overcome negative social reactions to the skin disease. In Niebel's (1995) dismantling study there was some suggestion that the addition of these methods improved effect sizes beyond those of relaxation and habit reversal for scratching, although group comparisons were generally nonsignificant. Table 19.2 gives an overview of a group treatment program for atopic dermatitis developed by Stangier et al., (1996). It integrates social skills and communication training with applied relaxation training and self-control of scratching. As already mentioned, the program was more effective in improving skin condition at 1-year follow-up than standard medical care or dermatological education (Ehlers et al., 1995).

ADJUSTMENT DISORDERS

Psychological Consequences of Dermatological Disorders

Very few dermatological conditions are life-threatening, like melanoma, or have a progressive course with a declining physical state, like scleroderma and epidermolysis bullosa. This is probably why the emotional distress caused by these disorders is often underestimated by physicians (Whitlock, 1976). Research indicates, however, that the somatic, social, and emotional effects of skin disorders require considerable coping resources and can lead to significant emotional distress and psychosocial impairment. Cassileth et al. (1984) showed that patients with various skin disorders displayed mental health impairment comparable to patients with cancer, diabetes, arthritis, and kidney disease.

Skin disorders can be considered as stressors that may exceed the individual's coping resources (Cohen & Lazarus, 1979). Like other chronic diseases, skin disorders threaten physical and psychological well-being, for example through physical discomfort, frequent hospitalization, social disapproval, or impact on self-esteem. Because the patient can only influence the course of the disease to a limited extent, subjective lack of control and helplessness are commonly experienced (Felton & Revenson, 1984). Figure 19.2 summarizes factors that may be important in explaining psychological maladjustment to dermatological disorders, using Leventhal's self-regulation model (Leventhal, Nerenz, & Steele, 1984; Leventhal, Suls, & Leventhal, 1993) as the general framework. The Leventhal method assumes that an implicit cognitive representation of threat posed by the illness determines which coping strategies the patient will choose. In patients who manage to adapt well to the disorder, perceived threat, coping efforts, and the appraisal of coping results form a negative feedback circle of self-regulation. Patients who perceive failure of their coping efforts (loss of control) perceive further threat and are likely to respond with coping behaviors that are maladaptive such as heightened attention to the skin or to negative social reactions, avoidance behavior, or habitual self-monitoring. These maladaptive coping reactions lead to symptoms of anxiety and depression and elicit positive feedback circles that maintain or increase the perceived threat (see dashed lines in Figure 19.2). Figure 19.2 shows that three types of threat are relevant in dermatological disorders, physical threat, social threat, and threat to self- and body image.

Physical Threat

Many dermatological disorders are accompanied by severe itching. In laboratory studies (Arnetz & Fjellner, 1985) as well as in clinical research with dermatological patients (Gupta et al., 1989, 1994; Stangier & Gieler, 1998) a close relationship between depression and itching has been observed. The distressing vicious itch-scratch circle has been described in the previous section. Patients with chronic skin disorders such as atopic dermatitis often do not perceive effective ways of controlling itching except scratching, and they form negative catastrophic cognitions like "The

itching will never stop" or "The itching will get worse and worse" (Ehlers, Stangier, Dohn, & Gieler, 1993). They develop anticipatory anxiety of the next itching attack analogous to the fear of pain (McCracken, Faber, & Janeck, 1997). This can lead to hypochondriacal self-monitoring and the expectation that the disease could spread further, along with anxiety and tension. If the patient does not perceive ways of influencing the course of the skin disorder, feelings of helplessness can develop into depressive reactions. All of these ineffective coping responses may increase the intensity of the itching further (Hermanns & Scholz, 1992). Analogous considerations apply to skin disorders that are accompanied by severe pain.

Social Threat

Sadly, patients with skin disorders commonly experience negative social reactions to their skin. These are not only based on aesthetic aversion. Skin diseases

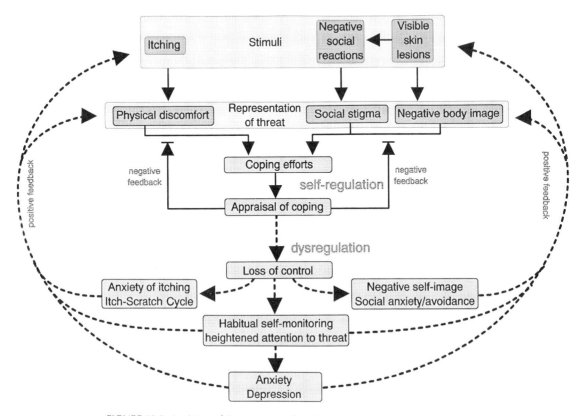

FIGURE 19.2. Anxiety and Depression in the Adjustment to Chronic Skin Disorders

are frequently misinterpreted as being infectious, probably because of associations with diseases such as plague and leprosy and more recently AIDS (Doka, 1997). Negative social reactions range from expression of compassion, ambivalent reservedness, and maintaining distance from the stigmatized person to open rejection (Bosse, Fassheber, Hünecke, Teichmann, & Zauner, 1976). Furthermore, dermatological patients often encounter discrimination at work and in public life (Jowett & Ryan, 1985). If the patient is unable to cope with these negative social responses, they can lead to negative self-evaluation, especially in patients who have excessively high standards in their personal behavior and appearance (Wessley & Lewis, 1989). Additionally, the experience of some negative social reactions may lead to a general fear of being rejected by others. These patients will tend to misinterpret neutral reactions of others to their skin condition as hostile and disapproving "staring," thus increasing the perceived threat. Patients with such social concerns usually avoid either specific situations associated with visual exposure of the skin such as contact with strangers, public sauna and bathing, and sexual activities (Ginsburg, 1995) or show more generalized avoidance. Although avoidance in the short term helps to reduce distress, it prevents patients from correcting the belief that others will reject them (Clark & Wells, 1995). Patients with social concerns will also focus their attention on the visible cutaneous symptoms and engage in repeated body checking and rumination about the threatening emotional and social consequences (Gupta, Gupta, & Habertman, 1987). Thoughts typically revolve around the occurrence of an impending rash and its consequences on social perception by others, which increases public self-consciousness. As a result of this preoccupation with outward appearance and heightened vigilance toward social attention and disapproval, patients may develop the belief of being "disfigured" (Jowett & Ryan, 1985).

Threat to Self- and Body Image

Cutaneous alterations are often perceived as a stigma that reduces personal attractiveness (Jowett & Ryan, 1985; Leichtman, Burnett, & Robinson, 1981). The impact on body image depends largely on the localization and morphological characteristics of the cutaneous alterations. Patients with psoriasis are often severely distressed by the visible cutaneous symptoms on arms, legs, and scalp, which consist of deep red patches covered by silvery scales (Ginsburg & Link, 1989). Due to widespread inflamed pustules and subsequent facial scars, acne frequently causes social anxiety and depression, especially in adolescence, when self-esteem and social relationships are greatly influenced by outward appearance (Koo et al., 1994). Emotional problems due to visible cutaneous symptoms have also been reported in individuals with vitiligo, which is characterized by white flaws as a result of altered cutaneous pigmentation (Porter et al., 1987). In severe cases this subjective experience can develop into a conviction of being disfigured (Jowett & Ryan, 1985).

Definition of Adjustment Disorders

Adjustment disorders are characterized by clinically significant emotional or behavioral symptoms in response to a psychosocial stressor. The main symptoms include anxiety and depressed mood, but may also include physical complaints, social withdrawal, or work or academic inhibition (American Psychiatric Association, 1994). Adjustment disorders are associated with an increased risk of suicide attempts and suicide.

Prevalence

In dermatological outpatients the prevalence of adjustment disorders is generally high. As already mentioned, patients with a wide range of dermatological disorders score high on self-report instruments of anxiety and depression. Wessley and Lewis (1989) administered a structured clinical interview and a self-rating instrument to assess psychiatric symptoms as well as the impact of skin disease in 173 dermatological outpatients. They found that clinically relevant psychiatric symptoms were associated with a high impact of the skin disease in 30% of the sample. Hughes et al. (1983) investigated 196 dermatology outpatients and 40 inpatients using a mental health questionnaire. Of the patients with visible skin lesions affecting the face or hand, 70% reported increased psychiatric symptoms. Over all, about 20% of the total sample displayed symptoms of an adjustment disorder. The prevalence of psychiatric symptoms was elevated in patients with acne, eczema, psoriasis, and alopecia areata. Suicidal ideation has been found in 6% of patients with psoriasis (Gupta, Schork, & Gupta, 1993) and may be increased in patients with acne (Cotteril & Cunliffe, 1997). Specific patterns of association may exist between dermatological disorders and certain psychiatric symptoms. Lyketos et al. (1985) found that urticaria was primarily associated with anxiety disorders, whereas alopecia areata was primarily associated with depression. Schmidt-Traub and Bamler (1997) observed a significant association of allergies of the immediate type and panic disorder.

However, the prevalences reported in these papers may overestimate the true proportion of adjustment disorders because patients with primary emotional symptoms are included in the samples. Wessley and Lewis (1989) found that the subgroup of patients with preexisting psychiatric symptoms accounted for 10% of the dermatological outpatient sample. It is therefore important to assess the sequence of the manifestation of the dermatological disorder and of the emotional problem.

Clinical Assessment

Until recently there has been a lack of self-report instruments for the assessment of the sources of threat and the degree of adjustment problems in chronic skin disorders. A number of short questionnaires have been developed to assess life quality in specific disorders including acne, psoriasis, and atopic dermatitis (Finlay, 1997). Furthermore, several questionnaires focus on specific aspects of certain dermatological disorders such as stigmatization in psoriasis (Ginsburg & Link, 1989; Gupta & Gupta, 1995). However, these questionnaires do not allow for a screening of a range of adjustment problems and a comparison of different skin conditions. The Adjustment to Chronic Skin Diseases Questionnaire (ACS) has been developed to measure specific problems in the adjustment to chronic dermatological disorders and has been validated on a large heterogeneous dermatological sample (Stangier, Ehlers, & Gieler, 1998).

Treatment

Consensus has developed that a combination of interventions to improve abilities to cope with the disease represents the most favorable treatment approach for patients with chronic dermatological disorders. Usually the treatment is delivered in groups so that patients can support each other emotionally and provide encouraging models for successful coping for each other (Folkman et al., 1991). An additional component of the interventions is patient education providing patients with information to cope with illness-imposed demands (Devins & Binik, 1996). Structured group programs have been developed and evaluated for atopic dermatitis (Cole et al., 1988; Ehlers, Stangier, & Gieler, 1995; Niebel, 1995), psoriasis (Bremer-Schulte et al., 1985; Price, Mottahedin, & Mayo, 1991; Zachariae et al., 1996), acne (Hughes et al., 1983), herpes genitalis (Drob, Bernard, Lifshutz, & Nierenberg, 1986), and malignant melanoma (Fawzy et al., 1990, 1993). Positive effects on measures of anxiety and depression and, in most studies, on medical outcomes were observed. The treatment components of these programs that are designed to cope with the physical discomfort associated with the disorder such as relaxation, guided imagery, and self-instructions have been described in the previous section on psychological factors influencing skin disorders.

Some recent programs (Ehlers et al., 1995; Niebel, 1995) have also included interventions designed to address the social threat involved in these disorders. However, if a patient suffers from an adjustment disorder, these interventions may not suffice, and methods established as effective in the treatment of depression and social phobia may be useful. Systematic evaluations of these methods in adjustment disorders in dermatological patients are, however, largely lacking.

Research suggests that interventions designed to prevent depression such as cognitive restructuring, self-management, and problem solving training reduce emotional distress caused by chronic medical conditions (Devins & Binik, 1996). For example, maladaptive cognitions decreasing the perception of pleasant bodily sensations (e.g., "I must avoid exertion as it incites skin symptoms") and negative cognitions regarding the course of the disease and the self-image (Leventhal et al., 1984) that may contribute to the development of depressive symptoms in dermatological patients (e.g., "I am nothing more than a sick person. I will be disabled for my whole life") need to be identified and changed by cognitive restructuring. Analogous to the treatment of depression, pleasant activity scheduling (Lewinsohn & Libet, 1972) is likely to be beneficial to dermatological patients with adjustment disorders because these increase physical and emotional well-being and counteract the patients' increased attention to the skin.

The first step in modifying social anxiety and avoidance is to develop an appropriate understanding of the problem. Despite considerable distress, patients frequently display a tendency to deny social anxiety and to focus exclusively on their somatic symptoms. It is therefore necessary to present the social concerns as a natural consequence of the skin disorder and not as a personal failure. The acceptance of the psychological intervention can be increased if it is presented as an adjunct to the available medical and cosmetic treatment.

Elements of social skills training and the cognitive-behavioral treatment of social phobia are useful in modifying social anxiety and avoidance. Particularly stressful for patients are situations in which other persons demonstrate rejection or disgust due to the skin lesions, make critical comments on scratching, or just ask about the skin symptoms in a neutral way because they lack knowledge. Role plays allow the patient to simulate social situations and practice assertive behavior. Controlled studies (Fiegenbaum, 1981) and case reports (Roback, Kirshner, & Roback, 1981) have shown that exposure to avoided social situations can be useful in disfiguring diseases if patients are carefully prepared by specific training of social skills, relaxation, and self-instruction.

Video feedback is a useful technique to modify negative body image and self-evaluation in dermatological patients (Hünecke, 1993). The "frozen," static look of oneself that one sees in photos or in the mirror enhances a selective attention to cutaneous flaws and the subsequent development of the conviction that one is disfigured. Through video feedback the dynamic aspects of expressive behavior that play an important role in the judgment of attractiveness can be observed by the patients. In role plays and through video feedback dysfunctional cognitions indicating a negative body image and an overestimation of bodily attractiveness may become evident (e.g., "Only when I look perfect and flawless will I be accepted by others"). These dysfunctional assumptions can be modified by

methods used in the cognitive treatment of social phobia (Clark & Wells, 1995).

SOMATOFORM DISORDERS RELATED TO DERMATOLOGICAL COMPLAINTS

The importance of the skin in body image, sense of well-being, and self-esteem makes it particularly prone to misinterpretation that may lead to the development of somatoform disorders. Cotteril (1981) termed this group of disorders "dermatological nondiseases" because patients report dermatological complaints that cannot be fully explained by a diagnosable dermatological condition.

The following somatoform disorders are frequently related to dermatological symptoms (Wessley, 1990):

1. *Body dysmorphic disorder (BDD):* the preoccupation with an imagined or exaggerated defect in physical appearance
2. *Hypochondriasis:* the preoccupation with the fear of having a serious disease, based on the misinterpretation of cutaneous symptoms
3. *Chronic cutaneous dysesthesias:* persistent aversive cutaneous sensations not of organic origin, including somatoform pruritus, burning, or pain, which may be categorized according to *DSM-IV* as "Undifferentiated Somatoform Disorder"

While in the first two groups of disorders, body-focused anxiety is an important diagnostic feature, somatic symptoms are predominant in the third group and anxiety is only one of various triggering factors. In all somatoform disorders, obsessive-compulsive features as well as high rates of comorbid depression are found (Barsky, Wyshak, & Klerman, 1992). Moreover, there is not always a clear distinction between these symptoms and delusions. Patients with BDD or hypochondriasis are often not able to recognize that their concerns are exaggerated (Barsky et al., 1992; McElroy, Phillips, Keck, Hudson, & Pope, 1992). With cutaneous dysesthesias, transitions to delusions of parasitosis or chronic tactile hallucinosis are possible (Munro & Chimara, 1982).

Body Dysmorphic Disorder

Definition and Clinical Features

According to the *DSM-IV* (American Psychiatric Association, 1994), BDD is a "preoccupation with an imagined defect in appearance. If a slight physical anomaly is present, the person's concern is markedly excessive." BDD must be distinguished from objective impairments in appearance caused by disfiguring dermatoses such as severe forms of psoriasis or acne. In these cases it is more appropriate to diagnose an adjustment disorder.

An accurate diagnosis is difficult because patients are often ashamed to talk about the problem. They will tend to conceal their disfigurement conviction and rarely express their emotional strain. Rather, they can be recognized by their excessive use of medications (including steroids) and cosmetics or by their requests for inappropriate (e.g., surgical) treatment. In some patients, noxious self-treatment and manipulations (excoriations) may indicate extreme helplessness in coping with the perceived flaw.

The complaints can be related to the size or asymmetrical forms of body parts, but in most cases, skin (particularly on the face) and hair are primary concerns (Philipps, McElroy, Keck, Pope, & Hudson, 1993). Examples include concerns about wrinkles, spots, vascular marking, scars, acne, paleness or redness, extreme hair growth, or loss of hair. The patients usually try to cover up the perceived flaw by all means (e.g., with make-up). Typical characteristics of these patients are obsessive-compulsive rituals (particularly self-monitoring in front of a mirror), the avoidance of attention by others (safety behaviors such as turning the head away), and social withdrawal from situations in which others could perceive the flaw (Veale et al., 1996). Patients often seek reassurance from others that the flaw is completely covered up or "not so bad."

Prevalence and Comorbidity

The prevalence of BDD in the total population has previously been underestimated. In a college sample, self-ratings of *DSM* criteria showed a prevalence of BDD of 4% for women and 1% for men (Rosen, Reiter, & Orosan, 1995). The proportion of dermatological patients with BDD is assumed to be significantly greater. Stangier and Gieler (1998) assessed the complaints of 163 patients of a university dermatological outpatient clinic with a questionnaire and compared them with physicians' ratings. Approximately 9% reported disfigurement that was out of proportion with their physicians' ratings.

There is a high rate of comorbidity with affective disorders (77%) as well as anxiety disorders (70%), and there is a clear overlap with obsessive-compulsive disorders (Hollander, Cohen, & Simeon, 1993). BDD patients usually suffer from high emotional distress, with 40% reporting suicidal tendencies (Philipps et al., 1993).

Cognitive-Behavioral Model

The irrational belief that one is disfigured by a bodily flaw is explained by a bias in the processing of body-related information (Veale et al., 1996). Patients are thought to excessively and selectively attend to morphological deviations of the body that are often hardly perceptible to others, although they might be present to a minimal degree. The attentional bias is based on dysfunctional cognitive schemata that include unrealistic beauty standards and a negative body image, and possibly an additional increased sensitivity in the perception of aesthetic discrepancies. The belief that one is disfigured results in feelings of rejection and disgust regarding one's own body, as well as fear that others might see the "ugly" defect. The dysfunctional beliefs are maintained through avoidance behaviors and compulsive monitoring rituals, especially monitoring appearance in front of the mirror. Additionally, subjective feelings of rejection and disgust are used as evidence of the objective "ugliness" of one's own body (so-called emotional reasoning).

Clinical Assessment

In general, acceptance of psychological assessment is limited in somatoform disorders. Therefore, it is necessary to first develop a model of the problem and the treatment before conducting the assessment. The BDD Diagnostic Module (Philipps, 1991) of the Structured Clinical Interview for *DSM-IV* (First, Spitzer, Gibbons, & Williams, 1995) may help to diagnose BDD. The Body Dysmorphic Disorder Examination (Rosen & Reiter, 1996) and the Modified Yale-Brown Obsessive Compulsive Scale (Y-BOCS) for BDD (Hollander &

Phillips, 1991) are specific, semistructured clinical interviews that have been developed to measure severity of symptoms and collect more detailed information about the problem. Useful additional questionnaire assessments include measures of depression (e.g., Beck Depression Inventory; Beck, Ward, Mendelson, Mock, & Erbraugh, 1961) and social anxiety (e.g., Social Interaction and Anxiety Scale and Social Phobia Scale; Mattick & Clarke, 1998).

Treatment

There is growing evidence from controlled case studies (Marks & Mishan, 1988; Neziroglu & Yaryura-Tobias, 1993) and controlled group studies (Gomez-Perez, Marks, & Gutierrez-Fisac, 1994; Rosen et al., 1995; Veale et al., 1996) that exposure to anxiety-provoking social situations and response prevention of camouflage, checking behavior and reassurance seeking are essential components of an effective treatment of BDD. However, a significant difficulty is patients' limited motivation for a psychological approach to the problem, and many patients refuse exposure treatment. Reverse role play in which patients argue against their beliefs has been shown to be beneficial in overcoming overvalued ideas (Newell & Shrubb, 1994). Veale et al. (1996) suggest an intense motivational phase in which treatment is defined as a time-limited testing of a psychological model of the problem. Their treatment is designed for 12 group sessions and includes development of a psychological explanation and treatment model, exposure to critical social situations including response prevention, and training to shift attention away from preoccupation with feelings to the perception of environmental reactions (Wells, White, & Carter, 1997), as well as cognitive restructuring of beliefs related to the outward appearance as a measure of self-worth. Preliminary results from a controlled trial with 19 patients showed a reduction in BDD symptoms, depression, anxiety, and social anxiety. No follow-up data were reported.

McKay et al. (1997) showed that the maintenance of treatment effects improved when a 6-month maintenance program followed treatment. This program aims to improve response prevention and coping with relapses through intense telephone contact with the therapist. Because pharmacological treatment with serotonin reuptake inhibitors has also proven beneficial in some case studies (Hollander, Cohen, Simeon, & Rosen, 1994), more controlled research is needed to examine whether the effectiveness of behavior therapy may be improved by combination with pharmacological treatment.

Hypochondriacal Disorders in Dermatology

Definition and Clinical Features

Hypochondriasis refers to the belief that one has a serious disease or a fear of having a serious disease that persists despite adequate medical reassurance. Thus, the definition includes inappropriate illness conviction as well as so-called illness phobia (Marks, 1987). Due to their visibility and variability, cutaneous symptoms are particularly apt to trigger fear of illness and conviction of being ill. The content of hypochondriacal beliefs largely depends on cultural and social conditions. In the past a fear of syphilis was common due to the association of skin symptoms and infections. In recent years, infections with the HIV virus have become a focus of hypochondriacal concerns (Scragg, 1995), as early cutaneous symptoms of HIV infection may include a whole range of general dermatological symptoms such as erythema, eczema, exanthema, blister, and itching (Warner & Fisher, 1986). Another common focus of hypochondriacal concerns are allergies. These patients are firmly convinced that they have an allergy to a substance (e.g., a certain food or chemical substance in the environment) although allergologic tests are negative (so-called multiple chemical sensitivities syndrome; Salvaggio, 1994). Finally, hypochondriacal worries might also relate to other threatening skin conditions such as skin cancer (melanophobia) or parasitic infestation (parasitophobia) (Koblenzer, 1993). To our knowledge, however, no empirical data have been presented for these disorders.

The behavior of hypochondriacal patients depends on their particular beliefs. For example, patients who are firmly convinced that they are infected with HIV may avoid HIV tests altogether, whereas others who fear to be infected may demand repeated tests, excessively seek information about AIDS, and avoid sexual relationships.

Prevalence

An Italian study showed a prevalence of hypochondriasis of 4.5% in the general population (Faravelli et al., 1997). According to Barsky, Wyshak, Klerman, & Latham (1990), 5% of the patients in medical treatment show hypochondriacal symptoms. No data are available about the prevalence of hypochondriacal symptoms related to dermatological disorders. In a dermatological outpatient sample, 9% of the patients reported a consistent fear or conviction of having a severe disease in the absence of corroborating medical evidence (Stangier & Gieler, 1998).

Cognitive-Behavioral Models

A central aspect of hypochondriasis is the false interpretation of bodily sensations or symptoms as signs of a dangerous disease (Salkovskis, 1989; Warwick & Salkovskis, 1990). The dysfunctional belief leads to anxiety and dysfunctional behaviors that maintain the problem, for example, heightened attention to bodily changes, checking behavior, and reassurance seeking. The misinterpretation of bodily sensations stems from dysfunctional assumptions about health and sickness and is activated through relevant information, for example, through the media or experiences such as the illness of a relative. Barsky and Wishak (1990) call the disturbances in perception and cognitive interpretation of somatic symptoms in hypochondriasis "somatosensory amplification." According to their theory, hypochondriacal patients are hypersensitive not only to the perception of pathological sensations such as pain, but also to aversive sensations in general such as hunger or heat.

An important factor promoting the development of hypochondriasis related to dermatological symptoms is the visibility of the skin symptoms. It is easy for patients to form images of the exacerbation of these symptoms, and this might enhance the risk of forming dysfunctional preoccupation with the skin (Wells & Hackman, 1993). In addition, the development of compulsive self-monitoring and checking is facilitated by the accessibility of the skin (e.g., excessive checking in the mirror).

Clinical Assessment

The Whitley Index is a measure of the general severity of hypochondriasis (Pilowski, 1967). Self-monitoring forms the basis of psychological intervention. Patients should be instructed to keep daily recordings of somatic symptoms, thoughts, mood, behaviors (including medication use and general activities), and precipitating stressful events (Salkovskis, 1989).

Treatment

There are no studies relating specifically to the treatment of dermatological hypochondriasis. However, several controlled studies support the effectiveness of cognitive-behavioral therapy (CBT) in the treatment of hypochondriasis (Clark et al., 1998; Warwick, Clark, Cobb, & Salkovskis, 1996). Although these studies did not exclusively focus on patients whose hypochondriasis involved misinterpretation of dermatological symptoms, it is likely that the procedures generalize to this patient group. Patients received 16 sessions in which misinterpretations of symptoms were challenged and replaced with realistic interpretations of symptoms and signs, and underlying dysfunctional assumptions were restructured. This included discussion, education, and behavioral experiments, for example, to test the hypothesis that self-focused attention increased symptoms. Behaviors maintaining the problem were modified by response prevention for repeated bodily checking and reassurance seeking and graded exposure to avoided illness-related situations. Homework assignments included daily recording of negative thoughts, rational responses, and behavioral experiments.

An educational group treatment, based on Barsky's concept of somatosensory amplification, was also effective in reducing hypochondriacal fears (Avia et al., 1996). The six group sessions used practical exercises and information sheets, focusing on the following topics: inadequate and selective attention, the role of muscle tension/hyperventilation, environmental factors, stress and dysphoric mood, and the attribution of somatic signals.

Logsdail, Clum, & Yaeger (1991) presented the successful treatment of seven cases with AIDS phobia who received 7 to 10 treatment sessions, consisting of self-directed exposure to avoided situations and other cues triggering anxiety, and prevention of checking, cleaning rituals, and reassurance seeking. Scragg (1995) recommends the use of techniques derived from the treatment of obsessive-compulsive disorders for AIDS phobia, such as reducing reassurance seeking, behavioral experiments, exposure in imagination, and cognitive restructuring of dysfunctional beliefs.

Further evidence for the effectiveness of a combination of exposure to anxiety-provoking situations, imagery, and cognitive restructuring in skin-related hypochondriasis comes from treatment studies with patients reporting medically unexplained allergic symptoms. Ikemi, Nakagawa, Kusano, & Sugita (1970) used a modified form of autogenic training that included principles of hyposensitization and systematic desensitization. Individuals with food intolerance reactions and allergic contact dermatitis were instructed while in a relaxed state to progressively imagine contact with allergens in the absence of allergic reactions. The effects of the training were assessed with in vivo exposure to the allergen, and none of the six participants experienced symptoms. Similarly, Guglielmi, Cox, and Spyker (1994) used exposure and cognitive reconstructing for patients with multiple chemical sensitivities syndrome to reduce the avoidance of anxiety-provoking situations.

Undifferentiated Somatoform Disorders

Definition and Clinical Features

In general, the diagnosis of Undifferentiated Somatoform Disorders refers to physical complaints, lasting at least 6 months, that are below the threshold for a diagnosis of Somatization Disorder and include pain, gastrointestinal, sexual, and pseudoneurological symptoms. In dermatology this diagnostic category may also include somatoform itching ("pruritus sine materia"), burning, and pain. *ICD-10*, but not *DSM-IV*, notes that the diagnostic criteria might also be extended, however, to abnormal cutaneous symptoms such as "itching, burning, tingling, numbness, soreness, etc." (World Health Organization, 1992, p. 162). The diagnosis of a somatoform disorder requires that the symptoms cannot be fully explained by a medical condition. Distinguishing somatoform disorders from somatic illness is often difficult because itching is a principal symptom in many dermatological, internal, and neurological disorders that are not always easy to diagnose (Bernhard, 1994). It should be noted, however, that somatic factors, per se, do not exclude the diagnosis of a somatoform disorder (and vice versa).

Although itching and pain share several neurophysiological features (Bernard, 1994), somatoform itching has rarely been studied. A close relationship between depression and itching was determined in laboratory studies (Arnetz & Fjellner, 1985) as well as in clinical research with dermatological patients (Gupta et al., 1989, 1994; Sheehan-Dare, Henderson, & Cotteril, 1994; Stangier & Gieler, 1998). Somatoform symptoms are often seen as the consequences of a depressive disorder (Katon et al., 1982), but one has to bear in mind that depressive symptoms can be the result of aversive cutaneous symptoms such as itching (Morrison & Herbstein, 1988).

Koblenzer and Bostrom (1994) first proposed the term *chronic cutaneous dysesthesias* for patients who suffer from sensations such as burning (including glossodynia and vulvodynia) and hypersensitivity to cold and light that cannot be explained by somatic disorders, but rather by psychiatric disorders such as depression or borderline personality disorder. A distinction between dysesthesias and hypochondriasis is not always easy. Unpleasant sensations seldom arise without the conviction of a related illness. Therefore, a spectrum of illnesses exists with primarily cognitive symptoms of hypochondriacal preoccupation on one side and primarily somatic symptoms of undifferentiated somatoform disorders on the other side. In addition, transitions to delusions of parasitosis are possible (Munro & Chimara, 1982).

Prevalence

Stangier and Gieler (1998) found that a high proportion of dermatological outpatients reported dermatological complaints related to undifferentiated somatoform disorders that were also associated with increased levels of self-rated depression. Slightly over 10% of the patients reported pruritus; 7.7% reported cutaneous pain and 7.7% burning sensations that could not be fully explained by a physical condition. However, it is assumed that the true prevalence is lower, given that it is often not possible to rule out somatic origin.

Cognitive-Behavioral Model

One possible central factor in the development of somatoform disorders is a tendency toward somatosensory amplification (Barsky et al., 1990), that is, an increased sensitivity in perceiving bodily sensations and the tendency to interpret these as threatening. Furthermore, similar to models of hypochondriasis or panic attacks (e.g., Ehlers & Margraf, 1989; Warwick & Salkovskis, 1990), the increased attention to the skin, misattributions ("skin rash") and negative emotional reactions (fear of spread of itching or skin lesions) can lead to a vicious circle in which minor internal sensations rapidly increase in severity.

For itching there is empirical evidence that its perception and processing in the central nervous system depend on emotional and cognitive factors: The intensity of itching is dependent on attention and sense of control (Hermanns & Scholz, 1992), and merely imagining itching or similar sensations can lead to their occurrence (Bethune & Kidd, 1961). Furthermore, experimental studies with animals document that the release of histamine, one of the most important mediator substances in itching, can be classically conditioned (Djuric & Bienenstock, 1993). These findings suggest the possibility that itching can become a response to triggers other than mechanical, physical, or chemical stimuli through learning processes.

Clinical Assessment

Currently no specific instruments exist for measuring somatoform dermatological symptoms. Self-rating scales might be useful to assess emotional distress caused by the symptoms. The SCL-90R (Derogatis, 1977) includes subscales for somatization, anxiety, and depression that have been shown to discriminate patients with multiple chemical sensitivity from controls (Simon, Daniell, Stockbridge, Claypoole, & Rosenstock, 1993). Analogous to hypochondriasis, records of variation in symptoms (e.g., intensity of itch, redness of skin), thoughts, mood, behaviors (including medication use and general activities), as well as precipitating stressful events are an important source of information in psychological treatment.

Treatment

As many patients with somatoform disorders are convinced that they need somatic treatment, the development of a multicausal model of the symptoms that takes both somatic and psychological factors into consideration is of central importance. It is often

difficult to determine the relative importance of somatic and psychological factors in individual patients (Gieler, Stangier, & Ehlers, 1997). An acceptable and plausible rationale for psychological treatment is to increase the patient's ability to cope with the stressful somatic symptoms. It is not advisable to overemphasize the importance of psychological factors in the etiology of the disorder.

Specific approaches to the treatment of undifferentiated somatoform disorders have, until now, primarily been suggested by psychodynamic authors (Koblenzer, 1987). Within the framework of behavioral medicine the following treatment components appear promising but yet require systematic evaluation: self-observation to detect functional associations between symptoms and specific situations, cognitions, and behaviors; identification and modification of specific cognitive and behavioral reactions that aggravate symptoms (e.g., catastrophic thoughts, preoccupation with the symptom, passive withdrawal behavior, social deficits); relaxation and imagery to increase a sense of physical well-being (see section on psychological factors in dermatological disorders); self-instruction to improve coping with itching; suggestion and imagery to distract attention from the aversive symptoms; and increase of positive activities associated with pleasant body sensations (Lewinsohn & Libet, 1972). It should be noted, however, that comorbid anxiety disorders are frequently present and need to be addressed in treatment.

SELF-INFLICTED LESIONS

Manipulations of the skin that lead to lesions occur for many reasons. These include reflexive reactions (scratching in response to itching); operant reactions that are performed to achieve external advantages (e.g., social reassurance), including malingering or changes in internal state (e.g., reduction of tension); and factitious lesions due to various psychopathological states (Gieler, 1994). Two forms of factitious lesions are distinguished (Gupta et al., 1987) on the basis of their triggers and mechanisms.

1. *Parafactitious disorders* such as trichotillomania (repetitive hair pulling) and neurotic excoriations (compulsive picking or scratching of the skin) that occur in a repetitive, ritualized form (Stein

& Hollander, 1992). Important triggers include negative emotional states such as aggressive impulses, diffuse anxiety, and depression.

2. *Dermatitis artefacta*, a factitious disorder with predominantly physical signs and symptoms, is often associated with severe psychological disorders, particularly borderline personality disorder (Koblenzer, 1987). The skin lesions are self-inflicted to assume the sick role. A dissociative state is a common trigger.

Parafactitious Disorders

Definition and Clinical Features

This group of disorders includes self-inflicted cutaneous lesions that are produced in a repetitive, ritualized act. The individual fails to resist the impulse to manipulate the skin or hair and experiences relief while committing the act. The most researched disorder is trichotillomania, which often begins in childhood. In *DSM-IV* (American Psychiatric Association, 1994), trichotillomania is classified as an impulse-control disorder, but it has also been suggested to include parafactitious disorders in the spectrum of obsessive-compulsive–related disorders (Stein & Hollander, 1993). However, in contrast to OCD, manipulation of the skin or hair is not triggered by obsessions, and the act is not intended to ward off future harm. In childhood, trichotillomania is frequently episodic and has been classified as a habit disorder (Swedo et al., 1989). Trichotillomania shares several similarities with onychotillomania and onychophagia (excessive nail biting), which are also common phenomena in children. High comorbidity with affective and anxiety disorders exists in adolescents and adults (Swedo et al., 1989). Christensen, Ristvedt, and Mackenzie (1993) identified two kinds of triggers of hair pulling: first, negative affect such as sadness, anxiety, frustration, and tension associated with poor self-esteem; and second, sedentary and contemplative activities, such as reading, watching TV, and preparing for bed. Patients could be divided into two subgroups—patients with high negative affect associated with OCD (as well as depression and other anxiety disorders) and those who responded primarily to situational cues in the sense of an inadequate habit.

Neurotic excoriation is compulsive picking or scratching of the skin that leads to a reduction in tension. While some authors describe the rather egodystonic character of the rituals (Stein & Hollander, 1992), other authors emphasize the ego-syntonic emotions, particularly aggressive impulses, as a trigger (Fruensgaard, 1984). Excessive excoriations may also occur with somatic or "psychogenic" itching (Fried, 1994) or minimal symptoms of preexisting dermatoses such as acne (so-called acne excoriée des jeunes filles) (Koblenzer, 1987). This must be distinguished from irritant dermatitis that results from excessive hand washing in obsessive-compulsive disorders (OCD) (Rasmussen, 1985). Finally, excoriations can also occur together with delusions of parasitosis (Munro & Chimara, 1982). In conclusion, this is a very heterogeneous group of dermatological symptoms related to various psychiatric disorders.

Prevalence

The frequency of neurotic excoriations in dermatological departments is estimated to be 2% (Gupta et al., 1987). No systematic data on the prevalence of trichotillomania are available (American Psychiatric Association, 1994).

Models of the Disorder

No psychological models of the origin of parafactitious disorders have yet been presented. As negative emotional states seem to trigger the behavior and patients describe a sense of relief when performing it, operant conditioning (negative reinforcement) may play a role. Stein and Hollander (1992, 1993) assume a neurobiological basis for the disorder, that is, abnormal serotonergic neural transmission that may form the basis of a psychological dimension of compulsivity versus impulsivity.

Clinical Assessment

The Trichotillomania Symptom Severity Scale (Swedo et al., 1989) may be particularly useful in practice. It includes five 20-point scores related to average time spent pulling each day, average time spent pulling on the prior day, amount of resistance against the hair-pulling urge, degree of subjective distress, and interference with daily activities. It may also be useful to apply the Yale-Brown Obsessive Compulsive Scale (Y-BOCS). The adapted version for trichotillomania, however, showed limited validity due to the considerable phenomenological differences with OCD (Stanley, Prather, Wagner, Davis, & Swan et al., 1993).

Self-monitoring of self-destructive behavior (e.g., Welkowitz, Held, & Held, 1989; Azrin et al., 1980) has been proved to be a valid and sensitive measure for this group of disorders. Furthermore, the Cues Checklist (Christenson et al., 1993) is a useful instrument for identifying circumstances that initiate hair pulling.

Treatment

Habit reversal (Azrin & Nunn, 1973) is the most successful behavioral treatment approach for trichotillomania (Azrin et al., 1980; Friman, Finney, & Christophersen, 1984) and neurotic excoriations (Welkowitz et al., 1989). Usually this method includes the self-monitoring of the target behavior in diaries (time of occurrence, preceding situation, and intensity of or time spent with manipulation), awareness training to interrupt the automatic behavior, and the training of alternative responses (e.g., tensing all muscles) as described in the section on psychological factors affecting dermatological disorders. Patients are instructed to apply this technique in critical situations and to record the daily practice. It is possible that training in progressive muscle relaxation could be a useful addition to habit-reversal techniques, as the impulse to pull hairs or manipulate the skin is often associated with increased tension.

The dimensions of compulsivity versus impulsivity and ego-syntone versus ego-dystone may be important for the differential indication for self-control methods (Stein & Hollander, 1992). According to Christensen, Ristvedt, and Mackenzie (1993), these methods might be effective in neurotic excoriations characterized by an automatic habit disorder and the lack of clear affective trigger. In contrast, treatment approaches applied in OCD might be appropriate when negative, ego-syntonic affect is present.

Besides positive self-reinforcement of successful resistance to the impulse, improvement of the patient's perception of self-control seems to be important. Hollander (1958) reported that posthypnotic suggestions might be useful in the treatment of acne excoriée. He instructed the patients to recall the word *scar,* as a reminder of the ugly appearance of the face after scratching, as a cue for the interruption of scratching. Furthermore, methods of stimulus control and covert sensitization have also been reported in literature (for review, see Friman et al., 1984). In addition, contingency management has been employed in children by training their parents to reinforce attempts to resist hair pulling or scratching (Latimer, 1979).

Dermatitis Artefacta

Definition and Clinical Features

Cutaneous artifacts are defined as the intentional simulation of a dermatological condition by damaging the skin with chemicals or through mechanical or physical manipulations (burns, abscesses, edema, sepsis). On the basis of the pattern of clinical symptoms, experienced dermatologists can often easily determine whether lesions are self-inflicted (Gieler, 1994). Control over the symptoms can be conscious or dissociative but is usually kept hidden from others in order to simulate a somatic cause (Sneddon & Sneddon, 1975). Often there is a history of seeking treatment (preferably inpatient treatment) repeatedly at various hospitals, which usually ends due to direct confrontation with the self-infliction.

Like the parafactitious disorders, the factitious disorders are a heterogeneous group with complex psychopathological characteristics. They are related to a wide range of mental disorders, including mental retardation, psychosis, conversion disorder, depersonalization, personality disorders (most frequently borderline personality disorder), and suicidal tendencies (Consoli, 1995; Koblenzer, 1987). Often a history of traumatizing childhood experiences such as violence and sexual abuse can be identified. Conditions triggering the disorder include states of high affect that the patient seeks to control by producing physical symptoms (Koblenzer, 1987) or social and emotional isolation that the patient seeks to compensate for with attention by health professionals. Family conflicts or real or anticipated separation from significant others may trigger self-inflicted lesions that are intended to exert control over the relationships.

Prevalence

Although reliable data are unavailable and a high number of cases might be undiagnosed, the few studies available indicate that dermatitis artefacta is a rather rare disorder. In dermatological clinics the prevalence is estimated to be below 1% (Gieler, 1994; Gupta et al., 1987).

Models of the Disorder

Psychodynamic models have dominated attempts to explain factitious disorders. They interpret this disorder as an identification with a significant other who is perceived as hostile (Plassmann, 1994). Moreover, the behavior serves to stabilize emotional self-regulation. It allows the nonverbal expression of aggression and anger and at the same time the reduction of the resulting intolerable guilt feelings through pain. Finally, it can serve as stimulation in conditions of unbearable inner emptiness and furthermore increases the awareness of body in depersonalization.

Cognitive-behavioral interpretations focus on the instrumental character of autoaggressive behavior (Favell et al., 1982). Autoaggressive behavior is positively reinforced through the attention, support, and physical contact with others. Additionally it allows the reduction or avoidance of unpleasant situations (e.g., social isolation, overtaxing demands). Furthermore, the aversive sensations caused by the lesions may help to reduce a distorted perception of the body via depersonalization.

Clinical Assessment

Psychological assessment is generally not possible because the psychological etiology of the symptoms is denied.

Treatment

Behavioral treatment approaches primarily use operant methods of changing the self-destructive behavior. These include: reinforcement of non–self-destructive behavior or of behavior that is incompatible with self-destructive behavior, modification of critical situations (e.g. withdrawal of attention, overtaxing demands), and reinforcement of suitable interactions with the environment. These measures require extensive control over the environment, such as in inpatient treatment. Because psychotherapeutic treatment is usually refused, Klonoff, Youngner, Moore, & Hershey (1983) suggest the use of biofeedback in outpatient clinics. This approach meets the somatic treatment expectations of the patient on one hand and provides the feeling of control over the body on the other hand. Sneddon and Sneddon (1975) further recommend the use of relaxation training to improve body perception. However, it should be taken into consideration that the long-term goals of treatment should focus on the underlying psychological and social deficits of the patient, especially in cases with borderline personality disorder (Beck & Freeman, 1990; Linehan, 1990).

SUMMARY AND CONCLUSIONS

A review of literature shows the importance of psychological factors in dermatological symptoms and disorders. Psychological factors such as stress, anxiety, depression, and maladaptive behaviors may be involved in the onset, exacerbation, or maintenance of dermatological symptoms, but may also reflect a consequence of them. It is estimated that in more than one-third of the patients seeking dermatological treatment, psychological factors play a major role (Rook, Savin, & Wilkinson, 1984).

Substantial progress has been made in developing cognitive-behavioral treatments of dermatological disorders in which psychological factors play a role. Their long-term effectiveness has been evaluated for chronic dermatological conditions including atopic dermatitis, psoriasis, and genital herpes. Furthermore, psychological treatment approaches have been shown to be effective in psychiatric disorders associated with dermatological complaints including body dysmorphic disorder, hypochondriasis, and trichotillomania. Thus, for many dermatological patients, psychological treatment approaches may be a viable alternative to the widely used psychotropic drugs (for a review, see Gupta & Gupta, 1996).

However, the review also shows a number of areas that need to be addressed in future research. Despite the clinical significance of psychological factors in dermatological disorders, there is still a lack of diagnostic and nosological schemata (e.g., Folks & Kinney, 1992). Furthermore, there have been few attempts to link psychological aspects of dermatological symptoms to theoretical constructs developed in clinical psychology (Friedman, Hatch, & Paradis, 1993). This deficit is particularly evident in the research on adaptation to the social consequences of disfiguring and stigmatizing dermatological disorders. Although the incidence of adjustment disorders is suggested to be high, only a small amount of rather unsystematic research has yet been conducted on this problem.

Another problem that needs to be addressed is the acceptability of psychological treatments for dermatological patients. Most of the patients will initially consult a dermatologist, who will be confronted with a complex interaction of dermatological symptoms with psychological and social factors. The process of identifying psychological problems, motivating the patient for treatment, and finally referring the patient to a psychologist or psychiatrist can be a time-consuming process (Gieler et al., 1997; Koblenzer, 1987). An important implication of the research presented in this chapter for clinical practice is the need for a close collaboration of dermatologists, psychologists, and psychiatrists.

REFERENCES

Al'Abadie, M. S., Kent, G. G., & Gawkrodger, D. J. (1994). The relationship between stress and the onset and exacerbation of psoriasis and other skin conditions. *British Journal of Dermatology, 130,* 199–203.

Alexander, F. (1950). *Psychosomatic medicine.* New York: Norton.

Allen, K., & Harris, F. (1966). Elimination of a child's excessive scratching by training the mother in reinforcement procedures. *Behaviour Research and Therapy, 4,* 79–84.

American Psychiatric Association. (1994). *Diagnostic and statistical manual of mental disorders* (4th ed.). Washington, DC: Author.

Arnetz, B. B., & Fjellner, B. (1985). Psychological predictors of pruritus during mental stress. *Acta Dermatologica et Venereologica, 65,* 504–508.

Arnetz, B. B., Fjellner, B., Eneroth, P., & Kallner, A. (1985). Stress and psoriasis: Psychoendocrine and metabolic reactions in psoriatic patients during standardized stressor exposure. *Psychosomatic Medicine, 47,* 528–541.

Avia, M. D., Ruiz, M. A., Olivares, M. E., Crespo, M., Guisado, A. B., Sachez, A., & Varela, A. (1996). The meaning of psychological symptoms: Effectiveness of a group intervention with hypochondriacal patients. *Behaviour Research and Therapy, 34,* 23–31.

Azrin, N. H., & Nunn, R. G. (1973). Habit-reversal: A method of eliminating nervous habits and tics. *Behaviour Research and Therapy, 11,* 619–628.

Azrin, N. H., Nunn, R. G., & Frantz, E. E. (1980). Treatment of hairpulling (trichotillomania): A comparative study of habit reversal and negative practice training. *Journal of Behaviour Therapy and Experimental Psychiatry, 11,* 13–20.

Barsky, A. J., & Wyshak, G. (1992). Hypochondriasis and somatosensory amplification. *British Journal of Psychiatry, 157,* 404–409.

Barsky, A. J., Wyshak, G., & Klerman, G. L. (1992). Psychiatric comorbidity in DSM-III-R hypochondriasis. *Archives of General Psychiatry, 49,* 101–108.

Barsky, A. J., Wyshak, G., Klerman, G. L., & Latham, K. S. (1990). The prevalence of hypochondriasis in medical outpatients. *Social Psychiatry and Psychiatric Epidemiology, 25,* 89–94.

Baughman, R., & Sobel, R. (1971). Psoriasis, stress, and strain. *Archives of Dermatology, 103,* 599–605.

Beck, A. T., & Freeman, A. (Eds.). (1990). *Cognitive therapy of personality disorders.* New York: Guilford.

Beck, A. T., Ward, C. H., Mendelson, M., Mock, J., & Erbraugh, H. (1961). An inventory for measuring depression. *Archives of General Psychiatry, 4,* 561–571.

Benoit, L. J., & Harrell, E. H. (1981). Biofeedback and control of skin cell proliferation in psoriasis. *Psychological Reports, 46,* 831–839.

Bernard, J. D., Kristeller, J., & Kabat-Zinn, J. (1988). Effectiveness of relaxation and visualization techniques as an adjunct to phototherapy and photochemotherapy of psoriasis. *Journal of the American Academy of Dermatology, 19,* 572–574.

Bernhard, J. D (1994). *Itch: Mechanisms and management of pruritus.* New York: McGraw-Hill.

Bethune, H. J., & Kidd, C. B. (1961). Psychophysiological mechanisms in skin diseases. *Lancet, 12,* 1419–1422.

Blanchard, E. B. (1994). Behavioral medicine and health psychology. In A. E. Bergin, & S. L. Garfield (Eds.), *Handbook of psychotherapy and behavior change* (4th ed.) (pp. 701–734). New York: Wiley.

Bosse, K., Fassheber, P., Hünecke, P., Teichmann, A. T., & Zauner, J. (1976). Zur sozialen Situation der Hautkranken als Phänomen der interpersonellen Wahrnehmung (The social situation of skin patients as a phenomenon of interpersonal perception). In K. Bosse & P. Hünecke (Eds.), *Psychodynamik und Soziodynamik bei Hautkranken* (Psychodynamics and social dynamics in skin patients) (pp. 85–92). Göttingen, Germany: Vandenhoek & Ruprecht.

Bosse, K., & Hünecke, P. (1981). Der Juckreiz des endogenen Ekzematikers (Itching in patients with atopic dermatitis). *Münchener Medizinische Wochenschrift, 123,* 1013–1016.

Bremer-Schulte, M., Cormane, R. H., Van Dijk, E., & Wuite, J. (1985). Group therapy of psoriasis. *Journal of the American Academy of Dermatology, 12,* 61–66.

Brown, D. G. (1972). Stress as a precipitant of eczema. *Journal of Psychosomatic Research, 16,* 321–327.

Buske-Kirschbaum, A., Jobst, S., Wustmans, A., Kirschbaum, C., Rauh, W., & Hellhammer, D. (1997). Attenuated free cortisol response to psychosocial stress in children with atopic dermatitis. *Psychosomatic Medicine, 59,* 419–426.

Carney, O., Ross, E., Ikkos, G., & Mindel, A. (1994). The effect of suppressive oral acyclovir on the psychological morbidity associated with recurrent genital herpes. *Genitourinary Medicine, 69,* 457–459.

Cassileth, B. R., Lusk, E. J., Strouse, T. B., Miller, D. S., Brown, L. L., Cross, P. A., & Tenaglia, A. N. (1984). Psychosocial status in chronic illness. *New England Journal of Medicine, 311,* 506–511.

Christenson, G. A., Ristvedt, S. L., & Mackenzie, T. B. (1993). Identification of trichotillomania cue profiles. *Behaviour Research and Therapy, 31,* 315–320.

Clark, D. M., Salkovskis, P. M., Hackmann, A., Wells, A., Fennell, M., Ludgate, J., Ahmad, S., Richards, H. C., & Gelder, M. (1998). Two psychological treatments for hypochondriasis. *British Journal of Psychiatry, 173,* 218–225.

Clark, D. M., & Wells, A. (1995). A cognitive model of social phobia. In R. G. Heimberg, M. Liebowitz, D. Hope, & F. Schneier, F. (Eds.), *Social phobia: Diagnosis, assessment, and treatment* (pp. 69–93). New York: Guilford.

Cohen, F., & Lazarus, R. S. (1979). Coping with the stresses of illness. In G. C. Stone, N. E. Adler, & F. Cohen (Eds.), *Health psychology* (pp. 217–254). San Francisco: Jossey-Bass.

Cole, W. C., Roth, H. L., & Sachs, L. B. (1988). Group psychotherapy as an aid in the medical treatment of eczema. *Journal of the American Academy of Dermatology, 18,* 286–291.

Consoli, S. G. (1995). Dermatitis artefacta: A general review. *European Journal of Dermatology, 5,* 5–11.

Cotterill, J. A. (1981). Dermatological nondisease. *British Journal of Dermatology, 103* (suppl.), 13, 18.

Cotteril, J. A., & Cunliffe, W. J. (1997). Suicide in dermatological patients. *British Journal of Dermatology, 137,* 246–250.

Cunliffe, W. J., & Savin, J. A. (1984). The skin and the nervous system. In A. Rook, D. S. Wilkinson, & F. J. G. Ebling (Eds.), *Textbook of dermatology* (3d ed.) (pp. 2229–2255). Oxford, England: Blackwell Scientific.

Dalkvist, J., Wahlin, T.-B. R., Bartsch, E., & Forsbeck, M. (1995). Herpes simplex and mood: A prospective study. *Psychosomatic Medicine, 57,* 127–137.

Derogatis, L. R. (1977). *SCL-90-R: Administration, scoring and procedures.* Baltimore, MD: Clinical Psychometric Research.

Devins, G. M., & Binik, Y. M. (1996). Faciliating coping with chronic physical illness. In M. Zeidner & N. S. Endler (Eds.), *Handbook of coping: Theory, research, applications* (pp. 640–696). New York: Wiley.

Djuric, V. J., & Bienenstock, J. (1993). Learned sensitivity. *Annals of Allergy, 71,* 5–14.

Doka, K. J. (1997). *Aids, fear, and society.* Bristol, England: Taylor & Francis.

Drob, S., Bernard, H., Lifshutz, H., & Nierenberg, A. (1986). Brief group psychotherapy for herpes patients: A preliminary study. *Behavior Therapy, 17,* 229–238.

Ehlers, A., & Margraf, J. (1989). The psychophysiological model of panic attacks. In P. M. G. Emmelkamp, A. M. Everaerd, F. Kraimaat, & M. J. M. Van Son (Eds.), *Fresh perspectives on anxiety disorders* (pp. 1–29). Amsterdam, Netherlands: Swets & Zeitlinger.

Ehlers, A., Osen, A., Wenninger, K., & Gieler, U. (1994). Atopic dermatitis and stress: The possible role of negative communication with significant others. *International Journal of Behavioral Medicine, 1,* 107–121.

Ehlers, A., Stangier, U., Dohn, D., & Gieler, U. (1993). Kognitive Faktoren beim Juckreiz: Entwicklung und Validierung eines Fragebogens (Cognitive factors in itching: Development and validation of a questionnaire). *Verhaltenstherapie, 3,* 112–119.

Ehlers, A., Stangier, U., & Gieler, U. (1995). Treatment of atopic dermatitis. A comparison of psychological and dermatological approaches to relapse prevention. *Journal of Consulting and Clinical Psychology, 63,* 624–635.

Faravelli, C., Salvatori, S., Galassi, F., Aiazzi, L., Drei, C., & Cabras, P. (1997). Epidemiology of somatoform disorders—a community survey in Florence. *Social Psychiatry and Psychiatric Epidemiology, 32,* 24–29.

Farber, E. M., & Nall, L. (1993). Psoriasis: A stress-related disease. *Cutis, 5,* 322–329.

Faulstich, M. E., Williamson, D., Duchman, E., Conerly, S., & Brantley, P. (1985). Psychophysiological analysis of atopic dermatitis. *Journal of Psychosomatic Research, 29,* 415–417.

Fava, G. A., Perini, G. I., Santonastaso, P., & Fornasa, C. V. (1980). Life events and dermatological disorders: Psoriasis, chronic urticaria and fungal infections. *British Medical Journal, 53,* 277–282.

Favell, J. E., Azrin, N. H., Baumeister, A. A., Carr, E. G., Dorsey, M. F., Forhand, R., Foxx, R. M., Lovaas, O. I., Rincover, A., Risley, T. R., Romanczyk, R. G., Russo, D. C., Schroeder, S. R., & Solnick, J. V. (1982). The treatment of self-injurious behavior. *Behavior Therapy, 13,* 529–554.

Fawzy, F. I., Cousins, N., Fawzy, N. W., Kemeny, M. E., Elashoff, R., & Morton, D. L. (1990). A structured psychiatric intervention for cancer patients: 1. Changes over time in methods of coping and affective disturbance. *Archives of General Psychiatry, 47,* 720–725.

Fawzy, F. I., Fawzy, N. W., Hyun, C. S., Elashoff, R., Guthrie, D., Fahey, J. L., & Morton, D. L. (1993). Malignant melanoma: Effects of an early structured psychiatric intervention, coping, and affective state on recurrence and survival 6 years later. *Archives of General Psychiatry, 50,* 681–689.

Felton, B. J., & Revenson, T. A. (1984). Coping with chronic illness: A study of illness controllability and the influence of coping strategies on psychological adjustment. *Journal of Consulting and Clinical Psychology, 52,* 343–353.

Fiegenbaum, W. (1981). A social training program for clients with facial disfigurations: A contribution to the rehabilitation of cancer patients. *Journal of Rehabilitation Research, 4,* 501–509.

Finlay, A. Y. (1997). Quality of life measurement in dermatology: A practical guide. *British Journal of Dermatology, 136,* 305–314.

First, M. B., Spitzer, R. L., Gibbons, M., & Williams, J. B. W. (1995). *Structured clinical interview for DSM-IV axis I disorders.* Biometrics Research Department, New York State Psychiatric Institute, New York.

Fjellner, B., Arnetz, B. B., Eneroth, P., & Kallner, A. (1985). Pruritus during standardized mental stress. *Acta Dermato-Venereologica, 65,* 199–205.

Folkman, S., Chesney, M., Mckusick, L., Ironson, G., Johnson, D. S., & Coates, T. J. (1991). Translating coping theory into an intervention. In J. Eckenrode (Ed.), *The social context of coping* (pp. 239–260). New York: Plenum.

Folks, D. B., & Kinney, F. C. (1992). The role of psychological factors in dermatologic conditions. *Psychosomatics, 33,* 45–54.

Foreman, J. C. (1987). Neuropeptides and the pathogenesis of allergy. *Allergy, 42,* 1–11.

Freedman, R. R. (1987). Long-term effectiveness of behavioral treatments for Raynaud's disease. *Behavior Therapy, 18,* 387–399.

Fried, R. G. (1994). Evaluation and treatment of "psychogenic" pruritus and self-excoriation. *Journal of the American Academy of Dermatology, 30,* 993–999.

Friedman, S., Hatch, M., & Paradis, C. (1993). Dermatological disorders. In R. J. Gatchel, E. B. Blanchard, & C. Paradis (Eds.) *Psychophysiological disorders, research and clinical applications* (pp. 205–244). Washington, DC: American Psychological Association.

Friman, P. C., Finney, J. W., & Christophersen, E. R. (1984). Behavioral treatment of trichotillomania: An evaluative review. *Behavior Therapy, 15,* 249–265.

Fruensgaard, K. (1984). Neurotic excoriations: A controlled psychiatric examination. *Acta Psychiatrica Scandinavica, 69,* 1–52.

Garrie, E. V., Garrie, S. A., & Mote, T. (1974). Anxiety and atopic dermatitis. *Journal of Consulting and Clinical Psychology, 42,* 742.

Gaston, L., Lassonde, M., Bernier-Buzzanga, J., Hodgins, S., & Crombez, J.-C. (1987). Psoriasis and stress: A prospective study. *Journal of the American Academy of Dermatology, 17,* 82–86.

Gieler, U. (1994). Factitious disease in the field of dermatology. *Psychotherapy and Psychosomatics, 62,* 48–55.

Gieler, U., Stangier, U., & Ehlers, A. (1997). Psychosomatic dermatology. In T. Von Uexküll (Ed.), *Psychosomatic medicine* (pp. 751–763). Munich, Germany: Urban & Schwarzenberg.

Gil, K. M., & Keefe, F. J. (1988). Direct observation of scratching behavior in children with atopic dermatitis. *Behavior Therapy, 19,* 213–227.

Gil, K. M., Keefe, F. J., Sampson, H. A., McCaskill, C. C., Rodin, J., & Crisson, J. E. (1988). Direct observation of scratching behavior in children with atopic dermatitis. *Behavior Therapy, 19,* 213–227.

Ginsburg, I. H. (1995). Psychological and psychophysiological aspects of psoriasis. *Dermatologic Clinics, 13,* 793–804.

Ginsburg, I., & Link, B. (1989). Feelings of stigmatization in patients with psoriasis. *Journal of the American Academy of Dermatology, 20,* 53–63.

Ginsburg, I. H., Prystowsky, J. H., Kornfeld, D. S., & Woland, H. (1993). Role of emotional factors in adults with atopic dermatitis. *International Journal of Dermatology, 32,* 656–660.

Gomez-Perez, H. C., Marks, I. M., & Gutierrez-Fisac, J. L. (1994). Dysmorphophobia: Clinical features and outcome with behaviour therapy. *European Psychiatry, 9,* 229–235.

Gray, S. G., & Lawlis, G. F. (1982). A case study of pruritic eczema treated by relaxation and imagery. *Psychological Reports, 51,* 627–633.

Guglielmi, R. S., Cox, D. J., & Spyker, D. A. (1994). Behavioral treatment of phobic avoidance in multiple chemical sensitivity. *Journal of Behaviour Therapy and Experimental Psychiatry, 25,* 197–203.

Gupta, M. A., & Gupta, A. K. (1995). The psoriasis life stress inventory: A preliminary index of psoriasis-related stress. *Acta Dermato-Venereologica, 75,* 240–243.

Gupta, M. A., & Gupta, A. K. (1996). Psychodermatology: An update. *Journal of the American Academy of Dermatology, 34,* 1030–1046.

Gupta, M. A., Gupta, A. K., & Habertman, H. F. (1987). Psorasis and psychiatry: An update. *General Hospital Psychiatry 1987, 9,* 157–166.

Gupta, M. A., Gupta, A. K., Kirkby, S., Weiner, H. K., Mace, T. M., Schorck, N. J., Johnson, E. H., Ellis, C. N., & Vorhees, J. J. (1989). Pruritus in psoriasis: A prospective study of some psychiatric and dermatologic correlates. *Archives of Dermatology, 124,* 1052–1057.

Gupta, M. A., Gupta, A. K., Schork, N. J., & Ellis, C. N. (1994). Depression modulates pruritus perception: A study of pruritus in psoriasis, atopic dermatitis, and chronic idiopathic urticaria. *Psychosomatic Medicine, 56,* 36–40.

Gupta, M. A., Gupta, A. K., & Watteel, G. N. (1997). Stress and pruritus in atopic dermatitis. *Psychosomatic Medicine, 59,* 77–108 (abstracts).

Gupta, M. A., Schork, N. J., & Gupta, A. K. (1993). Suicidal ideation in psoriasis. *International Journal of Dermatology, 32,* 188–190.

Harris, J., & Sieveking, N. (1979). Case study in hyperhidrosis. *American Journal of Clinical Biofeedback, 2,* 31.

Hashiro, M., & Okumura, M. (1994). Anxiety, depression and psychosomatic symptoms and autonomic nervous function in patients with chronic urticaria. *Journal of Dermatological Science, 8,* 129–135.

Hashiro, M., & Okumura, M. (1997). Anxiety, depression and psychosomatic symptoms in patients with atopic dermatitis: Comparison with normal controls and among groups of different degrees of severity. *Journal of Dermatological Science, 14,* 63–67.

Haynes, S. N., Wilson, C. C., Jaffe, P. G., & Britton, B. T. (1979). Biofeedback treatment of atopic dermatitis. *Biofeedback and Self-Regulation, 4,* 195–209.

Hermanns, N., & Scholz, O. B. (1992). Kognitive Einflüsse auf einen histamininduzierten Juckreiz und Quaddelbildung bei der atopischen Dermatitis (Cognitive factors modifying histamine-induced itching and wheals in atopic dermatitis*). Verhaltensmodifikation & Verhaltensmedizin, 13,* 171–194.

Hollander, E., Cohen, L. J., & Simeon, D. (1993). Body dysmorphic disorder. *Psychiatric Annals, 23,* 359–364.

Hollander, E., Cohen, L. J., Simeon, D., & Rosen, J. (1994). Fluvoxamine treatment of body dysmorphic disorder. *Journal of Clinical Psychopharmacology, 14,* 75–77.

Hollander, E., & Phillips, K. A. (1991). *YBOCS modified for body dysmorphic disorder.* Unpublished manuscripts.

Hollander, M. B. (1958). Excoriated acne controlled by post-hypnotic suggestion. *American Journal of Clinical Hypnosis, 1,* 122–123.

Hughes, H., Brown, B. W., Lawlis, G. F., & Fulton, J. E. (1983). Treatment of acne vulgaris by biofeedback, relaxation and cognitive imagery. *Psychosomatic Research, 27,* 185–191.

Hughes, J., Barraclough, B., Hamblin, L., & White, J. E. (1983). Psychiatric symptoms in dermatology patients. *British Journal of Psychiatry, 143,* 51–54.

Hünecke, P. (1993). Entstellungsgefühle und strukturiertes Video-Feedback—Orientierende Befunde und Überlegungen für einen neuen psychotherapeutischen Ansatz (Disfigurement and structured video-feedback—preliminary findings and suggestions for a new psychotherapeutic approach). In U. Gieler, U. Stangier, & E. Brähler (Eds.), *Hauterkrankungen in psychologischer Sicht. Jahrbuch der medizinischen Psychologie* (Bd. 9) (pp. 81–92). Göttingen, Germany: Hogrefe.

Ikemi, Y., Nakagawa, S., Kusano, T., & Sugita, F. (1970). The application of autogenic training to "psychological desensitization" of allergic disorders. In W. Luthe & J. H. Schultz, *Autogenic therapy: Research and therapy.* (Vol. 4.) (pp. 228–233). New York: Grune & Stratton.

Jordan, J. M., & Whitlock, F. A. (1972). Emotions and the skin: The conditioning of scratch responses in case of atopic dermatitis. *British Journal of Dermatology, 86,* 574–585.

Jordan, J. M., & Whitlock, F. A. (1974). Atopic dermatitis, anxiety and conditioned scratch responses. *Journal of Psychosomatic Research, 18,* 297–299.

Jowett, S., & Ryan, T. (1985). Skin disease and handicap: An analysis of the impact of skin conditions. *Social Science and Medicine, 20,* 425–429.

Kanfer, F., & Karoly, P. (1972). Self-control: A behavioristic excursion into the lion's den. *Behavior Therapy, 3,* 398–416.

Katon, W., Kleinmann, A., & Rosen, G. (1982). Depression and somatization: A review. Part I. *American Journal of Medicine, 72,* 127–135.

King, R. M., & Wilson, G. V. (1991). Use of a diary technique to investigate psychosomatic relations in atopic dermatitis. *Journal of Psychosomatic Research, 35,* 697–706.

Klonoff, E. A., Youngner, S. J., Moore, D. J., & Hershey, L. A. (1983). Chronic factitious illness: A behavioral approach. *International Journal of Psychiatry in Medicine, 13,* 173–183.

Koblenzer, C. S. (1987). Psychocutaneous disease. New York: Grune & Stratton.

Koblenzer, C. S. (1993). Psychological aspects of skin disease. In J. B. Fitzpatrick, A. Z. Eisen, K. Wolff, I. M.

Freddberg, & K. F. Austen (Eds.), *Dermatology in general medicine* (4th ed.) (pp. 14–26). New York: McGraw-Hill.

Koblenzer, C. S., & Bostrom, P. (1994). Chronic cutaneous dysesthesia syndrome: A psychotic phenomenon or a depressive symptom? *Journal of the American Academy of Dermatology, 30,* 370–374.

Koehn, K., Burnette, M. M., & Stark, C. (1993). Applied relaxation training in the treatment of genital herpes. *Journal of Behaviour Therapy and Experimental Psychiatry, 24,* 331–341.

Köhler, T., & Weber, D. (1992). Psychophysiological reactions of patients with atopic dermatitis. *Journal of Psychosomatic Research, 36,* 391–394.

Koo, J. Y. M., Shellow, W. V. R., Hallman, C. P., & Edwards, J. E. (1994). Alopecia areata and increased prevalence of psychiatric disorders. *International Journal of Dermatology, 33,* 849–850.

Kraus, S. J. (1974). Stress, acne and skin surface free fatty acids. In P. M. Insel & R. H. Moos (Eds.), *Health and the social environment* (pp. 81–88). Lexington, MA: Heath.

Laidlaw, T. M., Booth, R. J., & Large, R. G. (1994). The variability of type I hypersensitivity reactions: The importance of mood. *Journal of Psychosomatic Research, 38,* 51–61.

Latimer, P. A. (1979). The behavioral treatment of self-excoriation in a twelve-year-old girl. *Journal of Behaviour Therapy and Experimental Psychiatry, 10,* 349–352.

Leichtman, S. R., Burnett, J. W., & Robinson, H. M. (1981). Body image concerns of psoriasis patients as reflected in human figure drawings. *Journal of Personality Assessment, 45,* 478–483.

Levenson, H. L., Hamer, R. M., Meyers, T., Hart, R. P., & Kaplowitz, L. G. (1987). Psychological factors predict symptoms of severe recurrent genital herpes infection. *Journal of Psychosomatic Research, 31,* 153–159.

Leventhal, E., Suls, J., & Leventhal, H. (1993). Hierarchical analysis of coping: Evidence from life-span studies. In H. W. Krohne (Ed.), *Attention and avoidance* (pp. 71–99). Seattle, WA: Hogrefe & Huber.

Leventhal, H., Nerenz, D. R., & Steele, D. J. (1984). Illness representations and coping with health threats. In A. Baum, S. E. Taylor, & J. E. Singer (Eds.), *Handbook of psychology and health* (Vol. 4) (pp. 219–252). Hillsdale, NJ: Erlbaum.

Lewinsohn, P. M., & Libet, J. (1972). Pleasant events, activity schedules, and depression. *Journal of Abnormal Psychology, 78,* 291–295.

Linehan, M. M. (1990). *Cognitive-behavioral treatment of borderline personality disorder.* New York: Guilford.

Logsdail, S., Lovell, K., Warwick, H., & Marks, I. (1991). Behavioural treatment of AIDS-focused illness phobia. *British Journal of Psychiatry, 159,* 422–425.

Longo, D., Clum, G., & Yaeger, N. J. (1988). Psychosocial treatment for recurrent genital herpes. *Journal of Consulting and Clinical Psychology, 56,* 61–66.

Luthe, W., & Schultz, J. H. (1969). *Autogenic therapy* (Vol. 2). Medical applications. New York: Grune & Stratton.

Lyketsos, G. C., Stratigos, J., Tawil, G., Psaras, M., & Lyketsos, C. G. (1985). Hostile personality characteristics, dysthymic states and neurotic symptoms in urticaria, psoriasis and alopecia. *Psychotherapy and Psychosomatics, 44,* 122–131.

Marks, I. M. (1987). *Fears, phobia and rituals.* Oxford, England: Oxford University Press.

Marks, I., & Mishan, J. (1988). Dysmorphophobic avoidance with disturbed bodily perception. *British Journal of Psychiatry, 152,* 674–678.

Marshall, P. S. (1993). Allergy and depression: A neurochemical threshold model of the relation between the illnesses. *Psychological Bulletin, 113,* 23–43.

Mattick, R. P., & Clarke, J. C. (1998). Development and validation of measures of social phobia, scrutiny fear and social interaction anxiety. *Behaviour Research and Therapy, 36,* 455–470.

McCracken, L. M., Faber, S. D., & Janeck, A. S. (1997). Pain-related anxiety predicts non-specific physical complaints in persons with chronic pain. *Behaviour Research and Therapy, 36,* 621–630.

McElroy, S. L., Phillips, K. A., Keck, P. E., Hudson, J. I., & Pope, H. G. (1993). Body dysmorphic disorder: Does it have a psychotic subtype? *Journal of Clinical Psychiatry, 54,* 389–395.

McKay, D., Todaro, J., Neziroglu, F., Campisi, T., Moritz, E. K., & Yaryura-Tobias, J. S. (1997). Body dysmorphic disorder: A preliminary evaluation of treatment and maintenance using exposure with response prevention. *Behaviour Research and Therapy, 35,* 67–70.

McMenamy, C. J., Katz, R. C., & Gipson, M. (1988). Treatment of eczema by EMG biofeedback and relaxation training: A multiple baseline analysis. *Journal of Behaviour Therapy and Experimental Psychiatry, 19,* 221–227.

Medansky, R. S., Handler, R. M., & Medansky D. L. (1981). Self-evaluation of acne and emotion: A pilot study. *Psychosomatics, 22,* 379–383.

Melin, L., Frederiksen, T., Noren, P., & Swebilius, C. B. (1986). Behavioral treatment of scratching in patients with atopic dermatitis. *British Journal of Dermatology, 115,* 467–474.

Miller, R., Conger, R., & Dymond, A. (1974). Biofeedback skin conductance conditioning in dyshidrotic eczema. *Archives of Dermatology, 109,* 737–738.

Moan, E. R. (1979). GSR biofeedback assisted relaxation training and psychosomatic hives. *Journal of Behaviour Therapy and Experimental Psychiatry, 10,* 157–158.

Morrison, J., & Herbstein, J. (1988). Secondary affective disorder in women with somatization disorder. *Comprehensive Psychiatry, 29,* 433–440.

Munro, A., & Chimara, J. (1982). Monosymptomatic hypochondriacal psychosis: A diagnostic checklist based on 50 cases of the disorder. *Canadian Journal of Psychiatry, 27,* 374–376.

Newell, R., & Shrubb, S. (1994). Attitude change and behaviour therapy in body dysmorphic disorder: Two case reports. *Behavioural and Cognitive Psychotherapy, 22,* 163–199.

Neziroglu, F., & Yaryura-Tobias, J. S. (1993). Exposure, response prevention, and cognitive therapy in the treatment of body dysmorphic disorder. *Behavior Therapy, 24,* 431–438.

Niebel, G. (1995). *Verhaltensmedizin der chronischen Hautkrankheit (Behavioral medicine of chronic skin disease).* Seattle, WA: Huber Verlag.

Öst, L. G. (1987). Applied relaxation: Description of a coping technique and review of controlled studies. *Behaviour Research and Therapy, 25,* 397–410.

Pariante, C. M., Carpiniello, B., Rudas, N., Piludu, G., & Del Giacco, G. S. (1994). Anxious symptoms influence delayed-type hypersensitivity skin test in subjects devoid of any psychiatric morbidity. *International Journal of Neuroscience, 79,* 275–283.

Pearson, D. J. (1988). Psychologic and somatic interrelationships in allergy and pseudoallergy. [Review]. *Journal of Allergy and Clinical Immunology, 81,* 351–360.

Perini, G. I., Fornasa, C. V., Cipriani, R., Bettin, A., Zecchino, F., & Peserico, A. (1984). Life events and alopecia areata. *Psychotherapy and Psychosomatics, 41,* 48–52.

Philipps, K. A. (1991). *Diagnostic module for body dysmorphic disorder.* Unpublished manuscript.

Philipps, K. A., McElroy, S. L., Keck, P. E., Pope, H. G., & Hudson, J. I. (1993). Body dysmorphic disorder: 30 cases of imagined ugliness. *American Jounal of Psychiatry, 150,* 302–308.

Pilowski, I. (1967). Dimensions of hypochondriasis. *British Journal of Psychiatry, 113,* 89–93.

Plassmann, R. (1994). Structural disturbances in the body self. *Psychotherapy and Psychosomatics, 62,* 91–96.

Porter, J. R., Hill-Beuf, A. H., Lerner, A. B., & Nordlund, J. (1986). Psychosocial effect of vitiligo: A comparison of vitiligo patients with "normal" control subjects, with psoriasis patients and with patients with other pigmentary disorders. *Journal of the American Academy of Dermatology, 15,* 220–224.

Price, L., Mottahedin, I., & Mayo, P. R. (1991). Can psychotherapy help patients with psoriasis? *Clinical and Experimental Dermatology, 16,* 114–117.

Rasmussen, S. A. (1985). Obsessive-compulsive disorder in dermatology practice. *Journal of the American Academy of Dermatology, 13,* 965–967.

Ratliff, R. G., & Stein, N. H. (1968). Treatment of neurodermatitis by behaviour therapy: A case study. *Behavior Research and Therapy, 6,* 397–399.

Rechhardt, E. (1970). *An investigation of psychosomatic aspects of prurigo besnier.* Monographs from the Psychiatric Clinic of the Helsinki University Central Hospital. Helsinki, Finland.

Ring, J. (1993). Atopic diseases and mediators. *International Archives of Allergy and Immunology, 101,* 305–307.

Roback, H. B., Kirshner, H., & Roback, E. (1981). Physical self-concept changes in a mildly, facially disfigured neurofibromatosis patient following communication skill training. *International Journal of Psychiatry in Medicine, 11,* 237–243.

Roca, R. P., Wigley, F. M., & White, B. (1996). Depressive symptoms associated with scleroderma. *Arthritis and Rheumatology, 39,* 1035–1040.

Rook, A., Savin, J. A., & Wilkinson, D. S. (1984). Psychocutaneous disorders. In A. Rook, D. S. Wilkinson, & F. J. G. Ebling (Eds.), *Textbook of dermatology* (4th ed.) (pp. 2257–2267). Oxford, England: Blackwell Scientific.

Rosen, J. C., Reiter, J., & Orosan, P. (1995). Cognitive-behavioral body image therapy for body dysmorphic disorder. *Journal of Consulting and Clinical Psychology, 64,* 263–269.

Rosenbaum, M. S., & Ayllon, T. (1981). The behavioral treatment of neurodermatitis through habit-reversal. *Behaviour Research and Therapy, 19,* 313–318.

Rubinow, D. R., Peck, G. L., Squillace, K. M., & Gantt, G. G. (1987). Reduced anxiety and depression in cystic acne patients after successful treatment with oral isotretinoin. *Journal of the American Academy of Dermatology, 17,* 25–32.

Salkovskis, P. M. (1989). Somatic problems. In K. Hawton, P. M. Salkovskis, J. Kirk, & D. M. Clark (Eds.), *Cognitive behaviour therapy for psychiatric problems* (pp. 235–276). Oxford, England: Oxford University Press.

Salvaggio, J. E. (1994). Psychological aspects of "environmental illness," "multiple chemical sensitivity," and building-related illness. *Journal of Allergy and Clinical Immunology, 94,* 366–370.

Scheich, G., Florin, I., Rudolph, R., & Wilhelm, S. (1993). Personality characteristics and serum IgE level in patients with atopic dermatitis. *Journal of Psychosomatic Research, 37,* 637–642.

Schmid-Ott, G., Jacobs, R., Jaeger, B., Klages, S., Wolf, J., Werfel, T. W., Kapp, A., Schuermeyer, T., Lamprecht, F., Schmidt, R. E., & Schedlowski, M. (1998). Stress-induced endocrine and immunological changes in psoriasis patients and healthy controls: An explorative study. *Psychotherapy and Psychosomatics, 67*, 37–42.

Schmidt-Traub, S., & Bamler, K.-J. (1997). The psychoimmunological association of panic disorder and allergic reaction. *British Journal of Clinical Psychology, 36*, 51–62.

Schomer, H. H., & Vergunst, J. R. (1992). Psychological factors in epidermolysis. *South African Medical Journal, 81*, 530.

Scragg, P. (1995). A critical analysis of morbid fear of HIV/AIDS. *Clinical Psychology and Psychotherapy, 2*, 278–284.

Sheehan-Dare, R. A., Henderson, M. J., & Cotteril, J. A. (1990). Anxiety and depression in patients with chronic urticaria and generalized pruritus. *British Journal of Dermatology, 123*, 769–774.

Silver, P. S., Auerbach, S. M., Vishniavsky, N., & Kaplowitz, L. G. (1986). Psychological factors in recurrent genital herpes infection: Stress, coping style, social support, emotional dysfunction, and symptom recurrence. *Journal of Psychosomatic Research, 30*, 163–171.

Simon, G. E., Daniell, W., Stockbridge, H., Claypoole, K., & Rosenstock, L. (1993). Immunologic, psychological and neuropsychological factors in multiple chemical sensitivity. *Annals Internal Medicine, 19*, 97–103.

Sneddon, I., & Sneddon, J. (1975). Self-inflicted injury: A follow-up study of 43 patients. *British Medical Journal, 3*, 527–530.

Stangier, U., Ehlers, A., & Gieler, U. (1998). Measuring adjustment to chronic skin disorders: Validation of a specific self-report measure. Submitted for publication.

Stangier, U., & Gieler, U. (1998). Somatoform disorders in dermatology. Paper presented at the Fifth International Congress of Behavioral Medicine, Copenhagen, Denmark.

Stangier, U., Gieler, U., Dietrich, M., Florin, I. (1988). *Verhaltenstherapeutische Ansätze bei Psoriasis vulgaris— Erste Ergebnisse einer kontrollierten Therapievergleichsstudie (Behaviour Therapy in proriasis vulgaris— preliminary results of a controlled treatment study).* In W. Schüffel (Ed.), Sich gesund fühlen im Jahre 2000 (pp. 445–451). Berlin, Germany: Springer.

Stangier, U., Gieler, U., & Ehlers, A. (1996). *Neurodermitis bewältigen: Verhaltenstherapie, Dermatologische Schulung, Autogenes Training (Coping with atopic dermatitis: Behaviour therapy, dermatological education, autogenic training).* Berlin, Germany: Springer.

Stangier, U., Ehlers, A., & Gieler, U. (1999). Measuring Adjustment to chronic skin disorders: validation of a specific self-report measure. Psychological Assessment (accepted for publication).

Stanley, M. A., Prather, R. C., Wagner, A. L., Davis, M. L., & Swan, A. C. (1993). Can the Yale-Brown Obsessive-Compulsive Scale be used to assess trichotillomania? A preliminary report. *Behaviour Research and Therapy, 31*, 171–177.

Stein, D. J., & Hollander, E. (1992). Dermatology and conditions related to obsessive-compulsive disorder. *Journal of the American Academy of Dermatology, 26*, 237–242.

Stein, D. J., & Hollander, E. (1993). The spectrum of obsessive-compulsive related disorders. In E. Hollander (Ed.), *Obsessive-compulsive related disorders* (pp. 241–271). Washington, DC: American Psychiatric Press.

Sternbach, R. A. (1966). Principles of psychophysiology: An introductory text and readings. San Diego, CA: Academic Press.

Swedo, S. E., Leonard, H. L., Rapoport, J. L., Lenanae, M. C., Goldberger, E. L., & Cheslow, D. L. (1989). A double-blind comparison of clomipramine and desipramine in the treatment of trichotillomania (hair pulling). *New England Journal of Medicine, 321*, 497–501.

Temoshok, L., Heller, B. W., Sagebiel, R. W., Blois, M. S., Sweet, D. M., DiClemente, R. J., & Gold, M. L. (1984). The relationship of psychosocial factors to prognostic indicators in cutaneous malignant melanoma. *Journal of Psychosomatic Research, 29*, 139–153.

Twerski, A. J., & Naar, R. (1974). Hypnotherapy in a case of refractory dermatitis. *American Journal of Clinical Hypnosis, 16*, 202–205.

Veale, D., Gournay, K., Dryden, W., Boocock, A., Shah, F., Willson, R., & Walburn, J. (1996). Body dysmorphic disorder: A cognitive behavioural model and pilot ranomised controlled trial. *Behaviour Research and Therapy, 34*, 717–729.

Warner, L. C., & Fisher, B. K.(1986). Cutaneous manifestations of the acquired immunodeficiency syndrome. *International Journal of Dermatology, 25*, 337–350.

Warwick, H. M. C., Clark, D. M., Cobb, A. M., & Salkovskis, P. M. (1996). A controlled trial of cognitive-behavioural treatment of hypochondriasis. *British Journal of Psychiatry, 169*, 189–195.

Watson, D. L., Tharp, R. G., & Krisberg, J. (1972). Case study in self-modification: Suppression of inflammatory scratching while awake and asleep. *Journal of Behavior Therapy and Experimental Psychiatry, 3*, 213–215.

Wekking, E. M., Vingerhoeb, A. J., van Dam, A. P., Nossent, J. C., & Swaak, A. J. (1991). Daily stressors and systemic lupus erythematosus: A longitudinal analysis, first findings. *Psychotherapy and Psychosomatics, 55*, 108–113.

Welkowitz, L. A., Held, J. L., & Held, A. L. (1989). Management of neurotic scratching with behavioral therapy. *Journal of the American Academy of Dermatology, 21,* 802–804.

Wells, A., & Hackman, A. (1993). Imagery and core beliefs in health anxiety: Content and origins. *Behavioural and Cognitive Psychotherapy, 21,* 265–273.

Wells, A., White, J., & Carter, K. (1997). Attention training: Effects on anxiety and beliefs in panic and social phobia. *Clinical Psychology and Psychotherapy, 4,* 226–232.

Wessley, S. C. (1990). Dermatologic complaints. In C. M. Bass (Ed.), *Somatization: Physical symptoms and psychological illness* (pp. 276–299). Oxford, England: Blackwell Scientific.

Wessley, S., & Lewis, G. (1989). The classification of psychiatric morbidity in attenders at the dermatology clinic. *British Journal of Psychiatry, 155,* 686–691.

White, A., Horne, D. J., & Varigos, G. A. (1990). Psycho-logical profile of the atopic eczema patient. *Australasian Journal of Dermatology, 31,* 13–16.

Whitlock, F. A. (1976). *Psychophysiological aspects of skin disease.* London: Saunders.

World Health Organization. (1992). *The ICD-10 classification of mental and behavioural disorders.* Geneva, Switzerland: Author.

Wu, S., Kinder, B. N., Trunnell, T. N., & Fulton, J. E. (1988). Role of anxiety and anger in acne patients: A relationship with the severity of the disorder. *Journal of the American Academy of Dermatology, 18,* 325–333.

Zacchariae, R., Oster, H., Bjerring, P., & Kragballe, K. (1996). Effects of psychologic intervention on psoriasis: A preliminary report. *Journal of the American Academy of Dermatology, 34,* 1008–1015.

Zeidner, M., & Saklofske, D. (1996). Adaptive and maladaptive coping. In M. Zeidner & N. S. Endler (Eds.), *Handbook of coping: Theory, research, applications* (pp. 505–531). New York: Wiley.

CHAPTER 20

MANAGEMENT OF STRESS AND ANXIETY IN SMOKING AND SMOKING CESSATION

Geir Smedslund

K. Gunnar Götestam

This chapter deals with anxiety, various symptoms of distress, negative emotions, and their relationships to smoking and smoking cessation. Despite widespread knowledge in the general population about the hazards of smoking (USDHHS, 1989), large numbers of smokers have found it hard to quit. Although most smokers want to quit smoking, most who make an attempt soon relapse. One reason for this is the high level of stress associated with abstaining from the drug nicotine. Nicotine dependence is the most common substance use disorder in the United States (Hughes, 1995). In this chapter we review findings regarding the relationship of stress and anxiety to smoking initiation, continuation, cessation, and relapse.

Anxiety and stress may influence the smoking process at different points. Distressed persons may be more prone to begin smoking as teenagers. As regular smokers they may smoke more than their less distressed fellow smokers. Distressed smokers may also have a harder time quitting because of severe withdrawal symptoms. If these hypotheses are confirmed, there are implications both for the prevention of smoking initiation and for smoking cessation programs. Both anxiety and smoking have genetic components, but are these components related? We have devoted a section to a short discussion about whether certain individuals are predisposed to become addicted to nicotine.

DIAGNOSTIC CATEGORIES

Nicotine is a stimulant that increases heart rate and blood pressure (Gilbert & Spielberger, 1987). Due to vascular constriction, peripheral blood flow is reduced.

Throughout this chapter, the *Diagnostic and Statistical Manual of Mental Disorders*, 4th edition (*DSM-IV*) (American Psychiatric Association [APA], 1994) is used. The *DSM-IV* uses the general category of Substance-Related Disorders with 11 subcategories, of which Nicotine-Related Disorders is one. Nicotine-Related Disorders is further divided into Nicotine Use Disorder (305.10 Nicotine Dependence) and Nicotine-Induced Disorder (292.0 Nicotine Withdrawal and 292.9 Nicotine-Related Disorder Not Otherwise Specified).

The *DSM-IV* provides texts and criteria for the generic aspects of substance dependence. Each substance, however, is associated with a specific withdrawal syndrome, with specific tolerance potential, intoxication syndrome, et cetera. In addition, the severity of dependence has been found to vary according to the specific substance. The concept of dependence syndrome with graded levels of severity was originally derived from work with alcoholics. The applicability and clinical utility of the dependence syndrome across a wider range of substances was examined as part of the *DSM-IV* field trials (Woody, Cottler, & Cacciola, 1993). When using a criterion count method to assess severity, it was discovered that persons cluster at different severity levels according to the drug on which they are dependent. While two-thirds of those fulfilling dependence criteria for heroin, opiates, or cocaine had high dependence severity, it was quite the opposite for nicotine dependence. Two-thirds of those with dependence on nicotine were in the low/moderate severity range. But only 13.3% of those who had used tobacco did *not* meet dependence criteria. In contrast,

46.7% of those who had used alcohol, 56.5% of those using amphetamines, and 58.7% of those using cannabis did not meet dependence criteria. Over 80% of those who had used tobacco six or more times met dependence criteria, yet among those who were dependent, 78% had mild or moderate dependence severity. Tobacco thus readily produces dependence, but it does not progress to severe levels of dependence as readily as cocaine, heroin, and most other drugs. Although it easily causes compulsive use, tolerance, and withdrawal, tobacco may be less likely than most other substances to get "out of control" and progress to severe dependence (Woody et al., 1993).

Nicotine Intoxication

Intoxication is a generic category of substance-induced disorders in *DSM-IV,* but it does not apply to nicotine. Nicotine intoxication rarely occurs and has not been well studied (APA, 1994).

Nicotine Dependence (Nicotine Use Disorder)

Lifetime prevalence of nicotine dependence in the United States has been estimated to be about 20%. The prevalence of nicotine dependence for current smokers lies between 50% and 80%. Tolerance to nicotine is manifested by the absence of nausea, dizziness, and other characteristic symptoms despite using substantial amounts of nicotine or a diminished effect observed with continued use of the same amount of nicotine-containing products (APA, 1994).

Nicotine dependence is commonly assessed with a short questionnaire developed by Karl Olov Fagerström, called the Fagerström Tolerance Questionnaire (FTQ) (Fagerström, 1978). The test has recently been slightly changed and renamed the Fagerström Test of Nicotine Dependence (FTND) (Fagerström, Schneider, & Lunell, 1993). The FTQ and FTND are practical, noninvasive instruments that have been shown to correlate with tolerance, withdrawal, nicotine self-administration, cotinine level, and success in smoking cessation (Pomerleau, Majchrzak, & Pomerleau, 1989).

The most common observable signs of nicotine dependence are tobacco odor, cough, evidence of chronic obstructive pulmonary disease, and excessive skin wrinkling. Smoking is also associated with use of caffeine-containing products like coffee, tea, and cola beverages. Since there is a high comorbidity of smoking and alcohol (ab)use, the latter may also be a marker of smoking.

Nicotine Withdrawal (Nicotine-Induced Disorder)

The prevalence of nicotine withdrawal after smoking cessation in the United States has been estimated to be 50%. Nicotine withdrawal may be very similar to alcohol withdrawal. "The essential feature of Nicotine Withdrawal is the presence of a characteristic withdrawal syndrome that develops after the abrupt cessation of, or reduction in, the use of nicotine-containing products following a prolonged period (at least several weeks) of daily use" (APA, 1994, p. 244). The withdrawal syndrome includes four or more of the eight criteria under B:

A. Daily use of nicotine for at least several weeks.
B. Abrupt cessation of nicotine use, or reduction in the amount of nicotine used, followed within 24 hours by four (or more) of the following signs: (1) dysphoric or depressed mood; (2) insomnia; (3) irritability, frustration, or anger; (4) anxiety; (5) difficulty concentrating; (6) restlessness; (7) decreased heart rate; (8) increased appetite or weight gain.
C. The symptoms in Criterion B cause clinically significant distress or impairment in social, occupational, or other important areas of functioning.
D. The symptoms are not due to a general medical condition and are not better accounted for by another mental disorder.

Craving is an important element in nicotine withdrawal and may account for the difficulty that individuals have in giving up nicotine-containing products. Other symptoms associated with nicotine withdrawal are a desire for sweets and impaired performance on tasks requiring vigilance.

DIFFERENCES BETWEEN SMOKERS AND NONSMOKERS IN STRESS, ANXIETY, AND DEPRESSION

Questions of great importance are whether symptoms of distress are related to smoking or smoking cessation if this is a causal relation, and in what direction the cause–effect relation flows. First, if there is a causal relation, then there should be differences in anxiety symptoms between smokers and nonsmokers and there should be a difference in prevalence of smoking between distressed and nondistressed people. Second, if symptoms of distress cause persons to smoke, then the symptoms must precede the smoking in time, and if smoking causes the symptoms, then the smoking must precede the symptoms in time.

Anxiety and Smoking

Psychiatric patients supposedly have higher levels of anxiety than people from the general population. Hughes, Hatsukami, Mitchell, & Dahlgren (1986) reported that psychiatric outpatients had higher smoking prevalence than either local or national population-based samples. In a nonclinical sample, Patton, Barnes, & Murray (1996) reported that teenagers who reported high levels of depression and anxiety were twice as likely to be smokers, after controlling for year level, gender, alcohol use, and parental smoking. Regular smokers were also twice as likely as occasional smokers to report high levels of depression and anxiety. In contrast, Kick and Cooley (1997) found that although current smokers had higher anxiety levels than nonsmokers, anxiety was not significantly related to current smoking. Studies by Canals, Domenech, and Blade (1996) and by Farley and Lester (1995) have not detected any relation between smoking behavior and trait anxiety. Houston and Schneider (1973) studied psychiatric patients and reported that smokers had higher scores on the Taylor Manifest Anxiety Scale than nonsmokers, but they did not find any correlation between anxiety and number of cigarettes smoked per day. Williams, Hudson, and Redd (1982) discovered in a study of manifest anxiety (using the TMAS) that smokers obtained higher scores than nonsmokers on significantly more items in which anxiety manifested as physical rather than psychological symptoms. They argued that physical stimulation

by nicotine may give rise to a lower threshold for anxiety in smokers. On the other hand, a study concerning differences in manifest anxiety with male medical students (using the IPAT Anxiety Scale Questionnaire) found that nonsmokers' anxiety scores were nonsignificantly higher than smokers' scores (Lakshminarayanan & Raguram, 1989). Fleming and Lombardo (1987) used a behavioral avoidance test to assess subjects with rat phobia and did not find any effect of smoking on reported or motoric anxiety.

In short, most but not all studies have reported that, as a group, smokers have more anxiety than nonsmokers. It also seems well documented that persons high on anxiety are more likely to smoke than persons with low anxiety. These findings are in accordance with the hypothesis that smoking causes anxiety. However, the data do not weaken the hypothesis that anxiety causes smoking or that some unknown variable causes both smoking and anxiety. However, a longitudinal study by Cherry and Kiernan (1976) lends some support to the hypothesis that certain personality characteristics are predictive of smoking initiation in adolescents who have not yet started smoking. These investigators identified all infants born in Britain during a particular week and followed them every 2 years. The Eysenck Personality Inventory was administered when the children were 16 years old, and smoking information was obtained at 20 years and 25 years. Those who were smokers at ages 20 and 25 were higher on the Extraversion and Neuroticism scales at age 16.

In sum, there seems to be some evidence that early personality differences cause some adolescents to start smoking and others to remain nonsmokers. The smoking-prone child is extroverted, anxious, frustrated, and antisocial. But most studies in this field have been cross-sectional, so one must be cautious about drawing conclusions.

Depression and Smoking

Depression, whether conceptualized as a trait, symptom, or diagnosis, is overrepresented among smokers (Hall, Muñoz, Reus, & Sees, 1993). Depressed smokers appear to experience more withdrawal symptoms when quitting, are less likely to be successful at quitting, and are more likely to relapse. Therefore, it has been recommended that unsuccessful smokers should be screened for and possibly treated for depression in order to help them to quit smoking (Hughes, 1994). In order to examine whether negative affect was a direct relapse precipitant, Hall, Havassy, and Wasserman (1990) interviewed a sample of cigarette smokers and reported that poor mood was related to relapse when subjects were questioned after the relapse occurred. When the same data were examined prospectively, the relationship disappeared. These data suggest that the occurrence of a lapse may distort perception of the situation in which it occurred. Also, after a lapse a report of poor mood may be used to rationalize failure to abstain.

Predisposition to Nicotine Addiction

The American Psychiatric Association reported in its practice guideline for treating patients with nicotine dependence that the heritability of smoking is as great as or greater than that for alcoholism (APA, 1996). Paulson (1992) argued that smokers with high intrinsic dopamine levels are more prone to addiction than smokers without these high levels. Pomerleau, Collins, Shiffman, & Pomerleau (1993) suggested that initial reinforcement consequences set the stage for subsequent nicotine use. They agreed that it is important to gain an understanding of the contribution of environmental and inherited factors to nicotine dependence, as well as of individual differences in susceptibility to cigarette smoking. Their review of recent animal research and laboratory studies of smokers and never-smokers suggested that vulnerability to nicotine dependence was related to high initial sensitivity to nicotine. While some persons experienced heavy aversive effects of initial smoking, they also seemed to experience a high degree of pleasurable effects, while at the same time developing acute pharmacodynamic tolerance to nicotine. Other persons seemed to be less sensitive; they experienced less aversive *and* less pleasurable consequences, and they did not develop acute tolerance to the drug (Pomerleau et al., 1993).

Personality Differences between Smokers and Nonsmokers

Differences in personality have important consequences for vulnerability to stress and anxiety as well as for managing these conditions. In the literature on personality differences between smokers and nonsmokers,

three basic personality dimensions have primarily been investigated. These are neuroticism, psychoticism, and extroversion/introversion. The three dimensions have been endorsed by Eysenck (e.g., 1986). Gilbert and Gilbert (1995) reported that smokers had more neurotic traits (depression, anxiety, anger) and scored higher on social alienation (psychoticism, impulsivity, unsocialized sensation seeking, low conscientiousness). They also discovered that nicotine intake to a large degree was used as self-medication for mental suffering.

In a review by Dienstbier (1989) it is suggested that extroversion has related somehow to a large capacity for catecholamine secretion from the adrenal medulla. Extroverted individuals seemed to have a low baseline of adrenaline (A), noradrenaline (NA), and dopamine (D) secretion and showed strong and rapid rises in these substances under periods of challenges. Introverted persons, on the other hand, had somewhat higher baseline catecholamine releases. They did not have the ability for rapid rises in A, NA, and D; in fact, they ran the risk of depleting their supplies of these neurotransmitters under stress. They also released cortisol from the adrenal cortex under stress. The exact relationship between neurotransmitters and smoking behavior is not well known, but nicotine certainly interacted with brain receptors related to reward and reinforcement.

Kassel, Shiffman, Gnys, Paty, & Zettler-Segal (1994) examined the degree of sensation seeking in daily smokers, occasional smokers, and nonsmokers. The results revealed that nonsmokers judged themselves as socially more inhibited and less fond of strong stimulation compared with the two smoking groups. Kassel et al. also reported that daily smokers had less self-control, were more impulsive, and had more problems with resisting temptations compared to nonsmokers and occasional smokers. Patton, Barnes, and Murray (1993) examined smoking and personality in 1,257 subjects, and they reported that smokers were most extroverted and also had the highest scores on the psychoticism scale. Male smokers were more neurotic than male nonsmokers and ex-smokers. Patil and Chengti (1987) also found smokers to be more extroverted than nonsmokers.

Grossarth-Maticek and Eysenck (1990) have constructed scales for the measurement of two personality types prone to develop cancer and coronary heart disease and a third scale predictive of staying healthy. Whereas the two disease-prone types have been related to a lack of autonomy or self-regulation, the healthy type was characterized by a high degree of these traits. Smedslund (1995) reported that there were fewer smokers among persons belonging to the healthy personality type than among the disease-prone types.

Although smokers consistently have been found to be more extroverted than nonsmokers, there are both extroverted and introverted smokers as well as nonsmoking extroverts and introverts. Nirmala and Swaminathan (1985) investigated these four groups, and they reported that extroverted smokers were more sensitive, restless, aggressive, and impulsive than extroverted nonsmokers. Introverted smokers were more moody, anxious, rigid, and antisocial than introverted nonsmokers. Nirmala and Swaminathan interpreted the results to mean that smoking may be equally hazardous to a person's mental health as it is to physical health.

It seems that different groups of smokers use nicotine for different reasons. O'Connor (1989) has suggested that extroverted smokers use the stimulating effect of nicotine on the CNS through deep inhalations. Introverted smokers, on the other hand, are interested in maintaining a high degree of concentration and attention. These smokers are directed toward what O'Connor labels the "motoric sensoric aspects of smoking." A similar categorization has been described by Balfour (1993), who points to the causal pathway by which nicotine interacts with brain receptors that usually react to acetylcholine. These receptors are found in the mesolimbic dopamine system, thought to be related to reinforcement and reward of behavior. The fact that both nicotine and other drugs affect this system seems to imply the existence of a general mechanism for drug dependence. Balfour distinguishes between so-called peak seekers and trough maintainers based on their plasma nicotine concentrations. Peak seekers favor short periods with high nicotine concentrations. Trough maintainers can also be called "stability seekers"; they want to avoid very high *and* very low plasma nicotine concentrations. For example, by smoking a cigarette once every hour, the nicotine concentration can be sustained at a very stable level. It has been shown that the mesolimbic system reacts very differently to the two types of

nicotine administration, and this may be related to the addictive nature of the substance.

A third classification was reported by Knott (1979). He makes a differentiation between "high-activation" and "low-activation" smokers. The latter are smokers who have the greatest need to smoke in situations with little external stimulation, characterized by monotony and boredom, while the former have greatest desire for smoking in high-stimulation situations characterized by anxiety and excitement. This group also scored significantly higher on measures of extroversion and neuroticism.

There seem to be many similarities between O'Connor's extroverted/introverted smokers, Balfour's peak seekers/trough maintainers, and Knott's high-activation/low-activation smokers. These classifications may be viewed in light of the theory of optimal arousal (e.g., Eysenck, 1983). Extroverts need much stimulation to maintain a high level of cortical arousal, while introverts prefer less stimulation to keep cortical arousal low.

Personal Space

Every person has a private sphere in which others cannot intrude without causing distress to the person. Kunzendorf and Denney (1982) operationalized this concept of personal space by instructing their subjects to tell a confederate to stop when he had reached a comfortable distance. This distance could thus be exactly measured. Under one condition the confederate smoked and under another condition he did not. On average, the smoking confederate was stopped at a greater distance, thus signaling discomfort due to the cigarette smoke. Another finding was that the number of cigarettes smoked each day correlated positively with the magnitude of ideal personal space; that is, smokers had a desire for larger personal spaces.

ACUTE EFFECTS OF NICOTINE ON STRESS AND ANXIETY

Acute changes following smoking include increases in heart rate, blood pressure, cardiac output, stroke volume, myocardial contractile velocity and force, coronary blood flow, myocardial oxygen consumption, arrhythmia induction, and electrocardiographic changes (U.S. Department of Health, 1979). The sympathomimetic effects of nicotine in increasing cardiac rate and myocardial oxygen demand are aggravated by concomitant inhalation of carbon monoxide, which reduces myocardial oxygen supply by elevating carboxyhemoglobin levels (Pomerleau & Pomerleau, 1989). In other words, nicotine *increases* the oxygen demand while carbon monoxide *reduces* the oxygen supply.

Sympathetic activation produces symptoms typically associated with stress and anxiety. There has been some laboratory research on the combined effects of experimentally induced stress and smoking. The typical study has involved a 2×2 factorial group design (smoking lit cigarette/smoking unlit cigarette ["sham smoking"] and relaxation/stress) (see, e.g., MacDougall, Dembroski, Slaats, Herd, & Eliot, 1983). The MacDougall et al. (1983) study discovered that the condition relaxation/sham smoking had a negligible effect on cardiovascular reactions, whereas relaxation/smoking or stress/sham smoking produced increases of about 15/9 mm/Hg in blood pressure and 15 bpm in heart rate. Subjects in the stress/smoking condition evinced blood pressure and heart rate elevations nearly twice as great.

A later study by the same research group examined individual differences in cardiovascular reactivity (MacDougall, Musante, Howard, Hanes, & Dembroski, 1986). Thirty smokers were given an initial test involving two repetitions of mental arithmetic and paced smoking while blood pressure and heart rate were monitored. The same tests were repeated 2 months later, and large and stable individual differences were observed in cardiovascular reactivity to both stress and smoking.

Smokers frequently report that smoking helps them relax. However, Fagerström and Götestam (1977) reported that muscle tonus actually increased after smoking. Smoking has acute effects on anxiety. It has been found that nicotine significantly increases firing rates in the nucleus accumbens and other central dopaminergic nuclei involved in the mediation of reward (Vaughan, 1990). Smoking reduces anxiety (Pomerleau, Turk, & Fertig, 1984), and withdrawal increases anxiety (Hughes et al., 1986). Gilbert and Spielberger (1987) found that smokers felt less anxious in social situations when smoking, although their heart rate increased. Significant increases in smoking have been reported in response to a variety of laboratory stressors, including stage fright (anxiety) (Rose, Ananda, & Jarvik, 1983). Pomerleau and Pomerleau (1987) used a within-subjects factorial design with two levels of stress (mental arithmetic with and without competition) and monitored degree of ad lib smoking in each condition. They reported increased smoking in the presence of stress/anxiety.

STRESS AND ANXIETY IN SMOKING CESSATION

What happens to anxiety during and following smoking cessation? The *DSM-IV* lists increased anxiety as a nicotine withdrawal symptom. Increased anxiety has been reported to follow smoking cessation in most but not all studies. Indeed, there is some evidence for a reduction in anxiety, compared with precessation levels, after the first few weeks of abstinence. West and Hajek (1997) reported in a study of 101 smokers that there was no increase in anxiety during 4 weeks of abstinence.

There are methodological problems with asking successful quitters and relapsers about their experiences of stress and anxiety during smoking cessation. Such retrospective assessments may be biased because the success or failure may influence the memory of the relapse episode. Prospective designs should be used to overcome these problems.

COPING WITH STRESS AND ANXIETY IN SMOKING CESSATION

More than 90% of smokers who quit do so without help from any formal smoking cessation program (Pechacek, 1984). Carey, Kalra, Carey, Halperin, & Richards, (1993) used a prospective design to evaluate the usefulness of Lazarus and Folkman's (1984) model of stress with respect to unaided smoking cessation. The model predicted that, compared with nonquitters, quitters would (1) report less perceived stress, (2) appraise more gains and fewer losses involved in quitting, (3) express greater smoking self-efficacy, and (4) use more adaptive coping strategies and fewer maladaptive coping strategies. The results supported most of the hypotheses but not all. Quitters and nonquitters did not differ with regard to what they expected to gain and lose as a result of quitting. As for coping strategies, all observed differences were in the predicted direction. Quitters used problem solving and cognitive restructuring more frequently than did nonquitters; nonquitters used more wishful thinking, self-criticism, and social withdrawal than did quitters.

Pharmacological Treatments of Nicotine Dependence

Pharmacotherapies can be divided into replacement therapy, antagonist therapy, therapies to make drug intake aversive, and nonnicotine medications that mimic nicotine effects (APA, 1996). By far the most common are the nicotine replacement therapies.

Nicotine Replacement Therapies (NRTs)

The rationale behind NRT is that nicotine dependence has psychological and behavioral as well as physiological components. Smoking behavior is performed in a large variety of settings, and associations between pleasurable activities and smoking have been learned through classical conditioning. The idea is that it is easier to deal with one component at a time. While working on breaking the links between activities and smoking, the smoker can still get daily doses of nicotine, decreasing withdrawal symptoms.

Nicotine Chewing Gum (Nicotine Polacrilex). The Food and Drug Administration (FDA) approved of nicotine polacrilex for prescription marketing in 1984 and in 1996 for over-the-counter marketing. Nicotine polacrilex delivers plasma nicotine levels somewhat lower than smoking levels but higher than levels achieved by wearing a patch. Nicotine gum has not been proven effective on its own for smoking cessation, but it has a significant effect when combined with behavioral and psychological interventions. Cepeda-Benito (1993) conducted a meta-analysis of the short-term and long-term effects of nicotine gum in combination with intensive treatment and brief treatment. Results indicate that the gum had both short-term and long-term effects in combination with intensive treatment, but only short-term effects in combination with brief treatment. Negative aspects of the gum were that it tasted bad, had some mild adverse effects, and compliance was low.

Transdermal Nicotine (Skin Patches). Nicotine patches were partly developed because of compliance problems with nicotine gum (Fagerström et al., 1993). In 1996 the FDA approved two types of transdermal nicotine patches for over-the-counter marketing. One type is packaged in three different strengths and with instructions for use. The strongest patch is to be used first, followed by the medium-strength patch and then the patch with the lowest strength. Some patches are designed to use for 24 hours, while other patches are designed to be worn for 16 hours. While the 24-hour patches work against craving upon awakening, the nicotine delivery of the 16-hour patches more closely resembles that of smoking cigarettes. The plasma nicotine levels achieved with transdermal delivery systems are much lower than those achieved by smoking, and also lower than levels achieved with nicotine gum. Because of this, the patch has a low abuse liability (Henningfield & Keenan, 1993). A reduction of tobacco withdrawal symptoms through the use of the nicotine patch has been observed in many studies (Jorenby et al., 1996; Transdermal Nicotine Study Group, 1991).

Nicotine Nasal Spray. Two new nicotine medications have been available by prescription since 1996 in the United States. Nicotine nasal spray has been available since the fall of 1997. This is a nicotine solution in a nasal spray bottle similar to those used with antihistamines. Nasal sprays produce droplets that average about 1 mg per administration. This formulation produces a more rapid rise in nicotine levels than does nicotine gum; the rise in nicotine levels produced by nicotine spray falls between those produced by nicotine gum and cigarettes (APA, 1996). Because of the rapidity with which nicotine is absorbed when given as a nasal spray, it might be effective for those for whom the other means of replacement are too slow. Sutherland et al. (1992) conducted a randomized, double-blind, placebo-controlled trial in which 227 cigarette smokers received 4 weeks of supportive group therapy. In addition, 116 subjects received active nasal nicotine spray and 111 subjects received a placebo spray. Each administration contained 0.5 mg substance. Results suggested that the active spray was effective. Twenty-six percent in the active group were biochemically validated as abstinent throughout the whole year, whereas this was true for only 10% of the placebo group. The main side effects of the nasal spray included irritation of the nasal passages and throat, rhinitis, coughing, and tearing, which were tolerated by many but not all patients.

Nicotine Inhalers. The nicotine vapor inhaler was approved for sale in the winter of 1998. These are plugs of nicotine placed inside hollow, cigarette-like rods. The plugs produce a nicotine vapor when warm air is passed through them. Absorption from nicotine inhalers is primarily buccal rather than respiratory. More recent versions of inhalers produce venous nicotine levels that rise more quickly than with nicotine gum but less quickly than with nicotine nasal spray, with nicotine blood levels of about one-third that of between-cigarette levels (APA, 1996).

Summary. In summary, it should be stressed that nicotine intake is highest and fastest for cigarettes, followed by nasal spray, nicotine inhaler, nicotine gum, and nicotine patch. The nicotine patch produces the most stable nicotine delivery. Nicotine replacements can double the rate of long-term smoking cessation, have low abuse liability, and are not associated with severe side effects.

Non-Nicotine Treatments

Lobeline Sulphate. Lobeline is a nontobacco drug that shares tolerance with nicotine on several measures. It has been included in several over-the-counter antismoking medications. The pharmacokinetics of lobeline in humans have not been reported (APA, 1996). Schneider et al. (1996) evaluated the effects of sublingually administered lobeline sulfate on tobacco withdrawal symptoms in abstinent smokers. Tablets containing 2.5, 5.0, or 7.5 mg were administered 3, 6, 9, or 12 times between 8:00 a.m. and 11:00 p.m. on the test day. Smoking was terminated at noon of the previous day. A statistically significant reduction of withdrawal symptoms occurred with increasing cumulative dosage. Maximum efficacy occurred with 7.5 mg taken 9 or 12 times. There were no clinically significant adverse events. It was concluded that further investigation of lobeline's potential as an aid in smoking cessation is warranted.

Bupropion. A sustained release formulation of the antidepressant bupropion hydrochloride was approved by the FDA and first marketed on a prescription basis for the treatment of nicotine dependence in 1997. An advantage for some patients is that it is administered in the form of a pill two times a day. Bupropion has been associated with a seizure risk of approximately 1 per 1,000 up to a dose of 300 mg per day.

Trials of antidepressant medications for smoking cessation have had mixed results. Currently, only bupropion has shown remarkable improvement with nicotine craving. Bupropion acts primarily as a noradrenergic mechanism and has some mild dopaminergic activity, which sets it apart from tricyclics and the other classes of antidepressants (Hyder Ferry & Pettis, 1995). Hurt et al. (1997) have provided evidence for a dose–response relationship between smoking cessation and bupropion. They conducted a double-blind, placebo-controlled trial of a sustained-release form of bupropion for smoking cessation. The 615 subjects were randomly assigned to receive placebo or bupropion for 7 weeks. At the end of 7 weeks of treatment, the rates of smoking cessation as confirmed by carbon monoxide measurements were 19.0% in the placebo group, 28.8% in the 100-mg bupropion group, 38.6% in the 150-mg group, and 44.2% in the 300-mg group ($p < .001$). At 1 year, the respective rates were 12.4%, 19.6%, 22.9%, and 23.1%. The rates for the 150-mg group ($p = .02$) and the 300-mg group ($p = .01$)—but not the 100-mg group ($p = .09$)—were significantly better than those for the placebo group.

Hyder Ferry and Pettis (1995) argued that bupropion's mildness of side effects and lack of abuse liability made it the first non-nicotine replacement option for smokers who are unable to quit smoking, and cite severe nicotine withdrawal symptoms and dysphoria as reasons for relapse.

Cotinine. There has recently been some debate about whether cotinine, the major metabolite of nicotine, has effects on tobacco withdrawal. Although one study discovered that cotinine apparently increased anxiety and tension (Hatsukami, Grillo, Pentel, Oncken, & Bliss, 1997), other studies have not reported this kind of effect (Hatsukami, Pentel, Jensen, Nelson, Allen, Goldman, & Rafael, 1998). The latter study found that cotinine appeared to antagonize the effects of nicotine in the alleviation of withdrawal symptoms at doses that resulted in levels that were three to four times higher than those attained from normal smoking.

From a psychological point of view, treatment of the underlying depressed mood in individuals suffering from major depression may result in increased self-esteem and confidence and allow such individuals to better use other cessation treatments. Alternatively, antidepressants may specifically reduce craving symptomatology associated with withdrawal, secondary to effects on central neurotransmitter systems parallel to those of nicotine (Hall et al., 1993). It is also conceivable that antidepressant medications not only counteract withdrawal symptoms but serve to maintain abstinence through direct and ongoing effects on central mechanisms of reward (Churchill, Pariser, Larson, & Dilsaver, 1989).

BEHAVIORAL STRATEGIES FOR SMOKING CESSATION

One essential aspect of behavioral strategies for smoking cessation is that one starts with a registration of smoking habits. This involves the recording of each cigarette. Each time a cigarette is lighted up, the smoker notes the time, the situation, the mood, and how good that particular cigarette tasted. This provides information about the smoker's specific smoking habits. The information is used later to prepare the smoker for risk situations in which he or she has to take special care.

Reasons for smoking can be grouped into some main categories. One category involves smoking to increase well-being. Another has to do with reducing stress and anxiety. When the smoker becomes aware of his or her risk situations and reasons for smoking, strategies to deal with craving have to be learned and rehearsed.

Education about Symptoms

Smoking withdrawal is associated with a characteristic withdrawal syndrome (described previously). The symptoms may be very unpleasant and lead the smoker into relapse. But educating the smoker before the quit date about these symptoms and emphasizing the fact that the symptoms will decrease during the first week and cease completely during the first month

(Shiffman & Jarvik, 1980) will usually make the symptoms more bearable to the smoker.

Learning Coping Strategies

Effective coping strategies are for the most part individualized. After collecting information about smoking habits, one particular smoker may, for example, learn that he is especially tempted to smoke at parties. One coping strategy may be to avoid all parties for some time until he feels assured that he can withstand the temptation. Or, knowing that craving for cigarettes lasts on average only about 4 minutes, this person may plan to go to the toilet or outside until the craving has passed before returning to the party. Another general coping strategy involves breaking habits. This can be done by switching hand and finger position while smoking. Another example is stopping to smoke while doing other things. For example, the smoker who is used to smoking in her car is encouraged to park the car, have a cigarette, and continue driving afterward. The smoking television viewer may be offered the suggestion that whenever he feels a desire to smoke during a program, he should go outside, have a smoke, and return to the TV program.

The counselor should always bear in mind that the smoker must decide for himself or herself to change or quit his/her smoking. The best way to make an individual *not* change is to try to force or persuade the individual to change (Brehm, 1966; Miller, 1983).

Coping strategies should be rehearsed before the quit date. The last weeks before the quit date should involve nicotine fading, that is, gradually decreasing nicotine intake. This may be done by switching to a brand with lower nicotine content than the person's usual brand and smoking fewer cigarettes during the day. Beaver, Brown, and Lichtenstein (1981) did not find that anxiety management added to the effect of nicotine fading.

Cognitive-Behavioral Treatment of Depression

In the treatment of depressive disorder there is evidence that patients at the low and moderate levels of depression respond best to cognitive-behavioral approaches and that patients with severe levels of depression respond faster to pharmacotherapy (Elkin et al., 1989). It may be that if smokers are too depressed, they lack the energy to attempt the methods taught and place themselves in situations in which they can be reinforced for carrying out the self-change plans. This suggests that smokers who are currently depressed may not do well with smoking cessation cognitive-behavioral treatments.

SUMMARY AND CONCLUSIONS

Tobacco smoking is the most prevalent behavioral disorder in the world today. The fact that millions of Americans continue to smoke despite knowledge of severe health hazards, increasing stigmatization, and restriction of locations for legal smoking is readily explained by the fact that smoking cessation is often accompanied by extreme stress. As a group, smokers show significant differences in basic personality dimensions compared to nonsmokers. Smokers are more neurotic, more extroverted, more impulsive, more sensation seeking, and less socially conforming than nonsmokers. These differences seem to precede smoking initiation because they predict which nonsmoking adolescents will later start to smoke. Among the more than 4,000 chemical substances in cigarettes, nicotine is the main psychoactive constituent (together with its main metabolite, cotinine). The psychopharmacological effects of nicotine vary as a function of dose and rate of administration in such a way that the smoker can use nicotine as a type of self-medication for anxiety and depression. Most smokers have nicotine dependence, which has psychological, behavioral, and physiological components. In recent years several new medications for treating nicotine dependence have been approved by the FDA, and several others that used to be available only on prescription have become over-the-counter products (Henningfield, Gopalan, & Shiffman, 1998). Countless cognitive-behavioral interventions have been developed over the last decades. They share some common features of assessment of individual smoking habits; setting a quit date; learning coping strategies; and close follow-up, especially in the first months after cessation. Programs that combine pharmacological and cognitive-behavioral treatment can help as many as

30–40% of smokers to achieve long-term abstinence. The advancement of computer technology makes it increasingly easy to reach large numbers of smokers with individual or group tailored interventions.

REFERENCES

American Psychiatric Association. (1994). *Diagnostic and statistical manual of mental disorders* (4th ed.). Washington, DC: Author.

American Psychiatric Association. (1996). Practice guideline for the treatment of patients with nicotine dependence. *American Journal of Psychiatry, 153*, 1–31.

Balfour, D. (1993). The pharmacology of nicotine in the CNS and its bearing on nicotine replacement therapies. *International Journal of Smoking Cessation, 2*, 3–9.

Beaver, C., Brown, R. A., & Lichtenstein, E. (1981). Effects of monitored nicotine fading and anxiety management training on smoking reduction. *Addictive Behaviors, 6*, 301–305.

Brehm, J. (1966). *A theory of psychological reactance*. New York: Academic Press.

Canals, J., Domenech, E., & Blade, J. (1996). Smoking and trait anxiety. *Psychological Reports, 79*, 809–810.

Carey, M. P., Kalra, D. L., Carey, K. B., Halperin, S., & Richards, C. S. (1993). Stress and unaided smoking cessation: A prospective investigation. *Journal of Consulting and Clinical Psychology, 61*, 831–838.

Cepeda-Benito, A. (1993). Meta-analytical review of the efficacy of nicotine chewing gum in smoking treatment programs. *Journal of Consulting and Clinical Psychology, 61*, 822–830.

Cherry, N., & Kiernan, K. (1976). Personality scores and smoking behavior. *British Journal of Preventive and Social Medicine, 30*, 123–131.

Churchill, C., Pariser, S., Larson, C., & Dilsaver, S. (1989). Antidepressants and cessation of smoking. *American Journal of Psychiatry, 146*, 1238.

Dienstbier, R. A. (1989). Arousal and physiological toughness: Implications for mental and physical health. *Psychological Review, 96*, 84–100.

Elkin, I., Shea, T., Watkins, J., Imber, S., Sotsky, S., Collins, J., Glass, D., Pilkonis, P., Leber, W., Docherty, J., Fiester, S., & Parloff, M. (1989). National Institute of Mental Health Treatment of Depression Collaborative Research Program: General effectiveness of treatments. *Archives of General Psychiatry, 46*, 971–982.

Eysenck, H. (1983). Psychophysiology and personality: Extraversion, neuroticism and psychoticism. In A. Gale & J. A. Edwards (Eds.), *Physiological correlates of human behaviour: Individual differences and psychopathology* (vol. 3) (pp. 13–30). London: Academic Press.

Fagerström, K. O. (1978). Measuring degree of physical dependence to tobacco with reference to individualization of treatment. *Addictive Behaviors, 3,* 235–241.

Fagerström, K., Schneider, N., & Lunell, E. (1993). Effectiveness of nicotine patch and nicotine gum as individual versus combined treatments for tobacco withdrawal symptoms. *Psychopharmacology, 111,* 271–277.

Farley, J., & Lester, D. (1995). Smoking and trait anxiety. *Psychological Reports, 76,* 858.

Fleming, S. E., & Lombardo, T. W. (1987). Effects of cigarette smoking on phobic anxiety. *Addictive Behaviors, 12,* 195–198.

Gilbert, D. G., & Gilbert, B. O. (1995). Personality, psychopathology, and nicotine response as mediators of the genetics of smoking. *Behavior Genetics, 25,* 133–147.

Gilbert, D. G., & Spielberger, C. D. (1987). Effects of smoking on heart rate, anxiety, and feelings of success during social interactions. *Journal of Behavioral Medicine, 10,* 629–638.

Grossarth-Maticek, R., & Eysenck, H. J. (1990). Personality, stress and disease: Description and validation of a new inventory. *Psychological Reports, 66,* 355–373.

Hall, S. M., Muñoz, R. F., Reus, V. I., & Sees, K. L. (1993). Nicotine, negative affect, and depression. *Journal of Consulting and Clinical Psychology, 61,* 761–767.

Hatsukami, D., Grillo, M., Pentel, P., Oncken, C., & Bliss, R. (1997). Safety of cotinine in humans: Physiologic, subjective and cognitive effects. *Pharmacology Biochemistry and Behavior, 57,* 643–650.

Hatsukami, D., Pentel, P. R., Jensen, J., Nelson, D., Allen, S. S., Goldman, A., & Rafael, D. (1998). Cotinine: Effects with and without nicotine. *Psychopharmacology, 135,* 141–150.

Henningfield, J. E., Gopalan, L., & Shiffman, S. (1998). Tobacco dependence: Fundamental concepts and recent advances. *Current Opinion in Psychiatry, 11,* 259–263.

Henningfield, J. E., & Keenan, R. M. (1993). Nicotine delivery kinetics and abuse liability. *Journal of Consulting and Clinical Psychology, 61,* 734–750.

Houston, J. P., & Schneider, N. G. (1973). Further evidence of smoking and anxiety. *Psychological Reports, 32,* 322.

Hughes, J. (1994). An algorithm for smoking cessation. *Archives of Family Medicine, 3,* 280–285.

Hughes, J. R. (1995). APA position statement on nicotine dependence. *American Journal on Addictions, 4,* 179–181.

Hughes, J. R., Hatsukami, D. K., Mitchell, J. E., & Dahlgren, L. A. (1986). Prevalence of smoking among psychiatric outpatients. *American Journal of Psychiatry, 143,* 993–997.

Hurt, R. D., Sachs, D. P., Glover, E. D., Offord, K. P., Johnston, J. A., Dale, L. C., Khayrallah, M. A., Schroder, D. R., Glover, P. N., Sullivan, C. R., Croghan, I. T., & Sullivan, P. M. (1997). A comparison of sustained-release bupropion and placebo for smoking cessation. *New England Journal of Medicine, 337,* 1195–1202.

Hyder Ferry, L., & Pettis, J. L. (1995). Two atypical cases of nicotine withdrawal treated with bupropion. Paper presented at the Sixteenth Annual Meeting of the Society of Behavioral Medicine, San Diego, California.

Jorenby, D., Hatsukami, D., Smith, S., Fiore, M., Allen, S., Jensen, J., & Baker, T. (1996). Transdermal nicotine replacement reduces tobacco withdrawal symptoms. *Psychopharmacology, 128,* 130–138.

Kassel, J. D., Shiffman, S., Gnys, M., Paty, J., & Zettler-Segal, M. (1994). Psychosocial and personality differences in chippers and regular smokers. *Addictive Behaviors, 19,* 565–575.

Kick, S. D., & Cooley, D. D. (1997). Depressive, not anxiety, symptoms are associated with current cigarette smoking among university internal medical patients. *Psychosomatics, 38,* 132–139.

Knott, V. J. (1979). Personality, arousal and individual differences in cigarette smoking. *Psychological Reports, 45,* 423–428.

Kunzendorf, R. G., & Denney, J. (1982). Definitions of personal space: Smokers versus nonsmokers. *Psychological Reports, 50,* 818.

Lakshminarayanan, T., & Raguram, D. (1989). Cigarette smoking and anxiety: A study of the medical students. *Indian Journal of Clinical Psychology, 16,* 24–25.

Lazarus, R., & Folkman, S. (1984). *Stress, appraisal, and coping.* New York: Springer.

MacDougall, J., Dembroski, T., Slaats, S., Herd, J., & Eliot, R. (1983). Selective cardiovascular effects of stress and cigarette smoking. *Journal of Human Stress, 9,* 13–21.

MacDougall, J., Musante, L., Howard, J., Hanes, R., & Dembroski, T. (1986). Individual differences in cardiovascular reactions to stress and cigarette smoking. *Health Psychology, 5,* 531–544.

Miller, W. R. (1983). Motivational interviewing with problem drinkers. *Behavioural Psychotherapy, 11,* 147–172.

Nirmala, M., & Swaminathan, V. (1985). Cigarette smoking and personality. *Social Defence, 20,* 25–29.

O'Connor, K. (1989). A motor psychophysiological model of smoking and personality. *Personality and Individual Differences, 10,* 889–901.

Patil, R., & Chengti, S. K. (1987). A study on smoking and personality characteristics of farmers of rural Gulbarga. *Indian Psychological Review, 32,* 47–50.

Patton, D., Barnes, G. E., & Murray, R. P. (1993). Personality characteristics of smokers and ex-smokers. *Personality and Individual Differences, 15,* 653–664.

Patton, G. C., Hibbert, M., Rosier, M. J., Carlin, J. B., et al. (1996). Is smoking associated with depression and anxiety in teenagers? *American Journal of Public Health, 86*, 225–230.

Paulson, G. (1992). Addiction to nicotine is due to high intrinsic levels of dopamine. *Medical Hypotheses, 38*, 206–207.

Pechacek, T. (1984). Modification of smoking behavior. In *Smoking and health: A report of the Surgeon General.* Washington, DC: Department of Health, Education, and Welfare, Public Health Service.

Pomerleau, C. S., Majchrzak, M. J., & Pomerleau, O. F. (1989). Nicotine dependence and the Fagerström Tolerance Questionnaire: A brief review. *Journal of Substance Abuse, 1*, 471–477.

Pomerleau, C. S., & Pomerleau, O. (1987). The effects of a psychological stressor on cigarette smoking and subsequent behavioral and physiological responses. *Psychophysiology, 24*, 278–283.

Pomerleau, O. F., Collins, A. C., Shiffman, S., & Pomerleau, C. S. (1993). Why some people smoke and others do not: New perspectives. *Journal of Consulting and Clinical Psychology, 61*, 723–731.

Pomerleau, O. F., & Pomerleau, C. S. (1989). Stress, smoking, and the cardiovascular system. *Journal of Substance Abuse, 1*, 331–343.

Pomerleau, O. F., Turk, D., & Fertig, J. B. (1984). The effects of cigarette smoking on pain and anxiety. *Addictive Behaviors, 9*, 265–271.

Rose, J. E., Ananda, S., & Jarvik, M. E. (1983). Cigarette smoking during anxiety-provoking and monotonous tasks. *Addictive Behaviors, 8*, 353–359.

Shiffman, S. M., & Jarvik, M. E. (1980). Withdrawal symptoms: First week is hardest. *World Smoking and Health, 5*, 17–21.

Smedslund, G. (1995). Personality and vulnerability to cancer and heart disease: Relations to demographic and life-style variables. *Personality and Individual Differences, 19*, 691–697.

Sutherland, G., Stapleton, J. A., Russell, M. A., Jarvis, M. J., Hajek, P., Belcher, M., & Feyerabend, C. (1992). Randomised controlled trial of nasal nicotine spray in smoking cessation. *Lancet, 340*, 324–329.

Transdermal Nicotine Study Group. (1991). Transdermal nicotine for smoking cessation: Six month results from two multicenter controlled clinical trials. *Journal of the American Medical Association, 266*, 3133–3138.

U.S. Department of Health and Human Services (USDHHS). (1989). Trends in public beliefs, attitudes, and opinions about smoking. In *Reducing the health consequences of smoking: 25 years of progress: A report of the Surgeon General* (pp. 171–258). Rockville, MD: Author.

U.S. Department of Health, Education, and Welfare (USDHEW). (1979). *Smoking and health: A report of the Surgeon General* (USDHEW publ. no. PHS79-50066). Washington, DC: U.S. Department of Health and Human Services.

Vaughan, D. (1990). Frontiers in pharmacologic treatment of alcohol, cocaine, and nicotine dependence. *Psychiatric Annals, 20*, 695–710.

West, R., & Hajek, P. (1997). What happens to anxiety levels on giving up smoking? *American Journal of Psychiatry, 154*, 1589–1592.

Williams, S. G., Hudson, A., & Redd, C. (1982). Cigarette smoking, manifest anxiety and somatic symptoms. *Addictive Behaviors, 7*, 427–428.

Woody, G. E., Cottler, L. B., & Cacciola, J. (1993). Severity of dependence: Data from the DSM-IV trials. *Addiction, 88*, 1573–1579.

CHAPTER 21

THE ROLE OF ANXIETY IN WEIGHT MANAGEMENT

Linda Wilcoxon Craighead
Carolyn Aibel

Obesity is a prevalent problem that poses serious medical risks. Approximately 24% of men and 27% of women in the United States are obese (Kuczmarski, 1992). While definitions of obesity vary, it is generally considered to be a body mass index (BMI) of 30, which is the equivalent of 25% above the ideal weight for a given height (Marcus et al., 1990). Research has linked obesity with such medical disorders as: hypertension, diabetes, osteoarthritis, and some forms of cancer (Jeffery, 1988; Pi-Sunyer, 1993). The link obesity may have with psychological disorders, however, is less clear.

Theories of obesity have tended to focus on psychological variables. Initially obesity was conceptualized within the framework of psychoanalytic theory, which posited that obesity reflected an underlying personality disturbance and that individuals were acting out this unconscious conflict through excessive eating. From this framework evolved the psychosomatic theory of obesity, proposed by Kaplan and Kaplan (1957). This theory suggested that obesity resulted from overeating that occurred in response to excessive emotionality (Webber, 1994). Although these theories and others like them have largely been abandoned, the idea that obesity may in part be a consequence of "emotional eating" continues to be a focus in obesity research and treatment.

As the field of psychology began moving away from traditional psychoanalytic theories and more into behavioral theories, so too did psychological theorizing on obesity. The overarching idea that obesity was primarily the result of other underlying, psychological problems was for the most part replaced by more contemporary theories. Behavioral theories emphasized the role of maladaptive eating habits, which

both produced and sustained obesity. Behavioral (and cognitive-behavioral) treatments based on these theories have been quite successful in modifying eating habits and are in fact the only empirically supported treatments for obesity (Wilson, 1995). Nonetheless, relapse following successful treatment remains a significant problem, and dropout and treatment failure remain common occurrences. The insufficiency of current (and past) theories and treatments based on those theories is readily apparent.

In recent years a greater focus has been placed on understanding the biological underpinnings of what had been thought to be more purely psychological problems. As a result, obesity came to be seen as more of a biological—that is, medical problem. Treatments in medical settings have proliferated (i.e., medically supervised liquid fasts and very-low-calorie diets, jaw wiring, and gastric bypass surgery) (Kral, 1995; Wadden, 1995). As with psychological treatments, these approaches boast numerous successes but must also acknowledge probably even more failures.

We are coming to see that obesity may best be understood as a biopsychosocial disorder: the result of a convergence of various factors, such as genetic make-up, cell metabolism, family environment, societal influences, and personal psychological issues. Seeing obesity within this framework highlights the complex nature of obesity and points out the heterogeneity that characterizes obese individuals. Thus, while early psychoanalytic theories may have been upstaged by more contemporary behavioral and biological theories, psychological factors continue to play an important role in understanding obesity. This chapter discusses several ways that a significant psychological construct, anxiety, may be related to the etiology and maintenance of weight problems and suggests ways to adapt cognitive-behavioral treatment of obesity to address specific anxiety issues that may be interfering with successful treatment.

ANXIETY ASSOCIATED WITH OBESITY

Studies of self-reported anxiety among obese individuals have yielded mixed results. Recently, Friedman and Brownell (1995) performed a meta-analysis of correlational studies of obesity and anxiety and concluded that the obese in general do not report higher levels of anxiety than individuals at normal weight. However, Friedman and Brownell noted that the lack of correlational findings may not be indicative of a lack of relationship between anxiety and obesity, but may instead be indicative of a complex relationship, one that underscores the heterogeneity in the obese population. In fact, a particular subgroup of the obese, *obese binge eaters*, do report elevated levels of anxiety and have significantly elevated rates of comorbid anxiety disorders.

Binge Eating and Obesity

In 1959, Stunkard identified binge eating as a distinct behavioral problem among the obese, but it has only recently been viewed as a separate psychological disorder. Binge eating disorder (BED), currently a provisional diagnosis in *DSM-IV*, is characterized by two or more weekly episodes of eating a large amount of food in a short period of time accompanied by a sense of loss of control. The binge eating must persist for a period of at least 6 months and must not be accompanied by inappropriate compensatory behavior (such as vomiting, fasting, abusing laxatives, or excessive exercise). In addition, the episodes must be associated with three of the following: eating more rapidly than normal; eating until uncomfortably full; eating when not physically hungry; eating alone; or feeling very disgusted with oneself, depressed, or guilty after overeating.

Among those presenting for weight loss programs, between 25 and 50% meet criteria for BED (Gormally et al., 1982; Marcus, Wing, & Lamparski, 1985; Marcus, Wing, & Hopkins, 1988). Although being overweight is not a criterion for BED, the majority of individuals with BED are at least somewhat overweight, and the severity of binge eating has been shown to increase with the degree of obesity (Telch, Agras, & Rossiter, 1988).

Individuals with BED appear to differ significantly from obese individuals who do not engage in binge eating. Rates of psychopathology (clinical diagnoses) among obese nonbingeing individuals do not differ from normal weight individuals, but among those with BED, rates of psychopathology are higher, similar to rates among individuals diagnosed with bulimia (Antony et al., 1994). The high rate of BED among individuals seeking weight loss treatment indicates that some assessment of binge eating is desirable, if only to be alert to the possibility that binge eating is the problem when an individual fails to respond well in a group program. To make a definite diagnosis of BED, a structured interview such as the Eating Disorders Examination (EDE; Fairburn & Cooper, 1993) or the Interview for Diagnosis of Eating Disorders—IV (Kutlesic et al., 1998) is recommended. When that is not feasible, a brief self-report measure, the Binge Eating Scale (BES; Gormally et al., 1982) may be considered, at least as a screen. Individuals scoring over 27 on the BES are likely to meet criteria for BED (Marcus, Wing, & Hopkins, 1988). A binge is defined as any episode in which a person feels unable to control what he or she is eating; this is a subjective feeling of being out of control. The difficulty is determining what constitutes an *objective binge*—a "larger than normal amount"—as *subjective binge episodes* do not count toward the twice a week frequency criterion needed to give a clinical diagnosis of BED. Guidelines for the EDE suggest that servings more than two to three times a typical serving size are considered "objectively large." However, even subjective binge eating or less frequent (subclinical levels of) binge eating can be quite distressing to an individual who is trying to lose weight and can interfere with successful treatment.

Further research is needed to determine if individuals with BED do more poorly in standard cognitive-behavioral weight loss programs or if they benefit but would do better in programs tailored more specifically to their needs. Early reports (Keefe et al., 1984; Marcus, Wing, & Hopkins, 1988; Yanovski, 1993) indicated that these individuals might do less well in weight loss treatment, be more likely to drop out of treatment, and be more likely to regain any weight they did lose once treatment ended. However, the only study (Marcus, Wing, & Fairburn, 1995) directly comparing cognitive-behavioral therapy (CBT) (specifically adapted to address binge eating) to a standard behavioral weight loss program (BWLT) reported both were equally effective in reducing binge eating at posttreatment and the improvements were maintained through follow-up. Notably, BWLT participants lost considerably more weight during treatment; they did regain some weight during follow-up, but their weight remained below those who received CBT (who stayed about the same weight throughout the study). It is important to note that all treatment in this study was provided in individual sessions. Group therapy is the norm in behavioral programs (usually due to issues of cost-effectiveness), but individuals do not get much attention for their specific problems. Thus, it is possible that group BWLT, particularly in groups including a mix of BED and non-BED obese individuals, would not be as effective as the individual treatment provided in that study.

Results from a series of studies by Agras and his colleagues (Agras et al., 1994, 1995, 1997) suggest that individuals who become abstinent from binge eating generally fare better in terms of both initial weight loss and maintaining weight loss than do those who continue to binge. Thus, it may be better for a client to stop, or at least substantially reduce, binge eating before focusing too heavily on weight loss. However, BED clients are encouraged to attend to some degree (watch portion sizes and choose low-fat foods and start a structured exercise program) to prevent gaining weight during the time they are gaining control over binge episodes. Regardless of whether binge eating or weight loss is the primary target of intervention, it appears that binge eating must be essentially eliminated or it will interfere with effective long-term control over weight.

Anxiety and Binge Eating

Comorbidity studies indicate that approximately 20% of obese binge eaters also suffer from anxiety disorders, most commonly social phobia and generalized anxiety disorder (Marcus et al., 1990; Schwalberg et al., 1992). In addition, obese binge eaters scored higher on a measure of trait anxiety than both normal

weight individuals and obese non-binge eaters (Antony et al., 1994). In fact, Webber (1994) found that obese binge eaters reported significantly higher trait anxiety than a sample of anxious patients. Thus, when individuals present for weight loss treatment, it may be useful to assess for comorbid clinically diagnosable anxiety disorders. Most weight loss treatments, however, are done in a group context and do not involve extensive clinical evaluation for screening participants. Thus, it is likely that the presence of a comorbid anxiety disorder may go undetected until later in treatment, when it becomes clear that an individual is not responding well. Whether weight loss treatment is likely to be less successful on average for participants with comorbid anxiety disorders or whether the treatment necessarily needs to be altered in a particular way for those with anxiety disorders has yet to be explored. A review of the literature on the comorbidity of anxiety with the eating disorders anorexia and bulimia concluded that anxiety disorders have little impact on treatment outcome (Cooper, 1995). It is therefore likely that this would also be the case in weight loss treatment, but further research is necessary to determine the degree to which this is true. It is likely that some anxiety disorders may interfere with treatment (at least for certain individuals); for example, obsessive-compulsive symptoms could keep a client from resuming a normal diet, agoraphobia could keep a client housebound where there is little to do other than eat, and generalized anxiety could be a trigger for overeating. Binge episodes may be related to dissociative symptoms, which are typically considered to reflect some type of anxiety. If obesity is being treated in a group context, a referral for treatment of the anxiety disorder concurrently with the obesity is recommended.

Aside from clinically significant comorbid anxiety disorders, the high trait anxiety reported by individuals with BED has various explanations and consequences. These individuals may feel anxious about engaging in binge eating behaviors. A binge is by definition an eating episode characterized by a sense of loss of control, and lack of control of any type is generally considered a stressor. Thus, this disorder (which seems volitional) actually feels avolitional. This "out of control" feeling is itself a source of anxiety. Another source of anxiety for obese binge eaters may come from their body image. Cash (1991) reports that, compared to obese non-binge eaters, obese binge eaters (matched on weight) report higher body dissatisfaction, evaluate their bodies more negatively, and are more preoccupied with their weight and appearance. Individuals preoccupied with their weight and appearance are also more attuned to, and more sensitive to, negative feedback from others concerning this topic. Thus, obese binge eaters are likely to experience both intrapsychic (internal) and interpersonal anxiety related to how others perceive their weight problems. The social feedback they receive is likely to do little to decrease their anxiety, as being overweight in our society tends to elicit criticism and scorn. For obese binge eaters then, anxiety may stem from the binge eating behaviors themselves, specifically feelings of being out of control, and from their negative evaluations of their weight and shape in a society that favors thinness.

ANXIETY THAT LEADS TO EATING

The relationship between anxiety and eating behavior appears to be quite complex. Anxiety is generally considered to suppress appetite, but it appears that this varies considerably among individuals and depends to a large extent on situational variables. The relationship between depression and eating behavior is similar in this regard. Typically, individuals who are depressed eat less (and lose weight), but a significant subset (labeled "atypical") of depressed individuals eat more and gain weight.

Wolpe's (1958) early work studying anxiety in cats pointed out two different ways in which anxiety and eating could be related. After being shocked in an experimental cage, the cats showed signs of anxiety when put inside the cage, and they refused to eat. However, when he then removed them from the cage and fed them from afar, gradually bringing them back to the cage, he was able to successfully eliminate the cats' conditioned anxious responses. Eating was thus the first response used to demonstrate reciprocal inhibition of anxiety. Wolpe later used other responses, notably relaxation, to alleviate anxiety, but his early work demonstrated that feeding in the presence of relatively weak anxiety responses facilitated the extinction of those responses. Given the latter, it is not surprising that many individuals learn to eat as a way to cope with low-level, "everyday" type anxiety even though eating may not be particularly useful in dealing with more severe anxiety or true anxiety disorders.

A later study conducted by Slochower (1976) evaluating the hypothesis that eating may be a way to calm anxiety found that inducing anxiety in a sample of obese subjects did lead to increased eating. Subsequent studies, however, have had difficulty replicating this finding (Steere & Cooper, 1993). This may in part be due to the dual role anxiety seems to play in relation to eating (as sometimes it acts as an inhibitor). In addition, it may be a consequence of the variability between hypotheses guiding the studies. Researchers investigating the way in which anxiety may lead to eating have differing views on the pathways by which this occurs. In particular, there seem to be three current hypotheses, which we will address in turn: First, anxiety disinhibits dietary rules; second, anxiety is misinterpreted as hunger; and third, eating is used in an attempt to alleviate anxiety (this is referred to as emotional eating).

Disinhibition

The literature on anxiety (sometimes referred to as stress) and eating responses has shown that among nondieting women, anxiety diminishes food intake, but among women dieters, anxiety increases food intake (Heatherton, Herman, & Polivy, 1991; Herman & Polivy, 1975; Mitchell & Epstein, 1996). This phenomenon of increased consumption by dieters is known as *disinhibition;* anxiety seems to undo the cognitive and behavioral checks dieters have placed on their eating, leading them to eat more. Although the mechanisms behind this phenomenon are unknown, it has been suggested that it may be a result of reliance on cognitive rather than internal regulation of eating (Herman & Polivy, 1975). Dieters regulate their intake according to cognitive rules; they ignore internal feelings of hunger and fullness (satiety). When cognitive control is disrupted by anxiety (or other variables), overeating is more likely because they have not been relying on fullness as their cue to stop eating.

If cognitive control is more vulnerable to disinhibition than control based on internal cues, a cognitive behavioral approach designed to reinstate eating in response to appetite cues may be useful for clients who experience frequent difficulties with disinhibition. Appetite awareness training (AAT; see Craighead &

Allen, 1995) is a treatment based on this concept. In AAT, clients are taught to focus on their internal hunger and satiety cues and learn to regulate their eating accordingly rather than relying as heavily on cognitive rules or environmental controls.

Misinterpretation of Anxiety

Some individuals are not aware of feeling particularly anxious, but they report feeling hungry all the time or feeling as if they need to eat even when they have just recently eaten. These individuals are probably experiencing some type of internal sensation, such as anxiety/arousal, that they are mislabeling as hunger. One indication may be reports of a fairly high level of trait anxiety and/or general muscle tension. The lack of differentiation between anxiety and hunger obstructs weight loss efforts. These individuals frequently feel aversive internal sensations that they label as hunger and then may eat in an effort to alleviate these sensations. Treatment must therefore increase awareness of elevated levels of anxiety and help clients discriminate between the two internal states.

In most behavioral weight loss treatments, clients must monitor their food intake. This allows clients and doctors (or therapists) to see what the client is really eating and is also helpful in identifying a client's problem areas. Craighead and Aibel (1998) recommend using an expanded form of self-monitoring that includes appetite (hunger and fullness) ratings in addition to listing the amount and type of food eaten and the emotional context in which the eating occurred. In this way, clients are prompted to pay closer attention to internal appetite levels and to see how those are related to internal emotional states.

At the beginning of treatment, it is difficult for clients to know whether they are physically hungry, just anxious, or have what some clinicians term "mouth" hunger (i.e., wanting to be eating/chewing a particular type of food). At least initially, many clients need to rely on the clock to guide their eating times, using a regular schedule of three meals and two or three snacks. If clients feel hungry but have eaten a reasonable meal or snack within the last 2 hours, they should assume they are not physically hungry and should use distraction or alternative activities to wait until their next scheduled time to eat. If, however, it has been longer than 2 hours, we suggest they have their snack or their next meal early to ensure that they do not get too hungry before eating. We refer to this as "the 2 hour rule."

Although clients may continue to use a schedule indefinitely to structure their eating, we have found that by using the expanded self-monitoring (i.e., drawing specific attention to appetite cues and emotional states), a large majority of clients are able to get back in touch with hunger cues and are better able to discriminate between physical hunger and other sensations (for further discussion, see Craighead & Allen, 1995).

Emotional Eating

Many overweight individuals, particularly those with BED, are already quite able to identify when they are anxious (as opposed to hungry), but also find that eating (and/or binge eating) soothes their anxiety. They have not been able to find anything else that works quite as well and/or is as easily available to them when they need it. Eating helps alleviate anxiety, as Wolpe first noted, and eating can also serve as a distraction that helps the person cope with feeling anxious. In addition, for some individuals severe binge eating can involve a trancelike state known as dissociation (see Abraham & Beaumont, 1982). In such a state, individuals are "numbed out"; they lose touch with their surroundings (derealization) and/or with themselves (depersonalization). These individuals have learned to escape from very uncomfortable feelings (e.g., anxiety) by dissociating and, for some, binge eating helps them achieve such a state. Heatherton and Baumeister (1990) propose that binge eating is used as "an escape from aversive self-awareness."

Arnow, Kenardy, and Agras (1992) studied overweight binge eaters and found that anxiety played a considerable role in triggering binges. They interviewed subjects about several things including thoughts, feelings, and physical sensations they experienced before, during, and after a binge, as well as typical triggers associated with binge eating. Thirty-seven percent of the subjects reported binges specifically triggered by anxiety, and 100% reported binges triggered by negative moods (e.g., depression, anger, or anxiety). In addition, one of the most common thoughts before a binge involved the clear intention to alter mood—"I'll feel better if I eat this." Thus, at least for obese binge eaters, "emotional eating" occurs, and it is a frequent trigger for binges.

While individuals may realize that in general they eat in response to emotions, they are typically not aware enough in the moment to catch themselves. Thus, treatment for emotional eating must include heightened awareness as to when emotional eating is happening, more creative problem solving to develop alternative coping strategies, and interventions to help motivate clients to use those alternatives. An excellent discussion of emotional eating that is appropriate for a layperson can be found in Harrar et al. (1996). Cognitive-behavioral interventions address this type of eating in a number of ways that have considerable overlap.

In AAT, Craighead and Aibel (1998) identify four maladaptive cycles that interact to maintain overeating and binge eating. One is the "emotional eating cycle," which is described as follows:

> When you begin eating because of emotions (not because you feel hungry), *you are not thinking about appetite in the first place so you are likely to eat past moderate fullness.* You are also more likely to break a diet rule (comfort foods are usually those which are "forbidden") which may trigger loss of control, becoming a "binge." Eating works in the short run so eating in response to emotions gets strongly reinforced; next time you are even more likely to feel like eating when you feel those emotions. Once this pattern is established, *you may at times "plan" to binge, deliberately deciding to eat a lot (ignore fullness) or eat "forbidden" foods* because you need to feel the numbing or the release of tension that is associated with a binge. Compensatory responses (feeling fat and dieting more strictly) help maintain the cycle. (Craighead & Aibel, 1998)

In AAT, clients learn to identify what is happening (which cycles are involved) each time they binge. The self-monitoring form used in AAT cues the client to circle the appropriate label(s) for the episode. For those who no longer binge, the focus becomes identifying the cycles involved in overeating episodes. Once the client can label episodes as emotional eating, problem solving is used to develop alternative strategies. Table 21.1 lists strategies that are recommended in AAT for emotional eating.

Similarly, Apple and Agras (1997) ask clients to cue themselves with the word "mood" as soon as they recognize that a negative mood exists; this is to re-

TABLE 21.1. Strategies to Stop the Emotional Eating Cycle

1. Monitoring your hunger will help you identify high-risk situations in which you are likely to begin eating for emotional reasons (when not truly hungry).
2. Develop new strategies to avoid high-risk situations, but do not limit your social life in ways that could create even more problems. You may need to find new ways to celebrate without food. You may need to work on increased assertion in setting up social situations that are lower-risk for you.
3. Use cognitive and behavioral strategies to develop alternatives to responding to emotions by eating. Cognitive strategies focus on changing the way you think. Focus on how eating (at least in large amounts) is not, in fact, working very well for you and it's time to try something different. You can use cognitive restructuring to challenge maladaptive thinking patterns that upset you so that you can feel better and have less need to eat. Behavioral strategies focus on developing alternative behaviors that are incompatible with eating (meditating, exercising, etc.) and developing escape plans (staying over at a friend's for the night) to get you out of high-risk situations.
4. In some situations, it feels like nothing but food will do. In those cases, it is okay to eat for comfort (everyone does this to some degree); you just must be particularly attentive to your fullness cues (which you normally ignore when eating for comfort). Occasionally, or even regularly, eating *moderate* amounts of favorite or comforting foods is not a problem and may prevent you from feeling deprived.

mind them that being in a negative mood increases their risk for binge eating and they need to take precautions. The client identifies the particular mood or feeling state and then tries to figure out the cause of the mood. Once clients are able to identify the source of their feelings and acknowledge that a negative mood puts them in a high-risk situation, they are better able to develop an action plan. It is also necessary to educate clients about the self-destructive nature of their emotional eating, so that they themselves desire to deal with negative moods in a constructive, self-nurturing way rather than the familiar but self-destructive way (i.e., overeating or binge eating).

Cognitive-behavioral treatments for BED utilize three methods to help clients cope with moods without eating. These methods would likely be equally helpful for clients who do not binge but who eat in response to emotions. The first method involves *substitution techniques.* Clients are asked to generate a list of pleasurable activities (aside from eating). Activities more incompatible with eating are best (e.g., knitting, taking a hot shower), but others (e.g., reading or working on a puzzle) are appropriate if the person can/will do them without eating. When such individuals have an urge to binge (or eat in response to emotion), they are to work their way down the list until the urge to binge (or eat) lessens. Specific anxiety-reducing activities may be particularly useful for clients for whom the prominent emotion is anxiety. Clients may have a relaxation or self-hypnosis tape to listen to for a specified period of time, they may learn to meditate or do yoga, or they may go for a 20-minute walk or work out with an exercise video.

The main problem with activity substitutions is that they take time, while eating can be done quickly, even while the client continues with other activities—which he or she thinks must be done (e.g., studying or work). Because this is often the root of resistance, it is important to encourage clients to challenge their belief that they cannot take the time to take care of themselves. In addition, it is important to help clients set priorities and be assertive about getting their needs met (e.g., taking a break at work, asking spouse to make dinner). Often clients suggest activities that may be incompatible with eating but are neutral or aversive (e.g., doing paperwork, washing windows). Although some of these may be useful, it is important to point out to clients that in the face of a strong urge to eat, such an activity is unlikely to be a deterrent. The list is of no use if in the moment clients feel unable or unwilling to choose any of the alternative activities. Many clients have a hard time accepting that they need to take the time to do pleasant things. If this is the case, cognitive restructuring is needed to deal with their difficulties in justifying self-nurturance.

The second CBT method is problem solving (see also Goldfried & Davidson, 1994). Problem solving typically involves the following steps: (1) identifying the problem very specifically and adopting a problem-solving mind-set, (2) brainstorming alternative solutions, (3) evaluating the practicality and effectiveness of each solution, (4) choosing one or a combination of solutions and deciding on a time period to try it out, (5) implementing the plan and evaluating the outcome, and (6) revising the plan if needed by going back and defining it more clearly and/or coming up with additional solutions. Most programs provide clients with a written form that facilitates learning this skill. Problem solving is helpful because clients typically are "stuck." They may have tried many approaches and run out of new ideas. Often they feel hopeless; if they are feeling hopeless, they are unlikely

to be able to problem solve effectively. In this case, clients can be instructed to stop and engage in cognitive restructuring related to those maladaptive beliefs before returning to problem solving.

The most common difficulty in problem solving is the generation of alternatives. Clients may continue to use old strategies that are not working because of the erroneous belief that if they just put their minds to it, the strategy would work (the old "it's just a matter of willpower" way of thinking). In our problem solving, we instruct, "Don't try harder, try different." The old strategies do not work because they are flawed; it's time for new strategies. Problem solving is especially effective in a group setting, where the members can provide fresh input (brainstorm) and challenge each other's negative notions about particular strategies. But problem solving can also be done individually with the doctor/therapist. In either case, clients are encouraged to identify a friend, a support group, or a professional whom they can go to (after treatment has ended) when they have a problem or experience a lapse and feel stuck. Some clients resist the idea of having to ask others for help, which again calls for cognitive restructuring.

Another common obstacle to effective use of problem solving is the clients' expectations that they should find one "perfect" solution that will work all the time. Clients tend to give up on solutions that helped but did not eliminate the problem or only worked part of the time. We suggest clients adopt the "fifty percent rule"—keep using any strategy that works more than 50% of the time or that improves outcome by at least 50%. This encourages both positivity and creativity. Unlike many other problem-solving situations in which a client is choosing among various alternatives, bingeing or overeating can often be reduced by using different solutions together, producing a synergistic effect that is better than any one solution.

The third CBT method is *cognitive restructuring*, which, as noted earlier, must often be used in combination with the first two strategies in order to get clients to effectively implement those more behavioral strategies. The typical steps, as listed in Apple and Agras (1997), are: (1) identifying the problem thoughts, particularly the core or "hot" thought; (2) gathering evidence to support the thought; (3) gathering evidence to dispute the thought; (4) coming up with a reasoned conclusion that counters the original thought; and (5) identifying a course of action based on a logical conclusion. Again, most programs provide clients with a written form to facilitate learning this skill. In the case in which anxiety is triggering eating, cognitive restructuring can be used to reduce anxiety directly as well as to counter the belief that eating is the best or only way to deal with anxiety. Depending on the severity of the anxiety problem, clients may need to be referred to individual treatment or be encouraged to use self-help programs like Craske, Barlow, and O'Leary (1992) describe.

We also recommend that clients develop written cue cards, which have the effective counterthoughts they have developed for their main reoccurring problem thoughts. These can facilitate remembering effective counters that were developed in the group setting. Many clients have difficulty doing countering when they are quite upset, so they find referring to the cards useful. In doing cognitive monitoring, some clients note they often know exactly what they should do right then, but they seem unable to choose to do what they know would help. In the moment, they feel rebellious, almost defiant and the thought is more like, "I just don't care!" If this occurs frequently, we use Linehan's (1993) techniques designed to cultivate a "willing" not "willful" attitude. She defines willingness as "accepting what is, together with responding to what is, in an effective or appropriate way—doing what works—doing just what is needed in the moment; willfullness is imposing one's will on reality—trying to fix everything, or refusing to do what is needed" (p. 103). In addition, when the anxiety that is triggering eating is about something that is very negative and/or is not much under the individual's control, problem solving and cognitive restructuring may be only minimally effective. In that case, Linehan's list of techniques to improve "distress tolerance" can be useful as the therapist helps the client develop better skills to tolerate some degree of anxiety without resorting to eating, pointing out that, in the long run, eating does not fix the problem, but increases anxiety about possible weight gain.

ANXIETY ABOUT EATING

For obese BED clients, and perhaps to a lesser extent for obese non-BED clients, there may be substantial anxiety around their problematic eating patterns (binge eating, overeating, emotional eating). They may consider their eating patterns abnormal or even "crazy."

Many clients are secretive about their problematic eating because they are anxious about what others would think if they knew about them. However, this anxiety about eating may, in fact, play a role in perpetuating their maladaptive eating.

Anxiety about eating stems from having many episodes of failure to control eating as desired. Situations involving eating seem dangerous to such individuals as they provide opportunities to overeat or binge (i.e., to fail again). The individuals may begin to avoid feared situations. This may mean skipping meals, avoiding shopping for food or preparing meals, or adopting a pattern of "grazing"—not actually sitting down for meals. Clients erroneously believe these strategies will minimize opportunities to overeat. Similarly, because of anxiety and worry about how much they usually end up eating later in the day, clients may deliberately not eat until midafternoon or later. This is derived from the usually mistaken belief that they will then eat fewer total calories in the day. Likewise, clients may choose not to eat when not very hungry, believing they are saving those calories for later. When individuals decide to eat only when they must (i.e., are really very hungry), they increase the likelihood of bingeing or overeating. Individuals who are very hungry may feel they are justified or deserve to eat more and/or they may be unable to recognize when they are just full (as opposed to stuffed).

Many individuals come to believe that certain foods are particularly "dangerous" (i.e., highly likely to trigger a binge or overeating episode), so they place unrealistic restrictions on the foods they will eat. For instance, they may not allow themselves to eat any candy, they may eat only frozen diet foods, or they may limit themselves to extremely small portions. In addition, many report not keeping any kind of appealing food in the house (e.g., sweets, fatty foods). Some ask their family members to lock up "junk foods," and others do not let themselves go grocery shopping. This type of thinking about food reflects an "addiction" model of compulsive eating and posits that abstinence from these "toxic" foods that trigger binge eating is required to gain control. This model is often presented in popular self-help approaches. Wilson (1993) reviewed the evidence for applying the addiction model to the treatment of eating problems, and he concluded that the differences between compulsive eating and substance abuse were so vast as to render the model ineffectual in dealing with eating problems. A behavioral or "moderate use" model seems more applicable to eating problems than an abstinence-oriented model because people must continue to eat on a regular basis. Nevertheless, for many individuals the abstinence model seems to have some intuitive appeal and continues to be their guide in dealing with problem food behaviors.

Unfortunately the avoidance strategies people use to cope with anxiety about overeating encourage the development of the very patterns that make an individual highly vulnerable to episodes of "loss of control." The more people limit their exposure to food, the less able they are to cope effectively with food when it is presented. Avoidance reinforces the idea that food (or at least certain foods) is dangerous. In contrast, having food successes, in which a person eats "normally" (withstands urges to overdo it), develops a sense of self-efficacy. People learn they do have control, and they develop better coping mechanisms for difficult situations.

Additionally, the more limits individuals impose on specific foods, the more likely they are to desire those foods. When presented with a "bad" food, their desire for the "forbidden" often overwhelms their good intentions. They give in and binge or at least overeat. This type of "loss of control" response that occurs as a direct result of self-imposed abstinence (or rigid rules) was first described in the treatment of alcohol problems as the abstinence violation effect (AVE) (Marlatt & Gordon, 1985), and the concept has been applied to binge eating (Grilo & Shiffman, 1994). Living by rigid food rules is even more difficult than abstaining from other substances because those can more easily be avoided or banished from one's environment. It is not actually an option for people to just "quit eating" the way they might stop using drugs, drinking, smoking, or gambling. Thus, moderate, controlled use strategies are necessary and usually more effective with eating problems.

In AVE the giving in initially reduces anxiety; the struggle is over, although the client has lost. In the end, however, giving in creates more anxiety; food has proven more powerful than the individual. Having lost control or failed in their efforts to follow their rules, individuals usually resort to imposing stricter rules and more food limits in an effort to reestablish control. These compensatory responses perpetuate the cycle and further entrench the idea that food is dangerous and something to be feared.

Clients who are anxious about eating must be educated about this cycle in which they are caught as well as the ways in which dieting, excessive restriction, and becoming too hungry may be contributing to their problem eating episodes. All cognitive and behavioral weight loss programs recommend that clients adopt a regular schedule of reasonable meals and snacks to counter the maladaptive eating strategies they have been employing. In addition, clients are encouraged to follow a heirarchical desensitization paradigm to gradually introduce feared or forbidden foods into their diet. Clients make a list of the feared foods, noting when they do eat these foods on their self-monitoring records, and then cross them off the list as they become comfortable with eating them. At least initially clients may need to eat these foods in controlled amounts in situations that are not conducive to binge eating or overeating (e.g., going out for an ice cream cone with a friend).

The present authors have found that including appetite monitoring in standard cognitive behavioral treatment is especially useful in countering many clients' fear of eating. Clients may be entrenched in their maladaptive eating patterns because they are afraid of, or because they have never considered, relying on internal appetite cues to guide their eating. Initially they do not believe they can rely on those cues, as it appears that they have clearly not been responding appropriately to appetite in the past. However, we point out that their prior maladaptive dieting strategies have made it virtually impossible to respond appropriately to appetite. With a better understanding of appropriate eating habits, they can now learn to tune in to their appetite cues. Teaching clients to eat when they feel moderately hungry and stop when they feel moderately full affords them both a sense of control and a sense of normalcy; they feel they are learning to eat as others seem to eat—more naturally. Eating begins to feel more like a normal body function and thus less dangerous.

Appetite monitoring can be combined with food monitoring, but it can also be used by itself for clients who are not willing to monitor food or who find that writing down what they eat only serves to increase their anxiety about eating. This response is most common in clients who are very overweight, particularly those who suffer from BED, and clients who have failed in many efforts to lose weight (or keep the weight off); the very thought of writing down what they eat is aversive. Appetite monitoring is often less affectively charged than food monitoring for these clients, but it still draws their attention to their eating patterns and maladaptive cycles; it also encourages a healthy reliance on eating according to natural appetite cues.

ANXIETY ABOUT NOT EATING

Although many overweight individuals feel anxious about their eating, others may have almost the opposite reaction. Many obese individuals, particularly those who do not have binge eating problems, have more of a problem with the idea of not eating when (or what) they want to. For them the problem is not anxiety about eating or anxiety itself that causes a problem but it is anxiety about not eating, worrying about being hungry or contemplating intentionally restricting intake (Nagler & Androff, 1990; Pitre & Nicki, 1992).

This type of anxiety may stem from finding the sensation of being hungry particularly aversive. Nagler and Androff (1990) tested this hypothesis by asking a sample of female university students to either visualize a neutral/pleasant scene or a food scene in which they wanted to eat but were not allowed to do so because they were on a diet. The researchers found the strongest predictor of self-reported anxiety and urges to eat in response to the food scene was hunger susceptibility, a factor on the Three Factor Eating Questionnaire (Stunkard & Messick, 1985). This factor assesses how likely an individual is to eat in response to hunger and various external (food) cues. The results suggest that some individuals are particularly vulnerable to feeling anxious in food-related situations when they are trying not to eat. Individuals who find the experience of being hungry anxiety-provoking may go to great lengths to avoid even the possibility that they might become hungry and not be able to eat. They may therefore eat when not hungry or may eat more than they need to feel satisfied because they fear that they may not get a chance to eat later. If feelings of being "deprived" or of even moderate hunger give rise to anxiety, these individuals may be ambivalent about a weight control program.

They may be likely to drop out of traditional treatments because they are not able to tolerate restricting their food intake.

To deal with anxiety about not eating, we first recommend reassuring the client that feeling hungry is not necessary; in fact, it is cautioned against because aversive hunger states are common triggers for bingeing and overeating. We suggest clients always have a readily available food source (e.g., keeping pretzels at the office, carrying energy bars in their backpack). In this way, clients can feel assured that they will not be stuck in a situation in which they are hungry and unable to eat. Thus, they will not feel justified in overeating in an attempt to counter possible later hunger. Appetite monitoring may be particularly helpful for this type of client as it so clearly prompts the client that anything beyond moderate hunger is to be avoided.

Secondly, recent research suggests that it may be helpful to desensitize overweight individuals to feelings of hunger. Pitre and Nicki (1994) compared the effects of desensitization to "dietary restraint anxiety" and generic relaxation training. Participants received a single treatment session (of either desensitization or relaxation) and were told that in order to lose weight they needed to feel hungry and eat less. They then returned monthly for weigh-ins. After 6 months the desensitization group essentially maintained their weight, while the relaxation group gained significantly more, an average of 5.3 lb. These data suggest that while desensitization alone would not be a viable treatment for weight loss, it may be a useful adjunct for clients who identify feeling quite anxious about dieting or being hungry. We do not recommend that clients be encouraged to become quite hungry, but some may need to learn to tolerate moderate levels of hunger in order to be successful in even moderate calorie-restriction weight loss programs. If these fears cannot be addressed effectively, this type of client may need to focus, at least initially, on increasing exercise and working toward a goal of better fitness rather than attempting to diet.

ANXIETY ABOUT BEING OBESE

Earlier in this chapter we mentioned that obese binge eaters had more body image distortion and distress about their weight than did obese non-binge eaters.

However, obese non-binge eaters may also have significant anxiety about their weight. Indeed, in our society being overweight is so stigmatized that few individuals who are overweight are able to feel good about their size.

Research has consistently replicated the finding that being obese is stigmatizing. The obese are considered lazier, more immature, less competent, and more disturbed than their thinner counterparts (Kirschenbaum & Fitzgibbon, 1995). Children describe obese peers as lazy, dirty, stupid, and ugly (see Stunkard & Sobel, 1995). Stunkard and Sobel (1995) found that when presented with drawings of children who were normal weight, overweight, or had various handicaps (e.g., missing hands and facial disfigurement), children and adults both rated the overweight child as least likable.

Although prejudice and discrimination are common in our society, negative perceptions of weight are not felt and expressed solely by normal and underweight individuals. Overweight individuals are themselves prejudiced against obesity. Stunkard and Sobel (1995) reported that within their sample of obese individuals, not a single subject preferred being obese to being deaf, diabetic, or having heart disease. Eight percent even reported that they would rather have a limb amputated than be obese.

Negative body image and feelings of anxiety about being overweight are readily understandable given our society's prejudices, but in addition to being self-punitive, it probably makes it even more difficult for overweight clients to achieve their weight loss goals. First, overconcern with weight and shape has been hypothesized to be the major cause of excessively restrictive dieting that leads to binge eating (Fairburn, 1981). Clients who feel overly concerned about their weight are more likely to be drastic in their weight loss efforts. They tend to set up stricter (often unrealistic) rules about eating that they are unable to follow for any length of time. Such individuals will often fall prey to the AVE effect, described earlier. With clients we often refer to it as the "oh what the heck" phenomenon. Clients have only a small lapse in their eating plan, but they then give up and binge or continue to overeat. Perhaps they have a piece of chocolate, which they consider forbidden; having broken the rule already, they figure they may as well just have the whole bag. This reaction occurs, in part, as a response

to feeling hopeless that weight can ever be controlled as desired. Overweight individuals want the weight to disappear immediately. Because weight loss is inevitably too slow, they are vulnerable to the abstinence violation effect—giving up whenever they perceive they have overeaten at all.

Additionally, anxiety about being overweight and unattractive can serve as a trigger for emotional eating. Clearly eating because of anxiety about being overweight only exacerbates the problem, but this is difficult for individuals to grasp in the moment. For example, eating alleviates anxiety, so even anxiety that is a consequence of their eating may trigger further eating if they have no other effective coping mechanisms. In addition, anxiety about being overweight may work indirectly, increasing depression and thus rendering the individual more susceptible to eating in response to other emotions as well as anxiety.

Presently no measure specifically assesses anxiety about weight and shape. Measures of the affective component of body image come closest, but these reflect depressive as well as anxious feelings about weight and shape. Nevertheless, these measures provide a sense of how generally upset individuals are about how they look. We recommend using the Body Shape Questionnaire (BSQ; Cooper et al., 1982). This instrument measures the degree to which individuals are personally satisfied, socially comfortable, and internally preoccupied with their appearance. Considerable research exists on improving body image in anorexia and bulimia, where there is much evidence of distortion of and overconcern with body image. In reviewing the literature on body image in obese individuals, Rosen (1996) concluded that they also overestimate or distort their body size, are very dissatisfied and preoccupied with their weight, and avoid many social situations because of it.

Rosen, Orosan, and Reiter (1995) have developed an eight-session intervention to improve body image (not for weight loss) among the overweight that they showed was significantly more effective than a no-treatment control. At the end of treatment, 70% of those completing treatment were in the normal range on a measure of negative body image; the changes were maintained at 4-month follow-up. On average, participants' weight remained the same. Rosen (1996) notes that the intervention is entirely compatible with a weight reducing–focused program and can be presented simultaneously. Presumably, improved body image could enhance treatment directly by reducing anxiety about weight/shape (and thereby, emotional eating) as well as indirectly by supporting slower, more effective approaches to weight loss that are generally associated with better maintenance than more restrictive approaches. When the tendency to resort to drastic weight loss methods is reduced, binge eating is less likely to be triggered. In addition, reducing anxiety about weight may help individuals be less socially anxious and in turn less isolated and less likely to turn to food and perhaps more likely to participate in exercise activities. These researchers are presently evaluating the utility of combining the body image program with a weight loss program. The body image intervention includes self-monitoring of situations in which clients feel self-conscious, gradual exposure (desensitization) to the sight of the body and to avoided social situations, cognitive restructuring, exposure and response prevention to reduce behavioral rituals (checking appearance, asking for reassurance), and coping with stereotypes and prejudice about obesity by using self-protective strategies.

OBSESSIONS, RITUALS AND AVOIDANT BEHAVIORS RELATED TO FOOD AND WEIGHT

In addition to negative thoughts about weight and shape, many individuals who are dieting report obsessional thoughts or cravings related to specific foods. This phenomenon appears to be similar to what happens to individuals who experience other types of distressing, intrusive thoughts, as in obsessive-compulsive disorder. The harder individuals try to suppress distressing thoughts, the more the thoughts intrude. In weight loss, obsessions about foods typically occur when the individual finds a particular food is a trigger for binge eating and decides to completely avoid it. While this may work for some time, eventually the person begins to crave the forbidden food. As noted earlier in discussing the abstinence model of eating, the more people resist eating a particular food, the more the craving intensifies (at least in the short run). Unless they are able to force themselves to ride out the urge to eat (essentially exposure and response prevention), they will eventually give in and eat, and at that point, they will usually overeat, if not binge.

Some clients are able to learn to resist the urge, but typically the best solution is for clients to learn to eat moderate, very controlled amounts of the food, as discussed in the section on anxiety about eating. This helps challenge the dichotomous thinking in which they believe they can only abstain completely or overindulge. Some clients find they do better if they eat a small portion of the food each day. Other clients find this to be an unnecessary, difficult temptation. Regardless, we recommend that when individuals begin to obsess about a particular food, they eat a small amount in a controlled setting. We also encourage clients to focus on the taste of each bite. This usually helps clients recognize that while the food may be pleasant, it is not as wonderful as they are making it out to be in their imagination. Thus, occasional, small amounts are usually adequate to reduce specific food cravings. If, however, the cravings are particularly intense and the person is not usually satisfied with a moderate amount, a more formal form of exposure and response prevention may be used. Fairburn, Marcus, and Wilson (1993) recommend this be done in vivo but suggest it also may be done in imagery. The client eats a small amount of the food with the therapist present and may be asked to rate taste and satisfaction after each bite. Usually the client will note the clear decrease in satisfaction, a result of habituation. Many clients do not notice this habituation normally (particularly in binge eating situations) when they have "tuned out" their internal sensations. However, in a controlled, therapeutic situation, clients learn that moderate amounts can be eaten and the urge to eat more will diminish. They can learn to identify the point at which the pleasant sensation becomes more neutral and to notice if it even starts to turn into an unpleasant sensation. Even if clients do not experience the typical decrease in the urge to eat as they finish a moderate amount, they practice tolerating the urge to eat more while being prevented from eating more.

In addition to specific food cravings, some individuals (normal and overweight) have preoccupations, eating-related rituals, and body checking rituals that are similar to obsessive-compulsive behaviors. A structured interview is available (Yale-Brown-Cornell Eating Disorder Scale; Sunday, Halmi, & Einhorn, 1995) that provides an extensive list of preoccupations and rituals. This interview can be a useful way to elicit such information if one is concerned that a client may be having such difficulties. The treatment of these types of behaviors is better addressed in interventions for negative body image than those for weight loss—Rosen's (1996) intervention for obese individuals (described in the previous section) and Cash's (1996) intervention for normal weight women.

SUMMARY AND CONCLUSION

When overweight individuals present for weight loss treatment, it may be useful to assess comorbid anxiety disorders and to identify the roles anxiety plays in the individual's eating patterns. Clients can be assessed for the degree to which they: (1) have baseline anxiety, (2) eat to cope with anxiety, (3) are anxious about eating or have "forbidden foods," (4) are anxious about not eating, (5) have anxiety about their weight and shape, and (6) have obsessive thoughts about food and eating. Once the sources of anxiety have been identified, treatment for weight loss can be adapted to target these areas, which if untreated may thwart the behavioral changes needed to lose weight effectively.

Clients who report that they are hungry all the time may have high levels of anxiety or may be very stressed even if they do not label this arousal as anxiety. Such individuals may be misinterpreting their arousal as hunger, and they are eating to relieve aversive internal sensations. For these individuals it is important to treat their anxiety/stress either in conjunction with or prior to standard weight loss treatment. Learning to distinguish between anxiety or stress and physical hunger will allow them to focus on developing more adaptive ways to cope with anxiety without resorting to eating.

Other clients, particularly individuals with BED, may be able to identify when they are anxious, but may be using food to counter the anxiety. Treatment for this group of emotional eaters needs to focus on developing alternative coping strategies. By employing coping mechanisms that yield more positive results (i.e., lessening anxiety without inducing guilt or other negative self-feelings), clients may reduce the frequency of emotional eating episodes.

Obese BED clients, and perhaps to a lesser extent obese non-BED clients, may experience considerable anxiety about their problematic eating patterns (i.e., binges, overeating) and, as a result, adopt maladaptive eating patterns in their efforts to reduce overall intake. Standard behavioral instructions to eat regular meals and snacks are useful, and this anxiety typically decreases as the client gains more control over eating.

For some obese individuals, anxiety may be triggered by dietary restriction, that is, trying not to eat and worrying about getting hungry. If feelings of hunger or even the thought of being hungry is associated with feeling anxious, the client may be less likely to tolerate restricting food intake and more likely to drop out of a program or not lose weight. Desensitization to moderate hunger and/or being in food situations without eating may be useful. We do not recommend encouraging clients to become really hungry, but if clients learn to tolerate feeling slightly hungry, moderate calorie restriction becomes more viable.

Finally, the majority of obese patients suffer from anxiety about their weight and shape, and some have obsessions, rituals, or avoidance behaviors related to their eating/weight concerns. Although anxiety about being overweight is understandable given our societal values, it is harmful, unnecessary, and in some ways actually reinforces societal biases. Cognitive behavioral therapy to address issues of negative body image may help reduce anxiety about weight; individuals may then be less socially anxious and in turn less isolated and less likely to turn to food for comfort. These body image interventions also address problems with eating/food rituals and checking behaviors.

While research specifically addressing the role of anxiety in the treatment of overweight individuals is minimal, much has been written about the importance of attending to "emotional eating." Thus, anxiety may play a large role in the etiology and/or maintenance of weight problems. Further research is needed to investigate the precise role of anxiety and to identify important moderating or mediating variables. Nevertheless, for those who treat individuals for weight management, attention to the ways in which anxiety affects an individual's eating patterns can be quite useful. Once identified, the difficulties can be more directly addressed, paving the way for more successful weight loss.

REFERENCES

Abraham, S. F., & Beaumont, P. J. V. (1982). How patients describe bulimia or binge eating. *Psychological Medicine, 12,* 625–635.

Agras, W. S., Telch, C. F., Arnow, B., Eldredge, K., Detzer, M. J., Henderson, J., & Marnell, M. (1995). Does interpersonal therapy help patients with binge eating disorder who fail to respond to cognitive-behavioral therapy? *Journal of Consulting and Clinical Psychology, 63,* 356–360.

Agras, W. S., Telch, C. F., Arnow, B., Eldredge, K., & Marnell, M. (1997). One-year follow-up of cognitive-behavioral therapy for obese individuals with binge eating disorder. *Journal of Consulting and Clinical Psychology, 65,* 343–347.

Agras, W. S., Telch, C. F., Arnow, B., Eldredge, K., Wilfley, D. E., Raeburn, S. D., Henderson, J., & Marnell, M. (1994). Weight loss, cognitive-behavioral, and desipramine treatments in binge eating disorder: An additive design. *Behavior Therapy, 25,* 225–238.

Antony, M. M., Johnson, W. G., Carr-Nangle, R. E., & Abel, J. L. (1994). Psychopathology correlates of binge eating and binge eating disorder. *Comprehensive Psychiatry, 35,* 386–392.

Apple R. F., & Agras, W. S. (1997). *Overcoming eating disorders: Client workbook.* Albany, NY: The Psychological Corporation/Graywind.

Arnow, B., Kenardy, J., & Agras, W. S. (1992). Binge eating among the obese: A descriptive study. *Journal of Behavioral Medicine, 15,* 155–170.

Cash, T. F. (1991). Binge-eating and body image among the obese: A further evaluation. *Journal of Social Behavior and Personality, 6,* 367–376.

Cooper, P. J. (1995). Eating disorders and their relationship to mood and anxiety disorders. In K. D. Brownell & C. G. Fairburn (Eds.), *Eating disorders and obesity,* New York: Guilford.

Cooper, P. J., Taylor, M. J., Cooper, Z., & Fairburn, C. G. (1982). The development of the Body Shape Questionnaire. *International Journal of Eating Disorders, 6,* 485–494.

Craighead, L. W., & Aibel, C. (1998). *Manual for appetite awareness training.* Unpublished manuscript.

Craighead, L. W., & Allen, H. (1995). Appetite awareness training: A cognitive behavioral intervention for binge eating. *Cognitive and Behavioral Practice, 2,* 249–270.

Craske, M. G., Barlow, D. H., & O'Leary, T. A. (1992). *Mastery of your anxiety and worry.* Albany, NY: Graywind.

Fairburn, C. G. (1981). A cognitive behavioral approach to the management of bulimia. *Psychological Medicine, 11,* 707–711.

Fairburn, C. G., & Cooper, Z. C. (1993). The eating disorder examination (12th ed.). In C. G. Fairburn & G. T. Wilson (Eds.), *Binge eating: Nature, assessment, and treatment* (pp. 317–360). New York: Guilford.

Fairburn, C. G., Marcus, M. D., & Wilson, G. T. (1993). Cognitive-behavioral therapy for binge eating and bulimia nervosa: A comprehensive treatment manual. In Fairburn, C. G., & Wilson, G. T. (Eds.), *Binge eating: Nature, assessment, and treatment* (pp. 361–404). New York: Guilford.

Friedman, M. A., & Brownell, K. D. (1995). Psychological correlates of obesity: Moving to the next research generation. *Psychological Bulletin, 117,* 3–20.

Goldfried, M. R., & Davidson, G. C. (1994). *Clinical behavior therapy.* New York: Wiley.

Gormally, J., Black, S., Daston, S., & Rardin, D. (1982). The assessment of binge eating severity among obese persons. *Addictive Behaviors, 7,* 47–55.

Grilo, C. M., & Shiffman, S. (1994). Longitudinal investigation of the abstinence violation effect in binge eaters. *Journal of Consulting and Clinical Psychology, 62,* 611–619.

Harrar, S., Loecher, B., Konner, L. & Editors of Prevention Magazine Health Books (1996). In S. F. Faelten (Ed.), *Food and you.* Emmaus, PA: Rodale.

Heatherton, T. F., & Baumeister, R. F. (1990). Binge eating as escape from self-awareness. *Psychological Bulletin, 110,* 86–108.

Heatherton, T. F., Herman, C. P., & Polivy, J. (1991) Effects of psychological threat and ego threat on eating behavior. *Journal of Personality and Social Psychology, 69,* 138–143.

Herman, C. P., & Polivy, J. (1975) Anxiety, restraint, and eating behavior. *Journal of Abnormal Psychology, 84,* 666–672.

Jeffery, R. W. (1988). Dietary risk factors and their modification in cardiovascular disease. *Journal of Consulting and Clinical Psychology, 56,* 350–357.

Kaplan, H. I., & Kaplan, H. S. (1957). The psychosomatic concept of obesity. *Journal of Nervous and Mental Disease, 125,* 181–201.

Keefe, P. H., Wyshogrod, D., Weinberger, E., & Agras, W. S. (1984). Binge eating and outcome of behavioral treatment of obesity: A preliminary report. *Behavior Research and Therapy, 22,* 319–321.

Kirschenbaum, D. S., & Fitzgibbon, M. L. (1995). Controversy about the treatment of obesity: Criticism or challenges? *Behavioral Therapy, 26,* 43–68.

Kral, J. G. (1995). Surgical interventions for obesity. In K. D. Brownell & C. G. Fairburn (Eds.), *Eating disorders and obesity*. New York: Guilford.

Kuczmarski, R. J. (1992). Prevalence of overweight and weight gain in the United States. *American Journal of Clinical Nutrition, 55* (suppl.), 495S–502S.

Kutlesic, V., Williamson, D. A., Gleaves, D. H., Barbin, J. M., and Murphy-Eberenz, K. P. (1998). The interview for the diagnosis of eating. IV: Application to DSM-IV diagnostic criteria. *Psychological Assessment, 10,* 41–48.

Linehan, M. M. (1993). *Skills training manual for treating borderline personality disorder*. New York: Guilford.

Marcus, M. D., Wing, R. R, Ewing, L., Kern, E., Gooding, W., & McDermott, M. (1990). Psychiatric disorders among obese binge eaters. *International Journal of Eating Disorders,* 969–977.

Marcus, M. D., Wing, R. R., & Fairburn, C. G. (1995). Cognitive behavioral treatment of binge eating vs. behavioral weight control in the treatment of binge eating disorder. *Annals of Behavioral Medicine, 17,* S90.

Marcus, M. D., Wing, R. R, & Hopkins, J. (1988). Obese binge eaters: Affect, cognitions and response to behavioral weight control. *Journal of Consulting and Clinical Psychology, 56,* 433–439.

Marcus, M. D., Wing R. R, & Lamparskil, D. M. (1985). Binge eating and dietary restraint in obese patients. *Addictive Behaviors, 10,* 1163–1168.

Marlatt, A., & Gordon, J. (Eds.). (1985). *Relapse prevention*. New York: Guilford.

Mitchell, S. L., & Epstein, L. H. (1996). Changes in taste and satiety in dietary-restrained women following stress. *Physiology and Behavior, 60,* 495–499.

Nagler, W., & Androff, A. (1990). Investigating the impact of deconditioning anxiety on weight loss. *Psychological Reports, 66,* 595–600.

Pi-Sunyer, F. X. (1993). Medical hazards of obesity. *Annals of Internal Medicine, 119,* 655–660.

Pitre, J. J., & Nicki, R. M. (1992). Dietary restraint anxiety and its relationship to eating behavior. *Journal of Behaviour Therapy and Experimental Psychiatry, 23,* 77–80.

Pitre, J. J., & Nicki, R. M. (1994). Desensitization of dietary restraint anxiety and its relationship to weight loss. *Journal of Behaviour Therapy and Experimental Psychiatry, 25,* 153–154.

Rosen, J. C. (1996). Improving body image in obesity. In J. K. Thompson (Ed.). *Body image, eating disorders, and obesity*. Washington, DC: American Psychological Association.

Rosen, J. C., Orosan, P., & Reiter, J. (1995). Cognitive behavior therapy for negative body image in obese women. *Behavior Therapy, 26,* 25–42.

Schwalberg, M. D., Barlow, D. H., Alger, S. A., & Howard, L. J. (1992). Comparison of bulimics, obese binge eaters, social phobics, and individuals with panic disorder on comorbidity across DSM-III-R anxiety disorders. *Journal of Abnormal Psychology, 101,* 675–681.

Slochower, J. (1976). Emotional labeling and overeating in obese and normal weight individuals. *Psychosomatic Medicine, 38,* 131–139.

Steere, J., & Cooper, P. J. (1993). The effects on eating on dietary restraint, anxiety, and hunger. *International Journal of Eating Disorders, 13,* 211–219.

Stunkard, A. J. (1959). Eating patterns and obesity. *Psychiatry Quarterly, 33,* 284–295.

Stunkard, A. J., & Messick, S. (1985). The three-factor eating questionnaire to measure dietary restraint, disinhibition and hunger. *Journal of Psychosomatic Research, 29,* 71–83.

Stunkard, A. J., & Sobel, (1995). Psychosocial consequences of obesity. In K. D. Brownell & C. G. Fairburn (Eds.), *Eating disorders and obesity* (pp. 417–421). New York: Guilford.

Sunday, S. R., Halmi, K. A., Einhorn, A. (1995). The Yale-Brown-Cornell Eating Disorder Scale: A new scale to assess eating disorders symptomatology. *International Journal of Eating Disorders, 18,* 237–245.

Telch, C. F., Agras, W. S., & Rossiter, E. M. (1988). Binge eating increases with increasing adiposity. *International Journal of Eating Disorders, 7,* 115–119.

Wadden, T. A. (1995). Very-low-calorie diets: Appraisal and recommendations. In K. D. Brownell & C. G. Fairburn (Eds.), *Eating disorders and obesity*. New York: Guilford.

Webber, E. M. (1994). Psychological characteristics of binging and nonbinging obese women. *Journal of Psychology, 128,* 339–351.

Wilson, G. T. (1993). Binge eating and addictive disorders. In C. G. Fairburn & G. T. Wilson (Eds.), *Binge eating: Nature, assessment, and treatment*. New York: Guilford.

Wilson, G. T. (1995). Behavioral approaches to the treatment of obesity. In K. D. Brownell & C. G. Fairburn (Eds.), *Eating disorders and obesity*. New York: Guilford.

Wolpe, J. W. (1958). *Psychotherapy by reciprocal inhibition*. Stanford, CA: Stanford University Press.

Yanovski, S. Z. (1993). Binge eating disorder: Current knowledge and future directions. *Obesity Research, 1,* 306–324.

CHAPTER 22

ANGER CONTROL AS A HEALTH PROMOTION MECHANISM

Shani Robins

Raymond W. Novaco

Anger, a turbulent emotion ubiquitous in everyday life, is now substantially associated with cardiovascular disorders (Chesney & Rosenman, 1985; Friedman, 1992; Johnson, 1990; Siegman & Smith, 1994; Williams & Williams, 1993). The adaptive value of anger is unmistakable. It is well known that anger has utility for communicating threat (Ekman & Davidson, 1994), potentiating aggression toward meeting threat (Bandura, 1972; Cannon, 1932), and providing information for identifying priorities and expectations (Schwarz & Clore, 1990). Yet, there are numerous interpersonal and societal problems that result from this emotion and the violence that it subtends (Novaco, 1986), and, in regard to medical disorders, several decades of research have established a link between anger, hypertension, and coronary disease (Dembroski et al., 1985; Diamond, 1982; Siegman, 1992).

Enthusiasm for the study of anger was enhanced by its identification with medical disorders. After all, people have been dying as a result of anger and hostility for a rather long time. Mostly they have died from externally caused tissue damage inflicted by anger-induced behavior, as opposed to anger-induced internal disease processes. However, when it was established that some very desirable clientele (e.g., corporate executives) had anger problems that could be assessed and treated in medico-laboratory settings, the popularity of anger research grew exponentially.

The connection between anger and health is presented here in terms of anger being an adaptation-seeking response occurring within dispositional, interpersonal, and environmental systems. Both the functional and the dysfunctional roles of anger are described with regard to the dynamic interactions within and between these systems. The health implications of anger being experienced, expressed, or suppressed are discussed in that context. We focus primarily on the cardiovascular health relevance of anger, as it is in this medical area that the preponderance of research on anger-related dysfunction has occurred.

ANGER AND CARDIOVASCULAR DISEASES

According to a recent article in a widely read periodical (*U.S. News & World Report,* 1998), "heart disease is the nation's number one killer." The American Heart Association reported that over 50 million adults in the United States suffer from hypertension (defined as diastolic blood pressure greater than 90 mm Hg, systolic blood pressure greater than 140 mm Hg), and close to a million people die each year from coronary heart disease (CHD), of which more than half come from the hypertensive population (Kannel & Stokes, 1985; Kannel et. al, 1986). In 1995 the CHD mortality rate accounted for nearly half of all deaths (42%) in the United States and was greater than the mortality rates from cancer (538,455), accidents (93,320), and AIDS (43,115) combined (American Heart Association, 1995). Underscoring the current societal importance attributed to coronary dysfunctions, the 1998 Nobel Prize for medicine was awarded to Louis J. Ignarro and colleagues for their work on nitric oxide, a chemical that has far-reaching implications for treating hypertension and reducing the risk of heart attacks.

Among the originally considered risk factors for CHD were hypertension, cigarette smoking, cholesterol, parental history of CHD, gender (males at increased risk), racial differences (blacks at increased risk), and Type A behavior (cf. Siegler, 1994). When multiple risk factors are present for the same individual, the mortality rates from CHD increase considerably (Kannel et. al, 1986). For example, whereas hypertension alone may increase the mortality rate by a factor of 2 to 3, hypertension concurrent with even moderately high cholesterol levels and smoking behavior was found by Kannel et al. to increase the mortality by a factor of 10 to 15 depending on the levels of the added risk factors.

Because biological and historical factors accounted for less than 50% of CHD cases, researchers began shifting their attention to Type A behavior (Friedman & Rosenman, 1974; Rosenman, 1983) and later focused in particular on its anger/hostility component (Chesney & Rosenman, 1985; Dembroski & MacDougall, 1983). For the past two decades, hostility, anger, and aggression have been identified as being highly correlated with, and arguably among the primary contributors to, hypertension, CHD, and coronary arterial disease (CAD) (Diamond, 1982; Dembroski et al., 1985; Siegler, 1994). Although the link between anger and coronary deterioration is empirically robust, research has generated some mixed results as to whether it is anger *expression* (Kaplan, Botchin, & Manuck, 1994; Siegman, Dembroski, & Ringel, 1987; Williams, 1985), or anger *suppression* (Haynes et al., 1978; Haynes, Feinlieb, & Kannel, 1980) that contributes to coronary disease. However, with regard to hypertension, the preponderance of evidence indicates that it is the suppression of anger that is characteristic of hypertensive patients (Johnson & Gentry, 1992).

Coronary heart disease, caused by atherosclerotic narrowing of the coronary arteries, was linked to acute psychophysiologic reactivity in a seminal review by Kranz and Manuck (1984). It is facilitated by anger and anger's link to a high-hostile disposition through several pathways. One pathway includes fat being released into the bloodstream for energy during an anger episode but remaining unused and then converting to cholesterol. Increased cholesterol, in turn, contributes to blockage of the arteries (atherosclerotic plaque formation), and it is such arterial occlusion that increases blood pressure and contributes to hypertension and heart disease (Lichtenstein, Shipley, & Rose, 1985; Williams, 1994). This accounts for the evidence linking increased anger and hostility with elevated levels of cholesterol (Lundberg et al., 1989; Rosenman &

Friendman, 1974). In an early study comparing victims of mild heart attacks with controls (Jenkins, 1966), self-reports of frequent hostility were positively correlated with cholesterol levels for both groups, and interviewers rated the voices and facial gestures of heart attack victims as more aggressive than those of controls. High cholesterol intake from food contributes directly to arterial occlusion and is thus also positively correlated with heart disease, particularly in men who also demonstrate high scores on the Cook-Medley Hostility scale and elevated catecholamine levels (Suarez et al., 1991).

Another potential pathway between anger and arterial occlusion is that in which arterial damage or endothelial injury results from the turbulence of blood flow in cardiovascular reactivity (Clarkson, Manuck, & Kaplan, 1986; Krantz & Manuck, 1984). With each anger episode, blood rapidly rushes past the arterial walls, producing erosion in them. Clumps of platelets and cholesterol attach themselves to damaged spots on arteries and accumulate over time. As anger becomes more chronic and intense, arteriosclerotic plaque accumulates, blocking the blood's path to the coronary artery, which can lead directly to heart failure. Similarly, it has been conjectured that hypertension develops from increased vascular wall tension and structural adaptations associated with the effect of increased cardiovascular reactivity (Johnson, Gentry, & Julius, 1992).

In addition to these biobehavioral mechanisms, it has been suggested by Williams (1994) that depletion in brain serotonin has an important mediating role. Drawing on animal and human studies, he noted that increased brain serotonin produces a "nonhostile" autonomic balance—that is, decreased sympathetic outflow and increased parasympathetic outflow. He further linked brain serotonin deficiency to alcohol and nicotine use, whereby alcohol and nicotine consumption serves as a self-medication that releases serotonin to remedy the deficit in the brain. Fancifully he conjectured that the identification of a serotonergic basis for hostility might someday lead to precise measurement of "hostility syndrome" by laboratory assay. Another endocrine mechanism that has been conjectured to play a role in anger-related pathogenesis of cardiovascular disease is beta-andrenergic receptors (Shapiro, Krantz, & Grim, 1986; Suarez et al., 1997). Controlled research with animals offers promise for the attenuation of atheroscelerosis by beta-adrenergic blocking agents (Kaplan, Botchin, & Manuck, 1994). Lastly, associations between testosterone and anger, hostility, and aggression hypothetically contribute to the gender differences observed in hypertension (Vogele, Jarvis, & Cheeseman, 1997) and CHD rates, with males demonstrating twice the morbidity rates from CHD as females (Stoney & Engebretson, 1994).

Before proceeding further, some definitional clarity is needed. There are multidimensional psychological phenomena entailed in occurrences of anger (a subjective emotion), hostility (an attitudinal disposition), and aggression (behavior intended to cause injury or damage), and the equivocation of terms ("anger" and "hostility" have been used interchangeably, as have "hostility" and "aggression") and lack of definitional clarity that continue to occur in the literature (e.g., Houston, 1994) add confusion to an already complex puzzle. This confusion, which appeared early in the writings on essential hypertension (e.g., Alexander, 1939), was perpetuated by the popularity of the Cook-Medley Hostility Scale in the assessment of risk for coronary artery disease, as begun by Williams and his colleagues (Barefoot, Dahlstrom, & Williams, 1982; Williams et al., 1980). Although others have taken note of this mixing of terms (e.g., Spielberger et al., 1985), an important reason for this confusion went unnoticed: Research in psychosomatic medicine did not intersect with research on human aggression, co-temporaneously activated by the classic work by Dollard et al. (1939). Ever since anger, hostility, and aggression were distinguished by Buss (1961), not many aggression researchers would confuse "anger" with "hostility." Williams and his colleagues (e.g., Williams, Barefoot, & Shekelle, 1985) do not confuse these terms, nor do others (e.g., Smith, 1994). Far too often, however, there is conceptual slippage. Because these research fields have proceeded with little intersection, elementary distinctions and conventions in the aggression field are not so uniform in the health psychology/psychosomatic medicine field.

A SYSTEMS VIEW OF ANGER

At the outset, then, we wish to be clear definitionally: *Anger* is:

a negatively toned emotion, subjectively experienced as an aroused state of antagonism toward someone or something perceived to be the source of an aversive event. It is triggered or provoked situationally by events that are perceived to constitute deliberate harm-doing by an instigator toward oneself or toward those to whom one is endeared. Provocations usually take the form of insults, unfair treatments, or intended thwartings. Anger is prototypically experienced as a justified response to some "wrong" that has been done. While anger is situationally triggered by acute, proximal occurrences, it is shaped and facilitated contextually by conditions affecting the cognitive, arousal, and behavioral systems that comprise anger reactions. Anger activation is centrally linked to threat perceptions and survival responding. (Novaco, in press).

Aggression is behavior intended to cause psychological or physical harm to someone or to a surrogate target. The behavior may be verbal or physical, direct or indirect. Hostility is an attitudinal disposition of antagonism toward another person or social system. It represents a predisposition to respond with aggression under conditions of perceived threat. The relationship of anger to aggression is that anger is a significant activator of aggression and has a mutually influenced relationship with it, but anger is neither necessary nor sufficient for aggression to occur (cf. Novaco, 1998).

When people report anger experiences, they most typically give accounts of things that have "happened to them." For the most part, they describe events physically and temporally proximate to their anger arousal. As a rule, they provide accounts of provocations ascribed to events in the immediate situation of the anger experience, portrayed in the telling as being something about which anger is quite fitting. This can be viewed as a "proximity bias" in the understanding of anger, as opposed to a contextual perspective that would emphasize the embeddedness, interrelatedness, and transformationality of anger experiences (Novaco, 1993).

Researchers and clinicians alike have been seduced to attend to anger incident accounts. Clinicians, of course, are pressed with the situational imperative of needing to listen to a client who wants to talk. Researchers, particularly when focused on finding main effects rather than higher-order interactions, obtain anger self-reports based on daily diary data or classifications of open-ended descriptions, whereby respondents confine their accounts of the anger instigation to proximate situations. Assigning the causes of anger to discrete occurrences is uniformly the case in the community and student questionnaire studies, and it is the intrinsic character of lab studies.

The response to the question, What makes you angry? hinges on self-monitoring proficiencies and is often based on intuitions. Precisely because becoming angry involves a loss of self-monitoring capacity, people are not good or objective observers when they are angry; and because anger is very much a blaming reaction, people are inclined to point. Far less commonly do people disaggregate their anger experiences into source components, some of which may originate from distal sources and ambient circumstances, rather than from acute, proximal occurrences. Generally people do not attend to the cognitive and arousal residues of temporally distal circumstances nor to the ambient influences of the contextual surround. Nor do they recognize that their cultivated worldview provides the landscape for their anger.

In contrast to the more customary truncated view of anger, we have argued for a systems approach (Robins & Novaco, in press). We assume that the occurrence of anger is grounded in long-term adaptations to internal and external environmental demands that involve a range of environmental fields from the biological to the sociocultural. We are concerned with individual, group, and aggregate-level factors affecting anger as the person, group, or organization responds to demands pertinent to survival. Anger is viewed as having important adaptive functions in affecting behavior and thereby affecting the social and physical environmental systems in which the person has membership. Anger experiences are embedded or nested within overlapping systems, such as the work setting, the work organization, the regional economy, and the sociocultural value structure.

Emphasis is also given to interdependencies between systems and system components. Anger determinants, anger experiences, and anger sequelae are reciprocally influenced. For example, in a coercive family system, parental anger arises during disciplinary confrontations as an effort to control a child's antagonistic behavior. The parent's anger display can not only prompt further antagonistic behavior from the child but also models anger as a response to noncompliance or being thwarted, thus reinforcing the coercive character of the milieu.

The interrelatedness of system components provides for positive and negative feedback loops among the interdependent structures, which serve to amplify or counteract anger-related processes. An assumption of most systems is that they have a condition of equilibrium or a stable, resting state of homeostasis wherein their components are in balance. When a system moves away from equilibrium, negative feedback loops serve to counteract the deviation. This is the function of cognitive systems in self-monitoring anger reactions to achieve anger control. In contrast, anger reactions can be augmented by positive feedback, which is a deviation amplification effect. Anger displays in a situation of conflict tend to evoke anger and aggression in response, which then justify the original anger and increase the probability of heightened antagonism. Such anger/aggression escalation effects are well known in conflict scenarios, whether interpersonal or international.

Interventions proceeding from a systems model would examine the environmental, interpersonal, and dispositional subsystems that shape anger reactions. While recognizing that recurrent anger is often a product of long-term exposure to adverse conditions or to acute trauma, it can also be seen that anger is a product of agentic behavior. People who select high-conflict settings or recurrently inhabit high-stress environments set the stage for their anger experiences. Their anger response patterns may indeed demonstrate inertia. People who are habitually hostile create systemic conditions that fuel continued anger responding that is resistant to change. As interaction patterns and categorizations are schematized, anger is evoked with considerable automaticity in reaction to minimal threat cues. Thus, therapeutic focus on intrapsychic variables is transparently inadequate when the person remains immersed in anger-engendering contexts.

Intrapsychic, dispositional systems are the principal focus of psychotherapy, and, in that regard, anger has three main subsystems or domains: cognitive, physiological, and behavioral. Cognitive dispositions for anger include knowledge structures, such as expectations and beliefs, and appraisal processes, which are schematically organized. Anger schemata are mental representations about the environment–behavior relationship entailing rules governing threatening situations. Physiological dispositions for anger include high hormone levels (neurotransmitters) and low stimulus thresholds for the activation of arousal. Anger is marked by physiological activation in the cardiovascular, endocrine, and limbic systems and by tension in the skeletal musculature. Behavioral dispositions include conditioned and observably learned repertoires of anger-expressive behavior, including aggression but also avoidance behavior. Implicit in the cognitive labeling of anger is an inclination to act antagonistically toward the source of the provocation. However, an avoidant style of responding, found in personality and psychosomatic disorders, can foment anger by leaving the provocation unchanged or exacerbated.

Thus, it can be seen that these dispositional subsystems are highly interactive or interdependent. Anger-linked appraisals influence arousal levels, high arousal activates aggression and overrides inhibition, and antagonistic behavior escalates aversive events and shapes anger schemata and scripts for anger episodes as behavioral routines are encoded. In turn, the personal dispositional system interfaces with the environmental, such as when anger and aggression drive away pacific people, leaving one with angry and aggressive companions, who not only incite anger but from whom one continues to learn anger responding and anger-engendering appraisals, which further heighten arousal.

Anger and Physiological Arousal: Psycholinguistically Driven Intuitions

It has long been known that anger is accompanied by heightened levels of cardiovascular arousal, which has been identified as the mechanism that translates personality and behavior into cardiovascular disease processes (Siegman & Smith, 1994). Dr. John Hunter, a famous eighteenth-century British surgeon, is often quoted as having once remarked, "My life is in the hands of any rascal that chooses to annoy me." Indeed, he died suddenly while attending a hospital board meeting (Jenkins, 1978). Clearly this intuition preceded the landmark research by Barefoot, Dahlstrom, and Williams (1982) on the association of

hostility assessed in medical school with physician mortality 25 years later.

Since the time of the Stoic philosophers of the classical period, especially Seneca in Rome and Epictetus in Greece, anger has been considered an animal passion that needs to be controlled. Lakoff and Kovecses (1987) aptly assert that our very conceptualizations of anger rely on several metaphors, including one of anger being a dangerous animal that warrants containment. Linguistic evidence that we indeed conceive of anger this way includes mundane idioms such as "having a monstrous or ferocious temper," "arousing another's anger," and "unleashing" or "losing one's grip on one's anger." Lakoff and Kovecses argue that this metaphor is not merely a linguistic convenience, but rather defines our thinking about anger by importing to the domain of anger our conceptualizations from the domain of a dangerous animal. It is such psycholinguistic transfer across domains, Lakoff and Kovecses posit, that leads our intuition to prescribe that anger is something that needs to be controlled and contained (suppressed), just as a dangerous animal would be. Lack of such control can lead to instances of "growling" and "snapping at someone," as well as "biting their head off." A second metaphor that seems to promote suppression of anger is that of anger as an opponent, reflected in idioms such as "struggling," "battling," "wrestling" and "overcoming" one's anger rather than "surrendering to" or "yielding to" the anger.

Lakoff and Kovecses (1987) present a third metaphor highly relevant to cardiovascular functioning—that of anger being liquid heating in a closed container—that they believe predominates much of our thinking about anger, favoring its expression rather than suppression. Commonly used idioms in this regard include "bottling up your anger," "making your blood boil," being "red with anger," "losing your cool," "foaming at the mouth," being a "hothead," and being "under pressure." Correspondingly, idioms from this metaphor that specify ways of dealing with anger include "venting one's anger" and "letting off steam," or else the negative consequences of "flipping your lid," "blowing your top," and "exploding with rage."

The contrast between these metaphors, in terms of the expression versus the suppression of anger, parallels the inconsistencies in the literature regarding the health outcomes of these coping strategies (Suls & Wan, 1993). There is evidence that negative physiological outcomes result from expressing anger and positive outcomes result from suppressing it (e.g., Siegman, 1989; Williams, 1989); there is also evidence of positive physiological outcomes from expressing anger and negative physiological outcomes from suppressing it (Alexander, 1939; Diamond, 1982; Jamner et al., 1991; Julius, Schneider, & Egan, 1985; Manuck et al., 1985; Ragland & Brand, 1988).

Anger Expression and Cardiovascular Health

The adverse health consequences of anger have been established with regard to CAD and CHD largely for a personality style characterized by the expression of anger (Rosenman, 1985; Siegman, Dembroski, & Ringel, 1987; Siegman, 1994). Siegman (1994) argues that it is the expression of anger rather than the mere experience of anger that is significantly related to CAD and CHD. Some evidence suggests that particular types of anger have especially negative outcomes when expressed. Williams (1989), for example, suggests that it is a generalized, "hot," impulsive anger that gives rise to a positive correlation between anger expression and CHD. With regard to anger expression as a personality style, the Type A behavior pattern (TABP) has been the most widely studied individual difference factor, and the great attention that it received led to the later focus on anger and hostility, which soon (e.g., Williams, Barefoot, & Shekelle, 1985) dominated the research thrust, exemplified by the Chesney and Rosenman (1985) volume.

The TABP includes time urgency, competitiveness, impatience, accelerated pace of activities, and a propensity for anger and hostility. It has been demonstrated to be correlated with CHD and CAD in a multitude of studies (e.g., Rosenman et al., 1976; Rosenman, 1986, 1993) and across cultures (e.g., French-Belgium Collaborative Group, 1982). Reviews of this field can be found in Cooper, Detre, and Weiss (1981), Matthews and Haynes (1986), Booth-Kewley and Friedman (1987), and Siegman and Smith (1994). Intermittent failures to replicate the positive correlation between the global construct of TABP and coronary disease (cf. Scherwitz, 1989) led to evaluations

of each of its individual components. Among these components the anger/hostility dimension of the TABP was found to most clearly identify coronary-prone subjects (Dembroski et al., 1985, 1989; Shekelle et al., 1983).

The Type A hostility dimension pertains to an antagonistic interpersonal style that increases the likelihood of anger rather than to the actual feeling of anger. However, there is evidence that both the quality and quantity of anger of Type A's are pertinent. Physiologically, Type A's, in contrast to passive or anxious individuals, respond to competitive physical activity and stressful stimuli with increased physiological reactivity, entailing heightened levels of activation on three risk factors for coronary disease: norepinephrine (Friedman et al., 1975), testosterone (Williams, 1982), and systolic blood pressure (Manuck & Garland, 1979). At rest or during neutral tasks the blood pressure of Type A individuals is often similar to that of controls (Rosenman, 1987), which suggests that Type A individuals, like otherwise classified hostile individuals (Houston, 1994), are predisposed to react to life stressors with increased reactivity.

The original conception of the TABP was as a disposition potentiated by the social environment. This underlined the importance of an individual's milieu as an interacting factor in the anger–CHD association. The delineation of the interactions between this disposition and environmental conditions likely to manifest the hostility component are warranted, although research ethics issues weigh against achieving ecological validity in controlled experimentation. The more challenging and impactful the provoking stimuli are on the participant—that is, the more genuinely similar it is to real-life frustrations and anger-provoking events the greater the likelihood of real anger. Indeed, the Type A structured interview was designed to function as a provocation to elicit the behavior pattern (Chesney, Eagleston, & Rosenman, 1980).

Anger Suppression and Cardiovascular Health

Anger suppression can be functional in promoting interpersonal or social conciliation. For example, when there is a high probability of impending violence, it is prudent to restrain anger expression to diminish the likelihood of triggering a physical assault. Whether in a domestic, street, or occupational context, anger is adaptively muffled when physical retaliation can be expected or when a cool head is needed to solve a problem. In the short term, suppressing even the verbalization of anger may not only be interpersonally beneficial, but has been found as well to reduce, at least momentarily, physiological reactivity levels (Siegman, Anderson, & Berger, 1990). One might then expect negative correlations between anger suppression and coronary disease. Considerable evidence, however, demonstrates deleterious long-term health effects of suppressing anger (Johnson, Gentry, & Julius, 1992).

In terms of cardiovascular dysfunction, the suppression of anger is robustly correlated with sustained hypertension (Diamond, 1982; Goldstein, 1981), as are difficulties in expressing anger, hostility, and aggression (Esler, 1977; Jamner et al., 1991; Steptoe, 1981). The relation of the suppression of anger and aggression to elevated blood pressure has been observed for decades (Harburg et al., 1973; Miller, 1939; Schwartz, 1990). Ineffective anger management was found to predict higher baseline blood pressure and higher incidence of hypertension (Kahn et al., 1972), and, in large sample research, suppressed anger was positively correlated with CHD, an end-point consequence of elevated blood pressure (Haynes, Feinleib, & Kannel, 1980). Moreover, the extent of patients' Type A potential for hostility and "anger-in" (suppressing anger) predicted the patients who demonstrated both the greatest number of obstructed vessels and the most severe vessel stenosis, as well as the number of patients' obstructed heart vessels (Dembroski et al., 1985). However, Dembroski and Costa (1987) argued that anger-in is a *consequence* of CHD rather than an etiologic factor.

While studies of the relationship of anger to blood pressure have often been laboratory-based, seminal work in this area has been conducted in field settings, beginning with important studies by Harburg and Gentry and their colleagues, whose Detroit area studies illustrate the effects of anger as embedded in a larger physical and sociocultural milieu (Gentry, 1985; Gentry et al., 1982; Harburg, Blakelock, & Roeper, 1979; Harburg et al., 1973).

The pioneering study by Harburg et al. (1973), which reported on males only, basically found additive effects for three factors: (1) what they termed

"socio-ecological stress" (census tracts characterized by low socioeconomic status, high crime, high density, high residential mobility, and high marital instability), (2) race (black versus white), and (3) anger coping style (anger-in versus anger-out and also guilt). In assessments done by nurse-interviewers the highest diastolic pressures were found for those who lived in high-stress areas, were black, and who suppressed anger and felt guilty about it. The anger variable pertained to responses to scenarios of police harassment and housing discrimination. The environmental, biological, and coping style factors had additive effects on diastolic pressure. For a scenario of an arbitrarily angry boss, Harburg, Blakelock, and Roeper (1979) reported higher diastolic pressure for high-stress, resentful, anger-out young blacks.

Gentry et al. (1982) improved on the earlier methodology by basing the anger coping classification on the entire range of the five scenarios studied, by disentangling the contributions of the study's factors, and by also examining systolic pressure. It was found that the odds of being diagnosed hypertensive were higher for blacks, males, those under socioecological stress, and those with anger-in tendencies. They reported that "respondents in the highest risk category (black males residing in the high stress area who reported a low level of anger expression) had a 5.87 times greater risk for hypertensive disease" (p. 199). Gentry (1985) reported further that the effect of the suppressed anger coping style on blood pressure is potentiated by interracial hostility, job strain, and family strain, finding rather large differences (10 to 15 mm diastolic) between conditions.

More recently, in methodologically sophisticated research, Jamner and his colleagues have conducted a series of studies in natural settings, assessing blood pressure and heart rate in association with individual differences in hostility and its suppression. Jamner et al. (1991, 1993) and Shapiro, Goldstein, and Jamner (1995) used ambulatory recorders that measured blood pressure and heart rate during random intervals. Consistent with the previously described literature regarding anger suppression, findings suggested that increased levels of hostility (as measured by the Cook-Medley Hostility scale), when accompanied by a tendency to inhibit the expression of that hostility (as inferred by high scores on the Marlowe-Crowne Social Desirability scale), are associated with both greater increases of cardiovascular reactivity to provocative events and elevated blood pressure during resting periods between such events.

These results present a consistent link between the suppression of anger and increased hypertension. Several findings help account for this association between anger suppression, hypertension, and CHD. In one study, anger expression was found to shorten recovery times for returning elevated blood pressure to baseline levels (Hokanson, Burgess, & Cohen, 1963). Presumably, suppressing one's anger served to maintain ruminations beyond the instigating episode and consequently to maintain higher levels of hypertension. Converging evidence for this interpretation is provided by Wegner and Erber (1992), who found that active attempts to suppress thoughts produce hyperaccessibility for the target thoughts, particularly under conditions of high cognitive load. The argument is that disinhibition occurs when one's cognitive resources can no longer suppress unwanted thoughts. Actively inhibiting the processing of anger-evoking problems and traumas may not only leave them unresolved, but could also facilitate more frequent spontaneous retrieval of and rumination about those problems, thus increasing overall reactivity (Wegner et al., 1990).

Finally, residual arousal from anger events can transfer to future conflicts and further intensify the anger reactivity to instigating events (Zillmann, 1971; Zillmann & Bryant, 1974). Unexpressed anger is associated with exaggerated and more prolonged cardiovascular responses to a variety of stressful stimuli (Goldstein, 1981). Given the considerable empirical evidence about the deleterious consequences of both anger expression and suppression, one wonders why such a response would still be in our repertoire of evolutionary behaviors and why that predisposition would be so universally manifested across cultures. The next several sections offer an analysis of that seeming contradiction and suggest several adaptive functions that anger serves. The biological processes that subtend those functions are used to explain the negative coronary results of anger previously discussed.

Anger: An Evolved Adaptation

Anger, like other emotions, is one of many evolutionary adaptive responses for dealing with life stressors such as interpersonal antagonism and larger social conflict (Darwin, 1955; Ekman & Davidson, 1994; Lazarus, 1991; Novaco, 1976; Tooby & Cosmides, 1990). Evidence that anger is a species-wide predisposition includes the cultural universality of anger (e.g., Ekman, 1972, 1994; Scherer & Wallbott, 1986, 1994), as well as its appearance in the earliest stages of infancy (e.g., Lewis, Alessandri, & Sullivan, 1990; Sternberg & Campos, 1990). A critique of this position can be found in Averill's (1994) social constructivist arguments.

Neurophysiological evidence suggests that we have neural architecture (especially the limbic system) specialized for the processing of emotion and emotion–cognition interactions (LeDoux, 1984, 1989). The amygdala seems to be dedicated to detecting particular events and actions as threats (Aggleton & Mishkin, 1986). In parallel, higher-level cognitive reasoning further elaborates this information, in what are often termed *appraisal processes* (Lazarus, 1994; Ortony, Clore, & Collins, 1988). The perception that a stimuli is threatening is conjoined with the activation of sympathetic functions such as heart rate and respiration increases that prepare the body for a "fight-flight" response (Cannon, 1932).

If this elaborate neural architecture can be presumed to have evolved, then it is likely to have had one or more adaptive functions that facilitated its development. As with the eye's specialized function of encoding visual information and the thumb's specialized function of grasping, anger evolved because of its adaptive value in the interpersonal and social systems within which it is embedded (Carver & Scheier, 1990; Clore, 1992; Oatley & Jenkins, 1992). Such functionality would predict anger to be both ubiquitous and persistent. Among the adaptive functions of anger are its role in potentiating action and its value as a source of information.

From a survival point of view that acknowledges the inevitability of interpersonal conflict and social injustice, it is functional to have a system that energizes self-protection and the addressing of grievances. Anger activates the physiological mechanisms that prepare the body for the "fight" response and motivates persistence in dealing with adversity. In addition, anger provides information, both to oneself and to others (Novaco, 1976). In terms of the self, Schwarz and Clore (1988) elaborate this idea by positing that anger gives information useful for prioritizing and decision making. The intensity of anger, for example, can help focus and maintain attention on relevant goals and help one estimate progress toward those goals. In addition, when one is pressed to make a decision, anger provides a "how do I feel about it" cue that can be processed without the need for elaborate analysis (see Schwarz & Clore, 1988).

Regarding information for others, anger communicates perceived wrongdoing, threat of aggression, or intent of reprisal. The facial features associated with anger, as well as the interpretations of those expressions, have been found to be culturally universal (Ekman, 1972, 1994). Such information exchange prior to aggression can facilitate social and interpersonal negotiations toward conflict resolution and prevent the bodily harm that can result from escalation to violent confrontation.

Anger: A Vestigial Adaptation with Cardiovascular Disease By-Products

Cannon (1932) suggested that, although the physiological components of an anger response, such as increased blood flow, may be adaptive for survival in a short-term danger episode, the by-products of that response may wreak havoc on the body in the long term. Indeed, we have cited considerable evidence that the blood pressure reactivity component of the anger response is strongly correlated with CHD and hypertension. Those same anger mechanisms of sympathetic reactivity proven to be highly adaptive in our ancestral history are dysfunctional in modern environments (urban life, high-stress jobs, commuting),

In our ancestral environments, where the mechanisms for anger presumably evolved, the health cost–benefit ratio of an anger response was relatively low. The long-term health risks of cardiovascular disorders were unlikely to materialize given relatively short life spans. The benefits of anger, however, were high, especially during survival struggles, as anger's activation of aggression enabled vigorous engagement to prevent the loss of life or resources.

In today's industrial societies our appraisal of situations as conflicts or threats activates these same evolved anger mechanisms, often in response to challenges that do not threaten survival, such as freeway frustrations (Novaco, Kliewer, & Broquet, 1991). The

perceived hassles of daily life consequently result in near daily responses of anger in North American populations (Averill, 1982; Novaco, 1986). We are now living long enough to suffer the cumulative health damage of such responses.

INTERVENTIONS FOR ANGER DYSCONTROL

Research on the treatment of anger continues to lag behind the effort given to problems of anxiety and depression. There are multiple reasons for this, including the assault risk and other unsettling aspects of working with seriously angry people, the low frustration tolerance of angry clients who easily abandon treatment, the avoidant and distancing personality styles of chronically angry people, the entrenchment of anger and aggression based on their inherent instrumentality, and the typically impoverished social status and support systems of people who have anger and aggression problems (cf. Novaco, 1985, 1997). Nevertheless, some significant gains are being made in the realm of anger treatment, including some recent work with seriously disordered clinical populations (Chemtob et al., 1997; Renwick et al., 1997).

Generally the most commonly used approach to anger treatment has been cognitive-behavioral in orientation, and much of it has followed the stress inoculation (SI) framework pioneered by Meichenbaum for anxiety treatment in the 1970s (cf. Meichenbaum, 1985). In the anger field, CBT began with Novaco (1975, 1977) and was expanded by others, including Feindler and Ecton (1986) and Deffenbacher and his associates (e.g., Deffenbacher, 1994; Deffenbacher et al., 1995; Hazaleus & Deffenbacher, 1986), who are less tied to the SI framework. While methods of anger treatment will continue to evolve, the SI approach has had considerable favor, and it is important to test the efficacy of such work beyond university clinic populations (cf. Novaco & Chemtob, 1998; Novaco, Ramm, & Black, in press). With regard to cardiovascular disorders, there is a modicum of studies showing significant anger treatment gains, which we will present here. First, the basic components of anger treatment by the stress inoculation (SI) approach are described.

The Stress Inoculation Approach

The SI cognitive-behavioral approach to anger treatment involves the following key components: (1) client education about anger, stress, and aggression; (2) self-monitoring of anger frequency, intensity, and situational triggers; (3) construction of a personal anger provocation hierarchy, created from the self-monitoring data and used for practicing and testing coping skills; (4) arousal reduction techniques of progressive muscle relaxation, breathing-focused relaxation, and guided imagery training; (5) cognitive restructuring by altering attentional focus, modifying appraisals, and using self-instruction; (6) training behavioral coping in communication and respectful assertiveness as modeled and rehearsed with the therapist; and (7) practicing the cognitive, arousal regulatory, and behavioral coping skills while visualizing and role playing progressively more intense anger-arousing scenes from the personal hierarchy.

Provocation is simulated in the therapeutic context by imagination and role play of anger incidents from the life of the client, as directed by the therapist. This is a graduated exposure based on a hierarchy of anger incidents produced collaboratively by the client and therapist. This graduated, hierarchical exposure, done in conjunction with the teaching of coping skills, is the basis for the "inoculation" metaphor and is at the center of the stress inoculation approach. This SI approach to anger control was the foundation of the specialized anger therapy implemented in a controlled treatment trial with Vietnam veterans having severe PTSD and severe anger (Chemtob et al., 1997) and in a treatment project with hospitalized forensic patients who were mentally disordered, very angry, and seriously violent before and during institutionalization (Renwick et al., 1997). These two studies have further developed the therapeutic approach—the former by building in a conjunction with trauma and PTSD and the latter by expanding the treatment protocol for mentally disordered inpatients and developing of a treatment "preparatory phase" to address treatment resistance issues.

Anger dyscontrol is accompanied by a substantial loss of self-monitoring. Essential to re-instituting regulatory controls for anger and aggression is treating the central self-monitoring deficits. In that regard the clinician helps the patient to (1) monitor the cognitions that he or she typically experiences when threatened and which induce anger episodes; (2) identify signs of arousal, including its intensity, duration, and lability, in response to the perception of danger or threat; (3) recognize the role that anger reactions play, both as responses to sensing danger and as behaviors that create danger for others, thus escalating the threat potential of a situation; and (4) distinguish impulsive actions from more controlled responses. The cognitive, arousal, and behavioral domains of anger are segmented for self-monitoring. This attention to self-monitoring should be emphasized in psychotherapeutic regimens applied to cardiovascular problems.

Applicability of Anger Control Methods to the Treatment of Hypertension

An argument for the applicability to the treatment of essential hypertension of the cognitive-behavioral anger control methods was articulated by Novaco (1975). Although research in this area has been sparse, there is some evidence of effectiveness. Two hypertension intervention studies with community participants utilizing arousal reduction and CBT have obtained significant treatment gains. Chesney et al. (1987), in an elaborate component treatment design, found that SI procedures produced the greatest reductions in blood pressure, compared to blood pressure monitoring and other behavior therapy conditions. Moreover, these treatment group differences were greatest with regard to worksite blood pressure (as opposed to clinic measures), which calls attention to contextual factors. In a study of hypertensive treatment that focused on anger control intervention, Achmon et al. (1989) found significant decreases in blood pressure (clinic measures) for the anger SI treatment compared to controls, but less than the improvement found for heart rate biofeedback. Because the SI group had the most significant improvement with regard to anger control, perhaps home or work blood pressure measures might have produced different treatment group results.

A noteworthy study of anger and hypertension was conducted by Davison et al. (1991), who evaluated whether 7 weeks of relaxation therapy for anger re-duction would achieve physiological gains in male adults with borderline hypertension. Over the same period, control group participants received general in-formation for reducing hypertension such as exercis-ing regularly, reducing salt intake, and losing weight and had their blood pressure and pulse measured at each session. Anger treatment group participants were additionally given audio relaxation tapes to help guide their relaxation at home during the 7-week period. Pre- and posttreatment anger assessments in-volved Spielberger's State-Trait Anger Scale (STAS) (Spielberger, et al., 1983) and an Articulated Thoughts in Simulated Situations assessment (ATSS) developed by Davison et al. (1991) in which they verbalized their responses to prerecorded dramatic scenarios aimed at instigating anger. The verbalizations were transcribed and coded by two people, blind to experimental con-ditions, for the percentage of phrases that were angry, hostile, or aggressive. Treatment gains were evaluated in a pretest versus posttest design, and the association between anger and physiological reactivity was eval-uated by examining the correlation between anger re-duction and the level changes of blood pressure and pulse scores.

The results of the Davison et al. (1991) study were supportive of an anger–coronary connection as well as of treatment effectiveness. Prior to the intervention, no differences in anger, blood pressure, or pulse ex-isted between the two participant groups. Following treatment, participants in the specialized relaxation therapy demonstrated less anger than did controls on ATSS, although no such differences were found for the STAS. Most centrally, anger decreases on the ATSS were positively correlated with decreases in levels of systolic blood pressure and pulse. Interest-ingly this pattern was true for both treatment and con-trol participants.

Bennet et al. (1990) made a comprehensive evalu-ation of the effectiveness, relative to a control group, of two treatments aimed at diminishing Type A be-havior and anger. They additionally measured blood pressure and evaluated the relation between anger re-duction and blood pressure variation. The first treat-ment group, stress management training (SMT), was given eight, 2-hour weekly intervention sessions for general stress management training. The second treat-ment group, Type A management (TAM), received similar training, but methods for reducing Type A behaviors and anger in particular were emphasized. Anger was measured using the Spielberger Anger Expression Scale, and blood pressure was measured each week, both during rest and during the Type A Structured Interview (Rosenman, 1978). Scores were compared at baseline, post intervention, and at a 6-month follow-up. Both intervention groups dem-onstrated significant reductions in anger relative to baseline and to the control group, which actually had a slight increase in anger. TAM subjects demonstrated consistent reductions in anger-in, anger-out, and anger control, both at the 8-week and 6-month follow-up points. SMT subjects demonstrated only anger-in re-ductions at both time points. With regard to blood pressure, both treatment groups had significant re-ductions (7–9 mmHg) in resting systolic and diastolic blood pressure. Similarly, during the presumably stressful period of the SI interview, both interventions led to blood pressure reductions, with systolic drops averaging 12 mmHg and diastolic drops averaging 9 mmHg. Univariate analyses demonstrated that re-ductions in both anger-in and anger-out were signifi-cantly related to reductions in blood pressure.

These anger treatment studies are noteworthy in that they measure both anger and blood pressure reduc-tions. In terms of clinical goals, interventions should aim to reduce both the suppression (anger-in) as well as the expression (anger-out) of anger. Regarding the contextual perspective previously described, the inter-personal and social systems within which anger is em-bedded help define whether expressing or suppressing anger is behaviorally adaptive.

SUMMARY AND SUGGESTIONS

The evidence cited in this chapter clearly points to a robust association between anger and the deteriora-tion of coronary health. Anger expression seems to be a primary antecedent of CHD, whereas anger sup-pression seems to significantly contribute to hyperten-sion. Much of the data that bear out these conclusions seems to fall into one of two categories. Some of the evidence presented is epidemiological, demonstrat-ing positive correlations between measures of anger levels and of coronary reactivity as well as disease. The second major category of studies involves the experimental manipulation of anger in laboratory settings and the evaluation of the extent to which individual differences, such as high and low hostility, differentially contribute to changes in physiological reactivity, such as greater increases in blood pressure and heart rate. The laboratory research indicates that persons high in hostility are predisposed to react to conflicts with greater increases in blood pressure and consequently to be more prone to cardiovascular dysfunction.

For many clients, anger has come to be an "automatic" response, akin to the understanding of emotion as a "passion" that takes control of the personality (Averill, 1982). Anger reactions are thus experienced subjectively as being uncontrollable and inevitable. In contrast, a systems model emphasizes the capacity for long-term control of anger and of the systems within which anger is embedded. Interventions would therefore aim to modify systemic conditions to reduce dysfunctional anger reactions. Anger frequency, intensity, duration, and mode of expression are key response parameters for gauging its problematic effects on personal resource systems, such as health, interpersonal relationships, and occupation. Anger is diminished as one automatizes appraisals that are incongruent with anger, develops more adaptive alternative responses to environmental demands, chooses low-conflict environments, and maintains supportive social relationships. There is dynamic interaction between these interdependent components—a change in one component facilitates changes in others.

The systems perspective, with its emphasis on contextuality, suggests that clinical interventions for anger across client populations should give attention to variables other than the intrapsychic. Clinical models have imposed unnecessary boundaries on what are considered to be relevant factors that determine anger, influence its course, and show its effects. Perhaps because clinicians cannot easily "import" the physical and social environment into the therapy room, we have been entrenched in the world within the skins and skulls of our clients. However, through our clients' representations of those environments and through their efforts at behavior change aimed at optimizing well-being in those settings, we can give greater attention to the powerful factors that shape anger experiences.

REFERENCES

Achmon, J., Granek, M., Golomb, M., & Hart, J. (1989). Behavioral treatment of essential hypertension: A comparison between cognitive therapy and biofeedback of heart rate. *Psychosomatic Medicine*, *51*, 152–164.

Aggleton, J. P., & Mishkin, M. (1986). The amygdala: Sensory gateway to the emotions. In R. Plutchik & H. Kellerman (Eds.), *Emotion: Theory, research and experience* (vol. 3) (pp. 281–299). Orlando, FL: Academic.

Alexander, F. G. (1939). Emotional factors in essential hypertension: Presentation of a tentative hypothesis. *Psychosomatic Medicine*, *1,* 175–179.

Averill, J. R. (1982). *Anger and aggression: An essay on emotion*. New York: Springer-Verlag.

Averill, J. R. (1994). It's a small world but a large stage. In P. Ekman & R. J. Davidson (Eds.), *The nature of emotion* (pp. 143–145). New York: Oxford University Press.

Bandura, A. (1972). *Aggression: A social learning analysis*. Englewood Cliffs, NJ: Prentice-Hall.

Barefoot, J. C., Dahlstrom, G., & Williams, R. B. (1982). Hostility, CHD incidence, and total mortality: A 25-year follow-up study of 255 physicians. *Psychosomatic Medicine*, *55*, 59–64.

Bennett, P., Wallace, L., Carroll, D., & Smith, N. (1991). Treating Type A behaviours and mild hypertension in middle-aged men. *Journal of Psychosomatic Research*, *35,* 209–223.

Berkowitz, L. (1989). Frustration-aggression hypothesis: Examination and reformulation. *Psychological Bulletin*, *106,* 59–73.

Booth-Kewley, S., & Friedman, H. S. (1987). Psychological predictors of heart disease: A quantitative review. *Psychological Bulletin*, *101*, 343–362.

Buss, A. (1961). *The psychology of aggression*. New York: Wiley.

Cannon, W. (1932). *The wisdom of the body*. New York: Norton.

Carver, C. S., & Scheier, M. F. (1990). Origins and functions of positive and negative affect: A control-process view. *Psychological Review*, *97,* 19–35.

Chemtob, C. M., Novaco, R. W., Hamada, R. S., & Gross, D. M. (1997). Cognitive-behavioral treatment for severe anger in posttraumatic stress disorder. *Journal of Consulting and Clinical Psychology*, *65*, 184–189.

Chesney, M., Black, G. Swan, G., & Ward, M. (1987). Relaxation training for essential hypertension training at the worksite: I. The untreated mild hypertensive. *Psychosomatic Medicine*, *49*, 250–263.

Chesney, M. A., Eagleston, J. R., & Rosenman, R. H. (1980). The Type A structured interview: A behavioral assessment in the rough. *Journal of Behavioral Assessment, 2,* 255–272.

Chesney, M. A., & Rosenman, R. H. (Eds.). (1985). *Anger and hostility in cardiovascular and behavioral disorders.* Washington, DC: Hemisphere.

Clarkson, T. B. , Manuck, S. B., & Kaplan, J. R. (1986). Potential role of cardiovascular reactivity in atherogenesis. In K. A. Mathews, S. M. Weiss, T. Detre, T. M. Dembroski, B. Falkner, S. B. Manuck, & R. B. Williams (Eds.), *Handbook of stress, reactivity, and cardiovascular disease* (pp. 35–47). New York: Wiley.

Clore, G. L. (1992). Cognitive phenomenology: Feelings in the construction of judgment. In L. Martin & A. Tesser (Eds.), *The construction of social judgment* (pp. 133–164). Hillsdale, NJ: Erlbaum.

Cooper, T., Detre, T., & Weiss, S. M. (1981). Coronary-prone behavior and coronary heart disease: A critical review. *Circulation, 63,* 1199–1215.

Darwin, C. R. (1955). *The expression of emotions in man and animals.* New York: Philosophical Library. (Original work published 1896).

Davison, G. C., Williams, M. E., Nezami, E., Bice, T. L., & DeQuattro, V. L. (1991). Relaxation, reduction in angry articulated thoughts, and improvements in borderline hypertension and heart rate. *Journal of Behavioral Medicine, 14,* 453–468.

Deffenbacher, J. L. (1994). Anger reduction: Issues, assessment, and intervention strategies. In A. W. Siegman & T. W. Smith (Eds.), *Anger, hostility, and the heart* (pp. 239–269). Hillsdale, NJ: Erlbaum.

Deffenbacher, J. L., Oetting, E. R., Huff, M. E., & Thwaites, G. A. (1995). Fifteen-month follow-up of social skills and cognitive-relaxation approaches to general anger reduction. *Journal of Counseling Psychology, 42,* 400–405.

Dembroski, T. & Costa, P. T., Jr. (1987). Coronary-prone behavior: Components of the Type A pattern and hostility. *Journal of Personality, 55,* 211–235.

Dembroski, T. M., & MacDougall, J. M. (1983). Behavioral and psycho-physiological perspectives on coronary-prone behavior. In T. M. Dembroski, T. H. Schmidt, & G. Blumchen (Eds.), *Biobehavioral bases of coronary heart disease* (pp. 106–129). New York: Karger.

Dembroski, T. M., MacDougall, J. M., Costa, J. M., & Grandits, G. A. (1989). Components of hostility as predictors of sudden death and myocardial infarction in the Multiple Risk Factor Intervention Trial. *Psychosomatic Medicine, 51,* 514–522.

Dembroski, T. M., MacDougall, J. M., Williams, R. B., Jr., Haney, T. L., & Blumenthal, J. A. (1985). Components of Type A, hostility, and anger-in: Relationship to angiographic findings. *Psychosomatic Medicine, 47,* 219–233.

Diamond, E. L. (1982). The role of anger and hostility in essential hypertension and coronary heart disease. *Psychological Bulletin, 92,* 410–433.

Dimsdale, J. E., & Herd, A. (1982). Variability of plasma lipids in response to emotional arousal. *Psychosomatic Medicine, 44,* 413–430.

Dollard, J., Doob, L., Miller, N. E., Mowrer, O. H., & Sears, R. (1939). *Frustration and aggression.* New Haven, CT: Yale University Press.

Ekman, P. (1972). Universals and cultural differences in facial expressions of emotion. In J. Cole (Ed.), *Nebraska Symposium on Motivation, 1971* (pp. 207–283). Lincoln: University of Nebraska Press.

Ekman, P. (1994). Strong evidence for universals in facial expressions: A reply to Russell's mistaken critique. *Psychological Bulletin, 115,* 268–287.

Ekman, P., & Davidson, R. J. (1994). *The nature of emotion.* New York: Oxford University Press.

Engebretson, T. O., Matthews, K. A., & Scheier, M. F. (1989). Relations between anger expression and cardiovascular reactivity: Reconciling inconsistent findings through a matching hypothesis. *Journal of Personality and Social Psychology, 57,* 513–521.

Esler, M., Julius, S., Zweiffer, A., Randall, O., Harburg, E., Gardiner, H., & DeQuattro, V. (1977). Mild high-renin essential hypertension: Neurogenic human hypertension? *New England Journal of Medicine, 296,* 405–411.

Feindler, E. L. & Ecton, R. B. (1986). *Adolescent anger control: Cognitive therapy techniques.* New York: Pergamon.

French-Belgian Collaborative Group. (1982). Ischemic heart disease and psychological patterns: Prevalence and incidence studies in Belgium and France. In H. Denolin (Ed.), *Psychological problems before and after myocardial infarction.* Basel, Switzerland: Karger.

Friedman, H. (1992). *Hostility, coping, and health.* Washington, DC: American Psychological Association.

Friedman, M., Byers, S. O., Diamant, J., & Rosenman, R. H. (1975). Plasma catecholamine response of coronary-prone subjects (Type A) to a specific challenge. *Metabolism, 4,* 205–210.

Friedman, M., & Rosenman, R. H. (1974). *Type A behavior and your heart.* New York: Knopf.

Frijda, N. H. (1987). Emotion, cognitive structure, and action tendency. *Cognition and Emotion, 1,* 115–143.

Gentry, W. D. (1985). Relationships of anger-coping styles and blood pressure among black Americans. In M. Chesney & R. Rosenman (Eds.). *Anger and hostility in cardiovascular and behavioral disorders* (pp. 139–147). Washington, DC: Hemisphere.

Gentry, W. D., Chesney, A., Gary, H., Hall, R., & Harburg, E. (1982). Habitual anger-coping styles: Effect on mean blood pressure and risk for essential hypertension. *Psychosomatic Medicine, 44,* 195–202.

Goldstein, I. B. (1981). Assessment of hypertension. In C. K. Prokop & L. A. Bradley (Eds.), *Medical psychology: Contributions to behavioral medicine.* New York: Academic.

Harburg, E., Blakelock, E., & Roeper, P. (1979). Resentful and reflective coping with arbitrary authority and blood pressure: Detroit. *Psychosomatic Medicine, 41,* 189–202.

Harburg, E., Erfurt, J. C., Hauenstein, L. S., Chape, C., Schull, W. J., & Schork, M. A. (1973). Socio-ecological stress, suppressed hostility, skin color, and Black-White male blood pressure: Detroit. *Psychosomatic Medicine, 35,* 276–296.

Haynes, S. G., Feinleib, M., & Kannel, W. B. (1980). The relationship of psychosocial factors to coronary heart disease in the Framingham study. III: Eight year incidence of CHD. *American Journal of Epidemiology, 11,* 37–58.

Haynes, S., Levine, S., Scotch, N., Feinleib, M., & Kannel, W. (1978). The relationship of psychosocial factors to coronary heart disease in the Framingham Study. I. Methods and risk factors. *American Journal of Epidemiology, 107,* 362–383.

Hazaleus, S. L., & Deffenbacher, J. L. (1986). Relaxation and cognitive treatments of anger. *Journal of Consulting and Clinical Psychology, 54,* 222–226.

Hokanson, J. E., Burgess, M., & Cohen, M. F. (1963). Effect of displaced aggression on systolic blood pressure. *Journal of Abnormal and Social Psychology, 67,* 214–218.

Holt, R. (1970). On the interpersonal and intrapersonal consequences of expressing or not expressing anger. *Journal of Consulting and Clinical Psychology, 35,* 8–12.

Houston, B. K. (1994). Anger, hostility, and psychophysiological reactivity. In A. W. Siegman & T. W. Smith (Eds.), *Anger, hostility, and the heart* (pp. 97–115). Hillsdale, NJ: Erlbaum.

Houston, B. K., Smith, M. A., & Cates, D. S. (1989). Hostility patterns and cardiovascular reactivity to stress. *Psychophysiology, 26,* 337–342.

Jamner, L. D., Shapiro, D., Goldstein, I. B., & Hug, R. (1991). Ambulatory blood pressure and heart rate in paramedics: Effects of cynical hostility and defensiveness. *Psychosomatic Medicine, 53,* 393–406.

Jamner, L. D., Shapiro, D., Hui, K. K., Oakley, M. E., & Lovett, M. (1993). Hostility and differences between clinic, self-determined, and ambulatory blood pressure. *Psychosomatic Medicine, 55,* 203–211.

Jenkins, C. D. (1978). Components of the coronary-prone behavior pattern: Their relation to silent myocardial infarction and blood lipids. *Journal of Chronic Diseases, 19,* 599–609.

Johnson, E. H. (1990). *The deadly emotions: The role of anger, hostility, and aggression in health and emotional well-being.* New York: Praeger.

Johnson, E. H., & Gentry, W. D. (1992). Personality, elevated blood pressure, and essential hypertension: A research agenda. In E. H. Johnson, W. D. Gentry, & S. Julius (Eds.), *Personality, elevated blood pressure, and essential hypertension* (pp. 319–334). Washington, DC: Hemisphere.

Johnson, E. H., Gentry, W. D., & Julius, S. (Eds.). (1992). *Personality, elevated blood pressure, and essential hypertension.* Washington, DC: Hemisphere.

Julius, S., Schneider, R., & Egan, B. (1985). Suppressed anger in hypertension: Facts and problems. In M. A. Chesney & R. H. Rosenman (Eds.), *Anger and hostility in cardiovascular and behavioral disorders* (pp. 127–137). Washington, DC: Hemisphere.

Kahn, H. A., Medalie, J. H., Neufeld, H. N., Riss, E., & Goldbourt, U. (1972). The incidence of hypertension and associated factors: The Israeli ischemic heart disease study. *American Heart Journal, 84,* 171–182.

Kannel, W. B., Neaton, J. D., Wentworth, D., et al. (1986). Overall and coronary heart disease mortality rates in relation to major risk factors in 325,348 men screened for the MRFIT (Multiple Risk Factor Intervention Trial). *American Heart Journal, 112,* 825–836.

Kannel, W. B., Neaton, J. D., Wentworth, D., Thomas, H. E., Stamler, J., Hulley, S. B., & Kjelsberg, M. O. (1986). Overall and coronary heart disease mortality rates in relation to major risk factors in 325,348 men screened for the MRFIT. *American Heart Journal, 112,* 825–836.

Kannel, W. B., & Stokes, J. I. (1985). Hypertension as a cardiovascular risk factor. In C. J. Bulpitt (Ed.), *Epidemiology of hypertension: Handbook of hypertension* (vol. 6) (pp. 15–34). New York/Amsterdam: Elsevier Science.

Kaplan, J. R., Botchin, M. B., & Manuck, S. B. (1994). Animal models of aggression and cardiovascular disease. In A. W. Siegman & T. W. Smith (Eds.), *Anger, hostility, and the heart.* Hillsdale, NJ: Erlbaum.

Krantz, D. S. & Manuck, S. B. (1984). Acute psychophysiological reactivity and risk of cardiovascular disease: A review and methodological critique. *Psychological Bulletin, 96,* 435–464.

Lakoff, G., & Kovecses, Z. (1987). The cognitive model of anger inherent in American English. In N. Quinn & D. Holland (Eds.), *Cultural models in language and thought* (pp. 195–221). Cambridge, England: Cambridge University Press.

Lazarus, R. S. (1991). *Emotion and adaptation.* Oxford, England: Oxford University Press.

Lazarus, R. (1994). Appraisal: The long and the short of it. In P. Ekman & R. J. Davidson (Eds.), *The nature of emotion* (pp. 208–215). New York: Oxford University Press.

LeDoux, J. E. (1984). Cognition and emotion: Processing functions and brain systems. In M. S. Gazzaniga (Ed.), *Handbook of cognitive neuroscience* (pp. 357–368). New York: Plenum.

LeDoux, J. E. (1989). Cognitive-emotional interactions in the brain. *Cognition and Emotion, 3,* 267–289.

Lewis, M., Alessandri, S. M., & Sullivan, M. W. (1990). Violation of expectancy, loss of control, and anger expressions in young infants. *Developmental Psychology, 26,* 745–751.

Lichtenstein M. J., Shipley, M. J., & Rose, G. (1985). Systolic and diastolic blood pressures as predictors of coronary heart disease mortality in the Whitehall study. *British Medical Journal, 291,* 243–245.

Lunberg, U., Hedman, M., Melin, B., & Frankenhaeuser, M. (1989). Type A behavior in healthy males and females as related to physiological reactivity and blood lipids. *Psychosomatic Medicine, 51,* 113–122.

Manuck, S. B., & Garland, F. N. (1979). Coronary-prone behavior pattern, task incentive and cardiovascular response. *Psychophysiology, 16,* 136–142.

Manuck, S. B., Morrison, R. L., Bellack, A. S., & Polefrone, J. M. (1985). Behavioral factors in hypertension: Cardiovascular responsivity, anger, and social competence. In M. A. Chesney & R. H. Rosenman (Eds.), *Anger and hostility in cardiovascular and behavioral disorders* (pp. 149–172). Washington, DC: Hemisphere.

Matthews, K. A., & Haynes, S. G. (1986). Type A behavior and coronary disease risk. *American Journal of Epidemiology, 123,* 923–960.

Meichenbaum, D. (1985). *Stress inoculation training.* New York: Pergamon.

Miller, M. L. (1939). Blood pressure in relation to inhibited aggression in psychotics. *Psychosomatic Medicine, 1,* 162–167.

Novaco, R. W. (1975). *Anger control: The development and evaluation of an experimental treatment.* Lexington, MA: Heath.

Novaco, R. W. (1976). The function and regulation of the arousal of anger. *American Journal of Psychiatry, 133,* 1124–1128.

Novaco, R. W. (1986). Anger as a clinical and social problem. In R. J. Blanchard & D. C. Blanchard (Eds.), *Advances in the study of aggression* (vol. 2) (pp. 1–67). New York: Academic.

Novaco, R. W. (1993). Clinician ought to view anger contextually. *Behaviour Change, 10,* 208–218.

Novaco, R. W. (1998). Aggression. In H. Friedman (Ed.), *Encyclopedia of mental health* (pp. 13–26). San Diego, CA: Academic.

Novaco, R. W. (in press). Anger. *Encyclopedia of psychology.* Washington, DC: American Psychological Association.

Novaco, R. W., & Chemtob, C. M. (1998). Anger and trauma: Conceptualization, assessment, and treatment. In V. M. Follette, J. I. Rusek, & F. R. Abueg (Eds.), *Cognitive behavioral therapies for trauma* (pp. 162–190). New York: Guilford.

Novaco, R. W., Kliewer, W., & Broquet, A. (1991). Home environment consequences of commute travel impedance. *American Journal of Community Psychology, 19,* 881–909.

Novaco, R. W., Ramm, M., & Black, L. (in press). Anger treatment with offenders. In C. Hollin (Ed.), *Handbook of offender assessment and treatment.* London: Wiley.

Oatley, K., & Jenkins, J. M. (1992). Human emotions: Function and dysfunction. *Annual Review of Psychology, 43,* 55–85.

Ortony, A., Clore, G. L., & Collins, A. (1988). *The cognitive structure of emotions.* New York: Cambridge University Press.

Ragland, D. R., & Brand, R. J. (1988). Type A behavior and mortality from coronary heart disease. *New England Journal of Medicine, 318,* 65–69.

Renwick, S. J., Black, L., Ramm, M., & Novaco, R. W. (1997). Anger treatment with forensic hospital patients. *Legal and Criminological Psychology, 2,* 103–116.

Robins, S., & Novaco, R. W. (in press). Systems conceptualization and treatment of anger. *JCLP/In Session: Psychotherapy in Practice.*

Rosenman, R. H. (1978). The interview method of assessment of the coronary-prone behavior pattern. In T. M. Dembroski, S. M. Weiss, S. L. Shields, S. G. Haynes, M. Feinleib (Eds.), *Coronary-prone behavior.* New York: Springer.

Rosenman, R. H. (1983). Current status of risk factors and Type A behavior pattern in the pathogenesis of ischemic heart disease. In T. M. Dembroski & G. Blumchen (Eds.), *Biobehavioral bases of coronary heart disease* (pp. 5–17). New York: Karger.

Rosenman, R. H. (1985). Health consequences of anger and implications for treatment. In M. A. Chesney & R. H. Rosenman (Eds.), *Anger and hostility in cardiovascular and behavioral disorders* (pp. 103–125). Washington, DC: Hemisphere.

Rosenman, R. H. (1986). Current and past history of type A behavior pattern. In T. Schmidt, T. Dembroski, & G. Blumchen (Eds.), *Biological and psychological factors in cardiovascular disease* (pp. 15–40). Heidelberg, Germany: Springer-Verlag.

Rosenman, R. H. (1987). Type A behavior and hypertension. In S. Julius & D. Bassett (Eds.), *Handbook of hypertension. Volume 9: Behavioral factors in hypertension.* Amsterdam: Elsevier.

Rosenman, R. H. (1993). Relationships of the Type A behavior pattern with coronary heart disease. In L. Goldberger & S. Breznitz (Eds.), *Handbook of stress: Theoretical and clinical aspects* (2d ed.) (pp. 449–476). New York: Free Press.

Rosenman, R. H., Brand, R. J., Sholtz, R. I., & Friedman, M. (1976). Multivariate prediction of coronary heart disease during 8.5 year follow-up in the Western Collaborative Group Study. *American Journal of Cardiology, 37,* 903–910.

Scherer, K. R. (1993). Studying the emotion-antecedent appraisal process: An expert system approach. *Cognition and Emotion, 3/4,* 325–355.

Scherer, K., & Walbott, H. G. (1986). How universal and specific is emotional experience? Evidence from 27 countries on five continents. *Social Science Information, 25,* 1–14.

Scherer, K., & Walbott, H. G. (1994). Evidence for universality and cultural variation of differential emotion response patterning. *Journal of Personality and Social Psychology, 66,* 310–328.

Scherwitz, L. (1989). Type A behavior assessment in the Structured Interview: Review, critique, and recommendations. In A. W. Siegman & T. M. Dembroski (Eds.), *In search of coronary prone behavior: Beyond Type A* (pp. 117–148). Hillsdale, NJ: Erlbaum.

Schwartz, G. E. (1990). Psychobiology of repression and health: A systems approach. In J. L. Singer (Ed.), *Repression and dissociation* (pp. 405–434). Chicago: University of Chicago Press.

Schwartz, N., & Clore, G. L. (1988). How do I feel about it? The informative function of mood. In K. Fiedler & A. Forgas (Eds.), *Affect, cognition, and social behavior* (pp. 44–62). Toronto: Hogrefe.

Shapiro, A. P., Krantz, D. S., & Grim, C. E. (1986). Pharmacologic agents as modulators of stress. In K. A. Mathews, S. M. Weiss, T. Detre, T. M. Dembroski, B. Falkner, S. B. Manuck, & R. B. Williams (Eds.), *Handbook of stress, reactivity, and cardiovascular disease* (pp. 401–416). New York: Wiley.

Shapiro, D., Goldstein, I. B., & Jamner, L. D. (1995). Effects of anger/hostility, defensiveness, gender, and family history of hypertension on cardiovascular reactivity. *Psychophysiology, 32,* 425–435.

Shekelle, R. B., Gale, M., Ostfeld, A. M., & Paul, O. (1983). Hostility, risk of CHD, and mortality. *Psychosomatic Medicine, 45,* 109–114.

Siegler, I. C. (1994). Hostility and risk: Demographic and lifestyle variables. In A. W. Siegman & T. W. Smith (Eds.), *Anger, hostility, and the heart.* Hillsdale, NJ: Erlbaum.

Siegman, A. W. (1989). The role of hostility, neuroticism, and speech style in coronary artery disease. In A. Siegman & T. Dembroski (Eds.), *In search of coronary-prone behavior: Beyond Type A.* Hillsdale, NJ: Erlbaum.

Siegman, A. W. (1994). Cardiovascular consequences of expressing and repressing anger. In A. W. Siegman & T. W. Smith (Eds.), *Anger, hostility, and the heart.* Hillsdale, NJ: Erlbaum.

Siegman, A., Anderson, R. W., & Berger, T. (1990). The angry voice: Its effects on the experience of anger and cardiovascular reactivity. *Psychosomatic Medicine, 52,* 631–643.

Siegman, A. W., Dembroski, T. M., & Ringel, N. (1987). Components of hostility and the severity of coronary artery disease. *Psychosomatic Medicine, 49,* 127–135.

Siegman, A. W., & Smith, T. W. (1994). *Anger, hostility, and the heart.* Hillsdale, NJ: Erlbaum.

Smith, T. W. (1994). Concepts and methods in the study of anger, hostility, and health. In A. W. Siegman & T. W. Smith (Eds.), *Anger, hostility, and the heart* (pp. 23–42). Hillsdale, NJ: Erlbaum.

Smith, T. W., & Christensen, A. J. (1992). Hostility, health, and social contexts. In H. S. Friedman (Ed.), *Hostility, coping, and health* (pp. 33–48). Washington, DC: American Psychological Association.

Smith, T. W., & Pope, M. K. (1990). Cynical hostility as a health risk: Current status and future directions. *Journal of Social Behavior and Personality, 5,* 77–88.

Spielberger, C. D., Jacobs, G., Russell, S. F., & Crane, R. J. (1983). Assessment of anger: The State-Trait Anger Scale. In Butcher, J. N. & Spielberger, C. D. (Eds.), *Advances in personality assessment,* Vol. 2 (pp. 159–187).

Spielberger, C. D., Johnson, E. H., Russell, S. F., Crane, R. J., Jacobs, G. A., & Worden, T. J. (1985). The experience and expression of anger: Construction and validation of an anger expression scale. In M. A. Chesney & R. H. Rosenman (Eds.), *Anger and hostility in cardiovascular and behavioral disorders* (pp. 5–30). Washington, DC: Hemisphere.

Steptoe, A. (1981). *Psychological factors in cardiovascular disorders.* New York: Academic.

Sternberg, C. R., & Campos, J. J. (1990). The development of anger expressions in infancy. In N. Stein, B. Leventhal, & T. Trabasso (Eds.), *Psychological and biological approaches to emotion* (pp. 247–282). Hillsdale, NJ: Erlbaum.

Stoney, C. M., & Engebretson, T. O. (1994). Anger and hostility: Potential mediators of the gender difference in coronary heart disease. In A. W. Siegman & T. W. Smith (Eds.), *Anger, hostility, and the heart*. Hillsdale, NJ: Erlbaum.

Suarez, E. C., Shiller, A. D., Kuhn, C. M., Schanberg, S., Williams, R. B., & Zimmerman, E. A. (1997). The relationship between hostility and beta-adrenergic receptor physiology in healthy young males. *Psychosomatic Medicine, 59,* 481–487.

Suls, J., & Wan, C. K. (1993). The relationship between trait hostility and cardiovascular reactivity: A quantitative review and analysis. *Psychophysiology, 30,* 615–626.

Swan, G. E., Carmelli, D., & Rosenman, R. H. (1990). Cook and Medley hostility and the Type A behavior pattern: Psychological correlates of two coronary prone behaviors. In M. Strube (Ed.), Type A behavior. (Special issue). *Journal of Social Behavior and Personality, 5,* 89–106.

Syme, S. L. (1987). Coronary artery disease: A sociocultural perspective. *Circulation, 76,* 1112–1116.

Tooby, J., & Cosmides, L. (1990). The past explains the present: Emotional adaptations and the structure of ancestral environment. *Ethology and Sociobiology, 11,* 375–424.

Vogele, C., Jarvis, A., & Cheeseman, K. (1997). Anger suppression, reactivity, and hypertension risk: Gender makes a difference. *Annals of Behavioral Medicine, 19,* 61–69.

Wegner, D. M., & Erber, R. (1992). The hyperaccessibility of suppressed thoughts. *Journal of Personality and Social Psychology, 63,* 903–912.

Wegner, D. M, Shortt, J. W., Blake, A. W., & Page, M. S. (1990). The suppression of exciting thoughts. *Journal of Personality and Social Psychology, 58,* 409–418.

Williams, R. B. (1982). Type A behavior and elevated physiological and neuroendocrine responses to cognitive tasks. *Science, 218,* 483–485.

Williams, R. B. (1989). Biological mechanisms mediating the relationship between behavior and coronary heart disease. In A. W. Siegman & T. M. Dembroski (Eds.), *In search of coronary-prone behavior: Beyond Type A* (pp. 195–205). Hillsdale, NJ: Erlbaum.

Williams, R. B., Barefoot, J. C., Shekelle, & R. B. (1985). The health consequences of hostility. In M. Chesney & R. Rosenman (Eds.), *Anger and hostility in cardiovascular and behavioral disorders*. Washington, DC: Hemisphere.

Williams, R. B., Jr., Haney, T. L., Lee, K. L., Kong, Y., Blumenthal, J., & Whalen, R. (1980). Type A behavior, hostility, and coronary atherosclerosis. *Psychosomatic Medicine, 42,* 539–549.

Williams, R. B., Jr., Lane, J. D., Kuhn, C. M., Melosh, W., White, A. D., & Schanberg, S. M. (1982). Type A behavior and elevated physiological and neuroendocrine responses to cognitive tasks. *Science, 218,* 483–485.

Williams, R., & Williams, V. (1993). *Anger kills*. New York: Harper Perennial.

Zillmann, D. (1971). Excitation transfer in communication-mediated aggressive behavior. *Journal of Experimental Social Psychology, 7,* 419–434.

Zillmann, D., & Bryant, J. (1974). Effect of residual excitation on the emotional response to provocation and delayed aggressive behavior. *Journal of Personality and Social Psychology, 30,* 782–791.

CHAPTER 23

ANXIETY AND WOMEN'S HEALTH

Cheryl A. Frye

Risa B. Weisberg

A. Brooke Hinkson

Women's health concerns and anxiety management interface in numerous important ways. Anxiety disorders are more common in women than in men. The experience of these disorders may influence or be influenced by a female's hormonal or reproductive status, making the pharmacological treatment of anxiety disorders in women challenging. Further, difficulties unique to women, such as premenstrual syndrome (PMS), are often characterized by the experience of anxiety symptoms. Anxiety may also influence the health promotion or disease prevention measures taken by some women.

ANXIETY DISORDERS AND WOMEN

Prevalence

Anxiety disorders are approximately three times more prevalent in women than in men. Panic disorder and generalized anxiety disorder (GAD) are twice as common among women as they are among men (Blazer, Hughes, George, Swartz, & Boyer, 1991; Eaton, Dryman, & Weissman, 1991; Kessler, McGonagle, Zhao, Nelson, Hughes, Eshleman, Wittchen, & Kendler, 1994), and it is estimated that 75% or more of those with agoraphobia are women (Barlow, 1988; Bourdon, Boyd, Rae, Burns, Thompson, & Locke, 1988). Incidence of obsessive compulsive disorder (OCD) and social phobia are also estimated to be more common in women than men, with about 60% of those with OCD being female (Karno, Golding, Burnam, & Hough, 1989). The lifetime prevalence rate of social phobia for women is estimated to be 3%; for men it is 2.4% (Bourdon et al., 1988; Eaton, Dryman, & Weissman, 1991).

Possible Explanations for the Gender Differences in Anxiety Disorders

Biological and psychological factors have been implicated in the etiology of anxiety and may underlie gender differences in anxiety disorder prevalence.

Biological Factors

Biological factors, such as hormonal and neurotransmitter fluctuations during the menstrual cycle, pregnancy, postpartum, perimenopause, and postmenopause, may effect gender differences in the incidence and diagnosis of anxiety disorders. While a comprehensive review of this topic is beyond the scope of this chapter (see Fankhauser, 1997 for an excellent review), recent research has demonstrated that steroid hormones that vary over the menstrual cycle can have dramatic and direct interactions with the γ-aminobutyric acid (GABA) neurotransmitter system (Majewska, Harrison, Schwartz, Barker, & Paul, 1986; Majewska, 1992). One particular steroid, the progesterone metabolite 5α-pregnan-3α-ol-20-one (3α,5α-THP), is 50–500 times more effective at increasing the functioning of the GABA system than is the anti-anxiety drug valium (Majewska et al., 1986). Administration of 3α,5α-THP to laboratory animals decreases neuronal activation (Frye, 1995) and enhances analgesia and anxiety (Bitran, Hilvers, & Kellogg, 1991a,b; Frye & Duncan, 1994, 1995). Withdrawal from 3α,5α-THP is associated with overexcitation in the brain (Frye, Scalise, & Bayon, 1998) and anxiogenesis (Gallo & Smith, 1993). Preliminary data from women reveal similar effects of

3α,5α-THP on neuronal activity and anxiety (Freeman, Purdy, Coutifaris, Rickels, & Paul, 1993; Rosciszewska, Buntner, Guz, & Zawisza, 1986; Von Bardeleben & Holsboer, 1988).

3α,5α-THP is metabolized from ovarian or adrenal P, and circulating concentrations of 3α,5α-THP tend to covary with systemic P concentrations. 3α,5α-THP is increased in females compared to males. In women, 3α,5α-THP increases at ovulation and reaches its nadir during the perimenstrum. 3α,5α-THP levels are very high during pregnancy but are drastically lowered within minutes of parturition (Paul & Purdy, 1992). It has been proposed that endogenous variations in 3α,5α-THP may be related to perimenstrual or postpartum affective changes (Schmidt, Nieman, Danaceau, Adams, & Rubinow, 1998). Preliminary evidence suggests that 3α,5α-THP withdrawal may be associated with affective changes over the menstrual cycle (Freeman et al., 1992, 1990).

3α,5α-THP is also a neurosteroid that can be produced de novo by glial cells in the brain and directly interacts with the GABA system (Baulieu, 1997). Variations in neurosteroids influence the activation of neurotransmitter systems. Concentrations of circulating and central neurosteroids increase in response to previous prenatal stress (Bayon & Frye, 1998) and to ongoing environmental stimuli (Purdy, Morrow, Moore, & Paul, 1991). Although the role of neurosteroids in gender differences and hormonal fluctuations in anxiety disorders is just being elucidated, the existing literature convincingly demonstrates their intricate interrelationship with the environment, other neuromodulators, neurotransmitter systems, and affective behavior. Neurosteroids and other neuromodulators, hormones, or biological substrates may account in part for some of the gender, menstrual (van den Akker & Steptoe, 1985; Veith et al., 1984), stress-induced (Abplanalp, Livingston, Rose, & Sandwisch, 1977; Asso, 1978; Kubitz, Peavey, & Moore, 1986; Matteo, 1987), or psychological differences (Asso, 1978; Dennerstein & Burrows, 1979; Ivey & Bardwick, 1968; Moos et al., 1969; Woods, Most, & Dery, 1982) previously observed for anxiety. Although psychological factors are presumed to be reflective or responsive of changes in biological substrates, the precise physiological underpinnings of gender differences or factors relevant in anxiety of women have

yet to be elucidated. Greater progress will be made on the biological substrates of anxiety disorders in women when there is greater emphasis on research that addresses psychological factors in anxiety for women, treatment of anxiety disorders in women, relationship of anxiety and PMS, and anxiety related to female-specific concerns. Research progress in each of these areas is discussed in the remainder of this chapter.

Psychological Factors

The core psychological feature of anxiety is a sense of lack of control or helplessness. Anxiety or "anxious apprehension" has been defined as a cognitive-affective structure that is composed primarily of high negative affect; a sense of uncontrollability; and an inward, self-focus shift in attention (Barlow, 1988, 1991; Barlow, Chorpita, & Turovsky, 1996). According to this theory (Barlow, 1988, 1991) of anxious apprehension, depression, anxiety, stress, and excitement are viewed as a continuum. When a woman is faced with a new situation or challenge and is confident about her abilities to succeed, she may feel excitement. If she has a lesser sense of control over the situation, she may feel stressed. When the situation seems to be out of her control, she may feel anxious. If she begins to doubt she can ever control upcoming events, she feels depressed (Barlow, 1988; Rapee & Barlow, 1991). Thus, the experience of a stressor alone does not lead to anxiety; rather, the anxiety provoker is the perception that one may not be able to control the stressor.

The sense of uncontrollability in the experience of anxiety may help to explain gender differences in anxiety disorders. Women, more often than men, may experience opportunities to learn that they cannot control their environment. Evidence exists that boys' behaviors receive more response from their parents (Maccoby & Jacklin, 1974) and teachers (Dweck, Davidson, Nelson, & Enna, 1978) than do girls' behaviors. Researchers (Dweck et al., 1978; Maccoby & Jacklin, 1974) have found that while parents and teachers praise and scold boys according to their behavior, girls' actions are often ignored. Thus, from a young age, women may have more opportunities to learn that their actions do not control outcomes.

Differences in the coping mechanisms that men and women employ when anxious feelings occur may account for the greater prevalence of anxiety disorders in women. A number of studies have shown that men with anxiety problems tend to consume more alcohol than their female counterparts (Cox et al., 1993; Small, Stockwell, Canter, & Hodgson, 1984). Additionally, many male alcoholics have comorbid anxiety disorders (Hesselbrock, Meyer, & Keener, 1985). Men may experience feelings of anxiety as often as women but respond to these feelings through alcohol use, rather than agoraphobia or other physical avoidance.

It has been theorized that gender differences in the prevalence of depression are associated with men's propensity to engage in distracting behaviors, whereas women are more likely to ruminate about their feelings and their possible causes (Nolen-Hoeksema, 1987). Helping patients to engage in pleasurable activities is an effective treatment for depression. Thus, men's behaviors may dampen their negative mood. Women's rumination may amplify their depression, increasing their self-focus and self-blame. Because anxiety also includes a state of self-preoccupation or self-focused attention, this theory may apply to anxiety disorders as well as depression.

It is important to recognize that these explanations are not mutually exclusive. Rumination interferes with attention and concentration to external tasks. This, in turn, may lead to increased difficulty in controlling one's environment and hence lead to a greater sense of uncontrollability (Kuhl, 1981; Nolen-Hoeksema, 1987). Also, as previously stated, biological processes are closely related to social and psychological ones. It is possible that social roles and psychological states are formed around biological differences, and/or that biological differences may develop in an adaptive response to social roles.

Impact of Pregnancy, Postpartum, and Menstrual Cycling on Anxiety Disorder Symptoms

In addition to the greater prevalence of anxiety disorders among women, the nature of these disorders may be different for women than for men. There is evidence that women may experience more impairment associated with anxiety disorders. In an examination of patients at an anxiety disorders specialty clinic, female gender, low income, being single, and being a mother were each independently associated with more anxiety symptoms and more functional impairment (Shear & Mammen, 1995). Further, women may experience changes in anxiety symptoms during pregnancy, postpartum, and phases of the menstrual cycle. Research on the relationship of these hormonal and reproductive states and anxiety has focused almost exclusively on panic disorder and OCD.

Panic Disorder. Various researchers have examined the effects of pregnancy on panic disorder. Much of this research has been retrospective, in which women with preexisting panic disorder completed questionnaires about the relationship of pregnancy to their panic symptoms. A large percentage of women have reported that pregnancy was associated with a decrease in their panic symptoms (Northcott & Stein, 1994; Vileponteaux, Lydiard, Laraia, Stuart, & Ballenger, 1992). Pregnancy is thus often considered to be protective for women with panic disorder. It has been suggested that amelioration of panic symptoms during pregnancy may be related to CO_2. Changes in CO_2 may lower the "suffocation sensor" that is believed to be involved in the etiology of panic attacks (Klein, 1993).

Amelioration of panic symptoms during pregnancy does not appear to be a consistent occurrence among women, or within women across pregnancies. The majority of women who had more than one pregnancy indicated no consistent pattern of change in panic symptoms across pregnancies (Northcott & Stein, 1994). In the same retrospective (Northcott & Stein, 1994; Vileponteaux et al., 1992), many women reported amelioration of panic symptoms, but there were still many other women who reported no change (10–24%) or a worsening of their anxiety (14–33%) during pregnancy. Using retrospective interviews and chart reviews of women with preexisting panic disorder, 57% of women in this sample were noted to have experienced no significant change in panic during pregnancy (Cohen, Sichel, Dimmock, & Rosenbaum, 1994a). Two small prospective studies also failed to find strong evidence for a protective influence of pregnancy on panic. An evaluation of 10 panic disorder patients through pregnancy and postpartum revealed that 7 of the 10 patients continued to meet *DSM-III-R* criteria for panic disorder at all trimester visits (Cohen et al., 1996). Similarly, when 22 women with panic disorder were followed, the most common effect of pregnancy was no change in panic symptoms (Wisner, Peindl, & Hanusa, 1996).

Evidence has also been mixed regarding the relationship between the postpartum period and panic symptoms. Retrospective studies have often concluded that panic symptoms may worsen during the postpartum period (Northcott & Stein, 1994; Sholomskas et al., 1993). For example, 63% of women in a study of postpartum panic symptoms (Northcott & Stein, 1994) reported a worsening in symptoms during this time. Prospective studies, however, have more often found no change in panic symptoms during the postpartum (e.g., Cohen et al., 1996; Wisner, Peindl, & Hanusa, 1996).

Panic symptoms have also been thought to worsen during the premenstruum. Again, much of the evidence for premenstrual exacerbation of panic symptoms comes from retrospective studies (e.g., Breier, Charney, & Heninger, 1986; Sandberg, Fryer, & Endicott, 1986). Data from prospective studies are inconsistent. Half of the women with panic disorder prospectively reported at least a 100% increase in the frequency of panic attacks during the premenstrual phase (Kaspi et al., 1994). Increases in the severity of panic attacks during the premenstruum have also been reported (Cameron, Kuttesch, McPhee, & Curtis, 1988). However, no significant relationship between menstrual cycle and the experience of panic disorder has been reported (Cook et al., 1990; Stein, Schmidt, Rubinow, & Uhde, 1989). Interestingly, in one study in which no significant prospective menstrual variation was found, subjects retrospectively reported increases in their anxiety symptoms during premenstrual days (Cook et al., 1990).

Obsessive-Compulsive Disorder. Pregnancy and childbirth are also thought to significantly affect the course of OCD. As many as 69% of women with OCD have reported that the onset or worsening of their symptoms was related to some aspect of childbirth or pregnancy (Buttolph & Holland, 1990). Once again, the evidence for this association comes primarily from retrospective studies. In a retrospective study of female patients with OCD, 39% of those with children reported that the onset of their symptoms occurred

during pregnancy (Neziroglu, Anemone, & Yaryura-Tobias, 1992). Another recent retrospective examination (Williams & Koran, 1997) reported that pregnancy was associated with the onset of OCD in 13% of the women sampled. Of the women with preexisting OCD who became pregnant, 17% reported that their symptoms worsened. The majority of women (69%) in this sample, however, reported no change in symptoms during their pregnancy, and 14% reported improvement. Twenty-nine percent of these women reported postpartum exacerbation of symptoms.

As with panic disorder, it appears that OCD is not necessarily and consistently affected by pregnancy and the postpartum. However, for the women who do appear to suffer an exacerbation or onset of an anxiety disorder during pregnancy the symptoms may be particularly distressing. A chart review of 15 women with new-onset obsessive compulsive symptoms during the puerperium revealed that these patients, tended to experience disabling, intrusive, obsessional thoughts about harming their babies (Sichel, Cohen, Dimmock, & Rosenbaum, 1993). Further, these women avoided their babies due to thoughts of harming them. Thus, their symptoms may greatly have interfered with infant care.

Little research has examined the effects of menstrual cycling on OCD symptoms. One retrospective study (Williams & Koran, 1997) found that premenstrual worsening of OCD was described by 42% of the patients. Trichotillomania, a disorder thought to be related to OCD, has also been found to worsen during the premenstrual phase. In a sample of 59 women with trichotillomania, premenstrual exacerbation for hair pulling, urge intensity, and ability to control pulling was frequently reported. These women reported an alleviation of their symptoms during menstruation and shortly thereafter. The impact of pregnancy on hair pulling was less unidirectional, with both symptom exacerbation and lessening reported (Keuthen et al., 1997).

Conclusion. Much is yet unknown regarding the relationship between anxiety disorders and pregnancy, postpartum, and premenstrual phases. Research in this area has been complicated by a number of factors. Retrospective self-report studies have frequently concluded that panic symptoms ameliorate during pregnancy and exacerbate during postpartum and premenstrual phases. These findings have often failed to hold up when the relationships are examined prospectively. Pregnancy and postpartum have been associated with the onset and exacerbation of OCD. However, this exacerbation has not been found for the majority of women in all studies. Further, the relationship of OCD and women's reproductive stages is yet to be carefully explored prospectively. It is likely that sociocultural views of menstruation and pregnancy may influence retrospective self-reporting.

Research in this area has also frequently been complicated by changes in treatment during pregnancy and postpartum. For example, in one study (Cohen et al., 1996), six of the seven women experiencing no change in clinical status during postpartum also increased antipanic medication during the puerperium. In a chart review and retrospective interview study (Cohen, Sichel, Dimmock, & Rosenbaum, 1994b), 73% of the women who demonstrated a stable or improved course postpartum had been on pharmacotherapy by at least the third trimester of pregnancy. Some samples (e.g., Cohen et al., 1994b, 1996) include women who stopped or decreased antipanic medication during their pregnancy. It is possible that exacerbation of symptoms may be related to the effects of benzodiazepine withdrawal. Thus, it is difficult to determine what effect these reproductive stages have on anxiety, independent of medication.

The results are further confounded by the presence of both lactating and nonlactating women in the samples. Many of the postpartum studies (e.g., Cohen et al., 1994b, 1996) failed to report on whether or not participants were breastfeeding. One study reported that nearly one-third of the women in their sample were lactating during postpartum (Northcott & Stein, 1994). The authors concluded that weaning was mostly associated with no change in panic symptoms. However, they did not report on differences in postpartum panic symptoms between women who breastfed and those who did not. One researcher has suggested that lactation may cause suppression of panic, perhaps through the secretion of oxytocin, a neuropeptide linked to attachment behavior (Insel, 1992; Shear & Mammen, 1995). Thus, differentiation of lactating and nonlactating women in these studies may help clarify currently inconsistent results.

Further research is also needed to better understand the factors that may lead to exacerbation of anxiety during particular times in women's lives. Whereas women's hormonal and reproductive status may interact with the experience of anxiety symptoms, psychosocial changes occurring during these phases of women's lives may also lead to changes in anxiety. Pregnancy, for example, brings with it numerous psychosocial changes, in addition to hormonal and biological changes. The birth of a child, particularly a first child, leads to a major role change for a woman. A new baby may also bring related marital distress, problems with older siblings, and financial stressors. Further, the demands of infant care may contribute to anxiety symptoms in the mother. For example, sleep disruption has been found to have an adverse effect on anxiety disorders (Shear & Mammen, 1995). Lastly, little research exists on the relationship of reproductive stages to anxiety disorders other than panic and OCD.

Treatment of Anxiety Disorders in Women

The onset, continuation, or worsening of anxiety symptoms during pregnancy and postpartum has important treatment implications. The primary pharmacological agents used for treatment of panic disorder and OCD are tricyclic antidepressants (TCAs), selective serotonergic reuptake inhibitors (SSRIs), and benzodiazepines. The safety of these medications for fetuses and breastfeeding infants is uncertain. Although women of childbearing age are the primary consumers of antidepressants and anxiolytics (Blehar, 1995), women have often been excluded from studies of these medications. In particular, pregnant and lactating women have been systematically excluded from most psychopharmacological treatment studies, most likely due to ethical and legal concerns. Pharmacological treatment recommendations for pregnant women, therefore, are often made in the absence of empirical evidence (Blehar, 1995). In case studies, benzodiazepine use during pregnancy has been reported to be associated with numerous problems, including cleft palate, embryopathy, and developmental delays (Shear & Mammen, 1995). Clearly there is a need for more information about the effectiveness and safety of pharmacological anxiety treatments during pregnancy and lactation.

Fortunately, effective, nonpharmacological treatments have been empirically validated for most anxiety disorders. Cognitive-behavioral therapy (CBT) for panic disorder has been found to be effective for as many as 87% of patients (e.g., Craske, Brown, & Barlow, 1991; Klosko, Barlow, Tassinari, & Cerny, 1990). Exposure and response prevention, during which patients are exposed to feared situations and abstain from erforming anxiety-reducing compulsion, has a reported success rate of approximately 75% (Riggs & Foa, 1993). It has been recommended that pregnant women with anxiety disorders receive CBT as the first treatment method to reduce anxiety (Shear & Mammen, 1995). This recommendation can be taken a step further. Although women are often advised to discontinue psychopharmacologic treatment prior to or during pregnancy, many women may find it difficult to stop taking these medications (e.g., Cohen et al., 1994b, 1996). Women who discontinue benzodiazepines may be subject to withdrawal symptoms, perhaps just at the time they are most difficult to handle. Therefore, it is suggested that empirically validated CBT become the first line of treatment for women who have any plans of becoming pregnant within the next few years.

PREMENSTRUAL SYNDROME

Premenstrual syndrome (PMS) is often characterized by the experience of anxiety symptoms. Therefore, a chapter on women's health issues and experience of anxiety would not be complete without a discussion of PMS. However, the discussion of premenstrual syndrome is particularly controversial. Debates continue over numerous issues, including: Is this a disorder or a natural phenomenon? If it is a disorder, is it best understood as a psychological or as a biological problem? What should the disorder be called? What symptoms make up the syndrome? Thorough discussion of these issues is beyond the scope of this chapter, as it is our intention to focus on the relationship of anxiety to menstrual cycling. However, excellent reviews of the social, cultural, and historical perspectives of PMS are available (Figert, 1996; Gold & Severino, 1994).

General Definition

The term *premenstrual syndrome (PMS)* was coined in 1953 by Greene and Dalton (Gold, 1994). Katarina

Dalton's definition of PMS is "the recurrence of symptoms on or after ovulation, increasing during the premenstrum and subsiding during menstruation, with complete absence of symptoms from the end of menstruation to ovulation" (Brush & Goudsmit, 1988, p. 1).

Prevalence estimates have ranged from as many as 90% of all fertile women experiencing some symptoms of PMS (Andersch, Wendestam, Hahn, & Ohman, 1986). Mild to moderate symptoms occurring in about 20–40% of women and severe symptoms occur in only about 2–10% of women (Logue & Moos, 1986). Researchers examining PMS have used various definitions of the syndrome; thus, the characteristics of women's symptoms may vary across samples. In a particularly controversial attempt to standardize the definition of PMS, the syndrome was included in the research appendix of the *DSM-III-R* (1987) and the *DSM-IV* (1994). Termed "late luteal phase dysphoric disorder (LLPDD)" in *DSM-III-R* and "premenstrual dysphoric disorder (PMDD)" in *DSM-IV*, the key features are symptoms such as depressed mood, marked anxiety, affective lability, and decreased interest in activities. These symptoms must occur regularly during the last week of the luteal phase in most menstrual cycles during the course of at least 1 year. The symptoms remit within a few days of the onset of menses and are absent in the week following menses (American Psychiatric Association, 1987, 1994). In the research reviewed here, women are at times referred to as having LLPDD, PMDD, or PMS.

Psychosocial Influences

A paucity of research exists examining the influence of psychosocial factors in the etiology and maintenance of PMS. Menstruation myths and folklore are deeply imbedded in our culture and in many others (Figert, 1996). The role of societal and personal expectations on premenstrual symptoms must therefore be considered. One researcher examining these factors (Ruble, 1977) told a group of undergraduate women that they were premenstrual when they were not. This group exhibited significantly higher ratings for water retention, pain, change in eating habits, and sexual arousal compared with another group of women who were told they were not in the late luteal phase. Ratings of negative affect, however, showed no such difference. Thus, some but not all symptoms appeared to be related to suggestion and expectation.

Relationship of Anxiety and PMS

Women with LLPDD and severe premenstrual dysphoric changes have a higher rate of past mood and anxiety disorders than women without severe premenstrual syndromes (e.g., Endicott, Halbreich, Schact, & Nee, 1985; Harrison, Endicott et al., 1989; Pearlstein, Frank, Rivera-Tovar, & Thoft, 1990), with comorbidity rates being higher for depressive disorders than for anxiety disorders. However, in one sample of Italian women with prospectively confirmed PMS (Facchinetti, Romano, Fava, & Genazzani, 1992), current comorbid anxiety disorders were more common than affective disorders. Twenty-six percent of these patients met criteria for panic disorder with or without agoraphobia. Nine cases were diagnosed with GAD, seven had simple phobias, eight had social phobia, four had OCD, and five had a depressive disorder.

Physiological challenges have also provided evidence for a relationship between premenstrual syndrome and anxiety. Two challenges often utilized as physiological stressors in the study of panic disorder are lactate infusion and CO_2 inhalation. A review of the literature on lactate infusion (Cowley & Arana, 1990) concluded that 67% of patients with panic disorder, 10% of psychiatric patients without coexisting panic attacks, and 13% of healthy controls develop lactate-induced panic. Lactate-induced panic may be due to a learned phobic response to somatic symptoms (Ackerman & Sachar, 1974; Margraf, Ehlers, & Roth, 1986). Patients with PMS are also considered to be very sensitive to somatic cues and to react with psychological distress to physical symptoms occurring during the premenstrual phase (Facchinetti et al., 1992). Researchers have examined the response to lactate infusion in PMS patients. In two such studies (Facchinetti et al., 1992; Sandberg, Endicott, Harrison, Nee, & Gorman, 1993), women with PMS displayed an increased reactivity to somatic symptoms. In a sample of 35 women with PMS and 16 women without PMS (Facchinetti et al., 1992), lactate infusion was administered between 2 and 8 days prior to menses. Lactate infusion induced a panic attack in 63% of the PMS patients compared to only 13% of controls. Many of the women with PMS in this study

also had a comorbid anxiety disorder. Frequency of lactate-induced panic was not significantly different between patients with PMS only (64% of these panicked), patients with PMS and panic disorder (89% panicked) and patients with PMS and another anxiety or mood disorder (47% panicked). Further, self-reported discomfort in response to lactate infusion was not accounted for by the presence of comorbid anxiety disorders in PMS patients. The severity of PMS was related to a greater degree of discomfort in response to lactate infusion.

Lactate sensitivity was examined in 13 PMS patients who had no comorbid anxiety or depressive disorders and 7 controls with no history of anxiety disorders or panic attacks (Sandberg et al., 1993). Sodium lactate infusions were done 1 to 7 days prior to menses. Fifty-eight percent of the PMS patients were rated by a "blind" clinician as having had a definite panic attack during the infusion. None of the controls had panicked. There were also significant differences between patients and control participants in pre–post lactate change scores on anxiety ratings. History of major depression and history of at least one panic attack were not significantly related to a panic response within the patient group. Thus, in both of these studies (Facchinetti et al., 1992; Sandberg et al., 1993), women with PMS panicked in response to lactate infusion at a rate similar to that seen in samples of patients with panic disorder (Cowley & Arana, 1990).

Response to double-breath inhalation of 35% CO_2 in 14 women with LLPDD was examined by Harrison, Sandberg, et al. (1989). Sixty-four percent of the women with LLPDD responded with a panic attack as opposed to zero of the 12 control subjects. Patients with panic disorder have been shown to have similar vulnerability to 35% CO_2 inhalation (Fyer et al., 1987).

In summary, women with PMS have reacted to double-breath CO_2 and sodium lactate infusion in a manner similar to that of patients with panic disorder. These findings suggest that women with PMS may, in part, have a biological vulnerability similar to that of patients with panic disorder (Sandberg et al., 1993). Additionally, Sandberg et al., suggest that women with PMS may share a hypersensitivity to somatic symptoms with panic disorder patients.

Symptoms of PMS often include marked anxiety and irritability. As a result, it has been argued that premenstrual symptoms may affect the assessment of other psychological disorders (McLeod, Hoehn-Saric, Foster, & Hipsley, 1993). For example, premenstrual increases in symptom scores could result in mistaken assessment of the severity of GAD if patients are assessed without regard for menstrual cycle phase. The variability in scores across the menstrual cycle could influence the power of statistical tests used to assess treatment effects. In order to examine the effect of menstrual cycling on anxiety diagnosis, the Hamilton Anxiety Rating Scale (HARS; Hamilton, 1959) and the Hopkins Symptom Checklist-90 (HSCL-90; Lipman, Covi, & Shapiro, 1979) were administered to women with GAD and prospectively confirmed PMS, women with GAD but no PMS, and women with no PMS or anxiety disorder (McLeod et al., 1993). In the two groups without PMS the scales were administered without regard for the menstrual cycle. The patients with PMS were assessed during the premenstrual and follicular phases of their cycles. Patients with GAD and PMS had more severe scores on all subscales of the HSCL-90 and on the HARS during the premenstruum, although scores during both phases were within a clinical range. Additionally, scores obtained on both measures, during both phases of the cycle, were greater than those of nonanxious volunteers. During the premenstrual phase, scores from women who had GAD and PMS resembled the scores from women who had GAD without PMS. Scores during the follicular phase were greater than those of the non-anxious women, but lower than those from the GAD group who did not have PMS. Because many anxiety-related symptoms are more severe during the premenstruum than during the follicular phase in women with PMS, it is possible that a mistaken diagnosis of GAD could be assigned when patients with PMS are assessed. It is important to know whether women with PMS differ from nonanxious women not only premenstrually, but also during the follicular phase. If they do not, then GAD may not be the appropriate diagnosis. Additionally, because premenstrual scores on both the HARS and the subscales of the HSCL-90 differed from follicular scores, the inclusion of women with PMS in studies of GAD could lead to complications. Treatment studies in which weekly ratings are made could have increased variability that could lead to decreased ability of statistical tests to detect a between-group difference.

ANXIETY RELATED TO OTHER FEMALE-SPECIFIC CONCERNS

In addition to PMS, other concerns specific to women may be accompanied by the experience of anxiety. The experience of pregnancy and childbirth may be met with specific anxiety. Interviews at five prenatal clinics of 139 consecutive patients during the 31st to 33rd week of gestation revealed that 6% of these women were severely fearful of labor and delivery and 17% were moderately fearful (Areskog, Uddenberg, & Kjessler, 1981). Reports on a sample of 100 women referred to a psychosomatic outpatient clinic because of extreme fear of delivery indicate that 68% percent of these women requested cesarean section due to their fear of vaginal childbirth (Sjogren & Thomassen, 1997). "Phobic-avoidance of the baby" was found in 9 of 66 postpartum women hospitalized in a mother-baby unit (Sved-Williams, 1992).

PELVIC EXAMINATIONS

The pelvic examination is another experience that is unique to women and often associated with anxiety. Failure to comply with recommended routine gynecological care severely jeopardizes early detection of and intervention for cancer and noncancer health problems. Such problems include vaginal infections and sexually transmitted diseases, which can become health hazards if left untreated or treated incorrectly.

Physicians and Pelvic Examinations

Although the pelvic exam is considered to be a routine aspect of women's health care, the exam can be associated with negative experiences for patients and clinicians. There is a reluctance among some doctors to perform pelvic examinations (Domar, 1986). Physicians' reluctance to perform genital examinations is evident in examinations conducted on children, adolescents, and adults. In fact, a majority of physicians are reluctant to examine children's genitalia. A study of pediatricians compared the frequency with which male and female genitalia were examined compared to the ears, heart, and abdomen. Regardless of the child's sex or age, the ears, heart, and abdomen were examined 97% of the time. In contrast, female genitalia were examined 39% of the time and male genitalia 84% of the time. Both male and female physicians examined female genitalia half as frequently as male genitalia, with a trend to fewer genital exams as the children got older (Balk, Dreyfus, & Harris, 1982). This suggests that performing a pelvic exam produces anxiety in both the patient and the examiner; as a result, the exam is frequently deferred (Handel, 1985). Fifty percent of medical students surveyed reported that they thought they would experience greater anxiety examining sexual organs and that they would neglect the pelvic examination because of their discomfort (Mudd & Siegel as cited in Frye & Weisberg, 1994). Clinical observations of gynecological patients also indicate that they are reluctant to have pelvic examinations (Millstein, Adler, & Irwin, 1984).

Most literature pertaining to gynecological-related anxiety deals with new educational methods designed to reduce medical students' anxiety about performing pelvic examinations. Medical school programs recognize the anxiety felt by beginning obstetrics and gynecology students and are including novel training methods designed to alleviate student anxiety and increase doctor–patient communication. The method of using the anthropomorphic model "Gynny" has been suggested (Rakestraw, Vontver, & Irby, 1985), as well as encouraging medical students to mentally practice performing pelvic examination procedures (Rakestraw, Irby, & Vontver, 1983). Several research reports recommend when training students the use of professional patients rather than plastic models (Holzman, Singleton, Holmes, & Maatsch, 1977; Nelson, 1978). For example, studies have recommended trained women from the community (Leserman & Luke, 1982; Women's Community Health Center, 1976), female friends (Schneidman, 1977), or gynecologic teaching associates (Plauche & Baugniet-Nebrija, 1985; Shain, Crouch, & Weinberg, 1982). Using a human patient during instruction enables medical students to enhance the doctor–patient relationship and their interpersonal skills by alleviating the medical students' sexual embarrassment and anxiety (Billings & Stoeckle, 1977; Holzman et al., 1977; Lesserman & Luke, 1982; Shain, Crouch, & Weinberg, 1982). Another suggested teaching technique is providing residents with basic knowledge about female sexual problems so that the student will encourage open discussion of the patient's sexual practices and problems (Levine et al., 1978).

The use of the "educational pelvic" is also suggested to medical students and examiners who already conduct pelvic exams (Domar, 1986). The educational pelvic was designed to relieve patient anxiety by giving her knowledge and control during the pelvic examination. The goal of the educational pelvic examination is for the physician to perform a complete pelvic exam while instructing the patient on the procedure, reporting the results, and answering questions. There are three main objectives of the exam. The first objective is to inform the patient about the anatomy and physiology of the pelvic area. The second is to transfer some of the control over the examination from the physician to the patient. And the third objective is to give the patient the opportunity to address subjects such as problems in sexuality (Smilkstein, 1981). The educational pelvic exam reduces women's anxiety by alerting the patient about the next step in the exam along with reporting the findings. A patient also has control over the examination by being able to delay the exam at any point if she experiences discomfort or wants to ask a question (Smilkstein, 1981).

Women's Anxiety about Pelvic Exams

Some women may dread and postpone gynecological visits (Domar, 1986). There are several reasons why some women do not seek routine care. In general, women lack knowledge about their anatomy and possible pathology of their genitals (Miller, 1974). Some women also find the lithotomy position (lying on their back, feet placed in stirrups, and a drape over their body) embarrassing and uncomfortable (Miller, 1974; Osofsky, 1967). Feelings of overwhelming vulnerability and helplessness are among the most frequently reported complaints concerning the pelvic exam (Domar, 1986). Because a Pap smear is taken during a pelvic exam, many women fear discovering pathology (Domar, 1986; Miller, 1974). As a result of their fear, some women may postpone or avoid gynecological exams.

Previous research has examined women's qualitative responses about pelvic examinations. Between 35 and 85% of women polled have negative attitudes associated with pelvic examinations. One study reported that 85% of women indicated negative attitudes, including humiliation, dehumanization, and vulnerability, about their last pelvic exam (Weiss & Meadow, 1979). Sixty-six percent of women who visited a gynecological clinic reported that they feared the exam (Ivarsson, Rockner, Westin-Lindgren, & Olund, 1981). Fifty percent of women about to have a gynecological exam described the impending exam as a negative experience and 44% indicated feelings of degradation (Areskog-Wijma, 1987). Women often associate pelvic examinations with feeling anxious. In fact, one study reported that 80% of women experienced some degree of anxiety about pelvic exams (Osofsky, 1967). These data regarding women's negative attitudes and anxiety suggest that anxiety about pelvic examinations is common (Domar, 1986).

Adolescents describe fears regarding pelvic exams that are similar to adult women's concerns. One study reported that the most common concerns for adolescents about the exam were: "fear of the discovery of pathology; fear of pain; and embarrassment about undressing and about personal cleanliness" (Millstein, Adler, & Irwin, 1984). Never-the-less, it is important for adolescents to obtain routine gynecological care. The American Cancer Society predicts that "200,000 new cases of cervical intraepithelial neoplasia (CIN) will be diagnosed each year, many of them in adolescents" (Demarest, 1985). Adolescent reluctance to receive routine care is problematic because data suggest that women's past use of routine gynecological care is the best predictor of their current acceptance of routine gynecological testing (Burack & Lang, 1987; Howe & Bzduch, 1987).

The gender of the examiner influences women's reported anxiety about pelvic examinations. Many women have a strong preference for specific examiners (Domar, 1986). In a study conducted on college students' preferences for the gender of providers of genital exams, women reported preferring same-sex examiners (Faigel, 1983). In fact, women express their desire to be examined by a female gynecologist "ten times more often than a wish for a male gynecologist" (Areskog-Wijma, 1987). A similar study conducted on adolescents reported that some adolescents, like adult women and victims of sexual assault, prefer a female examiner to perform a pelvic exam (Seymore et al., 1986).

Patients' needs vary considerably depending on their gynecological, sexual, and assault histories (Jolicoeur & Frye, 1993). Specific populations such

as adolescents, victims of sexual abuse (Jolicouer & Frye, 1993), obese patients (Adams, Smith, Wilbur, & Grady, 1993), chronically mentally ill patients (Handel, 1985), and imprisoned women (McGaha, 1987) may be at greater risk of not receiving routine gynecological care. Women who are survivors of sexual assault view pelvic exams in a largely negative context. Jolicouer & Frye (1993) reported that women who had been sexually assaulted at some point in their lives had greater pre– and post–pelvic exam anxiety. Burgess (1981) found that victims of sexual assault by gynecologists develop an aversion to gynecological care.

Anxiety and stress are also closely related to gynecological symptoms (Deffenbacher & Craun, 1985). Stress and anxiety are correlated with difficulties in the female reproductive system (Siegel, Johnson, & Sarason, 1979; Stephenson, Denny, & Aberger, as cited in Deffenbacher & Craun, 1985) and vaginal infections (Williams & Deffenbacher, 1983, cited in Deffenbacher & Craun, 1985). One study found that anxiety management training resulted in reductions in anxiety, stress, and gynecological symptoms for students with gynecological problems (Deffenbacher & Craun, 1985).

Quantitative Pelvic Exam Anxiety Research

Pelvic exams are an important aspect of women's preventative health care. Although several studies have investigated various teaching techniques designed to reduce medical students' anxiety about performing pelvic exams, few studies examine women's anxiety about pelvic examinations. A majority of the research that does exist is retrospective and focuses on women's self-reported feelings of anxiety. Despite the implications that some women dread pelvic examinations, qualitative findings suggest that women may vary in the severity of their reported anxiety (Osofsky, 1967). The intensity of women's reported anxiety differs, ranging from mild to more severe anxiety. Some women report "dread" and "animosity" in reference to gynecological examinations. However, this finding is not quantified. Data suggest that patients' anxiety levels prior to routine pelvic examinations are elevated, compared to those patients about to have a colposcopy or infertility treatment (Miller, Hurley, Schwartz-Buzaglo, & Schreiber, 1992). These qualitative data indicate that women to various degrees perceive gynecological examinations as anxiety-provoking. It is possible that such anxiety may lead to avoidance of the feared situation and ultimately cause failure to comply with recommendations for routine gynecological care.

Although previous research suggests that anxiety intensity may be variable, only a few studies (Miller et al., 1992; Millstein, Adler, & Irwin, 1984; Seymore et al., 1986; Williams, Park, & Kline, 1992) have used a reliable and valid measure, such as the Spielberger State-Trait Anxiety Inventory (STAI) (Spielberger, 1983), to quantitatively assess pelvic exam anxiety. One study used the STAI to assess pre- and post-exam anxiety and to elucidate factors of pelvic examinations that were of particular concern to adolescents. Millstein et al. (1984) found that pre-exam anxiety for those having a pelvic exam was not significantly higher than the anxiety reported by a normative sample of high school females. However, almost half of the respondents in the Millstein study were not examined on the day of the questionnaire but gave retrospective responses (Seymore et al., 1986). Another group of researchers used the STAI to ascertain the influence that positioning (lithotomy or semi-sitting) had on adolescents' pre- and post-examination anxiety (Seymore et al., 1986). They found anxiety levels to be lower after the pelvic exam than prior to the exam. The STAI has also been used to assess post-examination anxiety levels of women wearing a newly designed examination gown (Williams, Park, & Kline, 1992). Additionally, the STAI has been used in the comparison between the anticipatory anxiety of women awaiting routine pelvic examinations and the anxiety of women awaiting a colposcopy or infertility treatment (Miller et al., 1992). This was the first study that compared pelvic examination anxiety to the anxiety experienced toward another procedure.

Hinkson & Frye (1993) utilized the STAI has also been utilized to compare undergraduates' pelvic exam anxiety to anxiety evoked by nongynecological visits occurring in a college health center (see Table 23.1). Pre- and post-visit STAI scores were compared in order to ascertain whether there were differences in pre- and post-exam anxiety levels. All participants had higher anxiety scores prior to being seen by the nurse practitioner than after they completed their visit. After their visit, women who indicated that their

TABLE 23.1 Mean State Anxiety Scores Using the Spielberger State-Trait Anxiety Inventory (STAI) of 99 College-Aged Women Prior to (Pre-) and Following (Post-) a Visit to Their College Health Center

TYPE OF VISIT	SCORE ON S-ANXIETY SUBTEST OF THE STAI
Irrespective of visit parameters	
pre-visit	39.0
post-visit	32.5*
Visits that included pelvic examination	
pre-exam	38.2
post-exam	29.0*
Visits that did not include pelvic examination	
pre-exam	39.2
post-exam	35.1
Visits that participant indicated was "urgent" and included a pelvic examination	
pre-exam	50.3
post-exam	35.2
Visits that participant indicated was "routine" and included a pelvic examination	
pre-exam	39.2
post-exam	30.5
Visits that participant indicated was "urgent" and did not include a pelvic examination	
pre-exam	39.5
post-exam	37.2
Visits that participant indicated was "routine" and included a pelvic examination	
pre-exam	38.7
post-exam	36.2
Post-exam scores by participants' perception of exam outcome	
problem was revolved	31.2
not sure if problem was resolved	41.3
problem was not resolved	38.4

*Indicates t-test scores are significantly ($p < 0.05$) higher prior to the visit (pre-visit) compared to after the visit (post-visit).

problem was resolved had lower anxiety scores compared with women who were ambiguous as to whether or not their problem was resolved. There were no effects of previous sexual activity, current sexual activity, or pregnancy history on pre- or post-visit anxiety scores. Interestingly, exam urgency was the most significant factor influencing pelvic exam anxiety. Women with walk-in gynecological visits had the highest pre-examination STAI scores. STAI scores were significantly higher for women being seen for a medical visit than for those with a gynecological visit. Independent of the reason for exam, patients who were seen for a walk-in visit had significantly higher post-exam scores than those seen for a routine, scheduled visit. Patients with medical visits, irrespective of exam urgency, obtained STAI scores most comparable to those from patients being seen for a walk-in visit. These results suggest that both examination type and examination urgency are prominent factors influencing exam anxiety.

The findings in these quantitative studies demonstrate that women do report some anxiety prior to a pelvic examination. However, it is important to note that the reported anxiety levels are comparable to the mean anxiety levels for the specific population being studied (Hinkson & Frye, 1993; Miller & Mangan, 1983). These findings are in contrast to the attitudes and feelings reported in many qualitative studies conducted years ago. In general the qualitative and quantitative data suggest that although pelvic exams may be anxiety-producing for some women, the anxiety is not paralyzing for most women and appears to dissipate after the examination is over.

Exhibiting Control during the Pelvic Examination

Because women's anxiety may prevent them from complying with recommendations for routine gynecological care, it is important that women are made aware of the methods that may alleviate their exam anxiety. Receiving education, choosing a provider, influencing exam procedures, creating a comfortable exam environment, and communicating with their provider may help women gain a sense of control over their examination.

Receiving education about the procedures that are conducted during a routine gynecological visit and the feelings that a woman may experience during the procedure may help decrease anxiety regarding exam expectations (Hinkson, 1993). In a study of 977 women, over 70% wanted to know more about their sexual organs, normal sexual functioning, sexual emotions, reasons for the pelvic examination, and the procedures involved in the exam. Over 68% felt that knowing more would make them feel more comfortable (Petravage, Reynolds, Gardner, & Reading, 1979). Knowing the gender of the practitioner ahead of time may also reduce pre-exam anxiety (Hinkson, 1993). As previously stated, several studies suggest women have a preference for a female examiner (Areskog-Wijma, 1987; Domar, 1986; Faigel, 1983; Seymore et al., 1986). However, if the examiner is a male, the presence of a chaperone during the examination may reduce exam anxiety. Twenty-nine percent of adult women and 46% of female teenagers preferred that a chaperone be present during a breast, pelvic, or rectal exam by a male physician. Thirty-six percent of adult women and 63% of female teenagers wanted a chaperone present during a first examination of these regions (Penn & Bourguet, 1992). The use of a chaperone may be beneficial when the patient is unfamiliar with the clinician conducting the exam, as research indicates that this situation is the greatest contributor to pelvic exam anxiety (Domar, 1992). In addition to reducing pelvic exam anxiety by obtaining information prior to the exam, there are several ways in which women can exert control over the exam environment to further alleviate their anxiety. Women can take a more active role during the examination by choosing their positioning during the exam. Some women find the lithotomy position embarrassing and uncomfortable (Miller, 1974; Osofsky, 1967), and other women find it to be the most emotionally difficult aspect of the gynecological examination (Harr, Halitsky, & Stricker, 1977). A semi-sitting position, in contrast to the traditional lithotomy position, is preferred by some patients and physicians (Seymore et al., 1986; Swartz, 1984). This position may provide more physical comfort for both the patient and the practitioner while allowing the opportunity for more communication as a result of patient physician eye contact (Piermattie, 1987).

Interaction and communication between the physician and patient during the exam may alleviate women's exam anxiety and provide the patient with a sense of control over the exam. Research indicates that women are curious about what the doctor is observing or finding during their pelvic exam, indicating a desire for more information and less mystery (Osofsky, 1967). The use of the educational pelvic exam reduces women's anxiety by alerting the patient about the next step of the exam along with reporting the findings. A patient also has control over the exam by being able to delay the exam at any point if she experiences discomfort or wants to ask questions

(Smilkstein, 1981). A study investigating how patients express their anxiety during gynecological exams and how gynecologists react to these expressions of anxiety encouraged women to express their concerns more overtly during a medical consultation because overt presentation of anxiety increases the chance that the patient's concerns will be explored by physicians (Weijts, Widdershoven, & Kok, 1991). This study also encouraged gynecologists to increase their awareness of covert ways in which patients may express anxiety, such as allusions to malignancies, pressure for rigorous medical intervention, and speech disturbances (Weijts, Widdershoven, & Kok, 1991).

ANXIETY AND COMPLIANCE

Women's anxiety about pelvic exams may prevent them from complying with recommendations for gynecological care. It is important to consider the attitudes and feelings regarding pelvic examinations that affect women's propensity for seeking care. One group of researchers studied women's noncompliant behavior toward receiving a follow-up Pap smear following an abnormal test and found that "noncompliers tended to be older, unmarried, have lower incomes, work outside of the home, be less educated, be less likely to have medical insurance, and be less likely to practice other types of health promotion behaviors" (Paskett, Carter, Chu, & White, 1990). The women who did not receive follow-up care reported anxiety about Pap smears and cervical cancer as their primary reasons for noncompliance. Other reasons given for their noncompliance were erroneous beliefs, family difficulties, embarrassment, fear, and transportation problems. Noncompliance with gynecological care can also be likened to noncompliant behavior in obtaining breast cancer screening. Small proportions of women receive annual mammograms (Rimer, Davis, Engstrom, & Myers, 1988). One study found women who felt they were less likely to develop breast cancer were more likely to comply with routine breast screening (Rimer et al., 1988). Failure to comply with recommended routine gynecological care severely jeopardizes early detection of and intervention for cancer and noncancer health problems such as vaginal infections and sexually transmitted diseases that can become health hazards if left untreated or treated incorrectly. Treatment for some gynecological infections is now available over the counter, so it is possible that women may attempt to use these medications to treat any new symptoms and therefore avoid professional gynecological care. Women who have no medical training and try to diagnose their own symptoms may jeopardize their own health. One study reported that women with no medical training were more likely to use over-the-counter agents inappropriately for pelvic inflammatory disease, bacterial vaginosis, urinary tract infection, and vaginal trichomoniasis (Ferris, Dekle, & Litaker, 1996). Annual gynecological exams, beginning in adolescence (Millstein, Adler, & Irwin, 1984), are integral for the maintenance of a woman's good health. Early detection of cervical and breast cancer is crucial considering cervical cancer is the second most common cancer in women and one in nine women will contract some form of breast cancer in her lifetime (Mass. Breast Cancer Coalition, 1992). Although impressive reductions in breast cancer (Smith & Hailey, 1988) and cervical cancer mortality have been demonstrated through regular screening programs (Rimer et al., 1988), studies have revealed that many women fail to comply with medical recommendations to receive routine gynecological care.

CONCLUSIONS

In conclusion, women's health concerns and anxiety management are linked in many ways. Although further investigation is needed on this multifaceted topic, the issues that have received the most research attention have been discussed in this chapter and include the following: First, the incidence of anxiety disorders is influenced by a female's hormonal and/or reproductive status. Women are more likely than men to be diagnosed with anxiety disorders, and the variations in women's endocrine status influence physiological systems that underlie anxiety. Women also experience variations in anxiety symptoms during times of the greatest hormonal changes, for example, pregnancy, postpartum, and phases of the menstrual cycle. Second, women's anxiety may be influenced by psychological or sociological status. Factors such as female gender, low income, being single, and being a mother are associated with more anxiety symptoms and greater functional impairment. Third, difficulties unique to women, such as premenstrual syndrome, are often characterized by the experience of anxiety symptoms. Women with severe premenstrual dysphoric changes have a higher rate of past mood and anxiety disorders than women without severe premenstrual syndromes. Fourth, in addition to PMS, other concerns specific to women, such as pregnancy and childbirth, may be met with specific anxiety. Fifth, anxiety about particular medical procedures, such as pelvic examinations, may influence the health promotion or disease prevention measures taken by some women. Review of these topics clearly indicates that women have unique issues surrounding anxiety; hence, research is warranted to further ascertain the nature of anxiety in the lives of women.

NOTE

Funding for CAF was provided by the Donaghue Foundation for Medical Research (96-10) and the National Science Foundation (95-14463). Technical support and instructive comments on the manuscript were provided by Meghan Lizotte and are greatly appreciated.

REFERENCES

Abplanalp, J. M., Livingston, L., Rose, R. M., & Sandwisch, D. (1977). Cortisol and growth hormone responses to psychological stress during the menstrual cycle. *Psychosomatic Medicine, 39,* 158–177.

Ackerman, S. H., & Sachar, E. J. (1974). The lactate theory of anxiety: A review and reevaluation. *Psychosomatic Medicine, 36,* 69–81.

Adams, C. H., Smith, N. J., Wilbur, D. C., & Grady, K. E. (1993). The relationship of obesity to the frequency of pelvic examinations: Do physician and patient attitudes make a difference? *Women and Health, 20,* 45–57.

American Cancer Society. (1989). *Cancer facts and figures: 1988.* New York: Author.

American Psychiatric Association. (1987). *Diagnostic and statistical manual of mental disorders* (3d ed.) (rev.). Washington, DC: Author.

American Psychiatric Association. (1994). *Diagnostic and statistical manual of mental disorders* (4th ed.). Washington, DC: Author.

Andersch, B., Wendestam, C., Hahn, L., & Ohman, R. (1986). Premenstrual complaints. I. Prevalence of premenstrual symptoms in a Swedish urban population. *Journal of Psychosomatic Obstetrics and Gynecology, 5,* 39–49.

Areskog, B., Uddenberg, N., & Kjessler, B. (1981). Fear of childbirth in late pregnancy. *Gynecological and Obstetric Investigation, 12,* 262–266.

Areskog-Wijma, B. (1987). The gynecological examination: Women's experiences and preferences and the role of the gynecologist. *Journal of Psychosomatic Obstetrics and Gynecology, 6,* 59–69.

Asso, D. (1978). Levels of arousal in the premenstrual phase. *Social and Clinical Psychology, 17,* 47–55.

Balk, S. J., Dreyfus, N. G., & Harris, P. (1982). Examination of genitalia in children: "The remaining taboo." *Pediatrics, 70,* 751–753.

Barlow, D. H. (1988). *Anxiety and its disorders: The nature and treatment of anxiety and panic.* New York: Guilford.

Barlow, D. H. (1991). Disorders of emotion. *Psychological Inquiry, 2,* 58–71.

Barlow, D. H., Chorpita, B. F., & Turovsky, J. (1996). Fear, panic, anxiety, and disorders of emotion. In D. A. Hope (Ed.), *Nebraska Symposium on Motivation: Perspectives on anxiety, panic, and fear* (vol. 43) (pp. 251–328). Lincoln: University of Nebraska Press.

Baulieu, E. E. (1997). Neurosteroids: Of the nervous system, by the nervous system, for the nervous system. *Recent Progress in Hormone Research, 52,* 1–33.

Bayon, L. E., & Frye, C. A. (1998). Endogenous variations in metabolites of progesterone and testosterone: The neurosteroids $3\alpha,5\alpha$-THP and 3α-diol are influenced by mating stimuli. Society for Behavioral Endocrinology Conference. New Orleans.

Billings, J. A., & Stoeckle, J. D. (1977). Pelvic examination instruction and the doctor–patient relationship. *Journal of Medical Education, 52,* 834–839.

Bitran, D., Hilvers, R. J., & Kellogg, C. K. (1991a). Anxiolytic effects of 3α-hydroxy-$5\alpha < \beta >$-pregnan-20-one-endogenous metabolites of progesterone that are active at the GABA$_A$ receptor. *Brain Research, 561,* 157–161.

Bitran, D., Hilvers, R. J., & Kellogg, C. K. (1991b). Ovarian endocrine status modulates the anxiolytic potency of diazepam and the efficacy of GABA-benzodiazepine receptor-mediated chloride ion transport. *Behavioral Neuroscience, 105,* 653–662.

Blazer, D. G., Hughes, D., George, L. K., Swartz, M., & Boyer, R. (1991). Generalized anxiety disorder. In L. N. Robins & D. A. Reiger (Eds.), *Psychiatric disorders in America* (pp. 180–203). New York: Free Press.

Blehar, M. C. (1995). Gender differences in risk factors for mood and anxiety disorders: Implications for clinical treatment research. *Psychopharmacology Bulletin, 31,* 687–691.

Bourdon, K. H., Boyd, J. H., Rae, D. S., Burns, B. J., Thompson, J. W., & Locke, B. Z. (1988). Gender differences in phobias: Results of the ECA community survey. *Journal of Anxiety Disorders, 2,* 227–241.

Breier, A., Charney, D., & Heninger, G. R. (1986). Agoraphobia with panic attacks: Development, diagnostic stability, and course of illness. *Archives of General Psychiatry, 43,* 1029–1036.

Brush, M. G., & Goudsmit, E. M. (1988). General and social considerations in research on menstrual cycle disorders with particular reference to PMS. In M. G. Brush & E. M. Goudsmit (Eds.), *Functional disorders of the menstrual cycle* (pp. 1–13). Chichester, England: Wiley.

Burack, R. C., & Lang, J. (1987). The early detection of cancer in the primary care setting: Factors associated with the acceptance and completion of recommended procedures. *Preventive Medicine, 16,* 739–751.

Burgess, A. W. (1981). Physician sexual misconduct and patients' responses. *American Journal of Psychiatry, 138,* 1335–1342.

Buttoph, M. L., & Holland, A. D. (1990). Obsessive-compulsive disorders in pregnancy and childbirth. In M. A. Jenike, L. Baer, & W. E. Minichiello (Eds.), *Obsessive-compulsive disorders: Theory and management* (pp. 89–95). Chicago: Year Book Medical Publishers.

Cameron, O. G., Kuttesch, D., McPhee, K., & Curtis, G. C. (1988). Menstrual fluctuation in the symptoms of panic anxiety. *Journal of Affective Disorders, 15,* 169–174.

Cohen, L. S., Sichel, D. A., Dimmock, J. A., & Rosenbaum, J. F. (1994a). Impact of pregnancy on panic disorder: A case series. *Journal of Clinical Psychiatry, 55,* 284–288.

Cohen, L. S., Sichel, D. A., Dimmock, J. A., & Rosenbaum, J. F. (1994b). Postpartum course in women with preexisting panic disorder. *Journal of Clinical Psychiatry, 55,* 289–292.

Cohen, L. S., Sichel, D. A., Faraone, S. V., Robertson, L. M., Dimmock, J. A., & Rosenbaum, J. F. (1996). Course of panic disorder during pregnancy and the puerperium: A preliminary study. *Biological Psychiatry, 39,* 950–954.

Cook, B. L., Noyes, R., Garvey, M. J., Beach, V., Sobotka, J., & Chaudry, D. (1990). Anxiety and the menstrual cycle in panic disorder. *Journal of Affective Disorders, 19,* 221–226.

Cowley, D. S., & Arana, G. W. (1990). The diagnostic utility of lactate sensitivity in panic disorder. *Archives of General Psychiatry, 47,* 277–284.

Cox, B. J., Swinson, R. P., Shulman, I. D., Kuch, K., & Reichman. (1993). Gender effects and alcohol use in panic disorder with agoraphobia. *Behaviour Research and Therapy, 31,* 413–416.

Craske, M. G., Brown, T. A., & Barlow, D. H. (1991). Behavioral treatment of panic disorder: A two-year follow-up. *Behavior Therapy, 22,* 289–304.

Deffenbacher, J. L., & Craun, A. M. (1985). Anxiety management training with stressed student gynecology patients. *Journal of College Student Personnel,* 513–518.

Demarest, C. B. (Ed.). (1985). Getting the most from the Pap smear. *Patient Care,* 63–85.

Dennerstein, L., & Burrows, G. D. (1979). Affect and the menstrual cycle. *Journal of Affective Disorders, 1,* 77–92.

Domar, A. (1986). Psychological aspects of the pelvic exam: Individual needs and physician involvement. *Women and Health, 10,* 75–89.

Domar, A. (1992). *The birth of the PEST: The development of a pelvic examination stress test.* (Unpublished manuscript.)

Dweck, C. S., Davidson, W., Nelson, S., & Enna, B. (1978). Sex differences in learned helplessness: II. The contingencies of evaluative feedback in the classroom and III. An experimental analysis. *Developmental Psychology, 14,* 268–276.

Eaton, W. W., Dryman, A., & Weissman, M. M. (1991). Panic and phobia. In L. N. Robins & D. A. Regier (Eds.), *Psychiatric disorders in America: The epidemiologic catchment area study* (pp. 155–179). New York: Free Press.

Endicott, J., Halbreich, U., Schact, S., & Nee, J. (1985). Affective disorder and premenstrual depression. In H. J. Osofsky & S. J. Blumenthal (Eds.), *Premenstrual syndrome: Current findings and future directions* (pp. 3–11). Washington, DC: American Psychiatric Press.

Facchinetti, F., Romano, G., Fava, M., & Genazzani, A. R. (1992). Lactate infusion induces panic attacks in patients with premenstrual syndrome. *Psychosomatic Medicine, 54,* 288–296.

Faigel, H. C. (1983). Gender preference towards providers of genital examinations and frequency of genital self-examination among college students. *Journal of American College Health,* 240–241.

Fankhauser, M. P. (1997). Psychiatric disorders in women: Psychopharmacologic treatments. *Journal of the American Pharmaceutical Association, 37,* 667–678.

Ferris, D. G., Dekle, C., & Litaker, M. S. (1996). Women's use of over-the-counter antifungal medications for gynecologic symptoms. *Journal of Family Practice, 42,* 595–600.

Figert, A. E. (1996). *Women and the ownership of PMS: The structuring of a psychiatric disorder.* New York: de Gruyter.

Freeman, E. W., Purdy, R. H., Coutifaris, C., Rickels, K., & Paul, S. M. (1993). Anxiolytic metabolites of progesterone: Correlation with mood and performance measures following oral progesterone administration to healthy female volunteers. *Neuroendocrinology, 58,* 478–484.

Freeman, E., Rickels, K., Sondheimer, S. J., & Polansky, M. (1990). Ineffectiveness of progesterone suppository treatment for premenstrual syndrome. *JAMA, 264,* 349–353.

Freeman, E. W., Weinstock, L., Rickels, K., Sondheimer, S. J., & Coutifaris, C. (1992). A placebo-controlled study of effects of oral progesterone on performance and mood. *British Journal of Clinical Pharmacology, 33,* 293–298.

Frye, C. A. (1995). The neurosteroid $3\alpha,5\alpha$-THP has anti-seizure and possible neuroprotective effects in an animal model of epilepsy. *Brain Research, 696,* 113–120.

Frye, C. E., & Bayon, L. E. (1998). Prenatal stress reduces the effectiveness of $3\alpha,5\alpha$-THP to block kainic acid-induced seizures. Neuroendocrine Workshop on Stress. *Hospital and Community Psychiatry.*

Frye, C. A., & Duncan, J. E. (1994). Progesterone metabolites, effective at the $GABA_A$ receptor complex, attenuate pain sensitivity in rats. *Brain Research, 643,* 194–203.

Frye, C. A., & Duncan, J. E. (1995). Estradiol benzoate potentiates neuroactive steroids' effects on pain sensitivity. *Pharmacology, Biochemistry and Behavior, 53,* 27–32.

Frye, C. A., Scalise, T. J., & Bayon, L. E. (in press). Finasteride blocks the reduction in ictal activity produced by exogenous estrous cyclicity. *Journal of Neuroendocrinology.*

Frye, C. A., & Weisberg, R. B. (1994). Increasing the incidence of routine pelvic examinations: Behavioral medicine's contribution. *Women and Health, 21,* 33–55.

Fyer, M. R., Uy, I., Martinez, J., Goetz, R., Klein, D. F., Fyer, A. I., Leibowitz, M. R., & Gorman, J. M. (1987). CO_2 challenge of patients with panic disorder. *American Journal of Psychiatry, 144,* 1080–1082.

Gallo, M. A., & Smith, S. S. (1993). Progesterone withdrawal decreases latency to and increases duration of electrified prod burial: A possible rat model of PMS anxiety. *Pharmacology, Biochemistry and Behavior, 46,* 897–904.

Gold, J. H. (1994). Historical perspective of premenstrual syndrome. In J. H. Gold & S. K. Severino (Eds.), *Premenstrual dysphorias: Myths and realities* (pp. 171–184). Washington, DC: American Psychiatric Press.

Gold, J. H., & Severino, S. K. (Eds.). (1994). *Premenstrul dysphorias: Myths and realities.* Washington, DC: American Psychiatric Press.

Hamilton, M. (1959). The assessment of anxiety states by rating. *British Journal of Medical Psychology, 32,* 50–55.

Handel, E. (1985). Deferred pelvic examinations: A purposeful omission in the care of mentally ill women. *Hospital Community Psychiatry, 36,* 1070–1074.

Harr, E., Halitsky, V., & Stricker, G. (1977). Patients' attitudes toward gynecologic examination and to gynecologists. *Medical Care, 15,* 787.

Harrison, W., Endicott, J., Nee, J., Glick, H., & Rabkin, J. G. (1989). Characteristics of women seeking treatment of "premenstrual syndrome." *Psychosomatics, 30,* 405–411.

Harrison, W. M., Sandberg, D. P., Gorman, J. M., Fyer, M., Nee, J., Uy, J., & Endicott, J. (1989). Provocation of panic with carbon dioxide inhalation in patients with premenstrual dysphoria. *Psychiatry Research, 27,* 183–192.

Hesselbrock, M. N., Meyer, R. E., & Keener, J. J. (1985). Psychopathology in hospitalized alcoholics. *Archives of General Psychiatry, 42,* 1050–1055.

Hinkson, A. B. (1993). *Women's anxiety toward pelvix examinations.* Unpublished undergraduate thesis. Wheaton College, Norton, MA.

Hinkson, A. B., & Frye, C. A. (1993, June). *Women's anxiety towards pelvic examinations.* Poster presented at the annual meeting of the Society for Menstrual Cycle Research, Boston.

Holzman, G. B., Singleton, D., Holmes, T. F., & Maatsch, J. L. (1977). Initial pelvic examination instructions: The effectiveness of three contemporary approaches. *American Journal of Obstetrics and Gynecology, 129,* 124–129.

Howe, H. L., & Bzduch, H. (1987). Recency of Pap smear screening: A multivariate model. *Public Health Reports, 102,* 295–301.

Insel, T. R. (1992). Oxytocin: A neuropeptide for affliation: Evidence from behavioral receptor autoradiographic and comparative studies. *Psychoneuroendocrinology, 17,* 3–35.

Ivarsson, G., Rockner, G., Westin-Lindgren, O., & Olund, A. (1981) Kvinnors installning till den gynekologista undersokningen. *Jordemodern, 11,* 391.

Ivey, M. E., & Bardwick, J. M. (1968). Patterns of affective fluctuations in the menstrual cycle. *Psychosomatic Medicine, 30,* 336–345.

Jolicoeur, M. R., & Frye, C. A. (1993, June). *History of sexual abuse/assault influences women's levels of anxiety during routine pelvic examinations.* Poster presented at the annual meeting of the Society for Menstrual Cycle Research, Boston.

Karno, M., Golding, J. M., Burnam, M. A., & Hough, R. L. (1989). Anxiety disorders among Mexican Americans and non-Hispanic Whites in Los Angeles. *Journal of Nervous and Mental Diseases, 177,* 202–209.

Kaspi, S. P., Otto, M. W., Pollack, M. H., & Eppinger, S. (1994). Premenstrual exacerbation of symptoms in women with panic disorder. *Journal of Anxiety Disorders, 8,* 131–138.

Kessler, R. C., McGonagle, K. A., Zhao, S., Nelson, C. B., Hughes, M., Eshleman, S., Wittchen, H. U., & Kendler, K. S. (1994). Lifetime and 12-month prevalence of DSM-III-R psychiatric disorders in the United States. *Archives of General Psychiatry, 51*, 8–19.

Keuthen, N. J., O'Sullivan, R. L., Hayday, C. F., Peets, K. E., Jenike, M. A., & Baer, L. (1997). The relationship of menstrual cycle and pregnancy to compulsive hairpulling. *Psychotherapy and Psychosomatics, 66*, 33–37.

Klein, D. F. (1993). False suffocation alarms, spontaneous panics, and related conditions: An integrative hypothesis. *Archives of General Psychiatry, 50*, 306–317.

Klosko, J. S., Barlow, D. H., Tassinari, R., & Cerny, J. A. (1990). A comparison of alprazolam and behavior therapy in treatment of panic disorder. *Journal of Consulting and Clinical Psychology, 58*, 77–84.

Kubitz, K. A., Peavey, B. S., & Moore, B. S. (1986). The effect of daily hassles on humoral immunity: An interaction moderated by locus of control. *Biofeedback and Self-Regulation, 11*, 115–123.

Kuhl, J. (1981). Motivational and functional helplessness: The moderating effect of state versus action orientation. *Journal of Personality and Social Psychology, 40*, 155–170.

Leserman, J., & Luke, C. S. (1982). An evaluation of an innovative approach to teaching the pelvic examination to medical students. *Women and Health, 7*, 31–41.

Levine, S. B., Resnick, P. J., Engel, I. M., Smith, D., Rosenthal, M. B., & Juknialis, B. W. (1978). A sexuality curriculum for gynecology residents. *Journal of Medical Education, 53*, 510–512.

Lipman, R. S., Covi, L., & Shapiro, A. K. (1979). The Hopkins Symptom Checklist (HSCL) factors derived from the HSCL-90. *Journal of Affective Disorders, 1*, 9–24.

Logue, C. M., & Moos, R. H. (1986). Perimenstrual symptoms: Prevalence and risk factors. *Psychosomatic Medicine, 48*, 385–387.

Maccoby E. E., & Jacklin, C. N. (1974). *The psychology of sex differences*. Stanford, CA: Stanford University Press.

Majewska, M. D. (1992). Neurosteroids—endogenous bimodal modulators of the GABA$_A$ receptor—mechanism of action and physiological significance. *Progress in Neurobiology, 38*, 379–395.

Majewska, M. D., Harrison, N. L., Schwartz, R. D., Barker, J. L., & Paul, S. M. (1986). Steroid hormone metabolites are barbiturate-like modulators of the GABA receptor. *Science, 232*, 1004–1007.

Margraf, J., Ehlers, A., & Roth, W. T. (1986). Sodium lactate infusions and panic attaches: A review and critique. *Psychosomatic Medicine, 48*, 23–51.

Massachusetts Breast Cancer Coalition. (1992). *Pamphlet: Women and breast cancer*. Available from the Massachusetts Breast Cancer Coalition. P.O. Box 383, Newton Highlands, MA 02161.

Matteo, S. (1987). The effect of job stress and job interdependency on menstrual cycle length, regularity and synchrony. *Psychoneuroendocrinology, 12*, 467–476.

McGaha, G. S. (1987). Health care issues of incarcerated women. *Journal of Offender Counseling, Services, and Rehabilitation, 12*, 53–59.

McLeod, D. R., Hoehn-Saric, R., Foster, G. V., & Hipsley, P. A. (1993). The influence of premenstrual syndrome on ratings of anxiety in women with generalized anxiety disorder. *Acta Psychiatrica Scandinavica, 88*, 248–251.

Miller, G. D. (1974). The gynecological examination as a learning experience. *Journal of the American College of Health, 23*, 162–164.

Miller, S. M., Hurley, K., Schwartz-Buzaglo, J., & Schreiber, P. (1992). *Post-traumatic symptomology and emotional distress in infertile women*. Paper presented at the thirteenth annual scientific sessions of the Society of Behavioral Medicine. New York.

Miller, S. M., & Mangan, C. E. (1983). Interacting effects of information and coping style in adapting to gynecologic stress: Should the doctor tell all? *Journal of Personality and Social Psychology, 45*, 223–236.

Millstein, S. G., Adler, N. E., & Irwin, C. E. (1984). Sources of anxiety about pelvic examinations among adolescent females. *Journal of Adolescent Health Care, 5*, 105–111.

Moos, R. H., Kopell, B. S., Melges, F. T., Yalom, I. D., Lunde, D. T., Clayton, R. B., & Hamburg, D. A. (1969). Fluctuations in symptoms and moods during the menstrual cycle. *Journal of Psychosomatic Research, 13*, 37–44.

Nelson, L. H. (1978). Use of professional patients in teaching pelvic examinations. *Obstetrics and Gynecology, 52*, 630–633.

Neziroglu, F., Anemone, R., & Yaryura-Tobias, J. A. (1992). Onset of obsessive-compulsive disorder in pregnancy. *American Journal of Psychiatry, 149*, 947–950.

Nolen-Hoeksema, S. (1987). Sex differences in unipolar depression: Evidence and theory. *Psychological Bulletin, 101*, 259–282.

Northcott, C. J., & Stein, M. B. (1994). Panic disorder and pregnancy. *Journal of Clinical Psychiatry, 55*, 539–542.

Osofsky, H. J. (1967). Women's reactions to pelvic examination. *Obstetrics and Gynecology, 30*, 146–151.

Paskett, D., Carter, W. B., Chu, J., & White, E. (1990). Compliance behavior in women with abnormal Pap smears. *Medical Care, 28*, 643–656.

Paul, S. M., & Purdy, R. H. (1992). Neuroactive steroids. *FASEB Journal, 6*, 2311–2322.

Pearlstein, T. H., Frank, E., Rivera-Tovar, A., & Thoft, J. S. (1990). Prevalence of Axis I and Axis II disorders in women with late luteal phase dysphoric disorder. *Journal of Affective Disorders, 20*, 129–134.

Penn, M. A., & Bourguet, C. C. (1992). Patients' attitudes regarding chaperones during physical examinations. *Journal of Family Practice, 35*(6), 639–643.

Petravage, J. B., Reynolds, L. J., Gardner, H. J., & Reading, J. C. (1979). Attitudes of women toward the gynecological examination. *Journal of Family Practice, 9*(6), 1039–1045.

Piermattie, L. A. (1987). Pelvic examinations in adolescence. *Patient Care, 21*, 156–162.

Plauche, W. C., & Baugniet-Nebrija, W. (1985). Students' and physicians' evaluations of gynecologic teaching associate program. *Journal of Medical Education, 60*, 870–875.

Purdy, R. H., Morrow, A. L., Moore, P. H., & Paul, S. M. (1991). Stress-induced elevations of gamma-aminobutyric acid type-A receptor-active steroids in the rat brain. *Proceedings of the National Academy of Sciences of the United States of America, 88*, 4553–4557.

Rakestraw, P. G., Irby, D. M., & Vontver, L. A. (1983). The use of mental practice in pelvic examination instruction. *Journal of Medical Education, 58*, 335–340.

Rakestraw, P. G., Vontver, L. A., & Irby, D. M. (1985). Utilization of an anthropomorphic model in pelvic examinations. *Journal of Medical Education, 60*, 343–345.

Rapee, R. M., & Barlow, D. H. (Eds.). (1991). *Chronic anxiety: Generalized anxiety disorder and mixed anxiety-depression.* New York: Guilford.

Riggs, D. S., & Foa, E. B. (1993). Obsessive-compulsive disorder. In D. H. Barlow (Ed.), *Clinical handbook of psychological disorders* (2d ed.) (pp. 189–239). New York: Guilford.

Rimer, B. K., Davis, S. W., Engstrom, P. F., & Myers, R. E. (1988). Some reasons for compliance and noncompliance in health maintenance organization breast cancer screening program. *Journal of Compliance in Health Care, 3*, 103–114.

Rosciszewska, D., Buntner, B., Guz, I., & Zawisza, L. (1986). Ovarian hormones, anticonvulsant drugs, and seizures during the menstrual cycle in women with epilepsy. *Journal of Neurology, Neurosurgery, and Psychiatry, 49*, 47–51.

Ruble, D. N. (1977). Premenstrual symptoms: A reinterpretation. *Science, 197*, 291–292.

Sandberg, D., Endicott, J., Harrison, W., Nee, J., & Gorman, J. (1993). Sodium lactate infusion in late luteal phase dysphoric disorder. *Psychiatry Research, 46*, 79–88.

Sandberg, D., Fyer, A. J., & Endicott, J. (1986). *Premenstrual changes in anxiety patients.* Paper presented at the annual meeting of the American Psychiatric Association.

Schmidt, P. J., Nieman, L. K., Danaceau, M. A., Adams, L. F., & Rubinow, D. R. (1998). Differential behavioral effects of ganodal steroids in women with and in those without premenstrual syndrome. *New England Journal of Medicine, 338*(4), 209–216.

Schneidman, B. S. (1977). An approach to obtaining patients to participate in pelvic examination instruction. *Journal of Medical Education, 52*, 70–71.

Seymore, C., DuRant, R. H., Jay, S., Freeman, D., Gomez, L., Sharp, C., & Linder, C. W. (1986). Influence of position during examination, and sex of examiner on patient anxiety during pelvic examination. *Journal of Pediatrics, 108*, 312–317.

Shain, R. N., Crouch, S. H., & Weinberg, P. C. (1982). Evaluation of the gynecological teaching associate versus pelvic model approach to teaching pelvic examination. *Journal of Medical Education, 57*, 646–648.

Shear, M. K., & Mammen, O. (1995). Anxiety disorders in pregnant and postpartum women. *Psychopharmacology Bulletin, 31*, 693–703.

Sholomskas, D. E., Wickamaratne, P. J., Dogolo., L., O'Brien, D. W., Leaf, P. J., & Woods, S. W. (1993). Postpartum onset of panic disorder: A coincidental event? *Journal of Clinical Psychiatry, 54*, 476–480.

Sichel, D. A., Cohen, L. S., Dimmock, J. A., & Rosenbaum, J. F. (1993). Postpartum obsessive compulsive disorder: A case series. *Journal of Clinical Psychiatry, 54*, 156–159.

Siegel, J. M., Johnson, J. H., & Sarason, I. G. (1979). Life changes and menstrual discomfort. *Journal of Human Stress, 5*, 41–46.

Sjogren, B., & Thomassen, P. (1997). Obstetric outcome in 100 women with severe anxiety over childbirth. *Acta Obstetricia et Gynecologia Scandinavica, 76*, 948–952.

Small, P., Stockwell, T., Canter, S., & Hodgson, R. (1984). Alcohol dependence and phobic anxiety states: I. A prevalence study. *British Journal of Psychiatry, 144*, 53–57.

Smilkstein, G. (1981). The educational pelvic examination. *Journal of Family Practitioners, 13*, 932–933.

Smith, P. C., & Hailey, B. J. (1988). Compliance with instructions for regular breast self-examination. *Journal of Compliance in Health Care, 3*, 151–161.

Spielberger, C. D. (1983). *Manual for the State-Trait Anxiety Inventory.* Palo Alto, CA: Consulting Psychologists Press.

Stein, M. B., Schmidt, P. J., Rubinow, D. R., & Uhde, T. W. (1989). Panic disorder and the menstrual cycle: Panic disorder patients, healthy control subjects, and patients with premenstrual syndrome. *Archives of General Psychiatry, 146,* 1299–1303.

Sved-Williams, A. E. (1992). Phobic reactions of mothers to their own babies. *Australian and New Zealand Journal of Psychiatry, 26,* 631–638.

Swartz, W. H. (1984). The semi-sitting position for pelvic examinations. *Journal of the American Medical Association, 251,* 1163.

van den Akker, O., & Steptoe, A. (1985). The pattern and prevalence of symptoms during the menstrual cycle. *American Journal of Psychiatry, 147,* 164–169.

Veith, J. L., Anderson, J., Slade, S. A., Thompson, P., Laugel, G. R., & Getzlaf, S. (1984). Plasma beta-endorphin, pain thresholds and anxiety levels across the human menstrual cycle. *Physiology and Behavior, 32,* 31–34.

Villeponteaux, V. A., Lydiard, R. B., Laraia, M. Y., Stuart, G. W., & Ballenger, J. C. (1992). The effects of pregnancy on preexisting panic disorder. *Journal of Clinical Psychiatry, 53,* 201–203.

Von Bardeleben, U., & Holsboer, F. (1988). Human corticotropin releasing hormone: Clinical studies in patients with affective disorders, alcoholism, panic disorder and in normal controls. *Progress in Neuro-Psychopharmacology and Biological Psychiatry, 12,* S165–S187.

Weijts, W., Widdershoven, G., & Kok, G. (1991). Anxiety-scenarios in communication during gynecological consultations. *Patient Education and Counseling, 18,* 149–163.

Weiss, L., & Meadow, R. (1979). Women's attitude toward gynecological practices. *Obstetrics and Gynecology, 54,* 110–114.

Williams, J. G., Park, L. I., & Kline, J. (1992). Reducing distress associated with pelvic examinations: A stimulus control intervention. *Women and Health, 18,* 41.

Williams, K. E., & Koran, L. M. (1997). Obsessive-compulsive disorder in pregnancy, the puerperium, and the premenstruum. *Journal of Clinical Psychiatry, 58,* 330–334.

Wisner, K. L., Peindl, K. S., & Hanusa, B. H. (1996). Effects of childbearing on the natural history of panic disorder with comorbid mood disorder. *Journal of Affective Disorders, 41,* 173–180.

Women's Community Health Center. (1976). Experiences of a pelvic teaching group. *Women and Health, 1,* 19–20.

Woods, N. F., Most, A., & Dery, G. K. (1982). Toward a construct of perimenstrual distress. *Research in Nursing and Health, 5,* 123–136.

AUTHOR INDEX

SUBJECT INDEX